The Big Book of Concepts

The Big Book of Concepts

Gregory L. Murphy

A Bradford Book
The MIT Press
Cambridge, Massachusetts
London, England

This book was set in Sabon on 3B2 by Asco Typesetters, Hong Kong. Printed and bound in the United States of America.

Library of Congress Cataloging-in-Publication Data

Murphy, Gregory L. (Gregory Leo)
 The big book of concepts / Gregory L. Murphy.
   p.   cm.
 "A Bradford book."
 Includes bibliographical references and index.
 ISBN 0-262-13409-8 (hc : alk. paper)
 1. Concepts. 2. Mental representation. I. Title.
BF443 .M87 2002
153.2'3—dc21   2001058683

To Jessica and Rachel, in alphabetical order.

Contents

1

Introduction

Concepts are the glue that holds our mental world together. When we walk into a room, try a new restaurant, go to the supermarket to buy groceries, meet a doctor, or read a story, we must rely on our concepts of the world to help us understand what is happening. We seldom eat the same tomato twice, and we often encounter novel objects, people, and situations. Fortunately, even novel things are usually similar to things we already know, often exemplifying a category that we are familiar with. Although I've never seen this particular tomato before, it is probably like other tomatoes I have eaten and so is edible. If we have formed a concept (a mental representation) corresponding to that category (the class of objects in the world), then the concept will help us understand and respond appropriately to a new entity in that category. Concepts are a kind of mental glue, then, in that they tie our past experiences to our present interactions with the world, and because the concepts themselves are connected to our larger knowledge structures.

Our concepts embody much of our knowledge of the world, telling us what things there are and what properties they have. It may not seem to be a great intellectual achievement to identify a bulldog or to know what to do with a tomato, but imagine what our lives would be like without such a conceptual ability (Smith and Medin 1981, p. 1). We might know the things we had experienced in the past—a particular chair, our bed, the breakfast we had today, our science teacher, etc.—but when we encountered new exemplars of these categories, we would be at a loss. When going into a new room and seeing a new chair, we would have to study it from scratch, attempt to determine whether it is alive or dead, what its function is, whether it will hurt us, or how it might help us. Instead, of course, we may not even consciously think "chair," but simply identify the object's category and plop down into it. By using our concept of chairs, we immediately draw the inference that it is appropriate to sit on this object, even if we have never seen anyone sit on it before. At a new restaurant, we read names of dishes such "gnocchi," "jerk chicken," and "pad thai" and feel we can decide which one we would prefer to eat, even though we have never had that exact meal, or even an example of that kind of meal at this restaurant. The speed and ease with which we identify objects as chairs or draw inferences about jerk chicken (too hot to have for lunch) can mislead us about how complex this process is and how much information we may have stored about everyday categories. The psychology of concepts is like other areas of psychology, in which a phenomenologically simple cognitive process, like understanding speech or walking, turns out to be maddeningly complex. Much of the excitement in the field arises from this complexity, as a topic that seemed to be fairly straightforward in 1960 has turned out to be a much deeper and richer scientific problem than researchers had expected.

The mental glue provided by concepts applies not only to the familiar categories of objects, like chairs and tomatoes, but also to a number of other domains that are of interest to psychologists, such as social and person categories, emotions, linguistic entities, events and actions, and artistic styles. For example, if we meet a new, highly talkative person and begin to suspect that he or she is a bore or instead a sociopath, our behaviors toward the person will differ accordingly. If told by someone else that the person is a lawyer or instead a priest, our behaviors will again differ. We rely on such categories to direct our behavior, sometimes despite more reliable information directly observed about the person.

The psychology of concepts cannot by itself provide a full explanation of the concepts of all the different domains that psychologists are interested in. This book will not explore the psychology of concepts of persons, musical forms, numbers, physical motions, and political systems. The details of each of these must be discovered by the specific disciplines that study them; to fully understand people's musical concepts will require much research into the psychology of music, rather than being predictable solely from what we know of concepts per se. Nonetheless, the general processes of concept learning and representation may well be found in each of these domains. For example, I would be quite surprised if concepts of musical forms did not follow a prototype structure (chapter 2), did not have a preferred level of categorization (chapter 7), and did not show differences depending on expertise or knowledge (chapter 6). Spelling out what categories people have of musical forms, what levels of abstraction there are, and what knowledge influences the concepts is primarily part of the psychology of music rather than the psychology of concepts. But once the basic elements of musical concepts are identified, the concepts will likely be found to follow the principles identified in other domains. In short, the psychology of concepts has much to offer other fields of psychology and cognitive science more generally.

Similarly, concepts are ubiquitous across different populations and ages—it is hard to see how any intelligent creature could do without them. It used to be thought that infants and young children were lacking in true conceptual abilities, which had to be onerously acquired over the preschool years. However, more recent research has found basic conceptual abilities in infants only a few months old (chapter 9), and preschool children now appear to have sophisticated conceptual abilities, even if they are lacking much of the conceptual content that adults have (chapter 10).

Another way that concepts infiltrate our everyday life and thoughts is through communication. When we talk, we are attempting to communicate ideas about the objects, people, and events that take place around us. Since we understand those objects, people, and events through concepts, our word and sentence meanings must make contact with conceptual representations. Not surprisingly, it turns out that many properties of concepts are found in word meaning and use, suggesting that meanings are psychologically represented through the conceptual system (chapters 11 and 12).

There is a real temptation for researchers in the field of concepts to get carried away on the "everything is concepts" bandwagon that I have started rolling here. (If I were more melodramatic, I could spin a fairy tale in which a person who has no concepts starves while surrounded by tomatoes, because he or she had never seen *those particular* tomatoes before and so doesn't know what to do with them.) Although in unguarded moments I do think that everything is concepts, that is not as restrictive a belief as you might think. Concepts may have a great variety of forms and contents, and this is part of what has made the field so complex. Across different people, levels of experience with the category, tasks, and domains, concepts may vary in a large number of ways. Although this is not itself a principle of the psychology of concepts, many examples of this variation will be seen throughout the book. Reconciling those differences, or at least understanding how different kinds of concepts are coordinated, is an important goal of this field, one that has not been fully accomplished yet.

The psychology of concepts, then, has the goal of understanding the representations that allow us to do all these things, most importantly, identifying objects and events as being in a certain category, drawing inferences about novel entities, and communicating about them. Although the field (and hence this book) concentrates on common object concepts, the principles involving concept formation and use are thought to be to some degree generalizable across different domains and settings.

How This Book Differs from the Book You Expected to Read

Most books and review articles that I know of on concepts have used an organization based on theories. The best example is the classic text by Smith and Medin (1981). After some preliminaries, it had chapters on the classical view of concepts, each of three probabilistic views, and then the exemplar view. Each chapter described the theory, presented evidence relevant to it, and then evaluated it. In 1981, this was an excellent organization. In 2001, however, this organization would have a number of problems. The first is that the field shows very little agreement on which theory of concepts is correct. One might have hoped that twenty years after Smith and Medin's review, the field would have sorted out many of the issues their book raised. However, there is as much, and perhaps more, dissension now as there was then. Focusing on theories, therefore, is not the best way to document the important progress that has been made in the psychology of concepts. Many interesting principles and generalizations have been discovered about concepts, and even if the field does not agree on the overarching theory that encompasses all of them, that does not deny that those discoveries have been a real advance.

The second reason not to organize this book around theories is that too many interesting questions do not fall easily into theoretical pigeonholes. Issues such as infant concept learning or conceptual combination are cohesive topics in their own rights, but they are difficult to parcel out to chapters on the classical theory or exemplar theory. If one were to divide up the parts of each topic that are most relevant to a given theory, one would have balkanized a previously coherent topic.

The third reason I have not followed the theoretical organization is that I am becoming increasingly uneasy about the particular theoretical disputes that have characterized the field. Much of the literature has compared exemplar and prototype theory (see chapter 3), but it seems fairly clear that both theories are wrong to a greater or lesser degree, and so focusing on them serves to reinforce this way of dividing up the field, when new ways of thinking may be required. In particular, I will suggest at the end of the book that a more inclusive approach may be needed, an approach that would be ill-served by organizing the book around distinguishing the different theories.

As a result, I have organized most of the book around phenomena or issues rather than theories. The book does begin theoretically, starting with the so-called classical theory of concepts and its downfall. The three main approaches to concepts are described in the next chapter, as a preparation for the discussions in individual chapters. As a result, chapters 2 and 3 should be read first (except perhaps by those already familiar with the field), and after that, readers may graze on the subsequent chapters in any order. Each chapter describes a particular topic or set of related phenomena and evaluates the explanations of those phenomena. At the end of each chapter, I discuss the implications of those phenomena and their explanations for the three main theoretical approaches discussed in chapter 3. The final chapter revisits the main theories and makes proposals for future directions. Thus, theoretical issues are by no means ignored in the book. However, one discovery I have made in organizing the book this way is that no theory has a ready explanation for all of the findings even *within* each specific topic. This helps to point out goals for researchers who take a given theoretical approach, but it also serves to point out the limitation of organizing the field primarily by the theories.

This book is not a complete reference work of our knowledge of concepts. It is a selective review, and I sometimes do deviate from the majority of the field in my choices of what I think is most significant or interesting. My goal here has not been to evaluate everything that has been done but instead to explain the most basic and exciting findings in the field and to try to draw some conclusions about how to explain them. I have attempted to take the "long view" and not to necessarily include the hot topics of this moment, much less the abandoned hot topics of yesteryear. For the most part, then, I have focused on the topics about which enough work has been done to draw a conclusion, rather than on topics that are still unsettled and perhaps of unclear future interest.

Terminology and Typography

In general, I try to use the word *concepts* to talk about mental representations of classes of things, and *categories* to talk about the classes themselves. However, in both everyday speech and the literature in this field, it is often hard to keep track of which of these one is talking about, because the two go together. That is, whatever my concept is, there is a category of things that would be described by it. Thus, when talking about one, I am usually implying a corresponding statement about the other. Writers in this field often say things like "four-year-olds have a category of animals," meaning "four-year-olds have formed a concept that picks out the category of animals." However, being too fussy about saying *concept* and *category* leads to long-winded or repetitious prose (like my example) with little advantage in clarity. When it is important to distinguish the mental representation from the category itself, I will be careful. In other situations, I will leave it to the reader to make the appropriate translation (e.g., from "having a category" to "having a concept that corresponds to a particular category").

Many writers also use typographic conventions to distinguish concepts (or categories) from the actual things. Obviously, a concept of a dog is not the same as a dog, and some authors indicate this by printing concept names in italics or small capitals. I have gone this route in the past, but I decided not to do so here. This issue is related to an underlying assumption about the relation of concepts and categories, so I will briefly explain why I have come to this decision.

In many cases, it is simply obvious whether one is talking about the concept or the object, and so the typographical convention is not necessary. In other cases, though, the ambiguity between the concept and the thing is intentional. Indeed, I am not always sure that authors get it right when they decide to capitalize the word. For example, suppose you learn that dogs bark. Have you learned that dogs bark or that DOG (the concept) has the property "barks"? From one perspective, you have learned about a property in the world, and so you have learned something about actual, lower-case dogs. From another perspective, you have changed your concept, and so you have modified your mental representation, that is, DOG. In fact, you have probably learned both. But when one follows such a distinction, choosing one typography implies that the other one is not intended. That is, if I were to say something about dogs, I would not intend you to understand this to be true of the concept of dogs, because I didn't write DOG. But often I, in fact, *would* intend to be making the statement about both: The parallelism between concepts and categories means that when you learn something about dogs, your concept of dogs has also changed, and so constantly making this distinction leads to false implications. So, I do not use a separate typography for concepts and real things, but instead simply say "the concept of dog" or the like when I want specifically to discuss concepts.

I follow standard practice in linguistics by italicizing cited words, as in "the word *dog* has one syllable." Things that people say are quoted.

A Note to Students

I have attempted to write this book at a level that an advanced undergraduate or beginning graduate student could understand. Although I assume general knowledge about experimental psychology and some familiarity with cognitive psychology, I have tried to start from scratch when it comes to concepts, so that little or no knowledge is assumed other than what has already been covered in the book. In fact, I have erred on the side of redundancy, so that chapters would be more self-contained. If you are not very familiar with the "traditional" literature of concepts (i.e., from the 1970s), then the first few chapters will be necessary reading. Even seasoned concepts researchers may be surprised to find themselves interested in these chapters, as it is often the most basic phenomena that are the most difficult to explain.

A student picking up this book might wonder whether there are still interesting questions to be asked in the psychology of concepts. Have the basic questions been answered, and are we only spelling out the details now? The book's conclusion is one answer to this question. Before getting there, however, I think I can safely say that the answer is "no." There are still important and surprising discoveries being made in the field. Many of these are coming through attempts to look at real-world concepts in greater detail, in which the findings are sometimes quite different from what would be expected from studies with artificial categories. Related to this is the benefit that concept research is receiving from connections to other areas of cognitive science such as psycholinguistics, reasoning, anthropology, neuropsychology, and problem-solving. Working out how concepts are influenced by and in turn influence processes in these other domains has been a fruitful and in some cases surprising enterprise. However, before a new researcher can engage in such cross-discipline interactions, he or she must understand the basic issues and findings in the field, and this is what the next few chapters discuss.

Some students may have more basic questions of the sort that one is reluctant to ask one's teacher or adviser. I find these illustrated in a letter written by an amateur student of astronomy to observers at the Mount Wilson Laboratory in 1933 (Simons 1993, p. 113):

Just a few lines to let you know that I am Interested in Astronomy. I have did quite a lot of reading on it and I am really interested in it. I have quite a bit of confidence in Materialism; I believe myself the whole Universe is substance. But what I would really like to know is will Astronomy get a person anywhere—is there any use in a person studying it. Will it put you in an unmentally condition?[1]

These are questions I have asked myself about the psychology of concepts as well. As to whether studying concepts will "get a person anywhere," it of course depends on where you want to get. I don't think it will get you a high-paying job in the new economy, but I think it may help you to understand a basic function of the mind. If you want to understand social thinking or perception or cognitive development, then learning about concepts will be a necessary part of your study. Another reason studying concepts may get you where you want to go is the incredible variety of research on concepts. It ranges from the mathematical models tested in artificial category-learning experiments to anthropological studies in rain forests to linguistic analyses of word and phrase meaning. It is possible to find your own niche within the study of concepts almost regardless of what your interests are. If you find one part of it (and of this book) too boring or too touchy-feely or too technical, you can wait a chapter or two and discover a topic and approach that are completely opposite.

The question of whether getting involved in this topic will put you in "an un-mentally condition," is a trickier one. Studying almost any question in psychology is bound to have its moments of mental unbalance, as past beliefs are called into question, and issues that were thought to be settled twenty years ago come back with renewed force. Overall, I believe that the risk is no greater here than in most areas of psychology. However, the risk of becoming unbalanced is clearly greatest in the prototype-exemplar theory debate, which shows little signs of abating after many years of controversy, so those who feel mentally vulnerable may wish to focus on other topics.

The writer of that letter concluded by saying:

But I know that the more you read up on it the more you get Interested.... Would you please give me some kind of basis to the Knowledge of astronomy?

My expectation is that the more you read up on concepts the more you will get interested in them as well, and the goal of this book is not so much to tell you all about concepts as to provide some kind of basis to your continuing acquisition of knowledge. That is, if you understand the sections on typicality and concept learning, for example, you should be able to pick up a contemporary paper on these topics and understand it. In serving that function, I hope that this book will have a shelf life that is longer than its function of describing recent discoveries, just as the Smith and Medin (1981) book could be used as background reading in the area for many years after its publication. The field has greatly expanded since 1981, covering many topics that did not really exist then; and much more has been learned about the topics that their book did cover. Therefore, this book is correspondingly bigger and more detailed than Smith and Medin's. My guess is that in twenty more years, it will be impossible to write a single-authored book that covers the same ground, because there will be more research than any one author and volume can handle. That is exactly why I have written this book now.

Acknowledgments

Is there any section of a book more boring than the acknowledgments? After one has searched in vain for one's own name, there is little point in continuing to read. Nonetheless, I owe a great debt of gratitude to a number of people and institutions who have supported the writing of this book, and I only wish that I could force every reader to read each name and fully understand the thanks that I owe to each and every one of them. That being impossible, I am forced to be brief.

First, I need to thank the University of Illinois, and especially its Center for Advanced Studies, for providing me with a sabbatical leave on which I researched and wrote most of the first draft of the book. The Beckman Institute, through its administrative and secretarial support (in the person of the invaluable Linda May), also made the writing much easier for me. The City University, London, provided a supportive home for me during that sabbatical and also for a month in 2000 when I did much revision and polishing. I am especially grateful to my host at City, James Hampton, for selfless efforts on my behalf.

Second, I am grateful to the National Institute of Mental Health for supporting my research reported in this book, as well as part of the writing itself (grant MH41704). Other funding from the National Science Foundation (a grant on which Brian Ross was principal investigator) was helpful as well (grant SBR97-20304).

Third, a number of very busy people took time out from their other duties to critique and comment on various chapters. The book is much better as a result, and would have been even better if I had taken all their advice. These people include Renée Baillargeon, Paul Bloom, Seth Chin-Parker, Herbert Clark, John Coley, James Hampton, Evan Heit, Devorah Klein, Barbara Malt, Arthur Markman, Kristine Onishi, Paul Quinn, Bob Rehder, Brian Ross, Paula Schwanenflugel, Edward Smith, J. David Smith, Sandra Waxman, Edward Wisniewski, and Karen Wynn. James Hampton, Kristine Onishi, Brian Ross, and especially Arthur Markman deserve combat pay for reading multiple chapters.

Fourth, I thank my former colleagues and students at Illinois, where I conceived and did much of the work on this book, for helping to create a stimulating and rich intellectual environment in which to work and write. If I list one name, I would have to list dozens, so I will just thank you all.

2
Typicality and the Classical View of Categories

The Classical View

When you were in junior high school or even earlier, you probably had a teacher who tried to get you to define words. Given a word like *wildebeest*, you might say "It's a kind of animal." Your teacher would not be satisfied with this definition, though. "A frog is also a kind of animal," she might point out, "Is it the same as a frog?" "No," you would reply sheepishly, "it has four legs and is about the size of a cow and has horns and lives in Africa." Well, now you're getting somewhere. My teacher used to tell us that a definition should include everything that is described by a word and nothing that isn't. So, if your description of a wildebeest picks out all wildebeest and nothing else, you have given a successful definition. (In fact, most definitions in dictionaries do not meet this criterion, but that is not our problem.)

Definitions have many advantages from a logical standpoint. For example, the truth or falsity of "Rachel is a wildebeest" is something that can be determined by referring to the definition: Does Rachel have all the properties listed in the definition—four legs, horns, and so on? By saying "Rachel is not a wildebeest," we are saying that Rachel lacks one or more of the definitional properties of wildebeest. And we could potentially verify statements like "Wildebeest can be found in Sudan" by looking for things in Sudan that meet the definition. Philosophers have long assumed that definitions are the appropriate way to characterize word meaning and category membership. Indeed, the view can be traced back as far as Aristotle (see Apostle 1980, pp. 6, 19–20). In trying to specify the nature of abstract concepts like fairness or truth, or even more mundane matters such as causality and biological kinds, philosophers have attempted to construct definitions of these terms. Once we have a definition that will tell us what exactly is and is not a cause, we will have come a long way toward understanding causality. And much philosophical argu-

Figure 2.1
Two concepts from Hull's (1920) study. Subjects learned 12 concepts like this at a time, with different characters intermixed. Subjects were to respond to each stimulus with the name at left (*oo* and *yer* in this case). Note that each example of a concept has the defining feature, the radical listed in the "concept" column.

mentation involves testing past definitions against new examples, to see if they work. If you can find something that seems to be a cause but doesn't fit the proposed definition, then that definition of cause can be rejected.

It is not surprising, then, that the early psychological approaches to concepts took a definitional approach. I am not going to provide an extensive review, but a reading of the most cited work on concepts written prior to 1970 reveals its assumption of definitions. I should emphasize that these writers did not always explicitly *say*, "I have a definitional theory of concepts." Rather, they took such an approach for granted and then went about making proposals for how people learned concepts (i.e., learned these definitions) from experience.

For example, Clark Hull's (1920) Ph.D. thesis was a study of human concept learning—perhaps surprisingly, given his enormous later influence as a researcher of simple learning, usually in rats. Hull used adapted Chinese characters as stimuli. Subjects viewed a character and then had to respond with one of twelve supposedly Chinese names (e.g., *oo* and *yer*). Each sign associated with a given name contained a radical or component that was identical in the different signs. As figure 2.1 shows, the *oo* characters all had the same radical: a kind of large check mark with two smaller marks inside it. Clearly, then, Hull assumed that every example of a concept had some element that was critical to it.

There are two aspects to a definition that these items illustrate. The first we can call *necessity*. The parts of the definition must be in the entity, or else it is not a member of the category. So, if a character did not have the check-mark radical, it would not be an *oo*. Similarly, if something doesn't have a distinctive attribute of chairs, it is not a chair. The second aspect we can call *sufficiency*. If something has all the parts mentioned in the definition, then it must be a member of the category. So, anything having that radical in Hull's experiment would be an *oo*, regardless of what other properties it had. Note that it is not enough to have one or two of the parts mentioned in the definition—the item must have all of them: The parts of the definition are "jointly sufficient" to guarantee category membership. So, it wouldn't be enough for something to be as big as a cow and be from Africa to be a wildebeest; the item must also be an animal, with four legs and horns, if those things are included in our definition.

Hull (1920) explicitly adopted these aspects of a definition (without calling them by these names) in one of the principles he followed in creating his experiment (p. 13): "All of the individual experiences which require a given reaction, must contain certain characteristics which are at the same time common to all members of the group requiring this reaction [i.e., necessary] and which are NOT found in any members of the groups requiring different reactions [i.e., sufficient]." (Note that Hull adopted the behaviorist notion that it is the common response or "reaction" that makes things be in the same category. In contrast, I will be talking about the mental representations of categories.) Hull believed that this aspect of the experiment was matched by real-world categories. He describes a child who hears the word *dog* used in a number of different situations. "At length the time arrives when the child has a 'meaning' for the word dog. Upon examination this meaning is found to be actually a characteristic more or less common to all dogs and not common to cats, dolls and 'teddy-bears.' But to the child, the process of arriving at this meaning or concept has been largely unconscious. He has never said to himself 'Lo! I shall proceed to discover the characteristics common to all dogs but not enjoyed by cats and "teddy-bears"'" (p. 6). Note that although Hull says that "Upon *examination* this meaning is ...," he does not describe any examination that has shown this, nor does he say what characteristics are common to all dogs. These omissions are significant—perhaps even ominous—as we shall soon see.

In the next major study of concept learning, Smoke (1932—the field moved somewhat more slowly in those days) criticized the definitional aspect of Hull's concepts. He says quite strongly that "if any concepts have ever been formed in such a fashion, they are very few in number. We confess our inability to think of a single one" (p. 3). He also quotes the passage given above about how children learn the concept of dog, and asks (pp. 3–4): "What, we should like to ask, is this 'characteristic more or less common to all dogs and not common to cats, dolls, and "teddy-bears"' that is the '"meaning" for the word dog' ... What is the 'common element' in 'dog'? Is it something within the *visual* stimulus pattern? If exact drawings were made of all the dogs now living, or even of those with which any given child is familiar, would they 'contain certain strokes in common' [like Hull's characters] which could be 'easily observed imbedded in each'?"

One might think from this rather sarcastic attack on Hull's position that Smoke is going to take a very different position about what makes up a concept, one that is at odds with the definitional approach described. That, however, is not the case. Smoke's objection is to the notion that there is a single, simple element that is common to all category members. (Although Hull's stimuli do have such a simple element in common, it is not so clear that he intended to say that all categories were like this.) Smoke says "As one learns more and more about dogs, [one's] concept of 'dog' becomes increasingly rich, not a closer approximation to some bare 'element'" (p. 5). What Smoke feels is missing from Hull's view is that the essential components of a concept are a complex of features that are connected by a specified relationship, rather than being a single common element. Smoke gives this example of a concept called "zum," which he feels is more realistic: "Three straight red lines, two of which intersect the third, thereby trisecting it" (p. 9). You may judge for yourself whether this is more realistic than Hull's Chinese characters. In teaching such concepts, Smoke made up counterexamples that had some of the components of the concept but not all of them. Thus, for a nonzum, he might make up something with only two lines or something with three lines but that did not intersect one another in the required way. Thus, he created a situation that precisely follows the definitional view: Zums had all the required properties, and for the items that did not, subjects had to learn not to call them zums. Thus, the properties of zums were necessary and sufficient.

In short, although Smoke seems to be rejecting the idea of concepts as being formed by definitions, he in fact accepts this view. The main difference between his view and Hull's is that he viewed the definitions as being more complex than (he thought) Hull did. I have gone through these examples in part to show that one can tell whether experimenters had the definitional view by looking at their stimuli. In many older (pre-1970) studies of concepts, all the members have elements in common, which are not found in the nonmembers. Thus, even if such studies did not explicitly articulate this definitional view, they presupposed it.

The work of Hull and Smoke set the stage for research within American experimental psychology's study of concepts. In addition to their view of concepts, the techniques they developed for concept learning studies are still in use today. Another influence that promoted the use of definitions in the study of concepts was the work of Piaget in cognitive development. Piaget viewed thought as the acquisition of logical abilities, and therefore he viewed concepts as being logical entities that could be clearly defined. Again, Piaget did not so much argue for this view of concepts as simply assume it. For example, Inhelder and Piaget's (1964, p. 7) theory relied on constructs such as: "the 'intension' of a class is the set of properties common to the members of that class, together with the set of differences, which distinguish them from another class"—that is, a definition. Following this, they provide a list of logical properties of categories which they argued that people must master in order to have proper concepts. (Perhaps not surprisingly, they felt that children did not have true concepts until well into school age—see chapter 10.) Piaget's work was not directly influential on most experimental researchers of adult concepts, but it helped to bolster the definitional view by its extraordinary influence in developmental psychology.

Main Claims of the Classical View

The pervasiveness of the idea of definitions was so great that Smith and Medin (1981) dubbed it the *classical view* of concepts. Here, then are the main claims of the classical view. First, concepts are mentally represented as definitions. A definition provides characteristics that are a) necessary and b) jointly sufficient for membership in the category. Second, the classical view argues that every object is either in or not in the category, with no in-between cases. This aspect of definition was an important part of the philosophical background of the classical view. According to the *law of the excluded middle*, a rule of logic, every statement is either true or false, so long as it is not ambiguous. Thus, "Rachel is a wildebeest" is either true or false. Of course, we may not know what the truth is (perhaps we don't know Rachel), but that is not the point. The point is that in reality Rachel either is or isn't a wildebeest, with no in-between, even if we don't know which possibility is correct. Third, the classical view does not make any distinction between category members. Anything that meets the definition is just as good a category member as anything else. (Aristotle emphasized this aspect of categories in particular.) An animal that has the feature common to all dogs is thereby a dog, just the same as any other thing that has that feature. In a real sense, the definition *is* the concept according to the classical view. So all things that meet the definition are perfectly good members of the concept, and all things that do not fit the definition are equally "bad" members (i.e., nonmembers) of the concept, because there is nothing besides the definition that could distinguish these things. As readers are no doubt thinking, this all sounds too good to be true.

Before confirming this suspicion, it is worthwhile to consider what kind of research should be done if the classical view is true. What is left to understand about the psychology of concepts? The basic assumption was that concepts were acquired by learning which characteristics were defining. However, unlike Hull's assumption (and more like Smoke's), it became apparent that any real-world concepts would involve multiple features that were related in a complex way. For example, dogs have four legs, bark, have fur, eat meat, sleep, and so on. Some subset of these features might be part of the definition, rather than only one characteristic. Furthermore, for some concepts, the features could be related by rules, as in the following (incomplete) definition of a strike in baseball: "the ball must be swung at and missed OR it must pass above the knees and below the armpits and over home plate without being hit OR the ball must be hit foul (IF there are not two strikes)." The use of logical connectives like AND, OR, and IF allows very complex concepts to be defined, and concepts using such connectives were the ones usually studied in psychology experiments. (There are not that many experiments to be done on how people learn concepts that are defined by a single feature.) Often these definitions were described as *rules* to tell what is in a category.

Bruner, Goodnow, and Austin (1956) began the study of this sort of logically specified concept, and a cottage industry sprang up to see how people learned them. In such experiments, subjects would go through many cards, each of which had a picture or description on it. They would have to guess whether that item was in the category or not, usually receiving feedback on their answer. For difficult concepts, subjects might have to go through the cards a dozen times or more before reaching perfect accuracy on categorizing items; for easy concepts, it might only take four or five run-throughs (blocks). Research topics included how learning depended on the number of attributes in the rule, the relations used in the rule (e.g., AND vs. OR), the way that category examples were presented (e.g., were they shown to the subject in a set order, or could the subject select the ones he or she wished?), the complexity of the stimuli, and so on. But whether this research is of interest to us depends on whether we accept the classical view. If we do not, then these experiments, although valid as examples of learning certain abstract rules, do not tell us about how people learn normal concepts. With that foreshadowing, let us turn to the problems raised for the classical view.

Problems for the Classical View

The groundbreaking work of Eleanor Rosch in the 1970s essentially killed the classical view, so that it is not now the theory of any actual researcher in this area (though we will see that a few theorists cling to it still). That is a pretty far fall for a theory that had been the dominant one since Aristotle. How did it happen? In part it happened by virtue of theoretical arguments and in part by the discovery of data that could not be easily explained by the classical view. Let us start with the arguments. Because this downfall of the classical view has been very ably described by Smith and Medin (1981) and others (e.g., Mervis and Rosch 1981; Rosch 1978), I will spend somewhat less time on this issue than could easily be spent on it. Interested readers should consult those reviews or the original articles cited below for more detailed discussion.

In-Principle Arguments

The philosopher Wittgenstein (1953) questioned the assumption that important concepts could be defined. He used the concept of a game as his example. It is maddeningly difficult to come up with a definition of games that includes them but does not include nongame sports (like hunting) or activities like kicking a ball against a wall. Wittgenstein urged his readers not to simply say "There *must* be something in common," but to try to specify the things in common. Indeed, it turns out to be very difficult to specify the necessary and sufficient features of *most* real-world categories. So, the definition we gave earlier of dogs, namely, things that have four legs, bark, have fur, eat meat, and sleep, is obviously not true. Does something have to have four legs to be a dog? Indeed, there are unfortunate dogs who have lost a leg or two. How about having fur? Although most dogs do have fur, there are hairless varieties like chihuahuas that don't. What about barking? Almost all dogs bark, but I have in fact known a dog that "lost" its bark as it got older. This kind of argument can go on for some time when trying to arrive at necessary features. One can find some features that seem a bit "more necessary" than these—abstract properties such as being animate and breathing appear to be true of all dogs (we are talking about real dogs here, and not toy dogs and the like). However, although these features may be necessary, they are not nearly sufficient. In fact, all animals are animate and breathe, not just dogs. So, features like these will not form adequate definitions for dogs—they won't separate dogs from other similar animals. Also, sometimes people will propose features such as "canine" as being definitional of dogs. However, this is just cheating. "Canine" is simply a synonym for the dog concept itself, and saying that this is part of the definition of dog is not very different from saying that the dogs all have the property of "dogginess." Clearly, such circular definitions explain nothing.

Wittgenstein's argument, which is now widely accepted in the field, does have a problem, however (Smith and Medin 1981): It is primarily negative. It says something like "I can't think of any defining features for games or dogs," but this does not prove that there aren't any. Perhaps it's just that we are not clever enough to think of the defining features. Perhaps there are defining features that will be realized or discovered in 100 years. This may be true, but it is incumbent on some-one who believes the classical view to explain what the defining features are, *and* why we can't easily think of them. If our concept of dogs is a definition, why are we so bad at saying what it is even when we know the concept? Why is it that we can use this definition for identifying dogs and for thinking about them, but the proper-ties we give for dogs are not definitional? The classical view has considerable trouble explaining this.

I used to think that the arguments against the classical view might be somewhat limited. In particular, it seemed likely to me that in certain technical domains, con-cepts might be well defined. For example, the rules of baseball are written down in black and white, and they look very much like the rules of old category-learning experiments (think of the disjunctive rule for a strike). Perhaps in the physical sciences, one will find classical concepts, as the scientists will have figured out the exact rules by which to decide something is a metal or a member of a biological genus. However, my own experience has always been that whenever one explores these domains in greater depth, one finds more and more fuzziness, rather than per-fectly clear rules.

For example, consider the following portion of a lecture on metals by a distin-guished metallurgist (Pond 1987). He begins by attempting, unsuccessfully, to get audience members to define what a metal is.

Well, I'll tell you something. You really don't know what a metal is. And there's a big group of people that don't know what a metal is. Do you know what we call them? Metal-lurgists!... Here's why metallurgists don't know what metal is. We know that a metal is an element that has metallic properties. So we start to enumerate all these properties: electrical conductivity, thermal conductivity, ductility, malleability, strength, high density. Then you say, how many of these properties does an element have to have to classify as a metal? And do you know what? We can't get the metallurgists to agree. Some say three properties; some say five properties, six properties. We really don't know. So we just proceed along presuming that we are all talking about the same thing. (pp. 62–63)

And in biology, biologists are constantly fighting about whether things are two dif-ferent species or not, and what species belong in the same genus, and so on. There is no defining feature that identifies biological kinds (Mayr 1982). In 2000, there was a dispute over whether Pluto is really a planet (apparently, it isn't, though it is too late to do anything about it now). Students in the town of Pluto's discoverer put up a web site demanding Pluto's retention as a full-fledged planet. Among their points was that the astronomers critical of Pluto's planethood "don't even have a definition of what a planet really is!" (Unfortunately, they did not provide their own defini-tion.) The very fact that astronomers can argue about such cases is evidence that the notion of planet is not well defined. The idea that all science consists of hard-and-fast logical categories, in contrast to those of everyday life, may be a romantic illusion.

One might well hope that legal concepts have a classical nature, so that definitions can be evenly applied across the board. One does not want judges and juries having to make decisions in fuzzy cases where there is no clear boundary between the legal and illegal. However, legal practice has found that in practice the law is sometimes very fuzzy, and legal theorists (e.g., Hart 1961) suggest that this is inevitably the case, because lawmakers cannot foresee all the possibilities the law will have to address, some of which do not exist at the time the law is passed (e.g., laws on intellectual property were written before the invention of the internet). Furthermore, since laws are written in language that uses everyday concepts, to the degree that these concepts are fuzzy, the law itself must be fuzzy. So, if one has a rule, "No vehicles in the park" (Hart 1961), does one interpret that to include wheelchairs? Maintenance vehicles? Ambulances? Bicycles? Although the law is stated in a simple, clear-cut manner, the fuzziness of the vehicle category prevents it from being entirely well-defined.[1]

Even artificial domains may have rules that are not particularly well defined. In 1999, Major League Baseball made a much publicized effort to clean up and standardize the strike zone, suggesting that my belief that strikes were well defined prior to that was a delusion. Perhaps the only hope for true classical concepts is within small, closed systems that simply do not permit exceptions and variation of the sort that is found in the natural world. For example, the rules of chess may create classical concepts, like bishops and castling. Baseball, on the other hand, has too much human behavior and judgment involved, and so its categories begin to resemble natural categories in being less well defined than the purist would like.

Empirical Problems

Unfortunately for the classical view, its empirical problems are even greater than its theoretical ones. One general problem is that the neatness envisioned by the classical view does not seem to be a characteristic of human concepts. As mentioned above, the notion of a definition implies that category membership can be discretely determined: The definition will pick out all the category members and none of the nonmembers. Furthermore, there is no need to make further distinctions among the members or among the nonmembers. In real life, however, there are many things that are not clearly in or out of a category. For example, many people express uncertainty about whether a tomato is a vegetable or a fruit. People are not sure about whether a low, three-legged seat with a little back is a chair or a stool. People do not always agree on whether sandals are a kind of shoe. This uncertainty gets even worse when more contentious categories in domains such as personality or aesthetics are considered. Is *Sergeant Pepper's Lonely Hearts Club Band* a work of art? Is your neighbor just shy or stuck up? These kinds of categorizations are often problematic.

Research has gone beyond this kind of anecdote. For example, Hampton (1979) asked subjects to rate a number of items on whether they were category members for different categories. He did not find that items were segregated into clear members and nonmembers. Instead, he found a number of items that were just barely considered category members and others that were just barely not members. His subjects just barely included sinks as members of the kitchen utensil category and just barely excluded sponges; they just included seaweed as a vegetable and just barely excluded tomatoes and gourds. Indeed, he found that for seven of the eight categories he investigated, members and nonmembers formed a continuum, with no obvious break in people's membership judgments.

Such results could be due to disagreements among different subjects. Perhaps 55% of the subjects thought that sinks were clearly kitchen utensils and 45% thought they were clearly not. This would produce a result in which sinks appeared to be a borderline case, even though every individual subject had a clear idea of whether they were category members or not. Thus, the classical view might be true for each individual, even though the group results do not show this. However, McCloskey and Glucksberg (1978) were able to make an even stronger argument for such unclear cases. They found that when people were asked to make repeated category judgments such as "Is an olive a fruit?" or "Is a dog an animal?" there was a subset of items that individual subjects changed their minds about. That is, if you said that an olive was a fruit on one day, two weeks later you might give the opposite answer. Naturally, subjects did not do this for cases like "Is a dog an animal?" or "Is a rose an animal?" But they did change their minds on borderline cases, such as olive-fruit, and curtains-furniture. In fact, for items that were intermediate between clear members and clear nonmembers, McCloskey and Glucksberg's subjects changed their mind 22% of the time. This may be compared to inconsistent decisions of under 3% for the best examples and clear nonmembers (see further discussion below). Thus, the changes in subjects' decisions do not reflect an overall inconsistency or lack of attention, but a bona fide uncertainty about the borderline members. In short, many concepts are not clear-cut. There are some items that one cannot make up one's mind about or that seem to be "kind of" members. An avo-

The Necessity of Category Fuzziness

The existence of unclear examples can be understood in part as arising from the great variation of things in the world combined with the limitations on our concepts. We do not wish to have a concept for every single object—such concepts would be of little use and would require enormous memory space. Instead, we want to have a fairly small number of concepts that are still informative enough to be useful (Rosch 1978). The ideal situation would probably be one in which these concepts did pick out objects in a classical-like way. Unfortunately, the world is not arranged so as to conform to our needs.

For example, it may be useful to distinguish chairs from stools, due to their differences in size and comfort. For the most part, we can distinguish the two based on the number of their legs, presence of a back or arms, and size. However, there is nothing to stop manufacturers from making things that are very large, comfortable stools; things that are just like chairs, only with three legs; or stools with a back. These intermediate items are the things that cause trouble for us, because they partake of the properties of both. We could try to solve this by forming different categories for stools with four legs (stegs), for chairs with three legs (chools), stools with backs (stoocks), stools with backs and arms (stoorms), and so on. But by doing so, we would end up increasing our necessary vocabulary by a factor of 5 or 10, depending on how many distinctions we added for every category. And there would still be the problem of intermediate items, as manufacturers would no doubt someday invent a combination that was between a stoock and a stoorm, and that would then be an atypical example of both. Just to be difficult, they would probably also make stools with no back, with very tiny backs, with somewhat tiny backs, . . . up to stools with enormous, high backs. Thus, there would be items in between the typical stools and stoocks where categorization would be uncertain.

The gradation of properties in the world means that our smallish number of categories will never map perfectly onto all objects: The distinction between members and nonmembers will always be difficult to draw or will even be arbitrary in some cases. If the world existed as much more distinct clumps of objects, then perhaps our concepts could be formed as the classical view says they are. But if the world consists of shadings and gradations and of a rich mixture of different kinds of properties, then a limited number of concepts would almost have to be fuzzy.

cado is "kind of a vegetable," even if it is not wholeheartedly a vegetable. The classical view has difficulty explaining this state of affairs; certainly, it did not predict it.

Another problem for the classical view has been the number of demonstrations of *typicality effects*. These can be illustrated by the following intuition. Think of a fish, any fish. Did you think of something like a trout or a shark, or did you think of an eel or a flounder? Most people would admit to thinking of something like the first: a torpedo-shaped object with small fins, bilaterally symmetrical, which swims in the water by moving its tail from side to side. Eels are much longer, and they slither; flounders are also differently shaped, aren't symmetrical, and move by waving their body in the vertical dimension. Although all of these things are technically fish, they do not all seem to be equally good examples of fish. The *typical* category members are the good examples—what you normally think of when you think of the category. The *atypical* objects are ones that are known to be members but that are unusual in some way. (Note that *atypical* means "not typical," rather than "a typical example." The stress is on the first syllable.) The classical view does not have any way of distinguishing typical and atypical category members. Since all the items in the category have met the definition's criteria, all are category members. (Later I will try to expand the classical view to handle this problem.)

What is the evidence for typicality differences? Typicality differences are probably the strongest and most reliable effects in the categorization literature. The simplest way to demonstrate this phenomenon is simply to ask people to rate items on how typical they think each item is of a category. So, you could give people a list of fish and ask them to rate how typical each one is of the category fish. Rosch (1975) did this task for 10 categories and looked to see how much subjects agreed with one another. She discovered that the reliability of typicality ratings was an extremely high .97 (where 1.0 would be perfect agreement)—though later studies have suggested that this is an overestimate (Barsalou 1987). In short, people agree that a trout is a typical fish and an eel is an atypical one.

But does typicality affect people's use of the categories? Perhaps the differences in ratings are just subjects' attempt to answer the question that experimenters are asking. Yes, a trout is a typical fish, but perhaps this does not mean that trouts are any better than eels in any other respect. Contrary to this suggestion, typicality differences influence many different behaviors and judgments involving concepts. For example, recall that I said earlier that McCloskey and Glucksberg (1978) found that subjects made inconsistent judgments for only a subset of their items. These items could be predicted on the basis of typicality. Subjects did not change their minds about the very typical items or the clear nonitems, but about items in the middle of the scale, the atypical members and the "close misses" among the nonmembers. For example, waste baskets are rated as atypical examples of furniture (4.70, where 1 is low and 10 is high), and subjects changed their minds about this item a surprising 30% of the time. They never changed their minds about tables, a very typical member (rated 9.83), or windows, a clear nonmember (rated 2.53).

Rips, Shoben, and Smith (1973) found that the ease with which people judged category membership depended on typicality. For example, people find it very easy to affirm that a robin is a bird but are much slower to affirm that a chicken (a less typical item) is a bird. This finding has also been found with visual stimuli: Identifying a picture of a chicken as a bird takes longer than identifying a pictured robin (Murphy and Brownell 1985; Smith, Balzano, and Walker 1978). The influence of typicality is not just in identifying items as category members—it also occurs with the production of items from a category. Battig and Montague (1969) performed a very large norming study in which subjects were given category names, like *furniture* or *precious stone* and had to produce examples of these categories. These data are still used today in choosing stimuli for experiments (though they are limited, as a number of common categories were not included). Mervis, Catlin and Rosch (1976) showed that the items that were most often produced in response to the category names were the ones rated as typical (by other subjects). In fact, the average correlation of typicality and production frequency across categories was .63, which is quite high given all the other variables that affect production.

When people learn artificial categories, they tend to learn the typical items before the atypical ones (Rosch, Simpson, and Miller 1976). Furthermore, learning is faster if subjects are taught on mostly typical items than if they are taught on atypical items (Mervis and Pani 1980; Posner and Keele 1968). Thus, typicality is not just a feeling that people have about some items ("trout good; eels bad")—it is important to the initial learning of the category in a number of respects. As we shall see when we discuss the explanations of typicality structure, there is a very good reason for typicality to have these influences on learning.

Learning is not the end of the influence, however. Typical items are more useful for inferences about category members. For example, imagine that you heard that eagles had caught some disease. How likely do you think it would be to spread to other birds? Now suppose that it turned out to be larks or robins who caught the disease. Rips (1975) found that people were more likely to infer that other birds would catch the disease when a typical bird, like robins, had it than when an atypical one, like eagles, had it (see also Osherson et al. 1990; and chapter 8).

As I will discuss in chapter 11, there are many influences of typicality on language learning and use. Just to mention some of them, there are effects on the order of word production in sentences and in comprehension of anaphors. Kelly, Bock, and

Keil (1986) showed that when subjects mentioned two category members together in a sentence, the more typical one is most likely to be mentioned first. That is, people are more likely to talk about "apples and limes" than about "limes and apples." Garrod and Sanford (1977) asked subjects to read stories with category members in them. For example, they might read about a goose. Later, a sentence would refer to that item with a category name, such as "The bird came in through the front door." Readers took longer to read this sentence when it was about a goose (an atypical bird) than when it was about a robin (a typical bird). Rosch (1975) found that typical items were more likely to serve as *cognitive reference points*. For example, people were more likely to say that a patch of off-red color (atypical) was "virtually" the same as a pure red color (typical) than they were to say the reverse. Using these kinds of nonlinguistic stimuli showed that the benefit of the more typical color was not due to word frequency or other aspects of the words themselves. Similarly, people prefer to say that 101 is virtually 100 rather than 100 is virtually 101.

This list could go on for some time. As a general observation, one can say that whenever a task requires someone to relate an item to a category, the item's typicality influences performance. This kind of result is extremely robust. In fact, if one compares different category members and does *not* find an effect of typicality, it suggests that there is something wrong with—or at least unusual about—the experiment. It is unfortunate for the classical view, therefore, that it does not predict the most prevalent result in the field. Even if it is not specifically disproved by typicality effects (see below), it is a great shortcoming that the view does not actually explain why and how they come about, since these effects are ubiquitous.

Revision of the Classical View

As a result of the theoretical arguments and the considerable evidence against the classical view, a number of writers have attempted to revise it so that it can handle the typicality data and unclear members. The main way to handle this has been to make a distinction between two aspects of category representation, which I will call the *core* and *identification procedures* (following Miller and Johnson-Laird 1976; see Armstrong, Gleitman, and Gleitman 1983; Osherson and Smith 1981; Smith and Medin 1981; and Smith, Rips, and Shoben 1974 for similar ideas). The basic idea is as follows. Although concepts do have definitions (which we have not yet been able to discover), people have also learned other things about them that aren't definitional. This kind of information helps us to identify category members or to use information that is not defining. For example, not all dogs have fur, so having fur cannot be part of the definition of the dog category. However, it is still useful to use fur as a way of identifying dogs, because so many of them do have it. Thus, "fur" would be part of the identification procedure by which we tell what actual dogs are, but it would not be part of the concept core, which contains only the definition. One could call "fur" a *characteristic feature*, since it is generally true of dogs even if not always true: Characteristically, dogs have fur.

Part of the problem with this proposal is that it is not clear what the concept core is supposed to do. If it isn't used to identify the category members, then what is it for? All the typicality effects listed above must arise from the identification procedure, since the category core by definition (sic) does not distinguish typicality of members. One proposal is that people use the identification procedure for fast and less reliable categorization, but that they will use the category core for more careful categorization or reasoning (e.g., Armstrong et al. 1983; Smith et al. 1974). Thus, when tasks involve more careful thought, with less time pressure than in many experiments, people might be encouraged to use the category core more. For example, Armstrong et al. (1983) found that people took longer to identify less typical even numbers than more typical ones (e.g., 4 is a more typical even number than 38 is). However, since subjects know the rule involving even numbers and are extremely accurate at this, they may use the category core to ultimately decide the question. Whether this argument can be extended to items that do not have such a clear rule, of course, needs to be considered.

In summary, on this revised view, the effects of typicality result from the identification procedures, whereas certain other behaviors (primarily categorization decisions) depend primarily on the concept core.

I will criticize this theory at the end of the chapter. However, there have been some empirical tests of this proposal as well. First, Hampton's (1979) study mentioned above also included a component in which subjects listed properties of different categories, and he attempted to separate defining from characteristic features. For example, subjects first said what properties they used to decide that something was a fruit. Other subjects then evaluated examples of fruit and similar objects to see which ones had the properties. So, they would have considered whether apple and avocado have properties such as "is from a plant," "is eaten," and "has an outer layer of skin or peel," which were mentioned by other subjects as being critical features. Hampton derived a list of necessary features for each category, by including the listed features that were found in all the category members. For example, all the items that his subjects identified as fruit had the feature "is eaten," and so this was a necessary feature. The question he next asked was whether these features were defining: If an item had all these features, would it be in the category? The answer is no. He found many cases of items that had all of these necessary features but were not considered to be category members. For example, cucumbers and garlic had all of the necessary features for fruit but were not considered to be category members. This, then, is another failure to find defining features of actual categories. Furthermore, Hampton found that when he simply counted up how many relevant features each item had (not just the necessary features, but all of them), he could predict how likely people were to include the item as a category member. But since all members would be expected to have the defining features (according to the revised classical view), the number of other features should not predict category membership. Thus, nondefining features are important in deciding category membership— not just core features.

In more recent work, Hampton (1988b, 1995) has examined the relationship between typicality measures and category membership judgments. According to the revised classical view, typicality is not truly related to category membership but simply reflects identification procedures. So extremely atypical items like whales or penguins are just as much mammals and birds, respectively, as typical examples are (Armstrong et al. 1983; Osherson and Smith 1981). However, Hampton's results in a number of domains show that typicality ratings are the best predictor of untimed category judgments, the ones that should only involve the core. These results appear to directly contradict the revised classical view.

One reason for the popularity of the classical view has been its ties to traditional logic (Inhelder and Piaget 1964). For example, how does one evaluate sentences of the sort "All dogs are animals" or "Coach is a dog and a pet"? Propositional logic tells us that "Coach is a dog and a pet" is true if "Coach is a dog" and "Coach is a pet" are both true. This can be easily accommodated in the classical view by the argument that "Coach is a dog and a pet" is true if Coach has the necessary and sufficient features of both dogs and pets. Surprisingly, there is empirical evidence suggesting that people do not follow this rule. Hampton (1988b) found that people are willing to call something a member of a conjunctive category (X AND Y) even if it is not in both components (X, Y). For example, subjects believe that chess is in the category sports that are also games, but they do not believe that it is a sport. So, chess seems to fulfill the definition for sport in one context but not in another. He also found (Hampton 1997) that subjects believed that tree houses are in the category of dwellings that are not buildings, but they also believe them to be buildings. So, on different occasions, people say that it does and does not have the defining features of buildings. Although very troublesome for the classical view, these examples have a very natural explanation on other views, as is explained in chapter 12.

A related advantage that has been proposed for the classical view is that it has a very natural way of explaining how categories can be *hierarchically ordered*. By this I mean that categories can form nested sets in which each category includes the ones "below" it. For example, a single object could be called Coach (his name), a yellow labrador retriever, a labrador retriever, a retriever, a dog, a mammal, a vertebrate, and an animal. These particular categories are significant because *all* yellow labs are dogs, all dogs are mammals, all vertebrates are animals, and so on. As we will see in chapter 7, this aspect of categories has been thought to be quite significant. The classical view points out that if all X are Y, then the definition of Y must be included in the definition of X. For example, all red triangles are triangles. Therefore, red triangles must be closed, three-sided figures, because this is the definition of a triangle. Similarly, whatever the definition of labradors is, that must be included in the definition of yellow labs, because all yellow labs are labradors. This rule ensures that category membership is *transitive*. If all As are Bs, and all Bs are Cs, then all As must be Cs. Since the definition of C must be included in B (because all Bs are Cs), and the definition of B must be included in A (because all As are Bs), the definition of C must thereby be included in A. The nesting of definitions provides a way of explaining how categories form hierarchies.

Hampton (1982) suspected that there might be failures of transitivity, which would pose a significant problem for the classical view. He asked subjects to decide whether items were members of two categories—one of them a subset of the other. For example, subjects decided whether an armchair is a chair and whether it is furniture. They also had to judge whether chairs are furniture (they are). Hampton found a number of cases in which an item was judged to be a member of the subset category but not the higher category—that is, examples of chairs that were not thought to be furniture. For instance, subjects judged that chairs were furniture and that a car seat was a chair; however, they usually denied that a car seat was furniture. But if a car seat has the defining features of chairs, and chairs have the defining features of furniture, then car seat must have the defining features of furniture. It should be pointed out that Hampton's task was not a speeded, perceptual judgment, but a more leisurely decision about category membership, which is just the sort of judgment that should involve the concept core. It is puzzling to the revised classical view that even such judgments do not show the use of definitions in the way that is expected. However, we will see later that this kind of intransitivity is easily explained by other views.

Finally, a theoretical problem with the revised classical view is that the concept core does not in general appear to be an important part of the concept, in spite of its name and theoretical intention as representing the "real" concept. As mentioned earlier, almost every conceptual task has shown that there are unclear examples and variation in typicality of category members. Because the concept core does not allow such variation, all these tasks must be explained primarily by reference to the identification procedure and characteristic features. So, if it takes longer to verify that a chicken is a bird than that a bluejay is a bird, this cannot be explained by the concept core, since chicken and bluejay equally possess the core properties of birds, according to this view. Instead, chicken and bluejays differ in characteristic features, such as their size and ability to fly. Thus, speeded judgments must not be relying on the category core. When this reasoning is applied to all the tasks that show such typicality effects, including category learning, speeded and unspeeded categorization, rating tasks, language production and comprehension, vocabulary learning, and category-based induction, the concept core is simply not explaining most of the data. As a result, most researchers have argued that the concept core can simply be done away with, without any loss in the ability to explain the results (see especially Hampton 1979, 1982, 1995).

Summary of Typicality as a Phenomenon

Before going on to the more recent theoretical accounts of typicality phenomena, it is useful to discuss these phenomena in a theory-neutral way. Somewhat confusingly, the phenomena are often referred to as revealing a *prototype structure* to concepts. (This is confusing, because there is a prototype *theory* that is a particular theory of these results, so sometimes *prototype* refers to the phenomenon and sometimes the specific theory. This is not an isolated case of terminological confusion in the field, as you will see.) A prototype is the best example of a category. One can think of category members, then, arranged in order of "goodness," in which the things that are very similar to the prototype are thought of as being very typical or good members, and things that are not very similar as being less typical or good members (Rosch 1975).

One way to illustrate this concept concretely is by the dot-pattern studies of Posner and Keele (1968, 1970), since it is very clear what the prototype is in their experiments. (Also, these are historically important experiments that are of interest in their own right.) Posner and Keele first generated a pattern of randomly positioned dots (see figure 2.2a) as the category prototype. From this pattern, they made

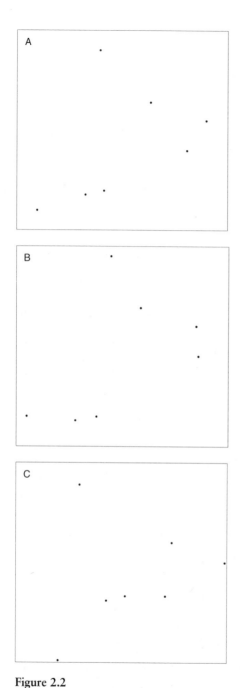

Figure 2.2
Dot patterns of the sort used by Posner and Keele (1968, 1970). 2.2a represents the initial randomly placed dots, the prototype. 2.2b represents a small distortion of the prototype, in which each dot is moved a small distance in a random direction. 2.2c represents a large distortion, in which each dot is moved a large distance. On can make indefinitely many such stimuli by generating a different (random) direction for each dot.

many more patterns of dots, by moving each point in the original pattern in a random direction. In some cases, they moved the points a small amount in that random
direction (as in figure 2.2b), and for other items, they moved the points a large
amount (as in figure 2.2c). These new patterns were called "distortions" of the
original. Here, it is clear that the prototype is the most typical, best member of the
category, because it was the basis for making the other patterns. However, it is also
the case that the distortions were all somewhat similar to one another by virtue of
the fact that they were constructed from the same prototype. Indeed, subjects who
viewed only the distortions of four prototypes were able to learn the categories by
noticing this similarity (they had no idea how the patterns were made). Furthermore, the prototype itself was identified as a member of the category in test trials,
even though subjects had never seen it during learning.[2] Finally, the items that were
made from small distortions were learned better than items made from large distortions. And when subjects were tested on new items that they had not specifically
been trained on, they were more accurate on the smaller distortions. Figure 2.2
illustrates this nicely: If you had learned that a category looked generally like the
pattern in 2.2a (the prototype), you would find it easier to classify 2.2b into that
category than you would 2.2c. In summary, the smaller the distortion, the more
typical an item was, and the more accurately it was classified.

This example illustrates in a very concrete way how prototypes might be thought
of in natural categories. Each category might have a most typical item—not necessarily one that was specifically learned, but perhaps an average or ideal example
that people extract from seeing real examples. You might have an idea of the prototypical dog, for example, that is average-sized, dark in color, has medium-length
fur, has a pointed nose and floppy ears, is a family pet, barks at strangers, drools
unpleasantly, and has other common features of dogs. Yet, this prototype may be
something that you have never specifically seen—it is just your abstraction of what
dogs are most often like. Other dogs vary in their similarity to this prototype, and so
they differ in their typicality. Miniature hairless dogs are not very similar to the
prototype, and they are considered atypical; St. Bernards are not very similar, albeit
in a different way, and so they are also atypical; a collie is fairly similar to the prototype, so it is considered fairly typical; and so on. As items become less and less
similar to the prototype, it is more and more likely that they won't be included in
the category. So, if you saw a thing with four legs but a very elongated body, no
hair, and whiskers, you might think that it was somewhat similar to a dog, but not
similar enough to actually be a dog. However, this is the point at which different
people might disagree, and you might change your mind. That is, as similarity gets

lower, there is no clear answer as to whether the item is or isn't in the category. Furthermore, as the item becomes more similar to other categories, the chance increases that it will be seen as an atypical member of that other category. You might decide that your friend's exotic, hairless pet is a weird cat instead of a weird dog.

In short, typicality is a graded phenomenon, in which items can be extremely typical (close to the prototype), moderately typical (fairly close), atypical (not close), and finally borderline category members (things that are about equally distant from two different prototypes). This sort of description summarizes the range of typicality that is often seen in categories. Researchers of all theoretical persuasions talk about category prototypes, borderline cases, and typical and less typical items in this way. However, this way of thinking about typicality should not make us assume that people actually represent the category by a single prototype, like Posner and Keele's original dot pattern, or the best possible dog. There are a number of other ways that they could be representing this information, which I will discuss in the next section and next chapter.

Theoretical Explanations of Prototype Phenomena

What Makes Items Typical and Atypical

What makes something typical or atypical? Why is penguin an atypical bird but sparrow a typical bird? Why should a desk chair be typical but a rocking chair less typical? One possible answer is simple frequency. In North America and Europe (where most of the research on this topic has been done), penguins are seldom if ever seen, whereas sparrows are often seen; there are a lot more desk chairs than rocking chairs, perhaps. This is one part of the answer, but things are not so simple. For example, there are some quite frequent items that are still thought to be atypical of their category. For example, chickens are a very frequently talked-about kind of bird, but they are not considered as typical as some infrequently encountered and discussed birds, such as the oriole or catbird (Rosch 1975) (e.g., I cannot say for certain that I have ever seen an oriole or catbird, but I see chickens fairly often). Similarly, handball is a much more typical sport than car racing (Rosch 1975), even though racing is more popular, is reported in the media, and so on. Mervis et al. (1976) found that simple frequency of an item's name did not predict its typicality. In fact, in the eight common categories they examined (birds, tool, fruit, etc.), none of the correlations of name frequency with typicality was reliably different from 0.

The best answer to the question of what makes something typical is related to the frequency of the item but is a bit more complex: Rosch and Mervis (1975) argued that items are typical when they have high *family resemblance* with members of the category: "... members of a category come to be viewed as prototypical of the category as a whole in proportion to the extent to which they bear a family resemblance to (have attributes which overlap those of) other members of the category. Conversely, items viewed as most prototypical of one category will be those with least family resemblance to or membership in other categories" (p. 575).[3] That is, typical items (1) tend to have the properties of other category members but (2) tend not to have properties of category nonmembers. For example, an oriole is of the same size as many birds, perches in trees, flies (common bird behaviors), has two wings (universal among birds), and so on. Therefore, even though orioles are not very frequent in my experience, I can recognize them as typical birds because they have frequent bird properties. In contrast, chickens, which I see much more often, are large for birds, white (not a very usual color), do not fly (not common among birds), are eaten (not common), and so on. So, even though chickens themselves are fairly common, their *properties* are not very common as properties for birds, and so they are atypical birds.

Rosch and Mervis (1975) supported this claim in a number of ways. Because their study is so important, I will discuss it in some detail. First, they examined a number of different natural categories[4] to see if they could predict which items would be typical or atypical. Rosch and Mervis selected twenty members of six general categories. Two examples are shown in table 2.1. They had subjects rate each item for how typical it was of its category, and that is reflected in table 2.1 in the order the items are listed (e.g., chair is the most typical furniture, and telephone the least typical). Then Rosch and Mervis had new subjects list the attributes of each of the items. The question was whether typical items would have more of the common attributes than would atypical items. However, there is a problem with just listing attributes, which is that people are not always very good at spontaneously producing attributes for items. If you were to look at such data, you would see that some subjects have produced an attribute for an item, but others have not. Is this because the latter just forgot, or weren't as careful in doing the task? In some cases, that seems likely. Furthermore, it is often the case that attributes listed for one item seem to be equally true for another item, for which it was not listed. For example, people might list "has four legs" for chair but not for bed. Because of this kind of problem (see Tversky and Hemenway 1984 for discussion), Rosch and Mervis asked judges to go through the list of attributes and to decide whether the attributes were true of all the items. So, if some subjects listed "has four legs" for chairs, the judges would decide whether it was also true for the other items of furniture. The judges also elimi-

Table 2.1.
Examples of items studied by Rosch and Mervis (1975), ordered by typicality.

Furniture	Fruit
chair	orange
sofa	apple
table	banana
dresser	peach
desk	pear
bed	apricot
bookcase	plum
footstool	grapes
lamp	strawberry
piano	grapefruit
cushion	pineapple
mirror	blueberry
rug	lemon
radio	watermelon
stove	honeydew
clock	pomegranate
picture	date
closet	coconut
vase	tomato
telephone	olive

nated any features that were clearly and obviously incorrect. This *judge-amending process* is now a standard technique for processing attribute-listing data.

Finally, Rosch and Mervis weighted each attribute by how many items it occurred in. If "has four legs" occurred in ten examples of furniture, it would have a weight of 10; if "is soft" occurred in only two examples, it would receive a weight of 2. Finally, they added up these scores for each feature listed for an item. So, if chair had eighteen features listed, its score would be the sum of the weights of those eighteen features. This technique results in the items with the most common features in the category having the highest scores. Rosch and Mervis found that this feature score was highly predictive of typicality (correlations for individual categories ranged from .84 to .91). That is, the items that were most typical had features that were very common in the category. The less typical items had different features. This result has been replicated by Malt and Smith (1984). Rosch and Mervis illustrated this in a clever way by looking at the five most typical items and five least typical items in each category and counting how many features they each had in common.

They found that the five most typical examples of furniture (chair, sofa, table, dresser, and desk) had thirteen attributes in common. In contrast, the five least typical examples (clock, picture, closet, vase, and telephone) had only two attributes in common. For fruit, the five most typical items had sixteen attributes in common, but the least typical ones had absolutely no attributes in common.

This result gives evidence for the first part of the family-resemblance hypothesis, but what about the second part, that typical items will not have features that are found in other categories? This turns out to be much more difficult to test, because one would have to find out the attributes not just of the target categories (say, fruit and furniture), but also of all other related categories, so that one could see which items have features from those categories. For example, if olives are less typical fruit because they are salty, we need to know if saltiness is a typical attribute of other categories, and so we would need to get feature listings of other categories like vegetables, meats, desserts, grains, and so on, which would be an enormous amount of work. (If I have not made it clear yet, attribute listings are very time-consuming and labor-intensive to collect, as individual subjects can list features of only so many concepts, all of which then must be transcribed, collated, and judge-amended by new subjects.) So, this aspect of the hypothesis is not so easy to test. Nonetheless, Rosch and Mervis were able to test it for two more specific categories (chair and car, Experiment 4), and they found evidence for this hypothesis too. That is, the more often an item had features from a different category, the less typical it was (correlations of −.67 and −.86).

Both of these studies are correlational. Like most studies of natural categories, the underlying variables that were thought to be responsible for the phenomenon (typicality) were simply observed in the items—the researchers did not manipulate them. As is well known, this leads to the correlation-causation problem, in which there could be some other variable that was not directly measured but was actually responsible for the typicality. Perhaps the most typical items were more familiar, or pleasant, or ... (add your favorite confounding variable). Thus, Rosch and Mervis (1975) also performed experimental studies of family resemblance that were not subject to this problem. They used lists of alphanumeric strings for items, such as GKNTJ and 8SJ3G. Each string was an exemplar, and subjects had to learn to place each exemplar into one of two categories. The exemplars were constructed so that some items had more common features (within the category) than others. Rosch and Mervis found that the items with higher family-resemblance scores were learned sooner and were rated as more typical than were items with lower scores. For these artificial stimuli, there is little question of other variables that might explain away the results for natural stimuli. In a final experiment, Rosch and Mervis varied the amount of overlap of an item's features with the contrast category. So, one item had only features that occurred in Category 1; another item had four features that occurred in Category 1, and one that occurred in Category 2; a different item had three features that occurred in Category 1, and two that occurred in Category 2; and so on. They found that the items with greater overlap with the other category were harder to learn and were rated as much less typical after the learning phase.

In summary, Rosch and Mervis's (1975) study provided evidence for their family-resemblance hypothesis that items are typical (1) if they have features common in their category and (2) do not have features common to other categories. Unfortunately, there is some confusion in the field over the term "family resemblance." I have been using it here as indicating both parts of Rosch and Mervis's hypothesis. However, other writers sometimes refer to "family resemblance" as being only the within-category component (1 above).[5] In fact, the between-category aspect is often ignored in descriptions of this view. It is important to note, though, that whatever name one uses, it is *both* having features common within a category and the lack of features overlapping other categories that determine typicality according to this view, and Rosch and Mervis provided support for both variables influencing typicality.

This view of what makes items typical has stood the test of time well. The major addition to it was made by Barsalou (1985), who did a more complex study of what determines typicality in natural categories. Using most of the same categories that Rosch and Mervis did, such as vehicles, clothing, birds, and fruit, Barsalou measured three variables. *Central tendency* was, roughly speaking, the family-resemblance idea of Rosch and Mervis, though only including within-category resemblance. The items that were most similar to other items in the category had the highest central tendency scores. *Frequency of instantiation* was the frequency with which an item occurred as a member of the category, as assessed by subjects' ratings. Barsalou felt that the simple frequency of an item (e.g., chicken vs. lark) was probably not as important as how often an item was thought of as being a member of the category, and frequency of instantiation measured this. *Ideals* was the degree to which each item fit the primary goal of each category. Here, Barsalou selected, based on his own intuitions, a dimension that seemed critical to each category. For example, for the category of vehicle, the dimension was how efficient it was for transportation.

Subjects rated the items on these dimensions and also rated the typicality of each item to its category. The results, then, were the correlations between these different measures and each item's typicality.

Barsalou's results provided evidence for all three variables. Indeed, when he statistically controlled for any two of the variables (using a partial correlation), the remaining variable was still significant. Strongest was the central tendency measure. The items that were most similar to other category members were most typical—the partial correlation was .71. This is not surprising, given Rosch and Mervis's results. More surprising was the reliable effect of frequency of instantiation (partial correlation of .36). Consistent with Mervis et al. (1976), Barsalou found that the pure frequency of any item (e.g., the familiarity of chicken and lark) did not predict typicality. However, the frequency with which an item occurred as a category member did predict typicality. This suggests that thinking of an item as being a category member increases its typicality, perhaps through an associative learning process (though see below).

Finally, the effect of ideals was also significant (partial correlation of .45). For example, the most typical vehicles were the ones that were considered efficient means of transportation, and the most typical fruit were those that people liked (to eat). This effect is not very consistent with the Rosch and Mervis proposal, since it does not have to do with the relation of the item to other category members, but with the relation of the item to some more abstract function or goal. Barsalou (1985) presented the results for each category separately, and an examination of the results shows that ideals were quite effective predictors for artifact categories like vehicles, clothing and weapons, but less so for natural kinds like birds, fruit and vegetables.[6] As Barsalou himself notes, since he only used one ideal per category, and since he derived them based on his own intuitions, it is possible that ideals are even more important than his results reveal. If more comprehensive testing for the best ideals had been done, they might have accounted for even more of the typicality ratings. Indeed, a recent study by Lynch, Coley, and Medin (2000) found that tree experts' judgments of typicality were predicted by ideal dimensions of "weediness" and height, but not by the similarity of the trees. Weediness refers to an aesthetic and functional dimension of how useful trees are for landscaping. Strong, healthy, good-looking trees are typical based on this factor. The importance of height is not entirely clear; it may also be aesthetic, or it may be related to family resemblance, in that trees are taller than most plants, and so tall trees are more typical. Surprisingly, the variable of centrality—that is, similarity to other trees (Rosch and Mervis's 1975 first factor)—did not predict typicality above and beyond these two factors.

These results suggest the need for further exploring how important ideals are relative to family resemblance in general.

The importance of ideals in determining typicality is that they suggest that the category's place in some broader knowledge structure could be important. That is, people don't just learn that tools are things like hammers, saws, and planes, but they also use more general knowledge about what tools are used for and why we have them in order to represent the category. Category members that best serve those functions may be seen as more typical, above and beyond the specific features they share with other members.

As mentioned above, correlational studies of this sort, although important to carry out, can have the problem of unclear causal connections. In this case, the frequency of instantiation variable has a problem of interpreting the directionality of the causation. Is it that frequently thinking of something as being a category member makes it more typical? Or is it that more typical things are likely to be thought of as being category members? Indeed, the second possibility seems more likely to me. For example, Barsalou found that typical items are more likely to be generated first when people think of a category. When people think of examples of weapons, for example, they hardly ever start with spears or guard dogs; they are more likely to start with typical items like guns and knives. Frequency of instantiation, then, could well be an effect of the typicality of items, rather than vice versa. Similarly, the effect of ideals might also have come after the category's typicality was determined. That is, perhaps the ideal of vehicles came about (or occurred to Barsalou) as a result of thinking about typical vehicles and what their purposes were. It is not clear which is the chicken and which is the egg.

Barsalou addressed this problem in an experimental study of the importance of ideals. He taught subjects new categories of kinds of people. Subjects in one category tended to jog (though at different frequencies), and subjects in another tended to read the newspaper (at different frequencies). Barsalou told subjects that the two categories were either physical education teachers and current events teachers, or else that they were teachers of computer programming languages Q or Z. His idea was that the joggers would tend to be perceived as fulfilling an ideal dimension (physical fitness) when the category was physical education teachers but not when the category was teachers of language Q; similarly, the newspaper readers would fit an ideal (being informed) when they were current events teachers but not when they were teachers of language Z. And indeed, amount of jogging influenced typicality ratings for the categories described as physical education teachers, but not for the category labeled teachers of language Q even though both categories had the exact same learning items. That is, the family-resemblance structures of the items were identical—what varied was which ideal was evoked.

This experiment, then, confirms part of the correlational study that Barsalou (1985) reported for natural categories. Ideals are important for determining typicality above and beyond any effects of family resemblance. A number of later studies have replicated this kind of result, and are discussed in chapter 6 (Murphy and Allopenna 1994; Spalding and Murphy 1996; Wattenmaker et al. 1986; Wisniewski 1995). Studies of experts have found even more evidence of the use of ideals (Medin, Lynch, Coley, and Atran 1997; Proffitt, Coley, and Medin 2000).

These studies do not show that family resemblance is not a determinant of typicality, but that there are also other determinants that Rosch and Mervis (1975) would not have predicted. Thus, I am not suggesting that their view is incorrect but that it is only a partial story, for some categories at least. They are clearly correct, however, in saying that frequency in and of itself does not account for typicality to any great degree (see also Malt and Smith 1982). Whether frequency of instantiation is an important variable is less clear. Barsalou's results do give evidence for its being related to typicality. However, since this variable has not been experimentally tested, the result is subject to the counterargument raised above, that it is a function of typicality rather than vice versa. This, therefore, is still an open issue.

End of the Classical View?
The classical view appears only very sporadically after this point in the book. To a considerable degree, it has simply ceased to be a serious contender in the psychology of concepts. The reasons, described at length above, can be summarized as follows. First, it has been extremely difficult to find definitions for most natural categories, and even harder to find definitions that are plausible psychological representations that people of all ages would be likely to use. Second, the phenomena of typicality and unclear membership are both unpredicted by the classical view. It must be augmented with other assumptions—which are exactly the assumptions of the nonclassical theories—to explain these things. Third, the existence of intransitive category decisions (car seats are chairs; chairs are furniture; but car seats are not furniture) is very difficult to explain on the classical view. The classical view has not predicted many other phenomena of considerable interest in the field, which we will be discussing in later chapters, such as exemplar effects, base rate neglect, the existence of a basic level of categorization, the order in which children acquire words, and so on. In some cases, it is very difficult to see how to adapt this view to be consistent with those effects.

In summary, the classical core has very little to do, as most of the interesting and robust effects in the field cannot be explained by cores but must refer to the characteristic features. This is true not only for speeded judgments, but even for careful categorizations done without time constraints.

In spite of all this, there have been a number of attempts to revive the classical view in theoretical articles, sometimes written by philosophers rather than by psychologists (Armstrong et al. 1983; Rey 1983; Sutcliffe 1993). This is a bit difficult to explain, because the view simply does not predict the main phenomena in the field, even if it can be augmented and changed in various ways to be more consistent with them (as discussed in the core-plus-identification procedure idea). Why are writers so interested in saving it? To some degree, I believe that it is for historical reasons. After all, this is a view that has a long history in psychology, and in fact has been part of Western thinking since Aristotle. (Aristotle!) If this were a theory that you or I had made up, it would not have continued to receive this attention after the first 10 or 20 experiments showing it was wrong. But our theory would not have this history behind it. Another reason is that there is a beauty and simplicity in the classical view that succeeding theories do not have. It is consistent with the law of excluded middle and other traditional rules of logic beloved of philosophers. To be able to identify concepts through definitions of sufficient and necessary properties is an elegant way of categorizing the world, and it avoids a lot of sloppiness that comes about through prototype concepts (like the intransitive category decisions, and unclear members). Unfortunately, the world appears to be a sloppy place.

A final reason that these revivals of the classical view are attempted is, I believe, because the proponents usually do not attempt to explain a wide range of empirical data. The emphasis on philosophical concerns is related to this. Most of these writers are not starting from data and trying to explain them but are instead starting from a theoretical position that requires classical concepts and then are trying to address the psychological criticisms of it.[7] In fact, much of the support such writers give *for* the classical view is simply criticism of the evidence *against* it. For example, it has been argued that typicality is not necessarily inconsistent with a classical concept for various reasons, or that our inability to think of definitions is not really a problem. However, even if these arguments were true (and I don't think they are), this is a far cry from actually explaining the evidence. A theory should not be held just because the criticisms of it can be argued against—the theory must itself provide a compelling account of the data. People who held the classical view in 1972 certainly did not predict the results of Rips et al. (1973), Rosch (1975), Rosch and Mervis (1975), Hampton (1979, 1988b, or 1995), or any of the other experiments that helped to overturn it. It was only after such data were well established that classical theorists proposed reasons for why these results might not pose problems for an updated classical view.

As I mentioned earlier, there is no specific theory of concept representation that is based on the classical view at the time of this writing, even though there are a number of writers who profess to believe in this view. The most popular theories of concepts are based on prototype or exemplar theories that are strongly unclassical. Until there is a more concrete proposal that is "classical" and that can positively explain a wide variety of evidence of typicality effects (rather than simply criticize the arguments against it), we must conclude that this theory is not a contender. Thus, although it pops up again from time to time, I will not be evaluating it in detail in the remainder of this book.

3
Theories

As described in the previous chapter, the classical view has taken a big fall. Into this vacuum other theories developed that did not assume that concepts were represented by definitions and so were not subject to the problems the classical view suffered. This chapter will consider the three main kinds of theories that arose after the downfall of the classical view. The goal here is not to comprehensively evaluate these theories, as that can be done only over the course of the entire book, after the complete range of relevant data has been presented. Instead, this chapter will introduce the three general approaches that are most current in the field and explain how they deal with the typicality phenomena that caused such a problem for the classical view.

The Prototype View

One of the main critics of the classical view of concepts was Eleanor Rosch, who provided much of the crucial evidence that revealed the shortcomings of a definitional approach to concepts. Rosch's writings also provided the basis for a number of the early alternatives to the classical view, all under the rubric of the *prototype view*.

A number of readers interpreted Rosch as suggesting that every category is represented by a single prototype or best example. That is, perhaps your category of dogs is represented by a single ideal dog, which best embodies all the attributes normally found in dogs. I gave such an interpretation in the previous chapter as one way of understanding the existence of typicality. For example, very typical items would be those that are similar to this prototype; borderline items would be only somewhat similar to this prototype and somewhat similar to other prototypes as well. (The dot-pattern experiments of Posner and Keele 1968, 1970, encouraged this interpretation as well, as their categories were constructed from a literal prototype.)

Rosch, however, explicitly denied that this was her proposal (Rosch and Mervis 1975, p. 575), though it must be said that her writing often encouraged this interpretation. She preferred to be open-minded about how exactly typicality structure was represented, focusing instead on documenting that it existed and influenced category learning and judgments in important ways.

The idea that a single prototype could represent a whole category is questionable. For example, is there really an "ideal bird" that could represent all birds, large and small; white, blue, and spotted; flightless and flying; singing, cackling, and silent; carnivorous and herbivorous? What single item could pick out penguins, ostriches, pelicans, hummingbirds, turkeys, parrots, and sparrows? It seems unlikely that a single representation could encompass all of these different possibilities (Medin and Schwanenflugel 1981). Furthermore, a single prototype would give no information about the variability of a category. Perhaps some categories are fairly narrow, allowing only a small amount of variation, whereas others have very large variation (e.g., compare the incredible variety of dogs to the much smaller diversity of cats). If each category were represented by a single "best example," there would be no way to represent this difference (see Posner and Keele 1968, for an experimental demonstration).

In short, the notion of a single prototype as a category representation, which I'll call the *best example* idea, has not been very widely adopted. Instead, the prototype view proposed by Rosch has most often been interpreted as a summary representation that is a description of the category as a whole, rather than describing a single, ideal member. The view I'll discuss was proposed by Hampton (1979) and was fleshed out by Smith and Medin (1981), although its roots lie in Rosch and Mervis (1975).

A critical component of the prototype view is that it is a *summary representation* (just why this is critical will be apparent when the exemplar view is discussed): The entire category is represented by a unified representation rather than separate representations for each member or for different classes of members. This may sound just like the single best example idea that I have just criticized, but you will see that this representation is considerably more complex than that.

The representation itself could be described in terms much like Rosch and Mervis's (1975) family-resemblance view. The concept is represented as features that are usually found in the category members, but some features are more important than others. It is important for weapons that they be able to hurt you, but not so important that they be made of metal, even though many weapons are. Thus, the feature "can do harm" would be highly weighted in the representation, whereas the feature "made of metal" would not be. Where do these weights come from? One possibility is that they are the family-resemblance scores that Rosch and Mervis derived (see previous chapter). That is, the more often a feature appears in the category and does not appear in other categories, the higher its weight will be. Unlike a best-example representation, this list of features can include contradictory features with their weights. For example, the single best example of a dog might be short-haired. However, people also realize that some dogs have very long hair and a few have short hair. These cannot all be represented in a single best example. The feature list would represent this information, however. It might include "short hair," and give it a high weight; "long hair," with a lower weight; and "hairless" with a very low weight. In this way, the variability in a category is implicitly represented. Dimensions that have low variability might have a single feature with high weight (e.g., "has two ears" might have a high weight, and "has three ears" would presumably not be listed at all). Dimensions with high variability (like the colors of dogs) would have many features listed ("white," "brown," "black," "orange-ish," "spotted"), and each one would have a low weight. Such a pattern would implicitly represent the fact that dogs are rather diverse in their coloring. This system, then, gives much more information than a single best example would.

One aspect of this proposal that is not clearly settled yet is what to do with continuous dimensions that do not have set feature values. So, how does one represent the size of birds, for example: as "small," "medium," and "large," or as some continuous measurement of size? If it is a continuous measurement, then feature counting must be somewhat more sophisticated, since items with tiny differences in size should presumably count as having the same size feature, even if they are not identical. Perhaps for such continuous dimensions, what is remembered is the average rather than the exact features. Another idea is that features that are distinctive are counted, whereas those that are close together are averaged. So, for categories like robins, the size differences are small enough that they are not represented, and we only remember the average size for a robin; but for categories like birds as a whole, we do not average the size of turkeys, hawks, robins, and wrens, which are too diverse. There is some evidence for this notion in category-learning experiments (e.g., Strauss 1979), but it must be said that a detailed model for how to treat such features within prototype theory seems to be lacking.

If this feature list is the concept representation, then how does one categorize new items? Essentially, one calculates the similarity of the item to the feature list. For every feature the item has in common with the representation, it gets "credit" for the feature's weight. When it lacks a feature that is in the representation, or has a feature that is not in the representation, it loses credit for that feature (see Smith and Osherson 1984; Tversky 1977). After going through the object's features, one adds up all the weights of the present features and subtracts all the weights of its features that are not part of the category.[1] If that number is above some critical value, the *categorization criterion*, the item is judged to be in the category; if not, it is not. Thus, it is important to have the highest weighted features of a category in order to be categorized. For example, an animal that eats meat, wears a collar, and is a pet might possibly be a dog, because these are all features associated with dogs, though not the most highly weighted features. If this creature does not have the shape or head of a dog, does not bark, does not drool, and does not have other highly weighted dog features, one would not categorize it as a dog, even though it wears a collar and eats meat. So, the more highly weighted features an item has, the more likely it is to be identified as a category member.

This view explains the failure of the classical view. First, no particular feature is required to be present in order to categorize the item. The inability to find such defining features does not embarrass prototype theory the way it did the classical view. So long as an item has enough dog features, it can be called a dog—no particular feature is defining. Second, it is perfectly understandable why some items might be borderline cases, about which people disagree. If an item has about equal similarity to two categories (as tomatoes do to fruit and vegetable), then people may well be uncertain and change their mind about it. Or even if the item is only similar to one category, if it is not very similar—in other words, right near the categorization criterion—people will not be sure about it. They may change their mind about it on a different occasion if they think of slightly different features or if there's a small change in a feature's weight. Third, it is understandable that any typical item will be faster to categorize than atypical items. Typical items will have the most highly weighted features (see Barsalou 1985; Rosch and Mervis 1975), and so they will more quickly reach the categorization criterion. If you see a picture of a German shepherd, its face, shape, size, and hair all immediately match highly weighted values of the dog concept, which allow speedy categorization. If you see a picture of a sheepdog, the face, length of hair, and shape are not very typical, and so you may have to consider more features in order to accumulate enough weights to decide that it is a dog.

Recall that Hampton (1982) demonstrated that category membership judgments could be intransitive. For example, people believe that Big Ben is a clock, and they believe that clocks are furniture, but they deny that Big Ben is furniture. How can this happen? On the prototype view, this comes about because the basis of similarity changes from one judgment to the other. Big Ben is a clock by virtue of telling time; clocks are furniture by virtue of being objects that one puts in the home for decoration and utility (not by virtue of telling time, because watches are not considered furniture). However, Big Ben is not similar to the furniture concept, because it isn't in the home and is far bigger than any furniture. Thus, concept *A* can be similar to concept *B*, and *B* can be similar to *C*, and yet *A* may not be very similar to *C*. This can happen when the features that *A* and *B* share are not the same as the features that *B* and *C* share (see Tversky 1977). On the classical view, this kind of intransitivity is not possible, because any category would have to include all of its superset's definition, and so there is no way that deciding that something is a clock would not also include deciding that it was furniture.

Smith and Medin (1981) discuss other results that can be explained by this feature-listing model. Most prominent among them are the effects of false relatedness: It is more difficult to say "no" to the question "Is a dog a cat?" than to "Is a dog a mountain?" I will leave it as an exercise for the reader to derive this result from the feature list view.

More Recent Developments

Unlike the other views to be discussed in this chapter, the prototype view has not been undergoing much theoretical development. In fact, many statements about prototypes in the literature are somewhat vague, making it unclear exactly what the writer is referring to—a single best example? a feature list? if a feature list, determined how? This lack of specificity in much writing about prototype theory has allowed its critics to make up their own prototype models to some degree. As we shall see in chapter 4, many theorists assume that the prototype is the single best example, rather than a list of features, even though these models have very different properties, for real-life categories, at least.

Feature combinations. The view taken by Rosch and Mervis (1975), Smith and Medin (1981), and Hampton (1979) was that the category representation should keep track of how often features occurred in category members. For example, people would be expected to know that "fur" is a frequent property of bears, "white" is a less frequent property, "has claws" is very frequent, "eats garbage" of only moderate frequency, and so on. A more elaborate proposal is that people keep track not just of individual features but configurations of two or more features. For example, perhaps people notice how often bears have claws AND eat garbage, or have fur AND are white—that is, combinations of two features. And if we propose this, we might as well also propose that people notice combinations of three features such as having claws AND eating garbage AND being white. So, if you saw a bear with brown fur eating campers' garbage in a national park, you would update your category information about bears by adding 1 to the frequency count for features "brown," "has fur," "eats garbage," "brown and has fur," "brown and eats garbage," "has fur and eats garbage," and "brown and has fur and eats garbage." This proposal was first made by Hayes-Roth and Hayes-Roth (1977) and was made part of a mathematical model (the *configural cue model*) by Gluck and Bower (1988a).

One problem with such a proposal is that it immediately raises the question of a computational explosion. If you know 25 things about bears, say (which by no means is an overestimate), then there would be 300 pairs of features to be encoded. (In general, for N features, the number of pairs would be $N * (N - 1)/2$.) Furthermore, there would be 2,300 triplets of features to encode as well and 12,650 quadruplets. Even if you stopped at triplets of features, you have now kept track of not just 25 properties, but 2,635. For any category that you were extremely familiar with, you might know many more features. So, if you are a bird watcher and know 1,000 properties of birds (this would include shapes, sizes, habitats, behaviors, colors, and patterns), you would also know 499,500 pairs of features and 166,167,000 feature triplets. This is the explosion in "combinatorial explosion." Not only would this take up a considerable amount of memory, it would also require much more processing effort when using the category, since every time you viewed a new category member, you would have to update as many of the pairs, triplets, and quadruplets that were observed. And when making a category decision, you couldn't just consult the 1,000 bird properties that you know about—you would also have to consult the relevant feature pairs, triplets, and so on.

For these reasons, this proposal has not been particularly popular in the field at large. Models that encode feature combinations have been able to explain some data in psychology experiments, but this may in part be due to the fact that there are typically only four or five features in these experiments (Gluck and Bower 1988a, pp. 187–188, limited themselves to cases of no more than three features), and so it is conceivable that subjects could be learning the feature pairs and triplets in these cases. However, when the Gluck and Bower model has been compared systematically with other mathematically specified theories, it has not generally done as well as the others (especially exemplar models), as discussed by Kruschke (1992) and Nosofsky (1992). In short, this way of expanding prototype theory has not caught on more generally. The question of whether people actually do notice certain *pairs* of correlated features is discussed at greater length in chapter 5.

Schemata.   One development that is tied to the prototype view is the use of *schemata* (the plural of *schema*) to represent concepts. This form of representation has been taken as an improvement on the feature list idea by a number of concepts researchers (e.g., Cohen and Murphy 1984; Smith and Osherson 1984). To understand why, consider the feature list view described above. In this view, the features are simply an unstructured list, with associated weights. For example, the concept of bird might have a list of features such as wings, beak, flies, gray, eats bugs, migrates in winter, eats seeds, blue, walks, and so on, each with a weight. One concern about such a list is that it does not represent any of the relations between the features. For example, the features describing a bird's color are all related: They are different values on the same dimension. Similarly, the features related to what birds eat are all closely connected. In some cases, these features are mutually exclusive. For example, if a bird has a black head, it presumably does not also have a green head and a blue head and a red head. If a bird has two eyes, it does not have just one eye. In contrast, other features do not seem to be so related. If a bird eats seeds, this does not place any restriction on how many eyes it has or what color its head is, and vice versa.

A schema is a structured representation that divides up the properties of an item into dimensions (usually called *slots*) and values on those dimensions (*fillers* of the slots). (For the original proposal for schemata, see Rumelhart and Ortony 1977. For a general discussion of schemata see A. Markman 1999.) The slots have restrictions on them that say what kinds of fillers they can have. For example, the head-color slot of a bird can only be filled by colors; it can't be filled by sizes or locations, because these would not specify the color of the bird's head. Furthermore, the slot may place constraints on the specific value allowed for that concept. For example, a bird could have two, one or no eyes (presumably through some accident), but could not have more than two eyes. The slot for number of eyes would include this restriction. The fillers of the slot are understood to be competitors. For example, if the head color of birds included colors such as blue, black, and red, this would indicate that the head would be blue OR black OR red. (If the head could be a complex pattern or mixture of colors, that would have to be a separate feature.) Finally, the slots themselves may be connected by relations that restrict their values. For example, if a bird does not fly, then it does not migrate south in winter. This could be represented as a connection between the locomotion slot (which indicates how the bird moves itself around) and the slot that includes the information on migration.

Why do we need all this extra apparatus of a schema? Why not just stick with the simpler feature list? The answer cannot be fully given here, because some of the evidence for schemata comes from the topics of other chapters (most notably chapter

12). However, part of the reason is that the unstructured nature of the feature list could lead to some peculiar concepts or objects being learned. Any features can be added to the list, and there are no restrictions on one feature's weights depending on what other features are. So, if I told you that birds are generally carnivorous, and you read somewhere that birds were generally vegetarian, you could simply list the features in your concept, say, carnivorous, weight = .80; and vegetarian, weight = .80. The fact that these two features both having high weights is contradictory would not prevent a feature list from representing them. Similarly, if I represented both the features "flies" and "doesn't fly" for birds (since some do and some don't), there is nothing to stop me from thinking that specific birds have both these features. The intuition behind schema theory is that people structure the information they learn, which makes it easier to find relevant information and prevents them from forming incoherent concepts of this sort (for evidence from category learning in particular, see Kaplan 1999; Lassaline and Murphy 1998).

Another argument often made about feature lists is that they do not have the kinds of relations that you need to understand an entire object. For example, a pile of bird features does not make a bird—the parts need to be tied together in just the right way. The eyes of a bird are *above* the beak, placed *symmetrically* on the head, *below* the crest. This kind of information is critical to making up a real bird, but it usually does not appear in feature lists, at least as produced by subjects in experiments. Subjects may list "has eyes," but they will not provide much relational information about how the eyes fit with the other properties of birds. Nonetheless, people clearly learn this information, and if you were to see a bird with the beak and eyes on opposite sides of its head, you would be extremely surprised. Schemata can include this information by providing detailed relations among the slots.

In short, a feature list is a good shorthand for noting what people know about a category, but it is only a shorthand, and a schema can provide a much more complete picture of what people know about a concept. For some purposes, this extra information is not very relevant, and so it may be easier simply to talk about features, and indeed, I will do so for just that reason. Furthermore, in some experiments, the concepts have been constructed basically as feature lists, without the additional relational information that a schema would include. In such cases, talking about feature lists is sufficient. However, we should not make the mistake of believing too much in the concepts we make up for experiments, which probably drastically underestimate the complexity and richness of real-world concepts. Schemata may be a better description of the latter, even if they are not required for the former.

The Exemplar View

The theory of concepts first proposed by Medin and Schaffer (1978) is in many respects radically different from prior theories of concepts. In the exemplar view, the idea that people have a representation that somehow encompasses an entire concept is rejected. That is, one's concept of dogs is not a definition that includes all dogs, nor is it a list of features that are found to greater or lesser degrees in dogs. Instead, a person's concept of dogs is the set of dogs that the person remembers. In some sense, there is no real concept (as normally conceived of), because there is no summary representation that stands for all dogs. However, as we shall see, this view can account for behaviors that in the past have been explained by summary representations.

To explain a bit more, your concept of dogs might be a set of a few hundred dog memories that you have. Some memories might be more salient than others, and some might be incomplete and fuzzy due to forgetting. Nonetheless, these are what you consult when you make decisions about dogs in general. Suppose you see a new animal walking around your yard. How would you decide that it is a dog, according to this view? This animal bears a certain similarity to other things you have seen in the past. It might be quite similar to one or two objects that you know about, fairly similar to a few dozen things, and mildly similar to a hundred things. Basically, what you do is (very quickly) consult your memory to see which things it is most similar to. If, roughly speaking, most of the things it is similar to are dogs, then you'll conclude that it is a dog. So, if I see an Irish terrier poking about my garden, this will remind me of other Irish terriers I have seen, which I know are dogs. I would conclude that this is therefore also a dog.

As in the prototype view, there must also be a place for similarity in this theory. The Irish terrier in my yard is extremely similar to some dogs that I have seen, is moderately similar to other dogs, but is mildly similar to long-haired ponies and burros as well. It has the same general shape and size as a goat, though lacking the horns or beard. It is in some respects reminiscent of some wolves in my memory as well. How do I make sense of all these possible categorizations: a bunch of dogs, a few goats, wolves, and the occasional pony or burro? Medin and Schaffer (1978) argued that you should weight these items in your memory by how similar they are to the item. The Irish terrier is extremely similar to some of my remembered dogs, is moderately similar to the wolves, is only slightly similar to the goat, and only barely similar to the ponies and burro. Therefore, when you add up all the similarities, there is considerably more evidence for the object's being a dog than for its being anything else. (I will describe this process in more detail later.) So, it is not just the number of exemplars that an item reminds you of that determines how you categorize it; just as important is how similar the object is to each memory.

How does this view explain the phenomena that the prototype view explained? First, this theory does not say anything about defining characteristics, so the problems for the classical view are not problems for it. Second, the view has a natural explanation for typicality phenomena. The most typical items are the ones that are highly similar to many category members. So, a German shepherd is extremely similar to many dogs and is not so similar to other animals. A dachshund is not as similar to other dogs, and it bears a certain resemblance to weasels and ferrets, which count against it as a dog. A chihuahua is even less similar to most dogs, and it is somewhat similar to rats and guinea pigs, and so it is even less typical. Basically, the more similar an item is to remembered dogs, and the less similar it is to remembered nondogs, the more typical it will be. Borderline cases are items that are almost equally similar to remembered category members and noncategory members. So, a tomato is similar to some fruit in terms of its having seeds, being round with edible skin, and so forth, but is similar to some vegetables in terms of its taste and how it is normally prepared.

Typical items would be categorized faster than atypical ones, because they are very similar to a large number of category members, and so it is very easy to find evidence for their being members. When you see a German shepherd, you can very quickly think of many dogs you have seen that are similar to it; when you see a chihuahua, there are fewer dogs that are similar to it. Thus, the positive evidence builds up more quickly when an item is typical (Lamberts 1995; Nosofsky and Palmeri 1997). The case of category intransitivity is explained in a way similar to that of the prototype view. For example, Big Ben is similar to examples of clocks you have seen in many respects. Clocks are similar to furniture exemplars in different respects. But Big Ben is not very similar to most furniture exemplars (beds, dressers, couches, etc.), and so it does not reach the categorization criterion. Whenever the basis for similarity changes, the exemplar model can explain this kind of intransitivity.

In short, the exemplar view can explain a number of the major results that led to the downfall of the classical view. For some people, this view is very counterintuitive. For example, many people don't consciously experience recalling exemplars of dogs in deciding whether something is a dog. However, conscious experience of this sort is not in general a reliable guide to cognitive processing. Indeed, one typically does not have conscious experience of a definition or a list of features, either. Access to the concept representation is often very fast and automatic. Second, some people point out that they feel that they know things about dogs, *in general*, not just about individual exemplars. This is a concern that will come up later as well. However, note that what you know about dogs in general may be precisely what is most common in the remembered exemplars. So, when you think of such exemplars, these general characteristics are the ones that come to mind. Finally, when you first learn a category, exemplar information may be all you encode. For example, if you went to the zoo and saw a llama for the first time, all you know about llamas would be dependent on that one exemplar. There would be no difference between your memory for the whole category and your memory for that one exemplar. If you saw another llama a few months later, you could now form a generalization about llamas as a whole (though the exemplar view is saying that you do not do this). But you would clearly also remember the two llama examples as separate items. When you saw the third llama, you might still remember parts of the first two llamas, and so on. The question is, then, when you have seen a few dozen llamas, are you forming a general description of llamas—as the prototype view says—or are you just getting a better idea of what llamas are like because you have more memories to draw on— as the exemplar view says? But at the very initial stages of learning, it seems that any theory would have to agree that you remember the individual exemplars, or else you would have no basis on which to form generalizations (see Ross, Perkins, and Tenpenny 1990, for a clever twist on this idea).

A final point is that the exemplar model requires that you have specifically categorized these memories. You can easily recognize a German shepherd as a dog because it is similar to other things you have identified as dogs. If you had just seen a lot of other German shepherds without knowing what they were, they couldn't help you classify this similar object. This requirement of explicit encoding will come up again later.

Similarity calculation. Medin and Schaffer (1978) were the first to propose an elaborate exemplar model of concepts. In addition to the exemplar aspect itself, they also introduced a number of other ideas that were taken up by the field. One aspect was the nature of the similarity computation used to identify similar exemplars. In the past, most researchers had considered similarity to be an additive function of matching and mismatching features (Tversky 1977). Medin and Schaffer, however, proposed a *multiplicative* rule, which had a number of important effects on how their model operated.

The first part of this rule (as for additive versions) requires us to identify which aspects of two items are shared and which are different. For example, consider Ronald Reagan and Bill Clinton. They share many aspects: Both are men, are

Americans, were born in the twentieth century, were Presidents of the United States, attended college, are married, and so on. They also differ in a number of aspects: Where they were born, their ages, their political philosophies, their presidential actions, whether they have been divorced, what kinds of clothes they wear, and so on. For each of these matching and mismatching features, we need to decide two things. First, how important is this dimension to determining similarity? So, how important is it for two people to have the same or different sex? How important is age or marital status? How important is political philosophy? We need to decide this so that trivial differences between the two men don't swamp our decision. For example, perhaps neither man has been to Nogales, Arizona, but this should not count as a very important similarity. Perhaps Ronald Reagan has never played bridge, but Bill Clinton has. This does not seem to be an important difference. Second, for the mismatching features, we need to decide just how mismatching they are. For example, the political philosophies of Clinton and Reagan are very different. Their ages are pretty different (Reagan was the oldest president, and Clinton one of the youngest), though both are adults, and so the difference in age is not as large as it could be. However, their typical clothes are not so different. Clinton differs from Reagan a great deal on political beliefs, then, moderately on age, and only a little on clothing.

In order to calculate similarity, we need to quantify both of these factors: the importance of the dimension and the amount of similarity on a given dimension. Medin and Schaffer suggested that the amount of mismatch of each feature should be given a number between 0 and 1. If two items have matching features, they get a 1; if they have mismatching features, they get a number that is lower, with 0 indicating the greatest possible difference on that dimension (this score is typically not given, for reasons that will become apparent). However, the importance of the dimension would be represented by raising or lowering that number. For example, suppose that Reagan's favorite color is yellow, and Clinton's is blue. These are very different colors, but this dimension is not very important. Therefore, Medin and Schaffer (1978, p. 212) suggest that we could still give this item a difference score near to 1. By not paying attention to a difference, you are effectively acting as if the items have the same value on that dimension. So, Medin and Schaffer's rule combines the importance of the dimension and the difference on that dimension in one score.

How similar are Clinton and Reagan, then? If we were to use a similarity rule like the one used by the prototype model described above, we would take the mismatch score of each feature and add it up for all the features (hence, an additive rule). Things that are similar would have many matches and so would have higher scores. Medin and Schaffer, however, suggested that we should multiply together the scores for each feature. Because the mismatch scores range between 0 and 1, a few mismatches will make overall similarity quite low. For example, suppose that Reagan and Clinton were identical on 25 dimensions but differed on 3 dimensions. And suppose that their differences on those dimensions were moderate, so that they received mismatch scores of .5 each. The overall similarity of Clinton and Reagan would now be only .125 on a 0–1 scale (25 scores of $1 \times .5 \times .5 \times .5$ for the three mismatching dimensions). This does not seem to be a very high number for two items that are identical on 25 out of 28 dimensions. If you work through a few examples, you will see that any mismatching feature has a large effect on diminishing similarity when a multiplicative rule is used. That is, mismatching features actively lower similarity on a multiplicative rule, but they simply do not improve it on an additive view. (You can now see why a similarity score of 0 is seldom given. If a dimension were given a 0, then the entire similarity of the two items is 0, since 0 multiplied by any number is always 0. That single mismatch would result in the two items being as different as possible.)

So far, we have been discussing how to decide the similarity of an item to a single other item. But what if you are comparing an item to a set of exemplars in a category? If you see an animal run across the road, and you want to decide whether to apply the brakes to avoid hitting it with your car, you might first try to identify what kind of animal it is (no point in risking an accident for a squirrel, you might feel) by comparing it to exemplars of other animals you have seen. So, you would compare it to cat exemplars, dog exemplars, raccoon exemplars, skunk exemplars, possum exemplars, and so on. Medin and Schaffer (1978) suggested that you add up the similarity scores for each exemplar in a category. So, if you have 150 exemplars of dogs in memory, you add up the similarities of the observed animal to these 150 items, and this constitutes the evidence for the animal being a dog. If you have 25 possums in memory, you add up the 25 similarity scores to get the evidence for possums, and so on. Loosely speaking, the category with the most similarity to the item will "win" this contest. If the item is similar to a number of categories, then you will choose each category with a probability that is proportional to the amount of similarity it has relative to the others. So, you might decide that such an animal is a raccoon on 60% of such cases but a skunk on 40% of the cases. For mathematical details, see Medin and Schaffer (1978) or Nosofsky (1984).

Because of the multiplicative nature of the similarity score, the Medin and Schaffer rule has an important property: It is best to be *very* similar to a few items, and it is unhelpful to be somewhat similar to many items. Imagine for example, that this animal was extremely similar to two other dogs you have seen, but not at all similar to any other dogs. The animal will have high similarity to these two items (near to 1.0), which would make the dog category have an overall similarity of almost 2.0. Now imagine that the animal shared three features with every possum you know (25 of them) and was different on three features with every possum. If the three mismatching features each have mismatch values of .25, then the animal would have a similarity of $1 \times 1 \times 1 \times .25 \times .25 \times .25$ to each possum, which is only .015625. When this is added up across all 25 possums, the total similarity for the category is only about .39—considerably less than the 2.0 for the dogs. Perhaps counter-intuitively, the two highly similar dogs beat out the 25 somewhat similar possums. This is because the mismatching features result in very low similarities, which cannot easily be made up by having many such examples. In short, *the Medin and Schaffer model says that it is better to have high overlap with a few items than to have moderate overlap with many items.* This property turns out to be a critical one, as the next chapter will reveal.[2]

Prototype advantages.   Some empirical results initially discouraged researchers from seriously considering exemplar approaches. One such result was the prototype advantage that was found by Posner and Keele (1968, 1970) and others. When subjects learned categories by viewing distortions of a prototype (see above), they were often better at categorizing the prototype than another new item. (Though they were *not* initially better at identifying the prototype than the old items, as is commonly repeated.) This suggested to many researchers that subjects had actively abstracted the prototype from seeing the distortions. That is, they had learned what the items had in common and stored this as a representation of the whole category. (Because Posner and Keele 1968, actually started with a prototype to make the category members, it is natural to think of subjects who are exposed to the category members doing the same process in reverse.) But from the above discussion, you can see that an exemplar model could easily explain this result. Perhaps the prototype is more similar to the learned exemplars than a new, nonprototypical item is. Since the prototype was the basis for making all the other items, it must be similar to *all* of them to some degree, but this is not true for an arbitrary new item.

Another result was more of a problem for the exemplar view. Posner and Keele (1970) examined categorization for items immediately after category learning and after a one-week delay. When tested immediately, subjects were most accurate for the specific items that they had been trained on (old items), next most accurate for the prototype, and less accurate for new items they had not seen in training. But when tested a week later, memory for the old items declined precipitously, whereas the prototype suffered only a slight decrement. Posner and Keele argued that if the prototype advantage were due to memory for old exemplars, it should have shown the same kind of decrement after a delay. They concluded that subjects formed a prototype during learning, and this prototype is somehow more insulated against memory loss than are memories for individual exemplars (perhaps because the prototype is based on many presented items, not just one). A similar effect was reported by Strange, Keeney, Kessel, and Jenkins (1970), and Bomba and Siqueland (1983) found the same effect in infants. There are other variables that have similar effects. For example, as more and more exemplars are learned for a category, the memory for old items decreases, but the prototype advantage generally increases (e.g., Knapp and Anderson 1984). If prototype performance is caused by memory for specific exemplars, how could performance on the prototype and old exemplars go in different directions?

An explanation for this kind of result was given by Medin and Schaffer (1978). First, consider why it is that in many cases with immediate testing, old exemplars are remembered best of all. This must be because when the item is presented at test, it results in the retrieval of itself. That is, when item 9 is presented at test, you remember having seen it before, and this makes you particularly fast and accurate at categorizing it. If you forgot this particular item, then it would no longer have this good performance, because it must be less similar to any other item than it is to itself. Over time, however, this loss of memory is just what happens. So, perhaps item 9 was a red circle over a green square. Even though you learned this item during the first part of an experiment, after a week's delay, this memory would be degraded. Perhaps you would only remember that it was a red circle over something green. Now when you get item 9 at test, it is not so very similar to its own memory, because that memory has changed. Similarly, if you learned 25 items as being in category A, your memory for each individual item will not be as good as if you only learned 4 items in this category. As you learn more and more, there is interference among the items which causes the exemplar memory for any one of them to be less accurate. This explains the decrements obtained in performance on old items.

What happens when you present the prototype (which was never seen during learning) at test? If it is an immediate test, the prototype is fairly similar to many items in the category, and so it is easy to categorize. However, it is not identical to any individual item, and so it is still not as fast as the old exemplars are. So, the advantage of old items over prototypes on immediate test is, according to the exemplar model, caused by the fact that the former has a perfect match in memory but the latter does not. (Note that this explanation relies on the exemplar model's weighting close similarity to one item more than moderate similarity to many items.) At delayed testing, the prototype is still very similar to a number of items. In fact,

Calculating Similarity According to the Context Model

Imagine that you have been learning categories made up of geometric figures printed on cards. Each figure is defined by shape, color, size, and position (left or right on the card). After you've learned the categories, suppose you're shown a new item, a large, green triangle on the left of the card. How do you calculate its similarity to the other items in order to decide its membership? The discussion in the main text gives the general outline of how this would be done. This box describes in a bit more detail how this is actually calculated in experiments that attempt to derive exact predictions for the context model.

Given the large green triangle on the left, one would have to compare it to each remembered exemplar. Suppose that you also remember seeing a large blue triangle on the right. We need to decide the matching and mismatching value for each dimension to see how similar it is. The two stimuli match on two dimensions, size and shape, and so these will be given values of 1.0. The two stimuli mismatch on two dimensions, and so these will be given values of s_c (for color) and s_p (for position). The s_c indicates how similar the green of one stimulus is to the blue of the other stimulus. If these are considered fairly similar, the value will be close to 1; if they are considered rather different, then the value would be closer to 0. The s_p correspondingly indicates how similar the left and right positions are. By using the multiplicative rule, we can calculate the entire similarity of these two stimuli as $1 \times 1 \times s_p \times s_c$. The problem is, how do we know exactly what s_p and s_c are so that we can come up with an actual number? In general, the answer is that these numbers will be calculated from the results of the experiment itself. For example, we can see how likely people are to categorize an item that is just like a learned item but differs in color; and we can see how likely people are to categorize an item that is just like a learned item but differs in shape; and so on. By using a mathematical modeling program, researchers in this area can put in the expected formulas for each item (i.e., how similar each test item is to each learned item according to the multiplication rule), and the program will provide the values of s_p, s_c, and the other similarities that make the model perform as well as possible. These are called *free parameters* of a model, because they are estimated from the data, rather than being stated by the theory in advance. (Other theories also have free parameters. For example, I said that prototype theory often has weights on how important each feature is for a category. These could be estimated from the data as free parameters, though they could also be directly measured through means analogous to those described in the next paragraph.)

Unfortunately, this is not entirely the end. Recall that Medin and Schaffer also discussed the possibility that some dimensions might be attended to more than others. Suppose, for example, that subjects never paid attention to the position of the figures for some reason, perhaps not thinking that it was relevant. Now, the value for s_p that we calculate by the above procedure would include *both* the intrinsic similarity of the items and the attention that subjects give to it. If subjects really ignored position, then s_p would equal 1—suggesting that the right and left positions were viewed as identical. That is, there is no way to separate the mismatch score from the amount of attention

continued

that people pay to that dimension, because both are being used by subjects to make categorization decisions. This is not necessarily a problem, but sometimes one does wish to know what the real similarities are, separately from knowing which dimensions subjects paid more attention to.

One way to handle this concern is to choose the stimulus differences so that they are known to be equally different in different dimensions. For example, by asking different subjects to provide similarity ratings, it might be possible to choose a size difference (values for the large and small items) that is psychologically the same size as the color difference (between the particular values of blue and green), which is also equal to the shape difference, and so on. The experimenter can ask subjects to rate the similarity of all the stimuli before doing a categorization experiment. Then he or she can choose stimulus values that are equated, or at least the relative values of s_p, s_c, and the rest can be measured. Unfortunately, this technique cannot tell us how much attention people pay to each dimension during learning—only how similar the stimulus values are perceptually. To discover any attentional differences, one must still estimate the s parameters from the main experiment.

Calculating the exact predictions for these models is not something that can easily be done with paper and pencil, as can be seen by this description. The actual calculations of the s values and therefore the model's precise predictions is almost always done in conjunction with a mathematical modeling program. In other cases, the properties of the models can be illuminated by proofs using the general form of the similarity rule (e.g., Nosofsky 1984; 1992). But these are not tasks for beginners.

because some of the specific information about the old items has been lost, they may now seem even *more* similar to the prototype than they did before. For example, suppose that the prototype was a red circle over a green triangle. This matched item 9 to a large degree, since the two differed only in the shape of the bottom figure. After forgetting, though, the memory for item 9 actually matches the prototype more than before, because there is no longer a conflict between the square in item 9, which has been forgotten, and the triangle in the prototype. In short, the effect of forgetting is to make the old test items less similar to their own memories, but it has less effect (or even the opposite effect) on the prototype.

Hintzman and Ludlam (1980) performed simulations of an exemplar model showing that the above explanation could in fact explain why exemplar memory and prototype memory have separate time courses. They showed that as forgetting occurred, old items became steadily less similar to the remembered exemplars, but prototypes retained their similarity to exemplars for the most part. (See also Hintzman 1986, for a more complete modeling effort.) In short, even if performance is based only on remembered exemplars, prototype effects will occur because prototypes are quite similar to a number of exemplars. One does not need to propose a summary representation of a category in order to explain prototype effects.

What Is an Exemplar?

For some time now, I have been discussing "exemplars" and the view of concepts based on them. However, I have not yet precisely said what these entities are. To some degree, this question has been left open by the proponents of this view. For example, suppose that I see a squirrel run across a lawn while I walk in to work today. Does this brief glimpse of a squirrel constitute an exemplar, even if I don't pay much attention to it? I have seen hundreds, perhaps thousands of squirrels in this way. Are all these exemplars stored in memory? (And are they stored *as* squirrels? As explained above, encoding the exemplar's category is required for it to influence categorization.) The exemplar view of concepts does not necessarily have an answer to this question, which is in part an issue of memory in general (not just concepts). It would have to say that *if* I did notice and remember that squirrel, then it could have an effect on the way I identify later animals as squirrels. If the squirrel is not encoded into memory or is forgotten, then it clearly can have no effect. But a theory of concepts cannot say exactly what everyone will and will not remember.

There is another, deeper question about exemplars, namely how an exemplar is to be defined. Consider this example. Suppose that I know a bulldog that drools a great deal named Wilbur. In fact, this bulldog lives next door to me, and so I have many opportunities to see him drool. I have seen other bulldogs, some of which appear to be drooling, and some of which do not. How do I decide, now, whether a friend of mine, who is complaining about her new dog's drooling, has a bulldog? According to the exemplar view, I would have to retrieve all the dog exemplars that I know that drool (no small number), and then essentially count up how many of them are bulldogs. But in retrieving these exemplars, how do I count Wilbur? Does he count once, because he is only one dog, or does each *encounter* with Wilbur count separately? Put in more formal terms, do I count types (Wilbur) or tokens (Wilbur-encounters)?

In terms of making an accurate decision, it seems clear that I should only count Wilbur as a type—he should only count as one dog. If I count up every Wilbur encounter as another exemplar, then the fact that a (drooling) bulldog lives next to me is having a large effect on my decision; if a labrador lived next to me, I would have many, many fewer such exemplars. However, which kind of dog happens to be living next door is not relevant to the question of whether a drooling dog is a bulldog. Or, to put it another way, how often I happen to see one particular bulldog should not greatly influence my decisions about bulldogs in general.

Nosofsky (1988) addressed this question in an experiment using colored patches as stimuli. The patches varied in how saturated and bright the colors were: The more saturated and bright colors tended to be in one category, and the less saturated and bright colors in another. He varied the frequency with which items were presented: One of the items was presented five times as often as the other items during learning. If each exemplar is considered as a type, then this frequency manipulation should not influence later category decisions. The fact that one color keeps reappearing would be like the fact that I live next door to Wilbur, not a relevant indication of the category in general. But if exemplars are defined as tokens, then stimuli that were like the more frequent item would be better category examples than stimuli that were like other, less frequent items, because there would be "more exemplars" remembered for the more frequent one. This is exactly what Nosofsky found. After learning, he showed subjects the items and asked them to rate their typicality. The more frequent item and other items that were close to it were rated as being more typical than the less frequent items. By this result, then, an exemplar is not an actual thing but rather the encounter with a thing. So, if I encounter Wilbur a hundred times, this creates 100 exemplars, not just one. Nosofsky also provided a simulation of the exemplar model, showing that it accounted for the results much better if it considered each presentation of the stimulus as an exemplar, rather than each type as being an exemplar.

Barsalou, Huttenlocher, and Lamberts (1998) raised a possible problem with this interpretation of Nosofsky's experiment. They pointed out that we do not know what subjects thought about the reappearing colors. Perhaps they thought that the stimuli were somehow different objects even if they looked identical. (It is difficult to know how to interpret the reappearance of these items, since they were color patches rather than objects.) Furthermore, as color patches are difficult to remember precisely, perhaps people did not realize that exactly the same item was being shown so often. Perhaps they thought that the colors were slightly different. If so, then they would naturally count them as separate exemplars.

Barsalou et al. performed a clever experiment in which they showed two groups of subjects the exact same stimuli during learning, but they varied whether subjects thought that each stimulus was unique, or whether they were seeing some of the items multiple times. Under most conditions, they found that this manipulation had virtually no effect on the concepts people formed; the very frequent exemplar had a strong effect in both conditions. That is, to return to my example, it makes no difference whether I think I'm seeing 100 different bulldogs or one bulldog 100 times—the effect on my concept of bulldogs is the same.[3] As Barsalou et al. point out, this has implications for prototype models as well as for exemplar models of concepts. In both cases, the theory needs to specify how units are counted up (how many features/exemplars have been viewed), and the empirical results suggest that it is *encounters* with objects that are most important, rather than the objects themselves.

The Knowledge Approach

The discussion of the final major theory is actually a bit premature for the present chapter. The prototype and exemplar models arose from the ashes of the classical view, and they were designed to account for the data that were so problematic for that view. The *knowledge approach* in contrast arose as a reaction to the two other approaches, and it is in some sense built upon them. As a result, we have not yet discussed the experimental results that led to this view, nor are we ready to do so now. A later chapter (chapter 6) provides a more detailed exposition of this account. Nonetheless, it will be useful to have this approach in mind when reading the next few chapters, and so I will give a somewhat brief description of this view now, without providing much of the experimental evidence.

The knowledge approach argues that concepts are part of our general knowledge about the world. We do not learn concepts in isolation from everything else (as is the case in many psychology experiments); rather, we learn them as part of our overall understanding of the world around us. When we learn concepts about animals, this information is integrated with our general knowledge about biology, about behavior, and other relevant domains (perhaps cuisine, ecology, climate, and so on). This relation works both ways: Concepts are influenced by what we already know, but a new concept can also effect a change in our general knowledge. Thus, if you learn a surprising fact about a new kind of animal, this could change what you thought about biology in general (e.g., if you learn that snails are hermaphrodites, your knowledge about sexual reproduction in general could be affected); and if something you learn about a new animal doesn't fit with your general knowledge, you may have cause to question it or to give it less weight. (Could snails *really* be hermaphrodites? Maybe you just misunderstood. Best to say nothing and hope they go away.) In general, then, the knowledge approach emphasizes that concepts are part and parcel of your general knowledge of the world, and so there is pressure for concepts to be consistent with whatever else you know (Keil 1989; Murphy and Medin 1985). In order to maintain such consistency, part of categorization and other conceptual processes may be a reasoning process that infers properties or constructs explanations from general knowledge.

Let me just give a simple example of the kind of knowledge involved here. One area of knowledge that is often studied in research from this perspective is that of biology. We know things about evolution, reproduction, physiology, and ecology, part of which we have just learned "naively" (on our own or informally from parents), and part of which we learned through more formal study. However, even young children seem to have basic ideas about biology (Gelman and Wellman 1991; Keil 1989) that they use in making judgments of the following sort. If a child sees a fuzzy, gray, tiny animal paddling around after a large, white, goose, the child may conclude that the animal must be a goose as well, even though it looks very different from other geese it has seen. Apparently, the child is using the logic: "Babies are smaller than their parents, and they often stick close to their parents. Any baby of a goose must itself be a goose. So, this much smaller animal could well be a baby, even though it looks rather different from the goose, and so it is also a goose." Of course, the child doesn't say this out loud, but there is reason to think that children are sensitive to notions of inheritance and parentage—basic biological properties that then influence their categorizations. In general, this approach says that people use their prior knowledge to reason about an example in order to decide what category it is, or in order to learn a new category.

In one description, this aspect of concepts was referred to as "mental theories about the world" (Murphy and Medin 1985), which is accurate enough if one understands that people's naive theories are incomplete and in some cases contradictory, given our incomplete knowledge and understanding of the things around us. The child in the above example doesn't have a complete theory of biology but does know some basic facts and principles that are partly integrated. Thus, this approach is sometimes called the *theory view* (or even the *theory theory* by those less easily embarrassed than I am). However, the term *theory* suggests to many something more like an official scientific theory, which is probably not an accurate description of people's knowledge (see, e.g., Gentner and Stevens 1983). This has caused some confusion about exactly what the approach is claiming, so I will tend to use the term *knowledge* rather than *theory*, to avoid this potential confusion.

Some of the discussion of schemata discussed in the prototype view is relevant here as well. For example, one reason given for using schemata for representing concepts was that they can represent relations between features and dimensions. This is just one way of representing knowledge about the domain. For example, we may know that animals without wings cannot fly, and so there may be a relation between the schema slot describing body parts and the slot describing behaviors that manifests this relation.

One of the studies on typicality described in some detail in the previous chapter was also a motivation for the knowledge view, namely, Barsalou (1985). Recall that Barsalou found that *ideals* are important to determining typicality. For example, something might be considered a good example of a weapon to the degree that it was an efficient way to hurt or kill people. This "ideal" weapon is not the average value of all weapons, because most weapons are less than ideal on this account (e.g., a knife requires close distance, accurate handling, and can only cut one person at a time). Barsalou found that items that were closer to the ideal were more typical than items that were farther away, and this was true even when family resemblance was first factored into the typicality judgment. This influence of ideals cannot, then, reflect just pure observation of the category, as a prototype or exemplar approach might claim. If people relied on the weapons they had seen or heard about, they would find only moderately effective devices to be the most typical weapons. Similarly, they would expect only moderately efficient people-movers to be good vehicles, since on average, vehicles are by no means ideal people-movers.

Where do these ideals for categories come from, then? Most likely they come from our knowledge of how each category fits in with other parts of our lives—its place in our greater understanding of the world. We know that vehicles are made *so that* people can be moved from place to place. Therefore, the most typical vehicles would do this in the best possible way. We know that weapons are created in order to hurt (or threaten to hurt) other people. Therefore, the most typical ones are the ones that do this in an effective way. Furthermore, we can apply our general knowledge to evaluate how well different vehicles and weapons actually fulfill these functions.

The importance of such knowledge can be illustrated even more by a kind of category that Barsalou (1985) called *goal-derived categories*. These are categories that are defined solely in terms of how their members fulfill some desired goal or plan, for example, things to eat on a diet, things to take from one's house during a fire, good birthday presents, and so on. For goal-derived categories, very little of the category structure is explained by family resemblance. For example, things to eat on a diet might include celery, sugar-free jello, diet soda, baked potatoes, baked fish, and skim milk. These items differ in many respects. They are much less similar to one another than normal food categories such as dairy products or meats, yet, they are all within the same category by being things that people eat while on a diet. Here, the ideal is something like having the smallest number of calories or the least fat. So, celery is an excellent example of things to eat on a diet, because it has virtually no fat and is extremely low in calories. Bread is a fairly good example, though it has somewhat more calories and fat. Fruit juice might be a moderate example, since it is low in fat but not particularly low in calories. And ice cream would be a bad example. Barsalou found that the most typical examples of goal-derived categories were the ones that were closest to the ideal. Family resemblance did not explain a significant portion of the variance. This is an extreme case in which an item's place in a larger knowledge structure is perhaps the most important aspect of category membership, and the "average" properties of the category members count for little. For example, the best food to eat on a diet would be a filling food with no calories, fat or other bad ingredients. However, these properties are by no means the most frequent ones of foods that people actually eat while on diets. So, this ideal seems to be imposed by our understanding of what the category is supposed to be, which is in turn driven by our understanding of how it fits into the rest of what we know about foods and their effects on our bodies. The ideal cannot be derived from just observing examples and noting the features that occur most. Although the goal-derived categories are an extreme example of this (because the members have very little in common besides the ideal), Barsalou found evidence for the importance of ideals in common categories as well (see previous chapter). Also, recall that Lynch et al. (2000) found a similar pattern for the category of trees; many other related examples will be described in chapter 6.

One of the themes of the knowledge approach, then, is that people do not rely on simple observation or feature learning in order to learn new concepts. They pay attention to the features that their prior knowledge says are the important ones. They may make inferences and add information that is not actually observed in the item itself. Their knowledge is used in an active way to shape what is learned and how that information is used after learning. This aspect of the theory will be expounded in greater detail in chapter 6.

One clear limitation of the knowledge approach should already be apparent: Much of a concept cannot be based on previous knowledge. For example, you might have previous knowledge that helps you to understand why an airplane has wings, how this relates to its ability to fly, what the jets or propellers do, and so on. However, it is probably only by actual observation of planes that you would learn where propellers are normally located, what shape the windows are, that the seats usually provide no lower back support, and so on, because these things are not predictable from your knowledge before learning the category. Or, in other cases, it is only after observing some category members that you know what knowledge is relevant and can only then use it to understand the category (see Murphy 2000, for a discussion). So, the knowledge approach does not attempt to explain all of concept acquisition by reference to general knowledge; it must also assume a learning mechanism that is based on experience. However, this approach has not incorporated any empirical learning mechanism. This may be seen as a shortcoming of the knowledge approach, or one can view the empirical learning process as simply being a different problem. That is, proponents of the knowledge approach are pointing out the ways that prior knowledge influences the learning of a new concept, and other aspects of learning are not part of the phenomena they are trying to explain. However, it should be clear that a complete account requires an integrated explanation of all aspects of concept learning. Furthermore, we should not necessarily assume that the empirical and knowledge-based learning components will be easily separable modules. It is possible that the two interact in a complex way so that one must study them together to understand either one (Wisniewski and Medin 1994). However, that discussion must await a later chapter.

Conclusions

It is too early in this book to evaluate these different approaches. However, it is worth emphasizing that none of them suffers from the problems of the classical approach. All of them actively predict that categories will have gradations of typicality and that there will be borderline cases. Unlike the later revisions of the classical model (discussed in the previous chapter; e.g., Armstrong, Gleitman, and Gleitman 1983), these theories claim category fuzziness as an integral part of conceptual processing, rather than an unhappy influence of something that is not the "true" concept. This is because similarity of items is inherently continuous. Category members will be more or less similar to one another and to their prototype, and this gradation of similarity leads to typicality differences, RT differences in judgments, and learning differences. Similarly, whether an item is consistent with one's knowledge in a complex domain is not an all-or-none matter but often a question of relative consistency. Thus, unlike for the classical view, typicality phenomena are not a nuisance to be explained away, but are rather inherent to the working of these approaches.

Another point to be made about each of these approaches is that they are not as entirely self-sufficient as one might like. For example, the prototype view does not deny that people learn and remember exemplars. Clearly, if Wilbur, the bulldog, lives next door to me, and I see him many times per week, I will be able to identify him and his peculiar attributes. And, as already mentioned, the first time one encounters a category member, the only prototype one can form would be based on that single exemplar. Thus, exemplar knowledge and prototype knowledge must exist side by side to at least some degree, according to prototype theory. The general claim of that theory, however, is that for mature categories, people rely on summary representations of the entire category rather than specific exemplars in making judgments about the concept.

Similarly, I pointed out that the knowledge approach focuses on one important (it claims) aspect of learning and representing concepts. However, it must admit that there is an empirical learning component to concepts, if only to explain the results of psychological experiments that use artificial stimuli that are removed from any knowledge. It is likely, then, that this view will have to be combined with one of the other views in order to form a complete theory of concepts. Finally, exemplar theorists might also agree that there must be a level of general knowledge that is separate from exemplar knowledge and that affects concepts and their use (though in fact most have not addressed this issue). For example, one could argue that facts such as whales being mammals are school-learned general facts, rather than something one learns from seeing many whale exemplars. But of course one does see whale exemplars occasionally too. So, in answering questions about whales, some information might come from the exemplars and some from general knowledge.

This mixture of different kinds of conceptual knowledge makes it difficult to evaluate the different theories. The result in the field has been to focus on certain experimental paradigms in which such mixtures would be expected to be less likely. However, for real-life concepts, we would do best not to assume that a single form of conceptual representation will account for everything.

APPENDIX: THE GENERALIZED CONTEXT MODEL

The body of this chapter has discussed the Context Model, proposed by Medin and Schaffer (1978), as the most influential version of the exemplar approach. However, in more recent times, Robert Nosofsky's enhancement of this, the *Generalized Context Model* or *GCM*, has been more widely cited and tested. This model has a number of different forms, as it has developed over years of investigation. The purpose of this appendix is to describe it in more detail and to give an idea of how it works. For more formal descriptions, see Nosofsky (1992) or Nosofsky and Palmeri (1997).

Overview

Recall that exemplar models argue that you categorize objects by comparing them to remembered exemplars whose categories you have already encoded. The more similar the object is to exemplars in a given category, the more likely it is to be categorized into that category. The categorization process can be thought of as having three parts. First, one must calculate the distance between the exemplar of interest and all the other exemplars. In the Medin and Schaffer (1978) model, this was done by the multiplicative rule described in the main chapter. In the GCM, this is done by a more general distance metric. Second, this distance metric is scaled in a way that has the effect of weighting close similarity much more than moderate similarity. Third, once one has all these similarities of the object to known exemplars, one must decide which category the object is in. This involves a fairly simple comparison of the exemplar similarities of the different categories involved.

The formulas involved in the GCM can be difficult if you aren't familiar with them. I personally am not a math modeling expert, and it has taken me some time to understand them (to the degree that I do). This chapter will help you begin to understand the model. However, to reach a fuller appreciation, I would recommend that when you read individual papers that describe this or other models, you resist the very natural temptation to skip over all the formulas. If you read these formulas and the authors' explanations of them in four or five different papers, you will eventually find (perhaps to your amazement) that you understand what they are talking about. So, don't give up just because it all seems so complicated here. I describe the three parts of the GCM in the following sections.

Distance Calculations

The basic idea of exemplar models is that an object brings to mind other similar exemplars. To measure this, the model calculates the psychological distance between the object to be categorized (usually called i below) and all the known exemplars, in order to identify which exemplars are going to be brought to mind.

In order to compare various stimuli, the GCM assumes that they have been broken into dimensions of some kind. This could be because they are items that have been constructed according to certain dimensions (color, size, position on a card, etc.) that subjects would be sensitive to. In other cases, one may have psychological dimensions of the stimuli that are derived from a scaling program, such as multidimensional scaling. For example, using multidimensional scaling, Rips, Shoben, and

Smith (1973) discovered that animals were thought to be similar based on their size and predacity. The scaling program provided the values of each item on each dimension, and these would be used to calculate similarity. The distance between any two objects is a function of how far apart they are on each dimension.

Equation (1) shows how the GCM calculates the distance between two items, i and j, when the dimensions of the objects are known. (Think of i as being the object to be categorized, and j one of the remembered exemplars.) It is essentially the same as the Euclidean distance between two points in space, from high-school geometry.

$$d_{ij} = \sqrt{\sum_m w_m |x_{im} - x_{jm}|^2} \tag{1}$$

For each dimension m of the items (either a physical dimension or one from a multi-dimensional scaling solution), you calculate the difference between the items $(x_i - x_j)$ and square it. Then this number is multiplied by the weight for that dimension (w_m). So, important dimensions will be counted more heavily than less important dimensions. (In the original context model, this was reflected in the mismatch values. The GCM more clearly separates psychological similarity from dimensional importance in categorization.) These numbers are added up for all the m dimensions, and the square root is taken. The main difference between this and simple Euclidean distance is the weighting of the dimensions. In calculating real distances, no spatial dimension is weighted more than any other. In the GCM, the w values for each dimension are a free parameter—that is, they are calculated from the data themselves rather than being specified by the model. Kruschke's (1992) influential ALCOVE model (based on the GCM to a large degree) provides a connectionist mechanism that actually learns which dimensions are important.

I should note that this particular form of the distance metric can vary in different studies. (Those who are just trying to get the basic idea of this model should definitely skip this paragraph.) Note that we squared the differences on each dimension and then took the square root of the sum. That is, we raised the distance to the power 2 and then raised the sum to the power 1/2 (that's a square root). Distance metrics in general raise the separation by some power and then the sum to one over that power. The number 2 is only one such number that could be used. We could have used the number 1—that is, raise the distances to the power of 1 (i.e., do nothing) and taken the sum to the power of 1/1 (i.e., do nothing again). This would give us the "city block" metric, in which the distance between two points is the sum of their distances on each dimension. This is called the city block metric, because one does not form hypotenuses for distances—one cannot cut through a city block.

To get from 40th Street and Second Avenue to 43rd Street and Sixth Avenue, one must walk three blocks north and four blocks west, resulting in seven total blocks (let's assume the blocks are squares). By Euclidean distance, the shortest distance connecting these points (cutting across) would be only five blocks. For some stimulus dimensions, the city block metric seems most appropriate, whereas for others, Euclidean distance works best.[4] And for still others, some number in between is most appropriate. Thus, this difference between dimensions can be made into a variable (usually called Minkowski's *r*), which is altered depending on the nature of the stimuli. So, you may see something like equation (1) with *r*s and 1/*r*s in it.

Turning Distances into Similarity

Unfortunately, we are still not done with deciding the psychological distance between two items. Research has shown that behavioral similarity between items is an exponentially decreasing function of their psychological distance (Shepard 1987). For example, if rats learn to produce a response to a certain colored light, other lights will elicit the same response as a function of the exponential distance between the test light and the original. The exponential function has the effect that things that are extremely close to the object have a large effect, which falls off very quickly as things become moderately and less similar. Recall that Medin and Schaffer (1978) used a multiplicative rule so that objects that are moderately different would have little effect on categorization decisions. The exponential function does the same thing.

As shown in equation (2), the distance scores derived from equation (1) are input to the exponential function, producing a similarity score, *s*.

$$s_{ij} = \exp(-c \cdot d_{ij}) \tag{2}$$

Note that $\exp(x)$ means to raise e to the xth power, e^x, and that $\exp(-x) = 1/e^x$. Therefore, the bigger x gets, the smaller $\exp(-x)$ gets. In equation (2), this means that the greater the distance between i and j, the smaller the similarity, since the distance is being negated. When distance is 0 (i.e., two stimuli are identical), *s* would equal 1.0; otherwise, *s* falls between 0 and 1. The variable *c* basically determines the spread of similarity by modulating the effect of distance. Sometimes people seem to pay attention to only very close similarity, and other times people take into account even fairly weak similarity. A high value of *c* corresponds to the former situation, and a low value corresponds to the latter. If *c* is very high, then the exemplar model is essentially requiring that an item be identical to a known exemplar, because any distance between i and j would be multiplied by a high number, resulting in a low similarity. If c is very low, then the similarity to all known items is used. Usually, c is a free parameter estimated from the data.

Making the Decision

In order to make a categorization decision, one has to decide which category exemplars are most like the object being categorized, i. If the object is similar to many dogs, a few cats, and one burro, then it is probably a dog. The GCM does this by looking at the object's similarity to *all* objects in every category, and then comparing the similarity of one category to that of all the others. In the previous sections, we calculated the similarity of the object to every other exemplar. If you were to add up all these similarity scores, you would know the total pool of similarity this object has to everything. The GCM uses something called the Luce Choice Axiom to turn this similarity into a response. The Luce Choice Axiom basically asks how much of the total pool of similarity comes from dogs, how much from cats, and how much from burros, and then turns those answers into response probabilities. Equation (3) calculates the probability that the object, i, will be placed into each category, J.

$$P(J \mid i) = \sum_{j \in J} s_{ij} \bigg/ \left[\sum_{K} \sum_{k \in K} s_{ik} \right] \tag{3}$$

The numerator is the similarity of i to all the members j of category J (as calculated in equation (2)). The more similar the item is to known exemplars in J, the higher this probability. The denominator is the similarity of i to members of *all* known categories (K), the total pool of similarity mentioned above. In English, then, equation (3) is the ratio of the similarity of i to all the things in J to the total similarity pool.[5] Continuing the previous example, if i is mostly similar to dogs, then perhaps $P(\text{dog} \mid i) = .75$, because dogs have 75% of the total similarity for this object. And perhaps $P(\text{cat} \mid i) = .20$, because the object is similar to a few cats. And because you once saw a very strange burro, $P(\text{burro} \mid i) = .05$. What the Luce Choice Axiom says is that you should call this object a dog 75% of the time, a cat 25% of the time, and a burro 5% of the time.

Note that this formula is probabilistic. It doesn't say that people will always categorize i into the category with the highest score. Instead, it says that their categorization will match the probability score. This behavior is not entirely rational. If it is 75 percent likely that i is a dog, then I should obviously categorize it as a dog whenever I see it, because it is much more likely to be a dog than a cat or a burro, based on my own experience. Any other response is much less likely. However, people tend to do *probability matching* in these situations, in which they give less likely responses a proportional number of times, rather than always choosing the most likely answer. This behavior is found in many choice tasks in both humans and other animals.

Later versions of the GCM have sometimes incorporated another parameter proposed by Ashby and Maddox (1993), called *gamma*, which relates to the probability matching phenomenon. To do this, the numerator of (3) is raised to the gamma power, and the inside term of the denominator ($\sum_{k \in K} s_{ik}$) is also raised to that power. (The exact value of gamma is usually a free parameter.) That is, once one has calculated the total similarity of i to a category, that similarity is raised to the power gamma. Gamma has the effect of varying the amount of determinacy in subjects' responses. When gamma is 1, the categorization rule has the characteristics mentioned earlier: Subjects respond proportionally to the probability. When gamma is higher, they respond more deterministically: They tend to choose the most likely category more. This is because the similarity values are less than 1, so raising them to a high power tends to decrease the small values almost to 0, thereby benefiting the larger values.

See how simple it all is? No? Well, you are not alone. Although all this may be confusing on first reading, if one simply focuses on one variable or equation at a time, one can usually understand how it works. Attempting to keep the entire GCM in one's head at a time is pretty much impossible, so do not be too discouraged if you don't feel that you get it. Especially at the beginning, you can probably only understand it piece by piece.

Although the GCM has been extremely successful in modeling results of categorization experiments, one criticism of it has been that it is too powerful. The complexity of the model and the number of parameters it has makes it very good at fitting data, even if the data are exactly what would be predicted by a prototype model (Smith and Minda 2000). Perhaps because it is a rather late addition to the model, gamma has struck some in the field as being a dubious construct. Some critics feel that it is simply a free parameter that lets the GCM account for data that could not previously be accounted for, without any clear psychological evidence that determinacy of responding is a variable that changes systematically. However, this level of argument is far beyond that of the present discussion. See the interchange between Smith and Minda (2000) and Nosofsky (2000) for discussion and references.

Whatever the criticisms of it, the GCM has been an extremely influential categorization model. What should now be obvious is that there is a lot more to the GCM than simply saying that people remember exemplars. There are many assumptions about how similarity is calculated, how decisions are made, and what variables affect performance that go far beyond the simple claim of exemplar representations of concepts. Thus, the model's successes and failures cannot be taken as direct evidence for and against exemplars alone.

4

Exemplar Effects and Theories

Seeing a striking similarity between a new dog and my golden retriever, I would be confident (if asked) that it was a dog, be hesitant to give it food that my dog (atypically for dogs) does not like, and slow to think of the possibility of it chasing cars, which my virtuous dog never does. Upon reflection I would acknowledge that a sample of one is a bit small, but this voice of rationality would, under many circumstances, come decidedly second.
—Brooks (1987), p. 142

Perhaps the most basic assumption of traditional views of concepts is that they are summary representations of a class of entities. The Classical View clearly embraced this assumption by proposing that concepts are represented as necessary and sufficient properties of the entire class. If all dogs have some features in common that are not in turn shared with other animals, then we can obviously give a summary description of this potentially infinite set of entities. When Prototype Theory criticized the Classical View, it attacked the necessity and sufficiency of the class's properties, but it did not question the notion that the representation of the dog concept is a description that applies to dogs in general. Indeed, a summary representation view is probably necessary in order to make sense of quantified statements (much beloved of philosophers and other proponents of the classical view) like "all dogs have four legs" or "no dog has lungs." How can such statements be represented within one's conceptual system except by a summary representation of dogs? Prototype theorists would argue that there are few features that all members of a category have, but their representations involve a general listing of features that most or many of the members have. And this list is a description of the category as a whole, rather than of particular members.

In this context, the proposal of Medin and Schaffer (1978) that concepts may be represented in terms of remembered exemplars was truly radical. Although proponents of this view may not, when pressed on the issue, claim that there are no summary representations (e.g., Smith and Medin 1981, p. 160), they do argue strongly that many phenomena usually ascribed to prototype representations can be explained by exemplar memories. The power of their arguments is often not fully appreciated outside of the field. To some people, the fact that children, say, can learn a word from one example and then apply it to a novel example shows that they must have formed a general representation of the word meaning rather than an exemplar-based representation. However, as reviewed in chapter 3, this is not correct. In fact, what is impressive about exemplar theory is how well it can explain generalization to novel examples and situations. And what is unique to exemplar theory is how it explains the *limitations* of that generalization—how properties learned of a class or set of exemplars are sometimes not extended to all category members. These limitations (discussed in the exemplar effects section below) are not part of our naive thinking about concept and word use, and the research revealing them is an important contribution to our understanding of concepts.

Chapter Organization
This chapter will discuss two rather different approaches to this issue. The first tradition, which I call *exemplar effects*, is the attempt to show that when people categorize an item, they use a particular remembered exemplar to make this decision. So, when I go to a store and identify something as a portable compact disc player, I may do so by accessing the memory of my own portable CD player, or another one that I've seen before that is particularly similar to this new one. My identification may be greatly influenced by even unimportant similarities, such as a manufacturer's label on the cover. Research on exemplar effects has generally not been formalized in mathematical or computational models. The second tradition, which I call *exemplar models*, involves the comparison of formal, usually mathematical models of category representation and the categorization process. Here, specific instantiations of exemplar theory are tested and compared to other instantiations or to prototype models. These models were introduced in the previous chapter.

The reason I separate these two traditions is twofold. First, the kind of experiment that is carried out in the two is quite different. In the exemplar effect tradition, experiments examine variables that influence the access of specific exemplars. The general goal is to show that the categorization of stimulus X involves retrieving a remembered exemplar Y. Exemplar model experiments usually do not show that one exemplar in particular was used to make this decision (in fact, they may claim that multiple exemplars were remembered). Instead, they attempt to compare the predictions of various models for how difficult it was to learn (or categorize) each stimulus in the set. Thus, the main dependent measure of interest is how well each model fits the results as a whole. This abstract description is no doubt somewhat difficult to follow at this point. However, the descriptions of experiments in the main sections of this chapter will illustrate the difference between the two.

Second, I separate these traditions because the most popular exemplar models contain many other assumptions about categories and processing than the use of instances. Indeed, the empirical success of exemplar models depends on both their assumption of exemplar memories and the multiplicative (or exponential) similarity rule that they use (Medin and Schwanenflugel 1981; Nosofsky 1992). Thus, an evaluation of exemplar models requires much more than a consideration of whether people use remembered exemplars—the models contain many more assumptions and claims about representation and processing. In fact, a full comparison of all these models is beyond the scope of this book, as it would quickly become extremely technical. However, the present coverage should give the reader sufficient background to read articles that make these comparisons.

Having said all this, it is still the case that demonstrations of exemplar effects should be taken as supporting exemplar models in general. Nonetheless, there is surprisingly little connection made between these two traditions in their respective papers. Although authors proposing specific models do tend to cite the papers showing exemplar effects, there is little attempt to model their results or to discuss the implications of the variables that have been shown to influence specific exemplar usage. This, then, is an area for future work to address.

Exemplar Effects

Work in other areas of cognitive psychology has shown the importance of remindings of specific instances in the development of cognitive skills. For example, Ross (1984) showed that when people learn how to solve a new kind of mathematical problem, they rely heavily on their memories for past examples in solving new problems. Often this memory is based on irrelevant properties of the problem. For example, we all remember algebra problems of the sort in which one train left a station at noon and travelled half an hour before meeting another train that had been travelling for an hour in order to reach the same point. Then we would have to answer questions such as when train 2 would reach the station or how fast train 1 was travelling, and so on. As a result, when we hear a new problem about trains leaving stations, we are likely to start writing down formulas like Distance = Speed × Time. If it turns out that the question is *not* of the sort requiring this formula, we may spend considerable time trying to answer it this way first, because of our memories for past train problems. Ross showed that the memory of specific learning examples can have deleterious effects on the performance of later problems, if that later problem is superficially similar to an example of the "wrong" type (for a review, see Ross 1989).

This logic underlies many of the experiments on exemplar effects in categorization. The idea is that by manipulating how similar an item is to a remembered exemplar— even similarity that is irrelevant to the classification task—one may be able to influence which category subjects think the item is in. Exemplar reminding could have two effects on category use. First, it might occur during learning. When you are learning about a new kind of animal, you might be reminded of other animals you have seen. This reminding could influence what you think this kind of animal is generally like. That is, the reminding could influence the category representation you initially form. Second, reminding may occur in categorization. So, if you see a curled-up animal in your neighbor's chair that looks just like your curled-up cat, you may very quickly identify it as a cat (even though when it uncurls, it turns out to be a ferret). Here you already know all about cats; the effect is not on forming new generalizations about cats but on identifying them. I discuss these two kinds of effects in order.

Exemplar Effects in Learning

In the very early stages of learning, often all that you know are a few exemplars. If someone points at an animal and says "That's a zebra," and if you've never heard of a zebra before, you have little else to go on than this single exemplar. (Of course, you do have your more general knowledge of animals and mammals, which you are likely to access when thinking about this category—see chapter 6.) When you've seen two or three exemplars, you are in a better position to form an idea of the category as a whole, rather than relying on the possible idiosyncracies of just one zebra. Nonetheless, given that you have only seen three zebras, you are also likely to remember all three of them fairly well. Even theories that do not talk about exemplars agree that people have episodic memories of encountering objects and events, and these memories can be a source of conceptual inference and judgment.

However, theories that focus primarily on summary representations (see chapter 3), like prototype theory, have little to say about how specific exemplars might be the basis for judgments about the category as a whole. There have been a few experiments looking at this process during learning itself. Before describing some of the more interesting such studies, it is important to remind ourselves not to take an overly simplistic view of exemplar effects. It was common in the 1970s and early

1980s to view exemplar effects as being essentially the advantage of old items over new ones. That is, the degree to which people were faster at categorizing exemplars that they had studied over those they had not (assuming the items had been equated for typicality, and so on) was assumed to reflect exemplar knowledge. This reasoning was used to predict that when the difference between old and new items disappeared, categorization could not be proceeding via exemplars. However, as we have already discussed (in chapter 3), the difference between old and new items can disappear even in exemplar models. As Hintzman and Ludlam (1980) pointed out, exemplars are forgotten over time, in bits and pieces. When part of an exemplar is forgotten, it may no longer have an advantage over a new item, even if both items are categorized by being compared to what is remembered of previously viewed exemplars. As a result, the old-new difference, which was the focus of considerable early attention (Homa, Sterling, and Trepel 1981; Posner and Keele 1968) is no longer considered to be a valid measure of whether exemplars are used. (More specifically, the presence of such an advantage is not necessary to indicate use of exemplars.)[1]

Ross, Perkins, and Tenpenny (1990) carried out an ingenious study of exemplar reminding in learning. They taught subjects two categories: two social clubs, each of which had different members. Initially, subjects learned only about two members of each club, to ensure that they had detailed information about each exemplar. Then subjects were tested on new items. These items were constructed so that they would be likely to remind subjects of one of the old items. Furthermore, the test item shared a feature with *both* of the members of its category. Ross et al. reasoned that if subjects were in fact reminded of one original exemplar, then they would notice the shared feature with that item, but not the feature that was shared with the other item.

Let's go through a more detailed example. Imagine that you learned about the following two members of Club X:

Shirley	*Julia*
likes ice cream	likes Westerns
bought nails	bought a swimsuit

Now you are presented with a new person to categorize. Different groups received slightly different items here:

likes sherbet / likes cowboys and Indians
bought wood
bought towels

If you received the version that had "likes sherbet," you would be reminded of Shirley. Then you might also notice that Shirley bought nails, and this person bought wood. Apparently, Club X members like carpentry. However, if you received the version that had "likes cowboys and Indians," you might be reminded of Julia, who likes Westerns, and then you might notice that Julia bought a swimsuit, and this person bought towels. Apparently, Club X members like to swim or go to the beach. Of course, both statements about Club X are equally true, given the exemplars you have seen.

In the third phase, Ross et al. (1990) gave their subjects new items to rank on how much they would be liked by Club X members. Among the items were "chisel" and "sunglasses." They found that subjects who read the "likes sherbet" item (and were reminded of Shirley) ranked chisel above sunglasses; subjects who read the "likes cowboys and Indians" item (and were reminded of Julia) ranked sunglasses above chisel. This is surprising, because the rest of the features were the same across the two groups: All subjects read an item that had *both* "bought wood" and "bought towels." Nonetheless, by manipulating a feature that made one or another exemplar memorable, Ross et al. showed that subjects made different generalizations about the category. They argued that when one exemplar reminds you of another, you pay attention to their common properties and may start to think that these properties are characteristic of the category as a whole. That is, it's not just that the test item reminded some people of Shirley, but that in being reminded of Shirley, certain commonalities were reinforced. Other items had different commonalities with this test item, but because those items were not brought to mind, their commonalities were not noticed.

Ross et al. argued that these effects are not consistent with most prototype or exemplar models. The only difference between the two conditions was one feature (likes sherbet/cowboys and Indians) that was unrelated to the critical comparison (like chisels/sunglasses). Thus, the same number of total features that were related to chisels or to sunglasses was presented in the two cases. If subjects had represented the two clubs as a list of features, weighted by their frequency, there is no clear reason why changing the unrelated feature should have an effect on features that were not varied (chisels and sunglasses). Similarly, if subjects made their judgment by examining the remembered exemplars, they would have found equal numbers of exemplars that contained information related to chisels and to sunglasses. Although reminding of specific exemplars is necessary to explain these results, Ross et al. say, one needs to assume that this reminding led to a generalization about the whole category. So, when the test items reminded subjects of Shirley, they thought something like "this club is interested in carpentry." Thus, both exemplar information (in the reminding) and summary information about the entire category (the generalization) is used. These conclusions were reinforced by follow-up experiments of Spalding and Ross (1994).

A different technique was used by Medin and Bettger (1994). They presented a set of seven items to subjects and then asked for recognition judgments. The items varied on four dimensions, and across the items there was a most frequent or typical value on each dimension. Furthermore, during the recognition test, items that had many typical values were recognized (even in some cases if they had never been seen) more often than items that had few typical values. (Past research has also found that category typicality predicts recognition in memory experiments; e.g., Franks and Bransford 1971.) Thus, although only one category was involved, this may be a form of category learning.

In their Experiment 2, Medin and Bettger varied the order in which the items were presented so that different similarities would become apparent. In the *adjacent* condition (I've changed their names), the items were presented so that three items in a row had two particular features. For example, all three might be green and large. In the *separated* condition, these items were separated, with other items between them. In the test, a new item that had the two critical features was quite often falsely recognized as having been seen in the adjacent condition, but less so in the separated condition. This effect was found even though the adjacent group was more accurate in general than the separated group was. When similar patterns occur in adjacent items, people apparently notice them and encode them as part of the category representation. But since the same exemplars were involved in both conditions, this result is puzzling to exemplar theories.

This effect of adjacency of exemplars cannot be explained by prototype models that assume that a category representation is a list of features weighted by their frequency (Hampton 1979; see chapter 3). At the end of an experiment, the prototype would have no information about the order in which the exemplars had been viewed, and both groups received the exact same exemplars. Similarly, exemplar models do not worry about the order of items. Although forgetting occurs for exemplars over time, that would not explain the greater weight given to items appearing together. This effect, then, is similar to the Ross et al. (1990) finding that when one exemplar reminds you of another, you are more likely to weight its common features. Adjacent items are by their nature reminiscent of one another: A subject may still have the earlier item in working memory when the next item is encountered. As a result, any commonality between them is more likely to be encoded and thought of as relevant to categorization. However, this commonality is apparently connected to a more general category representation, since it is not a property of any single exemplar. In short, such exemplar effects in category learning are a challenge to most theories of concepts.

Exemplar Effects in Categorization
According to exemplar models of categorization, people decide what a new item is by accessing already-known examples and relying on them. In some sense, this can be thought of as relying on analogy (Brooks 1987): Although I don't know for sure that this object is a pen, I know that I have something that looks just like it, which I have used as a pen for some weeks, and so I can infer that it also is a pen, will write, probably has blue ink, and so on. In most formal models of exemplar learning, though, the use of one particular exemplar is not the focus. When I see a pen, I access a large number of remembered entities (not just one), and it is the sum total of their categories (weighted by their similarity to the item) that predicts my categorization. Nonetheless, there has been considerable empirical interest in the importance of one or two closely related exemplars, and how they might affect categorization. This is the topic of the current section—how one or two very similar exemplars might influence categorization.

The emphasis on very similar or "close" exemplars has both a theoretical and a methodological purpose. First, Brooks (1987) has argued that when a known item is almost identical to the test item, one cannot help but be reminded of it. Furthermore, such remindings are almost always going to be valid and helpful, even if they are based on superficial features. So, if I see an animal that looks almost exactly like Wilbur, a bulldog I am familiar with, I can be extremely sure that this is also a bulldog, with typical bulldog properties, even though to be completely certain of my categorization I would have to verify the animal's parentage. Extremely close similarity is very difficult to achieve with things that are in different categories, and so it is an excellent cue for category membership even when it is not a very principled basis for decision. Of course, Brooks notes (pp. 163f), it is possible for somewhat similar items to be in different categories, as in cases such as whales and sharks. However, it would be extremely surprising to see something that looked just like a particular sperm whale but turned out not to be a whale at all.

The methodological reason for focusing on close similarity is that it allows us to know exactly which item is responsible for the categorization. So, if a test item has been manipulated so that it is in one condition very similar to exemplar 1 and in another condition very similar to exemplar 2, then the difference between the conditions in categorizing the item may be attributed to the access of exemplar 1 vs. 2 (assuming other variables are held constant, of course). This approach to evaluating exemplar use is more direct than the modeling approach to be discussed in the second part of this chapter.

The most prominent studies of exemplar effects have included a series of experiments done by Lee Brooks and his colleagues. I will only discuss a couple of these demonstrations, but there is considerably more evidence of the same sort. Brooks's approach combines work from the memory literature (especially work on implicit memory and the memory for surface details) with categorization research. As a result, a number of the studies that he and his colleagues have carried out have not been categorization studies per se, even though they related the results to categorization theory (e.g., Jacoby, Baker, and Brooks 1989; Whittlesea 1987), and I will not be focusing on these.

To demonstrate the basic effect that these studies have shown, I begin with a study using a real-world set of categories and subjects. Brooks, Norman, and Allen (1991) studied how physicians categorized skin diseases based on slides of examples, taken from the photographic files of actual dermatologists. The subjects were advanced residents or general practitioners, rather than dermatologists, but these doctors see many cases of skin problems, and the diseases chosen for study were all among the 20 most common skin disorders.

In the study phase, subjects were shown slides of various skin diseases, which were correctly labeled with their diagnoses. The subjects merely had to rate how typical each item was of its category (to ensure that they examined each one closely). Then in the test phase, subjects were shown slides of examples from the same categories and had to select which disease it represented from a 3-choice set of options. Some of these slides were the previously studied items; others were from the same categories but did not look superficially similar to the studied item; still others were from the same categories but did look superficially similar. By varying the precise item shown during learning, this variable was not confounded with item differences. That is, for one subject, picture 10 would be similar to the studied example of psoriasis, say, but for another subject, picture 10 would be dissimilar to the studied example. So, the overall typicality of the picture was controlled for in this comparison.

Quite surprisingly, Brooks et al. found a consistent 10–15% difference between the similar and dissimilar items in their experiments: The doctors were significantly more accurate in identifying the slides that were superficially similar to a studied slide. Furthermore, this difference held up when the study and test phases were separated by a week and was found for both general practitioners and residents. The effect was also found when the experimenters took steps to slow down subjects' judgments and make them actively consider all the alternatives in the multiple-choice test. Perhaps less surprisingly, there was also a noticeable advantage in categorizing the slides that had been viewed during study, compared to new ones. This also may indicate some exemplar memory. What is particularly impressive about this study is that it involves actual categories, as identified by their everyday users, and it shows an effect size that is "clinically important" (p. 284) rather than just statistically significant. Indeed, on first reaction one might be somewhat concerned about these results: Will you be totally misdiagnosed by your physician, simply because your skin looks similar to that of a recent patient with a different problem? Probably not: In a full medical diagnosis, the physician would have other information besides the visual appearance of part of your skin, such as your medical history, any events that coincided with the problem, whether it itches, how long it has been present, and so on. In many cases, this would distinguish cases that are borderline from the perspective of purely visual information.

Theoretically, Brooks et al.'s (1991) study seems to show that subjects are using similar exemplars in order to categorize items. Thus, slides that were quite similar to a previously studied item activated the memory of that item and its categorization, and this information was difficult to ignore.

Other studies have used the more typical artificial materials, with more carefully controlled dimensions. Allen and Brooks (1991), for example, used pictures of cartoon animals presented against an environmental background (e.g., a desert or an arctic scene). In this study, subjects were taught a rule by which items could be categorized. Although items varied on five features, only three of them were relevant: One category was associated with angular bodies, spots and long legs; the other with rounded bodies, lack of spots and short legs. If an item had at least two of the three critical features for a category, then it belonged in that category. Subjects were explicitly told this rule (in the condition I'll be discussing), so there was no need for them to rely on exemplars.

Allen and Brooks first taught the subjects eight items, giving considerable information to individuate each item. For the test phase, they constructed items that were very similar to the test items and that were either in the same or a different category. For example, by keeping the background environment and noncritical features the same but changing one critical feature, a new item could be extremely similar to a test item but be in a different category. (The backgrounds themselves were not predictive of category membership but were used to vary similarity among exemplars.) Such items were *bad matches*, because they were similar to something in a different category. By changing a different feature, the test item could be very similar to a test item but in the same category—a *good match*. The results showed that even though subjects knew a rule by which to categorize the items, they made more than 20% more errors on the bad matches than on the good ones. That is, subjects seemed to be relying on the learned exemplars. Allen and Brooks found that this effect persisted even when subjects were warned about the bad matches, and when they were asked to be very careful in their decisions. Similar results were found in RTs to categorize the items. When subjects were confronted with these results, they did not show much awareness that they had been fooled by similar items. Similar results were found with a slightly different stimulus construction by Regehr and Brooks (1993).

In order to obtain this effect of the bad vs. good matches, it is necessary that the test item immediately bring to mind a learned exemplar. If the item is presented as a list of verbal features, the effect essentially disappears (Allen and Brooks 1991, Experiment 2), in part because every list of features looks much like any other, and so there is no specific reminding. Especially when subjects know the category rule, they can focus on some features and ignore the others. However, when a stimulus is a complex visual scene, it is difficult to ignore irrelevant properties that might bring to mind a very similar exemplar. More generally, it seems to be necessary that each item be a coherent individual (Regehr and Brooks 1993), rather than a mere collection of properties. To the degree that one item is holistically like another, it is likely to bring the other to mind. This phenomenon is often not present in many categorization experiments, which use stimuli such as strings of letters and numbers, circles with diameter lines, cards with a number of colored geometric shapes on them, or any kind of list. Most effective in inducing reminding is a picture of a whole object or scene, in which a complex item is globally similar or different to another item. See Regehr and Brooks (1993) for detailed discussion.

A very different kind of methodology was used by Malt (1989) in her study of exemplars in categorization. Her reasoning was that if people are using a close exemplar to categorize items, then there should be some effect of this on the exemplar itself. If I categorize something as a dog because it reminds me of Wilbur, this should result in activation of my Wilbur exemplar. Therefore, Malt used a priming technique in which she looked to see if there was such activation after an item was categorized. First, she constructed categories of items using pictures of animals from wildlife books. She selected the items in pairs, so that one item would be considered to be very close to another item. During learning, subjects learned categories with only one of these paired items. They had to learn the items' names, to ensure that they had encoded each exemplar fully. At test, they had to categorize pictures of the old items as well as new ones that were similar to one of the old ones. In the critical trials, subjects first categorized a new item (e.g., a sperm whale) and then categorized its similar, already-learned item (e.g., a sei whale). If subjects had accessed the old item when categorizing the new one (e.g., if they thought "this looks like that other whale, which was in category 1"), then they would be faster to respond to the old item when it appeared. In a control condition, the new item was unrelated to the old one (e.g., a jackrabbit preceded the sei whale), and so no priming would be expected.

In her first experiment, Malt (1989) made up categories that were essentially arbitrary. Her reasoning was that these categories could only be learned by memorizing the exemplars; furthermore, she told subjects to classify new items by putting them in the same category as the most similar learned item. In these circumstances, Malt found large exemplar priming effects. When subjects classified a new item, the most similar old item was classified much faster, compared to the control condition. This experiment served to validate the measure. The question is whether the same priming would occur with more realistic categories and without these special instructions. In later experiments, Malt found evidence for such priming, though it was considerably smaller than when exemplar use was forced. Malt proposed that the weaker effects resulted from the mixture of different strategies: Some subjects were using similar exemplars to make their decisions, and others were using prototype information. In one experiment (using artificial categories), she separated subjects based on how they said they performed this task in a postexperiment interview. Subjects who claimed to use exemplars had 562 ms of priming, whereas those who reported a prototype strategy had a −16 ms priming effect.

In short, Malt's study gives some evidence for exemplar usage but also evidence for different processes of categorization. Why were her effects apparently weaker than those of Brooks's studies described earlier? One reason is probably that the level of similarity between the old and new items was less in her studies. For example, a sperm whale and a sei whale are clearly similar, but they are not nearly identical. This seems to be true of most of her natural categories (e.g., raccoon-badger; moose-caribou; musk ox-mountain goat) and is clearly true of her artificial stimuli (similar items were created by making one item smaller, changing the features slightly, and mirror-reversing the old item). It seems likely that if the pairs had been extremely similar, more exemplar usage could have been found. Of course, this raises the question of just how similar different exemplars typically are in real life, which will be addressed in the evaluation of the exemplar effect approach. Another reason for the somewhat weaker findings of exemplar usage may be that Malt's learning procedure emphasized the category prototypes as well as exemplar learning. In one case, she told subjects what the prototypes of the two categories were, and she also asked subjects to judge the typicality of each item as part of the learning phase, which might have emphasized the prototype structure of the category.

A related reason for Malt's mixed results is that the categories she used probably had a greater amount of perceptual commonality than in the Brooks studies. She did not include the large number of irrelevant features (and background) used in Allen and Brooks (1991) or Brooks et al. (1991), which probably resulted in less perceptual resemblance within their categories, and the items in Malt's naturalistic categories had a holistic similarity (the prototype of one category was like a river otter, and of the other was like a buffalo) that may have been more compelling than the featural overlap (two out of three features) in Allen and Brooks's study. So, prototype learning could have been more successful in her categories.

I mention all these possible factors, because they all bear on the question of when and why exemplars will be used in categorization. As Brooks et al. (1991) discuss, the holistic similarity of old to new items is probably very important. But by the same token, when members of a category are *all* holistically similar, there may be less reliance on memory of individual exemplars and greater reliance on a summary prototype. Brooks's results showing extremely strong exemplar effects may reflect in part a difference between perceptual resemblance and rule application: Subjects may prefer to rely on perceptual resemblance whether it is to a particular exemplar, or to a prototype that represents the category as a whole. In Allen and Brooks (1991) and Brooks et al. (1991), the perceptual resemblance was strongest to a particular exemplar, but in Malt's case, resemblance to a prototype was also fairly strong. These speculations have not yet been systematically tested.

Explanation of Exemplar Effects
The results of Brooks's studies give quite strong evidence for the use of exemplars in classification. Although Malt's (1989) results were more equivocal, they nonetheless did suggest that subjects are using exemplars in making categorizations, at least a substantial proportion of the time. How are we to interpret these effects? One way is within the normal confines of exemplar models of categorization. That is, Category A is represented by a set of exemplars that have been learned to be its members, and similarly for Category B. These learned exemplars are accessed in order to make a decision about new items. There is a somewhat different way of looking at these results, however, which I would like to propose. It is not a model of categorization

per se, but a connection between the findings summarized above and another memory phenomenon, namely *implicit memory*.

I will not give anything like a review of the implicit memory literature here (see Roediger 1990). In a nutshell, implicit memory is a usually unconscious and long-lasting memory for the precise details of a stimulus, often acquired as part of some activity carried out on it. Implicit memory is a particularly important aspect of skill learning, in which particular ways of processing stimuli and carrying out actions may be acquired without conscious awareness that they have been learned (e.g., Kolers and Ostry 1974; Poldrack, Selco, Field and Cohen 1999). The exemplar effects documented by Brooks and his colleagues are very reminiscent of these implicit memory effects. Indeed, this is not surprising, because he and those colleagues have published other papers that have been important demonstrations of implicit memory (most notably, Jacoby 1983). In addition to the research described above, this group has published other related experiments on how category structure affects the perception of briefly presented stimuli (Jacoby, Baker, and Brooks 1989; Whittlesea 1987), which is a standard test of implicit memory.

First, let me say why I think that the exemplar effects are examples of implicit memory, and then I will discuss the implications of this interpretation for a theory of concepts. The findings of exemplar effects are similar to implicit memory in a number of ways. First, the exemplar effects are not necessarily conscious. Allen and Brooks (1991) found that over half of their subjects did not identify exemplar similarity as a variable influencing their performance, and those who did often did so only after considerable prompting by the experimenters. Second, the effects are long-lasting. Brooks et al. (1991) found effects of similarity of items a week after initial learning. Homa and Vosburgh (1976, as reported in Homa 1984) found an advantage of old over new items (in dot pattern categories) that persisted for 10 weeks after initial learning. Third, the effects are often based on apparently "irrelevant," perceptual information. For example, Allen and Brooks varied the background environment that an item was depicted in, which was irrelevant to categorization (the same background occurred once in each category); Brooks et al. varied features that were not related to category membership. These irrelevant properties nonetheless influenced categorization, analogously to the way typeface or voice influences implicit memory in word completion or identification tasks (Church and Schachter 1994; Roediger and Blaxton 1987). Fourth, there is apparently an independence between exemplar effects and more "analytic" category memory. For example, even though they showed exemplar effects, Allen and Brooks also showed that subjects learned the category rule and that this influenced their categorizations. So, use of similar exemplars did not mean that other information was not also used. (This is likely also true for Malt's results, though it is not clear that individual subjects used both.) This result is analogous to findings that explicit memory and implicit memory can be present in the same items (indeed, this is usually the case shortly after learning). In the implicit memory literature, it is common to demonstrate that implicit memory is present even after explicit memory (e.g., recognition) has decreased to chance levels, but that does not seem to have been done here. Finally, implicit memory is often described as a kind of perceptual or motor *tuning*: As a result of processing a stimulus, people get better at processing stimuli of that sort. Speeded categorization is clearly consistent with that description, and the results there are similar to results when the task is simple identification of the stimulus (Whittlesea 1987).

These parallels are not all equally strong. There needs to be further evidence for the independence of exemplar effects and other category knowledge, for example. The reference to perceptual tuning is at this point more analogical than empirical. Nonetheless, there is an overall similarity of these exemplar effects to implicit memory phenomena that is striking. If this similarity stands up to further examination, what would it mean?

In implicit memory, much of the theory has to do with input and output processing (the final similarity noted above). One can think of these phenomena as extremely specific practice effects. For example, if you hear a list of words, you become more practiced at understanding those words when spoken by that speaker, and this ability can long outlast your propositional memory of which words were on the list (Church and Schachter 1994; Roediger and Blaxton 1987). It is your speech-processing and comprehension processes that have become altered implicitly, not your knowledge of which words were spoken (which is explicit). By the same token, then, perhaps it is not the concept representation that is being manipulated by these effects, but your *access* to the representation. When you have categorized a given item a number of times as being in Category A, you have practiced a certain way of making Category A categorizations. When a new item appears that is strikingly similar to this old one, your practiced categorization takes over. A new item that is not so similar does not benefit from the specific practice on the old item.

If this view is correct, it suggests a possible distinction between the content of the concept and the access to the concept that may not be entirely keeping with exemplar theory, or, indeed, most theories. That is, the exemplar effect, in spite of its name, may reflect tuning of the classification process rather than storage of a specific exemplar. The *content* of the concept may or may not include things like the irrelevant background information of Allen and Brooks, or the irrelevant features of Brooks et al. (1991), *even though* those features affect the access of the concept—just as one does not consciously remember or use the typeface of a book when talking about the plot or characters. Although memory of the typeface does affect our reading processes (Kolers and Ostry 1974), it is not part of the propositional content of the book. Similarly, if I get extremely good at recognizing a particular dog, Wilbur, in a particular context (say the back seat of his owner's car), through having considerable experience in categorizing Wilbur in this setting, this does not mean that I will necessarily use that setting or specific properties of Wilbur in making inferences about dogs, or in talking about dogs, or in other, higher-level concept uses. It does mean that if I see a similar kind of animal in the back seat of the same model automobile, I will be faster to think it is a dog. But such implicit effects may not affect more conscious concept usage.

In saying this, I am not trying to downplay the importance of exemplar effects. They are striking and counterintuitively strong, as Brooks (1987) discusses. However, if the interpretation I am giving is correct, then their importance may be primarily about the access to concepts rather than the content or use of concepts once categorization is achieved. If this view is correct, then exemplar effects may not be coming about through a representation of stored exemplars. (Indeed, it seems rather unlikely that specific exemplars are still explicitly represented a week after learning the concepts in an experiment, much less after 10 weeks as in Homa and Vosburgh's 1976 study.) What I am suggesting is a somewhat novel distinction between the access to concepts and their content, which is not something that is recognized by either prototype or exemplar theories as traditionally proposed, and so this proposal needs further development and test.

Theoretical Evaluations: Exemplar Effects

Because these effects are empirically distinct from the many tests of exemplar models to be considered in the second main part of this chapter, I will address how the different models address these results before going on.

Exemplar Models

Given the name, one would not be surprised at the conclusion that exemplar models are highly consistent with exemplar effects. However, this seems to be more true for the effects on categorization than for the effects on learning. The learning effects are somewhat difficult for exemplar models to explain, Ross et al. (1990) point out, because virtually the same exemplars are presented in their different conditions. The only difference between the conditions is one feature that does not figure in the critical feature being questioned. However, depending on which exemplar the manipulated item is most similar to, different generalizations about the category are made. This shows that exemplars are used, Ross et al. argue, but that subjects are also forming more abstract descriptions of the category, such as "Club X members do carpentry work" or "Club Y members go to the beach," which is not consistent with exemplar models. One might think that the manipulated items are simply strengthening all the items that are thought of as similar to it, but Ross et al. rule out this explanation.

Although I have been focusing in this book on the most popular exemplar models, those based on Medin and Schaffer's (1978) context model, a different kind of model, Hintzman's (1986) MINERVA 2, may be more successful. Although this model stores individual exemplars, it does not just compare a test exemplar to them and then calculate the probability of its being in a given category. Instead, the model's output is a sort of generalization of the stimulus, based on which items it is most similar to. Part of the output is the category name, which is used to determine categorization. Hintzman argues that this output is the sort of category abstraction that prototype models talk about (p. 422), and he suggests that such abstractions might indeed be separately stored as facts about the category (though MINERVA does not actually have any capability for doing this).[2] If correct, this proposal would include both the exemplar reminding and generalization mechanisms that Ross et al. argue are needed. Whether this version of his model would actually produce the Ross et al. generalizations is not yet known, however.

Similarly, Medin and Bettger (1994) point out that simple exemplar models cannot explain their effects, because the same exemplars are used in both conditions—only the order has changed. However, more elaborate models that allow attention to be focused on specific dimensions might be able to explain their results if attention is drawn to properties that are repeated in adjacent items. (Note that exemplar theories that we've been considering, such as that of Nosofsky 1986, do not make use of attention in this particular way. However, it would not be a very great change to their models to do so. A more recent article by Kruschke and Johansen 1999, does incorporate rapid shifts of attention, though it does not address the data we are considering.) I am not so sure that this mechanism would explain Medin and Bettger's results, however. In their experiment, only three adjacent items had the critical subpattern that was repeated. If attention were drawn to this subpattern by this repetition, subjects would then notice that it did not recur in the subsequent stimuli.

This might in fact cause inhibition of the pattern. Obviously, exact predictions would depend on how quickly attention was drawn to the critical dimension, how this affected learning of subsequent items, and how attention would shift as a function of new items that do not follow the pattern. It is certainly possible that some setting of these parameters would be consistent with the results. It does not seem so easy to me to explain why it was that subjects were better in old-new recognition of the adjacent than the separated conditions. Here, *all* of the dimensions were relevant to performance, and so shifting attention across dimensions would not explain the results. Medin and Bettger found this effect simultaneously with the subpattern preference just discussed, so both effects would have to be handled simultaneously. In summary, exemplar reminding in learning has not, to my knowledge, been adequately explained by any exemplar model.

In terms of exemplar effects in categorization, exemplar models are in very good shape. So long as the exemplar storage includes irrelevant information as well as the features predictive of categorization, the effects of exemplar similarity found by Malt and by Brooks and colleagues can be readily explained. That is, the test item will evoke similar exemplars in memory, and their categories will determine the classification decision. However, it is also possible that a simpler proposal would explain these results. In the usual exemplar model, a test stimulus is compared to *all* stored exemplars, which all have an effect (however tiny) on the categorization decision. A simpler idea is that only the closest stimulus or highly similar stimuli influence categorization. Because the Brooks and Malt experiments generally manipulated only a single similar stimulus, there is no particular need to incorporate a comparison to other stimuli in the model. Recent criticisms of exemplar models have also suggested that single-exemplar retrieval is a more plausible alternative to the more elaborate exemplar models (J. D. Smith and Minda 2000; and see Malt et al. 1999).

I have suggested above that there is a different possible explanation, based on implicit memory. Perhaps the main weakness of exemplar theory is its claim that exemplars are remembered for rather long periods of time (which it must claim in order to explain the long-lasting old-new or similarity effects). Of course, people do remember single episodes or objects for very long periods of time when they are particularly compelling, unusual, or interesting. However, it seems more doubtful that people have an explicit memory of dot patterns seen in an experiment that were not seen or used for 10 intervening weeks. This is more an intuition than an empirical argument, however, and it is possible that some weak exemplar memory does persist for weeks at a time, even for rather uninteresting stimuli used in psychology experiments. However, there is no evidence for this separate from the old-new item difference, so it is also possible that some form of nonpropositional skill-learning is accounting for this kind of exemplar effect.

Prototype Theory

Prototype models have the opposite problem from exemplar models when faced with the Ross et al. (1990) and Medin and Bettger (1994) data. They do not have any problem accepting generalizations like "Club X members like carpentry," but they find it difficult to explain how subjects form such generalizations if they don't remember individual exemplars. For example, if subjects simply added up the features presented for Club X, both conditions would have equal numbers of carpentry-related properties. The difference comes about because two items are similar on an unrelated feature, which causes their carpentry-based similarity to become more salient. However, if people did not remember these separate exemplars, this reminding could not occur.

As I have pointed out numerous times, prototype models do not claim that people never remember exemplars. Clearly, they do have episodic memory for individual items. The claim is, however, that the category-level information is stored as an abstraction separate from exemplar memory. So, it is not that prototype theory does not have the representations to explain these effects: It admits of both exemplar memory (which it says little about) and category knowledge (which is where the generalization would be stored). The problem is that prototype theory has not talked about the kind of reminding effects that Ross and colleagues have demonstrated. But if it is recognized that even prototype theory does not insist on amnesia for exemplars, it seems that there is room to incorporate this kind of reminding account. Prototype theorists have not actually done so, to my knowledge, and so this is a shortcoming of this view as a learning model.

Prototype theory is less able to be modified to account for the exemplar effects in categorization, however. The importance of idiosyncratic properties in classifying items is not predicted, since such properties would be infrequent and have very low weights in the prototype representation. The fact that the bad matches actually cause subjects to make the incorrect categorization suggests that these "irrelevant" properties are having a functionally significant effect, even though they would not be in the prototype.

The implicit memory story that I proposed earlier is one possible answer for the prototype view. However, this idea is not without its complications either. By suggesting that a classification process is getting tuned by exposure to specific exemplars, one is making a distinction between classification, which is a form of skill learning greatly affected by individual exemplar information, and the propositional concept representation, which is not. In most prototype and exemplar models, the representation of the concepts is used both to classify the items (e.g., the feature list is used to make categorization decisions, as proposed by Hampton 1979, and Smith and Medin 1981), and as the repository of knowledge about the concept, to be used in induction, decision making, and so on. By referring to implicit memory, we are now separating these two functions, to at least some degree. Thus, my experience in identifying Wilbur in the back seat of a car may change the way I classify similar objects in similar settings, but it may not change what I think about dogs in general. Such a modification would be an important change to prototype theory, since some of the earliest evidence for it involved speeded categorization data (see Smith and Medin 1981). In part, it would suggest that much of the research done on categorization is not telling us about other aspects of conceptual representation. Clearly, this all needs to be worked out in a more detailed way if prototype theorists are to take this route to explaining exemplar effects. However, it is also possible that there are independent reasons to make the distinction between category access and the rest of conceptual knowledge.

Finally, it may be useful to defend prototype theory against one interpretation of the exemplar effects in categorization. Allen and Brooks (1991), it will be remembered, found that exemplar similarity had an effect even when there was a rule that could be used to classify the stimuli. It would be easy to identify this rule with a prototype, since it was a kind of family-resemblance rule in which two out of three critical features had to be present. That is, one could conclude that exemplar effects were found even with a prototype that could be used. However, prototypes are not really numerical rules of this sort. For each item in the Allen and Brooks experiment, subjects had to evaluate all three features and decide which category had the majority votes. In real life, however, members of a category often have numerous features in common. This is not the case in the Allen and Brooks stimuli, in which most items had a third of their features associated with the wrong category.

For example, imagine that you went to the grocery store, which had both tomatoes and carrots available in the vegetable section. Let us say that tomatoes are usually round, red, and about 2 inches in diameter, whereas carrots are orange, long (i.e., having a carrot shape) and 5 inches in length. If your grocer followed Allen and Brooks's design, then there would also be the following examples available, in addition to these prototypes. Try to identify each one:

1. round, red, 5 inches
2. round, orange, 2 inches
3. long, orange, 2 inches
4. long, red, 5 inches
5. long, red, 2 inches
6. round, orange, 5 inches

You would identify items 1, 2 and 5 as tomatoes (obviously!), because they each have two of the tomato features, and the other three would be carrots, having two of the carrot features. However, if you actually tried to categorize these items, even though you are quite familiar with the features of carrots and tomatoes already, you probably found it somewhat difficult to decide that "long, red, 2 inches" indicates a tomato, because it has two tomato features. I did, anyway.

I mention all this in part because there seems to be an assumption in the field at large that any rule of this sort is like a category prototype, as will be seen in the next section. Although the "best two out of three" rule sounds something like the prototype model we have been discussing, it appears to be significantly more difficult than the prototypes of many natural categories. Thus, although these researchers intended to pit prototype and exemplar effects against each other, these prototype effects may not have been as strong as those to be found in real-life categories (see later discussion of category structure in exemplar model experiments), or even as those in the experiments of Malt (1989), which found a more balanced use of exemplars and prototypes.

One might also question how much close similarity of exemplars there are in the world. For some categories, such as kinds of insects, say, we might be hard pressed to tell any difference between category members, and so close similarity would likely be the rule. For other categories, such as personality types, paintings, or faces, close similarity could be very infrequent. Clearly, people can identify novel items that are not extremely similar to any previously known exemplar, and so showing that close similarity can have a very strong effect does not mean that it is the typical way that items are classified.

Knowledge Approach

The knowledge view has little to say about exemplar effects of either variety. As has already been pointed out, it needs to be augmented by a number of memory and learning components in addition to its focus on knowledge effects. It seems likely that the effects discussed in the present chapter will come from those other components. However, one could also point out that even these effects of specific exemplars sometimes reveal the use of knowledge. For example, consider the Ross et al. (1990) demonstration that subjects use remindings to rate the typicality of new features. If the critical item reminded subjects of one person, subjects concluded that the club members like carpentry, and if the item reminded them of another person, subjects concluded that club members like the beach. These generalizations, however, were knowledge-based ones. In the dependent measure, subjects rated the typicality of new features that they had never seen before, so the effects were not caused by empirical observation alone. Instead, subjects appear to be drawing inferences about why people in a club like certain things. If one club member buys a swimsuit, and another buys a towel, then these people may be going to the beach or a swimming pool. Subjects reasonably infer that such a person would need sunglasses (the critical feature rated at the end of the experiment), even though this feature was not present for any of the observed club members. Although not requiring great intellectual insight, this is still an inference based on prior knowledge. Of course, people made this generalization based on activating similar exemplars during learning. However, it would be wrong to think of these generalizations as mere collections of observed features, since they require inference to a novel feature.

In short, although the knowledge approach does not have much to say about these effects, the learning effects at least may require world knowledge for a complete explanation.

Tests of Exemplar Models

The second main part of this chapter will consider the voluminous literature on comparisons of exemplar models and (usually) prototype models of categorization. Indeed, such comparisons have formed the bulk of published research on adult concepts in the past twenty years or so, though there seems to be a welcome lessening of the flow recently. Ever since the seminal paper of Medin and Schaffer (1978), researchers have done numerous experiments attempting to tell whether people are using a summary representation (some form of prototype) or are relying on learned exemplars instead. The review here must be highly selective. In particular, I do not discuss most work within the tradition of exemplar theory that addresses the details of models, comparing different learning rules, similarity parameters, tasks, and so on. Instead, I will focus on studies that compared different approaches.

It may be thought that in summarizing and evaluating this work, I will now be telling which model is correct. After all, these experiments were designed specifically to compare the two approaches. Although the results discussed here will certainly be probative in regard to choosing a model, these experiments are not the be-all and end-all. A problem of this whole field is that there has been such an emphasis on this kind of critical experiment in category learning that the models are not tested in other areas, such as the basic level, conceptual development or word meaning. As will be seen in other chapters, the theories that do best within the range of experiments presented here do not always seem to be fully adequate in other domains. Thus, I am not giving away the end of the story by placing this chapter early in the book.

How to Tell the Difference between the Models

There is clearly an enormous difference between prototype and exemplar models. One says that people learn a summary representation of the whole category and use that to decide category membership. Category learning involves the formation of that prototype, and categorization involves comparing an item to the prototype representation. The other view says that people's category knowledge is represented by specific exemplars, and categorization involves comparing an item to all (or many) such exemplars. Thus, conceptual representations and the processes of learning and categorization all differ between these two models.

Nonetheless, it is not that easy to tell the models apart. The reason for this is that under many circumstances, the models make similar predictions. To understand the reason for this, let us return to the findings of Rosch and Mervis (1975). They discovered that the natural categories they studied had a family-resemblance structure. The most typical items were similar to other category members and were dissimilar to nonmembers. The less typical items were not as similar to other members and were somewhat similar to nonmembers. If we were to develop categories like this and use them in an experiment, the exemplar and prototype views would make identical predictions: The typical items should be learned more easily, and atypical items less easily. A prototype should be categorized quite fast during test, even if it had not been seen during learning. Why is this? Roughly speaking, the exemplar view predicts it because the typical test items are similar to more learned exemplars—and this is most true for the prototype. Atypical items are similar to fewer category members and are more similar to nonmembers. Thus, the pairwise similarity of exemplars predicts the usual effects of category structure. Prototype models explain these results by noting that typical items are more similar to the prototype (by virtue of having more of the typical features), and so are learned faster and categorized more easily after learning.

In general, it is very difficult to develop family-resemblance categories that will distinguish the two models in a simple learning experiment. The differences between their predictions are often so small that they cannot be empirically distinguished.

To avoid this problem, most of the experiments testing these two approaches use unusual category structures, in which the models' predictions deviate considerably. The result of this strategy, however, is that the structures no longer look like the natural categories described by Rosch and Mervis. (Whether this is seen as a drawback or not depends on which view one subscribes to.) One way to do this is to create specific items that are not very similar to the (putative) category prototype but that are nonetheless similar to one of the items in that category. Thus, prototype theory would predict that these items should be quite difficult to learn or categorize, whereas exemplar theory may not, since they are similar to a category member. Another way to test the two theories is to see whether people's learning seems subject to a constraint that is found in one but not the other theory. In particular, as will be discussed in detail, prototype models require that every item be more similar to its category's prototype than to the other category's prototype, but exemplar theory does not. This difference can allow a critical test of the two theories. However, the emphasis on atypical items or unusual category structures carries a cost in ecological validity that concerns some.

Linear Separability

Perhaps the main constraint that has been studied is that of *linear separability*, which applies to prototype models. As described in chapter 2, the generic prototype theory suggests that items are compared to a category description, the matching features identified, the weights of those features added up, and the item categorized positively if that sum is greater than some criterion. This process of adding up the weights and comparing the result to a criterion means that it doesn't make any difference which particular features are in an item, so long as their weights are large enough.

Let's take a hypothetical example. If as a young child, I only saw pigeons on the grass and robins flying, and I learned that these were both birds, what would I think when I first saw a flying pigeon? According to prototype theory, I should be very glad to categorize it as a bird, because both the pigeon shape and flying have been associated to the bird concept, and both would have fairly strong weights. According to exemplar theory, though, this should be a less typical bird, because it is not that similar to either the walking pigeons or flying robins that I've seen in the past (never having seen a flying pigeon before). So, prototype theory allows me to treat each feature as independent, and to associate it with the category separately from the others. In contrast, an exemplar-based concept doesn't store information about category features per se, but about specific individuals. Therefore, an item might not be very similar to a known individual even if it has "typical" features. Such items should be relatively difficult to categorize using exemplars.

Let's consider another example. Suppose that I am learning about mammals. Typically, mammals are land animals, often with four legs, usually larger than insects but smaller than trees. However, there are exceptions, such as whales, which can be extremely large, are water animals, have no arms nor legs, and so on. According to prototype theory, such exceptions should be very difficult to learn and categorize, because they don't have the typical mammal features. According to exemplar theory, however, such items may not be so difficult to categorize if they are similar to a few other items known to be in the category (e.g., seals and dolphins).

In short, the concept of *linear separability* holds when a category can be determined by a summing of the evidence of independent features. So, if I say "It's got wings, it looks like a pigeon, and it's flying" and add up those facts independently, I will identify the item as a bird, because these features are all typical of birds. This may be contrasted with nonlinearly separable categories, which are often said to involve *relational coding*. Here, the separate features are not considered—instead, it is the configuration of a specific set of features (in our case, an exemplar) that is important. So, in the bird example above, it isn't good enough for something to look like a pigeon and to be flying, because I had never seen that particular configuration of properties before. Instead, it is pigeon features *plus* walking on the grass, or robin features *plus* flying that are learned and used.

The following description will not focus too much on the mathematical instantiations of these models (though some discussion is inevitable) but will attempt to give a qualitative understanding of why they act the way they do. For a more formal description, see Medin and Schwanenflugel (1981) or Nosofsky (1992).

Let's start by asking why it is that exemplar models predict that relational coding is more important than linear separability. Recall that the Medin and Schaffer (1978) model used a multiplicative similarity rule to identify similar exemplars. As I described, this means that very similar exemplars are weighted very heavily, and moderately similar exemplars are not weighted much at all. Therefore, if a test item is very similar to an atypical member of a category, it can be categorized quite reliably, even if its features are not generally found in the category. Conversely, an item with very typical features would not necessarily be categorized easily if it is not similar to some specific items—that is, if its particular configuration of features had

Table 4.1.
Medin and Schwanenflugel (1981) Category Structure for Experiment 1.

Linearly Separable Categories

Category A				Category B			
D1	D2	D3	D4	D1	D2	D3	D4
1	0	1	1	1	0	0	1
1	0	1	0	0	0	1	0
1	1	0	1	0	1	0	0
0	1	1	0	0	0	0	1

Nonlinearly Separable Categories

Category A				Category B			
D1	D2	D3	D4	D1	D2	D3	D4
1	0	0	0	0	1	1	0
0	1	1	1	1	0	0	1
1	1	1	0	0	0	0	0
1	0	1	1	0	0	0	1

not been seen before. To put it simply, because the similarity rule is multiplicative rather than additive, exemplar models do not rely on the summation of independent features and so do not require that categories be linearly separable. Prototype theory does rely on this summation, and so it does require linear separability.

This difference may be better understood in the context of an example, taken from Medin and Schwanenflugel (1981), who first discussed linear separability in regard to human concept learning. Consider the top two categories in table 4.1. As before, D1–D4 indicate stimulus dimensions (like shape, color, etc.), and 1 and 0 indicate values on those dimensions (like square and triangle; red and green; etc.). So, 1011 might indicate a square, red, small figure on the left, and 0100 a triangular, green large figure on the right. The top two categories are linearly separable, because it is possible to give a weight to each feature (the 1 or 0 on each dimension) so that all the items in Category A have a higher score than all the items in Category B. In particular, if we ignore D4 (i.e., give it a weight of 0), and equally weight the value of 1 on all the other dimensions as 1.0, the items in Category A would all have sums of 2, and the items in Category B would have sums of 1. Or to put it another way, members of Category A have two out of three 1s on D1–D3, whereas Category B has two out of three 0s. Medin and Schwanenflugel's stimuli were geometric figures, so to learn these categories would be to learn that Category A generally was, for example, green triangles on the left, and Category B generally was blue squares on the right, with size being irrelevant. Each stimulus would have two of these three properties, as the table shows.

In contrast, the bottom two categories in table 4.1 are not linearly separable. How do we know this? It turns out to be somewhat difficult to ascertain that categories are *not* separable in general, because one must prove that no way of weighting the dimensions will result in higher scores for Category A than for Category B. And how is one to know that *no* possible way of weighting the dimensions would lead to this result? There are complex mathematical analyses that could be done, but in practice, researchers in the area take the following approach. Consider the first two items in Category A: On every dimension, they are opposite. Similarly, consider the first two items in Category B: These are also opposite in every respect. By putting these opposites in the same category, the experimenters are ensuring that no way of weighting the features could lead to a high score for both stimuli. For example, Category A tends to have the 1 features, but the first item in the category has only one such feature, a 1 on D1. Therefore, if we wish to include this item in the category, we must give a fairly high weight to D1. But as we weight D1 more and more, the second item is going to suffer, because it does not have a 1 on this dimension. Suppose then that we weight D2 more to make up for this. Although this will help the second item, it will hurt the first item, which is opposite on that dimension. In short, if you find weights that will help one item (i.e., ensure that it is in the category), they will of necessity hurt its opposite. So, there is no way to assign weights to features that will result in both the first and second items being in the same category. (One could use a very low criterion that would admit both items, but then one would not be able to exclude the members of the other category.)

Consider the nonlinear categorization problem from the perspective of prototype theory. Presumably, the (best-example) prototype of Category A would be 111? and that of Category B would be 000? (the question mark indicates that the last dimension is uninformative, since the values are equal in the two categories). However, the first item in Category A is actually more similar to the prototype of Category B, and the first item in B is more similar to the A prototype. As a result, if subjects are forming prototypes, these categories should be very difficult to learn, whereas it should be considerably easier to learn the linearly separable categories. Of course, subjects might eventually learn the nonlinearly separable categories, but this would presumably be through memorization of the stimuli or some other less preferred strategy, after prototype formation had failed.

The question, then, is whether linearly separable categories are easier to learn, as prototype theory predicts. Before revealing the results, it is important to point out that Medin and Schwanenflugel controlled for many irrelevant differences between the two structures. Both structures had eight stimuli, divided into two categories and used the same stimulus dimensions and values on those dimensions. Furthermore, the overall number of shared features was constant across the two structures. For example, notice that in D1 of the linearly separable categories, Category A had three 1s and one 0; Category B had three 0s and one 1. This is also true of the nonlinearly separable categories. That is, the same number of 1s and 0s is found in each category on each dimension in the two structures. Clearly, it would have been possible to make a very easy structure of one kind and compare it to a difficult structure of the other kind. The comparisons made here, however, hold constant the number of shared features in each category.

Medin and Schwanenflugel (1981) found no difference between these two structures. Subjects went through the items 16 times, and 66% learned them in the linearly separable condition, and 72% in the nonlinearly separable condition. The overall numbers of errors during learning were also nearly equal.

In their second experiment, Medin and Schwanenflugel varied the instructions given to subjects. They were told either to try to learn what the categories were like in general (a prototype approach) or to try to learn each individual item's category (an exemplar approach). They also used a new category structure that they thought would make the nonlinearly separable categories even easier. In this structure, there were a number of pairs of very similar items (differing only on one feature) in the nonlinearly separable categories, but fewer such items in the linearly separable categories. If similarity to exemplars aids in learning, then it should actually be easier to learn the nonlinearly separable categories. This is in fact what was found. The instructions did not influence the difference in learning difficulty between the two categories, though subjects told to focus on exemplars did make fewer errors overall.

Medin and Schwanenflugel achieved similar results (typically little difference between the two structures) in two further experiments. In addition, the experiments of Wattenmaker et al. (1986) and Murphy and Kaplan (2000) found very similar results in their comparable conditions. (As will be discussed in chapter 6, they also found a way to reverse this effect, though it is premature to discuss that here.) In short, it seems clear that subjects were not particularly sensitive to the constraint of linear separability. If they had been trying to form prototypes, then they should have learned the linearly separable categories sooner than the nonlinearly separable categories, yet this result was never found. If anything, the results seemed to slightly favor the nonlinearly separable categories. Clearly, this is very bad news for prototype theory.

More recent research has put this finding in a different light, however. J. D. Smith and Minda (1998) examined learning of linearly separable and nonlinearly separable categories in individual subjects, across the entire learning period. After each segment of learning (56 trials), they fit an exemplar model and a prototype model to each subject's data, and they mapped the success of these models across the learning process. Perhaps surprisingly, they discovered that prototype models generally had an advantage in the first few blocks of learning. With further experience, prototype models tended to do less and less well, with exemplar models having a substantial advantage when learning was complete. Smith and Minda argued that subjects began the task attempting to form prototype representations of the two categories they were learning. However, over blocks, this strategy turned out to be less than optimal (especially for the nonlinearly separable categories). Furthermore, with repeated exposures of a small number of stimuli, subjects were eventually able to memorize the items, which was always a successful strategy. Thus, exemplar models may be correct in the final representation of the categories, but this representation may only be reached after an initial, unsuccessful attempt at prototype learning, and exemplar learning (for these stimuli) may only be possible when the stimuli are seen over and over again.

Smith and Minda (1998) proposed an interesting model that combines prototype and exemplar ideas. They suggest that in addition to prototype learning, subjects may be memorizing individual exemplars. When they recognize an exemplar as being familiar, they use its stored category to help them respond. The exemplar portion is different from the context model (and many successor models), because it does not say that an individual exemplar is compared to all the category members in a rather complex way. Instead, if that particular exemplar has been stored, then it affects its own categorization but not the categorization of the other items. Smith and Minda (1998, 2000) argue that such a model accounts for the full range of learning data better than the usual exemplar models, and that the memorization process is simpler and psychologically more plausible than the usual exemplar-comparison process.[3]

Generic Exemplar vs. Prototype Experiments

I have focused on the question of linear separability because it has received much attention and because it is a principled way of distinguishing prototype and exemplar models (though I should emphasize that it is specifically exemplar models like the context model that are supported here, because they emphasize relational similarity). However, there have been many other contrasts of exemplar and prototype models in the literature, which differ in the specific models they consider. An early example is that of Reed (1972), who compared eighteen different models of category learning in his experiments. Unfortunately, he did not include an exemplar model like the ones discussed here, as the context model had not yet been developed. In their seminal paper, Medin and Schaffer (1978) constructed a number of category pairs for subjects to learn. They then derived predictions for the context model and a prototype model for how difficult it would be to learn each item in the learning set, and how subjects would categorize new transfer items after learning. In particular, they predicted that items similar to other items in the same category should be easy to learn. Prototype theory predicted that items with the most typical features should be easy to learn. Each theory was fit to the data so that optimal stimulus weights could be derived. (Recall that prototype theory weights each feature on its importance, and the context model has values for each mismatching feature in its similarity computation.) Overgeneralizing somewhat, the results tended to show that exemplar theory fit the overall data better than prototype theory (e.g., correlations between models and data of .99 vs. .81 in Experiment 2 and .98 vs. .92 in Experiment 3). The context model also made some predictions about which specific transfer items should be easiest, and these predictions often held ordinally but were not always reliable. Overall, though, the paper showed that the exemplar model could do quite well in predicting the data, with the prototype model alway a bit worse, even if not significantly so.

A good summary of other attempts to compare the two models can be found in Nosofsky (1992), who fits these models (as well as others) to 13 different experiments. The context model provides a better fit to the data than the prototype model we have been discussing (the "additive prototype" in his terms) in 10 out of these 13 cases. Other experiments were not specifically designed to contrast prototype and exemplar models but to investigate a more specific phenomenon (such as base-rate neglect or frequency effects; see chapter 5). However, many such papers have compared exemplar and prototype models to attempt to account for their data, and generally—though not always—prototype theory comes out second best (see, e.g., Estes 1986; Kruschke 1992; Medin, Dewey, and T. Murphy 1983; Medin and Smith 1981; Nosofsky 1986, p. 55; Nosfosky 1988—though not all of these have considered exactly the same versions of the models discussed here). In short, prototype theory has not done very well in explaining the results of these kinds of experiments.

Evaluation of Exemplar vs. Prototype Experiments

Since the two models are so directly contrasted in these studies, I will consider the implications for them together, rather than in separate sections as in most chapters. When taken as a whole, the contrasts of exemplar and prototype models favor the exemplar models fairly heavily. There are exceptions, but in many of those, the two are quite close. For example, in Estes's (1986) Experiment 1, the prototype model (what he calls the *feature model*) accounted for virtually the same amount of variance as the exemplar model (actually slightly less). However, it had one advantage, namely that the parameters of the feature model could be used in all the conditions he tested, whereas the exemplar model's parameters had to be fit to the particular condition. Thus, Estes felt that prototype formation was probably occurring to some degree in this experiment. However, in his Experiment 2, Estes used categories that could not be learned by independent feature associations (i.e., they were extremely nonlinear). Here the feature model could not begin to explain the results. This kind of result is typical: Prototype models do well on occasion, but in other conditions they are dreadful.

Clearly, the exemplar approach is strongly supported by this kind of finding. And although I am going to criticize these kinds of experiments, let us not lose track of the fact that criticism of support for the exemplar approach is not the same as support for prototypes. Exemplar models do well in these situations, and they deserve credit for it.

That said, there are some serious questions that can be raised about the kinds of experiments discussed here. Let us consider, for example, the Medin and Schwanenflugel (1981) design shown in table 4.1. There are two rather troublesome aspects of this design. First, the categories are quite small (which is true of many experiments using artificial categories—not just the ones under discussion). It seems likely that exemplar learning would be greatly enhanced under these conditions. Many natural categories are very numerous (just to pick some examples out of the air: book, table, doctor, tree, store, house, lecture, mother), and it is not entirely clear whether one can generalize from these artificial experiments to the learning of real categories that are orders of magnitude larger.

Second, and of potentially more theoretical interest, the category structure in this experiment is extremely weak. (J. D. Smith, Murray and Minda 1997, have made a very similar point, though I will be attacking it in a different way.) Let us first consider the linearly separable category. Medin and Schwanenflugel (1981) point out that there is a prototype for each category: 111? and 000? (the question mark indicating that there is no typical feature on D4). However, these prototypes are not particularly strong. In any single example, a third of the features are "wrong" (typical of the incorrect category). Furthermore, although it is easy for us to point out that D4 is not diagnostic of category membership, subjects do not know this when they start (and they don't get to look at table 4.1 as we do). Thus, from their perspective, the categories overlap quite a bit: Half of any item's features are irrelevant or misleading.

The nonlinearly separable categories are, if anything, less realistic. Clearly, there is something very peculiar about having items that are *opposite in every respect* being in the same category. What kind of category has items in it that are—literally—totally different? Now, one could respond to this by saying "This is only your intuition about what kinds of categories are good. However, the results *show* that the nonlinear categories are perfectly good—just as good as the linear ones, if not better. So, perhaps your idea about what is a good category is not correct." Although this answer is very polite, it is not totally convincing in light of the overall results of Medin and Schwanenflugel's Experiment 1.[4] Although they did not find much difference between the two structures, subjects had great difficulty learning the categories. Keeping in mind that there are only eight items to be learned, it is remarkable that 34% of the subjects did not learn the linearly separable categories and 28% did not learn the nonlinearly separable categories after 16 blocks (16 blocks is a lot). In their Experiment 2, with a different structure, and more learning blocks (20), almost all subjects reached criterion. However, Medin and Schwanenflugel's later experiments again led to very poor learning. In Experiment 3 there were only six items, and 47% and 28% did not learn the linearly and nonlinearly separable categories. In Experiment 4, fewer than 40% learned the categories, each with only three items. (Nonetheless, the Experiment 4 structure was later modeled by Kruschke 1992.) To be fair, there were a number of aspects of these experiments that could have led to difficulty in learning—not just the category structure.[5] However, the point stands that these categories were not learned even though they were extremely simple, with three item types apiece. This horrible performance is not characteristic of real-world category learning. The question, then, is whether results obtained under these circumstances tell us about category learning and representation more generally. I will address this point more completely later. In the meantime, I would like to note that the literature has generally not worried very much about the great difficulty in learning such categories. This problem has only seldom been mentioned at all (Murphy and Allopenna 1994; J. D. Smith et al. 1997), and some of the references to the linear separability findings have in fact been somewhat inaccurate in their descrip-

Table 4.2.
Category Structure from Medin and Schaffer (1978), Experiment 2.

Category A					Category B			
D1	D2	D3	D4		D1	D2	D3	D4
1	1	1	0		1	1	0	0
1	0	1	0		0	1	1	0
1	0	1	1		0	0	0	1
1	1	0	1		0	0	0	0
0	1	1	1					

tion of the nondifferences. For example, rather than concluding that "humans have little trouble with categories that systems employing linear generalization functions cannot learn (Medin and Schwanenflugel, 1981)," as Hintzman (1986, p. 425) did, one might have concluded instead that humans cannot learn *either* linearly or non-linearly separable categories.

Let me take another example. Medin and Schaffer's (1978) paper was the original impetus for the exemplar view, and its procedures have been borrowed heavily. Their first experiment used categories that contained opposites (and only three items per category), as in the bottom structure in table 4.1. The authors themselves pointed out that these categories may be rather artificial, given that they contained such opposites (and again, not all subjects learned to categorize the six items within 20 blocks). As a result, they constructed a new category structure for their later experiments, shown in table 4.2. This structure has been extremely popular in the literature. It was also used by Medin and Smith (1981), Medin, Dewey, and T. Murphy (1983), and even as recently as Lamberts (2000). (Since I first wrote this discussion, Smith and Minda 2000, have independently written in detail about this structure. We made some similar remarks, and I have incorporated some of their other points here.) It is often noted in this context that the structure is linearly separable and can be learned by a rule. All you need to do is to ignore D2, and the other dimensions follow a two-out-of-three rule: If there are two 1s, it's an A, otherwise it's a B. So, like the Medin and Schwanenflugel example, one dimension is irrelevant, and of the remaining dimensions, a third have atypical features in most items. (Actually, part of the difficulty here is that D2 is slightly predictive of Category A. So, this particular way of weighting the dimensions would be rather difficult to learn, even according to prototype theory, since it isn't the case that D2 is irrelevant on its own.) It may not be surprising, given all this, that in 16 blocks, only

56% of Medin and Schaffer's (1978, Experiment 2) subjects learned the categories. Lamberts's (2000) Experiment 1 is even more informative in this regard, because he did not stop subjects after a set number of blocks, but required them to continue until they were perfect. It took subjects an average of 38 blocks to reach this performance, which is extremely long for learning to categorize only 9 stimuli into 2 categories.

I am dwelling on the details of these experiments and their results because I think that it is important to understand the potential problems with the category structures and in turn with the overall results of the experiments. However, I do not wish to be taken as saying that these experiments were badly designed or are of little interest. In fact, their interest is apparent from the literature that has sprung up around them. I believe that they will continue to be the basis for further work and ideas. What is less clear, however, is what the results of these experiments tell us about everyday category learning. Their general finding is that exemplar models do better than prototype models. However, there are two respects in which these categories do not seem representative of many real-world categories: 1) They have very weak structures, and 2) people have great difficulty in learning them, in many cases not learning them at all.

The issue of weak structure was also addressed by J. D. Smith et al. (1997; and J. D. Smith and Minda 2000), who performed a quantitative analysis of the within-category and between-category similarity of items, suggesting that in studies of linear separability, both of the category structures compared (as in table 4.1) had very weak structures given the possible category structures that one could have constructed with the same number of features. The weak structures may have required subjects to learn exemplars, given the inefficiency of prototype representations.

A different approach to evaluating the category structure in these experiments is to refer to studies of natural categories. As discussed in chapter 2, Rosch and Mervis (1975) and Rosch et al. (1976) obtained information on category structures of everyday categories through feature listings and ratings. Before briefly reviewing them, it should be pointed out that such studies tend to underestimate the amount of information in a category, because people tend not to list "obvious" features (and the more obvious, the less likely they are to appear), and because many features are not easily verbalizable. So, although members of the cat family have a distinctive head shape, this is not easy to put down in words. Writing "cat head" does not seem very informative, and so one does not tend to find such features in the listing of cat or tiger, for example.

In spite of these caveats, an examination of feature lists shows that natural categories have many features listed in common. Rosch and Mervis (1975) describe features for superordinate categories, like furniture, vegetable, and clothing, which are the level of natural categories that have the weakest within-category structure (see chapter 7). For each of these categories, they sampled 20 items, ranging in typicality from prototypical items to atypical items that many people might not actually judge as being in the category (e.g., telephone for furniture; elevator for vehicle; foot for weapon; necklace for clothing). They found that there was sometimes a feature common to all category members (though not a truly defining one, since it would also be found in other categories), but more generally there was "a large number of attributes true of some, but not all, category members" (p. 581). For example, there was at least one property true of 18, 17, 16, and 15 members of the categories. The categories had 5 properties on average that were true of 9 of the category members. In short, although there were many differences among the items, there were also many commonalities. This was especially true in Rosch and Mervis's analysis of the 5 most typical items in each category. Here they found an average of 16 properties that were true of *all* 5 items. The 5 least typical items had hardly any properties in common, but these were in some cases dubious category members anyway.

The point I am trying to make here is that even in natural superordinate categories, which have fairly weak structure, there is considerable commonality among the items—and a very high degree of commonality among the most typical items. This is not found in most of the studies described in this chapter (indeed, in many studies of artificial concepts in general). It is possible, then, that prototype models could work much better with natural categories in which category members share 9–16 features, rather than 0–3, as in these artificial categories.

Further evidence of category structure can be found in Rosch et al. (1976), who had their subjects judge which properties are true of an entire category, thereby producing fewer properties overall, but presumably properties that are nearly universal. Because these features lists are available (in an unpublished note that was widely distributed), unlike the complete lists for Rosch and Mervis (1975), we can also examine how many of the features were found in other categories. For example, the category tool had three features listed as common to nearly all tools, none of which was listed as features of clothing or furniture. The category of saws had those same three tool features but also had seven features that were nearly universal to all saws—only two of which were found in other tools. Thus, if you found a tool that has teeth, is sharp and cuts things, you would be pretty sure it was a saw. (Again, even more telling features like a saw's shape were not easily verbalizable and were not listed.) Overall, Rosch et al. (1976) reported 9.4 features common to basic-level categories on average.[6] In short, even by what I believe is a conservative measure (because it depends on easily verbalizable features), there is considerable richness to these categories. This is in marked contrast to the categories (whether linearly separable or not) shown in tables 4.1 and 4.2, which are notable for their within-category diversity and between-category overlap.

Mervis and Crisafi (1982) took a different approach to measuring the level of similarity of items within and across categories. They took the category hierarchies used by Rosch et al. (1976) and gave subjects pictures of items from the same or different categories. Subjects rated the similarity of the depicted items on a 1–9 scale. The authors discovered that items from the same basic-level category (e.g., two different kinds of chair) were rated as quite similar, 6.9, whereas items from different categories in the same superordinate (e.g., chair and table) were rated only 3.3. Thus, there seemed to be considerable similarity of items within categories and little between categories, again rather unlike stimuli used in many experiments.

In short, it seems clear that the experiments reviewed in the previous section do not have the same level of category structure as do most natural categories, as shown by existing studies that have examined them. Of course, it is not to be taken for granted that these studies (e.g., Rosch et al. 1976; or Mervis and Crisafi 1982) have shown us a complete and accurate picture of category structure in the wild. It is possible that they have stimulus sampling problems, or that their measures have difficulties, or that there are other kinds of categories that are quite different from theirs, even if they are accurate within the domains they tested. However, it should be noted that the literature comparing prototype and exemplar models does not make this claim, nor does it try to relate the category structures used to real categories in most cases. There simply seems to be the assumption that the categories being tested are appropriate. (Recall, however, that these strange structures were not chosen arbitrarily but because theories generally make the same predictions for categories with a strong family-resemblance structure, and so weaker or unusual structures were tested.)

The second problem I raised above is that learning is so poor in many of these experiments. This is another sign that the categories are not very much like most natural object categories. Categories like chair, tree, table, dog, cookie, spoon, television, and so on, seem to be quite easy to learn compared to the categories in such experiments. Children do not have to take classes in the difference between chairs, couches and tables, and few people study examples of these categories over and over again in order to master them. Indeed, much work in conceptual development uses a technique in which a *single* object is indicated to a child along with its category name, and then the child is tested on what he or she has learned. Although this method is not really comparable to category learning as discussed in the present chapter, what is remarkable is that children do form very good hypotheses about the categories based on one or two examples (see Carey 1982 and chapter 10). Nonetheless, when these same children grow up to take Introductory Psychology and as a result end up in category-learning experiments, they have inordinate difficulty in learning categories that have only four or five members (e.g., the ones in tables 4.1 and 4.2). This suggests the possibility that the categories used in such experiments may be different from the ones that they learned rather more easily as children.

What are the implications of these difficulties? In general, the issue is that it is difficult to generalize from the learning of categories that have a weak structure to those that have a much richer structure. It is possible, for example, that one could very easily learn the category of chairs by forming a prototype of them, which would be different enough from any table or couch that one would be likely to see. If so, then perhaps people do form prototypes in such circumstances. It does not follow from this, however, that the same kinds of strategies will be successful in learning categories that have weak structures, whose prototypes are not very different from one another. In order to learn the categories in these experiments (both the linearly separable and nonlinearly separable, I would argue), subjects must essentially memorize most of the items. Naturally, one does not find differences between the two structures in such a situation. It is instructive, for example, that Estes (1986) found that a feature-based model could predict learning quite well when it was possible to do so, but not when the features were made independently nonpredictive of the category (Experiment 2). However, all research on natural object categories that I know of has found independently predictive features, though no doubt there are some that have different structures.

Why don't subjects appear to form prototypes in these experiments when it is possible to do so, as in the linearly separable categories of table 4.1? First, it should be pointed out that the prototypes that are discussed in these comparisons are not exactly the ones that I described in chapter 2. There I said that each feature received a weight depending on its frequency in the category (which increases the weight) and outside the category (which decreases the weight). However, the prototypes used in these experiments are simply the modal value on each dimension within the category (see Medin and Schaffer 1978; Medin and Schwanenflugel 1981; Nosofsky 1992). For example, in the categories shown in table 4.2, the modal prototypes would be 1111 in Category A and 0?00 in Category B. This is considerably less information in the category prototype than the weights that were proposed by Smith and Medin (1981), based on the family resemblance work of Rosch and Mervis. (Furthermore, if one had the weights, it would be obvious that each feature is only weakly associated to its category.) In some cases, this modal prototype turns out to have the same predictive power as the feature frequency version—if every feature occurs equally often in its category and for some smaller (but equal) number of times in the other category, for example. However, in other cases, the modal prototype is much less informative than the feature weighting would have been. In short, it is not obvious that the tests of prototype theory used in these experiments adequately reflect the more elaborate version that prototype researchers have proposed.

However, I suspect that even with a more complex prototype theory, one would find that in many cases there is little sign of prototype learning. Because the features are generally so weakly associated to the categories, and some dimensions must be totally ignored, it is possible that subjects simply conclude that there is little generality to the items within each category and so use a different strategy. As I mentioned earlier, J. D. Smith and Minda (1998) found evidence that subjects start out trying to learn prototypes but eventually end up using an exemplar strategy in typical experiments with artificial categories.

Stepping back a moment, I want to reiterate my earlier comment that these criticisms do not themselves provide support for prototype theory. I am suggesting that it might do better in cases in which there is stronger category structure. However, that has not in fact been demonstrated, and it is clearly not doing better with these structures, whatever their problems. Although defenders of prototype theories tend to complain about the category structures used to support exemplar models, they need to show that prototype theory will do better with other category structures. And for the most part, this has not been done (though see below). So, exemplar theory still has the advantage as of this writing. And it will be difficult to distinguish the two theories if stronger category structures are used, because they have such similar predictions about category learning in those cases. This suggests that different techniques will need to be applied to cases where the category structures are more like those involving natural categories. A good example is Malt's (1989) study of priming, which used real animals that could be learned moderately easily (3.1 blocks in Experiment 3). Recall that she found that when one could not learn the categories by using prototypes, there was considerable priming from similar exemplars, suggesting an exemplar categorization strategy. When the categories could be learned with prototypes, however, she obtained much weaker exemplar priming effects. She argued that some subjects were using exemplars and some were not. In short, her results suggest first, that the two theories can be distinguished when one does not rely completely on learning data, and, second, that when category structures are strong, the evidence for exemplars may be less than in the cases used in the traditional studies of prototype vs. exemplar learning.

This second conclusion was also drawn by J. D. Smith et al. (1997), who directly contrasted strong and weak category structures. In their second experiment, they used the Medin and Schwanenflugel nonlinearly separable structure as well as another nonlinearly separable structure with more attributes, which had greater structure (i.e., more within-category similarity). Contrary to most practice, they fit the data of their individual subjects rather than just group data. For their new structure, they found that half of the subjects were best fit by a prototype model and half by the Medin and Schaffer exemplar model. The prototype subjects were characterized by an advantage of the prototype over the normal typical items, but very bad (below chance) performance on the very atypical item. (In order to make the category nonlinearly separable, there must be at least one atypical item that cannot be correctly categorized by similarity to a prototype.) The exemplar subjects showed no prototype advantage and moderately good performance on the very atypical item. For the Medin and Schwanenflugel design, however, Smith et al. found that 81% of the subjects were best fit by an exemplar strategy. In short, they replicated the results of the earlier study but argued that they were in part due to the very weak category structure. When there is a stronger structure, some subjects appear to be learning prototypes and others appear to be learning exemplars. Surprisingly, when the data from all subjects in a condition were combined, the exemplar model predicted the results much better than the prototype model did. Even though there were equal numbers of subjects who were best fit by prototype and exemplar models, the *combined* data were fit best by the exemplar model. Smith et al. suggest that past results almost unanimously in favor of exemplar models might have been different if individual subjects had been examined (Maddox 1999 makes a similar point; and see Hayes and Taplin 1993; Malt 1989).

A final point made by Smith et al. (1997) is that it is quite surprising that some subjects simply do not seem to learn the atypical items. Subjects who were classified as prototype learners were making mistakes on the atypical item even at the end of extensive training. It is unclear why, if exemplar theory were correct, it should be so difficult to learn which category an item is in, after many blocks of training. It cannot be that subjects can't learn the individual exemplars. Medin et al. (1983), using the categories shown in table 4.2, found that it was easier for subjects to learn a name for each item than to learn the two categories (as did Malt 1989, with a different structure). This reinforces the concern that there is something not-very-categorical about these categories and also makes one wonder why subjects could not just memorize which exemplars are in which category if exemplar memory is the basis for normal categorization. It seems likely that they were attempting to form a coherent picture of the category, in which there were general properties true of most category members.

I have noted that exemplar models do not claim that people learn and remember everything about every example (see Medin et al. 1983, p. 612, for discussion). It is a concern, then, that most exemplar theories do not incorporate partial encoding or forgetting into their models. The array-based models of Estes (1994) and Hintzman (1986) do include forgetting, but the more popular models based on the context model typically don't (e.g., Kruschke 1991; Lamberts 1997; Medin and Schaffer 1978; Nosofsky 1984; 1986). How then can they explain the results of category-learning experiments in which subjects clearly do not always remember the exemplars? Usually, the slack is taken up by the weights on the dimensions that are assigned by the context model (and/or the sensitivity parameter in the GCM). So, if subjects only learned about or remembered dimensions 1 and 2 in the category, then the other dimensions would have very low weights, or their mismatch values would be very close to 1, so that it would have little effect in the multiplicative similarity computation. Although this is an effective way to model the data, it must be pointed out that it simply does not seem psychologically accurate: Memory effects are modeled by a process that does not represent memory. In the most extreme example of this, Nosofsky and Zaki (1998) modeled the category learning of severe amnesics without positing any differences in their memory representations of exemplars from those of normal controls (relying instead on the sensitivity parameter, c, described in the appendix to chapter 3). Exemplar models of this type would be greatly improved by incorporating more realistic memory assumptions.[7]

Other Views
The knowledge approach has little to say about the exemplar vs. prototype issue (which may be one reason that some researchers have preferred to work within that framework!). However, it is worth pointing out that knowledge in general is usually thought of as being something like a summary representation. For example, if you know certain things about animals, why they reproduce, how their physiology is related to their behavior, how animals relate to their environment, and so on, this is usually thought of as being knowledge about animals as a whole, or perhaps birds or mammals, or (if it is quite specific knowledge) about red foxes or chameleons. Knowledge is not usually thought of as being a fact you know about a particular chameleon you saw once and a specific dog you noticed, or the set of a dog, a chameleon, a chicken, and two squirrels. Instead, we usually think of knowledge as being the sort of things you know about mammals in general. If that is correct, then it may

be harder to integrate the knowledge approach with an exemplar model of specific category learning.

Conclusion

Some writers have concluded that one cannot readily resolve the exemplar-prototype question. Most notably, Barsalou (1990) provided a very detailed analysis of different possible exemplar and prototype models, concluding that there was no specific pattern of performance that could be accounted for by only one kind of theory. I agree with most of Barsalou's analysis, but I am not sure I draw the same conclusion. One reason is that there are many *possible* models of each type, but in fact, only a few of those versions have been seriously suggested. And this is for good reason. Although one could construct a prototype-like model that acts as if it represents individual exemplars, why would one do so? Why not just conclude that people are remembering the exemplars? Furthermore, although two models might account for categorization data equally well, there could be different kinds of data that would distinguish them. For example, Barsalou argues that if prototype models kept track of pairs, triplets, and larger n-tuples of features, they could show certain exemplar effects. That is, rather than only storing facts about individual features, like robins usually have red breasts, have beaks, and fly, this model would also store the frequency of has-beaks-and-flies, red-breasts-and-has-beaks, red-breasts-and-flies, red-breasts-and-has-beaks-and-flies, and so on. Such a model might be able to account for some categorization results normally thought to be explainable only by exemplar models, such as nonlinear category learning, making it difficult to distinguish the two approaches. However, we can also test the assumption that learners encode the pairs and triplets of features—in fact, it seems unlikely that they do so (see chapter 5; Murphy and Wisniewski 1989). Other measures beyond categorization performance per se, such as exemplar priming (Malt 1989), may also be able to give independent evidence for the assumptions of different theories.

Another point that Barsalou makes, which is now gaining wider attention, is that exemplar models are inherently more powerful than traditional prototype models. Because the exemplar models maintain the representations of all the observed items, they have all the information about a category that could possibly be used. So, if they store 40 category members, they have 40 known configurations, on which any number of operations can be carried out. In contrast, prototype models lose information by accumulating it into a single summary in which the co-occurrence of particular features is lost. Thus, exemplar models can easily mimic a prototype abstraction process, but not vice versa. This makes any comparison of the two approaches more complex to carry out, since even if subjects are truly using prototypes, an exemplar model can often do a very good job of accounting for the data.

As I stated earlier, this chapter cannot be the end of the exemplar-prototype debate, as there are many more phenomena in the psychology of concepts that need to be considered before a final decision can be made. Here I have been focusing on studies of category learning and categorization that pit the two models against each other, but a complete model of concepts must also account for phenomena such as conceptual combination, hierarchical structure in categories, and so on.

Exemplar models have the edge in the current battle of category-learning experiments—certainly so if one just counts up the number of experiments in which exemplar models outperform tested prototype models. With such a preponderance of evidence, it seems likely that something like exemplar learning may well be going on in those experiments. The main question about this work arises in attempting to generalize from it to natural concepts. As I have pointed out, the experimental categories differ from natural categories in a number of ways that seem very pertinent, including size (number of exemplars), differentiation (category structure), and apparent difficulty of learning. It is certainly possible that people use exemplars to learn categories like those presented in table 4.2 but do not do so for larger, well-differentiated natural categories that do not have a small number of exemplars that appear over and over again. Although my own intuition is that this is probably the case, there is little evidence that actually supports this view, and so such criticisms must be taken with a large grain of salt. However, one can also turn this around and state it as a goal for exemplar theory—to more convincingly demonstrate that the principles identified in experiments of this sort hold up in the learning of natural categories.

It may be significant that the few studies that looked at individual learners have found that they differ in their learning strategies. Both Malt (1989) and J. D. Smith et al. (1997) found that some subjects showed a clear prototype pattern of responding whereas others showed a clear exemplar pattern. J. D. Smith and Minda (1998) found that individuals seemed to shift from a prototype to an exemplar strategy within the experiment. This suggests that both kinds of learning may be an option for people, depending on the category structure (see J. D. Smith et al. 1997) and probably a variety of task and personal variables. That is, stating this debate as "prototype vs. exemplar models" may itself be an error. Perhaps the issue should be discovering when people form generalizations and when they rely on exemplars, rather than deciding which model is correct and which incorrect.

5

Miscellaneous Learning Topics

Readers may wonder why a well-organized book should have a "miscellaneous" chapter. That is the kind of question that answers itself, I suppose, but nonetheless there is an answer based on the overall structure I have followed here. The book is generally organized around major phenomena in the psychology of concepts. However, there are some topics that have received considerable attention in the field that do not fit so neatly into the major divisions of this book because they are specific phenomena that don't merit their own chapter. Also, there are some interesting methodological questions that don't relate to one particular phenomenon but could be used to address many of them. It seems unwise to omit discussion of all such topics simply because they don't fit into the structure of the rest of this book, hence the present chapter.

There is no particular order or relation between the topics in this chapter, so readers should feel free to pick and choose among them as they like. Although it might have been possible to shoehorn these sections into other chapters, there would have been considerable damage to the cohesion of those discussions, so I feel that the present organization is a bit more honest, if ungainly.

"Base-Rate Neglect" in Category Learning

Typically, when people learn categories, they are sensitive to the frequencies of both exemplars and properties within the category. For example, when one item occurs more than others, it is generally considered to be more typical and is categorized faster than less frequent items (Nosofsky 1988). As Rosch and Mervis (1975) showed, when a feature occurs more often in a category, items that possess it are learned faster and have greater typicality (and see Spalding and Murphy 1999). In this respect, there is plenty of evidence that people are sensitive to how often things occur in categories. In fact, category learning in general depends on people noticing the base rates of different properties of category members (that birds often fly but mammals usually don't, etc.). Nonetheless, there are some systematic exceptions to this observation that have received a certain amount of attention in the literature. These exceptions have been called the *inverse base-rate effect* (Medin and Edelson 1988) or *apparent base-rate neglect* (Gluck and Bower 1988), and they are the topic of this section. However, I put the phrase "base-rate neglect" in quotes in the section heading, because it should be remembered that this phenomenon occurs only in specific circumstances, and people are normally quite sensitive to the base rates of properties in categories.

To illustrate this phenomenon, consider the stimulus structure used by Gluck and Bower (1988). These categories were diseases, and the exemplars were patients who had each disease. The exemplars were made up probabilistically. That is, given that a patient had disease X, there was a given probability that the person would have symptom 1, a different probability for symptom 2, and so on. One disease was rare, and one was common, in that the common disease occurred three times as often as the rare disease. The symptom structures were as follows:[1]

	Rare Disease	Common Disease
Symptom 1	.60	.20
Symptom 2	.40	.30
Symptom 3	.30	.40
Symptom 4	.20	.60

The numbers here represent the probability of each symptom occurring, given the patient had that disease. For example, patients with the rare disease would have symptom 3 30% of the time.

This is something of a strange category structure, because it is possible (indeed, likely) for the exact same set of symptoms to be produced by the two different diseases. For example, a patient might have symptoms 2 and 3 and be in either the rare or common disease category. There is no way for the subject to tell for sure what disease a person has (in fact, even though we know the category structure, there is no way for us to know either). Indeed, a patient might not have *any* of the symptoms, due to the probabilistic nature of the categories. One can assume that these categories are difficult to learn (Gluck and Bower do not report learning data).

Gluck and Bower's (1988) main interest was in people's judgments about symptom 1. After subjects were trained on the categories, they were asked what percentage of patients with symptom 1 had the rare disease. In reality, the answer was 50%, because although symptom 1 is the most frequent feature within the rare disease, the common disease occurred three times as often. So, 3 times the rate of occurrence of symptom 1 in the common disease (.20) equals the frequency of symptom 1 in the rare disease (.60). Subjects, however, judged the feature to be in the rare disease category 67% of the time. This is the result that would be expected if subjects were ignoring the differences in category frequencies (hence the name "base-rate neglect").

Medin and Edelson's (1988) result was qualitatively the same, but they used deterministic (rather than probabilistic) categories and obtained category judgments on test items rather than measuring frequency. To make an analogy to the design given above, they essentially showed that an item with symptoms 1 and 4 would be more likely to be categorized into the rare disease category, even though it was in fact more likely to be in the common disease category, because of the large base-rate difference.

Why do subjects think that the critical symptom (1 above) is actually more indicative of the rare category? In a clever series of experiments, Kruschke (1996) has argued that it is a function of the order in which the categories are learned, plus shifts of attention to critical features. Kruschke points out that when one category occurs three or more times as often as another category, subjects will learn the more frequent category first. They will have more opportunities to observe its features and to learn from getting feedback on their categorizations. He argues that when subjects learn the common category, they have learned that it often has symptom 4, fairly often symptom 3, but hardly ever symptom 1, for example. Now when learning the rare category, subjects will tend to focus on the features that distinguish it from the already-learned common category. For that category, the most distinctive feature is symptom 1. Thus, this symptom becomes particularly strongly associated to the rare disease category.

To test his theory, Kruschke (1996) taught subjects categories that were equally frequent—but he taught some categories first, for 9 blocks, and then taught all the categories together for 9 blocks. His reasoning was that if it is the contrast between learned and unlearned categories that causes subjects to focus on a distinctive feature, the same result should be found in this condition, even though the categories are all equally frequent in the second phase. He found that subjects preferred the later-learned category for items that contained its distinctive feature, even when they were actually equally associated to the two categories. (It was not just that people preferred the later-learned category overall; the distinctive feature had to be present.) In another experiment, he showed that a feature must be distinctive to be subject to base-rate neglect. If the feature is frequent in both the rare and common categories, it does not produce the effect. The feature must be frequent within the rare category and less frequent within the common category.

These results support Kruschke's view that the base-rate neglect phenomenon occurs because of attention shifting from the common category to the most predictive features of the rare category. Without such a shift, he argues that learning models cannot explain the result. He developed a prototype model that incorporated this shift and explained the results (see an exemplar model with the same kind of attentional shift in Kruschke and Johansen 1999).

Feature Correlations in Concepts

Eleanor Rosch's writing on concepts greatly emphasized that conceptual structure is based on the structure of the environment. In particular, she argued that objects in the world do not have random collections of properties but instead are structured: "The world is structured because real-world attributes do not occur independently of each other. Creatures with feathers are more likely also to have wings than creatures with fur, and objects with the visual appearance of chairs are more likely to have functional sit-on-ableness than objects with the appearance of cats. That is, combinations of attributes of real objects do not occur uniformly. Some pairs, triples, or ntuples are quite probable, appearing in combination sometimes with one, sometimes another attribute; others are rare; others logically cannot or empirically do not occur" (Rosch et al. 1976, p. 383). In short, Rosch argued that categories contain clusters of correlated attributes that are fairly distinct from other clusters.

Whether the environment truly possesses such clusters is difficult to say (and is something that cannot be answered by doing psychology experiments, which can only measure people's perceptions of the environment). However, it does seem clear that our concepts consist of such clusters of correlated attributes. These are in fact the prototype concepts that have been found in empirical studies of natural concepts. That is, there are many features of birds that are predictive of birds but of few other animals. Birds tend to have wings, to fly, to have feathers and a beak, to migrate south in winter, to eat seeds, and so on. Not all of these features are true of all birds of course, but it is still the case that if you know that an animal lives in a nest and has wings, you can be more certain that it migrates south in winter than if you knew that it lives in a burrow and has paws. In short, the prototype structure of concepts is one way of representing these clusters of correlated features. When features are all connected to the same prototype, then they are all at least somewhat correlated. And the features that are very highly weighted in that prototype are probably highly correlated. For example, feathers and beaks are highly weighted in birds, and they are also highly correlated, as almost all birds have both.

In short, prototypes themselves represent feature correlations (note that in this section I shall be using the term *prototype* primarily to refer to the category structure rather than to the theory). However, there is a somewhat different possibility for encoding feature correlations, namely that they are directly represented in the concept. For example, Smith and Medin (1981, pp. 84–86) suggested that highly correlated features are associated together by a "correlated" link that indicates that when one feature is present, the other should be expected as well. As I have indicated, if two features are both quite frequent within a category, such a link would probably not be necessary, because one can infer that the features co-occur. However, there may be other features that are not universal within a category but nonetheless go together very frequently. For example, for birds, "is small" and "sings" seem to be correlated, even though many birds do not sing and presumably most are not small (relative to other birds). Perhaps, then, these two features are linked, so that when one sees a small bird (but not a large one), one would be likely to conclude that it sings.

There have been a number of experiments devoted to the question of whether such feature-feature correlations are in fact noticed by subjects and used in making categorization judgments. Before we discuss the evidence for this, however, it is important to reemphasize that these studies are not tests of Rosch's idea of concepts consisting of clusters of correlated attributes. The literature has sometimes presented the articles discussed below as testing the Roschian position, but, as I have pointed out, it is prototype concepts themselves that are the evidence for her notion. People do not have to explicitly link "beak" and "feathers" to represent their relation beyond including them both as frequent features of birds.

What we are asking, then, is whether, *within* a concept, some of the features are more correlated than others, and if people learn this information and use it in conceptual tasks. Malt and Smith (1984) obtained properties for members of six different superordinate categories (e.g., different kinds of birds, clothing and flowers) and asked subjects to rate how much each property applied to each category. For example, how much does "is black" apply to robins, seagulls, owls, penguins, and so on? They discovered that within each superordinate category, there were many features that were significantly correlated. Some of these correlations do not seem particularly interesting, such as the negative correlation between "is large" and "is small" within birds. However, others involved substantive correlations such as the positive correlation between eating fish and having a large beak, or, for furniture,

the correlation between having springs and being sat on. The number of such correlations was higher than would be expected by chance, and so Malt and Smith
argued that there was considerable structure within these concepts.

Malt and Smith next asked whether there is an effect of the property correlations
on the typicality of category members. For example, consider a bird that has the
features "is small" and "sings." In addition to being typical features, these are also
correlated. When judging this bird's typicality, then, does it gain an advantage by
having this correlated pair? Does the correlated pair make the item more typical
than one would expect based on its individual features? Malt and Smith calculated a
family resemblance score for each item (robin, seagull, etc.) by adding up the number
of features it had, weighted by how frequently each feature appeared in its superordinate category. They found (as one would expect from Rosch and Mervis's 1975
results) that these scores predicted the typicality of category members quite well
(correlations of .56 to .79).[2] Importantly, no significant improvement was achieved
in analyses that included information about correlated features (e.g., that increased
typicality for items that had both "sings" and "is small"). Typicality could be predicted by individual features just as well as by individual features plus correlations.

Malt and Smith (1984) also examined the possibility that correlations work sub-
tractively. For example, perhaps when a bird is small but doesn't sing, it is less typical than would be expected by its individual features, because it violates the positive
correlation of these features. However, they found no evidence for this idea either.
In short, Malt and Smith found little evidence that such correlations are used in
determining category structure in their study of typicality.[3]

In a final experiment, Malt and Smith presented subjects with items that differed
only in feature correlations. Each item was a list of features, like "has a beak, is
small, lays eggs, breathes, sings." Some cases, like the one just given, contained a
correlated feature pair (is small-sings), and others were identical except that one
member of the correlated pair was replaced with another feature that was not
involved in a correlation but that was equally frequent (e.g., "is small" might be
replaced with "eats bugs"). Subjects viewed pairs of such items and had to decide
which one was more typical. Malt and Smith found that subjects chose the item with
the correlated pair 61% of the time, which was greater than the 50% expected by
chance. Thus, there was some evidence that subjects were aware of and could use
the correlated features.

As a whole, the overall picture of the use of feature correlations is not very positive. For example, Malt and Smith found no effect of the feature correlations in
determining typicality of six different superordinate categories. The one positive

piece of evidence they found occurred when the *only* difference between items was that of feature correlations—subjects had no other basis on which to make a choice, since the items were identical in terms of family resemblance. Furthermore, by presenting the items simultaneously and forcing subjects to choose one of them, this procedure made the feature correlation much more salient than it would have been if each item had been presented separately. Consider this analogy. Imagine that color normally plays no functional role in your decision about whether something is a chair. However, if you were presented with two identical chairs that differed only in their color and were required to choose the more typical one, you would obviously have to make your decision based on color. And if there is any consistent basis for choosing one color over another (e.g., one is more attractive, one is more familiar, or when forced to think about it, you realize that one color is found slightly more often in chairs), then people might well agree on which chair is more typical. Similarly, although Malt and Smith's subjects agreed (a bit higher than chance) that the correlated item was more typical when forced to choose between a correlated and uncorrelated item, this is not very compelling evidence that an *individual* item is affected by the presence of the correlation. Given all the negative evidence in Malt and Smith's paper, then, correlations do not seem very critical.

Murphy and Wisniewski (1989) used an experimental approach to this question. They taught subjects family resemblance categories in which a pair of features always co-occurred (whenever one feature occurred, so did the other one). After subjects studied the items, they were tested on items that either preserved the correlation or else separated the formerly correlated features. Murphy and Wisniewski found no reliable effect of such correlations in three experiments. However, they performed a similar study with features that subjects would expect to be correlated, such as, for a weapon, "blinds you temporarily" and "emits a bright light." These were knowledge-based correlations, in that they could be explained by knowledge prior to learning the categories. Here there was some evidence that subjects were using the correlation. In fact, in their Experiments 3A and 3B, Murphy and Wisniewski found that subjects "learned" such correlations even when the features were not particularly correlated in the stimuli. Subjects rated items higher when they had the two correlated features than when the correlation was broken, even though the correlated features did not occur together any more often than other features in the category.

Murphy and Wisniewski concluded that subjects are not very good at learning these pairwise feature correlations based on statistical evidence. When subjects are trying to learn the two categories, they are attempting to learn how each feature is related to the category; trying to encode the feature-to-feature associations would require considerable effort. In general, if one knows N features about a category, one would have to consider $N \times (N - 1)/2$ correlations. For example, if one knew 25 facts about birds (a large underestimate), then there could possibly be $25 \times 24/2 = 300$ feature correlations. This is a large number of correlations to have to attend to, or even to learn without attention. In contrast, one's knowledge will only connect some of those features, and so using knowledge to identify feature correlations can simplify this problem considerably. A perusal of the feature correlations discovered in Malt and Smith's (1984) study shows that many of them are related to more general knowledge: eats fish-near sea, large wings-large, and flies-lives in trees (positively correlated), and small-large, small-large wings, can't fly-lives in trees, and near sea-eats insects (negatively correlated). Perhaps only such features, which are represented in more general domain knowledge, have an effect on typicality (as Malt and Smith themselves suggest). Unfortunately, it may be difficult to test the use of these correlations in natural categories, since it may be hard to find real category members that do not preserve the correlations (e.g., birds that eat fish but do not live near water, or small birds with large wings).

In a recent study, Chin-Parker and Ross (in press) confirmed that subjects do not learn feature correlations during category learning. However, when subjects performed an induction task during learning, in which they predicted unknown features, they did acquire the correlations. Thus, whether feature correlations are learned probably depends on the kind of processing done when encountering category members. If you are focusing on learning the category per se, you will probably not notice the correlations, but if you focus on feature relations, you can do so.

Having drawn this fairly negative conclusion about the importance of feature correlations, I must discuss an important paper that has sometimes been taken as providing evidence that people do learn feature correlations. Medin et al. (1982) performed two kinds of experiments to test people's sensitivity to feature correlations. In one kind, they presented subjects with the items from one disease category to study. In those items, two dimensions were perfectly correlated. For example, the patients who had the symptom "splotches on the skin" also had "high red blood cell count" (and vice versa). But when the patients in this category had "skin rash," they also had "high white blood cell count" (and vice versa). So, skin condition and type of blood symptom were perfectly correlated. At test, subjects rated items that preserved this correlation (splotches-red blood cell) higher than those that broke the correlation (splotches-white blood cell).

Table 5.1.
The stimulus structure of Medin, Altom, Edelson, and Freko (1982).

Terrigitis				Midosis			
D1	D2	D3	D4	D1	D2	D3	D4
1	1	1	1	1	0	1	0
0	1	1	1	0	0	1	0
1	1	0	0	0	1	0	1
1	0	0	0	0	0	0	1

Note: Each row depicts an exemplar of Terrigitis and an exemplar of Midosis. The Ds indicate stimulus dimensions, and the 1s and 0s indicate values on each dimension, in this case, disease symptoms. D3 and D4 are the "correlated" dimensions.

Such results do show that subjects learned these correlations. However, because there was only one category to be learned, this situation is rather different from the one investigated by the studies described above and from natural categories. For example, Murphy and Wisniewski found that when subjects learned two categories, they did not notice perfectly correlated features of this sort. When learning multiple categories, people are primarily learning how features are related to the different categories, not how they are correlated within the categories. However, in Medin et al.'s paradigm, there is nothing else for the subjects to learn besides how the features are related to one another: There were no categories to learn to distinguish. Subjects studied the nine items for 20 minutes, and it is perhaps not surprising that under such circumstances, they learned which dimensions were perfectly correlated. However, if subjects had been given a category-learning task, it seems less likely that they would have learned the relations between the dimensions.

Medin et al. (1982) recognized this possible problem, and they performed a final experiment in which items were in two different categories, using the category structure shown in table 5.1. However, these categories did not use feature correlations of the Roschian kind being discussed here. Recall that Rosch et al. (1976, p. 383) mentioned examples like "Creatures with feathers are more likely also to have wings than creatures with fur, and objects with the visual appearance of chairs are more likely to have functional sit-on-ableness than objects with the appearance of cats." However, Medin et al.'s correlated attributes, Dimensions 3 and 4 in table 5.1, do not fit this description. As you can see, the properties in Dimensions 3 and 4 occur equally often, both overall and within the category. (There are equal numbers of 1s and 0s on each dimension in each category.) Furthermore, it is not the case that a 1 in Dimension 3 tends to go with some value in Dimension 4: Across all items, the two dimensions are orthogonal (uncorrelated). In fact, each of the four possible combinations of these dimensions (11, 10, 01, 00) is equally frequent. This is quite different from the usual case in which some features are more frequent in the category than others, and some features tend to co-occur with others in order to form distinct categories. The relation between Dimensions 3 and 4 is complex. In the Terrigitis category, if there is a 1 on D3, then there is a 1 on D4 (and vice versa), but if there is a 0 on D3, then there is a 0 on D4. In the Midosis category, if an item has a 1 on D3, then it must have a 0 on D4 (and vice versa), but if it has a 0 on D3, it must have a 1 on D4. Following Rosch et al.'s example, imagine we used bird features in such a structure. Then one category would have things with wings that live in nests *or* with no wings that live in a burrow. The other category would have things with wings that live in a burrow *or* no wings that live in a nest. This kind of structure is more like the "exclusive or" (XOR) rule than the correlations found in natural categories. (This is not to deny that such categories occasionally exist, as in legal rules, the tax code, or equally unpleasant settings.)

Subjects in Medin et al.'s Experiment 4 studied these items for ten minutes in order to learn the categories, and they received five more minutes of study if they could not categorize them correctly. Then they were tested on old and new test items. Medin et al. found that subjects tended to categorize the new items according to the relation of Dimensions 3 and 4. When these dimensions were 11 or 00, subjects tended to categorize the item as Terrigitis; otherwise they tended to categorize it as Midosis.

Clearly, then, subjects can learn and use these relations between features in category learning. However, the complex nature of the correlation does not seem to be the same sort that has been claimed for natural categories, and so it is not possible to generalize this result to them. Furthermore, it should be noted that subjects *had to* learn the correlation in order to learn the categories, because (1) the features in Dimensions 3 and 4 were not individually predictive of category membership; and (2) the other dimensions were not sufficient to categorize the items (e.g., 10_{-} occurred in both the Terrigitis and Midosis categories, as did 01_{--}). Again, this is unlike natural categories in which one generally does not need to learn the correlation of features within a category in order to learn the category (one can learn that birds fly and live in trees and not have to learn that the two features are correlated). In fact, Malt and Smith's (1984) results suggest that this is just what people do learn in natural categories.

All of the above is not a criticism of the Medin et al. (1982) demonstration, but is an argument against taking it as answering this question about whether people learn feature correlations in natural categories, which is how it has often been interpreted. In natural categories, the features are correlated in clusters of related features, rather than the orthogonal structure shown in table 5.1. Furthermore, the features are independently predictive of the category. In such situations, it seems likely that people will learn the individual features rather than the correlations, as suggested by the results of Malt and Smith, and Murphy and Wisniewski. As remarked earlier, there are so many possible pairs of correlated features in natural categories that it is difficult to see how one could consider them all. One of the benefits of categories is that they allow us to reduce the information structure of the correlations in the environment. Instead of storing the facts that wings go with feathers, and feathers go with nests, and nests go with beaks, and wings go with beaks, and wings go with nests, and feathers go with beaks, and so on, we can store the facts that wings, feathers, nests, and beaks are all properties of birds, which implicitly represents the feature-to-feature correlations.

Theoretical Implications

What does this conclusion say about the different theories of concepts? Exemplar models would predict that the correlations should be preserved and used, because these correlations would be found in individual exemplars. For example, when categorizing something as a bird, one would retrieve bird exemplars that are small and sing, but one would not have stored exemplars that are large and sing (since they are so rare). A large, singing bird, then, would be considered less typical. (Indeed, it is as a test of exemplar theory rather than of feature correlations that Medin et al. 1982, present their experiments.) Thus, if one accepts my conclusion from the studies of Malt and Smith, Murphy and Wisniewski, and Chin-Parker and Ross that such feature correlations are not represented and used in category learning, then this is a problem for exemplar theory. Counteracting that is the finding in Medin et al.'s experiments that the relations among their features were noticed (see also Wattenmaker 1993). However, given the concerns that learning these correlations was absolutely necessary to complete the task and that very long study times and few exemplars were used, this is not very strong evidence. Thus, exemplar theory falls a bit short here.

Prototype theory does not normally represent feature correlations, though it could be modified to do so, as Smith and Medin (1981) proposed. The general negative findings of such correlations (in prototype-like categories, rather than the XOR-like categories) is therefore consistent with most prototype models.

Finally, the knowledge approach gained support from Murphy and Wisniewski's finding that feature correlations were noticed and used when the features were items that would be expected to co-occur. Contrary to exemplar model predictions, this effect was found whether or not the features actually did co-occur. Similar results were found by Barrett et al. (1993, Experiment 1) with children. To the degree that these experiments show that prior knowledge is influencing the learning of new categories, they are supportive of the knowledge approach.

Category Construction

In the majority of experiments on categories and concepts, subjects are required to learn novel categories. Typically, the experimenter designs pairs of categories and then has subjects go through item after item, until they correctly categorize them. Obviously, the experimenter decides which items are in which category, according to a rule or the requirements of the stimulus design. However, there is another way by which people can acquire categories, which is that they can spontaneously notice that items are in a separate category. Most of us have consciously noticed this, as when we find ourselves thinking "What is this new kind of dog that I see around nowadays?" (usually some annoying miniature breed), or "Look at the interesting flowers that they have out in the desert here," or "What is this music I've started to hear on the radio that has only bass and drums, and complex rhythms?" When we encounter items that don't seem to fit very well into our current categories but that form a coherent set, we have noticed that there is a new category that we are not familiar with. This is an example of *category construction*—the learning of a new category that you formed on your own, without an experimenter or teacher telling you what is in the category. Because of the absence of feedback, this is sometimes called *unsupervised learning*. (Note that what I call category *construction* is different from what is usually called category *learning* in that only the latter involves feed-back. However, this terminology is not yet universal.)

This process is one that is probably most important in childhood, when children notice the categories around them but may not yet have words to describe them or may not have received any feedback telling them that the things are indeed in the same category. Merriman, Schuster, and Hager (1991) have shown that children do form categories on their own and then will quickly learn a new word that refers to that category. Mervis (1987) has suggested that this is a typical way that children

Table 5.2.
The stimulus structure of Medin, Wattenmaker, and Hampson (1987).

Category A				Category B			
D1	D2	D3	D4	D1	D2	D3	D4
1	1	1	1	0	0	0	0
0	1	1	1	1	0	0	0
1	0	1	1	0	1	0	0
1	1	0	1	0	0	1	0
1	1	1	0	0	0	0	1

Note: This structure consists of a prototype (the first exemplar in each category) and other items that differ from the prototype by exactly one feature.

learn words—first noticing the category and then learning what it is called. Furthermore, as we shall discuss in chapter 9, experiments on infants often require them to form their own categories. That is, the infant is exposed to things that are members of a category (or two—see Quinn 1987) and is expected to notice that they are all the same kind of thing, even without any instruction or feedback from the experimenter or Mommy. Impressively, they do so. As adults, we already have concepts for most of the things we encounter, and so we may not notice this process working unless we travel, encounter a recent invention, or otherwise expose ourselves to new kinds of entities.

Although I haven't yet said much about how category construction works, one would expect that it should be like category learning in important respects. For example, if you held a prototype theory of categories, you would probably expect people to form prototype concepts; if you held an exemplar view, you would expect people to notice the similar exemplars and to think that they were in the same category. Surprisingly, neither prediction is correct, according to standard experiments. When people are asked to form categories, they form categories that are unlike natural categories. In a seminal paper, Medin, Wattenmaker, and Hampson (1987) gave subjects items that fell naturally into two categories. As shown in table 5.2, each category had a prototype, and its items differed from the prototype in only one feature. Thus, there were two clear clusters of similar items. Each item was printed on a separate card (in some experiments, they were pictures, in others, each feature was a phrase), and subjects were asked to divide them into the groups that were best or most natural. Surprisingly, when given items that fit this design, subjects virtually always divided them up based on one feature. That is, if the stimuli were pictures of objects, they would choose one dimension (e.g., size or body pattern) and divide the items up into categories that differed in that dimension (large vs. small, or striped vs. plain).

This *unidimensional* strategy is very robust to differences in stimuli and instructions. Medin et al. (1987) attempted to persuade subjects to form family resemblance categories (i.e., using all or many of the features, rather than just one) in a number of ways and were generally unsuccessful. For example, in one experiment, they made stimuli that had three different values on every dimension. They used bugs with tails that were long, short, and medium, in equal numbers, and similarly for the other dimensions. Then they required subject to form two equal-sized categories. So there is no way that they could use a single dimension to make the categories, right? Wrong: "... a subject might put the drawings with short tails in one category, those with long tails in another category, and then closely scrutinize the figures with medium length tails for any differences in tail length. Inevitably there were tiny differences and a subject could use these to assign two medium length tails to the 'long' category and two to the 'short' category" (Medin et al. 1987, p. 259). Regehr and Brooks (1995) also tried to prevent subjects from creating unidimensional categories by using complex geometric stimuli that could not be easily divided on single dimensions. Nonetheless, they found that subjects arbitrarily identified parts of the stimuli as dimensions and then used this to form two categories. So, the bias toward unidimensional categories is extremely strong. It used to be thought that preschool children did not use single dimensions in related sorting tasks, but recent evidence has suggested that they also are likely to sort items unidimensionally, at least, when there is any consistency to their sorting (see Thompson 1994; Ward et al. 1991).

Based on such results, Ahn and Medin (1992) suggested a two-stage model of category construction. In stage one, subjects choose a salient dimension on which to divide up the stimuli. If there are stimuli left over after this division (generally because information has been omitted from some exemplars, or because there are features in the middle of the extreme values), then they use a similarity strategy to add the stimuli to the categories already made. So, if they first divide up items according to color, but some items do not have any color, then subjects will try to put them with items that are similar to them on other dimensions. Ahn and Medin were able to provide strong evidence for this strategy using a variety of category structures more complex than the one in table 5.2 (and more complex than we wish to delve into here).

This model does not answer the question, however, of why people make categories that are so different from those of everyday life. As we have already discussed (e.g., chapter 2, but this has been assumed in almost every discussion in the book), categories do not have defining features that determine precisely what is in and what is out of the category. And even the most ardent classical theorist has never suggested that there is a single overt feature that can define natural categories. For example, subjects list many properties for categories like bird, car, chair, doctor, movie, breakfast foods, and so on. There is no single property by which one can identify them with any confidence. Furthermore, a category defined by a single attribute would be very uninformative. If we simply thought of birds as "things with wings," for example, we would not know that birds tend to fly, live in nests, have two feet, fly south in winter, and so on—all we would know is that they have wings. The power of categories is in part the fact that features seem to go together; as Rosch et al. (1976) pointed out (see previous section), properties tend to occur in correlated clusters, and this is what makes having a category useful. So, if I see something fly briefly across my window, I may identify it as a bird and could then infer that it has two legs, that it lives in a nest and lays eggs, even though I have not directly observed any of these properties. Thus, my concept of birds is multidimensional and rich, which gives it inductive power. Unidimensional categories are obviously not rich and have no inductive power: Since you need to observe the single feature to classify the item, and there are no other features, there is no further information to be gained from categorization.

If they are so unhelpful, why then do people make unidimensional categories? Part of the answer seems to be that this is an ingrained strategy that is taught in our education system for solving problems. For example, standardized tests put great emphasis on discovering the one property common to a number of disparate items. Science progresses by isolating and identifying the single causes of phenomena where possible. Finding such causes and ignoring the other, irrelevant variables is a major part of Western schooling, as discussed in chapter 10. A unidimensional category is one that can be logically explained and defended: *All* of the ones in this category are green, and *all* of the ones in the other are red. Furthermore, such a strategy can be done without having to learn very much about the items. In some respects, then, I am suggesting that it is an artifact of the particular task that has been given to college-educated American subjects. They interpret the task as one of finding the critical feature, and so they find one. In part as a result, some subjects do not even study the items very carefully, but instead immediately start to divide them into categories based on the first few items they encounter (Spalding and Murphy 1996).

A surprising manipulation has been found to reduce the unidimensional sorting strategy. Regehr and Brooks (1995) found that if subjects did not see all the items at once while they were sorting them, they were more likely to form family resemblance categories. They had subjects put the items into two piles, in which only the top item of each pile was visible (I am glossing over some details here). Here, subjects tended to put each item into the pile of the exposed item that was most similar to it overall. Under these circumstances, the fact that all of the items in each category may have shared a single dimension would have been less salient (literally invisible, since all items could not be seen), but the overall similarity of a new item to the exposed category member would have been quite salient. Thus, structuring the task so that the emphasis is on pairs of stimuli can create family resemblance sorting.

Although this bias is, I believe, an important part of why unidimensional categories are formed, it is also the case that finding the family resemblance structure of a set of items is not always very easy. If you were to examine stimuli that correspond to the structure in table 5.2, you would not immediately notice the category structure (a point made by Regehr and Brooks, as well). In fact, when I say "immediately," I am just being polite. You would most likely not notice it at all. When subjects are required to study the items on their own, or to view all the items four or five times on a computer screen, they do not spontaneously notice that there are two different kinds of things (Kaplan and Murphy 1999; Spalding and Murphy 1996). The category structure that is so obvious when presented in terms of 1s and 0s in table 5.2 is not at all obvious when translated into actual features. Indeed, I have given talks in which I present such items randomly arranged (in picture form), and I then arrange them into the correct categories. So far, no audience member has noticed the category structure before I revealed it. And even though I know the correct design, I find it difficult to arrange the items into the correct categories. One might think that this category structure is simply too weak, but Regehr and Brooks (1995) showed that adding more dimensions in the stimuli, thereby greatly increasing the family resemblance, also did not cause subjects to deviate from their unidimensional preference.

So, forming such categories without feedback is difficult. However, it is easier when prior knowledge connects the properties. Medin et al. (1987) suggested this first, by constructing items that represented people's personality traits. When the traits were all related, subjects constructed the family resemblance categories 70% of the time. However, it is not clear that this performance involved different dimensions, because some of the "different" traits seemed almost synonymous. For example, traits like "outgoing" and "exuberant" were values on two different dimensions. They are so similar, however, that subjects may not have perceived them as being different dimensions. If not, then subjects may still have been forming unidimensional categories.

Other attempts have used properties that are more clearly on different dimensions. Ahn (1990), for example, created categories of flowers using a design similar to that shown in table 5.2 (as well as others). She provided subjects with a causal explanation connecting the properties of the flowers, namely that one type of flower attracted a kind of bird, and the other attracted a kind of bee. The bird was said to like bright colors, be active at night, fly high, and lay eggs near water, and the bee was described as having the opposite preferences. After hearing this information, subjects divided the stimuli up into two categories. Under these conditions, subjects did form family resemblance categories a third of the time, identifying flowers that were brightly colored, blooming at night, found in trees, and near the water as one category. Control subjects formed family resemblance categories only 5% of the time. So, the prior knowledge had an effect. However, because subjects were given a causal explanation that explicitly linked the features of each category, this demonstration would not apply to a real-world case in which one has not already been given a description of the two categories.

Spalding and Murphy (1996) used features that subjects would be likely to connect on their own. For example, if a building was underwater, it also had thick walls; if it floated in the air, astronauts tended to live there. Although these are clearly not the same dimensions (wall type is not occupant type), people can easily identify the relations between them. Here, subjects did not receive any advance information about the category, but when the features could be connected in this way, they nonetheless used multiple features to form categories. When the features were unrelated, people predominantly formed unidimensional categories.

Thus, when people have some prior knowledge that relates the properties together, this appears to help them notice the category structure, and they are less likely to focus on a single property. Kaplan and Murphy (1999) found that prior knowledge was helpful even when it involved only a single feature per item. One does not need all of the features to be connected together in order for subjects to notice the category structure (though not surprisingly, the effect is stronger when all of the features are connected).

Why does prior knowledge increase family-resemblance category construction? Probably, the knowledge links the features, causing subjects to incorporate multiple features in the category. When one feature is noticed, others come to mind by virtue of the links. If you notice that some buildings float in the air, you may realize that astronauts could be part of the category too. If this explanation is correct, then other techniques that relate features together should also encourage subjects to form family resemblance categories. Lassaline and Murphy (1996) tested this prediction by getting subjects to relate the features together in a prior task, rather than using knowledge. In a first phase, some subjects were asked to answer questions about the items of the sort "If an item has property A, what kind of Y does it have?" For example, one set of stimuli was pictures of bugs. So, subjects might be asked "If a bug has curved antennae, how many legs does it have?" These questions asked subjects to relate the different dimensions of the items (here, antenna type to number of legs). A control group of subjects answered questions about individual dimensions, like "How many bugs have curved antennae?" and "How many bugs have 6 legs?" Both groups had to examine the features of the items in order to answer the questions, but only one group related the features together. After answering these questions, subjects were asked to divide the items up into categories. The subjects given the relational questions formed family resemblance categories the majority of the time, whereas the control subjects most often formed unidimensional categories.

This experiment is in some sense a concrete demonstration of the inductive power of categories discussed earlier. By asking subjects to make feature-feature inductions ("If it has A, which Y does it have?"), subjects noticed that there were clusters of properties that tend to go together and support such inductions. This observation helped to counteract the normal bias to create unidimensional categories in this task.

It should be mentioned that when very different category structures are used, subjects may be able to notice the family resemblance structure without the use of knowledge or a special task. Billman and Knutson (1996), for example, discovered that when subjects were shown highly structured items, they were able to detect it. Their stimuli (in Experiments 1 and 2) consisted of nine items of the form 1111___, nine items of the form 2222___, and nine items of the form 3333___. Here, the blanks indicate that various features could be introduced, in a nonsystematic way (e.g., 1111331, 1111112, 1111223, etc.). Because some aspects of the stimuli were repeated in exactly the same way on nine items, subjects noticed the repeated components and identified the relation between them. Their specific stimuli were pictures of animals at different times of day in different environments. Subjects might have noticed, for example, that there was one kind of thing that had long legs, spotted body, a curved tail, and was seen in the morning; and another kind of thing that had fat legs, a plain body, a furry tail, and was seen at night.[4] Presumably, the reason that their subjects were likely to notice the categories is because of the lack of exceptions in these patterns. That is, a given leg type always went with the same time of day, body type, and tail, whereas this is not at all true in the family resemblance structure shown in table 5.2, used by many of the researchers described above. Thus, one tentative explanation of the apparent difference in results is that subjects are better at spontaneously noticing the category structure when the critical features have no exceptions than when there is variability in the structure. Or, put another way, they are especially good at seeing the exact same configuration of properties repeated across items.

So, to summarize, the category construction task does not usually lead subjects to construct categories that are like natural categories. In part this seems due to a unidimensional strategy that these subjects have for solving problems of a certain kind. In addition to that, however, it is clear that subjects do not spontaneously notice the category structure even after many viewings of the stimuli (Lassaline and Murphy 1996; Spalding and Murphy 1996). It is only when properties are related together that the clusters that make up a family resemblance structure are noticed. This can happen either through the relations of prior knowledge (Ahn 1990; Kaplan and Murphy 1999; Spalding and Murphy 1996) or through inductions that relate the features (Lassaline and Murphy 1996). In real life, it is likely that both factors exist. When one notices a new animal, for example, one is likely to use prior knowledge to relate its physical characteristics to its habitat and behaviors. Furthermore, if one is trying to predict something about it (whether it will attack, whether it will fly away, or whether it will try to eat your garbage), one will notice relations between the features (things with sharp teeth and claws tend to attack, things with wings tend to fly away). Thus, the family resemblance structure of real categories is probably in part due to such attempts to understand and make predictions (inductions) about the world. Finally, when the categories are very highly structured (i.e., without any exceptions in the critical features), subjects can notice the structure. For any real categories that do have such strong structure, then, unsupervised learning may be fairly easy.

Implications

Without further assumptions, neither exemplar nor prototype views are happy with the massive bias toward forming unidimensional categories. According to both, family resemblance categories should be noticed, because they create clusters of similar items in the environment. Proponents of both theories would probably argue that the strong unidimensional bias is a task-dependent strategy that overrides the true category-construction processes that are found in the wild. If such a strategy is engaged, then the normal category-construction processes would not be able to work. What about the findings that relating the features together aids in the construction of the categories? This seems generally in keeping with prototype theory, because the knowledge or inductions will help to identify which features are associated with which prototype. That is, Lassaline and Murphy's questions would reveal that some bugs tend to have six legs and curved antennae, whereas others tend to have four legs and straight antennae. This would be just the information needed to distinguish two prototypes. It is not clear why these questions would affect exemplar processing. Perhaps they help in encoding the features of exemplars more than the nonrelational questions do.

Clearly, the findings in this domain give support to knowledge approaches, as the presence of knowledge, even in very small amounts (Kaplan and Murphy 1999), results in the construction of realistic categories. The absence of knowledge or other relational information leads to unrealistic unidimensional categories. Thus, the results here could be taken as showing that relating the dimensions together through background knowledge is an important part of our category-construction process, since most natural categories are not unidimensional.

One unanswered question concerns this task more generally. One could argue that it is only when given category construction as an experimental problem that the unidimensional bias is found: In a task of dividing up items into explicit categories, perhaps adults have a metacognitive strategy to use a single dimension. In contrast, in real life, we just notice new categories ("what *are* those dreadful little dogs?")— we are not given a set of items and asked to divide them up. If true, then the variables I've just discussed (knowledge, feature relations) may not really be necessary for category construction more generally, though the experiments certainly give evidence that they would tend to support the noticing of categories. So, before any firm conclusions are drawn about category construction in the real world, we may need a more realistic dependent measure to find out to what degree people spontaneously notice categories even when that is not their overt goal.

Category Use

The majority of research on concepts has focused on the process of learning to categorize. The most popular experiment by far is to construct two or more categories from artificial stimuli, and then get subjects to try to learn them by repeatedly categorizing items until they get them all correct. In such an experiment, categorization is often the only dependent measure. There are other uses of concepts that have received attention in the psychology of concepts, most notably category construction (just reviewed), induction (see chapter 8), and the use of concepts in communication (see chapter 11). However, within the experimental study of concepts, learning to classify items has a privileged place.

Brian Ross (1996, 1997, 1999) has pointed out that we often have extensive experience with real objects in addition to categorizing them. That is, I cannot only classify objects as beds, I have slept in them, made them, moved them, and so forth. When I made my bed this morning (this is a hypothetical example), I was not trying to classify it as a bed—I knew perfectly well that it was a bed. Nonetheless, it may be that in making it, I was learning something about beds or related items (sheets, pillows, what a bed looks like after you eat pizza in it the night before, etc.) that could influence my concept of beds. Of course, this would be especially true early in the course of one's experience with the category.

Contrast this situation with the typical category learning experiment. Here the object is often not really an object but only a visual display or list of phrases. Once one has categorized it, one has no further interaction with it. One never sleeps on a stimulus in a psychology experiment, nor straightens it up, nor moves it to a new home. Furthermore, there is usually nothing else *to* learn about the stimulus—no further meaningful interaction is possible. The red triangle is just a red triangle, and there is nothing else to learn about it. That is not true for real objects, which are extremely rich and highly structured entities, about which it is almost always possible to learn more than one knows now. No matter how much of a dog person you are, you could probably learn more about dog behavior, dog anatomy, dog diseases, dog training techniques, and so on. If you took your dog to a training class for a few weeks, you would be interacting with the dog in such a way that you might be learning much more about it, even if you could already perfectly categorize it as a dog.

Such interactions may change or augment the conceptual structures that represent the categories. One way to demonstrate this is to show that using category items can lead to changes in the categorization itself. That is, even when one uses the items for some purpose in a setting separate from the category-learning trials, what one learns will then be evident in later categorization. An example will make this clearer. One domain that Ross (1996) points out as particularly relevant is problem solving. When people solve problems, they often do so by first categorizing them as a particular type of problem. For example, students learn to identify problems as "Distance = Rate × Time" problems or quadratic equation problems, and so on. These categorizations lead to different solution procedures. However, as one solves problems over and over, one may learn different aspects of the problems that could later become important in identifying and solving them, especially by identifying properties that may not be evident through superficial contact.

In short, *category use* could be an important variable in how concepts are represented. I will use this term a bit ambiguously, to refer to use of specific exemplars or use of the category as a whole. As will be seen, thinking of the category itself is important, not just experiencing the exemplars. The typical case of category use as studied in experiments is that the learning exemplars are subjected to some other task in addition to category learning. This additional task, then, is the "use," and the question is how it influences the conceptual representation.

Ross (1996) used equations as stimuli, like the following.

$$a + \left(\frac{bx}{c}\right) = p \qquad \left(\frac{q + mx}{b}\right) = 2$$

Examples like the first were in one category. They consisted mostly of constants with letters from the beginning of the alphabet, had parentheses enclosing one term, and could be solved (for x) by the processes of subtraction, multiplication, and division in that order (called SMD). The second category had letters mostly from later in the alphabet, parentheses enclosing an entire side of the equation, and could be solved by multiplication, subtraction, and division in that order (MSD). Thus, there were a number of features by which subjects could learn to distinguish the categories. Ross's subjects all learned to classify the categories in a standard category-learning technique. However, one group also solved each equation for x after each categorization trial. This task did not give subjects any more information about the correct categorization of each item, so it was a use of the item outside of the category-learning process itself. Ross predicted, however, that subjects who solved the problems would become more aware of the differences between the two categories in the way the equations are structured and therefore solved—in other words, would become aware that one category was solved by SMD and one by MSD.

This prediction was tested with new items that varied both the superficial properties that predicted the categories (the letters used for constants and the placement of parentheses) and the deeper mathematical properties (whether solution was SMD or MSD). Ross found that subjects who solved the equations were significantly more sensitive to the mathematical properties of the two categories. It is important to recall that the mathematical properties were equally present in the items learned by both groups; what differed was that one group simply classified the items, whereas the other group also solved the equations, putting them to a use.

One concern about such experiments is that subjects who use the items have more experience with them, which could be accounting for the observed differences. To some degree this is not an alternative explanation. The point is that using items beyond classification will give information that could influence a variety of conceptual tasks. Such use will necessarily involve more time than no use. However, to ensure that it wasn't simply that subjects solving the equations were exposed to them longer,

Ross used a clever design in which he constructed equations with two variables, *x* and *y*. Although all subjects saw the same equations, some solved Category 1 equations for *x* and Category 2 equations for *y*; others had the reverse assignment. The equations were constituted so that solving for *x* in Category 1 used the SMD order, and solving for *y* in Category 2 had the MSD order. But the reverse assignment had different solution orders: Solving for *y* in Category 1 had the MSD order, and solving for *x* in Category 2 had the SMD order. In addition to the solution procedure, the equations also differed in surface characteristics such as placement of parentheses and use of different letters. In short, all subjects saw the same items and categorized them in exactly the same way. They all solved each equation as well. The only difference was whether they solved the Category 1 and 2 equations for *x* or *y*. Ross's test items were new equations that had only a single variable, *z*. These equations could be solved either by the SMD or MSD procedures. Ross (1996, Experiment 2A) found that the solution procedure influenced subjects' classification. That is, if the test equation could be solved by SMD, subjects in one group tended to identify it as Category 1 (because they solved for *x* in that category, in the order SMD), whereas other subjects tended to identify it as Category 2 (because they solved for *y* in that category, in the order SMD). Given that all subjects received the exact same exemplars for the two categories, and given that the categories could have been learned with the superficial features, this is an impressive demonstration of how using items can change a concept.

Later studies by Ross expanded these results significantly. Perhaps the effects of category use are specific to these equation categories, as equations are essentially constructions for problem-solving anyway. However, later experiments found similar results using disease categories, which are a popular kind of stimulus in category-learning experiments. Here, subjects learned to categorize described patients based on their symptoms. They also learned to prescribe medications for patients, based on symptoms as well. The symptoms that were critical to the prescription were treated as more important by subjects in categorization. For example, if a test patient had a treatment-relevant symptom from one disease and a treatment-irrelevant symptom from another disease, subjects tended to categorize them into the first category. When subjects were given the disease names and asked to generate the symptoms, they tended to mention the symptoms relevant to the treatment before those that were not used in the treatment (Ross 1997). Again, it should be emphasized that all the features were equally predictive of the categories. Nonetheless, when some features were involved in a later use of the item, they were learned better and were seen as more important to the category.

More recent work by Ross has shown that category use can be separated from the category learning process and still have an effect. For example, if subjects learn a category of diseases, and later learn the treatments, the features important to the treatments are more heavily used in categorization (Ross 1999, 2000). Importantly, however, the category itself has to be thought about during the use, or the effect is not found. For example, if subjects learn two categories, then use the items without the categories themselves being mentioned, the use does not affect later classification. In contrast, if the items are constructed so that subjects can't help but notice the categories of the items during use, then the use does affect later classification. This result is important in explaining how the effect of category use comes about, as will shortly be seen.

In summary, most category experiments look at a very limited situation, in which an item is presented, subjects guess its category, and then the item disappears. In contrast, there are many objects in the real world that people interact with more extensively—perhaps for many hours. What people learn in those interactions is apparently incorporated into their concepts and in turn affects categorization. Features that are salient in the interaction may become more salient in the concept, even if they are not more reliable or common than other features.

Implications

How are these effects to be explained? First, it should be clear that none of the major theories of concept learning talks about such uses of category members, and so none currently explains these results. What is not as clear is the question of how easily, if at all, the theories can be modified to incorporate such effects. For example, prototype theory allows conceptual properties to be weighted, and so it would be possible to weight the use-relevant features more highly. However, current versions of prototype theory determine feature weighting by the frequency with which the feature appears in the category and related categories. The theory would need a new mechanism to incorporate use effects. Similarly, exemplar models as they stand do not currently explain Ross's findings, because his experiments generally compared features that were presented equally often. For example, in the disease categories, "sore throat" and "fever" might have occurred equally often in a category's exemplars, but if sore throat determined what drug was prescribed and fever did not, subjects weighed the presence of sore throat more highly.

Some form of feature weighting might possibly account for these results. The fact that sore throats predict a given drug being prescribed makes sore throat seem more salient or important. These features are then relied on more in categorization. Thus, one might try to modify the exemplar representation by giving more attention to the use-relevant features, or perhaps even by encoding new features (such as the order of arithmetic operations in the equations, which subjects might not normally encode). Such a possibility could then be incorporated into the exemplar representation. The fly in the ointment is Ross's (1999, 2000) later experiments showing that subjects had to be thinking about the category during use in order for it to have a later effect on classification. On an exemplar account, it is hard to understand why the salient feature wouldn't be encoded into the exemplar memory in this situation. If subjects learned that a given item with the feature sore throat led to a particular treatment, this should increase the salience of sore throat in the exemplar representation, whether or not they are thinking of the disease category. The necessity of the category is more in keeping with prototype theory's assumption that features are associated to a summary representation. If the category is not active in memory, then it would not be surprising that the feature's weight in the prototype was unchanged.

This discussion (and see the articles cited above for more detailed analysis) is all a bit speculative, however, because none of the proponents of these theories has attempted to account for the results of category use, and so it is simply not known how the theories might or might not be able to account for these results. The same is true for the knowledge approach. However, it should be said that the general assumptions of the knowledge approach are quite sympathetic to these findings. The knowledge approach argues that what one knows outside of the concept influences how it is learned and then used. The concept is formed within the constraints of one's understanding of the world. Category use is a similar variable, in that it is an influence that takes place outside the category-learning situation itself, and yet it influences how the concept is represented. Research of the Medin group on tree experts (e.g., Medin et al. 1997) similarly suggests that people who actively work with category members develop representations that reflect their usual interactions with the objects, such that biologists and landscapers have rather different concepts of tree types. Continuing this analogy, studies of how knowledge influences categorization have shown that features that are important in background knowledge may have importance above and beyond their statistical relations to the category (e.g., Ahn et al. 2000; Lin and Murphy 1997; Wisniewski 1995), just as features involved in category use do.

I do not think that the category use demonstrations can simply be absorbed into the knowledge approach, but I nonetheless think that both are examples of a more general principle that concepts reflect more than the simple empirical predictiveness of properties. Just as the main models of concept learning need to address the use of knowledge, they also need to be modified to explain the effects of category use.

I have been defining category use as the interaction with category members separate from the category-learning procedure. This use does influence the representation of the category, as just discussed. Related effects are found when the actual learning of the category itself is done through close interactions with the exemplars, rather than through mere categorization training. Arthur Markman and his students (Markman and Makin 1998; Yamauchi and Markman 2000) have done a series of studies comparing traditional category-learning techniques with other ways of interacting with the category, most notably through inference. In an inference task, one is given an item with its category label. One of the features (e.g., color) is omitted from the item, and subjects are asked to predict the missing feature (e.g., is it red or blue?). Yamauchi and Markman (1998) found that such learning led to more complete representation of the category than traditional category learning, in which subjects provide the category label. They argued that inference caused subjects to encode all the dimensions of the stimulus and their relation to other dimensions (see also Lassaline and Murphy 1996). In contrast, category learning encourages subjects to focus on a single dimension of the stimulus or on the minimal amount of information necessary to get the category name correct. Popular categorization models had difficulty fitting their inference results in particular, although they did well on the category-learning data. Interestingly, Yamauchi and Markman found that if subjects performed an inference task followed by category learning, their representations were more complete than if they performed category learning followed by the inference task. Thus, the initial interaction with the items may have robust effects on later representations.

Markman's and Ross's work together suggest that researchers will have to broaden their approach to category learning, taking into account the richness of our interactions with the world. The traditional learning experiment has served us well since Hull (1920), but it is not the only way that categories are learned, nor the only one that can be studied in our experimental paradigms.

6
Knowledge Effects

Traditionally, studies of concepts have used materials that are as divorced as possible from outside knowledge. A survey of the literature would find stimuli such as geometric shapes, alphanumeric strings, patches of color, dot patterns, and schematic faces to be quite common. Although some of these stimuli have familiar elements, such as faces or geometric shapes, people's knowledge prior to the experiment could not have predicted what the concepts were. For example, nothing that one knows about geometry suggests that the to-be-learned concept should be red pairs of triangles, rather than single blue circles. Why are such categories so popular? There are two main reasons. First, researchers believe it is important in a learning experiment to use categories that the subjects do not already know. If subjects are already familiar with the materials, then the results would not just reflect learning but also their pre-experimental knowledge. In a study of category learning, then, artificial stimuli may be best. Second, by using very simple, even meaningless stimuli, some investigators feel that they are discovering general principles that will apply across many different domains. If the stimuli had been types of animals, for example, how could we be sure that the results would generalize to plants or furniture or economic principles? But when the stimuli are abstract items that are not related to any particular domain, the results may reflect basic principles of learning that would apply very widely.

It is not obvious that this reasoning is actually correct, however. It could be, for example, that the results of such experiments do not apply to more realistic situations in which people know something about the domain and do have expectations, right or wrong, about the concept. And just because the stimuli are simple and abstract does not mean that the results are especially generalizable. The history of cognitive psychology is based, one could argue, upon the finding that results from simple learning experiments (on rats, pigeons, or aplysia) do not give much insight into intelligent behavior and thought. Whether experiments on simple categorization could be the basis for explaining all concepts is an empirical question. However, if one is worried that experiments on learning animal categories would not generalize to learning about furniture, then how can we be sure that experiments on learning dot patterns generalize to both of them?

In contrast to the traditional assumptions, one could argue that the learning processes used for realistic concepts in familiar domains are not the same as those used for simple, artificial situations. It is not (or should not be) controversial to point out that there are important variables in real-world learning that are never identified or explored in the simple experiment, because they have been "controlled away" by the experimental design. In a more controversial sense, the results of the simple experiments may be actually wrong, in that people could be doing things in those situations that they do not do in real life. It is important to emphasize, however, that these are empirical questions. Some people love the elegance and control of the simple experiments, and some people find them boring. Discussions of which approach is correct have an unfortunate tendency to degenerate into personality clashes. This issue must be resolved not by argument but by research into what people do in the richer situations, which can then be compared to the results of the majority of past experiments on concepts, which follow the simple, abstract procedures. It is possible, and perhaps likely, that both approaches to understanding concepts will be necessary to paint the complete picture.

The present chapter, then, provides a review and discussion of a class of effects found in more realistic stimuli, in which some (but by no means all) of the richness of real-world stimuli is allowed into the laboratory and is examined. Specifically, this chapter examines the effects of background knowledge on concept learning and use, an issue that has not been a traditional part of the psychology of concepts but which has slowly grown in popularity since the mid-1980s (Carey 1985; Keil 1989; Murphy and Medin 1985).

Possible Benefits and Limitations of Prior Knowledge

Previous chapters have already reported a number of benefits of prior knowledge in concept learning and use. Nonetheless, it would be useful to step back and discuss some general ideas of why and how knowledge might be useful—or not—to put the whole enterprise into perspective. To start very simply, how might knowledge be related to or useful in concepts? One way some people summarize this possibility is to say something like "People have a theory of dogs, which is their concept of them." This gives the impression that the knowledge is sufficient to predict the existence of dogs and/or to account for all their properties, just as a scientific theory explains the existence of black holes, say. Such a situation is not impossible, as in some sciences it is possible to predict entities before they are actually seen. For example, Neptune was predicted to exist before it was actually discovered; and in subatomic physics, various particles have been predicted long before experiments could be devised to actually create and then detect them. However, I doubt very much whether people's knowledge is this powerful in most cases. If you have mundane knowledge of the seas, for example, it would not form a theory that would allow you to predict the existence of dolphins or sea slugs or sponges if you didn't already know that they existed. Instead, knowledge is almost always used in a post-hoc way to explain entities and apparent categories that one encounters. For example, if you saw a sea slug at the bottom of the ocean, you could use your knowledge to understand what kind of thing it was and what properties it probably has (e.g., gills rather than lungs). Therefore, I will focus here on the use of knowledge to *explain* a category when it is being learned, and use that as a framework to understand knowledge effects. (This discussion draws on material in Murphy 2000.)

Let's consider how a common category, birds, might be explained to some degree by everyday knowledge. Most people think of birds as being feathered, two-legged creatures with wings, which fly, lay eggs in nests, and live in trees. Why do birds have these properties? In asking this, I am not asking a question of evolution but of understanding why this particular configuration of properties exists rather than some other. With simple, mundane knowledge, one can explain many of these features. Let's start with flying. In order to fly, the bird needs to support its weight on wings. The feathers are important as a very lightweight body covering that also helps to create an aerodynamic form. Thus, wings and feathers enable flying. By virtue of flying, the bird can live in nests that are in trees, because it can easily fly into and out of the trees. This is a useful thing to do, because many predators are unable to reach the nests there. The bird needs a nest for brooding, and for the babies to live in until they are able to fly. Thus, flying can be partly explained by these desirable consequences.

This line of reasoning, which virtually any adult in our culture could perform, relies not on book-learning or courses but on everyday knowledge.[1] This knowledge may be incomplete or even wrong in detail (e.g., most people's ideas about how wings support a bird are probably wrong), but it is close enough to account for a number of generalizations about the world. For example, most things that fly have wings; almost everything with wings flies. The exceptions can be explained by the mundane knowledge as well. For example, ostriches have wings and do not fly, but this is easily explained by the tiny size of the wings relative to the size of the ostrich.

The surface area of the wings is manifestly unable to lift the ostrich's weight. So, even if people do not really understand the aerodynamic principles by which wings support a body, what they do understand (or believe) about them does a pretty good job in explaining why some things can fly and some cannot.

All I am claiming is that these particular properties of birds can be explained once one has noticed them. It might be possible for a physiologist, for example, to know some of the features and then to be able to predict others (e.g., predicting the internal structure of birds' bones, given observations of their flying and wing structure), but such a feat would be far beyond most of us. Instead, most people can provide a post-hoc explanation of why birds have the particular constellation of features they do. The post-hoc nature of such explanations makes them somewhat circular. One cannot just explain why a bird has wings. One must explain why it has wings, given that it flies, lives in a nest, lays eggs, and so on. But at the same time, the explanation for flying depends on knowing that the bird has wings, lives in nests, lays eggs, and so on. Rather than a logical chain in which unknown properties are deduced from known ones, each property can be explained by the other properties. These properties are in a mutually reinforcing or homeostatic relationship such that they conspire to support one another (Boyd 1999; Keil 1989). Such circularity would be anathema in science, but from the perspective of learners, circular explanations may still be useful.

There are some exceptions to the post-hoc nature of explanations. For example, if someone told you about a DVD player, they might say "It's like a CD player, but for movies." Or perhaps when you first saw a DVD inserted into a player, you thought something like that. Now you can bootstrap a concept of DVD players by drawing properties that you know from this related concept. However, this is only successful if you are told or observe the relationship between DVD and CD players— it is rather specific similarity between two categories rather than more general domain knowledge. Although this kind of similarity is probably very useful in many cases, I will be focusing in this chapter on broader domain knowledge.

Another shortcoming of explanations is their shallowness (Wilson and Keil 2000). Often one can explain a given property by referring to some underlying property or principle. But why that principle exists or where that underlying property came from is often totally opaque. For example, I can explain the fact that knives are made of metal by the fact that metal is hard and therefore helps the knife in cutting. But why is metal hard? Although I know that it is somehow based on chemical-physical properties, I don't really have a clue what they are. (NB: It is not necessary to write and explain them to me.) This shallowness of explanations seems typical. Like the doctor in Moliere's *Le Malade Imaginaire* who explained the effect of sleeping pills as arising from their "dormative virtue," we don't understand many properties more than one level down.

The question, then, is whether such knowledge will in fact be useful. If explanations are often applied after the fact and are rather shallow, can they really aid in learning and using concepts? Specifically, if one typically explains features after observing them, does knowledge arrive too late to help in initial learning? If one has to know that a bird has wings and flies in order to understand the connection between them, it looks as if one has already learned the critical features of birds. The explanation might make one feel a sense of understanding after the fact, but it may not have influenced the actual learning of the properties. If explanations are generally somewhat shallow, then how helpful could they be in using a concept, in tasks such as induction or communication?

In short, although it may seem intuitively obvious that our knowledge of the world will help us learn new concepts related to that knowledge, it is possible that the limitations on our knowledge will make it less than useful in many cases. Among those cases would be situations in which knowledge is incomplete or partially wrong, unfortunately not unusual circumstances for humans.

An Example of Knowledge Use

Before discussing actual experiments, let's consider a somewhat simplified example of how you might normally learn a new category, namely a trip to the zoo. This situation can be used to illustrate the specific uses of knowledge to be discussed and can be contrasted with the typical psychology experiment using artificial stimuli. Suppose that on a trip to the zoo, you encounter a new animal, the whingelow. The whingelow, let us hope, does not look anything like a dot pattern, a geometric figure on a card, or a string of letters. Instead, the whingelow probably looks much like other animals of its class. If it is a mammal, it likely has visible fur, four limbs, a symmetrical face with two eyes, a nose, two ears, and so on. Thus, the whingelow is unlike the stimuli in these experiments in just the respect that it *does* look like other kinds of things you know. Furthermore, if you find out (or can infer) that it's a mammal, then you can use your knowledge about other mammals to conclude that it has a four-chambered heart, gives birth to live young, and so on. This real-life situation, then, is exactly what the experimentalists described above were trying to avoid: The real-life concept learner is not in a pristine environment where past knowledge is useless—instead, the learner comes to the situation knowing much about similar kinds of animals and being able to use that knowledge to learn about the whingelow.

It must be emphasized that before your trip to the zoo, you did not already know what the whingelow was, perhaps never having heard about it. You might have known a lot about animals and mammals in general, however. So, this prior knowledge is knowledge about the entire domain (e.g., all animals must breathe) or about concepts related to the new one (e.g., the whingelow looks a bit like a wombat; animals in zoos are often endangered), rather than knowledge about the new concept itself. The question, then, is whether and how such knowledge might influence your learning about whingelows.

Before beginning, however, it is necessary to clarify some terminology. I refer here to *knowledge effects* as influences of prior knowledge of real objects and events that people bring to the category-learning situation. The word "knowledge" is polysemous, and it could also be used more broadly than I am here to indicate anything at all that one knows about a category. For example, once a subject in Posner and Keele's (1970) experiment had learned the dot-pattern categories, she could be said to have "knowledge" of the categories. But this is not the sort of knowledge that we are discussing in this chapter. The knowledge that we will investigate is the preexperimental information about the world, rather than what you know about the target concept in particular. (Sometimes I shall use the phrase *background knowledge*, which emphasizes this point.) As we shall see, such knowledge can have a powerful effect on learning.

Knowledge effects are to be contrasted with *empirical learning* of the properties of observed exemplars during learning. For example, at the zoo, you might see that most whingelows have an eye stripe; or you might remember a purple, mid-sized whingelow with two legs that whined. These observations would constitute empirical information about the category.

Researchers have suggested that knowledge is important in a number of different aspects of category use (Heit 1997; Murphy 1993; Murphy and Medin 1985). First, knowledge may be involved in defining the features of an object. For example, when you went to the zoo, you paid attention to the number of legs of the whingelow and incorporated this into your initial concept. But you didn't incorporate the location of the animal's cage or the time of day. These didn't seem to be important aspects of the concept of a whingelow, even though they were readily perceivable properties. It can be argued that it was your prior knowledge of animals that directed these judgments about what features to encode and use. In other domains, the features you ignored for whingelows might be very reasonable ones; for example, social events may exist at specific places or times of day even though animal concepts generally do not. Thus, one's domain knowledge could cause one to encode or ignore time of day when learning the new animal concept.

Second, knowledge could help people to learn the features of new categories. It is well known from memory experiments that it is difficult to learn arbitrary lists of things, but once those lists are formed into a coherent structure (e.g., a story or description), people learn the material much better. Thus, it could be easier for you to learn about the whingelow than about Rosch and Mervis's (1975) alphanumeric strings, because your prior knowledge about animals may aid learning the particular features of the whingelow.

Third, your knowledge could influence the kinds of categorization decisions you make after learning. For example, if you saw a smaller animal that was in the same cage as the whingelows, and that was hanging around one of the females, you might assume that this was a baby whingelow, even if it did not look identical to the adults (Mervis 1987). This is not due to your having learned (yet) what the babies look like, but instead would be explained by your broader beliefs about the behavior of juvenile animals. More generally, the way you categorize new objects may be partly dependent on your background knowledge, rather than solely on your experience with the category.

Finally, knowledge might also be used to guide inductions or inferences you make about a category. For example, if one of these (apparent) baby whingelows kept pestering one of the females, you might infer that it was attempting to suckle. Again, such an inference is not based on specific experience with that animal (or even with whingelows) but is an educated guess, based on your more general knowledge. This chapter will discuss each of these uses of knowledge in turn.

Knowledge Effects in Category Acquisition

Category Learning Experiments

Perhaps the simplest way to start this investigation is to ask, "Does it make any difference what you know when you are learning a new category?" Intuitively, the answer seems obviously to be "yes," but this answer is not one that you would receive from most theories of concept learning. For example, suppose that concept learning consists in forming a prototype, which is the set of features that are most distinctive of the category. Nothing in this process relies on knowledge—it is a matter of identifying the features of the category members and seeing which ones are the best indicators of the category (see chapter 3). This is a statistical process that does not depend on the identity of the features. Similarly, if learning the category amounts to learning individual exemplars, there is no obvious reason that background knowledge should be involved. And in fact, the main articles describing prototype and exemplar theories say little if anything about how background knowledge might be involved in category learning (Hampton 1979; Medin and Schaffer 1978; Nosofsky 1984; Reed 1972; Rosch 1973; Rosch and Mervis 1975). This is not to say that these authors would actively deny that knowledge is important but to point out that although we may have an intuitive belief that knowledge should influence category learning, the most prominent theories of category learning have not incorporated this idea.

A simple demonstration of the importance of background knowledge can be found in Murphy and Wisniewski's (1989) Experiment 4. In one condition, subjects learned *Coherent* categories. These were items in which the features were sensibly related to one another, or at least not contradictory. For example, subjects learned an animal category that usually had the features: lives in water, eats fish, has many offspring, and is small. In contrast, the *Incoherent* categories had features that did not make sense together, for instance, lives in water, eats wheat, has a flat end, and used for stabbing bugs. (These features were used to construct individual items and were presented as verbal descriptions. The details are not essential here, except to note that the concepts were formally identical—only the names of the features changed, not the structure of the exemplars or the feature distributions.) As can be seen, in the Incoherent condition, the features came from different kinds of domains (animals and tools), and even within those entities, they did not make much sense (if something is used to stab bugs, it should have a pointy end, rather than a flat one). And perhaps not surprisingly, Murphy and Wisniewski found that the Incoherent categories were learned less well than the Coherent ones. Subjects made more errors on test items, and they were less confident in their categorization decisions for Incoherent categories.

In short, a concept's content influences how easy it is to learn. If the concept is grossly incompatible with what people know prior to the experiment, it will be difficult to acquire. This conclusion, however, is not very impressive, since most concepts that people learn are not nearly as incoherent as those in the Incoherent condition. Pazzani (1991) asked a more interesting question, namely whether prior expectations could help people learn a category compared to a case in which they had no such expectations. Here neither category was incompatible with what is already known; one category was consistent with prior knowledge, and one was simply not related to any particular knowledge.

Pazzani (1991) used categories that were described by simple rules. His items were pictures of people performing actions on objects. Each picture showed an adult or child doing an action on an uninflated balloon that was either large or small and either yellow or purple. The action was to dip the balloon in a cup of water or else to stretch it. Pazzani compared two different kinds of categories, disjunctive and conjunctive. The disjunctive category was defined by the rule "the person must be an adult OR the action must be stretching the balloon." The conjunctive category was defined by the rule "the color must be yellow AND the balloon must be small." Considerable past research had shown that people find it easier to learn a conjunctive category than a disjunctive category, so that is what one would expect in this case as well.[2] Pazzani added another factor, however, which he believed would influence the result. He told subjects either that they were to try to learn "Category Alpha" or that they were to try to identify which balloons would inflate. He believed that the first condition would not activate any particular knowledge but that the second condition would bring to mind whatever people believe about inflating balloons. In particular, people may believe that adults are better able to inflate a balloon than children are and that stretching a balloon makes it easier to inflate. Thus, this knowledge would be expected to aid the disjunctive rule, which included these features. Subjects saw the pictures one at a time and had to say whether each one was in the category that they were learning. The dependent measure in the experiment was how many examples of the category they had to see before they were completely accurate in identifying category members.

When subjects received the Category Alpha instructions, Pazzani found the usual pattern of the conjunctive category being easier to learn than the disjunctive category (a difference of about 15 fewer trials). However, when the Inflate instructions were given, this result reversed; in fact, the disjunctive category was learned after only about 8 examples on average, whereas the conjunctive category was learned after about 28 examples (Pazzani 1991, figure 1). Clearly, the hint about balloon inflation greatly aided subjects in learning the category. Knowledge was useful in a more positive way than was demonstrated by the Murphy and Wisniewski experiment—namely, people used their knowledge to make hypotheses about a category's features, and since their knowledge was correct, concept learning was easier.

Pazzani's (1991) experiment has another implication as well. It is significant that a finding from many past experiments on category learning (starting with Bruner, Goodnow and Austin 1956), the advantage of conjunctive rules, could actually be *reversed* by the use of background knowledge. This suggests the somewhat disturbing possibility that the results of artificial experiments that do not make contact with prior knowledge may not hold in the situation where people have expectations about the category (which is probably the more usual case). That is, it is possible that results from experiments with dot patterns or geometric shapes will not apply to real-world cases in which people have background knowledge. This possibility will be discussed further in the chapter's conclusion.

Locus of the Knowledge Effect

Clearly, then, knowledge can help one learn a novel category. But there is considerably more to be investigated here. If one compares the traditional experiments with artificial stimuli (such as dot patterns) to natural categories, two differences are salient. The first is that the features themselves are different. The second difference is that the features of natural categories seem to hang together, whereas the features of artificial categories generally do not. In order to understand the knowledge effect, we need to discover whether either or both of these differences is responsible for it. The following experiments investigate these variables.

One possible reason for knowledge effects is that the features themselves may make learning easier. As noted earlier, in most experiments that do not involve knowledge, the stimuli have been themselves meaningless items, such as dots, geometric stimuli, and even letter strings (individual letters not having much meaning associated with them). Would using more meaningful stimuli in and of itself lead to an improvement in learning? Murphy and Allopenna (1994) compared categories that had relatively meaningless typographical symbols (like <, {, +, and !) as features to those that had meaningful phrases such as "lives alone" and "thick, heavy walls." However, these phrases were randomly assigned to categories, so that there was no overall rhyme or reason to them. Murphy and Allopenna did not find any difference in the difficulty of learning these categories; both were quite difficult. Thus, the mere meaningfulness of the features itself does not appear to be a very important aspect of the knowledge effect.

What did make an important difference in learning was how the features were related. When the features of a category formed a consistent set, the category was much easier to learn than when they were inconsistent or simply neutral. Consider the pair of categories summarized at the top of table 6.1. The features of these categories, both vehicles, can be described by a *theme* that connects them. The category in the left column seems to be a kind of jungle vehicle, and the one in the right column seems to be an arctic vehicle. That information was never given to subjects, but it is possible that during the course of learning they would realize that the features were related in this way, and this might in turn improve the learning process. Because these features could be integrated into a single theme, Murphy and Allopenna

Table 6.1.
Typical features of categories from Murphy and Allopenna (1984).

Integrated Categories	
Category 1	Category 2
Made in Africa	Made in Norway
Lightly insulated	Heavily insulated
Green	White
Drives in jungles	Drives on glaciers
Has wheels	Has treads
Neutral Categories	
Category 1	Category 2
Green	White
Manual transmission	Automatic transmission
Radial tires	Non-radial tires
Air bags	Automatic seat belts
Vinyl seats	Cloth seats

Note: Subjects would have learned a pair of integrated or neutral categories. Exemplars were constructed by selecting a subset of each category's features (shown above), along with some random features (not shown) that occurred in both categories equally often.

called this the *Integrated Condition*. Now consider the pair of categories summarized at the bottom of table 6.1. These categories are also vehicles, but their properties are no longer connected by a theme. There is nothing inconsistent about the features that appear together in the category—but there is no special connection between them, either. That is, there is no reason why being green should lead a vehicle to have a manual transmission rather than an automatic one, nor why air bags should go with vinyl seat covers rather than cloth seat covers. I will call this the *Neutral Condition*.[3] The category structures made from these features were identical—all that differed was how well the features could be related by a theme. The results showed that subjects could learn the Integrated categories in about half the time of the Neutral categories.

These findings suggest that knowledge helps learning because it relates the features in the category, rather than through the properties of the features themselves. Of course, it is likely that some differences in features are important, but more significant here is that the knowledge must relate the features to one another, and hence, to the category as a whole. Why is this helpful? Keep in mind that not every example from the category has the same features—one might have treads and be white, while another might be built in Norway and drive on glaciers. This variation in features makes the purely empirical learning process more difficult. One must learn multiple features, because every feature will not be present in every item, and an item might have an atypical feature. Learning these multiple features is easier if they can be related by a common knowledge structure. The knowledge could help subjects learn which features go with which categories and to remember that feature assignment at test. If you know that vehicle X is built in Norway, it's easy to learn that vehicle X goes on glaciers too.

In short, knowledge probably works by helping to relate features. Later, we will consider how using this knowledge affects the category representation.

Amount and Consistency of Knowledge

In the experiments discussed so far, the knowledge has generally been consistent with the entire category. For example, in Pazzani's (1991) experiment, the category was defined by the two features "adult OR stretch the balloon," and it was exactly these two features that were related to people's prior knowledge about inflating balloons. And in the Murphy and Allopenna experiments just described, all of the category's features were related to the theme. But this situation seems rather unrealistic. When you went to the zoo and saw the whingelow, you had some knowledge that explained some of its properties or that helped them make sense to you. But certainly others of its properties were not specifically related to that knowledge. The particular color of the whingelow, for example, or the shape of its nose, or the length of its fur might not have been related to any specific knowledge that you had. Yet, you might well learn from this experience that the whingelow is a kind of grayish animal, with a wide nose and short fur. Thus, even though you had knowledge about other animals and mammals that was relevant to learning about the whingelow, you probably also learned about properties that did not make contact with that knowledge. In the experiments discussed so far, there were no such properties. This raises the question, then, about whether knowledge is helpful in the more realistic situation. Perhaps when knowledge does not pick out most or many of the category's properties, it is not very useful.

Kaplan and Murphy (2000) investigated the situation in which some, but not all, of a category's features were not related to knowledge. Their categories were for the most part like the Neutral categories shown in table 6.1. However, every item had exactly one property that was related to a theme, such as arctic vehicle or jungle vehicle. These properties were different across items: One item had "green," another had "drives in jungles," a third had "is made in Africa," and so on. Thus, unlike the Pazzani or Murphy and Allopenna experiments, the majority of the features of every item were not related to specific knowledge. Furthermore, in order to realize that there was a theme related to the categories, subjects had to notice the relatedness of *different* features appearing in different exemplars (e.g., that one item's "green" was related to another item's "drives in jungles"). In previous experiments, the exact same feature was repeated across items (e.g., "stretch the balloon" in Pazzani's experiment). In spite of these apparent hindrances to noticing and using the knowledge, Kaplan and Murphy's subjects learned the categories significantly faster (in less than half the time) when these thematic features were present. Thus, we can conclude that background knowledge is helpful even when it is not related to all— or most—of a category's properties. This is a significant result, because it suggests that knowledge is likely to be useful even in complex settings in which one's knowledge is incomplete or imperfect.

Similarly, Murphy and Kaplan (2000) found that knowledge was useful even when it was not totally consistent. One popular way of making up items in a category-learning experiment (Medin, Wattenmaker, and Hampson 1987) is for each item to consist of N features, of which 1 feature is "incorrect" and $N - 1$ are correct. (As shown in table 5.2 of ch. 5, except for the first exemplar in each category.) For example, if there are six stimulus dimensions, each exemplar would have five correct features and one incorrect feature. By "correct" and "incorrect" here I mean simply that the feature is normally associated with the exemplar's category or a different category, respectively. To use a real-life analogy, I might make up an item that has wings, walks, lives in nests, lays eggs, and sings. Five of these features are associated to the category of birds, and one is associated to mammals. If the features in an experiment are derived from a theme, like those shown in table 6.1, how does the presence of the incorrect feature in each item affect learning? Because every item has a feature that is inconsistent with the rest of them, perhaps subjects will ignore the theme; perhaps the knowledge has to be almost perfectly consistent before subjects will rely on it.

Murphy and Kaplan found that even with this structure, Integrated Categories were easier to learn than Neutral Categories. Subjects were able to explain away or ignore the one inconsistent feature and still use the mostly accurate knowledge. Thus, knowledge does not have to be related to every feature in the category, and it does not have to be perfectly reliable in order to benefit learning.

Finally, it may be useful to ask *how soon* knowledge has its effect. Heit and Bott (2000) propose that knowledge will only be useful after a certain amount of learning, because it will take a fair amount of time to figure out which knowledge is relevant and is reliably associated to the categories being learned. And in their first experiment, they found no difference between knowledge-related and -unrelated features after one block of learning, but this difference did appear in later blocks. However, Heit and Bott's second experiment with different materials did find a difference after one block. Furthermore, Kaplan and Murphy (2000) also found a difference after one block of learning in their categories with minimal knowledge. In that case, each knowledge-related feature had been seen only *once*, and yet they were learned better than the more frequent knowledge-unrelated features.[4] It is likely that the time course of knowledge effects will depend greatly on the particular kind of knowledge present in the stimuli: A hint given in advance could affect the processing of the very first stimulus; a subtle knowledge difference that is not readily apparent could take a few blocks to reveal itself. However, there is certainly no general rule that considerable learning is required before knowledge begins to help.

So far, knowledge has been shown to aid in learning categories. However, background knowledge cannot be expected to always be correct. In some cases it may be vague, in others, wrong. (I am flouting convention here by referring to incorrect knowledge, which is an oxymoron. The point is that this information is exactly the same as information that is helpful—only it is wrong.) Clearly, knowledge may not be helpful in such cases. The degree to which "bad" knowledge hurts has not been very much investigated. Kaplan and Murphy (2000) found that when knowledge in a category was contradictory (i.e., features related to different themes were mixed together), subjects found the category about as easy to learn as categories in the Neutral condition (see bottom of table 6.1) that had no knowledge at all. Although the wrong knowledge obviously did not improve learning, it didn't hurt it relative to no knowledge (see also Murphy and Allopenna 1994). This rather surprising result has not yet been fully investigated.[5] The best guess is that when the knowledge is contradictory or misleading, subjects very quickly realize this and then simply ignore it. Thus, even though knowledge is generally helpful, people can apparently identify when it is not, by noticing internal inconsistencies and by receiving feedback.

In a series of experiments, Heit (1994, 1998) investigated how prior knowledge influences the way that new category examples—consistent or inconsistent with one's expectations—are processed. He posed the following thought experiment. Imagine that you are visiting a new country and have read some guide books on the people and sights there. The guide book has given some presumably stereotypical information on the character of the people of this country—say, that the people are typically friendly. When you go to the country, you will meet a number of people, and some of them are likely to be friendly and others not so friendly. How do you evaluate this information in coming to a conclusion about the character of the people? Given that you expected the people to be friendly, perhaps you should give greater weight to the people who meet this expectation—after all, the unfriendly ones are likely to be exceptions. Alternatively, perhaps you should give greater weight to the disconfirming information. These unfriendly people might surprise you and therefore draw attention to themselves. Thus, they might have a greater effect on your judgment about the people.

Heit's experiments followed this example in presenting to subjects descriptions of people in a new city, W. He manipulated subjects' expectations by using pairs of characteristics that would be expected to co-occur or not. For example, if a person was described as "shy," then one would expect the person to have the property "does not attend parties often" rather than "attends parties often." Heit manipulated how often pairs of features like "shy" and "does not attend parties often" co-occurred: They could be paired 0%, 25%, 50%, 75%, or 100% of the time. After viewing a number of these descriptions, subjects were asked to estimate percentages of the co-occurrences. For example, they were asked "if a person from city W was shy, how likely would the person be to attend parties often?" based on the exemplars.

Heit expected that subjects would be influenced by their prior knowledge in making these judgments. That is, they should give higher percentages for shy–does not attend parties often than for shy–attends parties often. Figure 6.1 illustrates this effect, by showing that high expectancies ($q = 90\%$) lead to higher estimates than low expectancies ($q = 10\%$) across the range of observed probabilities (the x-axis). However, the exact form of this effect should vary depending on which kind of example subjects pay more attention to. If people pay equal attention to examples that are consistent and inconsistent to their knowledge, then the effect should be equal across the observed co-occurrence of the pairs of features (as in figure 6.1a). If the congruent items (those consistent with knowledge) are weighted more, then the difference between consistent and inconsistent items should be largest at 50% and smallest at 0% and 100% (figure 6.1b). Because the evidence is most mixed at 50%, there is more "room" for knowledge to push up the congruent items and push down the incongruent ones. In contrast, if people attend to the incongruent items (those inconsistent with prior expectations), then the effect should be smallest at 50%. Attention to incongruent items would reduce the difference between the two item types, by pushing up their subjective frequency. The effect would again be found in

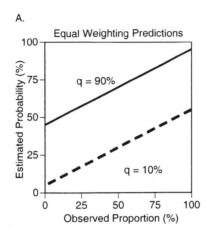

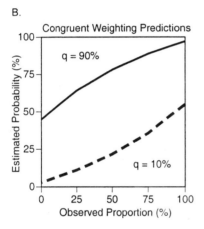
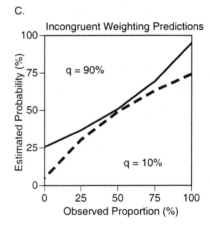

Figure 6.1
Predictions from Heit's (1994, 1998) weighting model. Each graph shows subjects' estimated probabilities of co-occurrence of pairs of items as a function of their actual co-occurrence (shown on the x axis), knowledge status (pairs expected to co-occur are solid lines; pairs expected not to co-occur are dashed), and form of weighting. In the equal weighting model, positive and negative exemplars are treated as equally informative. In the congruent model, positive evidence is weighted more heavily than negative evidence; in the incongruent model, negative evidence is weight more heavily. The congruent model shows the largest expectation effect when observed proportions are intermediate, whereas the incongruent model shows the smallest effect at intermediate proportions.

the middle, rather than near 0 or 100% (figure 6.1c), because it makes little difference how items are weighted when almost all the items are of one type. (Heit 1998 provides a mathematical model of the weighting process to support these predictions, which the interested reader should consult.)

Across many experiments, Heit found that congruent and incongruent items were weighted equally—that is, the effect of knowledge was constant from 0–100% co-occurrence (like figure 6.1a). However, Heit (1998) found one exception to this rule: When subjects were given a small number of items and a fairly long time to study each one (16 seconds), they tended to weight the incongruent items more, as shown in figure 6.1c. Here it can be seen that there is an overall knowledge effect; people tend to give lower ratings to the less expected feature pairs. However, this effect is smallest at the middle range of probabilities, because the incongruent items are weighted more (raising that curve) and the congruent ones less (lowering its curve).

Heit (1998) argued from these results that when people encounter an unexpected item, they spend more time thinking about it, perhaps attempting to explain its peculiar properties. And, indeed, he found that people studied the incongruent items longer when the study period was self-paced. This, then, is another effect of prior knowledge. It does not just aid category learning when it is consistent with the examples (as in the above experiments), but it also influences what subjects attend to when learning. It may seem paradoxical that it results in attention to items that disconfirm the knowledge, but this is probably a more efficient strategy for learning. There is no need to give special attention or weight to things that one already knows. Indeed, it is probably best not to think about them, since they do not teach anything new (see also Kruschke 1991). Instead, learning may be most efficient when it focuses on surprising events.

This section began with the question about whether knowledge would be helpful when it was not as complete and reliable as in the early experiments that investigated knowledge effects. The clear answer is "yes." When knowledge relates only some of the features, it still benefits learning; and when the knowledge was sometimes wrong, it still helped. In Heit's experiments, subjects were sensitive to both their prior expectancies and the observed level of co-occurrence of features— incorrect knowledge did not overwhelm the empirical data, nor was it ignored. Furthermore, even when the knowledge was plain wrong, it did not adversely affect learning, compared to no knowledge at all. Thus, the picture given by these studies is one in which learners use whatever amount of knowledge is present and useful but are not overly swayed by inaccurate expectations.

Interactions of Structure and Knowledge

In some cases, one might think of knowledge effects as being something that can be added to or subtracted from a category, much as one could print the stimuli in blue or red. And, indeed, many studies have added or subtracted knowledge by changing some features or prior information about the category. However, in an important study, Wattenmaker et al. (1986) argued that knowledge must be related to the structure of a category in order to be helpful. To see what they meant by this, I discuss their experiments in some detail.

Wattenmaker et al. began with the comparison of linearly separable and non-linearly separable categories described in chapter 4. To summarize this distinction briefly, linearly separable categories are those in which the evidence for the category can be simply summed together in order to make a decision. For example, if the members of category A are mostly blue, triangles, and tall, then one can assume that a blue, tall rectangle would be a member of category A, because the majority of its features are consistent with the category. (This is simplifying somewhat—see chapter 4.) In contrast, a nonlinearly separable category cannot be explained by such a rule. There is no way to simply sum up the evidence for individual features to decide whether the item is in the category. Typically, such categories are determined at least in part by specific configurations of features (e.g., blue-and-triangle might be associated to the category, although blue alone is not).

Table 6.2 gives an example of linearly separable and nonlinearly separable categories (from Wattenmaker et al. 1986). (Each row describes a category exemplar; the columns refer to different stimulus dimensions; and each 1 or 0 indicates a different value on that dimension. Keep in mind that in an experiment, these dimensions are turned into stimuli with colors, shapes, sizes, positions, and so on. Subjects do not get to see 1s and 0s as we do here, and so learning is harder than it often seems from such diagrams.) As can be seen, for the top pair of categories, each member of Category A has three or more 1s, but no member of Category B does. Therefore, a learner could acquire these categories by learning which features (the 1s) tend to go with Category A, and simply deciding whether each item has a majority of those features. In contrast, the category pair at the bottom of the table does not have any such rule. Although Category A does have more 1s than does Category B, exemplar B3 has a majority of 1s, and exemplar A1 has a majority of 0s. There is no way to simply add up the features to decide category membership. Instead, in order to learn this category, one must learn about individual exemplars (memorizing that A1 is a member of Category A, that B1 is in Category B, and so on), or one

Table 6.2.
Category structure used by Wattenmaker et al. (1986).

Linearly Separable Categories

Category A					Category B				
Exemplar	D1	D2	D3	D4	Exemplar	D1	D2	D3	D4
A1	1	1	1	0	B1	1	1	0	0
A2	1	0	1	1	B2	0	0	0	1
A3	1	1	0	1	B3	0	1	1	0
A4	0	1	1	1	B4	1	0	1	0

Nonlinearly Separable Categories

Category A					Category B				
Exemplar	D1	D2	D3	D4	Exemplar	D1	D2	D3	D4
A1	1	0	0	0	B1	0	0	0	1
A2	1	0	1	0	B2	0	1	0	0
A3	1	1	1	1	B3	1	0	1	1
A4	0	1	1	1	B4	0	0	0	0

Note: D1, D2, etc. refer to stimulus dimensions of each item. 1 and 0 refer to the values on those dimensions. Each exemplar is made up of four features, one from each dimension.

must learn about configurations of features (e.g., learning that only members of Category A have a 1 on D2 and a 1 on D4).

Wattenmaker et al. (1986) believed that whether a linearly separable or nonlinearly separable category would be easier to learn could depend on how the structure was related to knowledge that people bring to the learning situation. In some cases, the knowledge would suggest that the evidence should simply be summed up—consistent with a linearly separable category. In other situations, the knowledge would refer to configurations of features—consistent with a nonlinearly separable category. In their Experiment 1, they used personality features. They hypothesized that people are believed to be kind or intelligent or extraverted to the degree that they evince behaviors consistent with these characteristics. A kind person may not always be kind but is kind more often than not. Thus, personality categories might be particularly susceptible to a linearly separable form of categorization.

In their experiment, Wattenmaker et al. manipulated knowledge by the way they assigned features to their design. In the *trait* condition, the 1s and 0s in table 6.2 were replaced by actions that were consistent with a given personality. For example, the 1s on each dimension might be replaced by actions consistent with an honest person, whereas the 0s would be replaced by actions of a dishonest person. Pattern A1 in the linearly separable condition was: "Returned the wallet he had found in the park; Admitted to his neighbor that he had broken his rake; Told the host that he was late for the dinner party because he had overslept; Acted like he enjoyed shopping when his girlfriend asked him to go along with her to the store" (Wattenmaker et al., p. 169). The first three properties (1s) display honesty, whereas the last (a 0) is less than fully honest. Thus, in the trait condition, summing up the properties would lead to a simple rule such as "the people in Category A are usually honest." In the control condition, the dimensions were four different traits (honesty, talkativeness, cooperativeness, and cautiousness). Here, subjects would not be expected to sum up the features, because there is no personality category that corresponds to all these traits. That is, no prior knowledge structure says that people in a given category should be both honest and talkative, but not cooperative or cautious. So, a 1 on D2 was not related to a 1 on D4.

The results fit Wattenmaker et al.'s predictions. In the trait condition, the linearly separable categories were easier to learn. However, in the control condition, subjects found the nonlinearly separable category slightly easier to learn. Presumably, subjects were able to use their knowledge of personality types to combine the different actions in order to use a trait description of the category. In the nonlinearly separable case, this was not possible, and so attempting to use the trait was not very successful. In later work, Wattenmaker (1995) has suggested that social categories in general are interpreted as linearly separable, in part because we do not expect people to be entirely consistent in their behavior. Thus, social categories in general are flexible, in that they do not require specific configurations of features but usually just require some preponderance of evidence ("most of the time, Jessica's quite pleasant").

Wattenmaker et al. (1986) found that it was also possible to induce subjects to prefer a nonlinearly separable category. Without going into the details of their experiment, I'll describe a stimulus to illustrate it (based on their Experiment 3). Suppose that you are trying to learn about an occupation. Half of the members of this group work in the winter and half in the summer. Therefore, the season in which they work does not seem to distinguish this group from any other. However, later you realize that half of these people work indoors and half work outdoors. Now the season does seem relevant: The indoor workers should work in the winter, and the outdoor workers in the summer. This configural information is not the linearly separable sort, because it depends on how the two features are configured—"works indoors" is not predictive of the category by itself; it's predictive when it occurs with "works in winter" and not predictive otherwise. You can't simply sum up the evidence. Wattenmaker et al. (1986) found that when pairs of features made sense, as in this example, subjects found the nonlinearly separable categories easier to learn than the linearly separable ones. When the feature pairs did not make sense (i.e., were not predictable based on prior knowledge), then the difficulty of learning reversed.

In short, Wattenmaker et al. showed that which structure was more difficult depended on how it related to prior knowledge. Furthermore, prior knowledge was not always helpful. When it was well matched to the category structure, it did improve learning. But when it did not match that structure, it actually hurt learning in some cases. So, knowledge in and of itself may not be helpful unless it actually conforms to the category's structure. These results suggest that we should not think of prior knowledge as being an attribute of a category that can be simply added or taken away in the way that a single feature can. The utility of prior knowledge may depend in a subtle way on how the features related to knowledge are empirically structured. This is an important issue on which more work needs to be done.

Category Construction

As described in chapter 5, a very different way to study category acquisition is not to teach people the category but to let them try to discover it on their own—the *category construction* task. In real life, people notice distinctive classes of objects by themselves without someone telling them that these are different sorts of things, or instructing them in the name. In experiments of this sort, researchers have typically given the subjects a set of stimuli printed on cards and then asked them to divide them into the groups that are best or most meaningful. Quite surprisingly, adult subjects overwhelmingly choose a single stimulus dimension on which to divide up the cards rather than forming family resemblance categories (Ahn and Medin 1992; Medin et al. 1987; Regehr and Brooks 1995). For example, they might divide up the items based only on their color. Given that real-world categories like chair and rose seem to be family resemblance categories, this result is rather puzzling. You can't identify a rose simply by its color or its having thorns: You need to use many features associated with roses. The reasons for subjects' strong preference for unidimensional categories are discussed in chapter 5. Here I focus on the influence of knowledge on this task.

Perhaps if subjects had knowledge connecting the features, they might attend to more of the features when constructing these categories. Medin et al. (1987) had used pictures of bugs in their experiments, and they thought that if they impressed subjects with the idea that these were different species of bugs inhabiting different ecosystems, subjects might look for larger constellations of features rather than choosing just one, such as head shape. In one experiment, subjects were told that the bugs represented bottom dwellers and top dwellers of a pond. They were shown the two category prototypes and told that one was the "best adapted top dweller" and the other the "best adapted bottom dweller." Even with this help, 19 of 20 subjects used a single dimension to divide up the stimuli. That is, rather than noticing that a bunch of items were similar to one prototype and another bunch of items similar to the other prototype, they might put together all the items with the same head shape as prototype 1 and then all the items with the same head shape as prototype 2, ignoring the other dimensions. So, clearly, very general background knowledge about animals is not sufficient to overrule this unidimensional bias.

Ahn (1990) tried a more direct approach. She used features of flower categories that were clearly different, such as color and location, and provided subjects with a causal explanation connecting the properties of the two kinds of flowers, namely that one type of flower attracted a kind of bird, and the other attracted a kind of bee. The bird was said to like bright colors, be active at night, fly high, and lay eggs near water, and the bee was described as having the opposite values. After hearing this information, subjects divided the stimuli up into two categories. Under these conditions, subjects did form family resemblance categories a third of the time, identifying flowers that were brightly colored, blooming at night, found in trees, and near the water as one category. This result does demonstrate that knowledge can help people to identify category structure. However, the knowledge provided was somewhat arbitrary, in that the bird or bee just happened to prefer the prototypical features of the two categories, and subjects were given these descriptions that connected all the categories' features right before sorting. If, then, this sort of information is required to induce family resemblance categories, it would not be likely to be very helpful in more realistic settings.

Spalding and Murphy (1996) and Kaplan and Murphy (1999) used the stimuli like those described in table 6.1 in category construction experiments. They found that explicit instruction in the connection of the features is not necessary with these items, because subjects could spontaneously identify the relations between features. However, it was important to ensure that subjects first examine all the items. Spalding and Murphy (Experiment 3) found that if subjects were simply given cards and asked to divide them up, they discovered the family resemblance category 40% of the time when the categories were distinguished by themes (like the arctic and jungle vehicle). When subjects first read through all the items and then were asked to divide them up, 78% of the categories were family resemblance sorts. Thus, one reason why people often make unidimensional sorts in experiments may be that they do not study the items carefully enough to observe whatever structure is there. However, it should be emphasized that when there is no knowledge relating the features, examining the cards by itself is not helpful. In this condition, Spalding and Murphy found that no subject recovered the category structure.

Kaplan and Murphy (1999) essentially repeated their experiment with category learning described above, only using a category construction task. Recall that in their learning experiment, every item had only one feature that was related to the theme. All of the other features were neutral. In spite of the very small number of knowledge-related features in their stimuli, a third of the subjects divided them up into family resemblance categories. Control subjects who did not get these few knowledge-related features never made family resemblance categories. Thus, even a small amount of knowledge can lead subjects to pick out the category structure. One surprising result from their experiment was that when the categories had a thematic basis, subjects not only learned about the thematic features but also learned about the nonthematic features to some degree. Subjects whose categories did not have a thematic basis did not learn about either. The theme helped subjects notice the empirical structure of nonthematic features, which suggests an interaction between the empirical and knowledge-based learning processes.

These experiments demonstrate that knowledge may be helpful in people's spontaneous creation of categories. As described in chapter 5, the category construction methodology may be somewhat artificial, and so its results should be taken with a grain of salt. Nonetheless, the effects of knowledge demonstrated in these experiments suggest that knowledge may be used in more realistic situations as well. For example, suppose that you notice a tree with strangely shaped leaves that you've never seen before. You could make a new category that is essentially unidimensional: tree with such-and-such a leaf.[6] However, your knowledge of plants suggests that other properties are likely to be relevant, such as the location where the tree was found (forest, urban, mountain, near water), its size, the presence or absence of fruit, and so on. If the tree is in an unusual environment (say, a desert), you might try to make a connection between the strange shape of the leaf and the environment. Perhaps the leaves are small, to reduce water loss. In short, it is unlikely that you would stop at one dimension when trying to understand this kind of tree, and the other dimensions you consider would probably be the ones that your knowledge suggested were relevant.

The effect of knowledge in unsupervised category formation is important, because it indicates that feedback is not necessary to obtain the benefits of knowledge. In many situations one must form concepts without anyone available to provide instruction; in particular, it has been suggested that many of children's early concepts are initiated in just this way (see chapter 10). The somewhat surprising finding that even small amounts of knowledge can aid in this task (Kaplan and Murphy 1999) provides further evidence that children may benefit from knowledge when learning categories. That is, some have suggested that children do not know very much about biology or social categories or mechanical devices, and so their background knowledge could not help them very much. However, even a small amount of knowledge does improve category construction.

Knowledge in Categorization

The examples discussed up until now have all dealt with the initial acquisition of a category. However, knowledge may also influence a later-occurring process, namely the categorization of items into categories that are already known. An example of Douglas Medin's (Murphy and Medin 1985) will illustrate. Suppose you were at a party, and you heard that one of the guests had fallen into the pool. You might conclude that this person was drunk. But this is not because you have stored in your concept of drunks the feature "falls into pool." Instead, this event *can be explained by* the categorization of the person as drunk. Similarly, there are new inventions and newly seen objects that may not be very similar to anything we know, but which can be explained by their category membership. For example, suppose that you saw a construction worker holding a loud device that seemed to be shooting nails into some wooden studs. You might understand this machine to be a kind of electric hammer, even though it looks very different from other hammers you've seen. However, it fills the same function as a hammer and presumably was invented to fulfill the same purpose a hammer was invented for. In short, the machine would be explained if it were a hammer. As another example, consider a difficult medical diagnosis. (Diagnosis is a form of categorization, and patients with the same disease often do not have the same set of symptoms.) In a complex case, a patient may not look exactly like any single disease victim that the doctor is familiar with. However, perhaps the patient's symptoms can be explained by a particular set of disease categories (e.g., atypical hepatitis combined with a vitamin E deficiency). Doctors can make such diagnoses through reasoning processes that tell them that these diseases could explain the patient's symptoms and test results. All of these examples concern not the original learning of a category but rather the process of deciding whether something is or is not a category member.

In short, categorization may not always be based on simple matching of properties. It may be that background knowledge is more actively involved. There are many anecdotes of the sort just described, but there have been fewer tests of this hypothesis than in category learning. Most of these tests have been with natural categories, since these are ones for which subjects are most likely to have well-developed knowledge structures.

One study that examined categorization of this sort was performed by Rips (1989), who created a scenario in which an object or animal went through a transformation. In particular, he described to subjects something that was much like a bird. This animal, however, had the misfortune to live next to a toxic waste dump, where chemicals caused it to lose its feathers and develop transparent, thin wings. It also grew an outer shell and more legs. At the end of this metamorphosis, the creature appeared rather reminiscent of an insect. Rips asked subjects whether the animal was a bird or an insect and whether it was more similar to birds or insects. Subjects claimed that this stimulus was more similar to an insect but that it was still more likely to *be* a bird. That is, subjects felt that the change in outer appearance and even body parts did not constitute identity, but that the animal's inherent biological properties determined what it was. Apparently, then, this judgment was based on a domain theory about biology rather than on more superficial properties. Keil (1989) performed some very similar studies on children and adults using a surgical scenario, described in chapter 10. He found similarly that adults were not persuaded that transforming an animal would make a difference in its category membership, even when it ended up looking exactly like a different item. Children were somewhat more flexible: Before grade 2, they were generally willing to believe that a cat could be turned into a skunk, for example. However, even children at this age did not believe that an animal could be transformed into a plant or inanimate object.

Rips (1989) reported another influential study using a different kind of example. Imagine that there is a round object that is half way in size between a quarter (a U.S. 25-cent piece) and a pizza. Is it more likely to be a quarter or a pizza? There does not seem to be any way to tell based on empirical evidence. However, because people realize that coins are restricted in size by convention and law, whereas pizzas are not, Rips expected subjects to categorize it as a pizza. And in fact, this is what most subjects did.

Unfortunately, this study was found to be difficult to replicate, as Smith and Sloman (1994) discovered that the choice of the nonvariable category was found only when subjects were required to talk out loud and justify their answers. If they

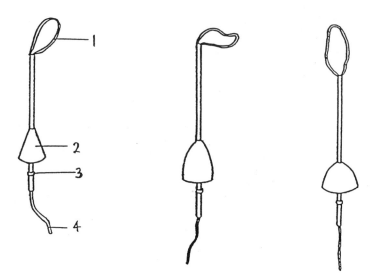

Figure 6.2
Pictures of the tuk category used by Lin and Murphy (1997). Subjects read descriptions of the item and were told what each of the numbered parts was. However, different subjects received different information about the objects and their parts, as explained in the text.

only had to make a categorization decision, they chose the variable and nonvariable categories about equally. Although this still indicates that people will use their background knowledge in making these decisions, Smith and Sloman argued that people use such knowledge only when encouraged to do so by the instructions of the task. In everyday life, they suggest, categorization of entities may not involve such knowledge at all, especially when it is done rapidly without much overt reflection.

Lin and Murphy (1997) attempted to find evidence for more automatic, less reflective use of knowledge, with speeded identification tasks that have been used in past categorization research (e.g., Murphy and Brownell 1985; Smith, Balzano and Walker 1978). These tasks would not be of the sort Smith and Sloman criticized, since they require fast, nonverbal responses. Subjects first learned about kinds of artifacts in a foreign country, such as the set shown in figure 6.2. Different subjects were taught different things about these items. For example, one group was told that the *tuk* displayed in figure 6.2 was used for hunting. The hunter would slip the noose (1) at the top over the animal's head, and pull on the loose end of the rope (4) to tighten it. The hunter held the tuk at the handle (3), and the hand guard (2) protected the hunter from animal bites and scratches. A different group read a very different story about the tuk. They were told that it was a fertilizing tool. The liquid

Consistent A   Consistent B   Control

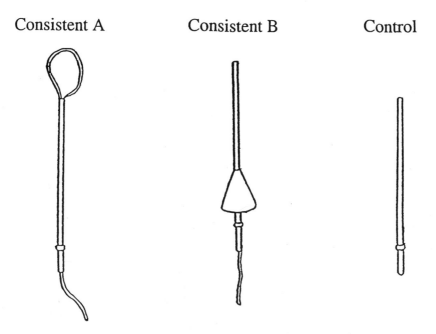

Figure 6.3
Test items used by Lin and Murphy (1997), differing in which critical properties are present in the object. The Consistent A item is consistent with one description of the tuk (the animal catcher), and the Consistent B item is consistent with the other interpretation (the fertilizer). The Control item has neither of the critical properties.

fertilizer was held in the tank (2), and the knob (3) was turned in order to let it flow out the outlet pipe (4). The loop at the top (1) was used to hang up the tuk in storage. Obviously, the two groups have very different background knowledge about this implement. However, they have both seen the same examples of tuks and have been given descriptions of the same parts. The question is, then, whether this difference in background knowledge will influence subjects' categorizations.

Lin and Murphy tested this question by creating items that lacked one or more of the parts of the originally seen tuks. As shown in figure 6.3, one item might lack the loop at the top, one might lack the triangular part in the middle, and another might lack both. The descriptions of the objects had been designed so that the most important part in one description should be relatively unimportant in the other description. For example, the loop at the top is critical for the hunting tool tuk, because it grabs the animal. In contrast, that part is not essential for the fertilizing tuk, because it only concerns the storage of the tool. The reverse is true of the triangular part (2), which is essential for holding the fertilizer but is only a convenience for the hunting tool. Lin and Murphy found that subjects' willingness to call these items *tuks* depended on the initial description. Those who learned the tuk as a hunting tool did not categorize the item with the missing loop at the top as a tuk; those who learned the item as a fertilizer did. These effects were also found in reaction times of speeded category decisions, even when subjects were given a response deadline, to make them go faster than usual. In fact, similar effects were found for subjects whose task was simply to decide whether the object, when presented briefly, had all of its original parts or not: Subjects were more likely to notice when a functionally critical part was missing than when a less important part was missing.

In short, although all subjects saw the same examples, they drew different conclusions about what parts of the object were most important. These conclusions influenced speeded categorization decisions, even though this background knowledge was not specifically asked about during the task. Palmeri and Blalock (2000) also found knowledge effects in speeded categorization, even when subjects were forced to respond very quickly. This result gives some confidence that Smith and Sloman's (1994) finding of limited knowledge effects is not universal. Recall that Smith and Sloman found that subjects only seemed to use their background knowledge when they were asked to justify their answers. In contrast, in Lin and Murphy's and Palmeri and Blalock's experiments, the results were found without such justifications being asked for, and under speeded instructions. (Especially noteworthy is the finding of knowledge effects on part detection, which is a simple, factual question.) Thus, some kinds of knowledge are probably directly incorporated into the category representation and used in normal, fast decisions about objects. Other kinds of knowledge, however, may come into play only when it has been solicited.

More generally, it seems unlikely that much background knowledge is called for when you walk down the street and see a pigeon, say, on the sidewalk. If the pigeon is clearly visible, and you've seen many of them before, you will identify it extremely quickly as a bird, without having to go through a long reasoning process. In other circumstances, however, overt reasoning using background knowledge would be called for. As described earlier, cases of medical diagnosis often require one to reason explicitly about how to explain the symptoms and test results observed. More generally, if you have to categorize something based on minimal perceptual information (e.g., a noise at the window), you might naturally rely almost entirely on background knowledge to arrive at an answer (a bird might have flown up to the window and then flown away; a dog couldn't get up there and then disappear so suddenly). In between these two extremes are cases in which knowledge might be somewhat involved or could speed up or slow down a decision. For example, if you were in the desert, you might have trouble identifying something on the ground as a pigeon,

Table 6.3.
Example of categories in Wisniewski (1995).

Mornek Category	Frequency	Plapel Category	Frequency
Installed near garbage dumps*	.50	Located in a nuclear plant*	.50
Found near mosquito-infested swamps*	.50	Found in the city water supply*	.50
Produces a poisonous substance*	.50	Has a red flashing light*	.50
Emits microwaves*	.50	Makes a loud beeping noise*	.50
Turned on by a dial	1.0	Turned on by a key	1.0
Box shaped	1.0	Barrel shaped	1.0

Note: Asterisks indicate knowledge-relevant features. Frequencies are the proportions of category items containing that feature.

because you would not expect pigeons to be there. Little is known about these in-between cases and how much knowledge is involved in the sort of everyday object categorization that people do so effortlessly.

Wisniewski (1995) addressed part of this issue by asking whether empirical information or background knowledge is more important in categorizing things when the two conflict. He constructed categories using features shown in table 6.3. In this example, subjects learned about two novel tools, *morneks* and *plapels*. Morneks tended to have the features listed in the left column, whereas plapels tended to have the features listed on the right. (Individual examples were made up by sampling from these features, plus some random features that occurred equally often in both categories.) Also, some features were quite typical of their category: They appeared in every example, as indicated by the 1.0 in the Frequency column. Other features occurred in only half the category items, as indicated by .50 in the Frequency column. The *knowledge group* was told that morneks are used for killing bugs, and that plapels are used for detecting toxic substances. The *ignorance group* (a name I have invented to emphasize the difference between conditions) was not given this information. This information about the function, then, is the background knowledge that Wisniewski manipulated. After learning, subjects had to categorize test items and say how confident they were in the category decision. If people use their background knowledge to categorize items, then there should be a difference between these two groups' performance on test items.

Some of the test items used are shown in table 6.4. The first type of item, the *atypical* test item pits the function against the statistical structure of the category. Two of the features (listed first here) are strongly related to the object's function:

Table 6.4.
Examples of Test Items for the Mornek Category (see table 6.3) used by Wisniewski (1995).

Feature Type	Functional Relevance	Feature Frequency
Atypical Test Item		
Emits microwaves	relevant to Mornek	.50
Installed near garbage dumps	relevant to Mornek	.50
Turned on by a key	irrelevant	0
Barrel shaped	irrelevant	0
Inspected once every 6 months	irrelevant	.50
Function Test Item		
Emits microwaves	relevant to Mornek	.50
Installed near garbage dumps	relevant to Mornek	.50
Inspected once every year	irrelevant	.50
Operates during the night	irrelevant	.50
Nonfunction Test Items		
Turned on by a dial	irrelevant	.50
Box shaped	irrelevant	.50
Inspected once every 6 months	irrelevant	.50
Operates during the day	irrelevant	.50

Emitting microwaves is a possible way of killing bugs, and garbage dumps are certainly a location where a bug-killer might be useful. The knowledge one might bring to bear on this item would support its being a mornek, the bug killer. However, two other features (listed next) were strongly associated with the plapel category. As table 6.3 shows, "turned on by a key" and "barrel shaped" occurred in *all* of the plapels and in none of the morneks. Thus, this is a very strong statistical clue to category membership. (The final feature was equally present in both categories.) Subjects in the ignorance group put this item into the mornek category only 43% of the time. However, subjects in the knowledge group were apparently more swayed by the relevant features, and they placed it into the mornek category 65% of the time. When two features were related to knowledge—that is, were closely related to the function of one category—they overruled the two features that statistically predicted a different category.

This contrast is also made by the two test items underneath. Here, the statistical properties of the features were held constant—all of them occurred in half of the learning items. However, in the *function* item, two properties were related to the object's function, but in the *nonfunction* item, none of the features was. These two differ, then, in the degree to which they relate to the knowledge underlying the category. Because these items are unambiguous, subjects almost always categorized them correctly. But Wisniewski found differences in how confident the subjects were about their answers. The knowledge group was more confident about the function items than about the nonfunction items, but the ignorance group showed no such difference (see also Wisniewski 1995, Experiment 1). Thus, the knowledge that subjects were given about the function influenced their categorization both for somewhat unusual exemplars (the atypical test item) and typical ones.

Locus of the Knowledge Effect in Categorization

There are two general ways that knowledge could be having its effect on categorization. First, when the knowledge is present during learning, it could be influencing the nature of the category representation. For example, Lin and Murphy (1997) proposed that when people learned their tools (see figure 6.2), they might have paid more attention to the features that were critical to the function. When the tuk was used for catching animals, they might have encoded more information about the loop at the top and elaborated their memory with inferences about how the loop worked, and so on. In contrast, when the tuk was used for fertilizing crops, this feature would not have received much attention and would have been represented in less detail. Second, it is possible that the knowledge is activated and used during the categorization judgment itself, after the learning period has ended. For example, at test, subjects in this experiment might have thought something like "that thing couldn't catch an animal, because it doesn't have the rope at the end, so it can't be a tuk." Here, it is not just that the initial representation of the category has been influenced—the underlying knowledge itself is actively used in making the categorization decision. Of course, it is possible that knowledge is used in both ways.

The criticism of knowledge effects by Smith and Sloman (1994) is about the second sort of use. It seems implausible to some researchers that when people see an object, they activate rather complex knowledge structures and then draw inferences about the object's identity. Object categorization is often quite fast (for familiar categories at the basic level, anyway), usually much less than a second, and it seems unlikely to some that much knowledge could be activated and used in that time. In experiments with time constraints on responding (Lin and Murphy 1997; Palmeri and Blalock 2000), it seems even less likely that the explicit use of knowledge is involved. Furthermore, Lin and Murphy found effects of background knowledge even in a task where functional importance is not relevant, namely part detection. Thus, their effects are probably due to knowledge influencing the categories' (and objects') encoding in memory.

Wisniewski (1995, Experiment 3) investigated this issue with regard to his categories by comparing groups that received the critical knowledge either before or after learning. The *early knowledge group* was given the information about the object's function during the learning trials, as in his other experiments. The *late knowledge group* went through the learning trials and was only told about the functions associated with the categories at their end. So, they could not have used this information to encode the properties of individual objects during learning, but they could still use this information in making their categorizations during the test phase. In fact, Wisniewski found that both groups seemed to use this knowledge. For example, both groups rated the function test items higher than the nonfunction test items, as described above (and see table 6.3). However, such differences were significantly larger for the early knowledge group. Knowledge was actively used during the categorization phase, as shown by the late knowledge group. But knowledge also influenced the learning of the exemplars, as shown by the greater use of knowledge for the group that received it prior to learning. Wisniewski's stimuli were verbal lists, so whether such results would extend to objects has yet to be seen.

Before the possible sources of knowledge effects in categorization can be fully understood, we will need more information about when and where such effects occur. It seems more likely that knowledge will actively be used during categorization when the decision is difficult, is slow, is based on little perceptual information, and in similarly straitened situations. It may be that the use of knowledge varies considerably both with category and with the pressures on the categorization task. When knowledge influences the initial encoding of a concept, however, that knowledge has been incorporated into whatever representation is used to later categorize items, and the categorization process cannot help but be affected by it.

A somewhat different case that might well be taken as demonstrating the use of knowledge in categorization is Barsalou's (1983, 1985) study of *ad hoc categories*. These are categories that are constructed in specific situations to describe a specialized class of objects that are of particular interest (see Barsalou 1991, for more detail). Examples include things to take on a camping trip, things to carry out of a burning house, ways to avoid being killed by the mafia, and ways to make new friends. Although these categories are of interest in a number of respects, for our purposes, the most important thing is that people can verify objects as being members of these categories, as well as being more or less typical members. For example, which of the following do you think are good examples of ways to avoid being killed by the mafia?

- move to South America
- have a garage sale
- take a bath only once a month
- change where you're living in Las Vegas
- change your identity

Most people would agree that the first and last items are both good examples of this category. "Change where you're living in Las Vegas" is a borderline member in my estimate. It is somewhat similar to "move to South America," but it would be unlikely to help you avoid the mafia for very long. The interesting point about these categories is that people can make such judgments with high reliability (Barsalou 1983) even if they have not previously learned the category or thought about the items in this way. I doubt that you learned item by item whether the things on this list were examples of ways to avoid being killed by the mafia. For most ad hoc categories, there is no learning period, per se. Instead, the phrase evokes a certain kind of meaning, which you can then apply to a new item. By reasoning about whether the new item fits this meaning, you can decide whether it's a category member or not. So, taking a bath only once a month may be off-putting, but you probably cannot think of a reason that it would deter a hardened mafia hit man who has been instructed to kill you. In contrast, by moving to South America, you might be out of range of the mafia's ability to find or harm you. These are not facts that you learned previously, but inferences you made at the time of decision. In short, category decisions about ad hoc categories are further evidence for the use of knowledge during categorization itself. Because these categories usually do not have any previous learning phase, the only way that knowledge could be influencing judgments is during the categorization process.

What clearly can be concluded from this discussion is that background knowledge affects not only initial acquisition of a concept but also later categorization judgments. People tend to positively categorize items that are consistent with their knowledge and to exclude items that are inconsistent, sometimes even overruling purely empirical sources of information. The details of how this works have not yet been established, largely because few experimental studies have been done, and most have not used objects but instead have employed verbal descriptions. Also, it seems very likely that how and when knowledge influences categorization will depend on the nature of the category and whether other cues are readily available. Working out the mechanisms of these processes is one of the more important tasks for this approach to concepts.

Knowledge in Feature Construction

Throughout this book, I have been talking about objects and concepts having certain features. For example, birds fly and have two legs, robins have red breasts, my pet bird Tweety sings, and so on. The reader may have wondered where these features come from—that is, not where do robins or their legs come from, but how is it decided that these particular properties are the ones that are part of the robin concept, as opposed to other properties? It is not too controversial to say that any object could be thought of as having an infinite number of features. For example, robins have two legs, but they also have a leg; they also have fewer than three legs, and fewer than four legs, and so on. Robins have a red breast; or, one could say that they have a red chest and red belly. Which, if any of these, should be features? Why is it that red breast gets to be the feature, rather than red chest plus red belly? Why isn't having fewer than four legs a feature? And I saw a robin on my lawn this morning. Should this fact ("found on my lawn this morning") become a feature of robins? Or should the property "robins can be found on lawns" or "robins can be seen in the morning" or "robins can be found in the morning in the United States" . . . or . . . "in the midwest" or "in Illinois?" Any object or event can be conceived of in many different ways, and it would be impossible to encode each one and store it as part of a concept.

We do not know very much, unfortunately, about which properties are encoded, or how this is determined. However, it has been argued that knowledge might play an important role in this process (Goodman 1965; Murphy and Medin 1985). One's prior knowledge of a domain provides a set of properties that can be used in encoding a new member of that domain. Indeed, it seems likely that in learning a new category, you compare it to similar categories and use features from or based on those categories to construct the properties by which to represent the category (Markman and Wisniewski 1997). This kind of comparison may not be a "knowledge effect," per se; it may only involve contrasting a new category to an old one from the same domain.

Schyns and colleagues (Schyns, Goldstone, and Thibaut 1998; Schyns and Murphy 1994; Schyns and Rodet 1997) have argued that features are in part defined by how they are related to category structure. In some cases, the features are so ambiguous that they cannot be reliably identified on simply examining a stimulus. Consider, for example, an X-ray. Often X-rays have a large number of spots and shadows on them that are of questionable importance. It is only experts who know that some spots are uninteresting structures ("You always get these shadows when you photograph through the ribs.") or artifacts of the procedure ("She probably moved a little while the X-ray was taken."), whereas others have special significance ("This series of spots could be an unusual growth."). When novices look at X-rays, they simply do not know which markings constitute coherent features, and which do not (Lesgold 1984). In these cases, category learning itself may be needed to identify the features. That is, learning to diagnose conditions from an X-ray does not just require learning which features predict which diseases but also requires learning which patterns are features and which are not.

There is evidence for this idea in the work of Schyns and Murphy (1994). They used blob-like stimuli with very ambiguous parts, such that subjects could not identify the critical features in advance. That is, they couldn't accurately determine which sections of a blob were a part. Subjects learned to distinguish two categories of such blobs. At the end of learning, they were now able to identify the correct features within the blobs, namely, the features that distinguished the categories, because they had learned that some aspects of the blobs were found in one category and some were found in the other. Control subjects who simply viewed the stimuli were not able to identify the same features—category learning itself was required. One might worry that the task, in which subjects were explicitly asked about the parts of the objects, might have been responsible for the results. Schyns and Rodet (1997) addressed this with a clever design in which they taught subjects categories in sequence. They proposed that subjects who formed features in the course of learning the first categories would find it easier to learn a second set that involved the same features. Here no explicit identification of parts or properties was required. The results supported their hypothesis.

In many situations, we assume that the features are obvious, and the only difficulty subjects have is in learning which features are associated with which categories. These experiments suggest that in some cases, the features are not readily available at the beginning of learning and that one goal of learning is to acquire the features themselves.

These examples, though, are not very knowledge-dependent in the way we have defined "knowledge" in this chapter. It was not general facts that people knew about the domains that determined the feature learning here, but instead the learning of the particular category that accounted for it. A more radical demonstration of knowledge-based feature creation was carried out by Wisniewski and Medin (1994). In their study, the stimuli were children's drawings of people. They divided up the pictures into two categories. One category had detailed drawings that also shared some superficial properties, such as curly hair on the people. The other category had

pictures of people performing some action; they also shared some superficial properties such as not smiling. In one experiment (1a), subjects were shown these two
collections of pictures and were asked to come up with a rule that separated the two
categories. Subjects were told either that one group of drawings was done by creative children and the other by noncreative children, or else that they were drawn by
children in Group 1 and Group 2. The use of these meaningful category names in
one condition was a way of activating knowledge structures that might be used in
interpreting the pictures.

Wisniewski and Medin examined the features that people produced as part of
their rules. They found that about half of the features listed by the subjects who did
not have prior knowledge (the Group 1/Group 2 subjects) were simple, concrete
features that were readily detectable in the pictures. One such rule was "all of the
characters have their arms straight out from their bodies, and they're also standing
very straight" (p. 241). In contrast, only 12% of the features of the knowledge
group were so simple. Instead, their features were more likely to be abstract, describing a whole class of properties (e.g., "drawings that show more positive emotional
expression"). In addition, the knowledge subjects were likely to make *hierarchical
features*, features that had both an abstract and a concrete component. In these cases,
the subjects would mention an abstract property of the features and then relate it to
a concrete feature: "There are many more details in each of them [drawings], things
like belts, pockets, and patterns on the clothes...." Here, the abstract feature of
"details" is mentioned and is related to more concrete properties.

Why did the knowledge group create these abstract and hierarchical features?
Wisniewski and Medin suggest that the prior knowledge created certain general
expectations about the properties. For example, subjects might expect that creative
children would make more detailed or unusual drawings. However, as discussed at
the beginning of this chapter, it is difficult to specify in advance exactly how these
general expectations would be instantiated. Unless you know a lot about children's
drawings, you might not immediately know whether one was particularly unusual
or detailed. Part of subjects' learning therefore was to relate the features observed
in the pictures to these general expectations (i.e., a post-hoc use of knowledge, as
described earlier). This process resulted in more hierarchical features being constructed, in which abstract expectations were linked to observed features. In contrast, when subjects did not have any particular expectation about the categories,
they were more likely to focus on concrete features, because they did not have an
abstract notion in mind at the beginning.

In their Experiment 2, Wisniewski and Medin (1994) asked subjects to provide a
rule to categorize the items after seeing each exemplar. Subjects would study a pic-

ture, say which category they thought it was in and why, and then get feedback on the answer. Subjects were told either that the pictures were done by farm kids and city kids or by creative kids and noncreative kids. Because subjects' initial guesses about the items were not particularly accurate, they were often forced to re-evaluate their rules and the features involved. Wisniewski and Medin identified a number of processes that subjects followed in making these revisions. One example was that subjects often reinterpreted a feature as supporting a different category. For example, one subject felt that the "perfect body proportionment" of a drawing indicated a creative child. When told that this was a drawing of an uncreative child, the subject decided that "perfect body proportions show lack of imagination." So, the same feature could be related to a different concept, via a different reasoning process. Another strategy that people used was to focus on new features that might overrule the feature that had led them astray. This is the kind of process that statistical theories of learning would propose—forming associations to the correct features, while weakening associations to other features. However, some of the processes were much more knowledge-related. For example, sometimes subjects changed their criterion for identifying a feature. Although a picture had seemed detailed, when told that its creator was not creative, a subject decided that "drawings done by creative children would be *more* detailed." Thus, the identification of the feature "detailed" changed as a result of learning. Finally, sometimes subjects reinterpreted the same property based on feedback. For example, one subject identified the clothing in a drawing as a "city uniform," but changed this to a "farm uniform," when told the drawing was done by a farm child. So, the feature itself changed as a result of new information.

These strategies suggest that subjects were not working from a pre-selected set of features that were obvious from the stimuli themselves. Different people focused on different features, and exactly what counted as a feature was rather flexible. Although a picture might seem detailed at first, later experience could change it to being thought of as not detailed. In fact, some subjects looked at exactly the same things and gave different interpretations. One drawing contained a series of dots on the front of the person's shirt. A subject who thought the drawing represented a creative child interpreted this as "buttons," reflecting a detailed picture. Another subject who thought it might be a city child's drawing interpreted the same dots as being a tie. By starting from different expectations, the subjects extracted different features from the pictures.

Wisniewski and Medin (1994) argued that the analysis of an item into features is a function of the stimulus itself, prior knowledge, and learning of the category. People do not view items in a vacuum—they have strong expectations about what the features will be. However, those expectations are flexible, and they change with actual experience with the category. Thus bottom-up and top-down processes combine to determine what features are associated with a category. And when this occurs, the feature may not be represented as a simple property, like "large" or "blue," but it may be a more complicated knowledge structure, such as "detailed, therefore contains buttons, pockets and shoes."

Wisniewski and Medin's article contains a number of arguments that challenge the usual assumptions by which category learning works. They propose a much more complex interaction of identifying features and learning the category than is normally proposed. Indeed, although their article has been published for a few years, the rest of the field has been somewhat slow to pick up on it, in part because the complexity of the process they describe. It is difficult to model concept learning when the features themselves are changing over the course of learning. Furthermore, one could criticize their study on the basis of ecological validity. To begin with, their categories did not actually correspond to pictures done by creative/noncreative or city/farm children (though their stimuli *were* real children's pictures and so were naturally occurring entities, unlike almost all the other experimental stimuli discussed in this chapter). There might, therefore, be some question as to whether the same results would be found when the categories were more accurate. In those cases, how flexible would the features have to be, and how often would they be revised during learning? Also, the learning situations that Wisniewski and Medin used were somewhat unusual, at least relative to learning tasks done in most concept experiments. In their Experiment 1, subjects looked at all the items (simultaneously) and then provided a rule for the categories. In Experiment 2, subjects were required not just to learn the categories, but to provide a rule after every example. These procedures are quite different from the usual categorize-plus-feedback experiment. These are valid concerns, but it would also be a mistake to take the typical category-learning experiment as a standard, simply because it is familiar to us by repetition. In the usual experiment, the stimuli are extremely simple (dot patterns or geometric figures), no information is given about an item other than its category membership, people go through example after example until they perfectly identify the categories, and so on. These characteristics are not particularly representative of real-world learning. Although these techniques have proved useful, it should be kept in mind that all experiments are to some degree simplifications, and the fact that Wisniewski and Medin's study has a different set of simplifications than usual is not in and of itself a criticism. Nonetheless, it would certainly be useful to have a replication of this work in other kinds of tasks, with other stimuli, and so on. As with any such ambitious project, it is necessary to replicate and extend it to new situations before its importance can be fully understood.

Since the above was written, an important step in this direction has been taken by Palmeri and Blalock (2000). Although they used Wisniewski and Medin's stimuli, they instituted a more familiar learning procedure and used speeded categorization judgments as their dependent measure. Half their subjects learned two categories of drawings as Group 1 and Group 2, and half learned them as drawings by creative and uncreative children. All subjects were tested on new pictures that matched the old ones either in terms of concrete features (like curly hair) or abstract features (detailed). The results suggested that the neutral category names led subjects to learn concrete features of the pictures, whereas the names referring to creativity led subjects to learn more abstract features. Perhaps surprisingly, these results held even when subjects were forced to categorize the pictures very quickly—within 500 ms. As discussed in the section on categorization, these results suggest that the knowledge influenced the way the pictures were encoded, as Wisniewski and Medin would have expected, rather than a slow reasoning process that operated at the time of categorization. Further work of this sort, especially using new materials, would be welcome.

To sum up, then, most work on concept learning has not said very much about where the object's features come from. By focusing on very simplified stimuli with perceptually obvious properties, this question has been largely avoided. But in real life, the relevant properties of an object or situation may have to be learned in addition to the concepts themselves. An anecdote may illustrate this (from Clark and Clark 1977, p. 486). A young boy misbehaved in some way, and his mother told him, "Young man, you did that on purpose." Later, he was asked what "on purpose" meant, and he replied "It means you're looking at me." Since the boy was told this when he was caught doing something, he inferred that the phrase referred to getting caught, rather than to the much more abstract feature of mental intention that actually determines purposeful actions. Children have to learn this kind of feature just as much as they have to learn the entire category. Learning the relevant properties for mental states is a very difficult task (Wellman 1990), in part because they are not visible. But learning the relevant properties for everyday objects and events may sometimes be difficult as well.

The work I have reviewed suggests that in learning one category it is very useful to already know the features of related categories. In other cases, the features are acquired as a function of category feedback—learning which items are in the category involves learning the features peculiar to that category. In still other cases, the features themselves may not be simple entities but are knowledge structures them-selves, in which general knowledge is related to specific properties. This possibility, which is perhaps the most interesting one, needs further exploration and analysis.

Knowledge in Induction

As described in chapter 8, one of the main functions of categories is induction. Once you know that something is a dog, you have a good idea that it will bark, it is not something you sit on, it has legs, it is male or female, it has a liver, and so on. In their simplest form, such inductions can be read off the concept representation. If you have represented the concept of dog as having the features: barks, has four legs, eats meat, is a mammal, and so forth, then when someone tells you that they have a dog, you can immediately infer that their pet barks, has four legs, eats meat, and is a mammal. This sort of induction does not require any particular knowledge other than the properties associated with the category. However, knowledge can be in-volved in induction in a more significant way. Because this work is covered in some detail in chapter 8, I will only review it briefly here.

In the standard category-based induction task, one is told that one category (or item) has a given property and then is asked whether the property would be likely to apply to another category (or item). So, the question is about the projection of a novel predicate from one category to another. Researchers have focused on two determinants of this process: the similarity of the two categories and their typicality to a more general category (Rips 1975). Knowledge relating the categories or the property to the categories is not part of the traditional view. Nonetheless, knowl-edge does influence this process.

Kalish and Gelman (1992) examined cases in which items were in two categories at once, such as *wooden pillows* or *fur bowls*. They asked children one of two questions about these kinds of items, which were presented as line drawings as well as being verbally labeled. One question required children to respond on the basis of the *kind* of item it was (pillow or bowl), and one required children to respond on the basis of the material of the item (wooden or fur). For example, children might be asked to decide which items were soft. Here they should pay attention to the mate-rial of the item. In another question, they might be asked whether an object should go into the bedroom or kitchen. Here, they should attend to the kind category. And in fact, children as young as 3 years old responded correctly for both kinds of questions. That is, they said that wooden pillows should go into the bedroom but were hard. Thus, the children knew which categories controlled which features (showing a very nice sense of conceptual combination to boot). Even though pillows are normally soft, wooden pillows are hard.

How did subjects know to use one category to make one kind of induction and a different category to make the other kind of induction *for the same item*? Kalish and Gelman proposed (pp. 1555–1556) that children were using knowledge of domains to tell them which features were critical to that domain. The reason pillows are hard or soft is because of the material they are made out of, and wood is by its nature a hard material. So, although pillows are normally soft, the domain of materials controls this judgment. In contrast, the functions of objects determine where they are placed in the home, and pillows are largely determined by their function. Thus, even wooden pillows would be placed in the bedroom.

Ross and Murphy (1999) compared inductions of different kinds of features from the same categories (see also Heit and Rubinstein 1994, described in chapter 8). They compared *taxonomic categories* of foods, such as fruits, to *script-based categories*, such as breakfast foods, which are determined by the time, location, or setting in which they are eaten. To do this, they constructed triplets of items: a target food, a taxonomic alternative, and a script alternative. For example, if the target food was cereal, then the taxonomic alternative might be noodles (both are breads and grains), and the script alternative might be milk (both cereal and milk are breakfast foods, but are not in the same taxonomic categories). Subjects made a forced-choice induction judgment. They were told that the target food had a certain property and then had to decide which of the alternatives was more likely to have that property. Ross and Murphy found that when the property was a biochemical one (possession of a given enzyme), subjects chose the taxonomic alternative 83% of the time; when the property was situational (when the food was eaten in a novel culture), subjects chose the taxonomic alternative only 29% of the time. That is, subjects preferred to draw inductions based on taxonomic relations for biochemical properties but based on script relations for situational properties.

This kind of result is a puzzle for most theories of induction, which claim that induction should depend primarily on the similarity of the categories involved. If that were correct, the type of property would not matter, yet these studies show that it does. Ross and Murphy's (1999) results suggest that subjects are engaged in complex reasoning, in which they consider not just how similar the categories are but exactly how they are related and how that relation in turn is relevant to the property being projected. The induction is considered strong to the degree that subjects can create a story that connects the property in the target category to the projected category (see also Lassaline 1996; Lin and Murphy 2000, Experiment 9). An even more radical effect has been found by Proffitt, Coley, and Medin (2000), who gave induction problems involving disease susceptibility to tree experts. For example, if oaks get a certain disease, would birches also be expected to get it? (They asked the question in a number of different ways, which I'm not distinguishing.) Proffitt et al. found that their subjects often did not simply rely on the similarity of the categories involved but would engage in long chains of reasoning about how a disease could or could not be transmitted from one type of tree to another. They referred to presence in the same ecological setting as well as to specific knowledge, such as how thick the bark is of different kinds of trees. These chains of reasoning went far beyond the similarity relations proposed by the most popular (knowledge-free) models of category-based induction.

All these examples, as well as others described in chapter 8, suggest that prior knowledge and reasoning are heavily involved in category-based induction. This fact has been hidden in most work in the field because most studies look at the induction of *blank predicates* that are chosen to be as uninformative as possible, often using fictitious or unfamiliar properties. In such cases, subjects can only rely on the overall similarity of categories and similar structural variables. But when the properties make contact with what one knows (as would almost always be the case in real life), people apparently use that knowledge to reason about whether the property should be projected.

Discussion of Models

This chapter has documented a number of ways that prior knowledge influences concepts. (And other chapters have reviewed knowledge effects in the context of their own specific topics, such as conceptual combination, conceptual development, and word meaning.) Indeed, knowledge appears to influence concepts at all stages that have been investigated: in identifying and constructing features that form the conceptual representations, at initial acquisition (in both supervised learning and unsupervised formation tasks), in categorizing novel examples, and in using concepts to make inductions. Later chapters will extend this list to include conceptual development and conceptual combination. These phenomena are consistent enough that a complete theory of concepts will have to explain them, and the effects are pervasive enough to suggest that it will not be possible simply to tack some knowledge onto a purely empirical theory. The knowledge will have to be integrated into the theory's processes of learning and use at various levels. That said, it is not clear that all the phenomena that are here being called "knowledge effects" form a single, coherent class. These effects may reflect knowledge of different sorts, may involve different interactions of knowledge with the other processes, and may have different constraints on how knowledge is used. Whether all these effects can eventually be incorporated into a single model is an empirical question, but one that we are still far from answering.

As usual, I will now discuss the three main theories' approaches to these questions. As will be seen, there is still much left to be answered as to how any of these theories will explain the results.

Prototype and Exemplar Models

As they are normally presented, neither prototype nor exemplar models have attempted to account for the knowledge effects described above. The problem is that these models start from a kind of *tabula rasa* representation, and concept representations are built up solely by experience with exemplars. Most of their attention has been directed toward empirical typicality and learning effects.

For example, in the prototype model (see chapter 3), subjects learn which features are associated to which categories by keeping a rough count of how often each one appears with category members. Features that are distinctive to a given category receive a higher weight than do features that are found in many categories. There is little need for prior knowledge in this process, as the features are assumed to be given directly by the stimuli, and knowledge is not necessary to keep track of the feature count. Similarly, in categorization, an item is compared to the feature list, resulting in a measure of how closely it matches the category representation. Knowledge is not used here, either, as the comparison process requires only the count of matching and mismatching features (Smith and Medin 1981).

Thus, the standard prototype model has no particular need for knowledge to account for the typicality effects that led to its creation, and so it has not incorporated knowledge as part of its learning and categorization mechanisms. The problem, then, is that the model cannot account for the data presented in this chapter that show that knowledge is in fact used. There is nothing in the prototype model, for example, that says that the shape of the whingelow is more important than its present location in identifying what kind it is. It does not provide any way by which features can be constructed, rather than simply observed (Schyns et al. 1998; Wisniewski and Medin 1994). There is no mechanism by which it can explain why categories related by a theme are easier to learn or construct than those that are not (Murphy and Allopenna 1994; Pazzani 1991; Spalding and Murphy 1996; Wattenmaker et al. 1986). In categorization, it does not have any mechanism by which to explain why some properties are more important than others that were equally often present in the learning set (Lin and Murphy 1997; Palmeri and Blalock 2000; Wisniewski 1995). It has no way whatsoever to explain how ad hoc categories are formed, especially since they do not follow the normal rules of family resemblance (Barsalou 1983). Finally, the prototype model does not explain the effects of induction just discussed.

The list is quite similar for exemplar models. The major exemplar models (Kruschke 1992; Medin and Schaffer 1978; Nosofsky 1984) do not have any way by which features can be constructed or interpreted; the experiments testing these models have almost always used simple, artificial stimuli with only a few features. Knowledge has no part in the learning or categorization rules used by these models, so without some modification, they cannot account for the learning and categorization effects of knowledge reported above.

Exemplar models have not generally been extended to explain induction, so it is worth considering whether they might be able to account for the results of Kalish and Gelman (1992), Proffitt et al. (2000), and Ross and Murphy (1999), described earlier. Suppose that induction from one category member to another involves the retrieval of similar exemplars. For example, imagine that you are asked whether property X of cereal is also true for milk or noodles. One way to answer this question is to retrieve examples of cereal and of milk and see whether they are similar (i.e., have the same properties). To the degree that they are similar, then, one might respond positively to this induction question. Such a rule is parallel to the categorization rule used by the Context Model (Medin and Schaffer 1978) and its descendants, and it would seem to predict many of the data found in classic studies of induction (e.g., the typicality and similarity effects of Rips 1975—see Osherson et al. 1990). By itself, however, this rule would not explain the knowledge effects shown here, because it would not predict reversals of inductions from cereal to milk, compared to inductions from cereal to noodles, for different properties. The similarity of cereal to milk would determine the same induction strength for all properties, and so this could not change depending on the property as Ross and Murphy (1999) and Heit and Rubinstein (1994) found. Although the similarity rule could perhaps be modified to be context-sensitive, it is not clear how to make similarity depend on the induced property in just the right way, unless one incorporated a reasoning process of the sort the knowledge approach includes. The ecological and causal-reasoning processes used by Proffitt et al.'s experts are clearly beyond the scope of this exemplar comparison process. So, the traditional exemplar model does not immediately predict knowledge effects in induction.

It is clear, then, that the traditional models will have to be augmented or modified in order to account for all these results. Some progress is being made on this front. Heit (1994) suggested that exemplar models could incorporate knowledge during learning by representing knowledge as a number of previously encountered exemplars. For example, in his experiment, subjects learned about how many people in City W were shy and often attended parties. Heit proposed that the subjects already knew people who are shy or not shy, and who often or seldom attend parties. That is, they already had some knowledge of how often these features co-occurred. Under the assumption that exemplars with the expected feature pairs are more frequent than the unexpected ones (e.g., that shy people typically do not attend parties), Heit found that an exemplar model could account for his results. This proposal, then, has the advantage of using a standard psychological model to represent both empirical learning and knowledge effects, although it does address only one form of knowledge influence.

Using exemplars to represent prior knowledge could work in some cases but seems implausible in others. The above example used a pair of features whose relation is already known, but sometimes the knowledge accessed is abstract or a generalization that is inferred from specific examples. For example, I can understand that a flying squirrel flies (or glides, really) because of the folds of skin between its body and limbs, because this mechanism is analogous to that used by other flying and gliding entities. However, other exemplars like birds, planes, parachutes, and so on, do not have these folds or this exact gliding capability—it is only by analogy or through a generalization of those exemplars that I can understand this new category. Thus, simply having exemplars would not be sufficient to explain the flying squirrel—a more powerful inferential or abstraction mechanism would be needed. As a thought experiment, consider the feature pairs: shy-often talks in videoconferences and shy-often talks in online chatgroups. Are they equally likely? The first seems much less plausible than the second to me, because I expect shy people to be more forthcoming when they are not physically present or perceptible to others. However, I do not have direct experience with shy people in either situation, and so I must rely on general knowledge to draw that inference, rather than on known exemplars. As will be discussed below, most representations of knowledge in psychology and artificial intelligence assume that knowledge is about whole classes of entities rather than about individuals: Wings are useful for flying because of the properties of wings in general and the laws of aerodynamics in general, rather than because of the properties of a lot of exemplars. This point is not to deny that Heit's proposal could well account for a subset of knowledge effects, but how widely it can be applied is less clear.[7]

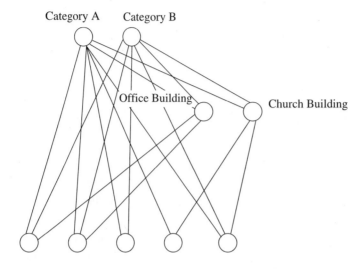

Figure 6.4
A simplified depiction of Heit and Bott's (2000) Baywatch model of category learning. The input features represent properties of the objects, and Categories A and B are the to-be-learned categories. The prior knowledge (PK) nodes are the already known concepts of church and office buildings.

In a later paper, Heit and Bott (2000) developed a connectionist model of knowledge effects. They had taught their subjects concepts of buildings reminiscent of churches and office buildings. The features related to these familiar concepts were learned significantly faster than those that were unrelated to the themes. They constructed a 3-layer connectionist model of this task, in which the input layer was the features used in the items, the output layer was the two categories, and the hidden layer contained the prior knowledge (PK) nodes of church and office building. As shown in figure 6.4, all of the input features were directly connected to the output nodes, initially at very weak levels; in addition, the input features related to the prior knowledge were strongly connected to the PK nodes. For example, if an input feature was "has candles," it would be connected to the church building node. The categories, then, could be learned through two routes: direct associative learning between the input and category (output) nodes, and indirectly through the PK nodes. (Note that this system is a prototype model, as it represents the strength of relations between features and categories, rather than configurations of features that might define an exemplar.)

During learning, this model learned empirically by associating the input features to the two categories (e.g., "has candles" was associated to category B). It also learned that the PK nodes were related to the categories, that category B was like a church and category A was like an office building. As a result, the model learned the knowledge-related features better than the neutral features, as the subjects did. "Has candles" directly activated category B and indirectly activated it through the church building node, whereas a neutral feature like "near a bus stop" activated its category only through the direct route. One might complain that the PK nodes were somewhat rigged, as they just happened to correspond to the two categories to be learned. However, Heit and Bott showed that if multiple knowledge nodes were present, only some of which were relevant to the categories, the model did not become confused. Because only the relevant nodes were consistently associated to the categories, only their links to the categories were learned; the irrelevant prior concepts had no effect.

This sort of model is a good start for explaining knowledge effects. Although it is unlikely that PK nodes of exactly this sort are generally available (normally, the concepts being learned are not as similar to known concepts), one can easily imagine other kinds of generalizations and relations among features that might be represented in hidden nodes and that therefore could aid category learning. One possible problem with connectionist models of this sort, as Heit and Bott (2000) and Kaplan and Murphy (2000) both note, is that they predict that knowledge will reduce learning of features that are not related to it: Learning some features comes at the expense of others. However, this result has not been empirically found in human concept learning. Surprisingly, unrelated features are learned equally well by subjects who do and do not have prior knowledge (Kaplan and Murphy 2000). This result is difficult to obtain in connectionist models that use error-driven learning. (Rehder and Murphy 2001 have recently developed a model that expands Heit and Bott's framework by using a more flexible representation of knowledge. It is able to learn knowledge-unrelated features while simultaneously showing the knowledge advantages found in experiments.)

Heit and Bott's (2000) model has considerable promise, then. Ultimately, a complete model of the learning process will have to do more to represent the relevant knowledge, perhaps through addition of an inferential mechanism of some kind. Furthermore, this sort of model is focused specifically on the learning of known features and, like all current models, does not address issues of feature construction, knowledge in induction, and the like. However, in order to develop a model that does all these things, we must first have a successful model that does one or two of them, and that is the goal for the field at present. Heit and Bott provide a useful discussion of various ways that knowledge could be incorporated into different kinds of models, and the interested reader should consult that article.

In short, we are just making a start at building theories and computational models that integrate empirical and knowledge-based learning. It might be useful to consider what a complete model would look like, so we can see the task ahead of us. Ignoring both practical and theoretical problems in developing such a system, how do the current data suggest that knowledge should be integrated into a learning model? First, an integrated model would have to represent a number of prior concepts at the beginning of the learning task, rather than modeling the learning of one or two concepts in a tabula rasa. Since similar concepts are a source of features and feature weights, they need to be present in order to give the new concepts a starting point. Learners also place special attention on properties that seem likely to be informative. So, in learning about a whingelow, the system must already know about other mammals in order to know which features to attend to and which generalizations to make from the observed examples. More difficult to implement, but probably also necessary would be a form of reasoning or inference engine. Somehow these models need to be able to use more general knowledge to draw inferences. These may not have to be very difficult or intelligent inferences, but, at the least, obvious ones such as "astronauts would live in a building in outer space, but divers would live in an underwater building." (However, it should be pointed out that the history of Artificial Intelligence tells us that such inferences are notoriously difficult to draw, so working models would probably have to confine themselves to a simple domain with only a small number of facts to deal with.)

Why is this whole reasoning apparatus necessary? Some researchers have suggested that weights on dimensions at the start of learning could represent some prior knowledge (Kruschke 1993). For example, perhaps one could give greater attention to shape than color, since shape seems to be a more important dimension for category learning. However, this kind of solution will not be sufficient, as different features are important for different categories (see Keleman and Bloom 1994). It cannot be a weight on the dimension itself, then, that accounts for this, because the weight would not change with different categories. (If you did not weight dimensions differently, you might pay a lot of attention to the present location of the whingelow, because present location is important for baseball positions. Then you would end up hypothesizing that whingelows are found only in the zoo, or only in San Diego, because that's the only place you saw them.) Especially for very new kinds of categories (space vehicles or very deep sea creatures, for example), the system could not rely on prior feature weights or exemplars but must be able to draw inferences from more general knowledge. Another problem with simply storing weights for each feature is that knowledge is also needed to tie together the features within a category. This can be seen in experiments that contrast the same features when they can be related together vs. when they cannot (Murphy and Allopenna 1994; Spalding and Murphy 1996; Wattenmaker et al. 1986). Such results obviously cannot be explained by feature weights, which are the same across conditions. However, it is also likely that frequently made inferences will be encoded into concepts so that they do not need to be drawn de novo every time.

General knowledge plus an inference engine could be used again during categorization. Knowledge would provide greater weight to some features of the item being categorized than to others, even if both were empirically found to be related to category membership. Furthermore, such knowledge could be used to infer unseen features (e.g., "that vehicle must have an engine, because it's moving on its own"). I should note, however, that the use of knowledge during categorization of well-learned categories is perhaps the least well demonstrated of the knowledge effects described earlier. If knowledge influences the learning process so that the representation of the concept is affected, it is not so clear that one must also access this domain knowledge during categorization—it could already be incorporated into the concept (see discussion of categorization above). For example, after seeing the whingelow, you could have encoded quite a bit about its shape and behaviors, but not so much about the time of day that you saw it or the number of them in the cage. If you did so, then when deciding whether another animal is a whingelow, you would not need to consult domain knowledge to decide whether shape or time of day are critical, because this information would already be implicit in the concept. Thus, it is possible that a formal system could get by without using knowledge during the categorization process itself, if it is incorporated during learning. Of course, this consideration would not apply to ad hoc categories (Barsalou 1983), which are essentially made up on the spot. Here, categorization is clearly a knowledge-intensive process, but perhaps these cases are out of the range of category-learning models.

The Wisniewski and Medin (1994) results are probably the most difficult for the prototype and exemplar models to accommodate. The root assumption of these models is empiricist: They assume that exemplars present their features to the learner, which then are associated to a category. This observation leads to a representation of the category in terms of the observed properties. The Wisniewski and Medin study undermines this whole perspective, however, by suggesting that the features are not always present in the observed items but can instead be *constructed*, in part as a function of prior knowledge. Similarly, the work of Schyns and colleagues (Schyns et al. 1998; Schyns and Murphy 1994; Schyns and Rodet 1997) has shown that the category-learning process itself helps to define what the features are. This makes it very difficult for both the exemplar and prototype views, because the features that are being associated to the category are a moving target. You can't count how often each one is associated to each category (or see which exemplars have which features) if the features themselves are changing from trial to trial.

How could this sort of effect be incorporated into the formal learning models? If one allows only a pre-set list of features such as "green," "square," "large," and so on, then there is no possibility of modifying them or adding to the set. In some sense, what these effects require is the entire perceptual system to be an input to the learning module. In Schyns's experiments, for example, the stimuli are rather ambiguous entities that could be perceptually divided in a number of different ways. The learning system needs to have access to the multiple representations constructed during perception, so that it can select among the possible ones in order to associate the correct one to the category. If one section of the blob keeps coming up in one category but not the other, this has to be identifiable as a coherent section in the perceptual system and then associated to the correct category by the learning component. (See Schyns 1991 for a related computational model.)

Even more complex are Wisniewski and Medin's findings with children's drawings, which reveal an interaction between the perceptual input and prior expectations of the category. The perceptual system must represent such drawings in a flexible enough manner that dots on the front of a shirt could be perceived as buttons by one subject and as a tie by another—the decision being made by knowledge that prompted the subjects to look for detail or city clothing. This system would be extremely complex, though, because not only does the knowledge influence the perceptual identification of properties, learning influences whether these encodings are maintained. That is, after identifying something as a detailed drawing, when a subject learns that it was not made by a creative child, he or she might decide that the drawing was not in fact detailed enough. So, there is a three-way interaction of the input, the prior expectation, and the feedback.

Unfortunately, very little of this fits in with current formal modeling. For proponents of prototype and exemplar theory, it can only be hoped that when such models are developed, the learning mechanisms and representations that they have proposed still have a place at the center of the learning process. But it is premature to say whether that will be the case or not, given that the field seems far from incorporating all these effects in any kind of model.

Knowledge View

There will be little suspense in concluding that something called "the knowledge approach" is the winner in a chapter entitled "Knowledge Effects." The phenomena reviewed in this chapter are exactly the ones that have caused some researchers to conclude that concept acquisition and use involves prior knowledge to a significant degree. It would be tedious to review all the phenomena and then point out that each one seems to require reference to domain knowledge. Therefore, in this section, I will consider more critically what the knowledge approach is and how it must handle the variety of effects discussed in this chapter.

As was mentioned in chapter 3, the knowledge approach is still somewhat incomplete. It has not been instantiated in a computational model to any significant degree, unlike the exemplar approach in particular. The statement that knowledge is heavily involved in many aspects of concept acquisition and use (as I have just reviewed) is now one that has extremely strong support. However, it takes much more than that statement to make a complete theory.

There are two reactions one could have to the kinds of results discussed in this chapter. The first, most aggressive approach would be to argue that the empirical theories are inadequate, since they do not account for the knowledge effects that have been demonstrated, and therefore they should be rejected. Instead, a new theory that relies more heavily on knowledge must be developed. This is certainly one possible conclusion, but at this stage, it seems premature for two reasons. The first is that the empirical phenomena discussed in other chapters, such as typicality, basic categories, and exemplar effects are extremely reliable, but they do not require prior knowledge. Clearly, people *can* learn categories in artificial and unfamiliar domains, and it is likely that at least some of the same learning mechanisms are involved in the learning of categories in knowledge-rich domains. Simply rejecting the more empirical approaches, then, provides no way of accounting for this commonality. Second, no knowledge-based approach has been proposed that could actually replace the empirical views. There is currently no general model based on domain knowledge, inference and reasoning, and so on, that can explain the sorts of results that the prototype and exemplar models have focused on. Given that, rejection of those models would be premature at this stage.

The second way to respond to the results presented in this chapter would be to try to fill in the gaps of the more empirical approaches. In the previous section, I argued that the learning models needed to be integrated with a knowledge base and reasoning process that used that knowledge during learning, categorization, and induction. The knowledge approach, then, could well be assigned the task of providing that component of a complete learning model; researchers in this approach should be saying what kind of knowledge people use, how it influences learning, how people use it during categorization, and so on. There are many gaps here that need filling. For example, we do not have anything like a taxonomy of different types of background knowledge and an understanding of how each type might influence learning (see Murphy 2000, and Wilson and Keil 2000, for discussion). And different research projects have drawn on different knowledge sources. For example, Wattenmaker (1995) activated knowledge structures by telling subjects that the items resembled categories that they already knew (see also Ahn 1990; Heit and Bott 2000; Wattenmaker et al. 1986, Experiment 6). In contrast, Pazzani (1991) evoked knowledge by using a pre-existing causal schema (see also Ahn 1998; Ahn et al. 2000; Rehder and Hastie 2001). Other studies have used categories that were "thematically related," in that the properties could all be related to a similar function or environment (e.g., Murphy and Allopenna 1994; Spalding and Murphy 1999). However, not all of these relations were clearly causal (e.g., arctic vehicles being white) or any other single type of relation. Although all these studies show the use of "knowledge," it is not at all clear that the knowledge involved is the same kind of thing, or that it is influencing learning in the same way. In short, this is a promising avenue for exploration.

A similar point could be made about categorization. I discussed above two different ways that knowledge might affect categorizations: (1) indirectly, by changing the concept representation during learning (i.e., before categorization); or (2) directly, by activating the knowledge during the category judgment. It is likely that both effects occur at least some of the time. For example, for fast visual categorization (as in Lin and Murphy 1997; Palmeri and Blalock 2000), the indirect influence seems most likely, but for ad hoc categories (Barsalou 1983) and the medical-experiment-gone-horribly-wrong categorization problems used by Keil (1989) and Rips (1989), it seems likely that the knowledge is used during the decision process itself. We now must ask what distinguishes these cases, and what the limits are of each kind of knowledge use.

Much of the research within the knowledge approach has been devoted toward showing that knowledge does indeed have an effect and that purely formal models of categorization are not sufficient. This point has been made very forcefully, and now it is necessary to go beyond it in providing explicit, detailed accounts of how knowledge is involved in these processes. More recent research has in fact been designed to differentiate hypotheses about how knowledge influences concept use (e.g., Heit 1994, 1998; Kaplan and Murphy 1999, 2000; Spalding and Murphy

1999; Wattenmaker 1995; Wisniewski 1995). If the critique of those traditional models of category learning that ignore knowledge is to go forward, however, it will be necessary for proponents of this view to provide similarly detailed models of their own. By the same token, proponents of formal theories need to develop their own models to provide an account of all the phenomena described here. This is in fact how the most recent proposals of Heit (1994; Heit and Bott 2000) developed.

The question that has yet to be answered is exactly how knowledge changes the learning process and the resulting concept representation. Early proposals (Murphy and Allopenna 1994) suggested that the knowledge simply *became* the category representation to some degree. For example, once you figured out "Category 2 is arctic vehicles" (see table 6.1), you didn't then devote attention to learning the category's properties or exemplars, but simply represented the category as arctic vehicles. On this account, then, knowledge pre-empted empirical learning. But later findings show that this proposal is clearly wrong—knowledge doesn't hurt the learning of statistical properties of the stimuli; in some cases, it may even help it (see especially Kaplan and Murphy 1999, 2000; Spalding and Murphy 1999). For example, subjects learn the frequency of features related to knowledge somewhat better than subjects do who do not have knowledge (Spalding and Murphy 1999). Theories of concept learning will need to be developed that can explain how knowledge simultaneously (1) greatly speeds category learning, (2) greatly aids learning of features related to the knowledge, (3) yet does not impair statistical learning of those features (or benefits it), and (4) does not hurt learning of features unrelated to knowledge. This is a surprising pattern of results, which is a challenge to all current theories.

Models from Outside Psychology

One place to look for inspiration on how to incorporate knowledge is the literature on machine learning in artificial intelligence (AI). More traditional learning algorithms have been called *Similarity-Based Learning* (SBL), because they learn categories based on the sharing of properties among items in the same class. These are analogous to the traditional prototype and exemplar models in psychology. SBL is contrasted with *Explanation-Based Learning* (EBL), which is related to the knowledge approach in psychology. In early EBL systems (e.g., DeJong and Mooney 1986), the computer started out with a bunch of knowledge, which could be thought of as premises. The system was exposed to a single category member, along with some kind of description of what the category was supposed to be (e.g., a tool to accomplish some function; a treatment for a particular disease). The system then used its knowledge to attempt to prove that the object was in fact in the category. The program could also generalize the proof so as to specify the range of observable properties that would satisfy it. This proof then became the representation of the category as a whole. In this way, the system would not have to go through a new proof with every new category member that was encountered, and it would not be misled by idiosyncratic properties of the learning exemplar.

This description may be a bit puzzling to psychologists, because it seems to assume that the system already knows what the category is, or else it could not have derived a proof, especially after observing only one exemplar. The system knows about the entire domain and also knows something about the function or goal of the category itself. (In Ahn, Brewer, and Mooney 1992, for example, subjects were provided with the purpose of the category before being exposed to the exemplar. In DeJong and Mooney 1986, the learning program already had a set of knowledge about human behavior and then had to learn a category from a narrative that exemplified a particular category of human behavior.) This situation still requires further learning, because even if one has general knowledge of a category, such as its function, one must still learn which particular properties are characteristic of it and be able to identify members based on perceptual properties. However, I think that it is fair enough to say that EBL models of this sort do not capture the typical situations in which one is confronted with objects and their category labels, or in which one has observed a number of objects and then realizes that they form a category. In most such cases, the learner does not already have a function available for the object. Also, learners can and do learn unexpected properties of objects as a result of induction from multiple examples.[8]

More recent models, however, have focused on situations that are somewhat more realistic, or, at least, somewhat more like psychology experiments. For example, Pazzani (1991) developed a computer program called Post-Hoc that simulated the performance in his experiment (described above). Post-Hoc developed hypotheses about the correct category representation by starting from its knowledge and then looking for relevant properties in the examples. For example, if the program was trying to learn the category of balloons that would inflate, it would then look for the properties of being stretched and being inflated by an adult. If a positive example had one of those features, it would be incorporated into the hypothesis about the category. It also had a fairly simple learning mechanism that would fix hypotheses that were found to be incorrect based on later evidence. Pazzani presented evidence that his model did account for important aspects of the human data.

Post-Hoc does have some interesting ideas for how knowledge-based learning may work, but it is incomplete in a number of respects. First, it only learns classical categories in which features are related by conjunction or disjunction. It would find it very difficult to learn many of the family-resemblance categories used in other experiments. Second, the model makes the strong claim that knowledge features are learned to the exclusion of other features (when the knowledge is correctly related to category membership). However, more recent evidence shows that people learn other features as well. For example, Kaplan and Murphy (2000) found that providing subjects with knowledge did make them focus more on the knowledge-related features. However, their learning of other features was exactly the same as that of subjects in the neutral group, and was fairly good overall. Wisniewski (1995) and Heit and Bott (2000) have also demonstrated learning of features unrelated to category knowledge. As noted earlier, this result is a puzzling one for many proposals of how knowledge influences learning, because it requires that knowledge speed learning and help some features but that the other features still be learned. This seems to be a realistic aspect of concept learning, since people learn not only knowledge-related features of everyday categories (e.g., birds have wings in order to fly), but also features that are not clearly related to that knowledge (e.g., birds have beaks).

IOU was designed by one of the originators of EBL approaches to learning, Raymond Mooney, to address some of these limitations of a purely knowledge-based approach. Mooney (1993) pointed out that prior theory can typically only explain some proportion of a concept's features, and that some other mechanism will be necessary to discover its other features. In the IOU (Induction Over the Unexplained) system, domain knowledge is first used to explain as much of the observed examples as possible. However, if this explanation does not result in correct categorization, it is augmented by an empirical learning system that learns additional features.

For example, suppose the system were trying to learn about cups, and it had the idea that cups are drinking vessels, but didn't know anything else about them (Mooney 1993). It would first attempt to explain as many features as possible based on its knowledge and the drinking vessel function (as in the usual EBL system). Now, some features of observed cups could be easily explained (cylindrical shape), but others might not be so easily explained, by the system, at least (their typical width and height). Furthermore, the explanation of a drinking vessel might pick out not only cups but also bowls and glasses. Therefore, the system must be exposed to cups and contrast categories, labeled with their category membership, in order to learn to separate cups from related items on an empirical basis. The explainable features are ignored in the empirical process, and only the unexplained ones are submitted to it. In one version of the program, the empirical learning component notices all the (unexplained) features that are common to the observed examples.

Mooney (1993) reviews how the model can explain aspects of psychological experiments, such as those of Wisniewski (1995) and Ahn et al. (1992). Indeed, the model is an important step in unifying empirical and knowledge-based learning. Like other EBL systems, it has the limitation that one must already have some description of the category to allow one to explain the observed features. It is not clear if the model will avoid the problems I raised for the Post-Hoc model. For example, it also seems to require that the explainable features be present in all items. IOU can certainly explain giving more weight to knowledge-related features, which are learned first; and it also accommodates the learning of purely empirical features. The model is not designed to accomplish unsupervised learning, but it does not seem impossible to adapt it to such a situation. Thus, this model has some promise, if it can overcome the issue of having to know the goal or other information about the category in advance. Although it does not address the more difficult issues of feature construction and induction, that is beyond any model at this time.

AI models hold promise for helping us understand the interaction of knowledge and empirical learning processes. Their main shortcomings as psychological accounts are twofold. First, they are sometimes not tested on psychological data but rather on in-principle problems, to see if they form reasonable categories. (This is less true with the particular models I have been reviewing in this chapter, which have addressed at least some psychological data.) Second, the models often have some assumptions that are psychologically implausible, for example, a reliance on predicate logic and classical rules in the knowledge component. These AI proposals are a good jumping-off point, but more specifically psychological theories of the interaction of knowledge and empirical learning still need to be developed.

Perhaps it is worth pointing out that these AI approaches all appear to be prototype models. That is, they produce descriptions that apply to the category as a whole, rather than learning individual exemplars. This is probably based on the belief that knowledge tends to be about whole categories rather than individual entities, and it is most convenient to represent it that way. In any case, these models therefore carry whatever positive or negative baggage that prototype models have in general.

Future Directions

I have been emphasizing the development of more complete models in this discussion, but there is still much psychological research to be done in order to increase our understanding of how knowledge effects work, and how they are integrated with empirical learning. At the present moment, the most critical question to my mind is the issue of how the learning process itself is changed by prior knowledge and how that in turn leads to changes in the category representation (see discussion at the end of the "Knowledge View" section above). The knowledge and statistical learning are apparently interacting in some way, but it is not obvious how.

As remarked in a number of places, there also needs to be further work done on knowledge in categorization, as the number of studies on this is somewhat slim, and important theoretical alternatives need to be distinguished. And finally, the influence of knowledge on feature construction is a fascinating question that has been little studied since Wisniewski and Medin's (1994) groundbreaking work.

In sum, there is still much to discover beyond the initial "does knowledge make a difference?" questions that motivated the earliest studies on this topic.

7

Taxonomic Organization and the Basic Level of Concepts

The people, objects, and events that we encounter every day do not each fit into a single category. Wilbur might simultaneously be a bulldog, a dog, a mammal, and an animal. At various times, he might be considered a pet, a friend, a guard dog, or even a weapon. People fit into many different categories such as being a woman, a reporter, a political conservative, a Yankees fan, a New Yorker, an African-American, a cousin, and so on. We identify people in terms of their gender, ethnicity, profession, and a host of social roles that our culture provides. We do not feel that one category is the only one or the best one ("Are you a woman or a reporter?"), though different categories are most relevant or useful at any given time. The same is true for events, as the same event might be thought of as seeing a comedy, going to the theater, spending an evening out, getting entertainment, going on a date, or (hopefully not) a fiasco. In some cases, the object or event can be viewed as simultaneously and equally being in these categories (e.g., Wilbur is both a dog and a mammal), and, in other cases, there is a shift of perspective involved (e.g., Wilbur is both a dog and a friend; the event was a date and a fiasco). Either way, most things are not solely in a single category but can be placed into a large number of different categories. The question arises, therefore, of how these categories are coordinated in our memories and behaviors. How do we decide which of these categories to use on any occasion? And is there a preferred category by which we think about any one thing?

In this chapter, I will not address all of the possible ways in which an object can be categorized. Instead, I will focus on one particular kind of category organization: the *hierarchical* structure of categories. In the above example, the categories bulldog, dog, mammal, and animal form a hierarchy or taxonomy—a sequence of progressively larger categories in which each category includes all the previous ones. That is, mammals include all dogs, which include all bulldogs. The hierarchical

This chapter owes a considerable debt to an earlier essay written with Dr. Mary Lassaline (Murphy and Lassaline 1997). I thank Mary for her contribution.

organization, which will be described in more detail shortly, has been suggested as a particularly important way of organizing concepts. In fact, when people are asked to categorize an object in a neutral setting without further instructions, they are very likely to provide one of the hierarchically organized categories, like bulldog or dog, rather than categories like friend, drooling animal, or something to be rescued in case of a fire. Thus, these taxonomic categories may be particularly important ones for thought and communication.

In addition to identifying hierarchical organization, psychologists have noted that one particular level of specificity of categories is important. For example, people normally call a Siamese cat "a cat," rather than calling it "a Siamese" or "an animal." There is something about the category cat that makes it just the right level of identification. Considerable effort has been expended to identify this especially useful level, called *the basic level of categorization*, in a number of different domains. This chapter presents the evidence for such a privileged level of categorization, along with explanations for what gives the basic level its advantages.

Hierarchical Structure of Categories

In order to illustrate the hierarchical structure of categories, I will refer to a category structure in the long-term memory of a fictional person, Rachel, shown in figure 7.1. To begin, we need to establish some terminology: The categories that are higher in the hierarchy are *superordinate* to the lower-level categories; the lower-level categories are *subordinate* to the higher-level ones. Note that some parts of the hierarchy are "deeper" than others, that is, have more levels. For example, Rachel knows two kinds of dogs but no kinds of deer; therefore, the hierarchy is deeper under the dog category. Finally, I should note that in order to save space, I have given each category only two subordinates. However, this is not an actual rule of hierarchies. In fact, Rachel likely knows many more kinds of animals and mammals than are shown in figure 7.1.

A hierarchy is a kind of network. That is, it has nodes (categories) connected by relations (indicated by lines in figure 7.1). However, a hierarchy is a special kind of network. To begin with, the only relation allowed between category members is the *set inclusion* relation. For example, the set of animals includes the set of fish, which includes the set of trout, which includes the set of rainbow trout. Set inclusion is sometimes called the "IS-A" relation (Collins and Quillian 1969), because the subordinate category "is a" superordinate: An oak is a tree, and a tree is a plant. In addition, for a network to be a hierarchy, any category can have only one immedi-

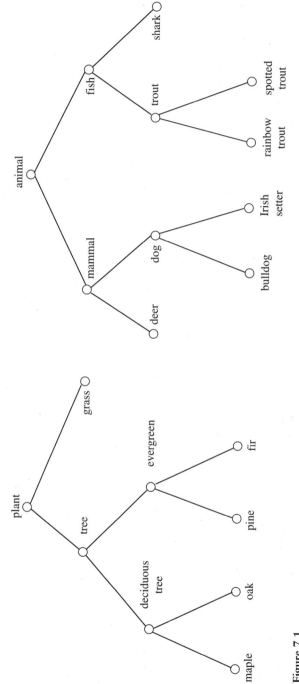

Figure 7.1
A simplified conceptual hierarchy. The lines represent IS-A links connecting concepts to their superordinates or subordinates.

ate superordinate; no node in figure 7.1 could have two lines leading to it from above. For example, deer can have mammal as its immediate superordinate, but it can't also have fish as an immediate superordinate.

The nature of the IS-A relation is also important in determining the properties of hierarchies. First, the IS-A relation is *asymmetric*. All dogs are animals, but all animals are not necessarily dogs. Second, the category relations are *transitive*: All pines are evergreens, and all evergreens are trees; therefore, all pines are trees. The transitivity of category membership leads to a similar transitivity of property ascription, called *property inheritance*. Every property true of the members of a category is also true of the category's subordinates. For example, suppose that all animals have blood. If this is true, then all mammals must have blood, and therefore all dogs have blood, and therefore all bulldogs have blood. Bulldogs, then, inherit the properties of dogs, and dogs inherit the properties of mammals. Property inheritance is directly related to the set-inclusion nature of the links. It is *because* all bulldogs are animals that the properties of animals must also apply to bulldogs.

These properties illustrate some of the power of hierarchical descriptions. If Rachel learns something about animals in general, she can now generalize this to all of the many categories that are under animal in the hierarchy. Or if she learns that a chow is a kind of dog, she can now generalize everything else that she knows about dogs to chows. By being able to place a category into its proper place in the hierarchy, one can learn a considerable amount about the category. So, even if Rachel has never seen a chow, she can assume that they have blood and bark—that they have all the properties common to dogs and other animals. Clearly, this is an important ability, since it allows one to immediately access knowledge about new entities that one hasn't had direct experience with.

Much of this section of the chapter will be devoted to discussing whether people really have and use such hierarchies. In order to discuss that, we need to specify what exactly counts as evidence for this hierarchical structure of concepts. Much work in developmental psychology has formed a very stringent set of criteria for this ability, based on the work of Piaget (Inhelder and Piaget 1964). However, Piaget's assumptions were based on theories of logic rather than empirical observations of how people use concepts, and so they seem in retrospect to be too stringent. For example, Piaget believed that if Rachel knows that all terriers are dogs, then she should be able to answer questions of logic and numerical reasoning of the sort "Are all dogs terriers?" and "Are there more terriers or more dogs?" Perhaps not surprisingly, Piaget and other researchers found that young children could be quite bad at answering such questions.[1] However, the uses of hierarchies that I described above do not necessarily require people to be able to answer such questions. For example, a child (or adult, for that matter) might not be able to reason about the number of bulldogs, dogs, and animals, but could still understand that if an animal has blood then a bulldog must also have blood.

What then, should constitute knowledge of a hierarchy and understanding of its relations? Markman and Callanan (1984) tentatively proposed that someone be able to identify an object at two different levels of categorization, for example, as a chair and as furniture. However, they then rejected this proposal, because such a person might not fully understand the inclusion relation, that all chairs are furniture. Perhaps the person only knows these two categories as independent kinds of groupings. In particular, they argue that the person should demonstrate an understanding of the asymmetry and transitivity of the relation.

For our purposes, the question of whether people *understand* the relation of class inclusion may be somewhat too strict. It is important to discover whether people organize their concepts in hierarchies that have these properties. However, it is possible that people do so but do not overtly understand the nature of these relations. For example, people may be able to infer that if animals have blood then bulldogs have blood—but not vice versa—without being able to articulate an understanding of the IS-A link or its asymmetry. The main criteria I will focus on will be the transitive nature of class inclusion and the corresponding inheritance of properties. That is, if someone understands that all bulldogs are dogs and all dogs are animals, then he or she should be able to infer that all bulldogs are animals. And if this is understood, then knowing that all animals breathe should allow one to infer that all bulldogs breathe. Someone who correctly represents this relation will not make property ascriptions with certainty in the opposite direction. That is, if all bulldogs have an omentum, it does not follow that all animals have an omentum. (However, it should be noted that for some properties such an inference could be reasonably made, even though it is not logically true. For example, if all bulldogs have a gene involved in the formation of the lungs, one might infer that all dogs or even all mammals have the same gene—see Osherson et al. 1990—in part because one does not expect such properties to vary much across related species. This is one reason why I am less concerned with the asymmetric aspect of class inclusion than Markman and Callanan 1984, were.) As will be seen, few of the studies of adults actually test subjects very carefully on whether they understand these relations in detail. This question is much more critical for the developmental concerns addressed in chapter 10. Instead, adult studies have focused on the issue of transitivity of category judgments, such as deciding whether a dog is an animal.

Psychological Status of Hierarchies

Hierarchical structure appears to be a universal property of all cultures' categories of the natural world (Berlin 1992). However, what is not clear is exactly how hierarchies are mentally represented. There are two main possibilities, which are not mutually exclusive. One possibility is that people's concepts are structured in memory much as in figure 7.1. That is, perhaps concepts are connected in hierarchical networks, and the connections are used in order to make inductive inferences and categorization judgments as described in the previous section. For example, figure 7.1 could illustrate the actual concepts that Rachel knows, with associations between the concepts indicated by the lines. In addition to what is shown in figure 7.1, there would also be properties associated with each concept. For example, perhaps linked to evergreens is the property "has needles," and linked to oak is the property "has lobed leaves." In this respect, then, the hierarchy is literally represented as a set of connections in memory, which would be consistent with many models of memory that argue that items are linked in large networks (e.g., Anderson and Bower 1973; Collins and Loftus 1975; Collins and Quillian 1969; Rumelhart and McClelland 1986). It is necessary to distinguish different kinds of links in order to indicate the hierarchical structure. The IS-A links (shown in figure 7.1) are the ones that specify the hierarchical structure, whereas other links would specify properties known about each concept, and still other connections might be made between related concepts or properties. But it is the IS-A links that constitute the hierarchical structure itself.

According to this view, the network would be used to make various category decisions. For example, in deciding whether a bulldog is an animal, one would locate bulldog in memory and trace upwards in the hierarchy until reaching the node for animal. At this point, the sequence of IS-A links would indicate that a bulldog is indeed an animal. Furthermore, information true of all animals would be stored with the animal concept, and only information distinctive to bulldogs would be stored at the bulldog node (Collins and Quillian 1969; Smith 1978). This assumption provides a kind of *cognitive economy*. By representing "breathes" with the animal node, one does not need to store the fact that mammals breathe, fish breathe, reptiles breathe, dogs breathe, deer breathe, bulldogs breathe, irish setters breathe, and so on. One does not need to store these individual facts because hierarchies provide for the inheritance of properties.

The second possibility for how hierarchies are psychologically represented is that the hierarchical structure of concepts results from a kind of reasoning process rather than being explicitly stored in memory. Suppose that all Xs are Ys, and all Ys are

Table 7.1.
Hypothetical features of categories that form hierarchical sets.

Category	Possible Hierarchical Feature Set
Animal	moves, breathes
Mammal	moves, breathes, has fur, gives birth to live young
Dog	moves, breathes, has fur, gives birth to live young, barks, has 4 legs

Zs. Now if I tell you that all Zs have six fingers, what does that tell you about Xs? A little thought will reveal that Xs must also have six fingers, since all of them are Zs. Thus, even though you clearly did not have the hierarchy stored in memory (before reading this paragraph), you could use the information about category inclusion to come to the correct answer. This suggests the possibility that people may not have a hierarchy directly represented in their heads but may still be able to infer category inclusion and then draw the appropriate inferences (see Randall 1976) through a reasoning process.

If people did not have the hierarchy stored in memory, how would they know that bulldogs are dogs and dogs are animals? One suggestion (Rips, Shoben, and Smith 1973) is that this information can be computed based on the properties that are known of a category. Recall that one version of the prototype view discussed in chapter 3 said that people learn properties that are generally found in the category members. So, to represent dogs, one would have a list of weighted features that are generally true of dogs (I will ignore the weighting here). In a hierarchy, the properties that are generally true of a category are also true of its subordinates; as a result, the more specific categories have the same features as the more general categories, with one or more additional features. Table 7.1 illustrates this. The right column presents the properties (or features) Rachel knows about each category in the left column, animal, mammal and dog (clearly, this is just an illustration—Rachel knows many more things about these categories). As one goes to more specific categories, the list of known features only increases. A subordinate has all the properties of its superordinate, plus some others that distinguish it. So, bulldogs have all the properties of dogs as well as some properties distinctive of bulldogs.

This example illustrates how one can look at the properties that are known of two categories and make a judgment about whether they are hierarchical. If X's features are a subset of the features of Y, then X is a superordinate of Y. For example, the features of animal are a subset of the features of mammal in the right column of table 7.1, and so animal is a superordinate of mammal. (It may be counterintuitive that fewer features means a bigger category, but remember that as more and more features are specified for a concept, it is being made more specific, and more objects are being ruled out because they don't have all the features.) If X has all the features of Y, plus some additional features, then X is a subordinate of Y. For example, dog has all the features of animal, plus some additional ones, and so it is a subordinate of animal. If X and Y have the same features, then they are the same category.[2] According to this view, then, we do not need to have IS-A links stored in memory— all we need to know is the properties of the category members, and we can infer the set inclusion relations from them. Note that this approach does not have cognitive economy, as features like "moves" are represented separately in each category.

In short, the category hierarchy could either be *prestored* or *computed* (Smith 1978). If it is prestored, then our memory is a network of IS-A links like that shown in figure 7.1. If it is computed, then hierarchical relations are not directly stored in memory but are calculated based on the properties of each pair of categories. In the 1970s, many experiments were conducted to discover which of these accounts of conceptual structure was most accurate (e.g., Chang 1986; Collins and Quillian 1969, 1970; Glass and Holyoak 1975; McCloskey and Glucksberg 1979; Rips, Shoben, and Smith 1973). Unfortunately, these experiments were not entirely con-clusive. Part of the problem is that it is necessary to make further assumptions about what memory structures and processes are used in any particular experimental task. Since neither theory completely accounted for all of the observed data, each was modified in order to be more complete. The result was that it became difficult to tell the two views apart. I will review here three relevant phenomena that were used to try to distinguish these two views. For readers wishing more information, the review in Smith (1978) is excellent.

If concepts are represented in a hierarchy of the sort shown in figure 7.1, then accessing conceptual relations should require one to use these hierarchical links. For example, deciding that a pine is a tree, one should first note that pines are evergreens (crossing one IS-A link) and then note that evergreens are trees (crossing another IS-A link). Because of the transitivity of set inclusion, this indicates that pines are trees. If it takes a certain amount of time to cross each IS-A link, Collins and Quillian (1969) reasoned, one could predict the response time to judge the truth or falsity of sentences: Subjects should be faster at verifying "A pine is an evergreen" than "A pine is a plant," because the former involves fewer IS-A links than the latter. Similarly, people should be faster at identifying "An evergreen is a plant" than "A pine is a plant." In general, the more IS-A links that need to be traversed in order to verify the sentence, the longer it should take people to verify that it is true. (Similar predictions can be made for false sentences such as "An evergreen is an oak," but they are more complex.) Because of the assumption of cognitive economy, one can predict that property questions should also take longer when more IS-A links are involved. For example, "A pine uses photosynthesis" requires one to infer that a pine is a plant (traversing many IS-A links) and to recall that all plants use photosynthesis. In contrast, "A pine has needles" requires only going up one IS-A link, to the evergreen node. Collins and Quillian found evidence for these predictions. When a sentence required traversal of only one IS-A link, subjects were faster to verify the sentence than when it required traversal of two links—both for category decisions and for property statements. This supported the notion that a taxonomic tree is indeed stored in memory.

Other researchers suggested a different explanation for such results, however. They argued that if people had stored mental descriptions of each category, categories closer in the taxonomic tree would generally have more similar descriptions. For example, as table 7.1 shows, dog shares many more features with mammal than it does with animal. If subjects were using feature lists to infer category relations, perhaps this similarity of the category representations could explain the effect that Collins and Quillian found.

Rips, Shoben, and Smith (1973) introduced a new factor, *typicality*, into the sentence verification paradigm. They compared category members that were more or less typical or representative of a superordinate category—for example, "A robin is a bird" vs. "An ostrich is a bird." Both judgments would require one IS-A link to be traversed (i.e., both robin and ostrich would be directly connected to bird as a superordinate), and so both should take about the same amount of time to evaluate. However, Rips et al. found that the sentences including typical terms, such as robin, took less time to verify than those including atypical terms, such as ostrich or goose, as reviewed in chapter 2. Rips et al. also found that for some items, people were faster at verifying category relations that crossed two IS-A links than a less typical category relation that crossed only one IS-A link. For example, people might be faster to verify "A dog is an animal" than "A dog is a mammal," because dog is a more typical animal than mammal. These results are inconsistent with the taxonomy represented in memory, as in figure 7.1, since it is impossible to verify that a dog is an animal without first going through the mammal category. Furthermore, the feature model could explain the typicality effect under the reasonable assumption that atypical members have fewer features in common with the category than typical members do (Rosch and Mervis 1975; see chapter 2).[3]

Another problem for the pre-stored view of hierarchies is cases of intransitivity. As described in chapter 2, Hampton (1982) has shown that people do not always follow the rules of transitivity that are found in a strict hierarchy. For example, his subjects verified that a car seat was an example of chair. They also agreed that chair is an example of furniture. But they denied that a car seat was a kind of furniture. If people were simply tracing the links in the IS-A hierarchy, they would not have denied this relation, since subjects did agree that each individual link was correct. However, intransitivity is compatible with the view that hierarchical relations are computed, with a few added assumptions. Car seat shares some features with chair (e.g., having a seat) but perhaps not very many, since it is not very typical. Similarly, chair shares some features with furniture, but probably different features than car seat shares with it (e.g., most furniture does not have a seat). As a result, a car seat may share very few features with furniture, and so subjects may not judge that it is a kind of furniture (see Hampton 1982, and chapter 2 for discussion). Randall (1976) found similar intransitivities in biological categories of a number of different cultures. Osherson et al. (1990) showed that subjects will make what they called an *inclusion fallacy* in inductive arguments. People believe that the argument "Robins have an ulnar artery, therefore all birds do" is stronger than "Robins have an ulnar artery, therefore ostriches do." If subjects believed the first argument, then by transitivity, ostriches should have an ulnar artery too, and so they should believe the second argument at least as much. But they don't, suggesting a failure of transitivity in reasoning about hierarchies.

Perhaps the greatest problem for the pre-stored view (and, indeed, the view that hierarchies are critical to conceptual structure) was found by Sloman (1998). He tested subjects on simple one-step logical inferences such as:

All metals are pentavalent.

Therefore, all iron is pentavalent.

Subjects had to rate the probability that the conclusion was true, assuming that the premise was true. To be sure that the results were not influenced by subjects' ignorance (conceivably some of them might not know that iron is a metal), he only used the probability ratings of subjects who said that the conclusion category was included in the premise category. Surprisingly, Sloman found that subjects did not rate the probability of the conclusion category as 1.0. Furthermore, Sloman (1993) found that subjects felt that arguments with typical items were stronger than arguments with atypical arguments, even though both were logically valid according to taxonomic rules. For example, the argument

Birds have an ulnar artery.

Therefore robins/penguins have an ulnar artery.

was judged as stronger when robin rather than penguin was used in the conclusion. But both should be maximally strong, since all robins and all penguins are birds.

Sloman (1998, p. 28) argued that people do not store and use hierarchies in the way envisioned by Collins and Quillian: "Inclusion relations are part of the set of rules that we can apply given the right conditions; not the set of relations that comprise memory structure." Instead, he argued that subjects compute the similarity (or typicality) of one category to its superordinate, and they are willing to draw inferences from one to the other to the degree that this similarity is high. This is clearly more consistent with the computed rather than the pre-stored view.

In my view, the feature models, which say that hierarchies are computed rather than prestored, have the edge in this battle (e.g., see McCloskey and Glucksberg 1979). The simplicity and elegance of a hierarchy like that found in figure 7.1 does not seem to be a property of human memory, as Sloman (1998) has demonstrated. Findings of typicality effects, intransitivity of class inclusion, and evidence from RT experiments all pose problems for the stored hierarchy view. People do not strictly follow cognitive economy in a way that organizes the information in memory so nicely. As I warned at the outset of this discussion, however, the evidence in this area is not entirely decisive. A list of features may also be insufficient to account for all the data. At least some category relations may be explicitly learned and represented. For example, children may learn that whales are mammals and store this fact explicitly in memory (Glass and Holyoak 1975)—if not in a network (like in figure 7.1), then perhaps as a feature of the concept. That stored fact could be used to help them answer questions about whales, rather than doing a comparison of the features of whales and mammals. In fact, storing that relation may be necessary, since whales are so different from most mammals that a feature comparison might not give the correct result. It seems most likely that some category relations are directly learned and stored (those that are not obvious, like the whale-mammal kind), whereas others are computed as needed. Although perhaps inelegant, this kind of mixed model may be the best explanation of the jumbled set of facts that people know about the world. Indeed, later versions of network models have allowed many violations of hierarchical structure and cognitive economy, taking on some of the assumptions of the feature models (e.g., Collins and Loftus 1975). Unfortunately, mixed models of this sort are very difficult to test, since they have different possible ways of representing any given piece of information one might test.

This somewhat confused state of current theory should not blind us to two important generalizations. First, people are able to learn and use taxonomic relations in order to draw inferences even if they are not perfectly logical in doing so. Second, people are able to reason taxonomically about novel materials that have not been previously stored in memory (as in the "All Xs are Ys" kind of example). This is useful for generalizing new facts about one category to its subordinates. Without such an ability, learning facts about the world would be much more onerous. In the next section, we'll discuss some important distinctions that have been made about different levels in the taxonomy.

The Basic Level of Categorization

As described earlier, any object can be thought of as being in a set of hierarchically organized categories, ranging from extremely general (e.g., entity) to extremely specific (e.g., eighteenth-century French upholstered dining room chair). An unknown object is most likely to be a member of a maximally general category, because members of general categories occur with greater frequency than do members of more specific categories. For example, there are more living things in the world than there are cats. Therefore, classification at the most general level maximizes accuracy of classification. Maximally specific categories, on the other hand, allow for greater accuracy in prediction than general categories. Given that something is a cat, you are able to predict more about it (its behavior, its appearance, its tendency to wake you up in the middle of the night when it knocks over a glass) than if you know only that it is a living thing (it might or might not have gills, produce leaves, or drink milk). Of all the possible categories in a hierarchy to which a concept belongs, a middle level of specificity, the *basic level*, is the most natural, preferred level at which to conceptually carve up the world. The basic level[4] can be seen as a compromise between the accuracy of classification at a maximally general level and the predictive power of a maximally specific level.

Initial Studies of the Basic Level

Roger Brown (1958a) first noted that people prefer to use a consistent middle level of categorization in speech. He pointed out that parents speaking to their children tend to use the same short, frequent names for things. For example, a parent might call a bulldog a *dog* or *doggie*, rather than an *animal* or *bulldog*. Brown proposed that parents use category names at a level that "anticipates the equivalences and differences that will need to be observed in most ... dealings with ... an object" (p. 16) and only supply a different name "in order to identify an immediately important property of the referent" (p. 17). For example, the name *chair* indicates that an object has a seat, a back, and legs, and is used to sit on, but *the new chair* or *the good chair* is in a different class, indicating that the child should treat it with care and probably not sit on it.

It may be that the psychologically basic level of categorization is a reflection of discontinuities in the world, suggesting a connection between the structure of people's concepts and the structure inherent in the world (see Malt 1995). Berlin (1992; Berlin, Breedlove and Raven 1973) studied folk classification by following native speakers of the Tzeltal language (spoken by Mayans in Mexico) through the jungle and asking them to name various plants and animals they came upon. He found that Tzeltal speakers tended to name plants and animals at a single level of scientific classification, that corresponding to the genus (pine, bass), rather than to a more specific (white pine, black bass) or to a more general (tree, fish) level. According to Berlin, people across all cultures have this same basic level, the genus. This proposal may be too rigid, however. For people who lack experience with a domain, a higher level is basic. For example, urban dwellers treat the life form—in this case, tree—as basic, rather than the genus, such as maple or elm (Dougherty 1978; Rosch et al. 1976), presumably because of lesser amounts of interaction with the natural environment (though see Coley, Medin, and Atran 1997). Second, people with extensive training may treat a more specific level as basic. I discuss changes in categorization with expertise in a later section.

In a series of highly influential studies, Eleanor Rosch and her colleagues (Rosch 1978; Rosch et al. 1976) developed a number of operational definitions of the basic level. First, the basic level of object categories was shown to be the most inclusive level at which category members possess a significant number of common attributes. When subjects were asked to list attributes possessed by categories at the superordinate, basic, and subordinate level (e.g., clothing, pants, and jeans, respectively) they only listed a few attributes for superordinate categories, and listed significantly more for both basic and subordinate categories. The number of attributes listed for subordinate categories was only slightly more than the number listed at the basic level. Subjects listed different kinds of attributes at the different levels, as well. The most frequent kind of attribute listed for superordinate categories was functional (e.g., keeps you warm, you wear it). Subjects listed noun and adjective properties at the basic level (e.g., legs, buttons, belt loops, cloth) and additional properties listed at the subordinate level were generally adjectives (e.g., blue).

In a second study, Rosch et al. found that basic-level categories are the most inclusive categories for which highly similar sequences of movements are made to category members. In this study, subjects were asked to write down the movements they make when interacting with objects that belong to superordinate, basic, and subordinate categories. As with the attribute listing study, subjects listed many more movements for basic and subordinate level categories (e.g., for pants: grasp with hands, bend knee, raise and extend leg, and eight others) than for superordinate categories (e.g., for clothing: scan with eyes and grasp). Similar results were obtained when subjects actually performed the movements associated with each category.

Additional studies were directed at determining the visual similarity of objects at different levels. Rosch et al. found that objects within basic and subordinate level categories had shapes that were more similar than objects within superordinate categories. They determined this by tracing the shapes of pictures of objects, and for pairs of shapes, computing the ratio of the area the two shapes had in common to their total areas. Furthermore, when the pairs of shapes were averaged to create a single shape, subjects could easily identify averages from the same basic and subordinate level concepts but often could not identify averages of superordinate concepts. These techniques are rather low-tech by current standards. They also involve a number of difficult assumptions, such as finding corresponding views of different objects. For example, a head-on picture of a cat would not be visually similar to a picture of a curled-up cat. And what views does one use to compare the picture of the cat and sock? Nonetheless, these studies at least demonstrate the intuition that members of basic-level categories share visual properties.

Rosch et al. (1976) concluded, then, that members of basic-level categories are similar to one another, and members of subordinates are only slightly more similar to one another. This finding has implications for psychological processes involving basic and subordinate concepts. For example, categories that have similar shapes should be easy to mentally represent as images. Rosch et al. tested this idea by presenting subjects with a category name and then asking them to identify a briefly presented picture of an object in that category embedded in visual noise (to make it harder to identify). Basic and subordinate level names helped identification more than superordinate names, suggesting that subjects can construct a mental image representing basic and subordinate categories, but not superordinate categories. In a related study, subjects were faster at verifying that a picture of an object was a member of a basic-level category than they were at verifying category membership for either subordinate or superordinate categories. For example, after hearing a category name and seeing a picture of a kitchen table, subjects were faster at verifying that the picture was a table than they were at verifying that the picture was furniture or a kitchen table. This result has been replicated in many other studies (e.g., Jolicoeur, Gluck, and Kosslyn 1984; Murphy and Brownell 1985; Murphy and Wisniewski 1989; Smith, Balzano, and Walker 1978). Finally, Rosch et al. found that people almost exclusively use basic-level names when asked to name pictures of objects. When shown a picture of a dog they call it *dog* (as I just did) rather than an *animal* or *bulldog*. In fact, subjects used basic-level names 1,595 times in the experiment, subordinate names 14 times, and superordinate names only once! There is evidently a very strong preference for the basic level. (For whatever reason, later studies have not found such a strong preference. Lin, Murphy, and Shoben 1997 found about 72% basic-level responding, with virtually all the remainder being subordinate names, similar to Tanaka and Taylor's 1991 results, described below. What is clear is that superordinate names are almost never used to refer to single items.)

There is also developmental evidence suggesting that basic-level concepts are privileged. Basic-level categories are the first categories that children can sort and the first categories that they name. Children also are able to learn novel basic categories before they can learn those at other levels in a category-learning experiment (see Anglin 1977; Horton and Markman 1980; Mervis and Crisafi 1982; Rosch et al. 1976; I will revisit this finding in chapter 10).

In summary, Rosch et al. (1976) found that basic-level categories were preferred to other categories or had some advantage in a number of respects. In many tasks, the basic level is spontaneously used by people or is easier to use than the other levels. Table 7.2 presents a list of such findings, which is not exhaustive. As it shows, the evidence for basic-level performance advantages is considerable. The question arises, then, how we can predict which category level will be basic, and what psychological principles underlie the observed preferences.

Metrics of the Basic Level

Rosch et al. (1976) argued that basic categories exist as inherently separable clusters of objects in the world. The basic level is the level at which objects are most differentiated in the environment. Rosch et al. suggested that one could find a metric for identifying the best categories, based on their structure. Their own suggestion was that basic-level categories maximize *cue validity*, the probability that a particular object belongs to some category, given that the object has a particular feature, or cue. For example, the cue validity for a winged thing being a bird is $P(\text{bird} \mid \text{wings})$, which is the probability that something is a bird, given that it has wings. To calculate this, you would have to know what proportion of things with wings are birds. Since categories are associated with many features, the total cue validity for the category is the sum of the cue validities of all the features possessed by category members: $P(\text{bird} \mid \text{wings}) + P(\text{bird} \mid \text{beak}) + P(\text{bird} \mid \text{lives in nest}) + \cdots$. (This *category* cue validity is no longer a probability, as it can exceed the value of 1.0.)

Table 7.2.
Empirical advantages of basic level categories.

Topic	Advantage (Reference)
Feature listing/ Similarity judgments	Basic categories much more informative than superordinates (Markman and Wisniewski 1997; Mervis and Crisafi 1982; Rosch et al. 1976; Tversky and Hemenway 1983, 1984)
Movements	Basic categories have many more movements in common than superordinates (Rosch et al. 1976)
Shapes	Basic categories have a common shape (Rosch et al. 1976)
Priming	Basic categories are more effective as primes for a visual comparison task than superordinates (Rosch et al. 1976)
Categorization	Pictures are identified as members of basic categories faster than as superordinates or subordinates (Jolicoeur et al. 1984; Lin et al. 1997; Murphy and Brownell 1985; Murphy and Smith 1982; Smith et al. 1978; Rosch et al. 1976; Tanaka and Taylor 1991)
	Basic categories are easier to learn (Horton and Markman 1980)
Word use	Basic categories are overwhelmingly preferred in free naming (Cruse 1977; Lin et al. 1997; Morris and Murphy 1990; Rosch et al. 1976; Tanaka and Taylor 1991; Tversky and Hemenway 1983)
	Basic names are more frequently used in text (Wisniewski and Murphy 1989)
	Basic names are the first acquired by children (Anglin 1977; Rosch et al. 1976)
	Basic names are more frequently used in talking to children (Anglin 1977; Callanan 1985)
	Children interpret novel words as picking out basic concepts (Callanan 1989; Golinkoff et al. 1995)
Word structure	Superordinate names are often mass nouns (Markman 1985; Wisniewski et al. 1996)
	Subordinate names often include basic-level names (Berlin 1992; Newport and Bellugi 1979; Rosch et al. 1976)
	Superordinate names in American Sign Language are composed of signs for basic-level names (Newport and Bellugi 1979; Rosch et al. 1976)

Note: This list of effects is somewhat simplified, in that the basic-level advantage can in some cases be altered by various manipulations. This list refers only to the simplest or neutral case.

Rosch et al. (1976) argued that superordinates have lower cue validity than basic categories, because they have fewer common attributes; for example, animals have fewer things in common than birds do, so there aren't as many cues that help you identify something as an animal as help you identify something as a bird. Subordinate categories were said to have lower cue validity than basic-level categories, because they share more attributes with contrasting subordinate categories than basic categories do with contrasting categories at the same level. For example, knowing that blue jays fly doesn't help much in identifying something as a blue jay, because many other birds fly. As a result, P(blue jay | flies) is quite low. In contrast, knowing that birds fly helps identify something as a bird, because not many other animals fly.

Contrary to Rosch's suggestion, cue validity alone cannot account for the basic level advantage (Murphy 1982). In fact, the superordinate level, being the most inclusive, actually has the highest cue validity. Because a superordinate includes lower basic-level categories, its cue validity can never be lower than that of the categories it includes. Consider the feature "has a tail" and the hierarchy of categories cat, mammal, animal. P(cat | tail) is lower than P(mammal | tail), because there are many mammals with tails that aren't cats, like dogs and mice. Since the mammals category includes all cats, as well as many other things with tails, if something has a tail, you can be surer that it is a mammal than a cat. Likewise, P(mammal | tail) is lower than P(animal | tail), because animal includes all mammals as well as other animals with tails that aren't mammals, like lizards and fish. For categories that are nested, cue validity will never be lower for a more general category than for one of the categories it includes. Cue validity is therefore maximized not at the intermediate basic level, but at the most general level (Murphy 1982).

An alternative possibility is that category validity can predict which level will be basic. Category validity is the conditional probability of possessing a feature given category membership, such as P(wings | bird). This is roughly opposite to the cue validity measure, and as a result, the converse of the argument raised against cue validity can be raised against category validity as a predictor of the basic level: Category validity tends to be highest at the least inclusive or subordinate level (Medin 1983; Murphy 1982), as more specific categories tend to have less variability in features. For example, P(tail | cat) is greater than P(tail | mammal), since there are proportionally more mammals without tails than cats without tails.[5]

A third probability metric for predicting the preferred level of categorization is *category-feature collocation*, which is essentially the product of cue and category validity (Jones 1983). The idea here is to combine the properties of the two previous metrics. However, it has been argued that this model is also inadequate, for reasons that go beyond the scope of this chapter (Corter and Gluck 1992). In part as a response to Jones's model, Corter and Gluck (1992) developed a metric that they called *category utility* and demonstrated that it can correctly predict the preferred level of categorization, as measured by reaction time to picture verification and naming experiments. Category utility combines three kinds of information in one measure: information about the base rate or frequency of occurrence of a category; the category validity of the category's features; and the base rates of each of these features. This measure is higher for categories that are more general (having a higher base rate) and that are very predictive of features. This metric is consistent with psychological explanations for the advantage of the basic level, as will be seen in the next section.

However, one problem with all of these metrics based on the frequencies of features in various categories is that it is often difficult to specify which features should be included (Murphy 1982; Murphy and Medin 1985). In deciding the cue validity of cat, should we include such features as "is larger than a beetle," "can be picked up," or "is less than 100 years old"? If not, how do we decide which features are included in the computation and which are not? One cannot simply accept any feature that is above a small frequency in the category, because some very silly features could be highly frequent (e.g., "doesn't own a raincoat" is true of almost all cats).

One answer is not to include all features that are empirically found in a category, but only those features that people psychologically represent for the category—for example, only the features that appear in subjects' feature lists of a category. However, this approach introduces a certain amount of circularity into the enterprise. The purpose of these metrics was to predict which categories would be psychologically basic, and if we now rely on data about psychological representations to make this prediction, we are using the representation to predict itself. Indeed, I believe that this is the reason that Rosch et al. believed that cue validity predicted the basic level. If one looks at feature lists, the basic level does have high cue validity. The reason is that people list features like "has a tail" for cat but not for mammal, even though more mammals than cats have tails. Thus, such lists cannot be a measure of environmental structure. (In fact, one can argue that Rosch et al.'s 1976 claims that basic categories match the structure of the environment could not have been confirmed by any psychological experiment, since people do not have access to environmental structures separately from their conceptual apparatus.) So far, the difficult question of how to determine which features are really in the environment has not been adequately addressed by metrics of the basic level, which may be one reason that they have received less attention than the psychological explanations to be described next.

In spite of the problems of many of these metrics of the basic level, we should not lose sight of the fact that it is possible to identify a basic level through performance measures (see table 7.2). There is little difficulty in identifying which level is psychologically basic; the problems arise in associating this with a measure of environmental structure. Therefore, I will focus on behavioral measures of the basic level from here on.

Psychological Explanations of the Basic Level

Given that there is good evidence for a preferential level of conceptual representation, a natural question is what psychological aspects of these concepts account for their preference. This is a difficult question to answer, because most of the evidence is correlational. That is, certain concepts have been found to be preferred, such as dog, table, shirt, and so on. To explain why these concepts are basic, we need to compare them to those of other concepts at different levels, such as animal, bulldog, coffee table, clothing, and so on, and see how they differ. The problem is that it is not clear which differences are causes and which are effects.

Consider one specific example. Basic category names are generally used more frequently, including in speech to young children, possibly influencing language learning (Callanan 1985). I have already mentioned Brown's (1958a) observation that parents are much more likely to call a dog a *doggie* than a *bulldog* or *animal*. Parents' choice of particularly useful names (and their consistency in using the same name over and over) might be influential in vocabulary learning, Brown suggested. One might argue from this that basic-level concepts are preferred because of their frequency or early age of learning—not because of their conceptual structure. However, such arguments can cut both ways. Why is it that parents decide to use the word *doggie* rather than another? What made them think that this (basic-level) name would be particularly helpful? Such preferences and frequency effects may themselves have causes in conceptual structure—perhaps parents use that name because it refers to a basic category.

In general, then, a variable that is related to basic-level structure could either be contributing to the basic-level phenomenon or could be a result of such structure. However, considerations of parsimony suggest that it is the conceptual structure that is primary. Basic concepts generally have many positive characteristics associated with them (e.g., have shorter names, are more familiar, are learned earlier, etc.). Rather than taking each characteristic as being coincidentally associated (it just so happens that the words that are learned first are the same as the categories that can be identified fastest), it is more parsimonious to argue that it is some underlying variable that causes the concepts to be the most useful. The simplest explanation is that useful concepts are used more often, learned earlier, have shorter names, are preferred in naming, and have other similar advantages, *because* they are useful. The main question, then, is what it is about basic-level concepts that makes them more useful.

Differentiation Explanation

The most frequently given explanation for the preference for basic concepts is a structural explanation, which I will call the *differentiation explanation*. I will focus my discussion on the version proposed by Murphy and Brownell (1985), which was itself partly based on Mervis and Crisafi (1982) and Rosch et al. (1976). On this explanation, basic concepts are said to be the most differentiated, which involves two properties: *informativeness* and *distinctiveness*.

The informativeness of basic concepts refers to the fact that such concepts are associated with a large amount of information (see the first three entries in table 7.2). As a result, when you know what basic concept describes an object, you know a great deal about the object. So, if you know that something is a dog, you can infer that it barks, has four legs, has fur, eats meat, is a pet, chases cars, and possesses a host of biological attributes (such as breathing, having a liver, having dogs as parents). Thus, dog is a very informative concept, since so many features are associated with it.

The distinctiveness of basic concepts refers to the fact that they are different from other categories at the same level. For example, dogs are fairly different from cats, horses, cows, raccoons, and other familiar mammals. These all look rather different from most dogs, they don't bark, most don't live in the home as pets or are used as guards, and so on.

There is descriptive evidence for the idea that basic concepts are highly differentiated. As already mentioned, Rosch et al. (1976) showed that subjects list many features for basic concepts, and only a few for superordinates. Basic concepts, then, are much more informative. Mervis and Crisafi (1982) asked subjects to rate the similarity of pairs of categories and found that basic concepts were highly distinctive relative to their contrast categories. That is, they found that people rated pants as quite different from other clothing such as socks and shirt. In fact, Mervis and Crisafi constructed a differentiation scale that combined informativeness and dis-

Table 7.3.
Differences among the category levels, according to the differentiation explanation.

Category Level	Informative?	Distinctive?
Superordinate	No	Yes
Basic	Yes	Yes
Subordinate	Yes	No
Atypical Subordinate	Yes	Yes

tinctiveness, and they found that basic-level categories were higher on this scale than were other categories.[6]

Where do superordinates and subordinates fall down according to the differentiation hypothesis? Subordinates are informative; in fact, they are slightly more informative than their basic concepts, because they are more specific (Rosch et al. 1976). However, they are significantly less distinctive. A kitchen table is not very different from a dining room table, and a coffee table is only slightly more different from both; a sedan is quite similar to a compact car and to a station wagon. In contrast, superordinates are very distinctive. Furniture in general is not very similar to tools or clothing or plants. However, superordinates are very uninformative— clothing differs considerably in its size, shape, material and specific use. Rosch et al.'s subjects could list very few features that were common to superordinate categories. In short, it is only basic concepts that are both informative and distinctive, as summarized in table 7.3.

Why is differentiation such an advantage? The informativeness component means that basic concepts are very useful; they communicate a lot of information. However, informativeness comes with a cost: When concepts are too specific, many more of them are needed to cover all the objects in a domain. If informativeness by itself were an unalloyed good, then people would form the most specific categories possible. In the limit, every object would have its own concept, and that would be the preferred level. This would clearly take up too much room in memory, and one would lose the ability to generalize across category members. Rosch (1978) argued that there is a need for *cognitive economy* to counteract the pressure to create ever smaller categories. (Note that this is a different form of cognitive economy than the one discussed by Collins and Quillian 1969, above.) In short, the conceptual system works better with a few fairly informative concepts rather than a very large number of extremely informative concepts. Distinctiveness works to limit the number of concepts. Nondistinctive concepts are harder to use, because it is difficult to tell them apart. (Try to learn the different kinds of sparrows in a bird guide, and you will see the problem with subordinates.) When objects are quite similar, therefore, they tend to be included in the same concept, rather than being split into finer groups. Of course, these principles do not ensure that there are *no* concepts at higher or lower levels than the basic level, but such concepts are less likely to be learned and used. We will return to the other levels of categorization later in the chapter.

Experimental Evidence for the Differentiation Explanation
Studies testing explanations of the basic level can be separated into those using novel artificial categories and those using familiar natural categories. I will discuss them separately.

Experiments with artificial categories.   One advantage of using artificial materials is that variables like familiarity and frequency of names, age of learning, and the like can be carefully controlled. In contrast, using natural materials requires the experimenter to simply accept the (usually unknown) variation in subjects' experience with different categories and names. An important finding in experiments using artificial materials is that robust basic-level advantages are usually found (Corter and Gluck 1992; Lassaline, Wisniewski, and Medin 1992; Murphy 1991; Murphy and Smith 1982). This strongly suggests that the preference is caused by the structure of the concepts rather than less interesting causes such as familiarity and characteristics of the names.

Murphy and Smith (1982) taught subjects hierarchies of tool concepts; an example of two of the basic-level categories is shown in figure 7.2. The hierarchies fit the differentiation explanation's assumptions (table 7.3): The superordinates were uninformative but distinctive; the subordinates were informative but nondistinctive; and the basic concepts were both informative and distinctive. The superordinates in this study were defined primarily by function, as are familiar artifact categories like clothing or vehicles. Murphy and Smith varied the order in which subjects were taught the different levels in order to discover whether the basic-level advantage could be reduced to a learning order effect. After all the categories were learned, subjects performed a timed categorization task, in which they heard a category name and viewed a picture. They pressed a button to indicate whether the picture was in the category indicated by the name. Rosch et al. (1976, Experiment 7) had found that natural basic categories were the fastest in such a task.

Murphy and Smith found that the basic-level concepts that they constructed were indeed the fastest in this task. The subordinate concepts were close behind, but the superordinates were considerably slower. Interestingly, a basic-level advantage was

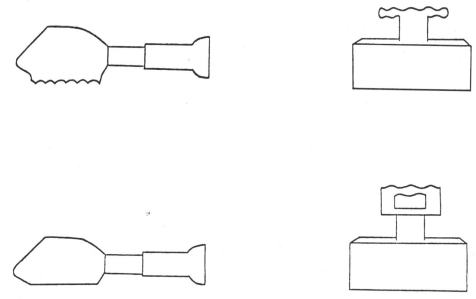

Figure 7.2
Artificial tools used as stimuli in the experiments of Murphy and Smith (1982). The two pictures on the left represent members of the same basic category, with the top one representing one subordinate, and the bottom one a different subordinate. The pictures on the right are a different basic category with its corresponding subordinates.

found regardless of which category level was learned first. Categories did benefit by being learned first, but this did not change the reaction-time ordering of the three levels. Of course, the order of learning in a single experimental session cannot be easily generalized to effects of learning order that take place over months and years in real-world categories, but the fact that order of learning did not change the relative speeds of the three levels suggests that the basic level cannot be completely reduced to learning order.

Murphy (1991) found more support for the differentiation explanation using even more artificial stimuli that did not resemble objects at all. Lassaline et al. (1992) used more variable categories and also found a basic-level advantage. In short, the finding of basic-level structure has been obtained in a number of studies using artificial stimuli and is robust to changes in stimuli.[7] Although there are inherent limitations in using categories that are artificially constructed and learned within a single experimental session, it is reassuring that the principles derived from natural categories are able to predict processing advantages in novel category learning in controlled experiments.

Experiments using natural categories.   Studies using natural concepts have not always been able to distinguish the factors that are proposed by the differentiation explanation from other possible factors. When different concepts are compared, they always differ on a number of variables. Nonetheless, the results of such studies support the differentiation explanation.

Murphy and Brownell (1985) examined atypical subordinates like penguin or boxing glove in a picture categorization task. Because such items are atypical, they are in fact distinctive: Penguins are not similar to other birds, and boxing gloves are quite different from other gloves. And because they are subordinates, such items are already informative. That is, unlike other subordinate categories, these atypical subordinates have both the properties of basic categories (cf. table 7.3), and so they should be easy to use. Contrary to the usual basic-level advantage, boxing glove should be preferred to glove and penguin to bird. And in fact, this is just what Murphy and Brownell found (see also Jolicoeur et al. 1984). (Note that this result should warn us against taking the word "level" too literally in talking about the basic level of categorization. Although penguin and robin appear to be at the same level in one sense—both are kinds of birds—the first is treated much like a basic category and the second is clearly a subordinate. Thus, it is probably best to think of individual categories, rather than an entire "level" of categories, as being basic or subordinate.) This evidence is particularly important, because it contrasts the category structure with other potential determinants of basic categories. For example, the word *glove* is much more frequent than the phrase *boxing glove*, is learned earlier, is shorter, and so on, and yet people are faster at categorizing boxing gloves as a boxing glove than as a glove. If the basic-level advantage resulted from some names being preferred to others (due to frequency, etc.), then glove would be the basic category for all kinds of gloves.

Murphy and Brownell (1985) further tested the differentiation explanation by experimentally manipulating the distinctiveness of subordinate categories. Consider a subordinate category trial that a subject might see in a typical experiment. First, the name "robin" appears on the screen. After a certain period of time, the name disappears, and a picture of a robin appears. This may appear easy to answer, but the subject must make sure that the picture is indeed a robin and not a lark or dove. (On some trials, difficult foils like these would appear.) Because subordinate categories like robin are not very distinctive, this decision is rather difficult. In contrast, if the category name had been at the basic level, "bird," then no difficult distinction would have been required. That is, if the picture were not a bird, it would have been something that looks quite different (perhaps a dog or snake). It is the similarity of robins to related subordinates, which are directly experienced on false trials, that makes it a difficult category to verify on true trials.

Murphy and Brownell reasoned that the distinctiveness of subordinates could be reduced somewhat by changing the nature of the false trials in this experimental design. In their Experiment 2, the false trials consisted of category names and pictures that were completely unrelated. So, if the category name were "robin," the picture on a false trial might be of a car or a hammer. Thus, subjects no longer had to worry about the distinctiveness of subordinates (or any category) in this experiment, because they no longer had to distinguish robins from larks, jays or doves— such false trials never occurred. It took subjects some time to realize the nature of the false trials that were being used, but by the end of the experiment, subjects were in fact *faster* at the subordinate level than at the basic level. Since subordinates are slightly more informative than basic categories, they actually become fastest when distinctiveness is equated across category levels. This result suggests that the lack of distinctiveness of the subordinates is responsible for their usual slowness in categorization tasks, as the differentiation explanation proposes.

The Other Levels

One might wonder why, if the basic level is so advantageous, people form concepts at different levels. Of course, it is not only the ease of thinking about a concept that determines whether it will exist. It is often useful to have extremely technical or detailed concepts that are not of great use on most occasions, but that are important for some specific endeavors. Experts in a field likely require much more specific, detailed concepts than novices do. If one becomes an expert on a subclass of insects, one can hardly call all of them *bugs*—precise categories will be necessary. But by the same token, extremely general categories may be useful as well. For example, sometimes one just wants "something to read" without caring whether it is a book, magazine, or newspaper. Scientists may find generalities that are true of all mammals or arthropods or animals. Such generalizations require categories that are more general than beetle and horse.

Subordinate Level Categories

Subordinate categories have not been the subject of much investigation. (This is less true in the study of children's concepts, as will be discussed in chapter 10.) However, studies comparing all three levels of categorization have suggested some ways in which subordinates differ from the higher levels. As already mentioned, subordinates are more informative than basic categories and are also less distinctive. What new information is added in going from the basic to the subordinate level? In general, subordinates seem to differ from their basic category in terms of perceptible details. That is, subordinates share the shape and general function of their basic category but provide additional information about specific details of the object (Tversky and Hemenway 1984). For example, different chairs tend to have the same parts: a back, a seat, legs, and possibly arms. A dining room chair tends to have a taller back and to be made out of wood. An armchair tends to be upholstered and (obviously) to have arms. An office chair tends to swivel rather than to have legs. In each of these cases, the basic shape, function and parts of most chairs are found in the subordinates, but there is a modification in some part or attribute, along with a consequent minor modification of function (e.g., an office chair allows you to swivel in order to work at different parts of your office). This is a typical way in which subordinates provide more information than their basic-level categories. This pattern has been proposed as a possible explanation for the basic-level advantage. In particular, it has been suggested that the fact that members of basic categories share distinctive parts (but other levels do not) could explain their processing advantages. However, at this point, the evidence seems to favor the differentiation explanation, as a basic-level advantage can be found when normal parts are not present in the stimuli; see Tversky and Hemenway (1984) and Murphy (1991) for discussion.

Because basic categories are more familiar and more generally helpful, there appears to be a convention in discourse that people name objects by the basic category label unless the information needed in the subordinate label is particularly relevant (Cruse 1977; Murphy and Brownell 1985). For example, if you were to tell someone, "My Jaguar is parked right outside," you would be taken as boasting of owning an expensive sports car. For most purposes, knowing that your *car* is parked outside would be sufficient; it is only when the information added by the subordinate is particularly relevant that it should be used (e.g., "We can't all fit in my Jaguar."). Even when there is no question of boasting, using the subordinate when it is not necessary seems peculiar. For example, if there were only one book on the table and you were to say "Could you hand me that paperback novel?" your addressee would wonder why you used this expression rather than *book*. Subordinate labels are useful, however, when there is a domain that contains many members of a basic-level category that need to be distinguished. While at the dog show, speakers should not refer to every animal as *dog*, or else confusion will result.

In short, subordinates generally indicate minor changes in the features from those usually expected in the basic category, but they preserve the general parts and functions associated with their basic category. They are useful in making fine distinctions when called for, but otherwise tend not to be used in discourse.

Superordinates

The superordinate level of categorization has been the subject of more research than the subordinate level. Much of this work has come about in the developmental literature, because young children have great difficulty learning superordinate categories (Horton and Markman 1980; Rosch et al. 1976). Although I cannot explore the developmental issues in depth here, I will describe some of the results of Ellen Markman's studies of superordinate categories in adults and children. Markman (1985) pointed out a somewhat surprising aspect of superordinate names: They are often mass nouns, rather than count nouns. Count nouns are words like *chair*, which can be pluralized and preceded by a number: *five chairs, all the dogs, some kettles*. In contrast, mass nouns, which usually refer to homogeneous masses or substances, cannot be directly counted or pluralized; all the following are ungrammatical in neutral situations: *five rices, all the muds, some waters*. (There are actually interpretations of these phrases that are grammatical, but they usually require assuming a missing element or an unusual interpretation—such as *waters* referring to oceans.) Mass nouns generally require a *classifier* preceding them in order to be counted, and it is the classifier that is pluralized: *five grains of rice, all the piles of mud, some pails of water*. Semantically, mass nouns often refer to substances like mud that cannot be easily separated into individual parts and so are treated as an indistinguishable whole.

Markman's discovery that superordinates are often mass nouns can be illustrated with the following examples from English: *furniture, jewelry, clothing, food*, and *reading material*. One would not say "I have only two furnitures in this room," but instead "I have only two pieces of furniture." However, the basic-level names for furniture are almost all count nouns. One can say "I have four chairs/sofas/tables/ lamps/beds/stereo sets...." That is, examples of furniture are not homogeneous masses like mud, but individual objects; yet, syntactically, *furniture* is a mass noun. This puzzling fact is not a quirk of English. In fact, Markman showed that it was true in a wide variety of languages from different language families. For example, 16 of the 18 languages she sampled treated the word corresponding to *food* as a mass noun, but none of the 18 languages treated *egg* as a mass noun, and only one treated *apple* as a mass noun.

Markman argued that this syntactic difference between superordinate and basic-level names reflects the way that superordinate names are normally used. In many cases, superordinates are used to refer to collections of a number of different items. For example, in talking about a single couch, one is very unlikely to refer to it in a form like "Let's move that piece of furniture." One would be much more likely to use *furniture* in referring to a couch, two tables and some chairs all at once, as in "Let's move the furniture before we begin painting." In fact, this property of superordinates has been verified in written text (Wisniewski and Murphy 1989): Basic-level names are most likely to be used to refer to single objects (70% of the time), whereas superordinates are more likely to be used to refer to groups or an entire class of objects (77% of the time). Markman's argument, then, is that this pattern of usage has the effect of making us think of superordinates as referring to multiple objects.

There are three main pieces of evidence (beyond the linguistic patterns just described) backing Markman's conjecture (and see chapter 10 for more discussion). First, when young children are taught new superordinates, they learn them slightly better when the superordinate is used as a mass noun during training (Markman 1985). Second, young children will sometimes act as if they think that a superordinate name must refer to multiple objects. For example, they might say that a group of animals together can be called *animal*, but will deny this of a single cow. When learning novel superordinates, even older children make this error (Markman, Horton and McLanahan 1980). Third, in work on adults, Murphy and Wisniewski (1989) showed that subjects were relatively faster at identifying objects at the superordinate level when they were presented in groups. When objects were presented in isolation, basic categorization was significantly faster than superordinate categorization, as usual. For example, a single couch would be categorized faster as a couch than as furniture. However, when the couch was shown as part of a living room scene, it was categorized equally fast as furniture and as a couch: Presenting objects in groups aided superordinate classification. In sum, there is evidence that the representation of superordinates may be different from that of lower levels of categorization. How these different types of representations are reconciled is not fully known.

In more recent work, Wisniewski, Imai, and Casey (1996) suggested that there is an important difference between superordinates that have mass names, like *furniture* and those that have count names, like *animal*. They argued that the mass superordinates refer to collections of objects that occur together (as in Markman's suggestion), but that count superordinates are taxonomic categories that are interpreted as describing individual objects. They provided evidence that exemplars of mass superordinates occur together more often than do exemplars of count superordinates. When people list features of items, they are more likely to list locations of mass superordinates, suggesting that the co-occurrence of such items is important. In contrast, people are less likely to list parts for mass superordinates, because parts are properties of individual items.

Thus, it may be that superordinate categories are not entirely homogeneous. There may be principled differences between them that can be predicted based on the properties of their names. Wisniewski et al. (1996) may take this conclusion to an extreme, however, in arguing that "… it is inappropriate to view a mass super-ordinate as a taxonomic category in which an object is linked to the category by an IS A KIND OF [IS-A] relation" (p. 292). Although they do find that members of mass superordinates occur together, for example, it is also the case that members of many taxonomic categories occur together (e.g., trees, cushions, grackles). Further-more, although mass superordinates had fewer parts listed than did count super-ordinates, they still had a fair number listed (8.1 parts per category, in comparison to 17.5 for count superordinates). Even mass superordinates give some information about individual category members (e.g., items of clothing are likely to be made of cloth, to be worn, to be colored; jewelry is likely to be made of some valuable material, to be worn on the outside of clothes). It seems more likely that there is a mixture of "taxonomic" properties (things that are true of individual items) and "collective" properties in superordinates, and the mass/count distinction corre-sponds to the relative amount of the two kinds of information rather than to a dis-tinct boundary.

Another important difference between superordinates and lower levels was noted by Rosch et al. (1976) and Tversky and Hemenway (1984). When subjects are asked to list the properties of different categories, they are very likely to list abstract or functional properties for superordinates. In contrast, specific categories are more likely to have parts and concrete properties listed. It seems likely that the abstract nature of superordinates is what encourages children to think of them as referring to groups of objects. For example, if children do not immediately see what is common to all furniture (which differ widely in shape and specific function), they may tend to interpret the word *furniture* as referring to the collection of sofa, bookshelves, table and chairs in the living room. It is only with greater experience and sophistication that they can perceive the underlying functional properties common to furniture.

In summary, subordinate and superordinate categories are opposites in many respects. Superordinates have only a few features in common, and these tend to be abstract, functional properties. Subordinates have many features in common, but most are also properties of their basic category; their novel properties tend to be minor perceptual or functional modifications of the typical properties at the basic level. These different category structures have the similar effect of making the two levels more difficult to use. They are both harder to learn, and children do not seem to know the correct meanings of either level right away. Speakers tend to avoid describing individual objects with names at either level. Nonetheless, both super-ordinates and subordinates are necessary for people to represent the groupings of entities in some situations.

The Basic Level in Nonobject Domains

The notion of a basic level within a hierarchical category structure was initially developed by researchers studying object concepts but has since been applied to a wide variety of nonobject domains, including person categories (Cantor and Mischel 1979), personality traits (John, Hampson, and Goldberg 1991), psychodiagnostic categories (Cantor et al. 1980), emotions (Shaver et al. 1987), actions and events (Morris and Murphy 1990; Rifkin 1985), scenes (Tversky and Hemenway 1983), and computer programming operations (Adelson 1985). In many of these cases, re-searchers found strong parallels between object and nonobject domains. Thus, the findings of a basic level are generalizable across diverse categories. However, there are also important differences between object and some kinds of nonobject cate-gories, making the interpretation of such differences difficult.

One problem with some of this research is that the category hierarchy and the categories themselves do not always seem to be ones that people normally use. For example, person categories that have been studied, such as committed person or sup-porter of the community orchestra may not be particularly widespread, and event categories such as going to a horror movie may not be a separate concept for many people. Part of the problem is that categories in some domains have no fixed names, making it harder to identify and study them. I am not saying that people do not have categories for personalities or events but that it can be difficult to know exactly what they are and what they should be called. In some studies, there have not been adequate measures taken to ensure that the tested categories are in fact the cate-gories that the subjects normally use.

Another point to keep in mind when comparing the organization of concepts in object and nonobject domains is that domains can differ in important ways. Objects have many concrete, perceptual features (e.g., is red, has legs), while nonobjects often possess more dispositional, abstract features (e.g., is greedy, is intended to entertain). Similarly, the concepts in these domains may not be organized hierarchically in every case. For example, John et al. (1991) studied trait categories such as being talented and being musical. However, it is unclear whether traits are organized hierarchically. Is being musical a kind of being talented? Or is being talented *part of* being musical? Although one can ask subjects to list features and to categorize traits in a way analogous to what Rosch et al. (1976) did with object categories and report analogous results, if the traits are not organized in IS-A hierarchies, then they could not have a basic level of categorization that is like that of object categories.

Researchers in some domains have developed nonhierarchical ways of relating different concepts. For example, Vallecher and Wegner (1987) have argued that actions can be conceptualized on different teleological levels. The same action could be thought of as pressing buttons, making a phone call, or initiating a friendship. Such goal-oriented categories do not form an IS-A hierarchy as found in object concepts: Pressing buttons is not a kind of phone call, but pressing buttons might be done in order to make a phone call, which might be done in order to initiate a friendship. The hierarchies described in this chapter, then, probably cannot account for all the ways people have of thinking about people, events, situations, scenes and other nonobject categories.

Although it seems safe to say that there are probably basic categories in many domains besides the much-studied realm of objects, it is also true that studies of those domains have not been as careful and deep as that of Rosch et al.'s original research. A more detailed review of studies of the basic level in nonobject concepts can be found in Murphy and Lassaline (1997).

Expertise

When Rosch et al. (1976) first proposed the concept of a basic level, they also noted that the specificity and nature of the basic level might well depend on a subject's expertise in the domain. In particular, they suggested that experts would know much more about categories at specific levels of abstraction. Thus, although categories like trees might well be salient for tree experts, more specific categories like maples and birches would be even more salient, because experts would know many features that are distinctive to these categories.

Although Rosch et al. did not explicitly test this hypothesis, the anthropological literature provided some evidence to support it. First, Rosch et al. themselves found that the basic level of their subjects' concepts of plants and animals was one level higher than that found in anthropological studies of people in nonindustrialized societies (Berlin 1992; Berlin et al. 1973). Subsequently, Dougherty (1978) compared the naming of different types of plants by Berkeley, California children with naming by Tzeltal Mayan children. She discovered that the American children named plants at a level higher than the biological genus (e.g., they used *tree* rather than *maple*), whereas Tzeltal children used genus-level names (like *maple*) very often. She concluded that "In terms of both the number of distinctions acquired and the specificity to which classifications can be extended, the eight-year-old Berkeley child lags well behind the six-year-old Tzeltal child. As Chamber's (n.d.) evidence shows the ethnobotanical knowledge of urban American adults may develop minimally beyond that of the eight-year-old child" (p. 75). In short, it seems that not only individuals, but whole societies or cultures may differ in their preferred level of categorization (see Malt 1995, for a review). These differences are domain-specific, however: Although urban citizens may well not have elaborate biological categories, they do have elaborate categories of colors, technological devices, legal terms, and so on. Our urban society generally is not familiar enough with biological kinds to classify them at specific levels, whereas isolated peoples living "closer to nature" clearly have much more knowledge about the natural environment, though they do not have as much knowledge about technology and science, for example. These are essentially expertise effects at the level of a whole culture.

The psychological literature has focused on individual differences in expertise and its influence on conceptual structure. Some of this literature has explicitly addressed the issue of hierarchical classification, but most of it has not. Nonetheless, even the latter has implications for understanding the basic level.

The most complete study of expertise and level of categorization was carried out by Tanaka and Taylor (1991), and I will discuss it in some detail. Their study is of particular interest for two main reasons. First, they examined categorization at the basic, subordinate and superordinate levels. Second, they used a within-subject design, in which they tested each subject in an area of expertise and in a domain outside that area. This design avoids problems of irrelevant differences between experts and novices that might explain the results. (For example, perhaps experts are smarter or more dedicated than novices, which could explain their different performance in an experimental task.) Their study examined the concepts of birdwatchers and dog experts for both birds and dogs.

First, Tanaka and Taylor asked their subjects to list features of categories at all three levels. In their novice domain, subjects listed many features at the basic level and fewer at the subordinate level. (For consistency, I will refer to the category level of dog, bird, cat, etc. as the basic level, even though the results will question whether this level is truly basic for all subjects.) In their domain of expertise, subjects listed more features at the subordinate level. For example, dog experts didn't list more features of dogs than bird experts did, but they did list more features of collies. In a free-naming study, Tanaka and Taylor showed subjects pictures of a variety of objects and asked them to give the first name that came to mind. Like Rosch et al., they found that people virtually never use superordinate labels. In their novice domain, subjects produced basic-level names the majority of times (76%). In their expert domain, subjects were fairly likely to produce subordinate names. This tendency was much more pronounced for bird experts, however, who used subordinates 74% of the time, compared to 40% for dog experts; both were higher than the subordinate labeling by novices. I'll return to the difference between dog and bird experts later.

Finally, Tanaka and Taylor tested their subjects in a timed categorization task. As a speeded perceptual task, its results may be more indicative of automatic processing, rather than conscious strategies that subjects might have used in the free-naming task (e.g., birdwatchers might feel they are expected to use the most precise name they know in a free-naming task, even if it was not the first name that came to mind). In the categorization task, subjects viewed a category name, followed by a picture. They responded true or false as to whether the object depicted was in the named category.

The results in the novice domain replicated those of Rosch et al. (1976): The basic category was fastest, and the subordinate category slowest. However, in the expert domain, the pattern was different: The basic and subordinate levels were equally fast, and the superordinate level was slowest. The primary difference in the results was that the subordinate level became much faster relative to the other levels in the expert domain. Thus, this finding is consistent with the results of Tanaka and Taylor's other experiments, in showing that expertise primarily benefits the subordinate level.

Tanaka and Taylor point out that this pattern is just what would be expected from the differentiation explanation of the basic level (Murphy and Brownell 1985). According to that explanation, subordinates are usually hampered by being relatively nondistinctive—they do not have many features that are unique. However, Tanaka and Taylor's feature listing results show that experts do know a number of features unique to subordinates—their subordinates *are* distinctive. Furthermore, subordinates are more informative than basic-level categories. As a result, experts' subordinates are much like their basic categories from the perspective of category structure. For experts, then, there may be no single level of categorization that is "basic" according to the classic definition. Birdwatchers can easily use the category bird, but they can also easily use the categories cardinal, plover, or kestrel.

Other studies of the relation between expertise and category structure have taken a somewhat different approach, namely, investigating how experts' advanced knowledge might influence their concepts. Typically, these studies have not examined different levels of categorization, so I will only describe them briefly here. They are relevant, however, because they address whether experts differ from novices primarily in specific or more general categories.

Chi, Feltovich, and Glaser (1981) examined the categories of physics problems formed by experts and novices. They discovered that novices (students who had done well in the introductory physics course) tended to group the problems based on superficial properties. For example, novices tended to categorize problems with inclined planes together, separately from problems with springs or those involving pulleys. In contrast, experts (advanced physics graduate students) categorized problems according to the physical principle involved in their solution. In some cases, this meant grouping together problems that involved rather different objects, such as a spring and an inclined plane. Although novices had taken the course that involved problems of this sort, they did not have the facility with theoretical knowledge that would allow them to see past the superficial similarities of the problems.

Murphy and Wright (1984) examined the feature listings of concepts from child psychopathology. Their subjects ranged from complete novices (college undergraduates with no experience with a clinical population) to experts with many years' experience in diagnosing and treating children with psychological disorders. Surprisingly, Murphy and Wright discovered that the categories of the novices tended to be more distinctive than those of the experts. The main reason for this was that novices only knew a few features of the category, which were usually superficially related to the category name. For example, they listed features such as "angry" and "hits other kids" for the category of aggressive-impulsive children, and they listed features such as "feels sad" for the depressed-withdrawn category. In contrast, experts in clinical psychology listed the features that they believe underlie many psychological disorders for more than one category. For example, all three categories of children were said to have the symptoms "feels sad" and "angry," not just depressed and aggressive children, respectively.

Together, the Chi et al. (1981) and the Murphy and Wright studies suggest that expertise may not only have the effect of making categories more distinctive, as Tanaka and Taylor (1991) found with bird and dog experts. Murphy and Wright found that experts knew both more distinctive features and more common features than the novices. Chi et al.'s results show that experts may notice underlying similarities between items that appear to be quite different. Thus, the influence of expertise on levels of categorization is probably complex. Experts may be able to identify objects more readily into specific categories than novices can, but they may also be able to notice commonalities across a domain that novices are not familiar with (e.g., the commonalities that allow spiders, shrimp, insects, and crabs to be grouped together as arthropods). The findings that experts have more abstract knowledge that unifies the instances of a domain does not conflict with the story derived from Tanaka and Taylor's results, but it does suggest a more complex effect of expertise that is not fully understood.

Thus, expertise may not be susceptible to a simple account like: "Experts' preferred level of categorization is lower than that of novices." It may be that some experts have different concepts or ways of organizing the domain than novices do, in which case their taxonomies could be different from novices'. Whether this happens probably depends on the nature of the domain and of expertise within that domain. For example, Tanaka and Taylor proposed that the differences between dog and bird experts they found may be due to the different nature of expertise of these two groups. Dog experts often tend to focus on one or two breeds of dogs that they raise and show, and they become extremely familiar with the properties of those breeds. In contrast, birdwatchers attempt to experience a wide range of birds and to identify many different species as quickly and reliably as possible. This difference in the nature of expertise might account for why the bird experts were more likely to supply subordinate-level names in the free-naming task. So, some experts may have deep knowledge about a few categories, whereas the others may have less detailed knowledge but be familiar with many more categories.

In short, there is considerable research still to be done on the nature of expertise and its effect on conceptual organization. Expertise may have some influence on the preferred level of categorization, but this influence will likely depend on the specific domain and on the nature of the expertise that subjects bring to it.

Empirical Conclusion

The hierarchical structure of categories is a well-established phenomenon, which has been identified in many different cultures. People rely on such hierarchies in order to be able to generalize their knowledge productively: Once you learn that all animals breathe, you don't need to relearn it for dogs, poodles, miniature poodles, and so on. Nonetheless, it is still not fully known whether this hierarchical structure is built into the conceptual system, in the form of taxonomies in the head, or is instead the result of an inferential process. There is considerable evidence against a purely pre-stored hierarchy, but it may well be that there is a mixture of different kinds of conceptual structures. Some concepts may be explicitly connected by IS-A links (e.g., whale and mammal), whereas other hierarchical relations may have to be computed (e.g., car seat and chair). The field is still awaiting an integrated model of all these phenomena.

Findings of a basic level provide a more consistent picture. Most experiments are consistent with the differentiation explanation of why basic concepts are preferred. This explanation is primarily a structural one: It refers to the number of features known about each category and their overlap with the features of other categories. It can be applied to any domain, once the features people know about the categories are determined. Perhaps it is worth emphasizing that this explanation is based on the structure of the information people know about the categories, not environ-mental structure per se. Although the properties of the environment will certainly strongly affect one's concepts of the world, we have seen a number of cases in which the basic level is influenced by expertise and cultural knowledge and interest. Thus, the differentiation explanation applies to what is known of the categories. The question of whether basic categories are basic "out there" in the world is one that psychology is not prepared to answer.

Surprisingly, given this overwhelming empirical support, some recent writers have taken to criticizing the overall notion of basic categories. For example, Mandler (1998, p. 289) complains that the quantitative measures for basic categories have been largely unsuccessful and points to findings about the variability of the basic level across domains and cultures as casting doubt on the whole concept of a basic level. (Mandler also argues that even Rosch et al. did not find the basic level where they expected it for biological categories. However, this seems an unfair criticism to make of the very first experimental study of the basic-level phenomenon. It isn't surprising that the authors' original expectations in advance of any data were in-correct for one of their domains. Furthermore, the problem for biological categories arises from the cultural differences discussed above, since Rosch et al. based their predictions on anthropological studies of nonindustrialized cultures. Those cultural differences confirm the differentiation explanation presented here rather than casting doubt on it.) However, such criticisms have not sorted through the entire set of evi-dence and explanations for basic categories given here and proposed an alternative account for them—they are entirely negative in character. In fact, the evidence for a basic level is extremely impressive. Reading between the lines, I suspect that such criticisms assume that the basic level is an immutable property of categories that is predictable from the "objective category" itself. Findings of different basic categories across cultures or development would therefore cast doubt on this notion. (However, it is also significant that every culture seems to have a preferred level of categorization, as concluded by Malt 1995, in a review of the anthropological literature.) As just discussed, basic-level structure is a psychological construct, which depends on what people know about the categories, and which can only be identified by behavioral tests. To be compelling, such criticisms need to be backed by alternative, concrete proposals for the phenomena Rosch, Mervis and their colleagues discovered. What is most impressive about the basic category construct is how it predicts advantages in many different tasks, as summarized in table 7.2. No other explanation has been offered that even attempts to account for these advantages.

Research outside the area of object categories has been less certain in demonstrating basic-level structure. In general, this does not seem to be a shortcoming of the theory of the basic level but rather a problem in identifying the categories that are actually known and used by subjects in each domain, especially when the categories do not have familiar verbal labels. Also, studies in other domains have often relied on a single task to measure basic-level structure, rather than repeating the process of converging operations used by Rosch et al. (1976). In some cases, studies have simply assumed that the concepts are hierarchically organized, rather than empirically demonstrating this. One goal for future work on basic categories is to elucidate the conceptual structures of new domains in a more complete way.

Theoretical Evaluations

Prototype Theory

When discussing feature models that might explain category judgments and the hierarchical structure of concepts (e.g., Smith et al. 1974), I was essentially providing the prototype theory for those phenomena. That is, concepts are thought to be represented by descriptions of their common components. One concept can be judged to be a subordinate of another if its features are a superset of the other's (see table 7.1). Because prototype theory thinks of categorization as being probabilistic, it does not claim that all of the features of the superordinate will be exactly found in the subordinate concept (Hampton 1993). Instead, it will only require that some criterion number of features (weighted by their importance) is necessary. Furthermore, typicality effects can be explained by the assumption that atypical categories share fewer features with their superordinates, as seems to be the case (Rosch and Mervis 1975). For example, an ostrich's features do not match the features of the category bird as well as a blue jay's features do, and so it is more difficult to categorize. This theory can explain the finding that it is often more difficult to make "long-distance" categorizations like bulldog-animal than closer categorizations like bulldog-dog, by making the reasonable assumption that the closer two items are in the hierarchy, the more features they share (assuming typicality is held constant).

In the above analysis, I have been assuming that category relations are computed rather than prestored. However, there is no reason that prototype theory could not be represented in a semantic network of the sort suggested by Collins and Quillian (1969), in which category relations are prestored. However, one would then need to make further assumptions, such as the IS-A links being weaker between atypical items and their superordinates, and one would also have to explain why long-distance categorizations are not always slower (e.g., why dog-animal is no slower than dog-mammal), if a network is being traversed. Since these phenomena are predicted very naturally by featural overlap, the notion of a prestored hierarchy seems less parsimonious at the present.

Basic-level structure does not appear to be a necessary prediction of prototype theory. The phenomenon is certainly consistent with prototype theory, however, as it can be explained by the number of features that a concept has and how many of those features it shares with similar concepts. Dog is a basic-level concept, then, because it is informative (i.e., has many features) and distinctive (i.e., does not share the majority of those features with bat, horse, mole, and other mammals). So, it is very easy to explain basic-level structure in terms of feature descriptions of the sort that prototype theory has proposed. However, there is nothing in prototype theory itself that predicts (so far as I can tell) that differentiation is such a critical variable. As Murphy and Smith (1982) pointed out, it could have been that the most abstract categories were easiest to use, because they have fewer features: Identifying something as a tool might have been easiest, because there are only a small number of features common to tools that need to be checked. (However, as mentioned above, the features at the superordinate level tend to be much more abstract than those at the lower levels, so a prediction based purely on the number of features is difficult to make.) Similarly, identifying something at the lowest level could have been easiest, because it would be expected to match an object most closely: A picture of a cross-cutting handsaw (one of Rosch et al.'s 1976 stimuli) is closest to the category description of cross-cutting handsaws, and less close to the descriptions of saws or tools.

In short, I think that one could have made very different predictions from proto-type theory about which level of categorization would be easiest if one had not known anything about the phenomenon in advance. So, basic-level structure per se does not appear to be a confirmation of prototype theory. However, the differentia-tion explanation I have offered is very easy to integrate into the weighted-feature prototype model (chapter 3) and so supports this approach in a general sense.

The Exemplar View

For the most part, exemplar models of concepts have not attempted to account for basic-level structure. Although the existence of basic categories is not generally said to pose a particular problem for exemplar models, accounting in detail for the per-formance advantages may be more difficult. More critically, the entire notion of hierarchical structure does not flow naturally from an exemplar view.

First, how can we explain the existence and advantage of the basic level in an exemplar approach? Recall that the exemplar view proposes that people remember instances of concepts and that when they retrieve a new instance, they access other instances that are similar to it and use their category membership to categorize the new item. The differentiation explanation given for the basic-level advantage seems general enough to fit an exemplar approach to concepts. For example, the factor of informativeness can be interpreted as the similarity of items within a category. The more similar the exemplars are, the more informative the category generally is, be-cause the more properties they will have in common. Similarly, distinctiveness can be interpreted as the dissimilarity of exemplars across categories. If particular dogs are different from particular cows, then these two categories are distinct from one another. So, the overall structural differences between categories is easy to describe in terms of exemplars.

At the same time, there are difficulties in specifying an exemplar-based *process* of categorization that leads to the basic-level advantage. Let's suppose you see Wilbur, a bulldog, and have to decide if it is a dog (the basic category). You will now re-trieve other items that are similar to Wilbur, most of which are presumably dogs, and few of which are other animals. Therefore, you should be fast to identify Wilbur as a dog. However, the exact same thing is true in deciding whether Wilbur is a bulldog. As described in chapter 3, exemplar models are sensitive to very close similarity to instances (e.g., via Medin and Schaffer's 1978 multiplicative similarity rule, or the Shepard exponential similarity rule, Nosofsky 1984). So, remembered items that are very close to Wilbur are given great weight, and those that differ in a few features have hardly any effect at all. Given this, the items that are highly similar to Wilbur would almost all be bulldogs, and so categorizing Wilbur as a bulldog would be quite easy. This would especially be true in a psychology experiment, in which a clear picture is shown of Wilbur in a canonical position, yet the basic-level advantage is consistently found in such experiments. If the exemplar view is to predict the basic-level advantage here, it must assume that items have very high (not just moderate) similarity to members of *other* subordinate categories, which add up to a higher similarity score for dog. That is, Wilbur must be quite similar to a dachshund or terrier in order to speed up basic-level categorization and slow down subordinate categorization. It isn't clear that this assumption is accurate. (For example, J. D. Smith and Minda 2000, have noted that in some psychology experiments, only a single, highly similar exemplar actually influences the decision of exemplar models. If this is true in natural categorization as well, then the exemplar model would not produce a basic-level advantage.)

Now consider superordinate categorization. If you are asked if Wilbur is an animal, you will retrieve very similar items and find that they are all animals. It must be at least as easy to categorize Wilbur as an animal as it is to categorize him as a dog, since all the dog exemplars you retrieved are also animals, and it is very likely that any nondog exemplars you retrieved (if any) are also animals. It is hard to understand, then, why an exemplar model would predict slower categorization at the superordinate level. However, superordinates are often the worst level in categorization tasks (e.g., Murphy and Brownell 1985).

One way out for exemplar models is to propose that the range of exemplars retrieved is different for different questions. For example, when asked about superordinates, perhaps subjects consider less similar instances than when asked about basic categories. Without some further justification, this proposal is very ad hoc. Why would subjects use this different strategy, which only results in slower, less accurate responses? Why not rely on close similarity for all decisions? Explaining categorization performance at different levels of categorization, then, is something of a puzzle for the exemplar model.[8]

The problem of exemplar models goes even deeper, however. In most experiments testing this view, subjects learn two categories and then are tested on old and new items. Thus, there is only one level of categorization, and every item is tagged with one category name. But in natural categories, each item is in many categories simultaneously. If I see a squirrel run across my path on the way to work, do I encode that as a gray squirrel, a squirrel, a mammal, an animal *and* an entity? This seems rather excessive. However, if I don't encode it as a mammal, then how do I decide how to answer questions like "Are squirrels mammals?" or to judge whether a picture of a squirrel should be categorized as a mammal? Exemplar theory requires that I retrieve instances similar to the test item and see whether they have the category name that is being tested. If I don't encode the squirrel on the path as a mammal, then wouldn't it later count as evidence against the proposition that squirrels are mammals?

This problem with exemplar models is illustrated by a recent article by Palmeri (1999), who investigated how different models, two of them being exemplar approaches, could explain hierarchical classification. Palmeri found it necessary to have different simulations of each model learn the different hierarchical levels, making a "virtual" hierarchy. That is, no single model actually learned that Wilbur is a dog and Wilbur is a bulldog; rather, different models learned these two facts. This further supports my claim that exemplar models as they currently stand are ill-equipped to handle hierarchies—and, indeed, any form of multiple categorization.[9]

In order to explain how people can answer questions about category membership, exemplar theory may have to claim that every exemplar in memory is encoded with all of the categories that it is a member of.[10] Although not a logical impossibility, this suggestion does not seem at all plausible. Furthermore, even if we do assume this, more work is needed to explain why there is a basic-level advantage in categorization tasks. If all squirrels are encoded as mammals, then any evidence that X is a squirrel will also be evidence that X is a mammal. One way out of this conundrum might be to assume that only one or two categories are encoded with each exemplar. It may be that most of the time you see squirrels, you encode them as "squirrel," but only occasionally as "gray squirrel" or "animal." When you retrieve instances that are similar to the test item in an experiment, you would get many that are identified as squirrels, but few as animals or gray squirrels, which could account for the basic-level advantage. This explanation is rather circular, however. We want our theory of concepts to explain the notion of a basic level. This explanation merely assumes that basic categories are better (for some unexplained reason) and therefore are encoded with instances more often. One could attempt to refer to other, nonconceptual variables as explaining why the basic category is most often encoded with the exemplar, such as word frequency and the like. However, these variables have generally been shown not to account for the advantage (Corter and Gluck 1992; Murphy 1991; Murphy and Smith 1982), so considerable work would need to be done to explain hierarchical classification on the exemplar view. Finally, if most squirrel exemplars are not encoded as mammals or animals, then how does one evaluate sentences like (as in Collins and Quillian 1969, and many experiments since) "All squirrels are mammals"? The exemplar representations would seem to give the wrong answer to this question, as most retrieved squirrel exemplars would not be coded as mammals.

Overall, then, there are many puzzles about how to account for hierarchical classification in general and the basic-level advantage in particular from the perspective of the exemplar view. It is too early to say that these results are incompatible with the view, but it is not too early to complain that insufficient attention has been given to these concerns by proponents of this theory. As hierarchical structure is a major component of human categorization, it is important for any theory of concepts to explain the existence of different levels of categorization, as well as the basic-level advantage.

The Knowledge View

The knowledge view is perfectly consistent with the idea that concepts are descriptions of some kind, and so it is also consistent with the feature-based explanation of hierarchical structure given here. The differentiation explanation of the basic level is not so easily related to the knowledge view. It is primarily a structural explanation. It refers to the number of features known about each category and their overlap with the features of other categories. It can be applied to any domain once the features of the categories are determined. Thus, it does not depend on complex knowledge structures about a domain, which is one reason why basic-level phenomena can be demonstrated with artificial stimuli and in many different domains. This ubiquity suggests that the basic level is not heavily dependent on knowledge (Malt 1995), and so it is not predicted by the knowledge view. On the other hand, the knowledge view also considers concepts to be summary representations, and so basic concepts can easily be conceived of as those with many features and with few features in common with other categories. That is, unlike the exemplar model, there is no particular difficulty in representing the relations between categories in a way that can accommodate basic-level structure. Furthermore, the knowledge view is certainly consistent with the notion that people often have general category knowledge of the sort "whales are mammals." So, it seems that the knowledge view does not explain the basic-category phenomena but is fully consistent with them.

The knowledge view expects there to be structural phenomena of concepts it does not explain. That view does not argue that everything is due to background knowledge—some of the basic content of a concept must be learned, and that learning process is no doubt subject to structural constraints that cut across domains.

There are however some signs even in this literature that knowledge has an effect. For example, effects of expertise and cultural variation show that different interests and amount of knowledge can affect the basic level. In our culture, people know less about biological kinds and so may have a higher basic level of categorization than do people from other cultures. Whether this is truly an effect of "knowledge" in the sense of domain-wide principles is not entirely clear, but it is clear that the environment itself does not completely determine the basic level.

Because domain knowledge tends to be about broad categories of things rather than specific items, it is perhaps more likely to have an effect on superordinate categorization. A. Markman and Wisniewski (1997) argued that superordinates share general frameworks or schemata rather than specific features. Consider vehicles for example. Although not all vehicles have wheels, they all have something that allows them to move over or through their medium. Not all have a steering wheel, but they all have some mechanism for turning. Although vehicles differ in what they primarily carry, they are all designed to carry something, from a single driver to many tons of oil. These kinds of generalities are abstract ones that relate to the overall function and place of vehicles in our society, which is what is captured by general domain knowledge. So, one cannot say whether a given vehicle will have wheels, but one knows that it will have wheels or wings or a hull or treads, and so on, because these parts are necessary to allow the vehicle to move. The general schematic structure of vehicles and other superordinates is tied to the knowledge we have about why such things exist and how they operate.

All this having been said, I should reiterate that the knowledge approach does not seem to be actually predicting the basic-level phenomena. Its proponents would probably argue that background knowledge is a precondition for category learning and use in general, but that it does not provide all the details of category structure. For example, people list properties such as "has four legs" for the category of dogs, but they do not list "is found in North America," "is not found in Antarctica," "will eat pork products on Fridays," "can be the same color as a bear," and other uninformative features. The knowledge view attempts to explain why people list features such as "has four legs" but not these (see chapter 6), and so it may be a necessary part of explaining the informativeness and distinctiveness of basic categories, even if it does not directly predict them.[11]

Conclusion

Of the three views, the prototype view seems to do the best in explaining levels of categorization phenomena, because summary representations most naturally explain the notion of category hierarchies and because the differentiation explanation proposed to explain basic-level structure is most easily construed in terms of concept prototypes. At this stage, it is simply not clear how exemplar models will either generate hierarchical structures or predict basic-level advantages in conceptual processing. What is surprising is that there seems to be no careful attempt to address these phenomena, even though they have been important ones in concept and semantic memory research for over 25 years.

More generally, it should be noted that none of these theories actually predicted (in the true sense of anticipating the results) basic-level structure and its explanation—the account was post hoc for every theory. The reason for this is that Rosch et al.'s (1976) findings were a genuine discovery. Previous writing in philosophy and psychology on concepts did not lead us to notice these generalizations and understand their importance. In this case, then, modern experimental psychology has made an important contribution to our understanding of concepts at a descriptive level, whatever theoretical explanation is eventually found to explain it.

8

Induction

One of the major uses of categories is to make predictions about novel items. If a friend calls me up and asks me to take care of her dog, as she cannot get home, I know pretty much what to expect. Even if I have never met that individual dog, I do know about dogs in general and what care they require. I don't have to ask whether I should water the dog, feed it, vacuum it, cultivate around its roots, launder it, and so on, because I already know what sorts of things dogs need. In fact, it is exactly this sort of inference that makes categories important. Without being able to make sensible inferences about new objects, there would be very little advantage in knowing that something is a dog or couch or tree. Categorization in and of itself is not useful—it is being able to apply category knowledge that is useful.

In the present chapter, when I talk about *category-based induction*, it is this sort of inference process that I am referring to, that is, the extension of category information to a new object or category. The term *induction* is quite broad, and it is also used to refer to other aspects of conceptual processing. Most notably, induction is the kind of reasoning that one uses when drawing conclusions about the category in general, for example, in deciding that dogs generally drool and have fur based on a few observed examples. (This is induction rather than deduction because it involves drawing an uncertain inference to the category as a whole.) So, the initial learning of a category is an inductive process. But the induction referred to here occurs with categories that are already known. In one kind of induction, the target is an individual object, like my friend's dog. In another kind, one is attempting to draw conclusions about one category based on knowledge of another category. For example, if I know that labrador retrievers are very friendly, will I conclude that golden retrievers are as well?

If one thinks of categories as grouping similar items, then the basis for induction is pretty clear. Since dogs are generally similar, when I think about my friend's dog, I can assume that it shares properties common to dogs, such as needing food and water, having teeth, or barking. Thus, similarity is behind much of the logic of induction. Categories whose members are extremely similar would have stronger inductive power than those that are less similar. For this reason, more specific categories usually allow stronger inductions than general categories. If I know that my friend has a pekinese, I can be more certain of what I will have to do than if all I know is that my friend has a pet of some kind that needs care.

Category-based inductions are extremely common in communication. In talking to people, we often refer to something by a simple category name and then assume that they can draw the necessary inferences. "I have to go home because of my dog" does not require any great effort to understand, because we know that dogs require a high level of maintenance and cannot be left alone indefinitely. Speakers assume that listeners will retrieve just this information about the category and use it to comprehend the sentence (see chapter 11). One would not expect to be able to say "I have to go home because of my couch" and get away without an explanation, because couches in general do not have the high maintenance property.

It is not always clear in real life how much of an inference is derived from category-based inference and how much comes about through information specific to the individual object. For example, if you see a slavering doberman pinscher leaping to the extent of its chain, snarling and barking, you may infer that it is aggressive. Some of this may be due to your knowing that it is a doberman, but some of it is clearly due to the properties of that particular animal. It is not known how those two sources of information are integrated, as most experiments look solely at category-level information, and the object is not described beyond its category membership. One exception was the developmental study of McCarrell and Callanan (1995), who used pictures of animals with properties such as large eyes, large ears, very long legs, and so on. They found that children drew inferences such as the animals with large eyes being able to see in the dark. In a second experiment, they manipulated whether the objects sharing such features were in the same category or not. For example, children might be shown an animal with large eyes and told that it could see well in the dark. Then they would be tested on animals that were similar except that they had small eyes, or that had large eyes but differed in some other dimension. Finally, sometimes the first kind of item had the same name as the target item, and sometimes the second item did. McCarrell and Callanan found that possession of the critical feature (large eyes in this case) was the most important factor in children's making the induction (seeing well in the dark); sharing the name had only a small effect. These results suggest that information about a specific object can override category-level information. For example, if the slavering, barking, snapping dog were an irish setter, you would probably conclude that this dog was very aggressive, even if you believed that irish setters are remarkably pacific. However, when the two sources of information, category and individual, are more ambiguous, it is not clear to what degree they are integrated.

Although information about an individual may overrule it, true category-based induction can be very important. In many cases, the property one is interested in is simply not perceptible, either at the moment or permanently. I drew the inferences about my friend's dog before ever seeing it. If I were interested in biological properties of this dog, such as whether it has a spleen, I would have to base my conclusion entirely on general category information, because it would take too much effort to test a particular dog for a spleen. In these cases, people must rely on category-based induction.

Research into category-based induction has typically used a kind of reasoning task in order to investigate what influences the kinds of inductions people make. The next sections describe this task, along with the basic results obtained. A subsequent section examines how multiple categories are used in making inductions when categorization is uncertain. Finally, much work on categorical induction has been done with children; this research is discussed in chapter 10.

Rips's Induction Task

The modern study of category-based induction begins with Rips (1975), and much of the subsequent research on the topic has used techniques based on his first experiments. Rips began with measures of category structure in the domains of birds and mammals. For simplicity, let's just consider birds. He started with multidimensional scaling solutions, or spatial representations, of the structure of the bird category (from Rips, Shoben, and Smith 1973). These solutions provided information about the similarity of the birds to one another and to the prototype of birds in general. These measures of similarity and category structure were the bases for his predictions of induction.

Another important aspect of Rips's task was his choice of unfamiliar or *blank predicates*. These are predicates that people do not already have very strong beliefs about. For example, do birds have sesamoid bones? Most people do not know what sesamoid bones are (though they can make general guesses), and so they cannot answer directly based on their existing knowledge. Blank predicates like "has sesamoid bones" may tell us about category-based inductions in general, without any influence of prior knowledge about the predicate. In contrast, suppose the question were about whether birds can fly. This predicate is something that people already have many beliefs about, and so they might rely on their present knowledge rather than on induction to answer questions about it. In the category induction task, subjects are told a fact involving blank predicates for one category (or category member) and then are asked whether the predicate applies to other categories (or members). Rips used a single predicate in this study, namely whether members of a category would catch an unknown disease. For example, if ducks had this contagious disease, would robins be likely to get it? How about geese? Subjects had to provide the percentage of members of each category that they thought would catch the disease. Thus, there are two main bases for drawing the induction: the *given category* (ducks in the example) and the *target categories* (robins or geese).

Rips found that people's willingness to extend this blank predicate to a new category was increased by two things: the typicality of the given category, and the similarity of the given to the target category. For example, inductions were stronger for the given category of robins than for eagles; and an induction from geese to ducks would be stronger than from geese to cardinals. The typicality of the target category had no effect.[1] Why do these variables affect induction? The similarity of the two categories is straightforward: If two things are similar, they are likely to share properties. If ducks catch some disease, geese are likely to as well, given how similar they are in many other respects. Less obvious is why typicality makes a difference. According to Rips, the typicality of the given category bears on whether the predicate is true of the entire category. "If a new property is known to belong to a typical instance, subjects assume that it will belong to less typical instances as well, for properties of typical instances tend to be widely shared. Conversely, if the property is known to belong to atypical instances, subjects are hesitant to assume that it could belong to more typical ones, since, by definition, many of the important properties of atypical instances are idiosyncratic ..." (Rips 1975, p. 679). (I would not say that less typical items have fewer common features *by definition*, but it certainly is empirically the case, as shown by Rosch and Mervis 1975, and as discussed in chapter 2.) In short, when a robin catches the disease, people may well think that this is a disease that all birds are subject to; when a duck catches it, they are less likely to think so. This argument is supported by later findings that "category coverage" is important, as I will discuss shortly.

It is worth emphasizing, then, that Rips's account has a categorical and noncategorical component. The similarity of the given and target items is not a question of what category or categories they belong to. Indeed, the given and target items could be individual objects not known to be in any category. However, the typicality question is obviously a matter of categorization. That is, the fact that robins are typical birds is relevant to the induction from robins to ducks, on Rips's account, even though the question does not mention or ask about birds in general. Most subsequent theories of category-based induction have also used these two components, one based on the items' similarity and one using category information.

One counterintuitive consequence of Rips's model is that the induction from X to Y is not in general the same as from Y to X (see also Tversky 1977). For example, the induction from a robin to a goose is more certain than the induction from a goose to a robin. Although the similarity between the two items is the same in both directions (in Rips's model, though not in all), robin is much more typical than goose is, and so it provides a better basis for induction. This prediction was confirmed by Osherson et al. (1990), as well by Rips.

For some reason, Rips's results did not generate much interest in category-based induction, and few studies were done on the topic for a number of years. The revival of interest in this subject was probably due to the work in developmental psychology of Gelman and Markman (1986), discussed in chapter 10. As this and subsequent work made clear that induction was a complex matter that children do not master immediately, greater interest in the processes of adult induction also arose. In any case, there is now a larger body of work on how categories and category structure influence induction in adults, much of it starting from Rips's initial methods and theory.

The Osherson et al. (1990) Model of Categorical Induction

One important set of studies was carried about by Osherson, Smith and their students, who developed a formal model of reasoning that was closely related to the Rips induction task. They generally presented arguments and asked subjects to judge their confidence in the conclusion.[2] Here are two examples of such arguments (from Osherson et al. 1990). Note that the premises are written above the line, and the conclusion below the line. So, in reading the argument out loud, one should read the line as saying "therefore."

(1)   Mosquitoes use the neurotransmitter Dihedron.
       Ants use the neurotransmitter Dihedron.
       _____
       Bees use the neurotransmitter Dihedron.

(2)   Grizzly bears love onions
       Polar bears love onions.
       _____
       All bears love onions.

These arguments again use blank predicates, as most people do not know what neurotransmitters different insects use, nor do they know whether bears like onions. Such arguments are an example of category-based induction because information is provided about some categories, and then the conclusions are drawn about other categories. The conclusion categories are typically categories at the same level and in the same domain as the premise categories (e.g., bees are like ants and mosquitoes in being a type of insect—or, at least, that's what subjects believe), or else are super-ordinates to the premise categories (e.g., grizzly bears and polar bears are types of bears). Argument (1), then, is like Rips's (1975) question in which one category was given and another from the same superordinate served as a target. However, Osherson et al. allow more than one category to be in the premise, as in (1), and this will generate important phenomena, as we shall see.

Osherson et al. developed a model of how people reason about such arguments, based on the similarity of the categories involved. The model has two main parts. The first is the similarity of the premise categories to the conclusion category. In (1), this would be the similarity of mosquitoes and ants to bees; in (2), this would be the similarity of grizzly bears and polar bears to bears. For cases like the latter, the similarity of categories to a more inclusive category was calculated as the average similarity of the items to the whole category. For cases like the former, the similarity they used was the highest of the similarities of the premise to conclusion categories. For example, if mosquitoes are highly similar to bees, but ants are not very similar, the overall similarity of the premises to the conclusions would be the highest one—in this case, the similarity of mosquitoes to bees. (Osherson et al. describe all this formally, and I am slightly simplifying their proposal for expository purposes.) The first component of their model, then, is the *similarity* of the premises to the conclusion.

The second component of their model is *coverage*—how well the premises cover the smallest category that includes all the items in the problem. For example, in (1), the smallest category would be insects; in (2), it would be bears. The basic predic-tion is that when the premises are distributed across this category, subjects can be-come more confident that the property is true of the entire category. For example, suppose you know that dolphins, cows, and rabbits all use Dihedron. You might feel pretty confident that mammals in general use Dihedron. In contrast, suppose you know that dolphins, whales, and seals use Dihedron. You would probably be less confident now that all mammals use Dihedron: You can't generalize from these examples to very different mammals.[3] In general, then, the more diversity there is in the premises, the stronger your induction should be. The important thing to note, however, is that coverage is important not only in making judgments about whole categories, like mammals, but also about individual subcategories. For example, in problem (1) the question is about a specific category, bees, rather than about insects as a whole. Nonetheless, the degree to which the premise categories, mosquitoes and ants, cover the insect category should influence the answer for bees. As coverage of the smallest superordinate category increases, the strength of the argument increases.

Osherson et al. show that their model can explain a number of interesting phenomena of inductive reasoning. I will present and analyze only a subset of the phenomena they describe.

Premise typicality. In general, the more typical the item or items in the premise, the stronger the argument is. So, (3) is stronger than (4):

(3) Robins have a high potassium concentration in their blood.

     All birds have a high potassium concentration in their blood.

(4) Penguins have a high potassium concentration in their blood.

     All birds have a high potassium concentration in their blood.

This result follows from the model because robins are on average more similar to other birds than penguins are (Rosch and Mervis 1975). Thus, the model's first factor, premise-conclusion similarity, is greater for (3) than (4).

Premise diversity. The more diverse the premise categories, the stronger the argument. So, (6) is stronger than (5):

(5) Hippopotamuses require Vitamin K.
     Rhinoceroses require Vitamin K.

     Humans require Vitamin K.

(6) Hippopotamuses require Vitamin K.
     Bats require Vitamin K.

     Humans require Vitamin K.

The smallest category including the premise and conclusion categories is mammals in both cases. Argument (6) has much better coverage of the mammal category than does argument (5). (Similarity to humans is no greater in (6), since bats are not at all similar to humans.) People judge arguments like (6) to be stronger, giving evidence for the importance of the coverage variable.

Premise monotonicity. If you add more categories (all of them being at the same level) to the premises, the argument gets stronger.

(7)   Foxes have sesamoid bones.
      Pigs have sesamoid bones.
      _____
      Gorillas have sesamoid bones.

(8)   Foxes have sesamoid bones.
      Pigs have sesamoid bones.
      Wolves have sesamoid bones.
      _____
      Gorillas have sesamoid bones.

As you add more categories, you must be increasing (or at least not decreasing) both the similarity of the premises to the conclusion and the coverage of the category. That is, with more categories, the diversity of the premises must be increasing, and so you are covering the category better.

The inclusion fallacy.   Finally, their model predicts a reasoning error similar to that of the conjunction fallacy of Tversky and Kahneman (1982). Argument (9) is judged to be stronger than argument (10):

(9)   Robins have an ulnar artery.
      _____
      Birds have an ulnar artery.

(10) Robins have an ulnar artery.
      _____
      Ostriches have an ulnar artery.

That is, people sometimes claim that the argument is stronger when the conclusion is a whole category than when it is a subset of that category. This must be an error, however, because if something is true of all birds, then it is true of ostriches as well. So, if robins having a property makes you think that birds have the property, you should think that ostriches have it at least as much. (Indeed, because it is possible for ostriches to have it without all other birds, like penguins or seagulls having it, you should probably be feel that (10) is stronger, though that is not logically required.)[4]

   This fallacy follows from the Osherson et al. model, however. The coverage of the premises of (9) and (10) are the same, because the premises are identical. However, the similarity of the premise and conclusion category are not the same: Robins are similar to birds in general but not very similar to ostriches in particular. Thus, (9) appears to be a stronger argument, even though (10) is logically entailed by it. This kind of fallacy will occur when the premise is very typical, and the specific conclusion (as in (10)) is very atypical. It is not that surprising that people do not follow logic: They hardly ever do. What is impressive is that the model can explain this kind of fallacy, along with the other phenomena of induction.[5]

This group has extended their work into related areas, often addressing issues in the psychology of reasoning rather than concepts (e.g., Osherson et al. 1991). Although beyond the scope of our discussion, such work gives greater evidence for the similarity-based approach they adopt for categorical inductions. Sloman (1993) extended this model with a more detailed representation of similarity that, he argued, obviated the need for coverage as a component in the induction process. However, his overall approach is actually fairly consistent with that of the Osherson et al. approach.

Although this chapter is not primarily focusing on developmental issues, it is nonetheless interesting to discover that the model can explain important aspects of children's inductive ability. López et al. (1992) examined many of the phenomena that Osherson et al. (1990) did (e.g., the typicality, diversity and monotonicity phenomena described earlier). They found that kindergartners (5-year-olds) demonstrated phenomena that relied primarily on the similarity component of the model. For example, they judged that inductions from dogs to all animals were stronger than those from bats to all animals. However, they did not show evidence of using the coverage component of the model. For example, as more premise categories were added, kindergartners did not find the argument to get stronger (cf. premise monotonicity above), nor did they use premise diversity.

By second grade (8 years of age), children did use the coverage component, in some situations at least. For example, they recognized that all animals would be more likely to have a property shared by cats and buffalos than one shared by cows and buffalos. However, even 8-year-olds did not use coverage when they were required to figure out the covering superordinate category on their own. That is, they used coverage when the target category was all animals but not when it was an individual animal. López et al. speculate that this could reflect the children's limited ability to categorize at the superordinate level (see chapter 10).

Thus, these results give evidence for the two processes Osherson et al. (1990) proposed as being involved in category-based induction. The similarity process is a very basic one, probably the same one used in categorization and typicality judgments, and therefore it is available for reasoning processes at an early age. López et al. (1992, p. 1075) suggest that the coverage computations may be too difficult for very young children to calculate, which is why they take longer to develop. An alternative possibility is that children do not understand the principle behind the use of coverage, that diverse evidence provides a stronger basis for inductions than does uniform evidence. One suggestion that this might be true is the finding that adults in some different cultures also do not appear to use the coverage component, even though they do use the similarity component (López et al. 1997). Coverage may be a specific piece of cultural knowledge or practice that needs to be acquired, rather than a cognitive universal that everyone eventually develops. Perhaps, then, kindergartners simply have not acquired this piece of knowledge, and second-graders have, to some degree. In any case, the developmental and cross-cultural results give general confirmation of the notion that two different processes are involved in category-based induction, as described by Osherson et al. (1990).

Limitations of the Osherson et al. (1990) Model

There has been some criticism of the Osherson et al. approach, however. These criticisms have claimed that global similarity is too broad a measure to account for subtler effects of induction, much like other arguments about the limitations of similarity in concept theory (see chapter 6). Most of these effects come about when predicates are not entirely "blank." Of course, the examples used above are not entirely blank in that people have some idea of what they mean, even if they do not know which categories have the properties. So, if I am asked to judge whether bees use the neurotransmitter Dihedron, I know that Dihedron is a neurotransmitter, and I know something about what neurotransmitters are and what they do. I know even more about "love onions" in argument (2) (this presumably refers to loving to eat onions rather than an emotional attachment, and I have some inklings about what bears might eat). To completely avoid any effect of knowledge, one would have to use phrases such as "has property *P*," which give no clue as to the property's nature. But such examples might not tell us much about real-world induction, since the properties of real categories are quite meaningful. So, it is important to know whether results from such experiments can be extended to familiar predicates.[6]

Heit and Rubinstein (1994) carried out an important study of how categorical induction depends on the predicate. They proposed that induction depends on the relation between the property and the basis of the similarity between the premise and conclusion categories. (They considered only the two-category case.) For example, animals can be similar because of their biology or because of their behavior and ecologies. Whales and sharks may have similar behaviors but are different in important aspects of their physiology and anatomy. In contrast, whales and rabbits share some important biological structures but are extremely different in most other respects. The Osherson et al. model relies on only one similarity measure to predict induction, and so the fact that items are similar or dissimilar in different respects is not relevant. Furthermore, the particular predicate used does not influence performance in their model (though note that they explicitly restricted it to blank predicates).

Heit and Rubinstein constructed arguments of the following sort:

(11) Given that tuna/rabbits have blood that contains between 2% and 3% potassium, how likely are whales to have blood that contains between 2% and 3% potassium?

(12) Given that tuna/rabbits usually gather a large amount of food at once, how likely are whales to usually gather a large amount of food at once?

Some subjects would see the questions with *tuna* and others with *rabbits*. Heit and Rubinstein predicted that when the predicate was a biological one, like (11), the induction would be stronger for biologically related pairs like rabbits and whales. But when the predicate was behavioral, like (12), the induction would be stronger for behaviorally related pairs, like tuna and whales. Because an interaction is being predicted, the overall likelihood of the conclusion (e.g., whales eating a large amount of food at once) is controlled for. The results confirmed their prediction (and see Ross and Murphy 1999 for another example).

A similar demonstration was carried out by Kalish and Gelman (1992). Because this is described in some detail in chapter 10, I will discuss it only briefly here. Kalish and Gelman gave children combined concepts such as wooden pillows and asked them whether they would be hard or soft. The two concepts conflicted in their implications for these properties: Pillows are soft, but wooden things are hard. Nonetheless, children could figure out which category should control the property, saying that wooden pillows are hard. This was not solely a bias toward wooden things (in this example), because the children said that wooden pillows would be kept in the bedroom, like other pillows. In general, whether a predicate can be generalized across category members depends on knowing the kinds of predicates that are appropriate for induction in each domain (what Goodman 1965 called *overhypotheses*). This, in turn, may require sophisticated knowledge and reasoning ability. Heit and Rubinstein (1994, p. 420) point out that it would be awkward to use different similarity metrics to try to account for each kind of property induction. Instead, they suggest that "prior knowledge could be used dynamically to focus on certain features when similarity is evaluated. In this conception, inductive reasoning is an active process in which people identify the features in the premise and conclusion categories that are relevant to the property being inferred." So, rather than judging overall similarity, as in the Osherson et al. model, people may more specifically focus on the particularly relevant way in which the categories are related. One way to think of this is that the similarity computation is based not on the concepts' total properties but on the properties that are specifically relevant to the predicate under question (Heit and Rubinstein, p. 421).

A somewhat different question investigated by Coley, Medin, and Atran (1997) turns out also to have implications for the Osherson et al. model. These authors asked whether induction shows a basic-level advantage. In particular, they asked whether one would find a pattern in induction similar to that in feature listing or other tasks investigated by Rosch et al. (1976; see chapter 7). In feature listing, for example, subjects list many properties for basic-level categories, and only a few for superordinates. Subordinates added only a feature or two to the basic categories. Thus, the basic level is a kind of "break point," because basic categories carry much more information than more general categories but little less than more specific categories. If induction follows the same pattern, then people should be willing to draw inductions for basic-level categories (like hammers) but not for superordinates (like tools). The strength of induction for subordinates (like claw hammers) should only be slightly greater than that for the basic categories.

Coley et al. first tested Itzaj Mayan Indians in Guatemala. The Itzaj, like many other traditional agricultural societies, seem to form their basic level for biological kinds at the genus. For example, they tend to identify a bird as a hawk rather than as a red-tailed hawk (species) or bird (lifeform). If the basic category hawk is the privileged level for induction, then subjects should be willing to draw inductions from one kind of hawk to hawks in general. However, they should be less willing to draw an induction from, say, hawks to birds in general. This is exactly the pattern that was found. When the Itzaj subjects were told that one category could get a disease, they inferred that other members of the species or genus would also get the disease. However, they did not infer that members of the lifeform or kingdom (animals and plants) would get the disease. Thus, the genus level—apparently the basic level—served as a break point for induction as just described.

Coley et al. (1997) also investigated the inductions of American college students. The picture here is a bit more complex, however, because most Americans have their basic level at a different level than do traditional societies. That is, for Americans, the basic level is bird, tree, or fish, instead of sparrow, oak, or trout (genera).[7] Rosch et al. (1976; and Dougherty 1978) argued that Americans' lack of knowledge about the genus categories makes these categories less distinctive. For example, most Americans do not know enough about trout, bass, and perch to be able to tell them apart very reliably. As a result, concepts at this level do not add much more information than the concept fish, and so they are subordinates, like claw hammer or dining room table. If one makes predictions based on Rosch et al.'s (1976) findings, then, the preferred level of induction for Americans should not be the genus level, as it was for the Itzaj, but should be at the lifeform level—bird, fish, tree, and so on.

In a number of experiments, Coley et al. found that this was not the case. Instead, the American subjects also showed a pattern in which the genus was the preferred level for making inductions. Although the pattern did not seem as strong as that for the Itzaj, it was clear that Americans did not prefer to draw inductions from, say, sparrows to all birds, as they should have if they preferred to draw inductions at their basic level. Coley et al. suggest that subjects may be able to recognize that different genera are biologically distinct, even if they do not know features that distinguish them. This is clearly related to the idea of an essence underlying biological kinds (Medin and Ortony 1989): People think that oaks are a coherent biological class with similar genetic, evolutionary, and physiological properties, even though they cannot say what those properties are. This belief drives their inductions, rather than the actual knowledge that they have about oaks. The unsolved question is exactly why they have these beliefs about oaks and hawks and salmon. One possibility Coley et al. propose is the structure of the names: *Oak* is a monolexemic name like *hammer*, and its subordinates have names that are modifications of it, like *bur oak* or *pin oak*. This pattern suggests that oaks are the basic kind rather than a higher or lower level.

In any case, one implication of these interesting results is that induction cannot be driven only by similarity structure. Rosch et al.'s feature-listing results show that American subjects know a lot of common properties of trees, but little more about oaks (to pick one example). Thus, according to Osherson et al.'s model, subjects should have been very willing to draw an induction from one kind of tree (say, oak) to another kind (say, maple), because oaks and maples would be very similar. But this did not happen. If Coley et al.'s (1997) explanation for their results is correct, it suggests that induction is at least partly determined by more general beliefs and expectations about the domain, rather than by simple similarity. Although Americans may not know enough about oaks and maples to distinguish them very well, they believe that they are biologically different, and this belief, rather than their perceived similarity, drives the induction decisions.

A more radical departure from the Osherson et al. model (and indeed the whole general approach to category-based induction) is seen in recent findings in which people appear to use an entirely different basis for making inductions. For example, Lin and Murphy (2001) found that people were willing to make inductions from one category to a very different one that was related by being found in similar situations, a *thematically* related item. For example, using the feature "having a new bacteria," they found that most subjects preferred to make inductions from cat to kitty litter over inductions from cat to lion; similarly, they preferred inductions from toothbrushes to teeth over toothbrushes to hairbrushes. If similarity were the primary basis for induction, subjects would have always preferred the taxonomically related items (cat-lion; toothbrush-hairbrush), which were much more similar. However, subjects apparently reasoned quite differently, thinking that bacteria are transmitted by spatial proximity, and so things that are close together will be more likely to share bacteria. Note that none of the previous studies discussed could have revealed this (or an analogous) result, since they only used taxonomically related items.

Recent work by Proffitt, Coley, and Medin (2000) gives a similar example. These researchers asked tree experts to make inductions about disease. That is, given that tree X had a disease, would tree Y or tree Z be more likely also to have the disease? The subjects also explained their decisions. Although the experts sometimes used similarity of the sort Osherson et al. would have expected, they also frequently used other strategies, such as reasoning about ecological relatedness ("trees X and Y are both swamp trees") or about specific mechanisms of disease and a tree's susceptibility to disease. Essentially, the experts appeared to be developing a causal explanation of how the disease might spread from one tree to another, rather than simply relying on category membership and similarity. López et al. (1997) report similar evidence in their study of the Itzaj Indians. One reason that these subjects did not show an influence of premise diversity (as reported above), they suggested, was that they were attempting to link the animals in the premises by ecological relations.

One might argue that such examples are simply outside the domain of the Osherson et al. model. That is, the predicates are not really "blank" for these subjects, and all sorts of knowledge is intruding that is not part of the situation the model attempts to explain. That may well be true, but it immediately raises the question of how often the fully "blank" situation actually obtains in real-world induction. Lin and Murphy's subjects were simply college students, rather than carefully chosen experts, and their materials were a wide selection of familiar categories. If thematic relations are more important than similarity in such a case, it seems likely that they will be involved in many real induction situations. And although Proffitt et al.'s tree experts were obviously experts, most of us do know quite a bit about the categories we make inductions about, and so we might have similar patterns of reasoning. Pure category-based induction may not be as common as one would think from the psychology experiments in the tradition of Rips (1975). In real life, other sources of knowledge and forms of reasoning may often be involved.

In spite of these limitations of overall similarity, the Osherson et al. (1990) model is a very useful one. In some cases, one does not know enough about the predicate to be able to focus on specific relations between categories. For example, if I know that apple trees will not grow near black walnut trees, I may infer that pear trees will not either. I don't know enough about why apple trees will not grow near black walnut trees (something about chemicals in the roots), and I don't know whether the properties of apple trees that create this problem apply to pear trees as well. Although I don't have the specific knowledge to answer this question, apple and pear trees seem generally similar enough to me that I would assume that it would not be wise to plant pear trees to replace my dying apple trees. Thus, similarity may be a good fall-back strategy when more specific knowledge is lacking.

How Many Categories Are Used in Induction?

Discussions of induction in categorization have often pointed out how important it is for everyday reasoning and behavior. For example, when you see an apple, you identify it as such and then can decide to eat it, because apples in general are edible. This is important, because you need not test every individual apple (e.g., by giving a little piece to a sibling to eat before you risk it yourself) but can generalize based on your knowledge of the category. (Note that we are now talking about using category knowledge to draw inferences about an individual object rather than a related category, as in most of the previous sections.) Such scenarios, which are commonly repeated in the categorization literature, are simplistic in at least two respects. First, what happens when you are not sure it is an apple? What if it is a funny-looking fruit, which could be an ugly apple or an unusual pear? Or what if it is simply too far away to be seen clearly, or the light is bad? Of course, in some cases you can do a little investigation in order to clarify the categorization, but in other cases you may not. For example, in categorizing people, you may not be able to tell very easily whether this person you have met at a party is just extraverted or is manic. After you buy a new car, it may be difficult to find out immediately whether the brakes feel funny because they are different from those in your old car, or because they are broken. Before you can find out, you may have to decide whether to take the car on a trip. In short, sometimes induction must be done when the category is not very certain. Saying that "when you categorize something as an apple, you know you can eat it" is true enough, but in many cases, categorization is ambiguous. This situation is not addressed in the majority of the induction literature, in which category membership is usually just stipulated—one is simply told "Flamingos have sesamoid bones," so there is no question of whether an individual object is a flamingo or not.

Second, how do people make judgments about properties that are not universal? Again, in studies of induction per se, properties are often stated as if they are universally true of all category members: "Birds have an ulnar artery," or "Polar bears love onions." But as discussed throughout the book, many of the most popular features of categories are not in fact universal. Although many birds fly, some don't; many chairs are made of wood or have cushions, but plenty do not. How people make inductions about such properties has not been investigated in the literature discussed so far. One obvious suggestion is to induce features with a strength proportional to their observed frequency in the category. If 90% of the birds we see fly, then one can infer that a new bird will fly with probability of .90; if 50% of cups are made of plastic, one can assume that a new, unseen cup has an even chance of being made out of plastic. Although people's predictions may not perfectly match the observed probabilities, they would be expected to be proportional to them.[8]

Although this proposal seems attractive, it may run into problems when combined with the first issue. What happens when the categorization itself is uncertain and the feature is not universal? For example, suppose you aren't sure that the object is an apple, and you want to know whether it will taste sweet. Now you can't just say that 50% of apples are sweet, because it may not be an apple. So how do you make an induction in such a case? The first specific answer to this question was suggested by Anderson (1991). Imagine that you want to know whether an object X has feature F, but you aren't sure what category it is in. Anderson's proposal was, roughly speaking, the following. For every category, you figure out the probability of items in that category having F. Then you figure out the probability that X (the object) is in each category. Finally, you multiply the corresponding probabilities together and add them up to get the probability that the object has F. (The probabilities represent disjoint events assuming that the categories are mutually exclusive, and so their sum is also a probability.) That is,

P(X is sweet) = the sum of {P(X is in category C) × P(something in C is sweet)}

where the sum is taken over categories.

To illustrate, consider the following example for the fruit case. You see an item, X, that is probably, but not certainly, an apple. Because it is a bit peculiar or cannot be seen very well, there is a possibility it is some other fruit or vegetable. Here are the relevant (fictional) probabilities:

P(X is an apple)	.60
P(apples are sweet)	.50
P(X is a pear)	.25
P(pears are sweet)	.90
P(X is a pomegranate)	.10
P(pomegranates are sweet)	.80
P(X is a brainfruit)	.05
P(brainfruit are sweet)	.05

The probability that X will be sweet, then, is the sum of the product of these probabilities; that is, the probability that it is an apple and apples are sweet, plus the probability that it is a pear and pears are sweet, and so on: $.60 \times .50 + .25 \times .90 + .10 \times .80 + .05 \times .05 = .6075$. Note that if you had only used the figure for apples, ignoring that uncertainty of categorization, you would have estimated a .50 probability that X is sweet. The sweetness of pears and pomegranates pulls up the probability, even though apple is the *primary* or most likely category. If pears, pomegranates, and brainfruit had 0 sweetness, the prediction would have been only $.60 \times .50 + 0 + 0 + 0 = .30$, less than the .50 probability for apples alone. Again, the reason is that the lack of sweetness in other categories pulls down the prediction. In Anderson's rule, each category contributes an amount proportional to how likely it is that X is in the category. Since X doesn't look much like a brainfruit, P(X is a brainfruit) is only .05, and so this category cannot influence the prediction much one way or another. But since X is fairly likely to be a pear, the properties of pears do influence the prediction substantially. By taking into account the uncertainty of categorization, the prediction is more accurate: If you just relied on the one category of apples, you would not use other information that is relevant. Note that as P(X is an apple) gets closer and closer to 1, the other categories have less and less effect.

All this arithmetic may make you think that the model is psychologically implausible. Clearly, people do not multiply all these probabilities and then add them up, all in their heads. However, Anderson is not claiming that people do these exact calculations—what he is claiming is that people will pay attention to two or three or more categories when they are uncertain which is the correct one. It may be that when you look at X and try to decide whether it is an apple, a pear, or whatever, the sweetness you associate with these categories is activated and influences your final judgment about how sweet X is.

Brian Ross and I have investigated whether and when people use multiple categories when making inductions. We have used two different methodologies in this endeavor, one of them somewhat artificial but allowing strict control over the probabilities of the properties involved, and the other more realistic. The first method (Murphy and Ross 1994) focused on the prediction aspect of categories and so attempted to eliminate problems due to category learning or memory, which are the usual focus of categorization research. To do this, we presented subjects with pictures showing objects and their categories, and then subjects were asked to make predictions about a new object. This technique meant that subjects did not have to learn and remember the categories. Murphy and Ross argued that this made it more likely that people would use a more complex rule like that suggested by Anderson. If memory or learning costs were too high, people might focus on a single category.

Figure 8.1 shows an example of the stimuli Murphy and Ross (1994) used. These geometric figures were said to be drawings that children made using a computer graphics program (this was in the days before children began making full-color science fiction movies on their PCs). (The pictures were actually in color rather than having different shadings, but I will write as if the pictures differed in shape and shading, to be consistent with the figure.) Each child was said to have drawn many such pictures, and the subjects were being shown a representative sample of them. Thus, the children are the categories, and the properties of their drawings are the features being induced. Subjects were given problems like the following. You might try to answer the questions yourself.

I have a drawing of a triangle. Who do you think drew it?

What is the probability that the child you just named drew that picture?

What shading do you think the triangle is?

What is the probability that this figure has the shading you just named?

Subjects gave probabilities from 0 to 100%.

Given the stimuli in figure 8.1, most subjects would say that Bob drew the triangle, since he drew more triangles than any other child. However, they were not very certain that Bob made this drawing (according to their answers to the second question), and so they might pay attention to the other categories when making their prediction about the triangle's shading. Bob's drawings are mostly black, and so people would be likely to predict that the new triangle is black. However, notice that John and Sam also drew a triangle. Furthermore, each of them drew a black figure as well. So, there is more evidence outside the category that this drawing is black. If people use not just the primary category but the alternative categories as well, they should raise their probability estimates. (John and Sam are analogous to

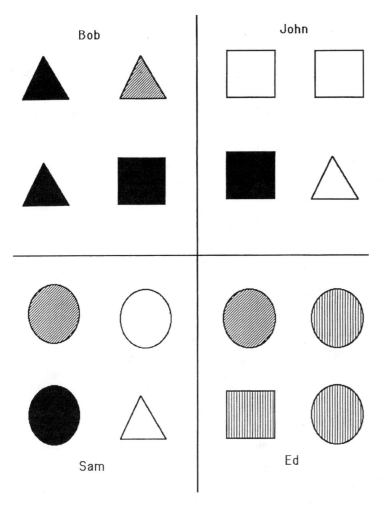

Figure 8.1
Example of Murphy and Ross's (1994) stimuli. The geometric shapes represent children's "drawings" using a computer draw program, and the shapes are representative samples of four children's drawings. Thus, the children are the category, and the geometric shapes are the exemplars.

the pear category in the earlier example.) Thus, this was called the *increasing* condition. But increasing relative to what? There were other questions that did not have evidence for the induction outside the primary category. For example, suppose you had a new square. Who do you think most likely drew it, and what shading do you think it has? Probably John drew it, and it is probably empty. However, note that Ed and Bob both have squares in their drawings, and they have no empty figures. So, this should not increase the probability that the square is empty. This is the *neutral* condition. If people pay attention to multiple categories, as Anderson (1991) argued they should, then the increasing condition should receive higher predictions than the neutral condition. In fact, it did not. People seem to be focusing only inside the primary category.

One might be concerned that it is the initial question "Who do you think drew [this figure]?" that is the problem. Perhaps it suggests to subjects that only one category is relevant. However, eliminating this question did not create a difference between the two conditions (Murphy and Ross 1994, Experiment 2). Another concern is that this is a null result. Perhaps subjects are simply not very good at making probability estimates, and so one does not see small differences. However, Murphy and Ross's Experiment 4 added another variable that would be expected to change subjects' probabilities: the base rate of the feature inside the primary category. In one condition, Bob had drawn three black figures, but in another condition, only two of them. Because this difference occurs inside the primary category, it would be expected to influence the results. In fact, it did have a very strong influence on subjects' inductions, but changing the features *outside* the primary category again had no effect. Over 11 experiments, Murphy and Ross found only some unusual conditions in which people used more than one category (see their article for details).[9]

Although such results may give important information about how people make inductions of this sort, one might be forgiven for believing that they are somewhat different from using everyday categories in which the information about whole categories is not displayed so readily. Furthermore, there might be important differences between these novel categories that subjects have not seen, and more familiar categories like tables, skunks, and trucks that people already know about. These concerns were addressed in later experiments by Malt, Ross, and Murphy (1995) and Ross and Murphy (1996). In their paradigm, subjects read scenarios involving different kinds of people. In most cases, there was uncertainty about one of the characters. For example, one story (Malt et al., table 1) described how the main character, Mrs. Sullivan, had read in the newspaper about a burglar who was robbing area homes. This put her into a bad mood, but she had to get ready for the visit of her grandchildren and a meeting with her real estate agent. At some point, she noticed a man walking up her driveway but couldn't see exactly who it was. Shortly after this, subjects answered questions about the story, some of which involved the man who walked up the driveway. The critical question was "What is the probability that the man who walked up the driveway will ring the front doorbell in the next 15 minutes?" If the man is the realtor, then he will probably ring the doorbell to talk to Mrs. Sullivan. But if the man is the burglar, he will presumably not ring the doorbell. (Both of these assumptions were verified independently.) So, if the subjects use both categories in making their predictions, they will reduce the probability they would give for the realtor alone, because of the influence of the burglar. Such a prediction needs a control condition, however. Therefore, another story was identical, except that Mrs. Sullivan read about a cable TV worker who was going to lay cable in the neighborhood, instead of about a burglar. Such a person would ring the doorbell before working in someone's yard (again, subjects verified this), and so he would not lower the probability. In sum, if subjects were attending to both categories in making their predictions, they should give higher probabilities to the story that mentions the cable TV worker than to the story that mentions a burglar as the secondary category.

In fact, Malt et al. (1995) did not find such an effect—people seemed to focus on the primary category. To try to increase people's use of the secondary category, Malt et al. included a condition in which the story reminded subjects that the person in the driveway might be the burglar/cable TV worker, shortly before the question was asked. This reminder did have an effect, but it was in making subjects change their mind about the primary category. That is, a number of people decided that the man walking up the driveway was probably the burglar, rather than the real estate agent. When only subjects who chose the "correct" primary category (in this case, real estate agent) were considered, there was no sign that the secondary category was used in making the prediction.

Using this kind of paradigm, Malt et al. and Ross and Murphy (1996) made a number of attempts to persuade subjects to use both categories. Most of them did not work. For example, emphasizing the uncertainty of the categorization in the story had little effect, even when a specific reason was given to doubt the categorization: If the story said that Mrs. Sullivan thought that the man walking up the driveway was probably the realtor, but she had thought he was taller, this did not lead subjects to use the burglar or cable TV worker. One variable that did have an effect was when the question itself was directly associated to the secondary category. For example, if the question said anything about cable wires, subjects then paid attention to the possibility that the man might be a cable TV worker; or if the question asked whether the man would check if the windows were locked (a typical burglar behavior), the burglar category was now used.

Ross and Murphy (1996) concluded that there is no capacity limitation or inability to use multiple categories in predictions—because of the few situations in which they do use them—but that people simply do not spontaneously think of doing so in most cases. When the question itself brings the secondary category to mind, people then do use it. In more neutral cases, however, people do not treat the uncertainty of their categorization itself as a cue to consider other categories. More recent research has looked at different ways to bring secondary categories to mind—see Murphy and Ross (1999) for details. At the present time, however, it seems that Anderson's (1991) idea that people will increase their predictive accuracy by using multiple categories is not correct. This suggests that categorization is even more important than one might think. That is, your initial categorization controls your behavior more than it ought to, especially when it is uncertain. In many situations, if you aren't sure whether something is a dog, but that is your best guess, you apparently will act as if this best guess were certain, not worrying about other possibilities. Although this sounds like a reasoning error, perhaps the relevant comparison is to ask how good people would be at making predictions if they did not use categories at all. That is, the overreliance on a single category is obviously not as accurate as using multiple categories. But before we say that categorization is leading people into error, we must consider what would happen if people did not categorize at all, and this is not really known. If people rely on a single categorization, and that is usually correct, then perhaps this is an efficient and generally useful way of making inductions.

Conclusions

Categorical induction is a critical aspect of our use of concepts, and yet it has received less attention than many other areas of the psychology of concepts (far less than concept learning, for example). One reason for this may be that researchers assumed that induction was a simple, straightforward process. If you know something is a dog, you know it has ears. What is tricky in such an induction? Well, nothing. However, the categories and properties used in induction are not always so simple, and not always so simply related. You may only have property information about related categories; you may not be sure what category the object is in; the property may not be universally true of the category; you may have other information about the object that influences the induction. It is in these less straightforward situations that interesting psychological issues arise.

Rips's work, and the subsequent development of models of induction by Osherson, Smith, and colleagues, and by Sloman, deal with situations in which it is not known whether a property is true of every member of the category: Although penguins get the disease, one doesn't know whether all birds get it, and one must then make a prediction about geese. According to the Rips and Osherson et al. models, category membership is critical to making these inductions, even if the category is not mentioned in the problem. That is, the typicality of penguin as a bird is important to determining the strength of induction, even if the problem doesn't mention "birds" per se. Furthermore, the other variable, similarity of the two categories (which is the only variable Sloman's model uses), is also a conceptual variable. That is, people use the similarity of the categories of penguins and geese to make the induction. Conceptual representations, then, are critical in both aspects of the induction process.

Research on induction has not generally been directed toward the issues of conceptual representation that have occupied much of the rest of the literature: There have been no comparisons of prototype and exemplar models so far as I know. Nonetheless, I will discuss the implications of the reviewed work for those models, in part to be consistent with the rest of the book, but in part because it is important for all these models to attempt to address such work and not restrict themselves to data on category learning.

Prototype Models

If read literally, almost all the work on category-based induction takes a prototype view of concepts. This is not to say that researchers on induction propose a specific category representation along with a learning rule. However, the talk about concepts is almost inevitably one in which a concept has a summary representation, usually described as a list of features, and the comparison of these representations leads to similarity judgments. For example, Rips's use of multidimensional scaling solutions treats each concept as a whole entity that is similar or dissimilar to other concepts. Osherson et al.'s (1990) model also treats concepts as individual entities. In later work, Osherson et al. (1991) obtained feature ratings for categories and then used these to develop a similarity measure, which in turn was used to predict induction. Sloman's (1993) model also used features associated to each category as the basis for predicting induction. These representations are just like the feature lists described by prototype theory (see chapter 3).

In all these cases, then, it is assumed that each category is associated with a summary representation that includes information about the typical features of the category—i.e., a prototype. As I will discuss shortly, this assumption may not be a critical claim for these theories. However, it is certainly striking that these papers never make reference to similarity of exemplars of these categories (a pattern that is also true of the developmental work on induction reviewed in chapter 10). Prototypes are extremely convenient sorts of representations for making inductions. If you want to know if a new X will be green or blue, you can look in your representation of Xs to see if the prototype has blue or green listed as a feature. If you want to know if Xs are green, given that Ys are, you can see how similar the prototypes of X and Y are and use this to make your prediction.

More recent research has suggested that the feature-list approach to induction may not be complete. Lassaline (1996) discovered that induction from one category to another was stronger when the two concepts could be aligned. That is, when the conceptual structures had analogous relations connecting the features, people found the inductions more compelling than when they had different relational structures. However, such findings are within the general modern approach to prototype theory that uses more structured representations than feature lists (e.g., schemata), as described in chapter 3. In general, then, the theories and results of category-based induction are quite compatible with the assumptions of prototype theory.

Exemplar Models

Given the previous conclusion, one might assume that induction is not very compatible with exemplar theories. However, it is not at all clear that that is true. It seems likely that the prototype talk one sees in papers of induction is to some degree driven by matters of convenience rather than by firmly held beliefs. When one talks about inductions from one category to another, it may simply be a convenient fiction that each category is represented by a summary representation. It would require long digressions to discuss category similarity in terms of many exemplars that may or may not contain the predicate of interest, and induction researchers may not care very much about the details of the representations, which their studies do not investigate per se. For their purposes, the question of exactly how the conceptual information is represented is not a pressing issue—all they need to know is that bears love onions, and however people represent that is largely irrelevant.

We should ask, then, whether we can imagine an exemplar model that would do the same things as the induction models described above. One of the components of such a model would be easy to represent: the similarity between the two categories.

When making an induction from robins to penguins, the similarity of these two categories is an important variable. If the categories are represented through remembered exemplars, it would not be difficult (in principle) to represent category similarity as the average similarity of the exemplars of the two categories. That is, individual penguin exemplars would not in general be very similar to individual robin exemplars. However, robin exemplars would certainly be similar to cardinal exemplars. Thus, the overall similarity of robins to cardinals would be higher than that of robins to penguins by this method (which certainly seems to be the correct answer). So far, so good.

It is less clear, however, how to deal with the typicality component of the induction models. Recall that Rips and Osherson et al. argued that the typicality of the premise category to its superordinate (loosely speaking) was an important variable. People make stronger inductions from robins to penguins than from penguins to robins, because the properties of robins are more likely to be true of birds as a whole. Unfortunately, as discussed in the conclusion to chapter 7, exemplar models have so far failed to provide an account of hierarchical category structures. For example, how would an exemplar model represent the fact that all robins are birds? If it explicitly encoded both category names for each exemplar, then every exemplar would have to be encoded with *many* category names, given that most objects are in many different categories (e.g., robin, bird, vertebrate, carnivore, animal, migratory bird, object, thing, etc.). If only categories that were originally encoded with the object were represented (so, if you thought of the robin as a robin and an animal, only those two categories would be represented), this would be problematic in making induction computations.

For example, if one had to decide whether penguins use the neurotransmitter Dihedron, given that pigeons do, one would now have to decide on the typicality of pigeons to the bird category. The first problem is how one would know that bird is the direct superordinate of robin and pigeon, if category information is represented through individual exemplars. If not every exemplar of pigeons and penguins is encoded as a bird, how would one know that birds are the lowest superordinate that includes them both? Second, one would then have to compare all one's pigeon exemplars to all one's bird exemplars (and the same for penguins) in order to derive the typicality of penguins as birds. This would again run into a problem if not all bird exemplars were encoded as birds. But if all bird exemplars *were* encoded as birds, this computation would be a very onerous one, since I for one have encountered many pigeons and many more birds in my life, and calculating the similarity of all pigeons (and then all penguins) to each of the remembered birds could take a very long time. One possible solution to this is to follow up Sloman's (1993) proposal, which does away with the typicality component of the induction models. That would leave the much more tractable similarity component.

There is a more basic problem with the exemplar approach, however, which is how it is to deal with generalization such as "All birds have sesamoid bones," which are often given to subjects during induction tasks—and which one often reads in articles or textbooks or hears in the classroom. If one has a summary representation of birds, it is computationally simple merely to add this fact to that representation. If the representation of birds is a thousand exemplars, then it is unclear how to represent such information, since one would presumably not update every single exemplar with this new fact. Yet if it is only encoded for a subset of exemplars, this does not represent the notion that *all* birds have the property. Thus, using exemplar models to explain induction suffers from the lack of the development of this approach to knowledge representation more generally.

In summary, the details of exemplar models of induction have not been worked out very well, and there are some questions about whether this approach will be able to handle the main results. Furthermore, like prototype theory, exemplar models have no mechanism to explain the knowledge effects that have been found.

Knowledge Approaches

The results of Heit and Rubinstein (1994), Kalish and Gelman (1992), Coley et al. (1997), Ross and Murphy (1999), and Proffitt et al. (2000) all show that background knowledge is an important determinant of induction. People do not seem to be using simple empirical procedures to make predictions but filter the empirical evidence through a complex set of beliefs and expectations about the categories. One might draw an induction from category X to category Y if they are similar in respects that are relevant to the predicted property, but the same categories might not support induction of a different property. As Heit and Rubinstein pointed out, the feeding behavior of rabbits simply does not provide useful evidence about the feeding habits of whales, even if one can draw physiological inductions from rabbits to whales. Coley et al. showed that how much people know about categories can be less important than their beliefs about the nature of those categories. Although American subjects may not be able to reliably tell a maple from an oak, they nonetheless believe that the two are importantly different and therefore do not draw inductions from one to the other. Such beliefs can cancel the similarity effects that are the basis of the Osherson et al. or Sloman models. People are apparently attempting to draw a kind of explanation for why something has a given property.

When their knowledge of the category and background knowledge converge on the induction, it will be quite strong. However, as Proffitt et al. and Lin and Murphy (1999) have demonstrated, sometimes the basis of induction changes from being similarity-based to relying on very different kinds of explanations. For example, ecological relationships among organisms may be as (or more) important as their taxonomic similarity for some properties, such as carrying a disease. Thus, people may draw inductions from a forest animal to forest trees in spite of enormous taxonomic differences. Although such inductions are still technically categorical (i.e., they concern the entire categories of willows and deer, or whatever), they evidently go beyond pure category similarity, which is the focus of most accounts of category-based induction.

Although background knowledge appears to win when it is placed in conflict with overall similarity (Coley et al. 1997), one might think of induction as forming a continuum from general causal explanations to more specific ones. That is, robins and eagles are likely to share many biological properties by virtue of their general biological relatedness (caused by a partially shared evolutionary history). However, if one can adduce more specific evidence for a given property (e.g., the property is related to migration, and both robins and eagles migrate), then one can make the induction even more confidently. Without such specific knowledge, people can fall back on overall similarity and shared superordinate categories, which are generally good predictors of shared properties. However, the fact that similarity in different respects changes induction (Heit and Rubinstein 1994; Kalish and Gelman 1992; Ross and Murphy 1999) suggests that the simple similarity approach is not a more basic or universal explanation for induction, but rather a fallback strategy when specific explanations are lacking.

As the induction literature includes robust effects of both knowledge and category structure, it is clear that neither the structural approaches (prototype and exemplar views) nor the knowledge approach will provide a complete account of induction.

9

Concepts in Infancy

It is not that common for reviews of the psychology of concepts to consider children's concepts at much length. For example, Smith and Medin (1981) did not have a chapter on development, nor did they discuss developmental issues very much as a part of other topics. I believe that there are two compelling reasons for paying attention to development, however. The first is that the development of concepts speaks to central questions of cognitive science. In fact, if there is a single main theme to cognitive science, it would be the question of how people come to have knowledge. Philosophers since Plato have treated the acquisition of concepts as a central question of epistemology. Much controversy in linguistics, psychology, and philosophy concerns which aspects of our knowledge are learned and which are innate. The present chapters will not be focusing on very broad questions of nature vs. nurture, but the findings they review on the acquisition of concepts will play an important role in eventually answering those questions.

The second reason for considering developmental evidence is that it may place constraints on our theories of adult competence and performance. Finding out how conceptual structure begins and how it develops may tell us about what structure is likely to be present in the adult, and how it is organized. Of course, reasoning in the reverse direction is just as valid. In making proposals about children, one must be constrained by proposals for what adults know. For example, the prototype notion of adults' concepts that arose in the 1970s was largely inconsistent with Piagetian theories of children's concepts, leading many developmental researchers to investigate different questions than had been raised in the Piagetian paradigm.

Having given this justification for the centrality of development, perhaps I should now apologize for having only two chapters on this topic. In part, the reason for this is that there is little developmental work on some topics that have been the focus of this book (e.g., conceptual combination and formal learning approaches). However, a more pressing problem is limitations of time and space that prevent me from addressing this topic at greater length. Indeed, one could easily write a book of the present length that only considers conceptual development. Thus, the present review is necessarily selective. I have divided the developmental work into two main chapters. The first chapter will consider infancy, the development of concepts from birth through shortly after the first year of life. The second chapter will consider later conceptual development, generally from the toddler stage through early school years. Because the behavioral and linguistic skills of infants differ so much from those of older children, very different kinds of studies have been designed to study their conceptual abilities, as you will see.

Methodology in the Study of Infant Concepts

A story that hardly needs repeating nowadays is the one of how psychologists over the past twenty years have radically changed our conception of infancy. We used to think of infants as passive creatures who had little capacity, did little besides cry, and were just waiting for development to bring them into a more mature stage in which real cognition could begin. In contrast, nowadays infants are thought to be active, rapidly developing creatures who have fairly sophisticated theories about the world. This change has come about through the development of methodologies that measured infants' understanding in spite of being unable to speak, follow instructions, or even to control their limbs to any great degree. Because these methodologies are the basis for everything we now know about infant cognition, and because they are so different from the other methods discussed in the book, I spend considerable time in explaining them before discussing the more substantive issues. They are in fact a fascinating example of scientific ingenuity, and so their story is an interesting one in itself.

The basic problem is to find out what an infant knows about its world, given its behavioral limitations. To take an example that is not from concepts, consider the notion of object permanence (as reviewed in Baillargeon, Spelke and Wasserman 1985). Piaget had originally argued that infants do not believe that objects exist permanently until the age of 9 months or so. Before that, when an object disappeared, it was as if it was out of existence from the infant's perspective. Piaget made this claim based on the fact that before 9 months, infants did not search for an object when it was hidden under a blanket or behind an occluder. Later researchers realized that it might be difficult for the infant to organize and carry out a search for an invisible object, even if the required actions (lifting the blanket or knocking over the occluder) were physically possible for the child. But how could they discover what the baby understood about the object except through overt search behavior?

Consider the following experiment (which is a simplified version of a number of studies of the sort done by Spelke or Baillargeon). An infant is held on a parent's lap or in a seat, looking at a small stage. An object enters the stage, moves back and forth to capture the baby's attention, and then goes behind a wooden screen. The screen is then lowered, and the object is not there! Amazed, the baby gazes at the scene for some time (perhaps looking for the object). How do we know the child is amazed? There must be a control condition in which the child would not expect the object to be there. In this condition, the object enters the stage, moves back and forth, and then returns offstage, without ever going behind the screen. Now, when the screen is lowered, the child looks, but not for as long as when the object had disappeared behind the screen. From this difference in looking time, we draw the inference that the child was more surprised when the object went behind the screen, and therefore that the child expected the object to still be there.

This kind of experiment uses a naturally occurring behavior that infants can easily control, namely, looking. Infants tend to look at things that are novel, surprising, or salient. As a result one can test what their expectations are about the world by creating situations that would be surprising if they had such-and-such a belief but not if they lacked that belief. As we shall see, the same kind of reasoning is central to testing infants' category learning. Some have criticized the preferential looking measure as only indicating that a child can tell the difference between two situations and therefore as being unable to reveal knowledge or conceptual abilities (e.g., Haith and Benson 1998). However, this reflects a misunderstanding of the technique. If the only way to distinguish situations X and Y is via a particular fact or belief, then even a very coarse measure that shows discrimination of these situations will a fortiori show the presence of the belief. Indeed, most cognitive experiments on adults are simple yes-no judgments indicated by the press of a button, rather than detailed verbal reports or complex motor responses. Thus, although critics may always question exactly what the basis for the discrimination may be, the fact that preferential looking is such a simple measure does not limit its usefulness for revealing possibly complex knowledge, any more than choice reaction-time experiments on adults do.

Dishabituation Techniques

As a general rule, infants will also look longer at objects and events that are new.[1] If the same object is displayed over and over again, an infant will decrease its looking over time (though if the object is very interesting, it may take some time for this to happen). This is the process of *stimulus habituation*. For example, if one were to present a picture of a bunny to the infant, it might look at it for 5 or 6 seconds before looking away. If the bunny were presented again, it might look again for 5 seconds. If this process were repeated for six trials, however, even the glamour of a bunny would begin to pale, and the infant might just glance at it and, having discovered that it is the same old bunny, look away. If the picture is changed on trial 7 to something entirely different, say a person's face, the infant may now increase its looking considerably from that of the previous trial, a process called *dishabituation*. This is due in part to the interest in the face, but also perhaps in part to surprise that the bunny is no longer there and has been replaced by something new. Of course, it is possible that the child was going to look more on trial 7 anyway, for some irrelevant reason having to do with its attention span, or noises in the lab, or some other irrelevant factor. Thus, it is important to have a control group that continues to see the bunny. If the children viewing a bunny on trial 7 look only for 2 seconds, and the children viewing a face look for 6 seconds, this is strong evidence that children can tell the difference between the bunny and the face, and that they identify the face as being a novel stimulus (though see below).

This *dishabituation technique* is an extremely flexible methodology for testing perception, memory, and concepts in infants. For example, a child will obviously not dishabituate to a new stimulus if it looks the same as an old one. Dishabituation, then, could be used as a perception test to see which stimuli look the same and which look different to infants at different ages. Similarly, the child's memory can be tested by inserting a delay between the test trial and the final habituation trial. If the child has forgotten that it had seen bunnies, it will not look longer at the face than at a bunny, because both will seem new to it.

This technique can be extended to the study of concepts as well. Suppose I want to know whether infants can learn the concept of bunny rabbits. I wouldn't do the experiment described above, because that shows that children can learn one particular bunny, but it does not reveal that they have learned a concept. In the concept version, I will present the infant with a *different category member* on every trial—in this case a different picture of a bunny. Thus, the infant will not be learning about a single object, but about a whole category. (I will assume that the infant doesn't already have the concept of bunnies, though this will be questioned later.) A schematic of the stimulus displays is shown in table 9.1. In the habituation or familiarization phase, many different bunnies are shown. At the test trial, I will present a *new* bunny (not seen before) to half the subjects, and a member of a contrast category to the other half. Note that the test bunny must be new, because the other picture will be new, and we do not wish our comparison to be a memory test of a specific item, but a test of category membership.

Table 9.1.
Sequence of trials in a single-exposure dishabituation task.

Habituation or Familiarization Trials	
Trial 1	bunny 1
Trial 2	bunny 2
Trial 3	bunny 3
Trial 4	bunny 4
Trial 5	bunny 5
Trial 6	bunny 6
Test Trial	
Trial 7	bunny 7 (control group)
	or mouse 1 (experimental group)

Note: In a similar design, there would be two test trials, one containing bunny 7 and one mouse 1, and each infant would receive both, the order balanced over subjects.

What should this contrast category picture used in the dishabituation trial be? In theory, it could be anything that is not a bunny. For example, I could use a person's face, as in my earlier example. However, this would not be very informative about what the infants learned. There are many differences between whole bunnies and a human face, and it would not be clear what the nature of the category was that the child learned. Thus, it would be better to use a comparison item that is close to the bunny category without actually being a bunny—say another small mammal, such as a cat or mouse (as shown). If children dishabituate (look more) to the picture of the mouse, say, then we can be fairly sure that they have identified what is common to bunnies in particular, enough to distinguish them from a similar category. Note that we can never conclude more from this test than the particular comparison that we make. So, if we find dishabituation to a mouse, we know that the child can distinguish bunnies from mice, but we do not know whether they could have distinguished bunnies from cats, say, though of course one can make reasonable inferences. Researchers in this area sometimes summarize results of such studies by saying things like "Infants can learn the bunny category at 6 months of age," but we should be careful in keeping track of which comparisons were actually tested, since infants might be able to distinguish bunnies from some categories but not from others that were not tested. Indeed, when researchers have made multiple comparisons, it is not unusual to find patterns such as infants being able to tell dogs from birds but not dogs from cats (Quinn, Eimas, and Rosenkrantz 1993).

Before we can conclude that the infants have noticed the commonality to the presented bunnies and the difference between them and the tested mouse, we must show that the bunnies themselves are distinguishable. Imagine, for example, that I presented you with color patches that were all a very similar shade of red—in fact, all within a range of one nanometer in frequency. Then I might test you on something that was also within that nanometer or something that was well out of it (in fact, kind of orange-ish). You might easily identify the color outside of that range as being different and the one inside the range as being the same color, but it would be wrong to conclude that you had learned a color *category*—in fact, the learning stimuli probably looked like exactly the same color patch to you. A category is a set of different items that are equivalent in some respects, not a repetition of what seems to be the same item. Because infants' perceptual abilities are rather different from those of adults, we cannot just assume that a dozen pictures of bunnies that look different to us also look different to the infants. To babies, the pictures could all look like grayish blobs with pinkish long blobs at the top.[2] In that case, infants were not really learning the category but were learning what to them was a single stimulus. To rule out this possibility, it is usual to do a control experiment in which category members are compared. In this test, one subject might learn bunny 1 (six presentations) and then be tested on bunny 1 vs. bunny 7; another subject might learn bunny 2 and then be tested on bunny 2 vs. bunny 3; and so on. If the bunnies all look alike to infants, they will respond similarly to the repeated and the new bunnies. If they can tell the difference among bunnies, they will habituate to the old bunny but dishabituate to the new one.

There is one aspect of the dishabituation technique just described that is problematic for a mundane reason. Note that the comparison being made is a between-subjects one. As shown in table 9.1, half of the infants view a new example of an old category (bunny 7), and half get a member of a new category (say, mouse 1). The problem is that infant looking data are quite variable. Infants in general are highly variable creatures, and it is not at all unusual for them to fall asleep, start to cry, or fuss during the experiment. If they obviously have stopped participating, then they can be removed from the study (and it is not unusual to lose 20% or more of one's infant subjects for crying or sleepiness). However, if they are just not paying much attention or are getting tired, they may not produce very good data, but one does not have sufficient reason to remove them from the experiment. The result is that it can take many subjects to get enough data to find a between-group difference in looking time. And because it is usually expensive to test infants, this can be a real problem, rather than just an annoyance. (Infants are expensive because they often require many experimenters to run the study—see below; parents must be reimbursed for travel costs; personnel are needed to find infants of the correct age and contact their parents to bring them in; safety and health regulations must be followed; and so on. For example, as a researcher using primarily college undergraduate subjects, I do not feel the need to keep a supply of diapers of various sizes on hand, nor do I keep toys and children's books to occupy my subjects or their siblings before the experiment. And I lose very few of my subjects due to crying.)

There are two ways to address this problem. One is to test all subjects in the habituation and dishabituation condition. For example, on trial 7, half of the subjects will see a new bunny and half a mouse; then on trial 8, the conditions will be reversed. Thus, every subject provides a habituation trial (the one with the bunny) and a dishabituation trial (the one with the mouse). Unfortunately, those subjects who receive the habituation trial second are not really in the same condition as those who receive it first. That is, after getting a mouse on trial 7, the bunny on trial 8 is now somewhat novel again, and so this may not be a pure habituation trial. Some researchers therefore always put the new item last, though this now creates a confounding of condition with trial.

A way to do the experiment more efficiently is to use a different kind of test, called a *paired preference procedure*, which also relies on dishabituation. In this paradigm, the child is simultaneously given two items to look at, and the amount of time spent looking at each item is measured. Of course, if the baby has been seeing one picture alone for seven trials, the sight of two pictures by itself might be so fascinating as to wash out any category effects that one could expect. Therefore, these experiments typically present pairs of items during the familiarization phase as well, as shown in table 9.2. During familiarization, pairs of bunnies are presented, and at test, a new bunny and a new contrast category member are presented. (The left-right position of the two items on the test trial would of course be counterbalanced over subjects. In some studies, there are two test trials, the second one reversing the positions of the pictures, as some children have strong position preferences that add considerable noise to the data.)

Infants now have the choice of looking at a novel bunny or at a novel mouse. If they have learned the bunny category well enough to distinguish it from mice, then they will presumably prefer to look at the mouse.[3] This dependent measure is a within-subjects design, in that each subject provides a score for what percent of the time he or she looked at the novel item. If this novelty score is significantly higher than 50%, we can conclude that the infants learned the category (well enough to distinguish it from a mouse or whatever). However, because infants often look at both pictures somewhat, average preference scores are usually no more than about 65%.

Table 9.2.
Sequence of trials in a paired-preference (dishabituation) procedure.

	Picture Location	
	Left	Right
Habituation or Familiarization Trials		
Trial 1:	bunny 1	bunny 2
Trial 2:	bunny 3	bunny 4
Trial 3:	bunny 5	bunny 6
Trial 4:	bunny 7	bunny 8
Trial 5:	bunny 9	bunny 10
Test Trial		
Trial 6:	bunny 11	mouse 1

Note: The left-right location of the bunny and mouse on the test trial would be varied across subjects.

How exactly can one tell where the infant is looking? Typically, there is an experimenter behind the screen where the pictures are displayed (these may be projected by a slide projector, or they may be physical pictures placed on the screen). The experimenter looks through a small hole in the screen and can see whether the baby is looking at either picture (or is dozing or looking at the ceiling, etc.). By pressing one of two buttons connected to timers, the experimenter times how long the baby is looking at each picture. However, it is possible that the experimenter could be biased by knowing which of the pictures is the more novel one. For example, suppose that the baby is looking only somewhat to the left, perhaps near the edge of the left picture. Does this count as looking at the item or not? If the experimenter expected the baby to look more at the left picture, then he or she might well decide that this is just what was expected, and score the infant as looking. If the experimenter thought the baby would look more at the other picture, then he or she might be a bit more conservative. To avoid this problem, it is now de rigeur to have two different experimenters—one who runs the habituation phase, and one who runs the test phase. The second experimenter does not know which items have been used in the first phase (e.g., in the design shown in table 9.2, the experimenter would not know whether the infant had seen bunnies or mice in the habituation period), and thus, he or she could not be biased. There is sometimes a third experimenter needed as well, to change the displays or to handle other equipment, which makes these experiments rather difficult to organize.

There are a number of other aspects of the experimental design that need to be discussed, unfortunately, in part because they were not always followed in early studies on concept acquisition, and so it is important to be on the lookout for design shortcomings. First, there should normally be some kind of counterbalancing of stimuli so that the same item is not used over and over as the test item. Typically, one cycles the stimuli through the different conditions, so that subject one gets bunny 11 as the test item (see table 9.2), subject two gets bunny 10, subject three gets bunny 9, and so on. Similar reasoning applies to the mouse stimulus. However, even with this cycling through of items, there is a potential problem: What if infants just prefer to look more at mice than at bunnies? If that is true, then we could spuriously find evidence that children dishabituate to the mouse, not because they have learned the bunny category, but because they simply prefer to look at the mouse picture. (Note that this would also apply to the simpler one-stimulus dishabituation procedure shown in table 9.1.)[4] Perhaps the easiest way to handle this problem is simply to use mice as the familiar category for half the subjects. Thus, for some subjects, the mouse is the new category (and so should be looked at), and for others, it is the familiar category (and so should be ignored). As a result, any preference for a single item would be equated across conditions.

If the researcher wants to know only whether infants can learn to categorize bunnies, though, this solution is not useful, since half the subjects would have learned the mouse category. Another way to deal with the preference problem is simply to do a separate test in which other infants are allowed to choose which picture to look at. That is, without any categorical training, infants are shown a bunny and a mouse (Trial 6 in table 9.2 without any preceding trials). If they look at them about equally, then they do not prefer one over the other, and the results of the main experiment cannot be due to preference. If the amount of looking is not equal, then it is appropriate to do a statistical comparison to show that the dishabituation is greater than could be explained by any preference (Quinn and Eimas 1996). In some cases, this can save otherwise dicey results. If my category-learning experiment found only a small, nonsignificant preference for the mouse in the table 9.2 example (say, 55% looking), the results might be saved if my preference test shows that infants greatly prefer to look at the bunny. If infants looked at the mouse only 35% of the time in the preference test, then the difference between 55% (after category exposure) and 35% (prior preference) might be significant.

Sequential Touching Techniques

A different technique has been used for older infants and young toddlers, namely sequential touching of real objects. At a certain age, infants are no longer very interested in sitting still and looking at pictures but instead demand the opportunity to move about and directly manipulate things. For these children, measures of passive looking would not be successful. A different measure is to give children a number of objects (almost always toys) that come from different categories. The objects are placed within reach of the child, who is videotaped during this interaction. The order in which the objects are touched and manipulated is coded from the tape.

This task can be thought of as halfway between the looking tasks described above and more active object-sorting tasks used for older children. That is, older children can be asked to put together objects that are "the same kind of thing." If they are good subjects, they will separate different categories of objects. Younger children, however, either do not understand this question very well or find it too difficult to remain on task, and so they typically cannot correctly sort objects into different groups. (As will be discussed in the next chapter, they will sometimes make structures out of the toys, which are clearly noncategorical responses.) In the sequential touching task, then, the objects are placed in front of the child, who is not given any specific instructions. Surprisingly, children will sometimes touch all or most of a category's members before they touch the members of the other category (Starkey 1981). Of course, this could also happen by chance if the child were just reaching out blindly for any attractive item. Therefore, various statistical procedures are used to identify how often a string of category members would be touched in a row if the child were responding randomly. Above-chance sequential touching of a single category is then taken as evidence that the child has that categorical distinction.

For some reason, this task is seldom done in a context of category *learning*. Instead, all the cases I have read of it have been directed toward testing to see if children have a given category (e.g., mammals or dogs or furniture) prior to coming to the laboratory.

The issues of experimental design here have to do primarily with stimulus selection and placement. Clearly, there may be concerns about preferences here (if children prefer to play with vehicles, then they may pick up the vehicles first), similar to those mentioned above for looking preferences of younger infants. Similarly, the objects should be placed in a random or well-distributed manner, so that spatial biases do not affect the touching patterns. Neither of these points gets as much attention as I would like in the method sections of papers reporting such studies.

Let me mention here a technique that is superficially similar to the present one, namely an object-examination task. In one such study, by Oakes, Coppage, and Dingel (1997), infants were in a high chair with a tray, and an experimenter placed an object in the tray, bringing the child's attention to it. The child was given 30 seconds to examine the toy, upon which it was removed, and another toy was put on the tray. These interactions were videotaped, and the amount of time the infant actively examined the toy was measured. This technique is similar to the sequential touching one in that actual objects are used, and children are encouraged to handle them. However, the logic here is just like the dishabituation task, as the child encounters only one stimulus at a time, eventually losing interest in objects that are like the previous objects. Oakes et al. performed a dishabituation test, in which, after presenting a string of sea animals, a land animal was introduced, to see if children would examine it more. Thus, many of the same design issues discussed in that task apply here.

Methodological Summary

The techniques used in these studies are doubtless clever, and it is to be hoped that new, equally clever techniques will be added in the future. Nonetheless, they do all have their limitations as well, which must be understood in evaluating experimental results. The first point, which is true of all these methods, is that positive results are much more interpretable than negative results. If children dishabituate to the new category, or if they touch one category's objects before another's, this is an indication that they see some commonality to one category and a difference to the other category. But when infants fail to distinguish the categories, the conclusions are not nearly as clear.

Let us focus on the dishabituation techniques. If infants do not dishabituate, one possibility is that children did not know or did not learn the category, and so did not show the novelty preference. However, it is possible that the infant did learn the category but simply does not find the new item (e.g., the mouse) to be particularly interesting or importantly different. Although the preference control test can rule out a priori biases (e.g., if children just don't like to look at mice), it is still logically possible that an infant could tell the difference between old and new stimuli but still not find the difference to be enough to re-engage its attention. Indeed, the entire task may be getting very boring to the infant. (For example, if I had spent two hours at a large exhibit of Monet paintings, I might not stop and look much at a Cézanne outside the exhibit, even though I can tell the difference between the painters.) Another issue is that lack of dishabituation could mean either that the category was not abstracted (e.g., the infant did not identify the commonalities of the bunnies) or that the novel test item is not novel enough (e.g., the infant does not see the mouse as being different from rabbits). If the novel item is very different, then the second possibility may be implausible (e.g., if the test is bunnies vs. motorcycles). However, since the evidence of category learning is solely found in performance on the dishabituation test, there is no logical way to know from any single experiment whether the category was not learned or the test was too difficult.[5] Just as a positive result is limited by the comparison items, so is a negative result. Thus, rather than say "Infants can't learn the category of bunnies," we ought to say something like "Infants didn't learn to distinguish bunnies from mice." Of course, null results can become more interpretable in the context of similar studies that achieve positive results, so that one may draw an inference about the cause of the noneffect.

One strength of the dishabituation technique, however, is that it has been found to be robust in a variety of contexts.[6] As a test of memory, for example, it usually seems to work. If you present a single item over and over again, subjects habituate to it and then dishabituate to a new item. In category-learning experiments, significant effects are almost always in the direction of the new item being preferred, giving further evidence for the robustness of the paradigm. One may be justified, then, in interpreting null results as occurring for more interesting reasons than simple insensitivity of the paradigm. For similar reasons, the examination procedure of Oakes et al. (1997) is probably fairly robust, though it does not yet have as much of a track record, and so its strengths and weaknesses have not yet been empirically identified.

The sequential-touching technique seems to be on thinner ice in this regard. Part of the problem is that it does not involve a specific task, as the object-sorting task given to older children does. So, if you tell a child to put together items that are the same, and the child puts together a block, a person and a flower, one can generally say that the child has not created a category and has failed the task (for whatever reason). However, if one simply puts objects in front of a child, with no instructions, it is unclear what it means when the child does not sequentially touch objects from the same category. The child wasn't *asked* to distinguish the categories, so it is not a task failure in the same sense. Furthermore, it may be that the child is well aware of the category distinctions but has some other basis for touching the objects, such as thematic relations (e.g., touching a boy and a dog, because the boy owns the dog), spatial relations, or idiosyncratic associations. If the child plays with the toys, then the sequence of touching will have more to do with his or her playing schema at the time, which may involve connecting the items by a story or common activity rather than by category membership.

Part of the problem with sequential touching is that we do not have independent evidence for how the touching is controlled. In looking preference, there are dozens of experiments showing a novelty preference after repeated presentations. Thus, when we apply this technique to category learning, we can feel pretty confident that new category members will cause dishabituation, since new items generally do cause dishabituation in perception and memory experiments. However, there is little such independent evidence of sequential touching in memory or perception experiments. We are on considerably weaker ground, then, when it comes to null results in this paradigm. Although positive results probably do show that children have made a distinction among the items, the null results could simply reflect that there is some other basis for touching that is more salient to the children.

The Domain of Infant Categorization

As I have mentioned, infants are learning much about their world during the first year of life. In fact, it is worth pointing out that many studies on infant cognition may turn out to be studies of concepts, even though their authors do not identify them as such. This point is made by Baillargeon (1998) in discussing children's knowledge of the physical world. When they are born, infants' understanding of physical objects is very limited. Although they may have very basic knowledge of objects, this knowledge is incomplete, in that they are not always surprised to see objects disappear when they shouldn't, maintain their position with inadequate support, move without adequate force exerted on them, and so on. Over their first year of life, they develop more complete expectations for what objects should and should not do. Baillargeon (1998, p. 507) has described this as a process of acquiring event and object categories. Event categories refer to coherent classes of actions and their consequences, in which, for example, something stops moving if it hits a larger obstacle, or something falls to the ground if it is pushed off a surface. When we say that children are learning principles of physics, this may amount to learning typical event categories. That is, they may learn, through myriad examples, that when the spoon is pushed off the table, it falls to the ground with a pleasing clatter. This is a physical fact (gravity makes things fall unless they are supported) that is also an event category (push X off table, X falls). Thus, category learning may be a central part of children's knowledge of their physical world, rather than being a separate psychological component. Although I will focus from here on out on experiments that have specifically investigated categorization, it is useful to keep in mind that much of an infant's accumulating knowledge could be thought of as category learning.

One question that is surprisingly ambiguous in this field is whether one is investigating infants' actual concepts or their concept-learning skills. Experiments on younger infants often assume the latter, though those on 1-year-olds and older often focus on the former. However, there is often no clear attempt to distinguish these possibilities. For example, consider the bunny-mouse experiment described above (see tables 9.1 and 9.2). It is possible that the infants have seen bunnies or mice before. Imagine for the sake of argument that they have, and in fact have developed these categories prior to coming in to the lab. Now what is happening in the habituation phase is that the child is identifying the pictures as being of bunny after bunny (though presumably not using the name *bunny*). After seeing so many examples of the same known category, the infant now is relieved to get a mouse, a member of a different category. Alternatively, imagine that the infant has never seen either a bunny or mouse before. Now, the child is clearly *learning* a new category by seeing example after example. After this learning process, the mouse can be identified as a new entity. In experiments using familiar stimuli, it is often not entirely clear which of these situations is the case, or whether some combination of them is true. For example, suppose that the child has seen a few bunnies and a few mice but has never formed stable categories around these experiences. Nonetheless, the earlier viewings may aid the child in quickly acquiring the new category in the habituation phase. It would be naive to deny (in advance of any evidence) that pre-exposure to the items used in the experiment might affect the learning process. And since pictures and toys are often used in these studies, we must also admit that the child's experience may come from television, picture books, or toys, as well as from actual exemplars of the items. Articles on infant categorization often contain statements of the sort "Of course, children would not know these categories prior to the experiment," or "These categories must be purely perceptual, since infants have no knowledge of [the stimuli]." However, these comments are often made on intuition and are often not given any empirical backing. The distinction between learning a novel category and being exposed to items that have already been categorized (or at least are familiar) is so critical a one that it is surprising that it has not been more explicitly tested.

Basic Categorization Abilities

With this large number of preliminary matters out of the way, we may now turn to questions of the psychology of infant categorization. Not surprisingly, the first studies of this question adapted techniques from then-current experiments on adults and older children. In the 1970s, the main questions of interest in adult work surrounded the abstraction of categories and the circumstances under which prototype-based categories would be learned. Research on infants (which lagged behind the adult work by a number of years then) asked whether the same kinds of phenomena might be found in infants. As discussed in chapter 3, the results of these experiments on adults can be interpreted either in terms of prototype theory or exemplar theory. The early infant papers on this topic did not acknowledge exemplar theory very much, and so I will tend to use a prototype-like description of the results, following their conclusions. However, it should be kept in mind that exemplar models can explain the same data, as explained in detail in chapters 3 and 4.

Studies of Artificial Concept Learning

One of the first studies that can be connected to the adult literature is that of Bomba and Siqueland (1983). Taking their cue from the studies of Posner and Keele (1968, 1970), they used dot-pattern categories. As will be recalled from chapter 2, these categories are usually formed by selecting a pattern of nine or so dots that have been randomly placed onto a matrix. This is the prototype, and learning exemplars are constructed by moving each of the dots a set distance in a randomly chosen direction. Subjects view these examples, usually mixed in with examples of other categories during a learning phase. Adult subjects, of course, overtly categorize each item and receive feedback on their responses. Infants, however, simply view items from a single category and then are tested on category members vs. nonmembers in a dishabituation task.

Bomba and Siqueland's study used the paired-preference procedure to study infants' concept learning. Their stimuli followed the adult model fairly closely, except that they did not use *random* dot patterns, but patterns that fit geometric concepts such as circle, triangle, and square. Thus, one prototype was a dot-outline of a triangle, and the exemplars were distortions of this triangle. This aspect of the experiment is unfortunate, since there might well be something distinctive to good geometric figures of this sort that cannot be generalized to other patterns. Although Bomba and Siqueland showed that infants did not prefer to look at the prototypes more than the distorted exemplars, there might still be some difference in the *learning* of the category, when the category is based on a simple geometric figure. (If there is an effect, it is probably that of making learning a bit easier for the infants—see Younger and Gotlieb 1988.)[7]

Bomba and Siqueland showed that 3- and 4-month-old infants could learn these categories: When they viewed distortions of a square, say, they then preferred to look at the triangle prototype over the square prototype—neither of which had been seen before. In short, infants clearly acquired the category and could distinguish it from other categories, even at this very early age.

Adult studies have found that a prototype is generally categorized more accurately (and rated as more typical) than are new exemplars. As discussed in chapter

2, it is often reported that the prototype is categorized more accurately than items that were actually learned. However, this is usually not the case with immediate testing on adults, though it may occur when there is a delay before test or when there are many exemplars in the learning phase. Bomba and Siqueland found quite comparable results. Immediately after viewing members of a category, infants did not prefer an old category item to the category prototype (Experiment 4). However, when they instituted a three-minute delay between the habituation and the preference test (Experiment 5), infants now preferred to look at the old item. Presumably, the precise details of individual patterns were forgotten to some degree during the delay, yet there was memory for the category as a whole. As a result, the prototype seemed more familiar to the infants, and so they preferred the old item. (Remember that in the dishabituation task, rejecting the prototype suggests that babies found it familiar.) Finally, when the number of exemplars was increased (Experiment 7), infants looked at the old item more than the prototype. This set of results, then, is strikingly similar to the general findings in the adult literature, suggesting that children form both memories for old items and an overall category representation (though again see exemplar accounts in chapter 3, and Hintzman and Ludlam 1980).

One interesting difference between the infant and adult experiments is that in the adult version, subjects are given the explicit task of learning the categories, and they receive feedback on their categorization decisions. Infants simply look at the category members, and yet they learn the categories. As discussed in chapter 5, adults do not always do so well in an "unsupervised learning" task of this sort.[8] Of course, in the real world, an infant is unlikely to see example after example of the same category members. Instead, it might see a spoon, a bowl, Daddy, the dog, the spoon again, the bowl again, the spoon on the floor, the dog licking the spoon, the lights on the ceiling, the spoon being put back in the bowl, and so on. To learn a category like spoons, the baby must notice the similarity of spoons across many different encounters, interspersed among many different category members. Although this very naturalistic situation has not been studied in experiments, there have been attempts to use a more realistic situation in which infants view two or more categories at a time.

Quinn (1987), also using the geometric categories of Bomba and Siqueland (1983), asked whether infants would be able to learn categories of this sort when they did not see only items from a single category. Perhaps the diversity of items would so confuse the infants that they would not notice the similarities among some of the items. Quinn constructed three types of learning sets. One group, *Cat-1* (I

Table 9.3.
Basic design of Quinn (1987).

Cat-1 Group		
Trial 1:	square 1	square 1
Trial 2:	square 2	square 2
Trial 3:	square 3	square 3
Cat-2 Group		
Trial 1:	square 1	square 1
Trial 2:	triangle 1	triangle 1
Trial 3:	square 2	square 2
Trial 4:	triangle 2	triangle 2
Cat-1 + Group		
Trial 1:	square 1	square 1
Trial 2:	ellipse 1	ellipse 1
Trial 3:	square 2	square 2
Trial 4:	rhombus 1	rhombus 1
Test Pair for all groups:		
	square 4	diamond

Note: The Cat-1 group actually had 6 familiarization trials, and the other two groups had 12–6 for each category.

have changed the names a bit from Quinn's) was exposed to members of a single category (e.g., distortions of a square); *Cat-2* was exposed to members of two categories (e.g., distortions of squares and triangles); and *Cat-1+* viewed distortions of one category plus other items that did not form a category (distortions of many different geometric figures). The design is shown schematically in table 9.3. The Cat-1 group saw fewer items than the other groups, but they were all from a single category; Cat-2 and Cat-1+ saw the same number of items, but they differed in their coherence, as the Cat-2 stimuli could be divided into two groups of similar items. If infants' learning abilities are limited to very simple and straightforward situations, they would likely only learn in the Cat-1 case. However, if they are able to extract regularities from disparate items, they might be able to learn categories in the other cases as well. The test of category learning was again a paired-preference procedure in which a novel item from a viewed category (e.g., square) was paired with a novel item from an unfamiliar category (e.g., diamond).

Quinn found that even 3- and 4-month-old infants were able to learn the categories in the Cat-1 (replicating Bomba and Siqueland 1983) and Cat-2 conditions. However, they did not learn in the Cat-1+ condition. Interestingly, performance in the Cat-2 condition was actually better than in the Cat-1 condition, suggesting that seeing the two categories together made them more distinctive. Clearly, the infants were not disturbed by seeing members of different categories mixed together, so long as the items had systematic variation. When the noncategory members varied randomly (Cat-1+), the diversity was apparently too much for the babies, interfering with category learning.

Quinn also found (Experiment 3) that subjects in the Cat-2 condition showed a large prototype effect—they preferred to look at an old (already seen) category member over the never-seen prototype. Those in the Cat-1 condition preferred the prototype to the old item. Similar to Bomba and Siqueland's results, then, when the number of items is smaller (6 in Cat-1, as opposed to 12 in Cat-2), subjects do not prefer to look at an old item. However, a more intriguing possibility is that learning multiple categories at once may lead infants to forget some stimulus-specific information and to retain category-level information.

Similar results have been found by Younger and Cohen in an experiment using drawings of simple animals rather than dot patterns. These investigators created stimuli in which some properties tended to co-occur, creating two distinct clusters of items. For example, in one learning set (see Younger and Cohen 1985, table IV), animals appeared in one of two types. One type had a giraffe-like body, a feathered tail, and webbed feet; another type had a cow-like body, a fluffy tail, and club feet. The animals also differed in their ears and number of legs, which did not correlate with the other items. To test whether the infants noticed the two distinct kinds of objects, Younger and Cohen tested them on items that had attributes consistent with the clustering (giraffe body and feathered tail) and items that were inconsistent (giraffe body and fluffy tail). Using the single-presentation dishabituation procedure, Younger and Cohen found that 10-month-old infants dishabituated to the inconsistent attribute pairing but not to the consistent one. That is, the infants apparently had learned that a given body type tends to occur with a given tail type, and any violation of this surprised them. Furthermore, they learned this while being simultaneously exposed to two different categories, rather than just a single one repeated over and over. Finally, it is also impressive that they learned such relations even while other stimulus dimensions were varying randomly (ears and number of legs).[9]

Later work by Younger and Cohen focused on the learning of specific correlated attributes—not just the learning of whole categories. However, finding evidence for the learning of specific correlations in categories turns out to be difficult even in adults (see chapter 5 for discussion), and the demonstrations for infants were not entirely convincing, for two reasons. First, in some cases, the correlations did not seem to be based on a sufficient amount of evidence for the child to form a generalization. For example, in some experiments, the correlations were represented by only two to four items total during the habituation period (see tables VII and VIII of Younger and Cohen 1985, which is a very useful summary of their work). Although infants sometimes were sensitive to the correlations in later tests, this is most likely to be explainable as the similarity of a test item to specific exemplars that had been learned during habituation, since two or four items do not provide a reliable basis on which to extract a correlation that distinguishes two categories. Also, when testing for feature correlations, it is critical to make sure that the test items do not differ in the frequency or typicality of individual features, but differ only in the pairing of those features. However, in some experiments (see Younger 1992, table 1), the frequencies of the test features during learning were not equated.

A second problem which plagues the question of feature correlations is useful to discuss because it also has more general importance. This is the problem of feature definition. For example, Younger (1992) used faces as her stimuli, varying the dimensions of nose width, eye spacing, and hairline (full or receding). In order to discover whether subjects (of any age) are learning feature correlations, it is necessary to be sure that they are extracting the same features that have been used to design the stimuli. Unfortunately, for pictorial stimuli, this cannot be easily guaranteed. For example, older subjects may interpret faces in terms of intelligence, friendliness, or emotional expressiveness. Even if subjects do not use such criteria, they may have other ways of perceptually analyzing faces that are more holistic and less analyzable as individual features. For example, perhaps some faces have more open space and others are more crowded; in some faces, the features are fairly triangular (wide eyes, small mouth), whereas in others, they are more rectangular (narrow eyes, wide mouth). It is important to understand that even though we as experimenters may design stimuli to have three features of such-and-such a kind, it is not necessarily the case that the subjects will analyze the stimuli as having exactly those three features. And if they don't, then we cannot discover whether they are learning feature correlations, because we have not manipulated the correlations of the features that they were using.

This argument was first made in an insightful paper by Kemler (1981). She focused on the fact that infants may not have the same perceptual abilities that adults do. So, even if we construct stimuli that have a certain structure that is apparent to adults, we cannot simply assume that it is apparent to infants. (It is for such reasons that research on adult sensitivity to feature correlations almost always uses verbal features that are clearly separated—e.g., Medin et al. 1984; Murphy and Wisniewski 1989.) Kemler's argument applies to any investigation in which knowing the exact identity of features is critical to the effect, not just feature correlations (e.g., questions of whether subjects are counting or averaging features in prototypes; Strauss 1979).

However, in spite of this rather daunting problem, we should not ignore what can be learned from the studies just reviewed, since most of them do not require us to know the exact features that infants see in the stimuli. The dot-pattern studies showing that infants can learn prototype categories are not subject to this problem. All we need to know is that the distortions are all somewhat similar to the proto-type, which is in fact confirmed by the results. In studies of typicality, all we need to assume is that the typical items are more similar to the prototype than are the atypi-cal items; we do not need to know the precise features the items differ in. Similarly, the Younger and Cohen (1985) finding that children will separate two categories of artificial animals is impressive, even if we cannot be entirely sure of what features they were using: The infants learned that there are two distinctive kinds of things in this experiment, in spite of considerable variability. Third, studies using real cate-gories to be described next do not require us to know the exact features that are being extracted. (This is a good thing, because it is not fully known what features are extracted from them in adult object perception, either.) Here, the stimuli are selected from actual categories, like chairs and dogs, and whatever the natural vari-ation among those items is, and however they are perceived, the primary interest is in whether infants can acquire them.

To summarize this section, infants seem able to learn one or two categories during a brief session without much difficulty. They also distinguish prototypes from other items, especially when there is a memory load that interferes with memory for spe-cific old items. Prototypes are treated as if they were familiar, which is exactly what would be expected if children learned the categories. Thus far, then, infants' basic category-learning abilities seem qualitatively similar to those of older children and adults. Furthermore, those abilities could be used to learn categories of physical events or other important concepts from a very early age.

Studies with Natural Categories

A later, but now more popular, approach has been to study infants' acquisition of natural categories. The main goal of this work is to discover whether and at what age children can learn categories of different types, and what variables influence this acquisition. Although perhaps less driven by questions of basic categorization pro-cesses, this work seeks to discover what actual concepts infants could be learning.

The eventual hope (by no means accomplished yet) is to link up the findings here with research on older children's categorization.

A number of studies have found that infants can learn single categories of animals. Cohen and Caputo (1978) found that 12-month-olds could learn the category of dogs (as distinguished from an antelope). Roberts (1988) showed that 9-month-olds could learn the category of birds (as distinguished from a horse). Quinn et al. (1993) extended such findings to 3-month-old infants, using photographs of animals, rather than line drawings. Using the paired preference procedure, they found that their subjects could learn the categories cats or dogs, as distinguished from birds. However, they also got (Experiment 4) the rather puzzling result that when infants were exposed to cats, they could distinguish them from dogs, but when exposed to dogs, they could not distinguish them from cats. Quinn et al. found evidence that the greater variability of dogs might account for this result. Because dogs have been bred to have a wide variety of body shapes and sizes in order to serve various functions, they are considerably more variable than many other basic-level categories. Thus, in looking at pictures of a sheepdog, a dachshund, a beagle, and a St. Bernard, infants may not be able to extract the similarities that make them all dogs. When infants were shown a less variable set of dogs, they were indeed able to learn the category (as distinguished from cats).

Although infants can learn categories that more or less correspond to our basic categories, the categories that the infants extract may not actually correspond to the categories that adults know. The less variable dog category of Quinn et al. described above is one example. Similarly, Eimas and Quinn (1994) found that infants could learn the category of cats that is distinguishable from horse, but not so distinguishable from tigers or female lions.[10] By 6–7 months, infants were able to learn the cat category in a way that distinguished it from tigers and lions. So, either infants had developed the ability to learn a narrower category in those few months, or perhaps they learned more about one or more of these categories outside the laboratory.

Later investigations have focused on exactly what cues children use in distinguishing similar animals such as dogs and cats or dogs and horses. Quinn and Eimas (1996) covered up various parts of animals during familiarization and tested to see whether infants could still distinguish cats from dogs. They found that when the whole animal was visible, the categories were learned quite well. They were learned equally well when just the face was visible. But when just the face was covered up, the categories were not learned. This pattern suggests that the infants were abstracting face information rather than body information from the whole animal. A more high-tech version of this study was reported by Spencer et al. (1997), which avoided

Figure 9.1
One of the stimuli used by Spencer et al. (1997). This shows a hybrid stimulus with the head of a dog and body of a cat. Note that the color and texture have been harmonized so that there is no obvious discontinuity between the two parts.

the possibly distracting occluders in the Quinn and Eimas study. In this experiment, children viewed either cats or dogs during the habituation phase. Then they were tested on hybrid stimuli, created electronically using a graphics program. One hybrid stimulus had the head of a cat and the body of a dog, and another had the head of a dog and the body of a cat (see figure 9.1). If children had viewed cats during habituation, and if they had particularly learned the faces of the cats, they should now be more interested in the hybrid with the dog's head and cat's body than the reverse hybrid. And that is in fact what happened—the faces appeared to dominate the bodies.[11] Quinn and Eimas (1996) suggest that the use of faces may reflect a very early interest that infants have in looking at human faces, which can then be extended to learning about different animals. I should also point out that this might explain why infants were unable to distinguish cats from female lions in Eimas and Quinn's (1994) study, since they have very similar faces (cats and lions—not Eimas and Quinn).

All of these categories could be characterized as "basic-level" categories (see chapter 7) to a rough approximation. As Mervis (1987) noted for older children, we should not assume that the basic category is the same for children and adults. Information that distinguishes categories is often simply not known to infants, and so they will treat members of two different categories as if they are the same. An infant cannot know that lions live in Africa, that they are much larger than housecats (in experiments, the pictures are always roughly the same size), that they hunt in packs, and so on. From the infant's perspective, all that can be used to distinguish the categories is evidence that is readily perceptible in the immediate environment. Any categories that rely heavily on less available information cannot be completely learned. It would be no shock to find that infants cannot form categories of financial institutions or subatomic particles, since these are things that they simply do not have enough information about and cannot directly perceive. It is not surprising, either, that infants can acquire basic-level categories, since these generally have high levels of within-category similarity and low levels of between-category similarity. Although domestic cats differ in color and slightly in size, they are quite homogeneous and are very different from most other animals that an infant is likely to see in North America or Europe, such as dogs, birds, and insects.

One piece of evidence that infants find basic-level categories easier than superordinates is Waxman and Markow's (1995) finding that infants will habituate to items in the same basic category more than they will to items in the same superordinate. For example, if children were given four toy cars to play with, they attended to the final car much less than they did to the first car—the usual habituation result. But if they were given four vehicles to play with (a helicopter, airplane, van, and car), their habituation was much less.

There is another research program, however, that has argued that children's earliest concepts are of more general, superordinate-like categories. Jean Mandler and her colleagues have used the sequential touching paradigm to argue that children are sensitive to what they call *global* categories. These are broad categories similar to what might be called *superordinate* categories in other contexts, but these authors correctly point out that the infant's general categories will not usually correspond to adult superordinates (and see Mervis 1987) and conclude that they should not receive the same name. The sequential touching paradigm requires somewhat older infants than can be used in dishabituation tasks, since the children must have fairly accurate motor control and must resist the temptation to sweep all the objects off the table, and so on. But if it could be shown that these older infants have global categories but not basic categories, this would tell us much about the concepts of younger infants.

A typical experiment of this sort is as follows (Mandler, Bauer, and McDonough 1991, Experiment 1). The stimuli were toys or models of real objects. These objects were placed on a tray in a "haphazard" arrangement and were presented to the child with the instruction "These are for you to play with" or "Can you fix these up?" As described earlier, the order in which children handle the toys is coded and examined for sequences in which many items from the same category were touched one after the other. The children, who were from 19 to 30 months old, did this task three times: once with items that differed at a global level (animals and vehicles), and twice with objects that differed at the basic level. The basic-level tasks involved some sets that differed only a little (on the authors' intuitions), such as cars vs. trucks, and other that differed more, such as cars vs. planes. The results showed that children distinguished the two global categories (animals vs. vehicles), but the basic categories were distinguished only when there was high contrast (e.g., cars vs. planes). They did not distinguish the basic categories when the categories were more similar (e.g., cars vs. trucks or dogs vs. horses). Other experiments found that children can distinguish general categories such as land, air, and water animals, animals vs. plants, and kitchen items vs. furniture. Yet children could not distinguish cacti vs. trees (the subjects were from an area where cacti are common), tables vs. chairs, spoons vs. forks, or string musical instruments vs. horns. All of these would be considered basic-level contrasts.

Mandler and McDonough (1993) attempted to extend their results to younger children, aged 9–11 months. The sequential touching task was not used here, but instead they used a modification of the dishabituation task in which subjects are allowed to pick up and examine objects one at a time (similar to that of Oakes et al. 1997, described above). First, the babies would see four objects twice. On the 9th trial, a new category member was given, and on the 10th trial, a nonmember was given. The question was whether infants would increase their looking to a new member and an item from a new category. Note that this method tests each infant on both a control item (a new object that is from the same category) and the experimental item (a new object from a new category). (However, the order of testing these items was constant, rather than counterbalanced, which causes some problems in interpretation.) In discussing their results, I will focus primarily on whether the new category member (trial 10) was examined longer than the novel item from the old category (trial 9). (This comparison is the cleanest one possible, given the order problem, because both items have not been seen before.)[12]

Mandler and McDonough (Experiment 1) found that children could distinguish animals from vehicles and cars from airplanes in this task, but they could not distinguish dogs from fish. The authors concluded that children at this age possess global categories of animals and vehicles but not more specific categories. The distinction between cars and planes they attributed to the large amount of land and air traffic in San Diego, where the study was carried out. Later experiments showed that the babies could distinguish cars from motorcycles (a basic contrast) and birds from airplanes (global), but not dogs from rabbits (basic).

Overall, Mandler and colleagues have found considerable evidence that children distinguish broad domains of objects but less evidence that they can distinguish basic-level categories (though note a number of exceptions listed in the last paragraph). This finding is contrary to a very large body of evidence in studies of older children that children first acquire basic-level categories and only very slowly acquire superordinates (Anglin 1977; Horton and Markman 1980; Mervis 1987; Rosch et al. 1976). Furthermore, older children find it more difficult to learn novel superordinates than basic categories. We will review and evaluate that evidence in the next chapter. For the moment, I will only point out that it is puzzling that, if children form global categories first, at the age of 1 or so, they have so much trouble with global categories when older.

There is one obvious challenge to Mandler's proposal, namely, that studies of young infants' concepts (reviewed above) have found numerous examples of even younger infants being able to learn basic-level concepts. For example, infants have been shown to learn categories such as dogs (vs. cats and birds), cats (vs. dogs and tigers), horses (vs. giraffes and zebras), chairs (vs. couches, beds, and tables), and couches (vs. chairs, beds, and tables). The dot-pattern studies discussed above showed that children can learn arbitrary visual patterns that are not from different domains of knowledge. Furthermore, children can learn to distinguish different categories of human faces, which are clearly a low-level category (Strauss 1979; Younger 1992). How then can Mandler conclude that children do not have basic-level categories, based on her work with children who are considerably older than most of these subjects?

Mandler makes a distinction between *perceptual* and *conceptual* categories. Perceptual categories are those that are solely a representation of a stimulus quality. For example, suppose that an infant sees many examples of cats and then sees an example of a tiger. The infant may notice that the tiger has stripes and may find this very interesting, in part because none of the previous items had stripes.[13] Thus, it is the repeated shapes and patterns of the habituation stimuli that are being learned here. A conceptual category has to do with understanding objects as being "the same sort of thing" (Mandler et al. 1991, p. 268). Mandler et al. (1991, p. 267) refer to research showing that adults may have sophisticated knowledge or theories about categories, which often do not rely on perceptual resemblance.

This distinction is echoed in some of the other literature on this topic. For example, Eimas and Quinn (1994, p. 904) say that they "take the representations of infants approximately 15 months and younger to be perceptual and not conceptual in nature." More concretely, Quinn et al. (1993, p. 464) argue that "Young infants use surface features as the basis for categorization and presumably know little about dogs, for example, other than these characteristics. The conceptual representation of more mature individuals, being to a large extent defined and organized by higher levels of knowledge, permit inferences about function and properties not given by perceptual information, as well as descriptions of why all dogs constitute a particular kind of thing as well as a kind of animal." I think that these authors, dealing with infants, may overemphasize the depth of the knowledge that adults have about various kinds. I do not think that most people have very specific information about what makes a dog a dog in particular, other than rather vague ideas about genetics or evolution that apply to all animals. Nonetheless, I agree that an infant might learn to recognize pictures of giraffes without knowing anything else about them than perceptual information given in the stimuli presented.

The distinction between perceptual and conceptual categories is the basis by which Mandler and her colleagues explain the differences between their results and those with younger infants. For example, infants can easily learn to tell the difference between things that look like dogs and those that look like birds, say. However, this does not mean that they have a conceptual category for dogs—perhaps it is only perceptual. In the sequential touching task, they do not show knowledge of the dog category, suggesting to Mandler that this task is tapping conceptual categories rather than perceptual ones. Furthermore, when children distinguish animals and vehicles in the touching task, this must be based on conceptual information, Mandler et al. (1991) argue, because the items within the categories are not perceptually similar. In short, this view proposes that children have the ability to form perceptual categories from the first few months of life. However, they do not form conceptual categories, as revealed through sequential touching, until later, and those conceptual categories refer to broad domains, such as animals, plants, furniture, clothing, or other distinct entities that infants are familiar with. It is only later that conceptual categories for basic classes such as dogs or spoon are formed.

Global vs. Basic Categories

This distinction between perceptual and conceptual categories, along with the parallel claim that very general categories are learned first, forms a somewhat tangled set of arguments, in my view. Given the amount of attention that this issue has received in the recent literature, I will attempt to untangle it a bit and see which parts of it have support and which currently do not. However, even more than usual, this section represents my personal opinion rather than a summary of the field as a whole.

The notion of a perceptual category seems straightforward, in the sense that an infant (or anyone) could notice a set of perceptual commonalities among stimuli without knowing anything else about them. However, it should not be thought that a simple sensory discrimination can explain the infant data. It is likely, for example, that infants are not just learning about patterns of light and color in pictures but are also drawing inferences about the underlying structures of the things being presented. For example, in the Quinn-Eimas work, animals are shown in a variety of poses (e.g., cats standing and sitting), which greatly changes their visual configuration. The colors and textures of the items also vary across pictures (e.g., long-hair and short-hair cats; calicos vs. "tigers"). However, animals in different positions have a consistent underlying configuration (the skeletal structure) that may be inferred from such pictures. So, even this kind of "perceptual" discrimination may in fact be fairly sophisticated, rather than a simple common feature or image. Similarly, if subjects are learning about the internal facial properties of cats and dogs (Quinn and Eimas 1996), they cannot be learning simple properties such as "has eyes," "has a nose," and so on, because these are true of both cats and dogs. Instead, subtler perceptual properties are being abstracted. Thus, even if infants are forming purely perceptual categories, we should not think that this amounts to a simple discrimination of stripes/no stripes or four legs/two legs, and so on. Furthermore, "deeper" perceptual properties (about skeletal structure, for example) may be just the kind of information needed to form other kinds of generalizations about an animal, such as its behavioral dispositions.

One could even go further and argue that the global discriminations made by children could in part be due to complex perceptual discriminations. For example, animate objects tend to have certain high-level properties in common, such as being bilaterally symmetric, having eyes and a mouth, having limbs, having complex texture (hair, fur, feathers), being rounded, and so on—properties that older children clearly are aware of (Massey and Gelman 1988). In contrast, many artifacts lack these features and are much more regular than animate entities. For example, most of the artificial objects in view to me now have straight edges, with flat or extremely regular cylindrical surfaces (pens or cups), edges that meet perpendicularly, and so on. It is easy to look at a collection of a bird, a whale, a dog, and a lion and say that they are not perceptually similar, but this is to ignore the higher-level commonalities they have in contrast with tables or motorcycles. In short, global categories may have considerable perceptual underpinning.

Smith and Heise (1992) report a preliminary experiment showing just this possibility. They performed a dishabituation study with 12-month-old children showing that they could distinguish animals from vehicles, using toy representations. However, they also found that the children would distinguish the two categories based on cut-up pieces of the toys as well, even though wheels, eyes, and other tell-tale parts were removed. They suggested that the texture differences between vehicles and animals (even in manufactured toys) were responsible for this discrimination, since the parts would not themselves be members of a conceptual category (e.g., are not animate, do not share function, etc.). In a personal communication, Linda Smith reports that in another study, infants could distinguish parts of *real* living things vs. parts of artifacts, again suggesting a sensitivity to perceptual differences between global categories.

The notion of a conceptual category also seems intuitively straightforward, and I will certainly not dispute the claim that people have all kinds of knowledge about categories (see chapter 6). However, it is not clear that one can make a clear distinction between two qualitatively different kinds of category types here, in part because perceptual information is critical to much underlying knowledge. Much work on knowledge-based categories is based on connections between perceptible features and underlying mechanisms (see Kaplan and Murphy 2000; Madole and Cohen 1995; Medin and Ortony 1989). For example, although having wings is a perceptible feature, there is knowledge involved in knowing that wings aid an animal in flying, and they do so by supporting the body on air (a theory that is widespread, though not exactly correct). Of course, one can *see* a bird flying with its wings extended, and see it fold up its wings when it lands, so this information also has a perceptual correlate. It is hard to provide a conceptual explanation of birds' structure that does not have an outward manifestation of some kind. Thus, background knowledge is not truly separate from perceptible features, because it often serves to explain those features (see also Kemler Nelson 1995; Smith and Heise 1992). Finally, young children are very sensitive to the relations between an object's parts and its behavior (Madole and Cohen 1995; McCarrell and Callanan 1995), suggesting that they are actively linking perceptible properties with dispositional expectations.

In short, theories that talk about background knowledge in categories (at least, my own work: Kaplan and Murphy 1999, 2000; Murphy 1993, 2000; Murphy and Medin 1985) have emphasized an interaction between perceptual features and underlying background knowledge. On this view, it would be incorrect to claim that there are two different kinds of categories—one perceptual, and one conceptual. More likely is the view, proposed by Quinn and Eimas (1997), that perceptual categories form the basis for more elaborate, knowledge-driven categories by providing a representation that can grow to incorporate knowledge. For example, once one notices wings and flying, one is ready to develop a conceptual explanation of how animals fly, by linking the two. Exactly how much perceptual and conceptual information constrain one another is still a matter of controversy. Smith and Heise (1992) argue that conceptual and perceptual information are closely connected but that the perceptual information dominates, just as scientific data must dominate theory (and see Jones and Smith 1993—discussed in the next chapter—for an even stronger position). However, positions arguing for a balance between the two are also clearly possible.

How do we explain the data that suggest that 1-year-olds distinguish global categories but not (always) basic categories? First, I have already pointed out that the global categories tested may have a perceptual basis that children could be noticing. This possibility is strongly supported by more recent findings that 2- and 4-month-old infants can learn to distinguish mammals from birds and fish (Behl-Chadha 1996; Quinn and Johnson 1997), even though mammals are a very diverse superordinate category. Since it is very unlikely that young infants have any biological knowledge to distinguish mammals from birds, this appears to be evidence for a possible perceptual basis for this distinction.

I have attempted to explain why the global categories can be learned in some cases. But why then does this not extend to basic categories in many of the sequential touching tasks (e.g., Mandler et al. 1991)? At this point, I need to remind the reader of the comment about null results made at the beginning of the chapter (it seems like a very long time ago). When one does not find evidence of categorization in these tasks, one is in a much less certain position than when one does find evidence for it. Of course, null results in any task are less informative than positive results are, but as I explained earlier, lack of discrimination in the present tasks can reflect a number of different factors that are not directly related to conceptual structure. This is especially true for the sequential touching task, where it is not well understood what is controlling the order of touching. Arguing that global categories are learned first is arguing based on a strong belief in the validity of the null results of basic categories in this task. But given that basic categories are learned much earlier in other tasks, this null result is not very strong evidence. There is no particular reason to believe that sequential touching is getting at the true nature of conceptual categories any more than the dishabituation task is. If 9-month-old infants in a dishabituation task can learn that a series of photographed cats, in different positions, different hair length, different coloring, and so forth, form a category that is different than that of tigers, it is not clear that null results in a touching task should convince us that older infants cannot form this category, or that it is somehow less conceptual a representation. (I am focusing on sequential touching in part because the object-examination results of Mandler and McDonough 1993, did not in fact give much evidence for global categories preceding basic categories. They found that children could distinguish cars from both motorcycles and airplanes, which are both basic category distinctions. So, the evidence there was mixed.)

That is all fine and good, but it does not actually explain why some categories are responded to in the sequential touching task and some are not. I will offer two facts, which I believe explain many, though perhaps not all cases. First, note that the stimuli in the object examination task are not in fact category members (i.e., animals, vehicles, and so on) but are *toys* and *models*, of similar sizes, usually made of hard plastic. It seems likely to me that any child who sees an actual horse or two will never have any trouble distinguishing them from actual rabbits or dogs. The items in the examination task are much more similar than the real life objects would be, which may explain some of the null effects. (For example, perhaps all the toy animals can be played with in similar ways.) Of course, the photographs used in dishabituation tasks have a number of problems as well, though apparently they provide enough evidence to distinguish many basic-level categories.

The second factor has to do with the distinctiveness of the stimuli. In one of the first studies using this task, Starkey (1981) used mostly artificial stimuli, like colored shapes. He examined a number of different determinants of sequential touching, and one result he found was that the more distinctive the items in the two sets, the more likely babies were to distinguish them in their touching (p. 494). For example, the greatest amount of category discrimination was when the stimuli included little people and yellow ovals (differing on many dimensions) and the least category discrimination was found when the stimuli included red ovals that differed only in size. Although children could easily detect the size difference (a difference in length of 1.3 vs. 7.5 cm), this was not enough to cause them to touch one group before the other.

Thus, the distinctiveness of the items may be an important influence on performance in this task.

As a general rule, the sequential touching data of Mandler and colleagues' experiments show effects when the items are very distinctive. The separation of different global categories virtually always corresponds to very different stimuli (animals and vehicles, for example). Similarly, the basic-level categories that subjects distinguished were usually of things that are fairly different (cars vs. airplanes). In fact, Mandler et al. (1991, Experiment 1) found that as basic-level categories became more distinctive, children were more likely to distinguish them in their touching (see also Rakison and Butterworth 1998, Experiment 1). Although this may be a rather mundane observation, it is a bit different than the way Mandler et al. are interpreting this task, which is in terms of common category membership. For example, I think that it is very likely that 2-year-old children have concepts of forks and spoons and of chairs and tables—in fact, it is very hard for me to believe otherwise, since these are the objects they have encountered multiple times every day of their lives. Some 2-year-olds already have names for these things. Yet, 2-year-olds do not distinguish these categories in the touching task (Mandler et al. 1991, Experiment 5).[14] The reason, according to my proposal, is that although forks and spoons are easily identified as two different kinds of things by a child, they are also similar in their overall shape, material, functions, and, perhaps most important, in terms of the activities they afford in such a task. That is, both allow the child to pick them up by the handle, bang them around, chew on the ends, and so forth, with very similar experiences resulting. In contrast, animals and vehicles provide very different ways and experiences of interacting, and children apparently prefer to do those interactions in sequence. That is, they like to pick up and make some things hop and then pick up others and go "vroom-vroom" with them.

Does discrimination in a touching task imply a broad conceptual category distinguishing the items? Although it may, it might also be that the children are simply biased to touch and play with some objects more. If they would rather play with the vehicles presented, then they will be seen to distinguish vehicles from animals, even if they do not make any conceptual distinction between the two. They may just like to examine or push toys that move. As argued earlier, preferences indicate discrimination of some kind, but they do not imply category knowledge. In fact, it is possible that children would show this discrimination without knowing anything about animals or vehicles in general. If, for example, they represent a toy dog as having properties like "four-legged, hairy, eats, barks, runs" and a car as "has wheels, has doors, Mommy drives it, windows go up and down," then these two representations are extremely different. Children would be likely to treat two such objects differently even if they do not understand the difference between vehicles and animals more generally. In contrast, a representation of a toy cat (e.g., "four-legged, hairy, eats, meows, runs") would be quite similar to the representation of the dog, and so children may not treat them differently in this task, even if they do know that they are in different categories.

This proposal for understanding the differences between the sequential touching and dishabituation tasks is speculative, and no doubt there will be plenty of chances to disconfirm it in future experiments. However, I think the theoretically compelling story is one in which children's initial primarily perceptually based categories develop into more conceptual categories (Oakes et al. 1997; Quinn and Eimas 1997), rather than suggesting two separate systems. The latter would be extremely unwieldy, and eventually unhelpful, as it is necessary for even conceptual categories to be perceptually identified. (Indeed, Mandler 1992, argues that conceptual categories arise through a process of perceptual abstraction. Her story here is interesting and may well be true. What is not so clear is how that process is different from the process of learning basic-level categories, which she argues is not conceptual.) Even if it turns out that our concept of dogs is a deep, heavily intertwined body of knowledge, we must relate that knowledge to individual dogs by learning perceptual properties that correspond to dogs. Furthermore, we want to use our concept to make mundane predictions about dogs (such as having ears or howling at the moon), and so this mundane information about what a dog does and looks like has to be integrated with the concept. From this perspective, the suggestion that infants learn what dogs and cats are perceptually, but later form independent conceptual concepts by subdividing their more global concept of animals, seems psychologically highly implausible. Perceptual and conceptual information must be intertwined. Nonetheless, Mandler's writings have been important in raising the issue, which was often ignored, of the nature of infants' first concepts, and of how perceptual and conceptual information is integrated in the earliest concepts. She is right in asking us to think about the degree to which nonperceptual information is integrated into infants' concepts. Although her own proposals have been controversial, they have been instrumental in stimulating research to resolve these issues.

Two Warnings

I remarked much earlier in this chapter that much infant-categorization work makes little distinction between experiments in which infants learn categories and those in which infants respond on the basis of known categories. In some cases, it is clear that infants could not know the categories being taught in the experiment, but in other cases, it is possible or even likely that they have encountered these objects before, in person, in picture books, or on TV (e.g., common animals and artifacts). The sequential touching task seems most likely to be sensitive to the categories that the children already have. That is, if they look at a set of stimuli scattered haphazardly on a tray, and begin handling the items immediately, there is little time for their touching behavior to be influenced by learning from the display itself. In contrast, the dishabituation task allows concepts to be learned in the habituation phase, or it may reflect already-known categorical knowledge, or both. It seems possible to me that differences between the results of these tasks could reflect a difference between categories that children already know and categories that they have learned in the experiment. In this respect, then, the results of the experiments are not directly comparable, and further investigation into them is called for.

A second warning has to do with attributing adult categories to infants. Mandler and her colleagues were wise to use the term "global" categories rather than "superordinates," in order to explicitly note the potential differences between infants' and adults' categories. But throughout the literature there are many statements of the sort: "Based on our results, infants can learn the category of dogs/mammals/female faces at 7 months, but not at 3 months." However, attributing this categorical knowledge to infants is rather dangerous. It is a danger that investigators know about but do not always explicitly mention, which has sometimes led to rather optimistic appraisals of infants' knowledge. In an infant category-learning experiment, only a small number of pictures is shown. Furthermore, very atypical subtypes are generally not used—ostriches, penguins, vultures, and hummingbirds do not figure heavily in the bird stimuli of these experiments. Nor do they use unusual items, such as genetically deformed birds or chicks that naturally look very different from their parents, and so on. However, in adult categories, atypical members and unusual items can all be accommodated.

My point is that we should not forget the limitations of an experiment in which infants seem to learn a category based on a small number of typical items. From such a set, they no doubt can form a category that corresponds to very typical category members, but we should not expect that the extension of an infant's "bird" category is very close to that of an adult's. This general point has some more specific implications. For example, I think that such deviations are most likely to occur at the higher-level categories that generally do not have many properties in common, and whose properties are often rather abstract, functional kinds of things (Rosch et al. 1976; Tversky and Hemenway 1984). Thus, claims about children having a particular abstract category should be taken with a grain of salt until they are tested on a wide range of objects that adults would admit as being category members.

Quinn and Johnson (1997) presented a connectionist model that attempted to learn categories at the basic and superordinate level. Like other such attempts (Anderson and Murphy 1986), they found that the model was very likely to learn superordinate categories first. They tentatively suggested that infants may be able to form global categories based on perceptual properties, as part of learning more specific and useful categories. Although this is certainly an intriguing possibility, it should be noted that the model was tested on only one superordinate distinction— that of mammals vs. furniture. More importantly, the examples of mammals input to the model were limited. They did not include sea mammals, like seals, walruses, dolphins, and whales, nor flying mammals, like bats, nor primates, like chimpanzees and humans, but used all four-legged land mammals. Similarly, the furniture they input to their model did not include lamps, televisions, or atypical examples like rugs and trash baskets. Quinn and Johnson chose such stimuli for their simulation because they were comparable to studies with actual infants. However, when drawing conclusions, one must not be too quick to say that infants or a model were able to learn a category, if it only corresponds to a very typical subset of the items. If children can see a similarity between lions and dogs but not between lions and whales or between dogs and bats, then they do not have the category of mammal yet. In general, it is not clear how far the categories of infants extend beyond the core examples that have been displayed in the experiment. This is itself an interesting empirical question, and one that will likely receive further attention in the future.

Infants' Concepts and Object Individuation

I have reviewed experiments showing that infants can form concepts of some kind at very early ages. As just discussed, Mandler has questioned whether these are true concepts of the sort that adults form. A similar, but more specific question has been raised recently about whether children can use concepts as *sortals*. Sortals are the units we use to identify and count things in the world. For example, the concept of dogs is a sortal, because we can divide things into dogs and nondogs, and we can count how many dogs are in the yard. In contrast, a concept like redness is not a sortal, because we can't "count the red in the yard" (Xu 1997). There may be *some* red, but there aren't reds. The prototype example of sortals is objects, but concepts such as types of events are also sortals, in that we can count the numbers of parties or tantrums we had last year. Although we are less likely to do so, we can also count up parts of things, like legs or handles.

Research on infant cognition has been extremely interested in the question of what children understand about objects, especially their physical and temporal properties. The question of what constitutes an object is a difficult one for infants to figure out, and there is considerable development in their understanding of objects over the course of the first year of life. One issue, which seems trivial to adults, arises when incomplete perceptual information about objects is available. For example, imagine you see a person sitting at a table, such that you can see his legs and feet and his chest and head. You will undoubtedly conclude that there is a single, continuous person from head to feet, even though you cannot see the connection between the top and bottom of the person because of the table. Based on perceptual information and knowledge, you count these two parts as just being one thing. However, infants do not always draw such conclusions—they must gain experience with the world before they know enough to relate disconnected entities as being the same object (see Wilcox and Baillargeon 1998a).

Concepts provide one source of information about how to count things. For example, if you know that there are four dogs and three cats in the yard, then you know that there are (at least) seven animals in the yard. That is, you know that the dogs and cats cannot be the same objects, and so they must be counted separately. More generally, concepts may provide one way of individuating entities, which allows them to be counted (Xu 1997).[15]

Research has shown that infants can use spatiotemporal information to distinguish and count objects. For example, if they simultaneously see two things with space between them, infants understand that there are different objects involved. What is not so clear is whether they can use concepts—without the use of spatiotemporal information—to individuate them. Consider an experiment by Xu and Carey (1996). They had infants view an apparatus with a screen in the middle. From behind the screen came one object, say, a ball, which moved to the left side of the apparatus and then returned behind the screen. Then a different object, perhaps a bottle, moved from behind the screen to the right side of the apparatus and then returned behind the screen. This sequence was repeated multiple times. Finally, the screen was removed, revealing either the two objects previously seen (ball and bottle), or only one of them (the bottle). Clearly, the latter situation is surprising to adults, as the screen should have been concealing two objects. However, infants were not surprised until they were 12.5 months old.[16] Xu and Carey concluded from this that the younger infants could not use category information about the objects to distinguish them as sortals. That is, from the 10.5-month-old's perspective, there could just be a single object moving back and forth behind the screen. The infants don't notice anything funny about this, because they aren't using concepts like ball and bottle to represent the object, and therefore, they don't conclude that there must be two objects.

To be clear, Xu and Carey are not denying that 10-month-old infants can individuate objects; in other paradigms, based on spatiotemporal cues, they can. Furthermore, they are not denying that infants form a concept of some sort in dishabituation tasks of the sort I discussed earlier. What they are denying is that these infants can explicitly represent the object's category in such a way that they can identify which object is which. So, the infants did not notice that there was a ball that went to the left and a bottle that went to the right, but only that something went to the left and something went to the right. Of course, if infants could simultaneously see a ball on the left and a bottle on the right, they would realize that there are two different objects present. But this conclusion may be based on a spatiotemporal analysis, rather than using the information about the two concepts. Xu and Carey speculate that word learning may be the key that allows very young children to use concepts to represent individual objects and therefore to count and distinguish them.

Xu and Carey's conclusion has been controversial, however, as different paradigms have suggested that infants can use category information, or more generally, information about objects' features, to count objects. Wilcox and Baillargeon (1998a) proposed that the situation Xu and Carey used was too complex for children to count the objects. They point out that the experiment had two parts: an occlusion event, in which objects appeared and disappeared, and a revealing event, in which the screen is removed (itself a surprise) and one or more objects are revealed. Infants in this task will be surprised if they can relate the objects in the two events. That is, if they keep track of the objects involved in the occlusion event, identify the objects in the revealing event, *and* if they understand the relation between these two events, then they will be surprised when the number of objects changes. Wilcox and Baillargeon used a simpler kind of task in which objects move back and forth behind an occluder (i.e., no revealing part). The objects could either be identical or different. For example, a ball that moves behind an occluder could appear as a box on the other side and then change back into a ball when it passes back behind the occluder again. Alternatively, only the ball could move back and forth. In this task, the child only has to monitor a single kind of event and notice whether it is internally consistent, not compare two different kinds of events. A final, clever twist on this paradigm is that Wilcox and Baillargeon manipulated the width of the occluding screen. If the screen were wide enough, it could hold a ball and box behind it, and so it would not be surprising if the ball appeared on one side and the box on the other—there could simply be two objects involved. But if the screen were too narrow to hold both a ball and a box, then the event would be seen as surprising—*if* the child was encoding the objects' identities. That is, if the child thinks that the narrow screen event with the two objects is surprising, this implies that the child thought there were two separate objects that could not fit behind the screen.

Wilcox and Baillargeon (1998a) first replicated Xu and Carey's earlier result that 11.5-month-old children did, but 9.5-month-old children did not, notice the changing objects in the original kind of task, in which an occlusion event is followed by a revealing event. However, they found that 9.5-month-old, and indeed, 7.5-month-old children could succeed at the easier task (and a later experiment found that 4.5-month-old babies could; Wilcox and Baillargeon 1998b). That is, when the screen was narrow, children looked longer at the two-object condition, involving the ball and box. When the screen was wide, they looked equally often at the two- and one-object conditions. Wilcox and Baillargeon argued that young infants keep track of the object's category and can use this category to individuate objects.[17] When a ball and box are involved, infants think that two objects are present and are puzzled about how they could both fit behind the screen. If they thought that this was just one object, then the size of the screen would not make a difference. (Perhaps there was something irrelevant about the narrow screen that made infants look more in the two-object condition, you're thinking. However, when the objects were made smaller, so that they could actually fit behind the same narrow screen, infants no longer looked more at the two-object condition.)

Unfortunately, this controversy is still not resolved, as Xu, Carey, and Welch (1999) have provided more experiments suggesting that children are unable to use categories as sortals until 12 months of age. They argue that Wilcox and Baillargeon's experiments may involve form perception rather than true categories. Perhaps infants are seeing not two distinct objects, but rather a single object that changes from a ball to a box when it goes behind the screen. Therefore, this kind of experiment is not really asking infants to count objects but instead to notice whether a single object changes. (Renée Baillargeon has pointed out to me that this explanation is not consistent with the finding that the small objects do not show the same effect. That is, the small ball and small box which both fit behind the narrow screen are not looked at longer than a small ball that moves back and forth. If infants saw the object as changing when it went behind the screen, then they should have looked more at the small two-object display.) Xu et al. review other evidence that they argue is consistent with their claim that concepts cannot be used as sortals until 12 months or so.

Interested readers should consult the papers cited above, as well as a commentary by Needham and Baillargeon (2000) and reply by Xu and Carey (2000) for the present status of the issue. Xu and Carey's view is somewhat more difficult to prove in principle, because it requires a convincing null effect. That is, other researchers have demonstrated that children use featural information to distinguish objects, and Xu and Carey must show that those experiments do not really require the use of conceptual information or that the tasks do not reflect object individuation. However, at the same time, they must demonstrate that their own tasks do require these things, and that their own null results for children under 12 months are real. This is not to say that Xu and Carey are wrong, but that it is always more difficult to argue from null results than from positive ones. In order to decide whose account of the data is correct, further studies will have to be performed to better understand what infants are deriving from the different displays used in different experiments.

If Xu and Carey's view turns out to be correct, then what would this mean for the psychology of infant concepts? One could take a modest view that this would simply reflect infants' limited skill in using and thinking about concepts. That is, perhaps infants can form concepts but cannot maintain two different concepts in working memory and use them to keep track of how many objects are present, or where they are. The problem with sortals would be simply a matter of expertise in remembering and manipulating multiple concepts simultaneously. A stronger view is that children undergo an important cognitive shift at around 11 or 12 months, in which they become able to represent kind concepts symbolically. This is Xu and Carey's (2000, p. 286) interpretation. For example, Xu (1997) proposes that infants in the typical dishabituation task may be interpreting the stimuli as something like "'an *object* with cat-properties, an *object* with somewhat different cat-properties, … an *object* with cup-properties' with no commitment as to whether the first cat, the second cat, and the cup were numerically distinct objects" (pp. 380–381, ellipses in the original). The infant, then, has some memory of properties it has seen but cannot use these properties to form a whole concept and to distinguish a cat from a cup, for example.

Under this more radical view, it is unclear how language learning could take place. If children are not able to form consistent concepts in order to represent entities, how can they learn what things are called by what names? They could not learn something like "things with whiskers, fur, four legs, that say *meow* are called *cats*," because they wouldn't have the concept of those things to associate to the name. Xu (1997, p. 379) points out that the younger infants who knew the names of some of the objects succeeded in the task, which supports her view that babies are using kinds to distinguish the objects. What is not clear, though, is how babies go from not being able to distinguish kinds to being able to distinguish them, so that they may learn object names.

In short, it seems to me that the view that infants do not form concepts that can be used to identify objects before the age of 12 months has some theoretical problems. It is certainly possible that it is true, but the more gradualistic approach of the mainstream infant concept literature (Quinn and Eimas 1997) can more easily explain the transition from perceptual to conceptual categories to name learning. Research on both sides of this question is very active at the time of writing, and it is likely that we will soon have more data from which to derive a more detailed understanding of infants' use of categories to individuate and represent objects.

Conceptual Development in Later Infancy

Much of the debate on global vs. basic categorization and on sortals has surrounded a central question that has still not been answered very well, namely, whether the infant has simply noticed some similarity of the items, or whether it has identified them as being in the same category. Although any of the popular tasks is probably sensitive to category membership, the tasks may also be sensitive to other kinds of similarity that would not constitute categories as usually construed. In the real world, when an infant sees a dog approach, does it think something corresponding to "there's another dog—the kind that barks and licks you" (though not in English, obviously), or does it just think "that seems familiar—duck!"?

One difference between a real category and just perceptual similarity is that categories are expected to be collection points for information. That is, when one learns what a dog does (barking, drooling, running), this gets associated with the information about what a dog looks and sounds like, and eventually is associated with any deeper knowledge about dogs. (This is part of the reason I am rejecting the putative distinction between perceptual and conceptual categories. A category connects all the related information about a kind, and so should include both sorts of information.) If an infant learns a new fact about a particular dog, it might generalize that to new dogs, by virtue of identifying them as being in the same category. This more productive use of category membership, which is involved in induction, would then go beyond a simple perceptual recognition response. The problem, however, is how to get infants to demonstrate category knowledge—and not just similarity—

more productively, since they are not able to make more explicit or sophisticated overt judgments.

In a very clever study, Baldwin, Markman, and Melartin (1993) found evidence of such productive use of categories, for young children 9–16 months old. In their study, Baldwin et al. gave infants a toy to play with. This toy had a nonobvious property, which the children often discovered by playing with it. For example, a cylindrical can made a mooing sound when turned over; a doll's head could be separated from its body by pulling. Consider the case when an infant discovered this nonobvious and quite interesting property. If this can makes a mooing sound when turned over, would a new, similar can (but with a different color and pattern on the outside) also be expected to make such a sound? If the children turned over the can in an attempt to make the sound, this would be evidence not only that they saw a similarity between these objects, but that they drew an inference about this new object—that it would possess the same behavioral property as the familiar object. Essentially, this would show that children thought the object was the same kind of thing. In order to ensure that this was in fact an inference, Baldwin et al. disabled the second, test object, so that it did not in fact have the same property (the can did not moo; the doll's head could not be removed). Thus, the child's response could not be a function of the object's actual behavior during the test trial. Finally, in a control condition, the first object did not have the nonobvious property. So, the question was whether children would turn over the second can more often when the first can made the mooing sound than when the first can did not.

The authors found that children did indeed make the behavior corresponding to the nonobvious property (turning the can over, pulling on the doll's head), when the first object had demonstrated that property. Even the youngest children tested (9–10 months old) showed this ability. Therefore, the children were not simply noticing perceptual resemblance but were using that resemblance to infer hidden features and dispositions of the objects. This suggests true category knowledge. It would be difficult, however, to extend this kind of task much earlier, since the infant's motor coordination is not very good at, say, 3 or 4 months (and they might also forget the property, or forget what they planned to do with the object, etc.). Nonetheless, this study is a good beginning at the important attempt to better understand the nature of children's concepts. (I should also mention that it provides a methodological model for other work in this area; I would encourage students to read it for the details of design and scoring.)

A final issue that may be becoming of greater interest is a return to more basic questions of category learning. The first studies in infant concepts (Bomba and

Siqueland 1983; Younger and Cohen 1985) examined simple questions of whether infants could learn fuzzy categories, whether they showed a prototype advantage, and so on. Since then, there has been a focus on which real-world categories infants can and cannot learn, leading to the global-basic category and sortals debates. However, there is still much to be learned about how infants form their new categories. Two recent findings illustrate this. Bauer, Dow, and Hertsgaard (1995) found that children performed better in a sequential touching task when the category members were prototypical than when they were not. Oakes et al. (1997) examined the role of category variability in learning, using an object-examination task. They discovered that children showed more categorical performance when the items in the category were less variable. This kind of study may allow a more complete understanding of how infants notice and learn new categories. What is interesting here is that most of the effects are similar to ones that can be found in the adult literature (cf. Mervis and Pani 1980, for the typicality result; Posner and Keele 1970, for variability). Thus, in spite of the enormous differences in motor skills, knowledge, and almost every aspect of cognitive development, the processes of infant concept learning do not appear to be very different from those of adults.

If I may end with a brief suggestion, it seems to me that much of the research in this area is too caught up with particular categories that children do and do not know, or can and cannot acquire. It is of course interesting and theoretically relevant to know whether children can acquire concepts such as mammals or wing chairs, because these relate to basic questions about what kinds of categories they notice in general. However, by focusing on particular discriminations (dog vs. motorcycle or dog vs. cat), the results can be overly influenced by specific properties of particular items that are not always very generalizable to other items. That is, after ascertaining that infants must be 6 months old to learn dogs vs. cats, one must also study dogs vs. horses, and dogs vs. ferrets, and dogs vs. skunks, and so on, to get a complete picture. But there would be no end to such possible comparisons—even after dogs have been taken care of, one would then have trees or pillows or cakes to study.

For this reason, I think there should be a more balanced use of real and artificial stimuli in infant categorization studies. Although random dot patterns and the like certainly have their limitations, it is usually very clear exactly what their physical properties are, and it is obvious that infants do not know the categories prior to the experiment. Thus, one can more purely manipulate variables such as category size, variability, similarity to contrast categories, and so on, without having to worry so much about whether the infant is already familiar with or has such-and-such knowledge about the category. More realistic items such as novel objects, animated characters, and computer-generated pictures are possible, limited only by the imagination of the experimenter. Both "perceptual" and "conceptual" issues may be explored with novel categories. By using such categories, one can investigate general properties of the learning mechanism that should generalize to a wide number of other domains, thus avoiding the necessity of testing all the dog-pillow, cake-tree, dog-tree, pillow-cake, and so on comparisons. In the adult literature, most of the results found in artificial category situations (e.g., typicality and prototype effects, basic-level phenomena, learning effects) are also found in more realistic situations.

Of course, none of this is to say that one should not study realistic categories, nor that it is unimportant to know more exactly the specific categories that children have acquired at different ages. But studies of artificial category learning can provide a more general perspective on the real-life acquisition of categories that has not been used as much as it could be in the infant literature.

Theoretical Implications

Prototype and Exemplar Views

The work on infants has not been directed toward distinguishing prototype and exemplar theories. The earliest research attempted, following Posner and Keele (1968), to discover whether children abstracted a prototype that was separate from exemplar memory. However, as discussed at length in chapter 3, these early attempts were not in fact capable of disconfirming exemplar theory. For example, although Bomba and Siqueland (1981) found that prototypes were recognized better than old items in some circumstances, this could be accounted for by an exemplar theory, under the assumption (particularly likely for infants) that memory for the old items had decayed to some degree.

I think it might be rather difficult to provide a careful test of prototype and exemplar models in infant category learning, because one would have to have an accurate notion of how the stimuli were represented. For example, if I showed adult subjects colored geometric shapes of different sizes, I could be fairly sure that they abstracted dimensions of color, shape, and size. These are then input into the similarity computations of the exemplar model or into the feature count of the prototype model (see chapter 3), allowing a comparison of each model's predictions to the actual learning data. In contrast, if I showed infants such stimuli, I would be on much less solid ground in the analysis of the stimulus dimensions. This is especially true because very young children may have problems separating stimulus dimensions (Kemler 1981). That is, whereas we see a colored shape as having two very different properties—its shape and its coloring—infants may perceive the same thing as a more holistic stimulus and therefore may not, for example, identify it as being particularly similar to something that has the same color but a very different shape (Shepp 1983).

This difficulty has not created any problem in showing that infants can in fact learn new categories and that such categories have a prototype-like structure. However, investigations into more specific models may require a better understanding of infants' perception of the particular stimuli used in a given experiment. Perhaps we could say more positively that there is nothing in the infant concepts literature that suggests that their basic categorization processes are different from what either prototype or exemplar theory would expect. Indeed, what is striking from the studies using artificial categories is how qualitatively similar the effects of category learning seem to be in infants and adults, suggesting that whatever theory is eventually agreed upon for adults may be broadly suitable for young children and infants as well.

Theory Approach

Infants have very little background knowledge. In fact, it has often been commented about the theory approach that it could not possibly explain infant concept learning, because infants do not have detailed background knowledge about the domains of the concepts they learn. It is certainly significant that infants of only 3 months can learn concepts of things about which they have no background knowledge, such as dot patterns. Clearly, the basic category-abstraction mechanism does not require a deep understanding of a domain in order to work, which is probably necessary to give the infant enough flexibility to learn concepts in a wide variety of domains.

At the same time, though, it is possible that children's background knowledge does affect their learning, as soon as they have such knowledge. I mentioned much earlier the suggestion by Baillargeon (1998) that learning about physical principles is in a sense learning categories of events. Similarly, the acquisition of "background knowledge" about broad domains is in part learning about general properties of large categories. For example, animals are likely to move, perceive their environments, breathe, eat, and so on. For adults, such facts are augmented by a great deal of more detailed biological knowledge, specifying the mechanisms and functions of these activities. However, the beginnings of this knowledge are found in the young child who expects to see a novel bird move about and eat a bug, but who would be amazed to see a piece of furniture do so.

It is simply not known yet how early children form these kinds of generalizations about broad domains, although this is an active research area in cognitive development, and so we will probably soon know more. A major challenge for the knowledge approach is to understand how simpler perceptual information becomes integrated with the more sophisticated knowledge of childhood and then adulthood. However, as mentioned above, sometimes perceptual knowledge shades into theoretical knowledge imperceptibly. For example, if an infant knows that an object with animal-like legs is likely to run around, is this a piece of perceptual knowledge (legs are associated with a certain kind of motion) or is it a fact about the world (legs allow the animal to move in a certain way)? Even if it begins as a perceptual association (a very high order one), one can see how it could easily be the basis of a more conceptual understanding. The documenting of such transitions is still in the future, though see Madole and Cohen (1995) for an interesting discussion.

One final point is about the very small amount of children's background knowledge. With such a sketchy understanding of biology, for example, how can this knowledge be helpful in acquiring categories? Although it is very risky to generalize from adult to infant studies, it is still intriguing that Kaplan and Murphy (1999, 2000) found that even one knowledge-related feature in each item could improve both category learning (with feedback) and category construction (without feedback—more analogous to the infant dishabituation paradigm). Thus, one does not need an advanced degree in biology before one's knowledge will help in learning new kinds of animals. It may be that even the very small amount that infants and young children know about a domain will help them to acquire new categories within that domain. For example, Madole and Cohen (1995) found that 18-month-olds could not learn a correlation between a part of an object and the function of a *different* part of the object. Yet the same aged children could learn correlations between a part and the function of the same part. This suggests that 18-month-olds had a primitive expectation how shapes and functions relate, which influenced their learning. To discover how early in infancy such expectations exist will probably require new tasks or experimental designs.

Conclusion

The basic processes of concept learning and use that we have seen in the chapters on adults can be seen as early as the first year of life. Very young infants can form categories, even going so far as being able to separate two intermixed categories without feedback (Quinn 1987). These concepts apparently have a prototype structure, much like adult concepts do (Bomba and Siqueland 1983). As early as 9 months, infants show signs of using conceptual knowledge productively, in terms of drawing inferences about new category members (Baldwin et al. 1993). Although some researchers have focused on possible limitations of infants' concepts (when used as sortals or nonperceptually), this should not distract us from the impressive conceptual abilities that infants unquestionably do demonstrate. This suggests that some important aspects of human conceptual structure arise from innate learning mechanisms rather than from education, acculturation, or experience. Indeed, it is possible that these basic concept-learning mechanisms are the ones young children use to learn about physical reality, social relations, and the world around them.

10

Conceptual Development

A chapter on post-infant conceptual development must cover a lot of territory. In fact, it must almost be a miniature version of the rest of the book, as many of the issues addressed in the adult literature have also been addressed in children. However, there are a number of questions specific to development that do not arise in thinking about adult concepts. The result is that this is the longest chapter in the book and the most difficult to organize. I begin with basic questions about whether children's concepts are radically different from those of adults, a position that was held for much of the last century. Answering this in the negative, I then present the developmental counterparts of many of the issues that have arisen in the adult work. I begin by considering the question of whether children have taxonomic concepts, understand taxonomic organization (like dog-mammal-animal), and have a basic level of categorization. Next is the central issue of whether children's concepts reveal category structure effects such as typicality. Much of the research on conceptual development has been phrased in terms of word learning, and so issues specific to learning the meanings of words are addressed at some length. The chapter ends with a treatment of knowledge effects and induction. With all this material, readers may wish to read the first section or two for background and then focus on the specific topic that they are interested in.

One way to try to unify all these topics would be to attempt to frame them in terms of a single theoretical issue of some kind (e.g., Piagetian conceptions of thought or classical vs. prototype theories). I have resisted this temptation, which I think would do violence to the details of the individual topics. However, one question that readers might wish to keep in mind when reading the chapter, which would help to tie the disparate topics together, is the question of how similar children's and adults' concepts are. Of course, children and adults differ in terms of the *content* of their concepts, as children simply don't have the knowledge and experience that adults do. But more important is the question of whether children's concepts have a different structure, follow different principles, or are qualitatively different in some way from those of adults. The first section of the chapter addresses one particular claim that the concepts of children and adults differ radically, but this kind of question could be raised in every section and is an important question in understanding cognitive development more generally. Because child concepts eventually develop into adult concepts, any qualitative difference between the two poses a problem in explaining development. Nonetheless, traditional theories of children's concepts did posit large differences in conceptual abilities, as the next section describes.

Traditional Views of Children's Concepts

As in so much of cognitive development, the work that inspired later research was done by Piaget and his collaborators. (In the case of conceptual development, Vygotsky 1965, was also influential.) Piaget's framework fell well within the classical theory of concepts. He took an explicitly logical perspective, in which objects are divided into well-defined sets and thinking about categories involves logical analysis or combination of those sets. In fact, the classic work by Inhelder and Piaget (1964) that influenced all later work on conceptual development was called *The Early Growth of Logic in the Child: Classification and Seriation*. Concepts and their manipulation were just part of the more general development of logical thought in Piaget's framework. Such a logical approach, based on set theory, required that one be able to specify exactly what is in every set—that is, it required that every set have a definition. Like other classical theorists (see chapter 3), Piaget never argued for this view of concepts, but simply assumed it. For example, Inhelder and Piaget gave the following definition: "the 'intension' of a class is the set of properties common to the members of that class, together with the set of differences, which distinguish them from another class" (p. 7). That is, they assumed that there are normally necessary and sufficient properties for each concept. In order to demonstrate that children know concepts, Inhelder and Piaget argued that they should be able to give an adequate definition of the concept and furthermore show skill in answering logical questions about it, using quantifiers such as *all* and *some*. It may not be surprising, then, to discover that they didn't think that children could fully form categories until they were quite elderly (by child psychology standards). As I have discussed at length elsewhere (see chapters 2 and 3), this classical theory of concepts has been abandoned, and there is no particular evidence that it is more true for children than it is for adults. In fact, later sections of this chapter will show that children's concepts also reveal typicality effects of the sort that helped to overrule the classical view in the adult literature. Thus, I will not spend more time discussing the problems with the classical view here. Readers who wish to find out more about the demise of the classical view in children's concepts should consult Anglin (1977), Markman (1989), Mervis and Rosch (1981), or other sources from that era.

Although Piaget believed that fully developed concepts are definitional, he argued that children's concepts often were not, and his theory of children's concepts is quite different from current thinking about concepts. Thus, it is important to evaluate his proposal and to understand the empirical results that led him to it.

The basic task that Inhelder and Piaget (1964) used for understanding children's concepts was an object sorting task. He assumed that if children had adequate (classical) concepts, they would sort items into groups that could each be defined by criterial features. Thus, if given a set of colored geometric tokens, children might divide them into groups according to shape or perhaps shape and color. If given a set of representational toys, they might divide them into animals and nonanimals, then divide the animals into four-legged and two-legged, and so on.

However, Piaget found that children often do not make such nice, *taxonomic categories* based on shared properties. Instead, they often gave two kinds of responses. First, young children sometimes built structures or made images out of the items. These could be complete pictures (e.g., arrange the items into the shape of a house) or could simply be a sequence of items that did not fit any definition. Often, pairs of items in the sequence would be related (e.g., the first two might be triangles, the second and third might both be green, the fourth and fifth might both be tiny, etc.), but the whole sequence would have little or no coherence. Such a sequence of pairwise relations that do not fit any overall definition is often called a *complex*. A second kind of response was when children put items together according to *thematic relations* (some writers call these complexes as well), based on their involvement in the same event or setting. For example, children might put a woman and a car together saying that the woman would drive the car; and they might group a dog and a bowl, saying that the dog would eat out of the bowl. Consistently sorting a dozen or more objects may be rather difficult for children, so later experiments have often used a *triad task*, in which one object is given (e.g., a dog), and then the child is asked which of two other objects it is like. One of these choices might be taxonomically related and one thematically related (e.g., a bone and a cow). In a well-known study using this task, children most often chose the thematic response (Smiley and Brown 1979). As thematic relations often relate items that are of drastically different kinds, this is not much like adult categorization. If children really believe that dogs and bowls are the same kind of thing, then their concepts are radically different from those of adults.

Although it took some time for writers in this field to notice this, children's concepts cannot plausibly be like either the complexes or the thematic responses that they make in such tasks (Fodor 1972). Imagine, for example, that children formed a category corresponding to dog-and-leash. They might do so because the leash is used only on the dog, and whenever the dog goes outside, it must have the leash on. Perhaps the dog even fetches its own leash. In short, the dog and leash are thematically related. If the dog and leash therefore formed a category, they would be treated as roughly equivalent in the child's thought and language. When talking about "the dog," the children would be referring to either the leash or dog, or perhaps both together; the properties of dog and leash would be joined together in their concept; inferences made about the dog would also apply to the leash; and so on. All this seems extremely unlikely and at variance with children's everyday behavior. They do not treat the leash like a dog, nor vice versa. For example, they never pet the leash or hang up the dog by the door. Similarly, they don't refer to their spoon and cereal by the same word; when learning facts about a bus, they don't attribute them to the bus driver. Fodor (1972) pointed out that we would have little idea what children were talking about if they actually formed categories like this, since our own words like *dog* refer to taxonomic categories that are qualitatively different from thematic categories. So, the sorting task does not seem to give a valid picture of children's categories.

To go beyond informal observation, Huttenlocher and Smiley (1987) did a careful examination of how children use their first words, to see if they could be interpreted as being thematic or complexive relations, rather than referring to a taxonomic category. For example, if children used the word for *spoon* only when there was food present, they might have a thematic category of spoon-and-food. Similarly, they looked to see whether children's words were used only as an integral part of some activity or situation. For example, perhaps children only use the word *ball* as part of a game in which they roll and catch balls. Thus, *ball* may not refer to a true category of objects for the child, but could be just a learned response during part of an activity. Huttenlocher and Smiley found that object names were overwhelmingly used to refer to correct objects or items that were similar to the objects. They did not find that words were generally limited to one or two activities or situations, with some understandable exceptions. For example, *shoe* was almost always used in conjunction with a foot, and *hat* was often used with the activity of putting on a hat. It is conceivable, then, that these words were understood as thematic relations (shoe-and-foot; or "say 'hat' as part of putting something on your head"), but it seems equally likely that it is just that these objects are discussed in a few restricted situations and so do not show cross-situational usage. That is, children simply do not think or talk about shoes very much except in the context of putting them on or taking them off, and so there is necessarily a correlation between their use of the words and certain situations. Overall, however, object names did not show a restriction to particular situations, actions, or associated objects in their analysis.[1]

If children's word use suggests that their categories are taxonomic, then why do they respond thematically in sorting tasks? Markman (1989) makes the important point that thematic relations are a necessary thing for children (and adults) to know. They need to know about what things go together, how objects are used in various events, what items can be expected in different situations, and so on. A child learns that presents, cake, candles, and guests are all likely to be found in a birthday party, and learning this is part of learning about parties in our culture; it is also of great interest to most children. Thematic information is thus one form of general knowledge that children must learn about; it is not an irrelevant or unimportant response. The unusual aspect of children's responding, then, is not that they know about and use thematic relations, but that they sometimes use them in preference to taxonomic responses when asked to choose things that are of the same type.

There are probably a number of reasons for children's preferences in the sorting and triad tasks. In some cases, a reason for children's thematic responses is the vagueness of the task. If children are given objects and told to group them together, it is not clear what they are supposed to be doing. In fact, some ways of phrasing the instructions, particularly, "put together the things that go together" seem to promote thematic responding. Waxman and Namy (1997) showed that 3-year-olds in a triad task were fairly likely to respond thematically (about 50% of the time) to the question "Which goes with" the target item, but were very likely to respond taxonomically (about 80% of the time) to the question "Can you find another one?" As we will discuss below at greater length, Markman and Hutchinson (1984)—and many others since—showed that giving the target object a name (e.g., *dax* or any unfamiliar name) greatly encouraged children to make taxonomic responses. The traditional task did not use names and so obtained more thematic responding. Another variable is that the spatial aspect of the sorting task might encourage children to form spatial structures. Markman, Cox, and Machida (1981) found that asking children to put the items into different bags, rather than grouping them on a table, increased taxonomic sorting. It may be, then that the usual sorting procedure encourages nontaxonomic responding. At the very least, it is not always a reliable measure of children's concepts. (Note that the experiments described in the previous chapter showed, using very different methods, that even infants can learn taxonomic categories. Of course, these studies had not been carried out when Piaget and Vygotsky were writing.)

Piaget's claim about a shift from thematic to taxonomic categories has two components. The first is that children's concepts are thematic or complexive. The second is that adults' responses in the sorting task are taxonomic. I have been discussing evidence casting doubt on the first aspect, but there is also evidence casting doubt on the second.

Vygotsky's student, Luria (published in 1976 but carried out in the 1930s), tested adults in a primitive part of Uzbekistan and found that they often grouped items thematically. For example, they would insist that an ax be grouped with wood, so that you could cut it, or that a boy be grouped with adults, so that he could run errands for them (those were the days!). Indeed, they characterized taxonomic choices (placing the ax with a saw) as "stupid" when asked about them (p. 54). However, there is no evidence that in real life these subjects did not understand taxonomic categories, or that they had any temptation to confuse axes with wood or children with adults. Their use of language was apparently normal. Similarly, Sharp, Cole, and Lave (1979) found that uneducated Mayan adults tended to make more thematic groupings than did Mayan children in the 6th grade or secondary school. Nonetheless, uneducated adults could use taxonomic relations when there were no competing thematic relations, as in a memory task. Thus, the preference to choose taxonomic categories in such tasks may be in part a result of Western education. That is, the notion of choosing objects that share a certain kind of semantic relationship is one that is developed in analytic thinking skills taught in school. Indeed, the many examples Luria gives suggest more that the subjects did not understand the nature of the question and task than that they didn't understand taxonomic categories.

Smiley and Brown (1979; see also Annett 1959) found that elderly Americans—but not college students—also made thematic choices in a triad task. The authors questioned their subjects, both children and elderly, and found that both populations were aware of and could state the taxonomic relations of the stimulus items, even though they chose the thematic ones. Apparently, they simply found the thematic relations to be more salient or interesting. (The taxonomic relations used in such tasks are usually rather weak ones at the superordinate level; see below.) This suggests, then, that thematic performance may not reflect deeper conceptual structure so much as subjects' idea of what the best answer is in this kind of task. College students, being in the midst of schooling, may be best able to identify what kind of answer experimenters are looking for. Finally, Lin and Murphy (2001) used strong thematic categories and found that adult college students often made thematic choices in a triad task. Most subjects demonstrated a strong personal preference, in which they would respond predominantly taxonomically or thematically. Lin and Murphy presented evidence that thematic groupings were not totally unmotivated, as they could also be the basis for inductive inference. For example, items that are usually found in the same place will therefore have some properties in common that unrelated items would not.

What should we make of all these results? It is now generally agreed that children and adults know about both taxonomic and thematic relations, but that their primary categories are formed on the basis of taxonomic relations. That is, they think of dogs as being the same kind of thing rather than being like leashes. Children's preferences for thematic responses were encouraged by aspects of the traditional tasks such as the vague instructions, lack of strong taxonomic categories, and the spatial nature of the sorting task. Even children who responded thematically were probably able to form taxonomic categories and would have done so under other circumstances. Clearly, the adults who respond thematically in these tasks are well aware of categories like animals or tools, even though they choose not to use them to sort the items. Although thematic relations are extremely important to learn about for some purposes (children do learn to get the leash when taking the dog for a walk), they are not the basis on which we form most of our categories, and so we will consider only taxonomic categories for the remainder of this chapter.

It should be clear, then, that the argument that children have very confused complexive or thematic categories—in contrast with adults' taxonomic categories—is wrong. Children can and do form taxonomic categories (as the rest of the chapter will document), and adults can also be sensitive to thematic relations.

Hierarchical Relations and Basic-Level Categories

There is more to taxonomic categories than the thematic-taxonomic debate would suggest, however. As described in some detail in chapter 7, adult concepts form an implicit hierarchy, a *taxonomy*, in which general categories like animals are superordinate to lower-level categories like dogs and beagles. This hierarchy can be revealed in beliefs such as all dogs being animals, and all beagles being dogs. Hierarchies are important in part because they provide inductive power: When you learn that all animals breathe, you can infer that all dogs breathe. Chapter 7 also discussed the evidence for one level being primary in thought and language, the so-called *basic level*. The present discussion overlaps a bit with chapter 7, to keep the chapters fairly self-contained. The focus here will be on whether children's categories have hierarchical structure and show a basic-level advantage, so for more general discussion of these topics, see that chapter.

Understanding of Taxonomic Relations

In a classic article, Markman and Callanan (1984) reviewed the topic of hierarchical classification in general and the question of whether children understand the class-inclusion relations of such hierarchies in particular. The authors argued that many tasks used to test children's conceptual hierarchies did not provide very strong tests. For example, showing that children understand that something is both a dog and an animal is not sufficient. They might think that dog and animal are the same category or overlapping categories at the same level. One must show that children understand that all dogs are animals, but that all animals are not dogs; and that if animals have hemoglobin, say, then dogs must also have hemoglobin. Although it would certainly be nice to have such evidence, one cannot in general require that children have metacognitive knowledge about something before crediting them with understanding that thing. Metacognitive knowledge often only develops long after the basic knowledge is acquired. Many of the tasks used to determine hierarchical classification do seem to require metacognitive knowledge. For example, children might be able to infer that dogs have hemoglobin if they learn that animals do. However, they are not very good at answering questions such as "Must all dogs have hemoglobin if all animals do?" which ask about the principle rather than just requiring children to use the principle (C. Smith 1979). Often such questions are peculiar ones to ask from the child's perspective, since the questioner is not really interested in actual properties of dogs but rather in whether a form of reasoning is valid. (More generally, such questions may seem a bit strange to the child since the adult should already know the answer—after all, it is she who has been doing all the talking about hemoglobin—and yet the question assumes that the child but not the adult knows the answer. One of the effects of schooling is to give practice in answering hypothetical questions of this sort.)

Inhelder and Piaget (1964) required extensive metacognitive skills before they would attribute knowledge of hierarchies to children. For example, they were particularly interested in numerical reasoning skills. Children were required to demonstrate that if all *A*s were *B*s, the number of *A*s present had to be less than or equal to the number of *B*s. However, children perform quite badly on such tasks, again in part because the questions themselves seem very peculiar to a child. So, if asked "Are there more roses or more flowers?" the child would generally compare the number of roses present to *other flowers* rather than to the total number of flowers including the roses. Rather than demonstrating lack of knowledge of set inclusion, this may reflect the child's generous attempt to interpret the question as being an interesting question instead of a tautology. That is, the adult could plausibly want to know whether there are more roses than daisies, but she would be rather weird if she were asking about the relative number of roses and the entire set of flowers. (Unfortunately for the child, the right answer is that the experimenter is rather weird.) More recent work, therefore, has focused on simpler and more direct tests of taxonomic categorization.

Blewitt (1994) pointed out that taxonomic knowledge can be separated into a number of different components. Two such components are the ability to form categories at different levels of abstraction and the willingness to include the same objects in categories at two different levels. Although we take for granted the fact that the same thing can be a dog and an animal, it is possible that children believe that these are mutually exclusive categories (see Markman 1989). Perhaps they think of dogs as dogs and not animals, and perhaps they think of cows, sheep, and horses as animals only (and not yet as cows, sheep, and horses). However, when Blewitt investigated 2- and 3-year-old children's concepts in well-known basic and superordinate categories, she did not find such examples. That is, children were generally willing to call monkeys both *monkey* and *animal*. In fact, she found (see her table 1) that the children were actually more likely to categorize into the correct superordinate when they were correct on the item's basic category name—the opposite of the pattern suggested above. That is, they were more likely to call a monkey an *animal* if they knew the name *monkey* as well. Although there are a number of anecdotes in which children reject one name for an item because they claim it has another name,[2] Blewitt's results suggest that children in general accept that the same object can be in two categories at different levels of generality. This is an important aspect of hierarchical classification, which assumes that categories are nested within one another, and hence that objects can be in multiple nested categories at once.

Another study focused on children's ability to use taxonomic structure to make inferences. I noted earlier that one important function of taxonomic categories is to allow induction down the taxonomic hierarchy. That is, if you learn that animals all have hemoglobin, then you can infer that dogs have hemoglobin. Johnson, Scott, and Mervis (1997) tested children for this ability using familiar subordinates (like apple juice) and unfamiliar subordinates (like banyan trees). For example, they were told that a banyan tree is a kind of tree, and then told that all trees have lignin. Then they would be asked if banyan trees have lignin. Three-year-olds were near chance in answering these questions, though 5- and 7-year olds were considerably better. At all ages, the performance was higher for familiar categories like apple juice than for unfamiliar ones like banyan tree, suggesting that the general reasoning ability to draw inferences from basic to subordinate categories was not very well established but instead depended on learning about specific categories. Thus, according to Markman and Callanan's (1984) analysis, these children did not have a general grasp of hierarchical classification at these levels. However, I have already mentioned that such puzzle-like questions are often difficult for children, requiring meta-conceptual knowledge to answer. (For example, the experimenter has just told the child that all trees have lignin and then asks the child whether banyan trees have lignin, even though the experimenter obviously knows much more about lignin than the child does. This is a strange thing to do in normal conversation. Pre-school children in particular may not understand how this game is played.) As the knowledge effect was found across all ages, including adults (there was no interaction of this effect with age), and as adults are not perfect on other simple hierarchy questions (Sloman 1998), it seems too stringent to require children to answer such questions perfectly before we give them credit for taxonomic organization. Clearly, *something* is developing, as performance on such questions improves drastically across ages, but it may be that what is developing is a better understanding of logical inference rather than conceptual organization.

Smith (1979) asked children (4-year-olds through 6-year-olds) a number of questions that required them to use taxonomies. She found that they were able to answer the simplest forms of the questions from the earliest ages she tested. For example, children could answer questions such as "Are all dogs animals?" or "Are some trees elephants?" However, the youngest children did not perform very well on questions like "All milk has lactose. Does all chocolate milk have to have lactose?" Smith provided evidence that children's errors often resulted from performance problems, such as confusion resulting from repeated testing on similar sentences. For example, 4-year-olds who performed 82% correct on the first half of one test scored at chance on the second half. Furthermore, children's answers often indicated that they correctly understood taxonomies but did not correctly understand the question. For example, when asked, "A tody is a kind of bird. Does a tody have to be a robin?" a child answered "Yes, or could be a robin or bluejay or sparrow" (p. 448). The child apparently did not understand the meaning of "have to be" in this context but did understand that a tody was like robins and sparrows in being a kind of bird. Another child who was asked "Are all women people?" answered "No, but all women are *some* people, and there's men too" (p. 451). The answer shows that the child did understand that people include both men and women. Strictly speaking, though, these children did not answer the questions correctly and would not have been given credit for understanding class inclusion in the Piagetian tradition.

What, then, can we conclude about children's understanding of taxonomies? Clearly, they do not have adult competence in answering questions and reasoning about hierarchies. However, they are able to categorize items at different levels and, to a lesser degree, draw inferences based on the hierarchies. There is, therefore, little evidence for a qualitative difference between children's and adults' concepts on this dimension, in spite of differences in overall performance. Research on hierarchical classification in children has had a difficult time addressing these issues because of the problems in interpreting the methodologies, which often call for explicit, meta-cognitive knowledge. Smith (1979) argues that children do have the ability to represent taxonomies, but their ability to apply that knowledge and to understand questions about it takes time to develop. A further problem is that children have a tendency to interpret category names as occurring at a single level of classification, for example, thinking that *bird* and *duck* are contrasting terms rather than super-ordinate-subordinate (see Clark 1993 for discussion). This preference for a single level does not mean that children cannot form more specific or more general categories, but it does mean that their first guesses of word meanings may not have a hierarchical structure. That preference is the topic of the next section.

Preferred Levels of Categorization

Research on adults has revealed a very consistent preference within members of a given culture for a single level of categorization, the *basic level* (see chapter 7). For example, most people would call a calico cat *a cat* rather than a superordinate (more general) name like *animal* or a subordinate (more specific) name like *calico*. A number of measures show that children acquire basic-level categories first. For example, they learn names for basic categories first (Anglin 1977). Rosch et al. (1976) suggested that the usual problems that children have on traditional object-sorting tasks could arise in part because such tasks had almost always used superordinate categories (e.g., requiring children to separate animals, vehicles, clothing, and people). Since such categories are harder for children to identify, it is not surprising that they formed complexes instead. If basic-level categories had been used, children might have formed perfectly good categories. Rosch et al. compared children's categorization at the basic and superordinate level using a triad task. For example, in the basic-level task they might have presented pictures of a cat, a different cat, and a car. In the superordinate task, pictures of a cat, a fish, and a car would have been presented. Children were asked to select the two items "that are the same kind of thing." Children made overwhelmingly taxonomic responses at the basic level (99% of the time) even at age 3, but were nearly at chance (55% correct) for superordinate trials, which would have required them to group items such as a cat and a fish. Unfortunately, this test was not quite correct, because the foil for the basic level was not from the same superordinate category. In the example above, to show that children are using the basic level, Rosch et al. should have used a cat, another cat, and a cow, say (i.e., all animals) (Mervis and Crisafi 1982). (This is because to identify something as a cat, one must distinguish it from other animals, which are the things most likely to be confused with it, rather than distinguishing it from a vehicle.) Nonetheless, this demonstration gives evidence that basic categorization is easier than superordinate categorization, because if children had simply been categorizing the items at the superordinate level, there would have been no difference between conditions—both conditions could be equally well distinguished at the superordinate level.[3] Rosch et al. (Experiment 9) got similar results using a sorting task, though with the same problem. (I refer to this issue below as the absence of *stringent foils*. Studies are somewhat inconsistent in whether they use the most stringent false items or not, and so I sometimes point out when a study does or does not have the appropriate tests for the different levels being compared. Most studies after Rosch et al.'s initial experiments do use stringent foils.)

Since Rosch et al.'s initial experiments, numerous studies using a wide variety of materials and methods have found a basic-level advantage in children's concepts. Mervis and Crisafi (1982) created artificial categories that fit a taxonomy of superordinate, basic, and subordinate categories (this was verified by adult ratings). They also performed a triad task, this time using stringent foils (that is, false items that were as similar as possible without being in the same category). They found that children were at ceiling for basic-level categories as young as 2.5 years old, but they did not get the superordinate task correct until age 4 and the subordinate level until age 5.5. Mervis and Crisafi did not teach children the categories, but instead tested their ability to identify categorical membership at the different levels. Horton and Markman (1980) found similar results in a sorting test of artificial stimuli (p. 713), but their main experiment was to actually teach categories to children, by modifying pictures of animals to make novel superordinate and basic categories. The superordinates were analogous to categories like ungulates and reptiles, and the basic categories were analogous to squid and salamander. Children learned basic categories better than they did superordinate categories. In a study with familiar objects, Callanan (1989, Study 1) labeled an object with a new name, such as *terval*, and then looked to see how children interpreted the name. Subjects were given items from the same subordinate, basic, and superordinate categories and asked whether they also were tervals. When simply labeling a single object (without other cues), children predominantly interpreted the word as indicating a basic category. Golinkoff et al. (1995) performed a similar picture-selection task in which the correct answer was either in the same superordinate or same basic-level category. Children were much more accurate at finding the taxonomic response when the correct item was in the same basic category (91%, Experiment 6) than when it was in the same superordinate category (39%, Experiment 2). Although Golinkoff et al. did not have the most stringent foil for the basic-level category, they did have a perceptually similar item as a foil in both cases (e.g., for a banana, the foil was a very similarly shaped quarter-moon). Finally, Waxman et al. (1997, Experiment 1) showed that when children were told a property of an item, they were most likely to assume that this property was true of the item's entire basic category, not just its subordinate and not its entire superordinate category. So, basic categories appear to be the most natural level for induction of properties.

I described part of Blewitt's (1994) study above. One finding that she did not emphasize was that children were significantly better at categorizing items into familiar basic than superordinate categories (e.g., in Study 1, 2-year-olds were 92% correct at the basic level but 64% correct at the superordinate level), using stringent foils in the test. Blewitt also asked children at the end whether something could really be in two categories at once (e.g., "Could this be both a monkey and an animal?"). She found that 2-year-olds seemed confused by this question (again, reflecting the problem of asking metaconceptual questions), but that some of them also gave interesting answers (p. 1286): "Asked about an object's superordinate label, these children would say, 'That's a (*superordinate label*), *and* it's a (*basic level label*).' Rather than being disturbed by multiple category membership, they seemed concerned to establish that the object in question was a member of its basic level category, whatever else it might be." That is, in the children's eyes, a monkey is first and foremost a monkey—its basic-level category—and only secondarily an animal.

Evidence about levels of categorization can also be found more indirectly. Klibanoff and Waxman (2000) taught children new adjectives, such as *curly* and *holey*.

They discovered that when the item used to teach the adjective was in the same basic category as the test items, 3-year-olds performed much better than when it was in a different basic category (but the same superordinate). Note that the children were not asked to categorize the object but simply to use the new adjective correctly. Waxman and Markow (1998) found an analogous result in 21-month-olds. Apparently, the greater coherence of basic categories aided the children in applying the adjective to a new concept.

Children's preference for the basic level is mirrored in their parents' speech. It is well known that parents tend to use basic-level terms when speaking to children (Brown 1958a, made the first observation; see Anglin 1977, for further evidence). Apparently, parents believe that children will understand these category names better than others. Furthermore, when teaching concepts at different levels, parents tend to use different strategies. Callanan (1985) found that parents used basic-level names when teaching superordinates, but not vice versa. Given that superordinates include very diverse kinds of objects, parents apparently feel it is necessary to make direct reference to those different objects, at the basic level. But when teaching basic categories, they did not make much reference to subordinates. Some writers have been tempted to trace the entire set of differences between basic and other category levels to such differences in parental labeling. However, this attempt does not explain the structural differences found between the different levels (see chapter 7), and it is essentially circular, because it does not say why the basic level has this precedence in parental naming and explanation. That must be explained by *their* parents having labeled things at the basic level, which was due to *their* parents, and so on, ad infinitum. This explanation also cannot explain the results of experimental studies reviewed above in which children showed a basic-level advantage for novel, artificial categories. I would argue that the parents' speech reflects two main determinants. The first is their own conceptual structures—that is, a cat is first and foremost a cat to them, and only later an animal or a tabby or whatever. The second is the parents' beliefs about what their children can most easily understand—beliefs that are apparently correct, according to the experimental evidence.

In sum, virtually every study that has either compared known categories or that has taught children new categories at different levels has found that the basic level is considerably easier for the child to learn. A number of studies not discussed above have also found the superiority of the basic level on their way to addressing other issues that were the focus of the study, some of them mentioned below. It would be tedious to review them all here. The impressive robustness of the results argues strongly that the basic-level advantage in children's concepts is real—not tied to a particular domain or type of experiment. Thus, children's concepts are much like adults' in their preference for a given level of categorization, which is reflected in learning, naming, and induction.

Subordinate-Level Categories

Although children generally learn basic-level categories earlier and are more accurate in categorizing with them, this does not mean that they do not learn categories at other levels. There has been relatively little work focusing on the more specific subordinate level. As pointed out earlier, Mervis and Crisafi (1982) showed that children did not extend category membership at the subordinate level until after being able to do so for basic and superordinate categories. Mervis, Johnson, and Mervis (1994) taught 3-year-olds subordinates of familiar basic-level categories (e.g., for shoes, they taught the children cleats and penny loafers). The subordinates were given novel names like "nup," and children had to learn to distinguish nups from members of their basic and superordinate categories (e.g., other shoes and clothing). Some of the subordinates had a salient attribute that distinguished them from other category members (e.g., cleats have little spikes on the bottom), and others did not. Mervis et al. found that the salient attribute made learning the subordinate much easier. When children did not correctly learn the subordinate category, they most often gave responses consistent with a basic-level interpretation (see their table 9). That is, when they failed to learn that "nups" were penny loafers, they would instead extend this name to all shoes, the basic category. They virtually never did this for all members of the superordinate category. Thus, the basic level again is more salient, though children were able to learn subordinate categories as early as 3 years, with some help (and see below).

Johnson et al. (1997, Study 2) taught children properties that were described as true of a novel subordinate category (like whelk, a kind of seashell), or of the basic category (seashell). On test items, even 3-year-olds were generally able to attribute subordinate properties to other subordinates and basic properties to the whole basic category. However, this tendency was by no means perfect, even for adults who were tested, suggesting that subjects may have been making up their own minds about how the feature related to the categories. (Although the authors assume that labeling a property at a given level should indicate that the property is only found at that level, in fact, people often extend a property to related categories, as research on induction has shown; see chapter 8 and below.) Overall, however, performance was fairly similar across ages, showing only a quantitative increase in the tendency to restrict properties to the labeled level.

In short, subordinates are harder for children to learn. This is no doubt largely due to the fact that subordinate categories are often very similar: The differences between penny loafers and regular shoes are slight, differing only in the presence of one or two features. We will see evidence for this suggestion in studies of linguistic labeling of categories.

Superordinate-Level Categories

Perhaps because they were originally the focus of the work of Piaget and others, superordinates have received greater attention from researchers in children's concepts than subordinates have. The most significant of these projects has been Ellen Markman's study of the possible *collection* structure of superordinates. Markman and her colleagues have pointed out that the difficult aspect of taxonomic structure for children may be dual identity. That is, the same object is both a chair and a piece of furniture. Coordinating these two categories could be difficult, because one has to think of the same object in two different ways.[4] Markman has pointed out that a similar dual-identity situation exists with collection terms, like *family, pile, army,* and *class.* That is, the same person is a boy and is in the family; the same object is a toy and is in the pile. This dual-identity situation is somewhat easier to understand, Markman argues, because it involves a part-whole structure. It is not that the boy *is* the family, but that he is part of the family; the object isn't the pile itself, but is part of the pile. Such collection terms are often determined by external relations among the objects rather than by the properties of the object itself. For example, the toy is part of the pile if it is touching the other members that together result in a connected heap of items. The boy is part of the family if he is the son or brother of other members of the family. It is not just the boy's intrinsic properties that determine whether he is in the family.

Markman has suggested that children may understand some superordinate terms as if they had collection meanings. A term like *furniture* could mean to the child not just something that is in the home having certain properties, but could refer to the entire collection of things typically found in the living room: couch, coffee table, lamp, rug, and so on, all together. The difference in interpreting furniture as being a class term (of the sort we have been discussing throughout this book) and a collection has to do with whether it refers to a single object or multiple objects. If one can describe a single chair as being a piece of furniture,[5] then it is a class term; if we can only describe the chair, couch, and table together as (some) furniture, then it is a collection term. Just as one soldier does not make an army, perhaps to the child one chair does not make furniture. On the face of it, then, the collection hypothesis suggests an important difference between children's and adults' concepts at the superordinate level, at least.

Markman, Horton, and McLanahan (1980) taught children from 1st through 12th grade (aged 6 through 17) novel categories at different levels of abstraction. To understand what they did, consider the diagram below:

High Level Category	C	C	C	C	C	C
Low Level Category	A	A	A	A	B	B
Objects	1	2	3	4	5	6

In this diagram, the items numbered 1–6 refer to pictures of objects (novel shapes or animal-like entities). Subjects were shown this display of pictures and then were taught the categories at the lower level (A and B—they did not see the letters in the diagram, which are for illustrative purposes). The experimenter pointed at items 1–4 and said "These are As" (actually, nonsense names were used, but I will ignore this). Then she pointed to items 5 and 6 and said "These are Bs." Finally, she pointed to all 6 items and said "These are Cs." Other subjects learned C first and then A and B. Note that this way of labeling the objects is consistent only with a class interpretation of the categories. If C were a collection term, then one could not say "These are Cs," but instead "These are a C." For example, if objects 1–6 were a family, one would say "These are a family," not "These are families." So, the syntax of the sentence directly indicated that A, B, and C were class terms, and that C was a superordinate to A and B.

After this learning, the children were asked questions of individual items like "Is this a C?" and performed tasks such as "Show me a C" or "Put a C in the envelope," with similar questions at the lower levels. For both behavioral and yes-no questions, children were fairly likely to answer incorrectly for the superordinate-level term (C) but were accurate for the lower-level terms (A and B). Furthermore, the most common error with C was to pick out the entire array of objects when asked to point to a C or put a C in the envelope, as if "a C" referred to multiple objects rather than just one. Errors at the highest level were quite common (more than 50%) through the 8th grade. Finally, Markman et al. found that if subjects were told during learning that As and Bs were a *kind of* C, the collection errors were greatly reduced, though still fairly common in 2nd graders. The kind-of relation is taxonomic: Mammals are a kind of animal.

This experiment, then, gives impressive evidence that children might prefer to interpret superordinate labels as referring to collections. They act as if *a C* refers to multiple objects, instead of a single object, just as *a family* does. However, we should be careful before extending this result to real-life superordinates for a number of reasons. First, all the objects and category names were unfamiliar and were taught in a single session. Second, there doesn't appear to have been any commonality among the items that were identified as being in the same superordinate category. Thus, it was not possible for children to give a simple class interpretation to the term (e.g., "The Cs are all curvy and reddish"). Real superordinates differ in whether they have common features that a child might notice. For example, animals probably have a number of common features that children might learn (even if they are not really true of all animals), but furniture is less likely to have such features (see Rosch et al. 1976). Children may be more likely to give collection interpretations when a superordinate does not have common features that allow a class interpretation (Wisniewski, Imai, and Casey 1996). If the child cannot see anything much in common to a couch, table, and lamp, then he or she will not be able to form a coherent class interpretation, and may instead assume that it is the grouping of the three that makes them furniture—i.e., a collection interpretation. Finally, the children did not get feedback on their interpretations and did not even hear the category labels very many times. However, it should be pointed out that in real life, superordinate names are very likely to refer to multiple objects rather than to just one (Wisniewski and Murphy 1989) and that parents are likely to describe superordinate terms as applying to many objects at once, rather than to individual objects. For example, Shipley, Kuhn, and Madden (1983) reported that parents used superordinate labels only 6% of the time when describing single objects but 47% of the time when describing multiple, diverse objects. Such patterns of speech might encourage children to think of superordinates as collections.

Clearly, however, we need more direct evidence of children's representations of real categories before embracing this hypothesis. Callanan and Markman (1982) tested children on real hierarchies such as toys (balls, dolls), cars (racing cars, VWs), and animals (horses, cows). Children were shown arrays of objects (e.g., balls and dolls) and were asked yes-no questions at both high and low levels, about individual objects ("Is this a doll?") and multiple objects ("Are these toys?"). They were also asked to carry out instructions like "Put a toy in the box." The results showed that for superordinates, children were more likely to make errors on singular questions than on plural questions; at the lower level, the pattern was slightly reversed. In the behavioral tasks, a similar pattern was found. That is, children found it difficult to say that a single doll was a toy, but less difficult to say that the dolls and balls (together) were toys.

In a second study, Callanan and Markman made statements about objects, and the children were asked to say whether the statements were "ok" or "silly." In one condition, just one object was shown, and a puppet made a statement about it, such as "This is a shovel" or "This is a tool." In the other condition, multiple exemplars were shown, and plural statements were made, such as "These are tools." Not surprisingly, children were more accurate about basic-level statements than about superordinate statements. More interestingly, there was an interaction in which singular statements were particularly difficult at the superordinate level but not at the basic level. Furthermore, children who correctly verified superordinates for plural statements ("These are tools") denied the same statement in its singular form fairly often ("This is a tool."). This study does involve metalinguistic judgments (namely, what sentences are sensible) that children find difficult, but it is still interesting that superordinates benefit from being phrased in the plural, but basic categories do not.

Callanan (1985) investigated how mothers taught children concepts at all three levels. She found that mothers were much more likely to use plural expressions when teaching superordinates than basic categories. In fact, a number of things that the mothers said would seem to promote the (incorrect) idea that superordinates are collections: "Furniture's a group"; "All of them together are vehicles"; and "A whole bunch of things together that you ride in are vehicles" (Callanan 1985, p. 514). Thus, parental input may encourage the interpretation of superordinates as being collective nouns.

Although there is clearly evidence for the collection view, there are also some problems with it. Some writers have noted that children do not treat superordinates as collections in their spontaneous speech. That is, they generally do not refer to a bunch of animals as "an animal," the way they would refer to a bunch of soldiers as "an army." One reason for this is that children only seldom name objects at the superordinate level. If they are directly asked whether a bunch of animals is "one animal" or "a lot of animals," they tend to correctly choose the latter (Macnamara 1986, p. 160), which is inconsistent with a collection interpretation of the category. Another reason to be skeptical of the collection idea is that adult superordinates are clearly not collections but classes, and it is difficult to see how a term that is interpreted as a collection could develop into a radically different kind of concept. For example, adults have no trouble accurately identifying an individual item as being an animal or piece of furniture.

Both of these concerns suggest that the child's understanding of superordinates is not entirely like that of a collection but is something of a hybrid. For example, in understanding the concept of furniture, children may notice certain features that are often found in individual pieces of furniture (being artifacts, having legs, being sat on, etc.), *as well as* noticing configural features that are typical of collections. For example, they may notice that the couch and chairs are all oriented toward a central coffee table in a typical living room. Since the word *furniture* is often used in reference to multiple objects in just this situation, it is not surprising that children encode this configural property, which is not true of an individual item but of the set of items. However, with greater experience in seeing and talking about furniture (e.g., lawn furniture, office furniture) that does not have this configural arrangement, this aspect of the representation will decrease, but the other, more reliable properties will remain. Furthermore, as children become better able to identify fairly subtle properties that are common to furniture (Bloom 1996), they may find these more accurate than the configural cues.[6]

In short, even if Markman's collection hypothesis is generally correct, it does not follow that there is a qualitative difference in children's and adults' representations of superordinates. Instead, both may be a mixture of taxonomic and configural (collection) properties, differing in the relative proportions of the two. One reason to take such a view is because adults show a residual effect of configural properties in some superordinates (Murphy and Wisniewski 1989a; Wisniewski et al. 1996), even though they clearly represent superordinates as classes. Thus the distinction between the two may be fuzzy.

Prototype Structure in Children's Concepts

As described in chapter 2, perhaps the most frequent single finding in concept research is that some items are considered more central to the category than others and therefore have advantages in speeded classification, learning, ratings, induction, and other tasks. It is not surprising to find, then, that similar findings are quite frequent in the literature on children's concepts. One does not usually ask children to rate the typicality of items, which is an abstract question that they may not understand very well. However, in simply asking children to categorize items, one finds that they are more accurate with typical items than with atypical ones (Anglin 1977; Bjorklund and Thompson 1983, p. 340; Hayes and Taplin 1993). In an implicit test using looking preference, Meints, Plunkett, and Harris (1999) found that 12-month-old children could correctly identify typical members of named categories but not atypical ones. For example, the babies might have been shown a picture of a dog next to a picture of a bird while hearing the sentence "Look at the dog!" They did look at the dog when it was a typical one, like an irish setter, but not when it was an atypical one, like a bulldog.

Like adults, children learn better if they are taught with typical items. Mervis and Pani (1980) created novel categories with artificial objects that varied in typicality.

Children were first taught the category names on one object from each category. This object was either a typical or atypical exemplar. When the children were tested on the other category members, they were found to be accurate when they had learned on the typical item (only 1.9 errors) but much less accurate when they had learned on the atypical item (7.5 errors). Furthermore, when children learned on the typical example, they were more likely to make errors for new atypical items than for new typical items. In a second experiment, Mervis and Pani had children return for multiple sessions of learning. Each day, subjects learned the categories by having either typical or atypical examples labeled and then were tested on the entire set of items. Learning was much easier when the typical items were labeled than when atypical items were labeled.[7] In fact, the difference in items was apparent to the children themselves: One child in the study who had only the atypical items labeled "finally generalized four of the categories. As soon as she did so, the child handed the experimenter the good examples of these categories and told her it would have been much easier if she had named these objects, instead of the ones actually named" (p. 519).

The phenomenon that children sometimes exclude atypical items from a category is to be expected by all modern theories of categorization. For example, the atypical items will resemble the prototype less than typical ones do. Furthermore, almost by definition, typical items will be more similar to exemplars of the category that children have encountered. Thus, children are similar to adults in terms of showing typicality structure. However, this finding also points out that the *content* of children's categories may deviate considerably from adults' versions of the "same" categories. For example, if children refuse to call worms or insects *animals*, they have a somewhat different concept of animal than adults do. Such differences may be a bit hard to track in a formal study, because they require very broad sampling of a category, which also raises problems of repeatedly testing a young child on the same categories over and over, when some of those would not normally be encountered. Mervis (1987) carried out a diary study on her son Ari's conceptual development in early childhood, in which she combined observation with more focused testing of his understanding of selected words. She found that Ari's initial concepts seldom corresponded exactly to the adult or correct category. "The great majority of his categories were at some point not perfectly matched to the adult categories. Most … were in an overlap relationship to the corresponding adult categories" (p. 217)— that is, most categories did not include all correct members and included some incorrect members. However, before being too hard on children for their inadequacies, we should also recognize that adult categories can also be inaccurate. Mervis points out (p. 218) that many adults have incorrect ideas of categories like

duck, bulldozer, and robin (e.g., many urban Americans unknowingly exclude juvenile and female robins). It can become a philosophical problem to decide whether
a 2-year-old and an adult have "the" concept of animals, say, when they mostly
overlap but also show important differences—and neither is technically correct. I
will take the pragmatic view that since the child and adult call the category by the
same name, and since the child's concept will presumably become the adult concept,
they can be called the "same concept." (Furthermore, it should be admitted that
adults can differ considerably in their concepts—Barsalou 1987; McCloskey and
Glucksberg 1978.) However, that does not deny the proposition that the adult and
child may have different representations for some concepts, and it is the job of developmental psychology to explain how one is transformed into the other.

As Mervis (1987, p. 202) pointed out, it is not at all surprising that such differences are found between children and adults or between different cultures: "only the
principles governing the determination of basic-level categories were predicted to be
universal (Dougherty 1978; Rosch et al. 1976). The actual categories formed on the
basis of these principles will vary because different groups notice or emphasize different attributes of the same object as a function of different experiences or different
degrees of expertise." Children often do not know the function or cultural significance of various object properties. Lacking such knowledge, they may categorize by
visual similarity, which will work in some but not all cases. The properties that are
most salient and interesting to the child may not be so interesting to adults. More
mundanely, children typically do not have the range of experience with category
members that adults do. Furthermore, the child may have false beliefs about objects,
based on plausible inference, or in some cases, misinformation from adults (Mervis
1987, p. 204). In short, it is not to be expected that the *content* of children's concepts is the same as adults', because children simply do not know the things that
adults do (Carey 1982).

Having said this, then, we need to keep in mind the possibility that children who
seem to share concepts with us may actually have somewhat different ideas. Mervis
(1987) calls children's first categories *child-basic categories* to distinguish them from
the adult versions. For example, her son used the word *duck* to refer to a wide variety
of water fowl, including geese, swans, and herons in addition to ducks, contrary to
the adult use of the term.[8] Only gradually did he get closer to the correct category,
in part as a result of learning the names for geese, swans, and other similar birds.

In another case, Ari learned to call a kitchen mixer by the name "mixer." Surprisingly, he spontaneously extended this word to pictures of an old-fashioned hand
water pump and a sewing machine. As Mervis's (1987) reproduction of these pic-

tures makes clear, there is an overall visual similarity to these items that explains this labeling. Furthermore, Ari had no way of knowing what the sewing machine actually does, and the picture had no size cues to show the difference in sizes between the mixer and pump. Thus, Ari's problem may have been in part ignorance of other objects, like sewing machines, in addition to incomplete mastery of the mixer category itself. The question arises, then, as to how incorrect concepts of this sort get corrected. Mervis suggests that Ari was most willing to change his labeling of such items when she provided a reason for it to be in a different category. For example, he called all felines *kitty-cat*, but accepted the word *lion* for lions when told that they said "roar" instead of "meow." However, he still accepted lions as being kitty-cats, and he also did not call female lions *lion*. In short, his early concepts were clearly not the same as those of adults. If Mervis's examples are typical, children's basic categories may be broader and more diffuse than those of adults, who can distinguish related categories more accurately.

This difference between children's and adults' concepts might lead us to question the conclusions about category levels drawn earlier. Although children may learn to call things *bird* before they learn to call them *animal*, if neither category corresponds to the adult category of bird and animal, it is slightly misleading to say that children have learned the basic category first—in fact, they have not learned either one yet. The question is, then, whether the child's preferred concepts, taken on their own merits, are closer to having the structural properties of basic concepts, or of some other level. I think there are three reasons to conclude that children's preferred concepts are basic. First, their preferred concepts are generally the ones that turn into adult basic concepts, and they have real difficulty with concepts that will turn into adult superordinates and subordinates. Second, the mistakes children make are often of the sort that they include items that should be excluded but that have the same shape and other important properties of the category—e.g., calling lions "kitty-cats" or geese "ducks." In general, commonality of shape is a property of basic-level categories, and so children's errors are in fact a natural result of assuming usual basic-level structure for a category that may not be entirely "basic." (Another way of putting this is that categories like duck and cat are not very good basic categories. Cats can be a basic category in our society in part due to the absence of lions, jaguars, and other nondomesticated felines. It is exactly such items that children make errors on, at the zoo or in picture books.) Third, experiments from artificial categories like those of Mervis and Crisafi (1982) and Horton and Markman (1980) reveal a strong basic-level advantage. This evidence is especially important because the materials are not subject to differences in knowledge and experience that affect children's natural concepts. When only conceptual structure is varied, one finds a clear basic-level advantage. Although there are certainly differences between adult and child concepts, the documented differences don't give us any reason to believe that children's preferred concepts are at an overall higher or lower level than those of adults.

In short, children's acquisition of categories is not a single, all-or-none affair, as it might seem from (adult) experiments in which intensive training occurs, and a subject must continue through learning until the category is completely learned. For children, the information about a category may come in haphazardly, as they often do not have multiple examples present simultaneously to compare. Furthermore, to the degree that a category requires cultural or theory-laden information that the child does not yet know (see Carey 1982), his or her acquisition of the concept is bound to be incomplete. However, in a broader sense, the child's concept learning seems comparable to that of adults. Children learn better if they are given typical items to learn from; they perform better on typical items; they generally learn basic concepts first. Thus, there appears to be considerable continuity between conceptual processes of childhood and adulthood. That is not to say that nothing develops, but that the structural principles of categorization operate similarly from childhood through adulthood.

Learning Words for Categories

In this chapter so far, I have been referring rather promiscuously to studies of word learning and use as well as to studies of concept learning per se. As described in chapter 11, there is a close relation between these two, and a strong argument has been made that the representation of word meanings is based on concepts (e.g., Clark 1982; Murphy 1991a). As a purely methodological point, it is easy to try to investigate a child's concept of dogs, say, by testing his or her use of the word *dog*. It is certainly possible, though, that word learning has some principles and determinants that are not related to conceptual learning, or that learning a concept is different when it is introduced as a word meaning.

Word learning is one of the most heavily researched and controversial topics in the field of cognitive development, and it is attracting an especially large amount of attention at the time of writing. The intricacies of word-learning could fill their own book (and they have—see Bloom 2000; Clark 1993), so it is necessary here to focus on the aspects that are most relevant to concepts and conceptual structure. These include the questions of how early word use reflects conceptual structure and how labeling a category by a word might change what children learn about it. Although there are some purely linguistic variables that must be mentioned, I will ignore the more linguistic aspect of word learning (e.g., the learning of mass vs. count markings for nouns, or thematic roles for verbs) and will continue to focus almost entirely on concrete nouns. Obviously, the learning of words for events, states and properties is a critical aspect of language acquisition, but studies of this do not yet make strong connections to the rest of the concept literature, and so I will not be reviewing them. Also, there are many controversies about word learning in particular that are not related to the categorical aspect of the word (e.g., the proposed Principles of Mutual Exclusivity and Contrast), which space precludes a discussion of. See Clark (1993) and Woodward and Markman (1998) for excellent reviews.

Problems of Induction

One of the most famous philosophical examples in cognitive science is that of a hypothetical linguist, described in Quine's (1960) *Word and Object*, who is trying to learn a language of some little-known "natives." In particular, he is trying to learn the language so that it can be translated into English. The linguist follows around native informants and notes their speech in various situations. He analyzes what aspects of the environment correspond to different utterances, and he then forms hypotheses about what the words mean. The linguist can test these hypotheses by trying out the different utterances in situations that do and do not correspond to their suspected meanings.

Quine has us imagine a case in which "A rabbit scurries by, the native says 'Gavagai', and the linguist notes down the sentence 'Rabbit' (or 'Lo, a rabbit'), as tentative translation, subject to testing in further cases" (p. 29). This case is often analogized to the situation of the child learning words (e.g., Bloom and Markson 1998; Markman 1989, among many others). The child is like a diminutive linguist who notes the words of these peculiar natives (parents and other children) and must arrive at hypotheses about what the words mean. As Quine is rather pessimistic about the ability of linguists to come to the true account of the meaning of the native words, this provides an interesting problem for the psychology of word learning, since, following the analogy, the same problems would apply to the child.

The word-learning literature often rephrases the problem in the following way. What is the problem with understanding *Gavagai*? Clearly, it means *rabbit*, doesn't it? No, the native could mean something like *white thing, animal, one thing, food*, or even *that means the huckleberries are ripe!* In fact, we could think of a very large number of such hypotheses for what the word means—if we had enough time, an infinite number of them. How is the child to rule out these hypotheses? If the child considers each one, one at a time, then he or she will take a very long time to learn what *Gavagai* means, or will never learn it. Quine suggests that it would be almost impossible for the linguist (child) to discover that *Gavagai* means undetached rabbit parts rather than rabbit. Furthermore, it would be a very difficult problem for the child to keep track of all these possible meanings and to check each one to see which are consistent with all the evidence of how the word is used. Yet, as we shall see, word learning is actually very fast.

This way of presenting Quine's problem, like many such translations of philosophy to psychology (see the discussion of Wittgenstein in chapter 2), is not exactly what Quine had in mind, however. Furthermore, Quine's assumptions underlying his example are very different from those of modern psychologists, and those assumptions are part of the reason why he found this problem. I examine the question of what Quine really meant in the box "Quine's *Gavagai* Problem," but this is a digression from the psychological questions of word learning, and so the less interested reader may skip it without shame. The discussion is more for those who are familiar with Quine's problem than for the newcomer.

How, then, are children able to figure out the meaning of a category label, given the large number of possible meanings that it could have based on a few examples? One popular answer is that the word-learning process is subject to a set of *constraints* that greatly restrict the hypotheses children consider. Since, according to Quine's analysis, empirical evidence itself cannot suffice to determine the word meaning (and this will be echoed to some degree by the problems of induction discussed below), the assumption has been that children must have some pre-existing biases that essentially tell them what kinds of hypotheses to consider as possible word meanings, biases that probably put "undetached rabbit parts" pretty far down the list as a possible word meaning.

Let's consider in more detail why we might need constraints. It is generally believed that no finite amount of evidence can allow someone to learn a word meaning (or any other inductive generalization) with perfect confidence. For example, suppose that I point to a green square and say "glark." If I do this for a number of green squares, you might eventually come to believe that *glark* means green square. Of course, you will have to rule out a very large number of more general meanings that are also consistent with this evidence, such as colored square, green thing, square, green geometric object, green thing with straight sides, and so on. And you will have to rule out more specific hypotheses, such as green square that is less than six inches tall, green square on a white background, and so on. These specific hypotheses are particularly hard to rule out because no finite amount of evidence will be able to rule out all narrower interpretations of the word than the correct meaning: There will always be some further condition on the word's use that you haven't tested yet. As a result, Goodman (1965) argued, most of our hypotheses about word meanings (and other generalizations) are not in fact fully justified by the kind of evidence we have. For example, perhaps *glark* means something as perverse as green square that is in North America. If you are an American or Canadian child, you will get a lot of evidence for *glark* meaning just green square, since you will always hear the word referring only to green squares, unless you leave the continent. Thus, in reality, you could never say for sure whether glarks are green squares or have some other property that simply has not been disconfirmed in your experience yet. The problem for psychologists, then, is why people generally come up with one or two of these hypotheses (like green square) but not others that are equally justified on the basis of the empirical evidence (like green square in North America). See Goodman (1965; and also Murphy and Medin 1985; and Shipley 1993) for more on general problems of induction.

The importance of constraints on word meanings, then, is that they direct children toward the kinds of meanings we have in our languages. Children don't come up with hypotheses like "green thing seen before noon when someone is pointing at it" even if this is consistent with all of their evidence for glarks. Such constraints only work, of course, because our languages have words for rabbits, squares, green things, computers, and the like, and not for green things seen before noon that someone happens to be pointing at. One might ask whether it is the constraint or this fact about the language that comes first. After all, if children find it very difficult to come up with complex hypotheses about a word's meaning, then such meanings might die out of the language, since children would not correctly learn them. The constraints (or some of them) could be self-fulfilling prophesies that act on the evolution of languages. Alternatively, the constraints could be embodied in the child's learning mechanism through evolution.[9] In either case, the constraints must be relative to a particular kind of language that the child is going to learn. There are possible languages for which the constraints discussed next would be maladaptive.[10]

Finally, as we shall also discuss, human caretakers are a bit savvier and more helpful than Quine's native. Parents take it upon themselves to speak to children in ways that they will understand. Sometimes parents even explain words to children, so that the induction problem based on examples is greatly reduced. They could certainly say "Glarks are only before noon," if that were really a critical feature that the child might not notice. The job of learning a new word is certainly a lot easier if

Quine's *Gavagai* Problem

In *Word and Object*, Quine did not actually worry too much about the kind of hypotheses concerning what *Gavagai* might mean that I described above. He believed that the linguist could quickly rule out *white thing* or *animal* as the meaning of *Gavagai*, by watching a few more examples and asking a few questions. So, he could point at a white rock and ask "Gavagai?" in order to test the whiteness hypothesis.[11] The problem of knowing whether *Gavagai* refers to animals or rabbits or white things is part of a more general problem of induction that Quine did not dwell on (in this example, anyway).

In fact, Quine was more worried about a situation in which the linguist might know almost exactly when the natives would and would not use the word *Gavagai* (which, of course, would not happen if he mistook it for *white thing* or *food*) but still might have the wrong meaning. Perhaps, Quine suggested, *Gavagai* refers to a stage of a rabbit's life. Or, perhaps *Gavagai* refers to "all and sundry undetached parts of rabbits" (p. 52). Such hypotheses might be virtually impossible to distinguish through observation, since one can hardly point at a rabbit without pointing at rabbit parts. A linguist might have to resort to carefully questioning the informants about exactly what they meant by *Gavagai*. For example, seeing the same rabbit twice would count as two rabbit-life-stages, but only one rabbit; thus the linguist could ask if he had seen one or two Gavagais to try to distinguish these hypotheses (p. 53). However, all such approaches assume that the linguist has accurately identified the other words involved in the question (in the native tongue) "How many Gavagais were there?" If the linguist cannot be sure that he has the meaning of a simple word like *Gavagai* right, how can he be sure about the rest of the words in that sentence, which are presumably even more abstract and difficult? And how could he be sure that he would correctly understand the answer?

Quine argued that this *indeterminacy of translation* meant that one could never be sure of the meaning of words in this foreign language, even if one became extremely accurate at identifying situations in which the different words could and could not be used. In fact, two different linguists might come to hypotheses about English translations for the language that were equally empirically valid but that were quite different.

So far as I can tell, the vast majority of the research on word learning does not concern itself with this deeper issue of Quine's indeterminacy of translation. That is, it worries more about the practical problem of getting a meaning that is empirically valid, so that *rabbit* is used to refer to rabbits and not to furry things, or all animals, or rabbits and their food, and so on. And, I think, there is good reason that the research does not worry about Quine's deeper question, because it is very unclear that it is in fact a real worry. Suppose, as Quine proposes, *Gavagai* refers to undetached rabbit parts, and the linguist simply records it as meaning *rabbit*. Are these in fact different meanings? Clearly, the phrases *rabbit* and *undetached rabbit parts* seem somewhat different in English, but if they both end up referring to all and only rabbits, then they both pretty much mean *rabbit*. Quine is playing on our intuitive sense that *rabbit* and *undetached rabbit parts* are different things (after all, the latter sounds weird, and the former

continued

doesn't) to suggest that there is an important difference. However, the difference is only stipulated by Quine; he never gives an account of meaning in which these are different.

There are other reasons for why we should be a bit skeptical about taking Quine's example at face value. Much of Quine's argument is based on his presuppositions about the nature of language and mind, presuppositions that are not widely shared by researchers today. For example, Quine takes an explicitly behavioristic perspective, focusing on the *stimulus meaning* of words (i.e., the sensory experiences that occasion their use) and relying on reinforcement to explain the acquisition of words (see sections 8, 9, and 17 of *Word and Object*). Such accounts of both word meaning and mental life are bound to be inadequate, because sensory stimulations do not form natural classes by which we can explain behavior (Fodor 1975). Quine himself (section 9) sets the stage for part of the argument, by talking about examples in which the native is pointing to a place where a rabbit once was (unknown to the linguist) and says "Gavagai!" The sensory qualities that cause uses like absent rabbits will not overlap with those that cause the labeling of an actual rabbit. Thus, one reason for Quine's skepticism about word translation (and by analogy, word learning) is that he starts with an overly empiricist approach to language and mind. It is less clear whether we should be as concerned about his problem with an overtly cognitivist, constructivist approach. Finally, perhaps it should be noted that Quine does not go very far in drawing this analogy to children's language learning himself. As best I can tell, he only mentions it once or twice, somewhat removed from the main discussion of the linguist (p. 94). Furthermore, elsewhere he seems to suggest that children learning the language don't have the same indeterminacy (pp. 71–72) as the linguist has, though this is also not entirely clear.

In short, I think that the issues that psychologists have been focusing on in the study of word meaning are not really the primary concerns that Quine had in *Word and Object*. He was worried about deep, subtle differences in meaning that might never be distinguishable by empirical evidence. Psychologists have been more worried about mundane problems of how the child comes up with the hypothesis (and then confirms it) of an empirically valid interpretation of *rabbit* based on a small amount of evidence. These are basic problems of induction that other philosophers (notably Goodman 1965) have discussed, and which are formidable in their own right. I think that Quine was a bit fast in passing over these problems, because children are not trained scientists who can carry out carefully designed tests of their hypotheses, and yet all normal children learn a language. These are in fact the main concerns of most studies of word learning. I think that psychologists have reinterpreted Quine's *Gavagai* problem as being this straightforward problem of induction rather than the more recherché problem he intended. To be clear, the interpretation commonly given of Quine does point out a critical issue in word learning; I am simply arguing that this was not Quine's intention when he described that problem.

someone just tells you what it means. Fortunately for children, that route is available for the hard cases, but unfortunately, it only works once they have already learned a fair amount of the language.

Word Biases

As described in chapter 11, most of the literature does not make a clear distinction between learning a word meaning and learning a new concept. The two go together in many experiments in which a new concept is taught along with a novel name. However, much of the recent literature on word learning has explored the possibility that learning a word meaning may involve processes that are not found in concept acquisition per se. That is, the presence of a word may cause children to form different concepts than they would form without a word. These word biases are one kind of constraint that children use to solve induction puzzles.

In the typical concept-acquisition study with adults, the subject is presented with items that are members of two or more categories. The subject is usually required to guess which category each item is in. A convenient way to do this is to have the subject say (or press a response key corresponding to) the category names. So, the subject learns which items should be called "dax" and which "kez," say. For most investigators, the category names are of no particular importance in and of themselves. It is probably a bit easier for subjects to remember the daxes and kezes than to remember "category 1" and "category 2," or just the left or right button. But the use of category names in and of itself is generally not something that researchers give much consideration to (an exception is Yamauchi and Markman 2000a).

From that perspective it is surprising to find that children learn concepts differently when names are present. Most of these studies are not full-fledged category-learning experiments of the sort carried out in the adult literature but are designed to resemble real word-learning experiences. When children learn a new word, they typically do not get many trials in a row in which they have to distinguish the correct and incorrect referents of the word, as in the usual adult experiment. More typically (it is believed), they see one example which they interact with for some time while an adult names it. Because these experiments are interested in the constraints operating on children's hypotheses, they often provide the child with very little evidence for the word meaning—often only one object—and then test what hypotheses the child formed by asking whether the word would apply to a number of other objects.

I mentioned above the finding that children often make thematic classifications (like dog-leash) when shown an object and asked to choose another that is the same kind. This result has caused considerable consternation in the field, because most nouns do not refer to thematic groupings but rather to taxonomic classes, in which similar things are grouped together. Thus, there has been some worry that children's choices in these tasks reveal that they have a different way of categorizing the world. An important paper by Markman and Hutchinson (1984; see also Markman 1989) showed that thematic choices are greatly reduced when children are given a category name. For example, in one study, they presented 2- to 3-year-olds with a target item such as a picture of a blue jay (bird). Below it were taxonomically and thematically related objects, such as a duck and a nest. In one condition, children were asked to find another one that is the "same as" the unnamed target item (the blue jay). In another condition, children were told that the blue jay was "a sud," and they were asked to find another sud. Children chose the taxonomic item 59% of the time when there was no name, but 83% of the time when there was a name. Another experiment, using older children, showed a similar effect when superordinate categories like vehicles and animals were used. Markman and Hutchinson replicated their findings with artificial materials that could be grouped by taxonomic or thematic relations. Waxman and Gelman (1986) found similar results with a picture-sorting task, which is more challenging than a triad task, where only two responses are possible.

Apparently, children have the hypothesis that a word (more specifically a count noun) applied to an object should pick out a kind of thing (i.e., class of similar things), rather than a relation. Thus, even though thematic relations are of great interest to children, the use of the word tells them that they are not relevant in this task. This is sometimes called the *taxonomic constraint* on learning word meanings (Markman 1989). Within the word-learning literature, this important finding has spurred new debates. For example, is the taxonomic bias with words something that children develop as a result of learning common nouns, or is it a predisposition that they bring to the earliest word learning? Waxman and Markow (1995) showed that even 1-year-old children gave evidence of the constraint, though this depended somewhat on their vocabulary development. Children who could produce no more than two words did not show the constraint, but those who could produce more than two words (on average, nine words) did. The directionality of this relationship is not clear at this point—the taxonomic constraint could be arising from early word learning, or it might be promoting it. (Note that production lags behind comprehension, so the children probably know quite a few more words than the above figures indicate.)

Another effect of providing a word is a *shape bias*. For example, suppose that you learn that a U-shaped, brownish wooden object is called a *sud*. Now if I give you a yellowish, wooden object of the same shape, would you call that a sud? What about an O-shaped brownish wooden object? Or a U-shaped brownish cloth object? Simply labeling one object does not provide enough evidence to narrow down the word meaning: Perhaps *sud* refers to the material of the object, or to the color, or to the position of the object on the table, and so on. Indeed, if you simply show children an object such as this without naming it, and then ask them to find other items that are like it, you will find that they give a variety of responses. Some children choose the objects with the same color, some with the same material, some with various combinations (e.g., items with the same shape and material). However, if the object is first labeled as a *sud*, and children are asked to find another sud, they pay considerably more attention to the object's shape (Landau, Smith, and Jones 1988). This effect is found in both 2- and 3-year-olds, but is rather stronger in the 3-year-olds. It is possible that this bias is really another side of the taxonomic bias found by Markman and Hutchinson (1984). That is, it may reflect the belief by children that items with the same shape are the same kind of thing, and the name may be cuing children to choose items that are the same kind of thing (i.e., in the same taxonomic class), as argued by Ward (1993) and Bloom (2000). Although color and texture are interesting to the child, they may not be reliable indicators of category membership.

Some evidence for this interpretation of the shape bias is given by two studies that have found limitations of it. Becker and Ward (1991) taught children the name of a new animal by presenting and labeling a drawing of it. The children were then tested on variations of the animal that differed in overall shape, the presence of appendages, texture, and other properties. The authors varied the shape in two different ways: In one case, the shape reflected internal organization, and in the other, it reflected a change in posture. For example, in one case a child would be taught that a snake-like thing was a diffle. Test items were snakelike or snail-like (having a large lump below the neck). Finally, one of the snakelike items took the same overall shape as the snail-like item, by curling its tail around. Becker and Ward found that children were much more willing to accept the curled item as a diffle than the snail-like item, even though they had the same overall shapes (outlines). That is, it isn't just that children's attention is focused on the silhouette or configural properties of the *picture*, but that they believed that the curled item was the same kind of thing, only in a different position.

Another limitation on shape bias was found by Jones, Smith, and Landau (1991). They began by replicating the preference for same-shape objects found in their past work: When a name was presented, their subjects chose same-shaped objects significantly more than when no name was presented. Their stimuli were geometric shapes constructed out of various materials like the wooden U-shaped object described above. In new experiments, they placed eyes on the objects. In this case, the shape preference began to break down, apparently because the children interpreted the stimuli as representing animals, and they expected animals to share both shape and texture. (See a related demonstration by Becker and Ward, described in Ward 1993; as well as Ward et al. 1991, Experiment 3.) Thus, there may be no simple "pay attention to shape" bias for named objects; instead, children try to pick out the same kind of thing as the object. They believe that objects with different shapes are the same kind of thing in most cases, but when shape differences can be explained through postural changes (Becker and Ward 1991), or when other variables important to identity are varied (Jones et al. 1991; Soja, Carey, and Spelke 1991), the emphasis on shape per se may be weakened. A final piece of evidence in favor of this proposal is the finding that giving children explicit instructions to choose the same kind (via a brief story) also fosters a shape bias (Ward et al. 1991).

The emphasis on kinds, and shape in particular, is perhaps part of the reason that names seem to be particularly related to basic-level categorization. As mentioned above, Callanan (1989) found that when an object was named for children, they were most likely to interpret it as referring to a basic-level category. The tendency for the basic-level preference can be overruled if children are shown diverse objects labeled by the same name (Callanan 1989) or if they are simply given only superordinate choices. Waxman and Kosowski (1990) showed that labeling an item (e.g., a cow) with a novel name made children more likely to pick two other members of a superordinate category (e.g., a fox and a zebra) from a display than when no name was given (see also Markman and Hutchinson 1984). Here there was no basic-level item to distract the children, and so the word was interpreted as having a superordinate category membership. Waxman (1990) replicated this finding at the superordinate level but found that providing a name actually lowered children's performance at the subordinate level. For example, when shown collies and told that they were called *akas* (a Japanese name) by a puppet, children were less likely to choose only collies as being *akas* than if they had only been told that the puppet liked these items and asked to choose others that the puppet liked. Perhaps this indicates that the child believes that collies and other dogs are all the same kind of thing, and so this is what the puppet must mean by *aka*.

There are probably other constraints on learning word meanings that will be discovered. For example, Hall and Waxman (1993) showed that children prefer to interpret names as referring to a kind of object rather than to a context-dependent concept like *passenger* or a life-stage of an object like *puppy*. When children learned the name of an animal that always appeared in a certain vehicle, for example, they interpreted the name as being that kind of animal, rather than "rider in the vehicle." It was only when given verbal information about the context ("It's a murvil, because it's riding in a car") did children incorporate that aspect of the situation into the meaning. Because this study did not compare a labeled to a nonlabeled condition (the object was always called *murvil*), it isn't clear whether this is a word effect in particular. However, the experiment illustrates the point that children may have a number of biases about what kinds of categories are out there and what kinds of meanings words are likely to have, and future work will probably focus on more specific constraints such as the one Hall and Waxman identified.

Parental Input

As I have already mentioned, parents typically do not simply label objects when they are teaching categories. For example, they may give an explanation for the categories, such as saying that vehicles move and carry people. They may also draw the child's attention to specific aspects of the object in order to clarify the category. Mervis (1987) suggested that her son was able to learn some new categories that were similar to categories he already knew only when some distinguishing feature was provided. Callanan (1990) found that parents mentioned more functional properties when describing superordinate-level categories and more perceptual features and parts when describing basic categories, matching the different kinds of properties associated with these levels (see chapter 7). Mervis et al. (1994) found that describing a property unique to the subordinate category helped children considerably in learning it.

Fairly subtle linguistic cues, such as the type of name given to an object, can help children learn what kind of category is being referred to. Recall that Waxman (1990) found that labeling subordinate categories with nouns actually reduced children's accuracy in choosing the correct subordinate category. Waxman suggested that children believe that subordinates should be indicated by adjective terms. For example, perhaps the child can tell that a collie looks different from a terrier but believes that they are essentially the same kind of thing. The child might accept a distinctive description for the collie but would not expect the collie to receive its own category name, at least without some justification. Waxman carried out an experiment similar to the one described above (i.e., teaching the children about akas), except that she used an adjective form in describing the objects. That is, the puppet described the category as *akish ones* instead of *akas*. Children who heard these adjective versions learned the subordinate categories better than children who heard no name; however, the adjective versions did not help superordinate categorization. Presumably, the children interpreted the adjective as referring to one or more properties of the collies—such as being hairy or long—rather than picking out a kind.

Waxman, Shipley, and Shepperson (1991) examined other types of information that children might use to learn subordinate categories. Before teaching the categories, they first taught them some information using a picture for each subordinate category. For example, they taught them that one kind of fish has fused teeth and changes color, but another kind has teeth on its tongue and swims fast to escape its enemies. Once children had this information, providing them with novel nouns no longer hurt their subordinate categorization, presumably because they now interpreted the fish as being different kinds. In another experiment, the researchers did not provide these facts but labeled the objects at *both* the basic and subordinate level, using a familiar basic-level name. For example, they would point out that the pictures were of fish, and then they would label each kind of fish with a novel name. Anchoring at the basic level overruled children's tendency to interpret the novel name as being at the basic level; now, the name helped children relative to the no-name condition.

Finally, Waxman et al. (1997) found that children greatly benefited from contrastive information used when teaching subordinate categories. For example, when teaching about kinds of dogs, children would be told that Noocs pull sleds. Then, pointing to a picture of another kind, children would be told, "See these? We call this kind Tesses. They help us find birds. They don't help us pull sleds like the Noocs. No! They help us find birds." Contrasting two categories this way made children much more likely to interpret a new feature taught for the Noocs as applying only to them.

It is interesting to compare the strategy that parents use in teaching categories to the standard adult concept-learning experiment. In that situation, subjects are given the category names and must guess which items are in which category. They are not given any hints about what dimensions are relevant, what the typical items in the category are like, what hierarchical relations exist, and so on. After all, that would give it all away! But when teaching children concepts, adults often give them extremely useful information. That is, descriptive studies like those of Callanan (1985) or Blewitt (1983) show that parents tend to use basic-level descriptions, and that when they use different levels, they tend to anchor them at the basic level. The experimental studies of Waxman, Markman, et al. show that this is in fact just the kind of help that promotes category learning in children. We should not be misled in thinking, however, that such help trivializes the category-learning process.

Certainly, it is a lot easier to learn what a collie is if someone tells you that it is a kind of dog and brings attention to its hair and the shape of its nose. Nonetheless, the learning does not stop there, as most of us eventually learn much more about such categories. Furthermore, sometimes the information adults give about the category is not even perceptually available in the stimulus (e.g., the fish's fused teeth, the lion saying roar, anchoring information such as mentioning that akas are all fish), so that does not always tell the child how to identify category members. That must still be learned. These linguistic cues help to identify the type and level of the category, which children then use in order to develop hypotheses about how wide or narrow the category is. Furthermore, we should also keep in mind that sometimes parents tell the children things that are strictly speaking inaccurate (such as the collection-like descriptions found by Callanan 1985). Thus, although adult input is probably very helpful, it is by no means letting the child completely off the hook when it comes to learning the category.

It is possible that helpful input from adults is not necessary for children to learn many of these words. Clearly, children can and do learn new words from simple ostension and interactions with rather unhelpful siblings and playmates. Bloom and Markson (1998) point to cross-cultural studies suggesting that some cultures do not engage in helpful "motherese" in talking to children, and are less likely to play labeling games as yuppie American parents are wont to do. Yet children in such cultures certainly acquire language perfectly well. However, to conclude that parental input has little effect would require a more careful comparison of the rate of vocabulary acquisition of different kinds of words in cultures that differ in this respect. Such studies do not seem to have been done. Based on the results described above, one might predict that children who get minimal parental input would have little trouble in learning basic-level category names but considerable trouble in learning category names at other levels,[12] and that they might be very delayed in acquiring atypical exemplars. Nonetheless, it appears to be an empirical fact that in North America, parents do introduce different kinds of categories in different ways and that these differences help children learn labels for those categories, even if they are not strictly necessary for learning (see Bloom 2000, for a more extended discussion).

Syntactic Constraints

Given the limitations on our present discussion, I will only mention a final constraint, which has been the subject of considerable research in the word learning literature. When children hear a new word, it is often in a linguistic context that helps to specify the meaning. That is, children don't usually just hear a category label like "Gavagai!" by itself but are more likely to hear a new word in a sentence, like "Look at the ungulate!"; "I'll chastise your brother when I find him"; and so on. Although such contexts may not appear to give very much information about the meaning of the word, they do help to narrow it down in a number of respects, if only from the syntactic information the sentences provide. For example, Roger Brown (1958b, pp. 250ff) showed children a picture of some hands kneading a peculiar substance in a distinctive container. He asked children if they had ever seen "a sib/some sib/some sibbing" when showing them this picture. Brown found that, depending on the exact syntactic form of this new word, *sib*, children took it to refer to the stuff in the picture, the action being performed, or the container holding the stuff.

Similarly, suppose that I point to an unusual green-haired monster and tell you "This is a fendle." You will probably take *fendle* to refer to this kind of monster. On the other hand, if I said "This is fendle," you will probably take *Fendle* to be a proper name for this particular monster. Even young children are able to use such information to interpret new words (Katz, Baker, and Macnamara 1974). In the realm of verbs, syntactic information can be even more informative, as a verb that takes direct or indirect objects (like *give* or *push*) is likely to refer to a different kind of meaning than one that is intransitive (like *sleep* or *sit*). Fisher (2000) reviews research showing that 2-year-old children will interpret a novel verb like *pilk* differently, depending on the sentence structure—compare (1) and (2) below—even when the sentences are illustrated by the same action.

Event: One person rolls another on a wheeled dolly by pulling it with a crowbar.

(1) She's pilking her over there.

(2) She's pilking over there.

The rest of the sentence gives cues as to whether pilking is a kind of action performed by one actor on a recipient or instead is a kind of event undergone by a single person.

Thus, syntactic variables (like the presence or absence of an article), and morphological variables (like verb vs. noun endings on words) can be used as cues about what the word may mean. Much research has investigated how soon and to what degree children can use information of this sort to interpret the meaning of a word. Obviously, children cannot use this information when learning their very first words, because they do not know the syntactic and morphological cues that determine the type of meaning. That is, when they are just learning their first words, they could not know that *some sib* is more likely to refer to substance than is *a sib*,

Table 10.1.
Examples of syntactic cues to word meaning (after Bloom and Markson 1998).

Syntactic cue	Usual type of meaning
article: a fep, the fep	individual category member
plurals: feps	multiple members of a category
mass nouns: much fep, some fep	stuff (not individuated)
verbs: Fran feps	one-participant action
verbs: Fran feps Lee	two-participant action
adjective: a fep thing	property
quantifier: fep dogs*	quantifier

* Note that the adjective occurs with an article, but the quantifier does not. Although quantifiers can occasionally occur with articles, they are most likely not to, as in *five dogs* or *some dogs*.

because they don't know the significance of the words *some* and *a* yet. However, even 2-year-olds can use some of this information (Katz et al. 1974). Furthermore, as I discussed above, such syntactic information may be relevant to children's hypotheses about what categories are being picked out, as shown in Waxman's (1990) study. Recall that she found that children were better able to learn subordinates when they were described in adjectival form (*akish ones*) than in noun forms (*akas*). However, 1-year-olds are not able to take advantage of such differences in word form (Waxman and Markow 1995). Although syntactic information is not perfect (e.g., some nouns like *redness* refer to properties rather than objects), it usually is helpful, especially in the kinds of simple sentences directed to young children (in which terms like *redness* seldom occur).

Further discussion of syntactic variables would carry us too far into language acquisition per se. However, it is clear that such information is used by children to help them solve the induction problem that arises from simply seeing an example of a category. Hearing that the item is "akish" may help children to understand which aspect of the item is relevant. Such syntactic constraints can be used very quickly, without further experience of the items, to help narrow down the word meaning. Table 10.1 gives a number of examples of syntactic cues and the types of meanings they typically pick out.

Fast Mapping
Before leaving the topic of word learning, it is worth emphasizing a significant difference between this literature and the adult category-learning experiment. In the

typical adult experiment, subjects are given many examples, but the categories are difficult to acquire, and much study is usually required to learn them. In the typical experiment on children's word learning, the child is given one or two examples, the name is used two or three times, and then the child is tested. This difference seems to reflect two different assumptions about the nature of categories: The adult work assumes that the categories are very overlapping and that considerable learning is necessary (and that opportunities for such learning exist); the child work apparently assumes that the categories are fairly trivial in themselves and that the problem is in narrowing down which of the possible categories is correct.

The assumption in the word-learning literature can be seen in a phenomenon called *fast mapping* (Carey 1978). Basically, this phenomenon is that a child hears a word used two or three times to refer to a novel object (e.g., "Can you hand me the koba? Thanks. Let's put the koba over here."), without any further explanation. The child may now infer what *koba* means, without any explicit training or discussion. This inference is helped if linguistic contrast is provided (as in "Can you hand me the chromium tray? Not the blue tray, the chromium one."), but this is not necessary (Heibeck and Markman 1987). After this rather minimal exposure to the word, children can remember it and pick out a koba a month later with no intervening use of the word (Carey 1978; Markson and Bloom 1997). Even if they are not perfectly accurate, kids often have some idea of what the word means, such as its referring to a kind of animal, a color, or whatever. Markson and Bloom (1997) suggest that fast mapping is not actually specific to word learning but includes other salient facts that are learned about an object as well. For example, children will also remember an item as "the thing my uncle gave me" a month later.

Such word learning is indeed impressive. No doubt this is one reason that children learn many words a day during their school years: It takes only a very few exposures for them to acquire the word meaning. (Of course, not all these words are category names of the sort that are the topic of this review.) However, this also points out the difference between the assumptions of the word-learning and the adult category-learning literature. For example, to test a child's understanding of *koba*, Markson and Bloom used items that were identical to the learning item and foils that were very different. Children did remember which item had been labeled as *koba* a month earlier, but it is not clear how children would extend the word to other similar, but not identical items, nor how much learning would be required if the word labeled a less obvious category (e.g., water mammals or a manure rake). It may be that the adult category-learning experiments do describe (closely enough) the learning of some kinds of categories, and that the single-example labeling of the word-learning literature describes (closely enough) how other kinds of categories are learned. However, the gap between these two literatures in terms of their methods and conclusions needs to be closed by more than such wishful assumptions.

Knowledge Effects

A major issue in adults' concepts is the way in which concept acquisition and use are influenced by background knowledge (see chapter 6). It has been argued that people actively use their knowledge to construct features, to focus on likely hypotheses of the concept's content, and in using concepts in induction. One possible weakness of this view, however, is the developmental psychology of concepts. Since the majority of our most basic concepts are learned during childhood, knowledge will only be a truly powerful determinant of concepts if it influences children as well as adults.[13] But some have argued that children do not know enough to allow such knowledge effects. They have not undergone schooling in physics or biology in order to use actual scientific theories to constrain their concepts of animals, plants, and inanimate physical objects. They haven't had courses in engineering to tell them how cars or computers work; they don't know enough physiology to understand disease; and so on. A contrasting view is that children have learned many important generalizations about the world, and they rely on those generalizations in acquiring and using concepts. Some of these generalizations may be simplified, and a few may be just plain wrong. But that doesn't mean that children don't use them or that they aren't generally justified in using them.

If children do not have enough reliable knowledge to aid their category acquisition, then they must rely on much simpler, purely empirical learning. For example, if they hear the word *cat* a dozen times, and for ten of those times, they can see whiskers, perhaps they conclude that cats have whiskers. If only once do they see a collar, then they do not conclude that cats wear collars. In short, if children cannot rely on knowledge, they must use an associative learning mechanism based on individual exemplars or feature-to-category associations. The discussion of constraints on word learning already casts doubt on a very strong version of this view: Purely empirical learning is not sufficient to explain children's interpretations of category names. Constraints such as the taxonomic bias and the shape bias influence children's hypotheses about what words mean. However, that literature does not tell us whether more specific knowledge, such as knowledge about animals, artifacts, or people, influences children's learning of concepts and word meanings. If we were to find that children cannot or do not typically use such knowledge, this would represent an important difference between children's and adults' concepts.

Knowledge in Word Learning

The word-learning literature reviewed above has already provided some examples of how children might use their knowledge in acquiring new concepts. For example, when an item has eyes on it, children attend to more features than just the shape, whereas they greatly emphasize the shape when there are no eyes (Jones et al. 1991; and see Ward 1993). This suggests that children have expectations about what features are relevant to animals that they use to direct their hypotheses in learning about new animals. Furthermore, if shape differences could be attributed to changes in posture, children did not pay attention to them (Becker and Ward 1991). In a clever study, Bloom, Markson and Diesendruck (reported in Bloom 2000), found that 4-year-olds would not call two same-shaped objects by the same name when they saw one of them used as a container for the other. So, children do not inflexibly rely on a given cue, even one as important as shape: They can use some aspects of the stimuli (e.g., presence of eyes, apparent function) to activate a more general knowledge structure (e.g., expectations about animals in general, the importance of function in artifacts) that will then guide further learning.

A very interesting study that was directed more specifically at knowledge effects was carried out by Kemler Nelson (1995). This used the common word-learning technique in which one item was taught to the child, who was then tested on new items. In this experiment, children were introduced to a novel artifact (an actual object, not a picture), called a *bindle*. The object was designed to be able to fulfill two different functions. One of these functions was demonstrated to the child, while the object's name was repeated. After this introduction, children were shown other objects that were or were not globally similar to the original training item, and that looked able or unable to perform the two functions (the functions of the test items were not explicitly demonstrated). Children had to say whether each test item was a bindle. Kemler Nelson's idea was that children would interpret the artifact as having been constructed to perform the function that was demonstrated and so would decide whether the object could perform that function as a criterion for judging whether the new objects were in the same category. The results strongly confirmed her predictions. Although global similarity also had an effect, the presence vs. absence of the demonstrated function was critical to deciding category membership for children as young as 3 years old. When children were asked to justify their decisions, they often mentioned the presence or absence of parts in the test objects. However, the parts they chose to mention were most often those related to the function they had seen.

This study is particularly well done because each object had two different functions, and so different children made very different decisions based on which function they learned. The children's decisions cannot be explained by simple similarity of test items to the learning item, since they all saw the same learning item but made different judgments. Similarly, the results cannot be attributed to the salience of a particular part or property—which parts were salient depended on which function children learned. Kemler Nelson concluded that children do not simply learn the function of the artifact or the superficial properties of the object but instead relate the superficial properties to the function in a sophisticated way, as an explanation of why the object is the way it is. This explanation then influences what other objects will be called by the same name. (For a similar study with adults, see Lin and Murphy 1997.)

Thus, a number of word-learning studies can be interpreted as indicating that children use domain knowledge to help in providing interpretations of word meanings when they first hear them. In this way, they seem much like adults. However, the main evidence in the adult literature for knowledge effects has been found in studies of concept learning in which consistency of the category with knowledge is directly manipulated. There have been relatively few studies of this sort on children, but they do provide some evidence for the use of knowledge in concept learning, and so they are the topic of the next section.

Artificial Concept-Learning Studies

One reason that there are relatively few concept-learning experiments of the sort done with adults is the assumption that children are less willing to sit cooperatively through the many blocks of learning that it takes to acquire a complex category structure. As experiments on adults sometimes require many, many blocks until the categories are learned, it is not possible to translate them directly into experiments with children. However, it is possible to use simpler structures or to not set such high criteria for learning in order to allow children to perform somewhat competently.

Barrett et al.'s (1993) Experiment 1 looked for evidence of children's use of knowledge in learning specific features of a category. They taught first- and fourth-grade children about two kinds of birds. The properties of the birds were communicated by showing children a schematic picture of each property while explaining it. For example, the bird's beak could be straight or rounded, and a picture of a straight or round beak was shown. The categories were constructed so that two of the four critical features of each category would be related in children's prior knowledge. In one category, the bird was said to have a big brain and to be able to remember all the places it has found food. In the other category, the bird was said to have a small brain and to only remember the last place it found food. (Children generally have the belief that brain size corresponds to intelligence.) Each category was made up of exemplars that had three of the critical features of the category plus some irrelevant features that were found in both categories. Importantly, the features that were expected to be related in children's prior knowledge were not any more correlated in the learning stimuli than any other features in the category were.

After viewing the category exemplars, children were asked to categorize test items. Some of the test items had both of the related attributes (big brain–good memory or small brain–bad memory), and some reversed the expected pairings (big brain–bad memory or small brain–good memory). However, the two kinds of test items had equal numbers of typical features overall. Barrett et al. found that children were more accurate in categorizing the items with expected feature pairings than those with reversed pairings (75% vs. 48%), even though the family resemblance of the two items was identical. The same effect was found in typicality ratings. This is similar to results found with adults (Murphy and Wisniewski 1989b).

These results suggest that children were actively applying their knowledge of animals to the categories they were learning. Brain size and memory were not empirically correlated, but children spontaneously connected the two and used them in making categorization judgments.

The Barrett et al. (1993) experiment focused on how children learned specific pairs of features. A more general question is whether knowledge can aid in the acquisition of the entire category. Much work on adult concepts suggests that it can (e.g., Kaplan and Murphy 2000; Murphy and Allopenna 1994; Pazzani 1991; Wattenmaker et al. 1986; see chapter 6). However, experiments on children's concept learning with and without supportive knowledge are rare. The only published papers I am aware of are those by Hayes and Taplin (1992) and by Krascum and Andrews (1998).

Hayes and Taplin (1992) taught 6- and 11-year-old children categories of different types of people, described by phrases such as "went to university" and "likes to watch TV." The stimuli varied on dimensions of place of education, type of holiday they preferred, place of work, and leisure activities. Formally, all these dimensions were treated the same way in making up the two categories. However, Hayes and Taplin hoped to selectively activate some dimensions more than others by giving their categories different names (similar to Pazzani 1991; or Wattenmaker et al. 1986). Some subjects learned the categories of people as doctors and secretaries; others learned them as indoor and outdoor people; and the control group learned them as the Smith and Jones family. Hayes and Taplin found that children learned the categories more quickly when the names were meaningful (i.e., not Smith-Jones). They also gave the children a variety of test items after learning, which enabled them to discover which dimensions the children had emphasized. They discovered that children emphasized the features relevant to occupation for the doctor-secretary categories but the features relevant to recreation for the indoor-outdoor people category, even though all subjects saw exactly the same exemplars during learning, and all the features were equally predictive.

Hayes and Taplin's study gives compelling evidence that children are able to use their background knowledge in learning new categories. They did so even when such knowledge was not necessary—the categories could have been learned solely by learning the prototype or exemplars (which is presumably what the Smith-Jones group used). However, the children used in the study were already beyond early childhood, with 6-year-olds as the youngest group. (Also, the categories taught to children already referred to known categories, like doctors and secretaries.)

Krascum and Andrews (1998) extended the age of subjects tested to 5 years old. They taught children two kinds of animals, wugs and gillies, represented by pictures. The two categories had identical outlines but differed in features that could be added to the outlines (tail, feet, etc.).[14] In one condition, the experimenter explained the function of the features to the children. Wugs were described as animals that like to fight, and their features were all related to fighting (e.g., claws used for scratching); gillies were described as animals that hide from the wugs in trees, and their features were related to this function. In a control condition, each feature was mentioned, but no function was given for it. After viewing four exemplars of each category, children were tested on the learning items and transfer items that had only one or two of the features. The children given the functions for the features performed much better than the children who only heard the features named, on all test items.

One possible problem with this result is that the descriptions of the functions may have encouraged or interested children more generally, rather than having their effect through knowledge per se. So, in a second study, Krascum and Andrews described functions for all the features. However, in the control condition, the functions did not form a unified whole but were independent. For example, instead of describing the wug's features as all deriving from their fighting, its horns were described as helping the wug to pick up leaves to make a bed, its claws were used for digging for ants, and so on. Roughly the same amount of information, then, was provided for each feature in the two conditions. Nonetheless, virtually identical results were found in this experiment, as the group with unifying knowledge performed much better, especially on the transfer items.

These results are comparable to demonstrations with adults that a unifying theme can greatly increase the speed of learning (see chapter 6). Thus, this work shows that children will indeed use knowledge in learning categories. They do not rely solely on associative learning or remembering exemplars, without paying attention to how the exemplars relate to what they already know. It should be noted that, like adults, children did not only learn the general theme: Wugs are fighters, gillies hiders. Krascum and Andrews showed in a pre-test that these themes alone were not enough to allow children to categorize the items (without a learning phase). Furthermore, children who learned the themes were also quite good at a recognition memory test on the learning items given at the end of the experiment—significantly better than children who did not receive functional information. Children used the knowledge, then, to help learn the categories (and items) better, rather than using it to bypass more detailed learning (for analogous adult data see Kaplan and Murphy 2000; and Spalding and Murphy 1999).

Although these studies are promising, there is a need for more experimental studies of concept learning in children analogous to the many adult studies that have been done in this area. Most experiments have used much simpler techniques and categories when teaching categories to children (e.g., naming one object; testing only category members that are virtually identical to the learning items), so that it is difficult to identify a developmental progression. Nonetheless, the evidence that is available all shows that children use prior knowledge in acquiring new categories, just as adults do. There is no evidence that they rely solely on associative learning because their knowledge is limited.

Studies of Known Categories

Most research done on effects of knowledge in children's concepts has studied children's natural concepts acquired outside the laboratory. Especially popular have been studies of biological categories, since children show considerable interest in different kinds of animals (though less in plants), and they also develop a body of knowledge about biology that might influence their concepts. Major studies have been done by Carey (1985) and Keil (1989), the latter to be discussed in some detail below. Earlier work by Chi examined how children's knowledge and expertise affected a number of cognitive processes, including memory and learning. In a study focused specifically on concepts, Chi, Hutchinson, and Robin (1989) compared children who were experts on dinosaurs with those who had some knowledge of dinosaurs but who were not as knowledgeable. When children were asked to sort pictures of 20 dinosaurs, some of the experts created hierarchies, such as first dividing the dinosaurs into plant- and animal-eaters, and then subdividing them into family types (like duckbills); none of the novices did so. Overall, the experts used more family groupings than the novices did. When asked to give reasons for their groups, the novices tended to mention explicit physical features. Experts were less likely to mention such features and were much more likely to mention properties that could not be directly observed in the pictures, such as the animals' diet, defense, and habitat. In short, children's knowledge directly influenced their classification.

Other studies have focused on common concepts that all children would be expected to acquire. Keil (1989) examined children's use of characteristic and defining features of *nominal kinds*, like lie, twins, factory, island, and uncle. These are concepts that (almost) allow simple definitions, of the sort "a lie is something that one says that is not true, in order to deceive someone else."[15] Children are not able to articulate definitions for such items. Here is an example of a preschooler (apparently, a future Chauncey Gardiner) trying to define *island* (pp. 62–64; C = child; E = experimenter):

C: You dance.
E: What kind of dance? Can you show me?
C: I can't ... I mean you can watch people dance like you put on a song.
E: So, whenever you put on a song and dance, that's an island?
C: Uhuh ... people watch.
E: What does an island look like?
C: People ... yup, people without clothes on—you can't.
E: You can't have clothes on an island?
C: No, but you can watch.
E: Is there an island in Ithaca [the location of the study]?
C: No.
E: Why not?
C: 'Cause it's not summertime yet.
E: You mean there can only be islands during the summer?
C: Yeah.
E: But it's summertime now.
C: Yeah.
E: So is there an island?
C: No.

This child's concept of islands seems to be based on prototypical images of the sort that might appear on TV or in stories: Islands are tropical locales (explaining the reference to summer), with scantily clad natives dancing the hula. There is little mention of water. Do these results show that children cannot learn concepts of this sort? This would certainly be consistent with the traditional, Piagetian view of children as being unable to acquire definitions like "an island is a body of land surrounded by water." (However, as I have pointed out, one cannot expect children to be able to verbalize the bases for their behavior, so part of the problem here is simply their inability to describe their true concept. Indeed, as Keil's studies show—see also Anglin 1977; Gelman 1988—children's explanations of concepts are often much less sophisticated than their actual judgments about category membership.) Alternatively, perhaps it is just that children have not been exposed to the critical features in a way that allows them to learn the concept. If they see a movie in which people sail to an island, where they climb palm trees to pick coconuts, swim, and dance the hula, it is not clear that the critical aspect of the island is the water. Surely, that is a lot less interesting than the coconuts and dancing. Movies are generally not very good at explaining the bases of categories. So, are children's troubles in such tasks due to a general problem with learning definitions, or to a simple lack of knowledge of what the critical features are?

To answer this question, Keil, in collaboration with Nancy Batterman, constructed stories that had some characteristic (typical) features of such concepts but lacked definitional features. For example, one story described a mean old man with a gun in his pocket who came to take away your TV, which your parents had said he could have. Children would be asked if he was a robber. The opposite kind of item, with the definitional features but not characteristic features, was also used. For example, another story described a place with apartment buildings and snow, surrounded by water. Children would be asked whether it was an island. Children at different ages were presented these stories, and their decisions were tracked across ages.

Keil and Batterman (see Keil 1989, ch. 4) found, not surprisingly, that children improved in the task with age. Kindergartners often attended only to the characteristic features, whereas fourth-graders often used only the defining features. There were noticeable differences in how "defining" different concepts were. Children attended to the defining features for moral terms (lie, robber) right from the beginning, whereas concepts like museum and church took some time to learn correctly, and were not completely attained by grade 4.

Keil makes the point that the differences between domains argue against the claim that children at a certain age are just unable to learn definitional features, as Piaget would have predicted. If children were unable to ignore typical features and focus on the most critical ones in grade 2, for example, as was the case for the concepts of news and museum, then they should not have shown the ability to correctly classify robber or twin when the characteristic features were atypical. Yet they could. In later studies, Keil (1989) showed that some of this development was consistent across concepts within a single domain. Children's performance on different meal concepts (like breakfast and dinner) or on various kinship concepts (like cousin and uncle) was highly correlated. Keil argued that this occurs because learning the critical features for one concept in this domain provides exactly the critical features for the other concepts. So, once one learns that breakfast is the morning meal (regardless of exactly what is eaten), one can easily learn that lunch is the midday meal (regardless of what is eaten). In contrast, performance in the domains of tools and cooking terms was less correlated. Presumably, this is because learning what a hammer is does not provide much helpful information about what a drill is, because different functions and properties are involved.

These studies provide some insight into how the child's acquisition of knowledge promotes the development of more accurate categories. However, the studies are also correlational, in that they simply follow the increasing accuracy of performance with age. It is not clear from them exactly what is driving the change in decisions about the different stories. Also, it is important not to get too carried away with the terms "characteristic" and "defining" features and the notion of a "characteristic-to-defining shift" (which Keil sometimes uses). We should be very careful in saying that children focus more on defining features in general, as if this were a well-defined (sic) class of features that are psychologically separate from characteristic features, and that for some reason, young children choose to emphasize the characteristic features but are later persuaded to emphasize the defining ones. The true story seems to be that at first children do not know enough about the domains to be able to identify the features that are most central to the categories. Many of the critical features of these terms are, in retrospect, rather bizarre ones that no one could blame a child for not thinking of. Who would ever have imagined that there would be a concept for the brother of one's parent OR the husband of the sister of one's parent (i.e., uncle)? Young children often don't even know these relations (i.e., that uncle Tony is the husband of the sister of their father), but they do have access to prototypical features such as uncle Tony's being avuncular, visiting on holidays, giving them birthday gifts, and so forth. In order to acquire such concepts, they must learn the principles behind the domain (of kinship, in this case), not just learn to attend to definitional features in some generic sense.

Keil has also carried out a number of other very interesting studies that investigate the basis on which children make classifications. These studies pit the appearance of the object against theory-based properties, such as its origins and internal organs. If children were learning categories in a primarily empirical way, then the appearances should win out in such tests. One paradigm was the *discovery procedure*, in which children are shown a normal picture of an object but then are told that scientists have discovered some surprising facts about it. For example, children would be shown a picture of a horse, which would be described as having the behavioral properties of a horse (it goes "neigh," people ride it). However, they would also be told that scientists examined the animal and found that it had inside parts of cows, cow blood, and cow bones. Also, they discovered that its parents were cows, and that its children were cows. So, the children would be asked, is it a cow or a horse? On other trials, the item was not a natural kind but an artifact. A key would be shown, but children would be told that it had been made out of pennies, and scientists discovered that it consisted of penny metal. Later, it would be melted down and made into pennies again. So, is it a key or a penny?

Children of all ages were not swayed by the "scientific" discoveries about artifacts. The thing that looks and is used like a key *is* a key, regardless of where it came from, or what material it is made out of. Children were sometimes swayed by the discoveries about natural kinds, however. By grade 2, children were siding with the scientists rather than with what the animal looked like. Kindergartners, however, tended to stick with the picture. Although the animal had cow blood, it looked like a horse, and it *was* a horse. Thus, by second grade (about 7 years 9 months old), children could overrule their perceptions of an object and attend instead to more theoretical underlying properties. Note that it was not that the older children were uncritically accepting of whatever the scientists claimed to find (as so many people are nowadays), because they did not use the scientists' findings about artifacts. Although 2nd and 4th graders did use their knowledge of biology to influence their decisions, they did not do so all the time—there was still considerable improvement in adults, who almost always followed the scientific discovery for the natural kinds (but virtually never for the artifacts).

Keil also used a *transformation procedure*, in which an item starts out life as a typical category member but then is transformed into something that looks different. For example, a raccoon is operated on to become very like a skunk, even going so far as to have a sack of "super smelly yucky stuff" implanted beneath its tail. A picture shown to the child would reveal that it now looks exactly like a skunk. But is it really a skunk, or is it still a raccoon? In contrast to the discovery procedure, the theory-based answer is now that identity has not changed from what it was originally thought to be (see also Wells 1930). The results were very similar to those of the discovery paradigm: Kindergartners generally tended to follow what the final picture looked like, whereas older children stayed with the original identity for the natural kinds. For artifacts, all children believed that the item had changed categories as a result of its transformation.

These results, then, suggest that school-age children are able to use their knowledge of underlying causal mechanisms to help make decisions about category membership. Kindergartners, however, do not perform so well. This could mean either that they are "seduced by percepts," that is, tied to the way that the item looks, or that they simply do not know enough to pay attention to the scientific properties. Evidence for the latter possibility was found in another experiment Keil did, in which objects were transformed into radically different kinds of objects (a porcupine turned into a cactus, for example). Here, even the kindergartners objected that the object had not changed. Also, note that because this paradigm pits two variables against each other (i.e., perceptual resemblance suggests one answer whereas scientific knowledge another), it does not provide an assessment of either source alone. Kindergartners might easily use knowledge when it is not contradicted by the item's present likeness.

It would be possible to interpret these results to indicate that children don't pay attention to perceptible properties, but instead are interested in deeper, theoretical properties. However, this would be an oversimplification. As Keil comments himself (e.g., p. 281), this kind of theory or background knowledge often works by relating underlying causes to observable, overt properties. For example, being a bird involves flying and having wings, because wings enable flying, and it is in the nature of birds (usually) to fly. Many of a bird's perceptual properties (wings, sleek body) are related to deeper, more underlying properties rather than being arbitrary. In real life, the perceptually available features typically reflect rather than contradict underlying causes. The importance of those experiments is in showing that children go beyond the appearance of features by connecting them to their knowledge as best they can.

Keil's book has much interesting discussion in it that I cannot do justice to here. It is particularly good in tying together the philosophical and psychological literatures. I recommend it to anyone interested in this topic.

Keil's studies, as well as others, have suggested to some researchers that children believe in *essentialism* of categories. As Medin and Ortony (1989) claimed for adults, children may infer hidden causes for overt events and in particular an essential property that makes a thing what it is. This is somewhat evident in Keil's (1989) transformation studies, in which children denied that something that looked like a horse was really a horse, because it started out as a cow. Although the picture shown was of an actual horse, children did not believe that the cow's essence could be removed by an operation or by feeding it horse food, and so on. Hirschfeld (1996) argues that children are also essentialists about race. For example, they believe that if a child is born to a family of one race but raised by a family of a different race, it will have the race of its parents. Gelman, Coley, and Gottfried (1994) suggest that children's assumptions about motion also reflect essentialism. When objects are seen to move on their own, this is treated as a property of their internal dispositions, even for transparent objects that appear not to have internal mechanisms. Hirschfeld and Gelman et al. suggest that essentialism arises from a strong tendency for children to give causal explanations for things, combined with domain-specific information that is consistent with internal explanations. For example, children know that animals have insides, and that these insides are in some respects related to their external behavior (e.g., eating, locomotion). Therefore, children find it natural to explain an animal's behaviors through internal causes.

Similarly, the fact that animals reproduce after their kind can be explained through the transmission of an essential characteristic, which adults might identify as a genetic code, but children might think of as being bits of the parents' blood, bones, and so on (Springer and Keil 1991). Children are not essentialists about everything, Gelman et al. (1994) argue, because other kinds of entities do not support internal explanations. Keil (1994) proposes that children have preferences for a few different kinds of explanations, such as mechanical, intentional, and teleological, and these preferences tend to "resonate with specific sets of phenomena" (p. 251), resulting in different kinds of specific explanations.

Gelman and Wellman (1991) proposed that a precursor to essentialism is an understanding that internal states and mechanisms are responsible for overt structures and behavior. For example, to succeed in Keil's transformation task, one must have the idea that there is something internal to the animal that determines its identity and that cannot be reduced to having a certain color skin, or even having a sack of super smelly yucky stuff. Because very young children do not have an advanced understanding of genetics and its influence on morphology, it is perhaps unreasonable to expect them to know about such essences early on (and, indeed, Keil found it difficult to demonstrate such thinking in 5-year-olds). Nonetheless, easier tests might show that even young children do have the precursors to essentialist thinking.

In one experiment, Gelman and Wellman (1991) simply asked children which of three objects had the same insides. They found that children as young as 3 were able to identify two objects from the same superordinate category as having the same insides (e.g., a pig and cow) over two items that looked very similar but were from different categories (e.g., a pig and piggy bank). In a different paradigm (readers who have recently eaten lunch may wish to skip to the next paragraph), they showed children a picture of an item and then asked them what would happen if you took out its insides or if you took away its outsides and left the rest. Children were specifically asked if it was still the same kind of thing, and whether it could behave normally. For example, if the item were a dog, the experimenter would ask if it was still a dog and could still bark and eat dog food. Four- and 5-year-old children identified the insides as more important for both identity and the behavior or function of the object. As a control, Gelman and Wellman also tested containers, where the insides are less critical (e.g., if you take the peanut butter out of a jar, it is still a jar). Children did not emphasize insides for such items.

It may be, then, that children's first understanding of essences is through recognizing that many kinds of things have internal structures that are responsible for their external appearance and behavior. However, it is also possible that children have acquired specific knowledge about the insides of such items that is not based on essentialism. Perhaps children recognize that without its insides, a dog's outsides could not move, eat, and so on, because they have some understanding of the function of bones and muscles. Such specific knowledge may not be telling us as much about the child's understanding of what makes something a dog as it is telling us that they understand that an animal without its insides is in very bad shape indeed. A dog that is missing its insides is not much of a dog, or in fact, an animal of any kind—it is just a pile of skin. In that sense, the Keil transformation study is a bit more conclusive, because it maintains a coherent living animal across transformations but questions its identity. But, as Gelman and Wellman point out, such questions about whether something is "really" in a category, are very difficult (for adults as well as children), and so are perhaps too high a criterion as an understanding of essences.

Gelman and Wellman's (1991) later studies looked at inborn potential as a determinant of category membership. Here they constructed cross-raising scenarios for animals and asked children whether the animals would have their typical properties. Such scenarios do not create the unsightly items missing their insides and so avoid the problems I just mentioned. In this experiment, children might be shown a picture of an immature cow, named Edith. They would be told that right after Edith was born, she was moved in with pigs, who raised her, and she never saw another cow. Then children would be asked to decide whether Edith would have a cow or a pig property, such as a straight or curly tail, when she grew up. The property was not visible in the picture. Children (4 and 5) generally chose the property associated with the animal's biological parents, rather than with its upbringing (e.g., saying that Edith would have a straight tail and would say "moo"). (Perhaps surprisingly, this result was very strong for behavioral properties like saying "moo," and not quite as strong for physical properties like kind of tail.) Thus, even 4-year-olds had some idea that animals are born with innate potentials from their parents, which may make up part of their idea of the category's essence.

An even more extreme version of an emphasis on insides and inborn potential may be children's understanding of race. Hirschfeld (1996, ch. 6) argues that children form ideas of different races of people, along with the assumption that they are different kinds, before they can reliably identify people's races. Their categories are based on having heard people identified as white or Asian or black or in having heard generalizations about such groups. It is only later that they can identify their classmates, for example, as being in these different groups. In this case, then, knowledge of perceptual properties lags behind the assumption that there are underlying differences between groups of people. Hirschfeld suggests that children's understanding of race is an extension of the essentialist tendencies documented in other categories.

Much of the recent research in conceptual development has focused on specific domains of children's concepts. In fact, this work is continuous with what might be called the development of knowledge in these specific areas. For example, how soon do children understand the nature of biological inheritance? Do they understand the germ theory of disease? Do they think of people as having enduring personalities or as only acting based on immediate causes? These kinds of issues are under study in many laboratories. They all relate to issues of categorization, because children's deeper understanding of a domain is tied to their categorization of the entities in it. For example, if children think that diseases are caused by a biological agent, then they may identify someone as having the disease who is infected with the agent whether or not they show symptoms. If they think of the disease as being simply the possession of certain symptoms, then they will categorize anyone with those symptoms as having the disease, even if they lack the virus or bacterium. This literature is too voluminous to be reviewed in any kind of detail here, and it is not that relevant to do so, because it would quickly get us into very specific details of those domains (e.g., Gelman and Wellman's 1991 comparison of children's understanding of the inborn potential of seeds vs. inheritance in animals). Nonetheless, it is a very active and interesting research area.

Domain Specificity

Some researchers have argued that knowledge can be divided into distinct domains, based on differences in phenomena and underlying principles. Children start out with expectations about these different domains, allowing them to quickly learn concepts within them, because they already have some inkling about what features will be critical for each domain. Proposals for such domains include numbers, music, animals, psychology, faces, and physical objects. For example, children's beliefs about objects include very basic information about objects being solid entities that take up space, that will fall if not supported, that continue to exist when out of sight, and so on. The basic principles of object existence and behavior are thought by some to define this as a domain that is qualitatively separate from other domains of knowledge, such as arithmetic or psychology. These domains are generally much more basic than the concepts like shoes or cows that we have been focusing on, though some of the domains suggested, such as animals, or people, may well intersect with them. However, even in those domains, the type of knowledge that is discussed is general principles of the sort that animals move on their own because of internal structures, rather than specific properties of categories of animals (e.g., that cows say "moo").

In order to explain why children distinguish such domains, it is often assumed that there is some innate cognitive structure that focuses their learning appropriately within the domain. Another possibility is that the information in the domain is inherently segregated to some degree, so that the domain can be formed as a result of experience. For example, music might be a separate domain, because the properties of music simply don't overlap much with the properties of objects, social events, people, and so on. This domain specificity may not always need to be attributed to cognitive structures then, but may in part be a function of the organization of experiences that young children are likely to have, given the nature of the domain. Finally, some authors argue that domain specificity only develops slowly, as children learn the basic phenomena and principles of the domain. For example, Carey (1985) argues this for biological knowledge, and she and her students (Johnson and Solomon 1997; Solomon et al. 1996) have proposed that young children's understanding of inheritance is not truly biological (i.e., domain specific), because it does not accurately separate biological from nonbiological properties.

The question of how domains arise—innately and otherwise—and whether this domain specificity is even a helpful concept would take us too far afield here. For discussions, see Carey (1985) and the book edited by Hirschfeld and Gelman (1994), especially the chapters by Spelke and Carey and by Keil. Also, R. Gelman (1990) specifically addresses both number and animals as possible domains. Much of this literature focuses on domains such as speech, number, or music, which may not be easily generalizable to everyday categories like chairs and cows.

One reason I am not delving further into this issue is that I have been taking a more general perspective in which "knowledge effects" are considered as a very general phenomenon. Some of the writers above would distinguish the knowledge of specific facts from the basic principles that are unique to that domain and serve to separate it from different domains (e.g., Solomon et al. 1996). However, as we have seen, mundane facts about the world greatly influence children's concept learning (and as we will see next, induction). For example, children know that doctors have university degrees and that animals with small brains are not as smart as animals with large brains. Neither of these is a basic principle of a domain, but both influence concept learning. I do not know of any data showing that deeper domain principles influence concept acquisition in a way that mundane knowledge does not, though this may be because this particular contrast has not been made. Nonetheless, it is clear that the knowledge children have about the world is influencing their concept learning and performance. If there are strongly separate domains of knowledge, then the principles in each domain certainly will influence it as well.

Induction

One of the main functions of concepts is to allow induction to new items. When we see a new dog, we know not to try to take its food away and that we should not yank its tail, even though we haven't seen what that dog would do under those circumstances. This is because we know certain properties that are often true of dogs, and we are willing to extend them to new dogs, unless there is reason not to do so. Furthermore, if we learn that our pet dog suffers from sleeping sickness, we may decide that all dogs are susceptible to sleeping sickness. As chapter 8 recounts, this aspect of induction, the extension of properties to other category members, is one of the major functions of concepts. As a result, children's inductive abilities have also been of considerable interest.

Children are willing to make inductions to new category members, suggesting that they use this function of categories very early on. (Indeed, their everyday behavior gives evidence of this, as they try to eat cookies, open books, and throw breakfast cereal, even when they have not seen those specific objects before.) In chapter 9, I discussed the study of induction in 9–10-month-olds by Baldwin, Markman, and

Melartin (1993). Some research that bridges the gap between these infants and older preschoolers is that of Mandler and McDonough (1996) on 14-month-old children. To begin, the experimenter demonstrated an action on a toy. For example, she pretended to give a toy dog a drink of water, or pretended to start a car with a key. The experimenter then gave the prop to the child and placed objects of the same or different categories on the table. For example, the child might be given the cup and then would have the choice of employing the action on a rabbit or motorcycle. Mandler and McDonough found that children much preferred to carry out the action on the item in the same category, even if the test item was not very similar to the training item (e.g., dog-fish).

Although these results do suggest that children saw a connection between the category members, they are somewhat clouded by the fact that the actions themselves were so familiar and may have already been known as properties of those categories. That is, the young children may have already believed that most animals drink or that most machines need to be turned on, and so it is not clear to what degree the results show induction of a new property or simple reminding of a known property. This possibility is strengthened by the finding in Mandler and McDonough's Experiment 3 that when drinking (for example) was demonstrated on a vehicle, children still preferred to carry it out on an animal. That is, they followed their initial preferences rather than category membership of the training item. Thus, children are clearly extending known properties to new animals, but are not so clearly making inductions about novel properties (cf. Baldwin et al. 1993, who did teach novel properties). As we shall see, it is somewhat easier to demonstrate induction of a novel property with older children, because one can teach them a novel property and ask them more directly about its presence in different categories. With younger children, the methodological problems still pose a difficulty in assessing their inductions.

Gelman and Markman (1986) showed that children's inductions were not just a matter of applying known properties to familiar items. They found that children will attribute novel properties to category members in preference to nonmembers that look quite similar. In a seminal experiment, they showed children a triad of drawings. The first two were in different categories, such as a bird (flamingo) and bat. Children were told a novel fact about each example, for example, that the bird feeds its babies bugs, and the bat feeds its babies milk. The third item looked like one object but was in the same category as the other object. So, for the above example, the third item was a bird that looked very similar to the bat. Children would be asked which property they thought this item had: "Look at this bird. Does it feed its babies bugs, like this bird, or does it feed them milk, like this bat?" Thus, category membership (both items being birds) was contrasted with perceptual similarity (the bird and bat looking similar). Gelman and Markman found that 4-year-olds tended to use category membership rather than perceptual similarity to make their inductions. Using a simpler procedure, Gelman and Markman (1987) extended this to 3-year-olds. Even preschool children, then, have the assumption that category members share nonobvious properties and will use category membership to make inductions. Clearly, this is further support for the hypothesis that children believe in category essences, as discussed above, since they were not basing their inductions on perceptual properties but instead on inferred deeper similarity of category members.[16]

Inductions should not always be drawn, however. For example, if you see a penguin for the first time, and it is sleeping, you should not conclude that penguins are all asleep; if you saw the penguin in the zoo, you would hopefully not conclude that all penguins are in a zoo. Some properties are inducible and some are not—and which properties are inducible depends on the nature of the category. For example, natural kinds tend to have properties of inner mechanism and origins in common, but not locations or functions. In contrast, artifacts and event categories may have location and function properties in common. Gelman and Markman (1986) found that children did not make the same kinds of inductions about superficial properties as they did about deeper ones. As we have seen, children extended biological or behavioral properties to items in the same category. But for properties like "weighs 100 pounds" or "is dirty," children did not rely on category membership. Some of them tended to use the perceptual similarity of the pictures, but in general the children were not very regular in such decisions. Children were not simply saying "They're in the same category, so they must be the same." Instead, they distinguished inducible from noninducible properties.

As part of her extensive study of expertise, Chi and her colleagues have also looked at inductions. Chi et al. (1989) showed children novel dinosaurs and asked them to provide any information they could about them. The more knowledgeable children were likely to make inductions based on category membership, such as: "He's pretty dangerous. [Why?] 'Cause he's a meat eater." That is, identifying the dinosaur as a member of a particular class allowed the children to infer an unobservable property such as being dangerous. In contrast, novices were more likely to make inferences based on observed attributes such as: "He could walk real fast. [Why?] 'Cause he has giant legs." Although such differences are important, it is not entirely clear whether they are due to background knowledge as defined here or simply to greater familiarity with the categories in question (e.g., knowing more meat-eating dinosaurs). Other studies have looked more specifically for evidence of domain reasoning that might be driving induction.

Gelman (1988) looked at different kinds of properties that could be reasonably attributed to natural kind and other categories. She found that 2nd graders (almost 8 years old) were noticeably better than preschoolers (4 years old) at distinguishing these different kinds of properties. For example, they were more likely to generalize properties like having certain chemicals inside to natural kinds, but to generalize functions to artifacts. Even the 2nd graders did not distinguish these properties very well, though, and it may be that the methodology of using unfamiliar properties (e.g., "has pectin inside" or "is used to make fumet") is too difficult for the children.

Kalish and Gelman (1992) went further into this issue by examining which properties children would derive from more complex cases that involved two different concepts. In particular, they looked at combinations of material and object concepts, like wooden pillows or glass scissors. If children identify one category as the "real" category for such objects (e.g., it's a pillow, regardless of what it's made of), then they should derive all their inductions from that category alone. However, if they have some idea of what kinds of properties arise from different kinds of concepts, then they should be able to distinguish these properties according to which concept controls them. For example, wooden pillows would have the texture and material properties of wood but would have the functional properties and shape of pillows. Kalish and Gelman cleverly chose categories and properties so that children's experiences could not tell the correct answer for their inductions: All wooden things are hard, but all pillows are soft. Therefore, children cannot rely on experiences with wooden things and pillows to decide whether wooden pillows are hard or soft. Because this task asked children about familiar properties, like whether something was hard or soft, it could be used even for young children. Kalish and Gelman found that children as young as 3 years old used the appropriate categories to make their inductions. For example, they said that wooden pillows were hard but would be found in the bedroom.

In a second study, Kalish and Gelman (1992) used the procedure of teaching a novel property for one object and seeing whether children would extend it to other objects. For example, children were told that glass scissors were "used for partitioning" and "will get fractured if put in really cold water." Although the children would not know what "partitioning" and "fractured" meant, they might be able to identify the first as a functional feature, and the second as a property of the material. Then the children were asked whether metal scissors or a glass bowl would have these properties. Correct responding would be to attribute the material property to the glass bowl and the functional property to the metal scissors. Three-year-olds could answer the object properties but not the material properties correctly; 4-year-olds performed above chance on both. Again, the difficulty for younger children is probably caused in part by the use of unexplained terms such as "partitioning." In fact, it is impressive that the 4-year-olds could answer these questions sensibly, when they did not know exactly what the words meant.

These results reveal a fairly sophisticated ability to identify the kinds of properties relevant to different categories. Even at young ages, children know enough about the relevant domains of different categories to be able to identify which properties are extendable and which are not. This extension is not achieved through surface similarity, as the Gelman and Markman (1986) results showed, though when surface similarity is not contrasted with category membership, it does have an effect too, as might be expected (see Gelman 1988). Although space precludes a description here, it should also be mentioned that induction as a reasoning process has also been studied in children, following the model of adult categorical induction developed by Osherson et al. (1990). Interestingly, children are able to use some of the principles Osherson et al. identify quite early, but others do not develop until well into school age. See López et al. (1992) for details.

More research is being done on what kinds of inductions children are likely to make. However, this work, like some of the categorization work described in the previous section, begins to melt into questions about what children know about specific categories and properties. For example, when do children learn about material categories and their properties? When do they learn which properties of animals rely on inheritance and which on environmental factors? The exact nature of the categories and children's interactions with them turn out to be important, as, for example, Gelman (1988) found that children were better at inductions for biological kinds than for substances (which are also natural kinds), like gold. Thus, there is no developmental milestone at which children become extremely adept at making just the right inductions. They must have specific knowledge of the particular domains in order to be able to separate the inducible from the noninducible properties.

Conclusions

Children do not have the facility in learning and using concepts that adults do. It is harder for them to learn concepts, and they often have misconceptions and errors that last for years (e.g., thinking that dolphins are fish or that an ostrich is not a bird). Nonetheless, children learn new concepts at an amazing rate, and many of our most essential concepts are to a large extent formed during childhood. At the beginning of the chapter, I raised the question of to what degree children's concepts and conceptual processes resemble that of adults. Overall, it is remarkable how qualitatively similar the basic processes of concept learning and representation seem to be in children and adults. Although the field of developmental psychology had traditionally focused on what were apparently major differences between children and adults (i.e., the work of Piaget, Vygotsky, and their followers), more recent work has shown that children are generally in the right ballpark. For example, they show effects of typicality in categorization and learning, just as adults do. They use hierarchical category structure fairly early, and show a basic-level advantage very similar to that of adults. They use knowledge in learning categories and in making categorical inductions, again like adults. One can get too carried away in such comparisons and end up thinking that children are just like adults. That is clearly not true. However, I think that for the most part, children's conceptual abilities are quite similar to those of adults. The differences seem to be due largely to (1) differences in experience with category members; (2) differences in domain knowledge; and (3) differences in processing capacity or fluency. I discuss these in turn.

Differences in experience cause a problem because children simply have not been exposed to the category members that adults have, and for learning large, difficult categories (like mammals, legal terms, and personality types), it is necessary to come into contact with the unusual, infrequent members in order to grasp the concept as a whole. North American children do not see ostriches and penguins every day, and when they do see them, category membership information may not be available. It therefore takes such children some time to learn that birds do not have to fly and that other features are more criterial. This is not a matter of cognitive ability but of having sufficient experience. Adults who travel often find out that features that they had assumed were true of all category members in fact are not ("In England, the beer is warm!"). Their categories may change as a result of this expanded experience, just as children's do, albeit less often.

Differences in children's knowledge are obviously related to their lack of experience. However, if we take "knowledge" as referring not just to anything that one knows, but to a somewhat coherent set of beliefs about a domain, it is clear that children gain not only experience with category exemplars but also an understanding of general principles and patterns in various domains. Some of this is due to parental input and education, but some is simply due to the child figuring things out on his or her own. Of course, early knowledge may not be very accurate (and the same is unfortunately true for adults), but it apparently influences category acquisition nonetheless. As a result of gaining knowledge about biology, social relations, materials, and so forth, children's concepts can become more sophisticated. However, the difference between children and adults on this dimension is not a qualitative difference in conceptual processes but a quantitative difference in how much children generally know.

Differences in processing capacity or fluency are not really the subject of this book, and I have little to say about them. I bring them up only to point out that one reason for developmental differences in concepts is that children simply do not learn as quickly as adults do. Their attentional capacities and learning strategies may also be somewhat different, or at least somewhat limited relative to adults' (see Schneider and Bjorklund 1998). Many studies have shown that children's working memory is less than that of adults and that their learning is generally slower. In the concept acquisition literature, such comparisons are not often made directly, though one can see adult advantages in the work of Hayes and Taplin (1993) and Markson and Bloom (1997), for example. It is somewhat controversial in the cognitive development literature whether differences in processing are the causes or effects of differences in knowledge. For example, perhaps it takes children longer to learn categories because they cannot encode and remember as many features about each exemplar during learning; alternatively, perhaps because their familiarity with such categories and their features is less (i.e., because their knowledge is less), they cannot remember the stimuli as well. Either way, it seems likely that processing capacity is the cause of at least some differences between children and adults. For example, perhaps the difficulty children have with atypical category members is due to their being unable to remember specific items (see Hayes and Taplin 1993). If more typical items are forgotten, there is less damage, because other items will be similar to them. If you forget that someone told you that a robin is a bird, you will still be able to identify it if you remember that cardinals and sparrows are birds. If you forget that an ostrich is a bird, you are pretty much out of luck.

The exact proportions of these causes for differences between children's and adults' concepts are unknown. And given the overall qualitative similarity between the two, perhaps it is not that important for us to worry about. However, for those who are interested in explaining development per se, such questions are of vital importance.

Exemplar and Prototype Approaches

The issue of exemplars vs. prototypes, which has dominated much of the adult literature, has had very little influence on the developmental literature. However, this is not because the question has been answered with respect to children. Instead, it is as if the researchers have decided that they have better things to do with their time and so have decided to focus on more interesting questions. (After reading the adult literature on this topic, many readers may agree.) In fact, almost all of the research on children seems to, at least implicitly, take a prototype view of concepts. That is, it assumes that there is a summary representation of a category that children quickly acquire and then update through further experience or in gaining domain knowledge. Whether children's performance could be accounted for by exemplar models is not generally addressed.

One reason for the lack of attention to the prototype/exemplar debate is the difficulty of getting children to perform in experiments that would provide an appropriate test of different models. Most tests of the exemplar approach involve subjects learning difficult categories (if the categories have a simple structure, all the theories make identical predictions) to a high criterion. The main data are how difficult it is to learn different items. Young children, however, do not wish to view a dozen exemplars over and over and over again, trying to learn categories that do not make any obvious sense: They may not even finish the experiment, or may never learn the categories at all. In fact, this kind of experiment is aversive enough that one might have ethical concerns about making young children go through it.

There were a few early studies of children's ability to form prototypes, which generally found that children seemed to abstract prototypes from viewed exemplars (e.g., Lasky 1974; Posnansky and Neumann 1976). They also found that the youngest children tested (6–7-year-olds) showed a smaller prototype effect than older children. However, whether this is due to differences in prototype abstraction or differences in attention or motivation is not clear. Lasky (1974) also concluded that children could not have been learning exemplars, because they did not show expected differences between old and new items. However, no study from this era tested a more recent exemplar approach, which does not necessarily predict very good memory for individual exemplars (see below).

There have been some more recent attempts to compare different models of children's category learning, perhaps the best one being that of Hayes and Taplin (1993), who also review the problems with previous attempts. They had 6- and 11-year-olds and adults learn two categories of figures described as Martians or Venusians. (Note that older children were used than in many of the studies described earlier in the chapter, in part, I suspect, because of the difficulty of this task.) After learning the categories (though the criterion was not perfect performance, as in adult studies), children were tested on old and new items, and their performance was compared to a prototype and exemplar model. Instead of one of the more familiar exemplar models, Hayes and Taplin used a simpler one in which the distance of an item to its nearest exemplar was used to predict performance.

With this comparison, Hayes and Taplin found that both models predicted the performance of 11-year-olds and adults pretty well. However, 6-year-olds showed little effect of near exemplars, and their performance could be accounted for by prototype distance quite well. The authors concluded that the younger children were not using exemplars, perhaps because they did not remember them very well, which was consistent with the finding that 6-year-olds did not perform better on old than on new items. Although this conclusion is tempting, it is still possible that one of the more powerful exemplar models such as the Generalized Context Model or Minerva (see chapter 4) would account for the results of all subjects. For example, perhaps the 6-year-olds do not really form prototypes but remember exemplars in partial form. If this were true, then they would no longer show an advantage of old items but might well show a prototype advantage (Hintzman and Ludlam 1980), as discussed in chapter 2. However, I should point out that the criticisms of exemplar models, described in chapter 4, such as their being too powerful, would apply here as well.

In short, there is little good information about whether children form prototypes, learn exemplars, or do both. The evidence suggests that younger children are more liable to rely on prototypes than are older subjects, but the most popular adult models have not been tested, and so no firm conclusion can be drawn. I suspect that the answer to this question will not come directly from developmental work, but is more likely to come through a consensus in the field as a whole about whether exemplars or prototypes (or some mixture) are the correct representation.

Knowledge Approaches

In contrast, the use of knowledge is shown in many studies of children's concepts. It can be found in artificial concept-learning experiments such as those of Barrett et al. (1993), Hayes and Taplin (1992), Kemler Nelson (1995), and Krascum and Andrews (1998). In such studies, children use their prior knowledge of a domain to understand what is central to category membership, and to decide how membership should be extended to other items. As in the adult studies, one does not need to highlight the knowledge or instruction for children to use it—they spontaneously draw on it in making their decisions.

Studies of natural concepts offer an even richer source of evidence for children's active use of knowledge. The transformation studies of Keil (1989), for example, show that children's background beliefs about natural kinds can override perceptual similarity in making category judgments. Even younger children may understand the importance of biologically critical properties that they believe are essential to animals (Gelman and Wellman 1991). In making inductions from known categories, children use such knowledge appropriately, forming generalizations over properties that are supported by the category (e.g., all birds might feed their babies the same way) and not over properties that are not supported (e.g., birds are not all clean or all dirty) (Gelman and Markman 1986; Kalish and Gelman 1992). In fact, there is probably more evidence for children using domain knowledge in category-related tasks than there is for adults—in part because the topic has been more studied, and is perhaps more surprising, in children.

A kind of backlash has arisen against the more knowledge-driven accounts of categorization in children. Jones and Smith (1993) provide a trenchant critique of the field, in which they propose that researchers are underestimating the importance of perceptual information in children's learning of concepts. Furthermore, they argue, many experiments that study such knowledge effects do not provide good perceptual information to children. Often there is only a photocopied, not very accurate line drawing of the item, which is much less detailed and salient than the actual item would be. Jones and Smith (1993, p. 114) argue against what they feel is the now prevailing view of concepts, that "our perceptual experiences as we encounter objects in the world are represented at the periphery of our concepts. At the center lies our nonperceptual knowledge: principally, beliefs about the origins and causes of category membership."

It is not obvious to me that the conceptual development field has indeed become very knowledge-driven. Clearly, there has been a very large increase in studies of children's knowledge of the world and how that influences their concepts. However, the simple fact that people are studying this issue does not mean that they do not think that perceptual information is important. Perceptual similarity was the basis of almost all categories studied since Hull (1920), and now that researchers have noticed a very interesting aspect of concepts that is not so perceptual, it is not surprising that there has been a change in research direction, if only to right past imbalances. One cannot infer from the proportion of researchers studying knowledge that researchers believe that knowledge accounts for that proportion of the psychology of concepts.

However, if researchers as a whole *have* been ignoring perceptual information, this is certainly a mistake. Although there are some cases in which knowledge and perceptual information conflict, in the vast majority of cases, they do not. Furthermore, children clearly learn to categorize items even when theoretically critical information is not available, which is much of the time. They can identify a dog from a photograph, without knowing anything about its DNA or parentage or physiology. In our experimental paradigms, it is often useful to contrast the two sources of information, but in real life, background knowledge must be generally consistent with perceptual information, or else it would change to become consistent. So, the fact that children, like adults, sometimes override the way that things look when they have other information that contradicts the perceptual information does not show that children don't normally learn and rely on perceptual information in categorization. Perceptual information is a critical part of concepts, and this is especially true for real-world, fast identification of objects, which relies on rich and detailed perceptual representations for their accuracy. Thus, Jones and Smith are right to tell us not to ignore perceptual information and to point out that such information may be richer in real-life objects than in reproductions.

That said, I think that the contrast between perceptual information and knowledge is not a real one. Most of the knowledge that researchers have studied relates perceptual features to underlying causes (Keil 1989). That is, knowledge is not a separate, independent aspect of the concept, but instead is something that connects the different properties that are known about the category. Birds have wings in order to fly, which allows them to live in nests in trees; televisions have screens on which to project images, which are received through a tuner, and which require electricity to operate. My knowledge suggests that if birds did not have wings (a perceptual feature),[17] they could not fly (a perceptible behavior); if the TV did not have a screen (a perceptual property), it would not allow us to see the signal its receiver gets. Perceptual properties are themselves explained by our knowledge rather than being separate from it. It is certainly possible that some researchers have fostered the impression that there is a dichotomy between perceptual information and underlying knowledge, especially when their experimental methodology contrasts the two. However, I would claim that there is no such dichotomy, and that the task of concept researchers is to explain how these two sources of information are coordinated and used in different tasks, rather than to try to say which one is more important. One might look to Kemler Nelson's (1995) study as a particularly good example. Here, children were found to have emphasized different perceptually present parts because of their inferences about the importance of those parts to the object's function. Rather than emphasizing knowledge at the expense of perception, Kemler Nelson showed how children's knowledge helped them to encode visible parts and use them in categorization. The parts that could be explained were more influential in the category representation than those that weren't.

Finally, at least some of the examples that Jones and Smith (1993) use to make their points are not examples of *knowledge* contrasting with perceptual information—at least, not as I conceive of these notions. For example, Jones and Smith give much attention to the induction experiments of Gelman and Markman (1986) and the many subsequent studies in that tradition. As reviewed above, children tended to say that, for example, two dissimilar birds would have the same property, rather than a visually similar bird and bat. It is important to understand that this task tests not domain knowledge but *category membership*. That is, subjects would be told that one critical item was a bird and the other a bat. The children had to decide whether the target bird would have the same property as another bird (sharing category membership) or as a bat (a different category). The children did not hear different facts or receive different information about the items, as one would do if one were manipulating knowledge (cf. Hayes and Taplin 1992; or Kemler Nelson 1995). So, it is incorrect to characterize such experiments as trying to show that knowledge is more important than perception, since it was category membership that was pitted against perception. (In fact, perceptual similarity was varied and was found to influence induction. Gelman and Markman 1987, found that perceptual similarity influenced induction when items were in the same category—e.g., were both birds— but not when the items were in different categories—e.g., bird-bat. Such results again suggest that perceptual information interacts with other sources of information, rather than competing with it.) It is certainly possible, as Jones and Smith argue, that if the pictures had been more realistic that children would have relied on perceptual information more than category membership. However, that is an empirical question.[18]

We should also keep in mind that perceptual information about items is often absent in one very common way of using concepts, namely linguistic communication. If I tell you a story of how my car broke down, you will use your knowledge of cars, background knowledge of mechanical devices, and many other assumptions about highways, human behavior, weather, and so on, in order to interpret the story. Unless I managed to film the episode, you will have to rely completely on your conceptual knowledge of these things to understand the story, since you will not have perceptual information about any of them. Children understand such stories and often enthusiastically tell stories and anecdotes on their own. If a child can become excited in hearing about a new puppy, it seems that the perception of how a puppy looks, feels or smells is not necessary to activate that concept. Again, that is not to say that perception is somehow peripheral but that there is nothing unusual or unnatural about using category knowledge when perception is not directly involved.

In sum, the knowledge-based approach has much to be happy about in developmental research. The exemplar and prototype views require further work, both in terms of accounting for present data and in the development of methodologies that can be effectively applied to children. If the usual category-learning study done on adults is not practicable with young children, then a new but equally precise method must be developed to gain a window on the exact nature of children's conceptual representations.

11
Word Meaning

Throughout much of this book, I have waffled on the question of whether I am talking about *concepts* or *words*. The two seem to be closely related. I can talk about children learning the concept of sheep, say, but I can also talk about their learning the word *sheep*. I would take as evidence for a child having this concept the fact that he or she uses the word correctly. On a purely intuitive basis, then, there appears to be considerable similarity between word meanings and concepts. And in fact, much of the literature uses these two terms interchangeably. In this chapter, I will address in greater detail the relation between concepts and word meanings, and so I will have to be somewhat more careful in distinguishing the two than I have been. (Let me remind readers of the typographical convention I have been following of italicizing words but not concepts.)

To discuss the relation between these two, one ought to begin by providing definitions for these terms, so that there is no confusion at the start. By *concept*, I mean a nonlinguistic psychological representation of a class of entities in the world. This is your knowledge of what kinds of things there are in the world, and what properties they have. By *word meaning*, I mean quite generally the aspect of words that gives them significance and relates them to the world. I will argue that words gain their significance by being connected to concepts. It is important to note, however, that this is not true by definition but needs to be argued for on the basis of evidence and psychological theory. And that is the main goal of this chapter. More generally, the goal is to say how it is that word meanings are psychologically represented.

As the reader will see, there is less new empirical material here than in most of the chapters of the book. Instead, the chapter is more of an essay in which I attempt to argue for a specific relation between word meanings and concepts. I begin by discussing notions of word meaning from psychology and linguistics and then propose a particular kind of relation between concepts and meanings. I attempt to support this proposal with theoretical and empirical evidence. Finally, I discuss some important topics from lexical semantics that are usually not addressed in psychological theories of word meaning, including polysemy and lexical modulation. These phenomena are critical to a complete explanation of how word meaning is related to comprehension, even though they have not received much attention in the psychological literature.

Different Conceptions of Word Meaning

The present chapter will not provide an introduction to the study of linguistic meaning. That is an enormous topic that has a huge literature in philosophy and linguistics, in addition to psychology, and a single chapter cannot even mention many of the topics in it, much less develop them in any detail. The focus of this chapter will be on how word meanings are psychologically represented. It will not address the meaning of larger linguistic structures (sentence, discourse, or story) except tangentially, and it will not consider controversies involving meaning in the philosophy of language. That said, I need to quickly review approaches to the study of meaning outside of psychology, in part to explain why it is that cognitive scientists from different perspectives have said things about meaning that seem at odds with what I propose. The reason, in brief, is that they have goals and assumptions that are not ours. In some cases, their enterprises are simply separate questions that do not conflict with the psychological ones. In other cases, however, it is likely that the two approaches will clash, and one will eventually have to give way (hopefully theirs). But resolving such disputes will not be the focus of this chapter.

One idea that people often have about word meaning is that it is a kind of "official" statement of the sort that is found in dictionaries. That is, when you have an argument with a friend over whether *berm* means a bank of earth or a small stream, you would look it up in the dictionary and find out that it means the former. Or you might have an argument over whether *data* is singular or plural, and check a style manual to decide the answer. From this perspective, the meaning is whatever is in the dictionary or other authoritative source. However, this kind of prescriptive meaning is not what we will be talking about, though it does have some importance. We will be talking about the meanings of words as people ordinarily use and conceive of them. So, if people typically misuse a word according to the dictionary or style manual, that is a problem for experts in usage. Psychologists are interested in the meaning of the word represented in the person's head—not what people are supposed to do.[1]

In linguistics and philosophy, *semantics* (a synonym for *meaning*, usually) is taken to mean the relation between language and the world. Typically, we use language to talk about real objects, people, events, and states. A theory of semantics, from this perspective, is one that explains how this connection between language and the world works. This approach is often called *referential semantics*, because it argues that words get their meanings by referring to real objects and events. One reason for framing the question of semantics this way is to explain the truth of sentences (see Dowty, Wall, and Peters 1981). That is, a statement is true just in case it corresponds to a situation in the world. Theories of semantics based on logic spell out that correspondence. For example, if I see you opening a gate and tell you "There's a mad dog in that yard," it would not be surprising if you were to step back and quickly close the gate. The reason for this is that there is a reliable (though not perfect) relationship between this sentence and a situation in the world in which a mad dog is to be found in a yard. The goal, then, is to explain the relationship between *mad* and various mad things, between *dog* and kinds of animals, between *in* and different spatial relations, and so on, such that the meaning of "There's a mad dog in that yard" corresponds correctly to a real-world situation of a certain kind of animal located within a yard. (Or if it doesn't correspond correctly, we could explain why you complained that I misled you.) For a good explanation of this aspect of meaning, see Chierchia and McConnell-Ginet (1990).

In order to explain the reliable connection between language and the world, many philosophical theories of semantics argue that word meaning is simply a relation between a word and the world. So, the meaning of *dog* is the set of dogs in the world. Actually, the theories are somewhat more complex than this, because the set of dogs in the world is changing all the time: New dogs are born and old ones die every minute. Furthermore, we may talk about hypothetical or fictional dogs, which would not be found in the world. Thus, the meaning of *dog* must be something more complex, like the set of all the dogs that ever existed and that will exist, or the set of all *possible* dogs ("If I had a dog, it would be brown"). In this case, as in many others, the meaning would be an infinitely large set of objects, since there is an infinite number of possible dogs.

Referential semantics is extremely popular in linguistics, but it is not acceptable as a psychological theory. The reason is that people do not know or have access to these sets of objects or events. Fortunately, I do not know all the dogs in the world, much less all dogs that ever existed or will exist, or all possible dogs. If understanding the meaning of "dogs have four legs" requires reference to the set of all possible dogs, then I can't possibly comprehend this sentence, because I can't know all possible dogs. This approach to meaning, then, is not suitable as a psychological theory (see Chierchia and McConnell-Ginet 1990; or Dowty, Wall, and Peters 1981;

for more detailed explanation and defense of referential semantics). It is possible that a psychological theory will turn out to be related to the referential theory. For example, whatever my meaning of *dog* is, perhaps it allows me to pick out any possible dog, even though my meaning is not actually the set of all possible dogs. If such a correspondence could be worked out, then separate linguistic and psychological theories might be compatible, even if they involve very different kinds of entities (infinite sets and relations in one case, some kind of psychological representation in the other).

The psychological approach assumes that people do not know about every example of each word they know. Instead, it assumes that people have some sort of mental description that allows them to pick out examples of the word and to understand it when they hear it. For example, I do not know all possible dogs, but I have some description of what *dog* means in my mental *lexicon* (or dictionary) that can be used to identify dogs. Furthermore, when people tell me things like "my dog bit me," I can understand them, because I can retrieve the mental descriptions of these words and combine them to result in a proposition that describes the meaning of the entire sentence. This description will be accurate enough in most cases for me to make contact between words and the world, as referential semantics assumed. That is, my mental descriptions of *mad* and *dog* are such that I can combine them to identify actual mad dogs and then talk about them. So, the goal of any psychological approach to word meaning is to specify that mental description associated with each word, which allows people to use it.

I want to remind the reader that my taking this perspective is due to our ultimate goal of explaining how people understand and produce words. If one has a different goal, such as explaining how words got the meanings they have, or how meaning relates to logical validity, one might take a very different perspective. In providing a conceptual theory, I am not saying that it exhausts all that needs to be said about meaning. In too many discussions of meaning, there are arguments in which writers show that X cannot fully account for some semantic phenomenon, and so they conclude that X is not part of a theory of meaning. My own guess is that many different kinds of perspectives will be required to explain all of meaning. The present perspective is the most appropriate one for addressing psychological issues.

Summary of the Conceptual View

My claim in this chapter is that word meanings are psychologically represented by mapping words onto conceptual structures. That is, a word gets its significance by

Word 1 <===> Concept 1

Word 2 <===> Concept 2

Word 3 <===> Concept 3

Word 4 <===> Concept 4

...

Word N <===> Concept N

Figure 11.1
The "word = concept" idea. There is a one-to-one mapping between words and concepts.

being connected to a concept or a coherent structure in our conceptual representation of the world. To put it another way, the meaning is built out of concepts. The way that this works can be somewhat complex, and specifying it is difficult, because (understating wildly) we do not know everything we would like to know about conceptual structure. As a result, whatever limitations there are in our understanding of concepts will be carried over onto our understanding of how concepts represent meaning. In order to clarify how the two are related, let me work through some very simple, wrong ideas, which will illustrate why the answer must be more complex.

One very simple idea about the relation of word meanings to concepts could be called the "words = concepts" idea, illustrated in figure 11.1. As the figure shows, every concept is connected to exactly one word, and every word has exactly one concept as its meaning. Clearly, this is oversimplified: There are synonyms and ambiguous words in which the mapping is not one-to-one (i.e., ambiguous words must be connected to two different concepts, and synonyms must be connected to the same concept). However, it would be fairly simple to allow these in our system, by listing ambiguous words twice, for example. A more serious problem with this version of the concept-meaning relationship is that there are many concepts that do not have a word to go with them. In fact, people have published books of concepts that do not have words but which ought to. Some examples that were distributed over an electronic bulletin board include:

ELBONICS: n. The actions of two people maneuvering for one armrest in a movie theater or airplane seat.

PUPKUS: n. The moist residue left on a window after a dog presses its nose to it.[2]

I, for one, was familiar with these concepts, though I never had a word for them before reading these suggestions. Another example I have used in my courses is the

Word 1 <===> Concept 1

Word 2 <===> Concept 2

Word 3 <===> Concept 3

Word 4 <===> Concept 4

    ...

   Concept N

   Concept N+1

   Concept N+2

    ...

Figure 11.2
In this view, every word corresponds to a single concept, but some concepts are unnamed, i.e., do not correspond to words.

clumps of dust that accumulate under beds or in closets of rooms that have wood floors. I typically find that about half the class has a name for these things (*dust bunnies* or *dust monsters* being the most popular), but about half does not. So, the mapping from concepts to words is incomplete. Although every content word must have a meaning (I will ignore primarily syntactic words like articles), this does not mean that every concept is connected to a word. So, words ≠ concepts.

A second view is illustrated in figure 11.2, in which every word is connected to exactly one concept, even though some concepts are not labeled by words. Again, ambiguous words are a problem here, as they have two meanings, and so must be connected to two concepts. There is no point in pretending that the meanings of *bank* are really a single concept. But if we agree to list ambiguous words twice, maybe this view is a reasonable one: Each word has one concept that represents its meaning. Here our ignorance of conceptual structure is something of a problem, since it is not entirely clear what "one concept" is. If our conceptual system is a highly interconnected set of facts and beliefs (as the knowledge view suggests, for example), then picking out a single concept could be difficult, since chopping the concept away from its connections would not correctly represent how it works within the conceptual system. Furthermore, couldn't it be that a word picks out *part of* a concept, rather than the whole thing? For example, it seems likely to me that the word *leap* refers to one part of an event concept (it talks about the jumping off but not the landing). A word like *toenail* probably refers to a subsection of a concept—a toenail is part of a toe and is probably represented within the toe or foot concept rather than being a fully independent concept. A final concern is that even unambiguous words often have a number of different, related senses. For example, *theater* can refer to the institution which puts on plays and the building in which one views the plays (e.g., "American theater is in the doldrums"; "I met her outside the theater"). These are clearly not the same thing—one is an institution and one is a building—even though they are highly related. We will be discussing this phenomenon in some detail below.

In short, we can't stick with the view shown in figure 11.2, even for unambiguous words. Taking a conceptual view does not require that there be exactly one concept that represents a word's meaning. Instead, we will have to be quite flexible about how concepts make up the meaning of a word, and much of the remainder of this chapter consists of a discussion of just this. For the moment, I would suggest the following principles for a conceptual approach to word meaning. First, word meanings are made up of pieces of conceptual structure. Second, an unambiguous word must pick out a coherent substructure within conceptual knowledge. (Ambiguous words pick out n coherent structures, one for each of their n meanings.) Third, when an unambiguous word has multiple related senses, the meanings are overlapping or related conceptual structures. For example, the two senses of *theater* discussed above are related by both containing information about plays.

Although it may seem that not much can follow from these principles, in fact, important parts of the psychology of word meaning can now be easily explained by referring to the psychology of concepts that we discussed earlier in the book. That is, principles of concept use will carry over to become principles of word meaning. Furthermore, there are a couple of corollaries that follow from these principles that are important, even if somewhat obvious. First, semantic content entails conceptual content. That is, if a word you know means something, that something must be part of your conceptual structure. Second, no semantic distinctions can be made that are not distinguished in conceptual structure. For example, you couldn't distinguish the words *chair* and *stool* if you didn't perceive the difference between these kinds of things and have that difference represented in your concepts of furniture.

One concern that people sometimes have about this psychological approach is the idea that conceptual representations are necessarily private—they are inside your head, rather than being publicly available. This is a concern because word meaning appears to be public, in that there is a meaning for the word *dog* in the language, which must be shared by all speakers in order to be understood. If everyone has his or her own private concept, then on what basis could we communicate (J. D. Fodor

1977)? This argument is to some degree correct, but it ignores the fact that people do not associate any old concept to a word. Instead, they learn through socialization which concepts go with which words. So, as a child, you learned that *dog* refers to a certain kind of animal. If you first developed the hypothesis that *dog* refers to any four-legged mammal, you would soon find yourself miscommunicating with people. They would not understand you when you referred to a sheep as *dog*, and you would not understand them when they said that all dogs bark, and so on. Thus, there is a social process of converging on meaning that is an important (and neglected) aspect of language (Clark 1996). The result of that process is that different people within a community relate words to very similar concepts. Even though my concept of dogs is an internal mental representation, it has been shaped to be the concept for the word *dog* by many years' interaction with other English speakers. This process of convergence can be seen experimentally when speakers are placed into a novel environment and need to make up words or descriptions for the new objects (Clark and Wilkes-Gibbs 1986; Garrod and Doherty 1994; Markman and Makin 1998). So the private nature of concepts does not prevent them from being the basis of communication.

Theoretical Arguments for Conceptual Representations

Why should we say that concepts are our representation of word meaning? There are empirical reasons based on experiments that I will discuss in the next section. However, there are also theoretical reasons for why this is the most likely representation. To understand why this is, we need to take a step back and consider why people have concepts. Concepts represent our knowledge of the kinds of things in the world. They allow us to identify a new object as a dog or a shoe, and they then allow us to infer unseen properties of the object, such as its likely behavior or function. They also help to explain the properties or actions of different objects. Thus, concepts provide critical information for our interactions with objects and our participation in events.

When we communicate, we use what we hear to control our interactions with the world. For example, if someone warns us "There is a mad dog in that yard," we can infer various actions that would be appropriate and inappropriate based on this information. We don't need to be actually bitten by the mad dog in order to take action; the linguistic warning obviates that necessity. It has often been argued that this aspect of language, communicating information critical to survival, is the reason that humans have evolved a highly sophisticated capacity for communication.

Since we represent our information about the world in terms of concepts, language needs to make contact with those concepts in order to be useful. For example, if someone tells you "Never approach a dog with your hand raised over its head" (good advice), this will only be useful to you if the word *dog* makes contact with your concept of dogs. That is, in a different situation, perhaps weeks or months later, you need to be able to categorize an object as a dog and then recall the advice that was given linguistically, and turn that information into behavior. You need to make a connection between the word *dog* and that dog, between the word *hand* and your hand, between the word *approach* and your present action of approaching, and so on. Since the way we represent the world is via our concepts (as just defined), the way to use linguistic information is to have it make a change in our conceptual structures. That is, the information in such a sentence would need to be added to our concept of dogs in order to be put into use.

For linguistic meanings to alter our knowledge of the world, it would be most efficient if they were directly connected to our concepts. In contrast, suppose that linguistic meanings were purely linguistic, that meanings were represented in "semantic features" that were not part of our conceptual knowledge, much like syntactic features probably are.[3] Now sentences would not influence our conceptual structures and therefore influence our interaction with the world, because they would only be representations in these linguistic features, and not in the concepts we use to interface with the world. In short, you would now go into the yard with the mad dog. (One might naturally attempt to augment this view by suggesting that meaning is purely linguistic but that those linguistic entities are connected to our conceptual structure as well, which allows language to influence our understanding of the world. However, the semantic features in this theory turn out to be completely redundant with the conceptual structures. They could be eliminated without any loss; Murphy 1991.)

Empirical Evidence for Conceptual Representations

We are not limited to purely theoretical arguments for this position: There is overwhelming empirical evidence for the conceptual basis of word meaning. The evidence discussed below follows a consistent pattern. I will identify a phenomenon that is found in the concept literature and then show that it is also found with words and/or in linguistic tasks. (Indeed, many of the experiments discussed up until this chapter have used words as their stimuli, although I did not draw attention to this aspect of them.) The argument, then, is that if a general property of concepts is also found in the use of words, this is evidence that the words are represented via those concepts. Although one such property might arise through coincidence, there is evidence for many such properties throughout the psycholinguistic literature. Indeed, I do not know of any phenomenon in the psychology of concepts that could conceivably be found in words that has not been found. If word meanings are not represented in terms of concepts, then they must be represented in terms of something else that just happens to have the exact same properties as concepts. By Occam's razor, I will conclude that word meanings are represented in terms of concepts.

Category Effects

This evidence directly reflects the use of categories in sentence comprehension. Federmeier and Kutas (1999) performed a reading study in which they sampled brain waves (*Event-Related Potentials*, or *ERPs*) while subjects read sentences. The materials consisted of sentence pairs that created an expectation for the final word. For example:

They wanted to make the hotel look more like a tropical resort. So along the driveway, they planted rows of . . .

Here subjects would have a strong expectation of the word *palms*. In one condition, the expected word was actually shown. In another, an unexpected word from the same category was shown, for example, *pines* for the above example. In the final condition, an unexpected word from a different category appeared, like *tulips*. When unexpected words appeared, the ERPs revealed a component known as the N400 (a negative wave occurring about 400 ms after the onset of the word), which often indicates semantic anomaly or an unexpected event. Importantly, the N400 was significantly less when the presented word was in the same category as the word that was expected; for example, the N400 was smaller for *pines* than for *tulips*, even though both were inconsistent with the context.

Federmeier and Kutas argue that the results are due to subjects forming an expectation for what word would appear at the end. The category effect reveals that this semantic expectation involves the category structure of semantic memory. That is, items in the same category are more related than are items in different categories. What is surprising about this effect is that it is found even though no categorization test was involved—only reading—and that the category relation was between the presented word and a word that was not actually shown. Category-level information, then, seems to be involved in sentence comprehension.

Typicality Effects

As chapter 2 reviewed in detail, there have been many demonstrations that not all category members are equal. This is revealed both in unclear category members (items that are not clearly in or out of the category) and in typicality structure. This kind of result is found with every type of stimulus that has been investigated. For example, it is found with dot patterns (Posner and Keele 1970), alphanumeric strings (Rosch and Mervis 1975), patches of color (Nosofsky 1988), geometric shapes (Medin and Shaffer 1978), and so on. Thus, it is a phenomenon that is not specifically tied to linguistic materials by any means. Nonetheless, typicality gradients have been found in innumerable tasks using linguistic stimuli.

For example, Rosch's first studies of typicality were of color names (see Rosch 1973b), where she found that there is a small range of hues that is prototypical of a color term, and other hues are perceived as being less typical even if they are clearly in the category. There are also unclear members that are not definitely in or out of the category (is teal a kind of blue or green?). Such findings led her to find similar results for superordinate categories like vehicles, weapons, and clothing (Rosch 1975). At the same time, research in semantic memory was finding that words like *bird* and *animal* had typicality structure that greatly influenced their use. Rips, Shoben, and Smith (1973) found that it took longer to verify sentences like "An eagle is a bird" than "A robin is a bird," where eagle is less typical than robin. This result has been replicated many, many times since then. In a clever task, Rosch (1977) asked people to generate sentences that included category names (like *bird*). She then took those sentences and replaced them with typical or atypical category members (like *robin* and *goose*). She found that the sentences replaced with typical members were rated as much more natural than the ones with the atypical members.

These experiments mostly involved various kinds of judgments, such as sentence verification or ratings. However, typicality also influences naturalistic sentence processing tasks. For example, in language production, people are more likely to produce a typical item before an atypical item. Kelly, Bock, and Keil (1986) asked subjects to repeat sentences, after a delay. Often subjects made slight errors in repeating the sentence. When a sentence contained two category names, the errors were more likely to involve placing the more typical item first. So, subjects were more likely to say "The child's errand was to buy an apple and lemon at the fruit stand" than "The child's errand was to buy a lemon and apple at the fruit stand." The authors argued that the sentence planning process was sensitive to the typicality of concepts, which in turn influenced the accessibility of words. That is, *apple* comes to mind before *lemon*, because it is a more typical fruit.

Garrod and Sanford (1977) examined the comprehension of anaphoric noun phrases based on category relations. For example, if I am talking about a thief, I can later say "The criminal escaped," and you would understand me to be talking about the same thief. This is because a thief is a kind of criminal, and so it is likely that I am talking about the same person. Garrod and Sanford compared examples like the following:

(1)   A tank came roaring around the corner.
       The vehicle nearly flattened a pedestrian.

(2)   A bus came roaring around the corner.
       The vehicle nearly flattened a pedestrian.

Here, *the vehicle* in the second sentence refers to either the tank or bus mentioned in the first sentence. Clearly, a bus is a much more typical vehicle than a tank. Garrod and Sanford predicted that it would be more difficult to understand the anaphoric relationship between these terms when the antecedent was atypical. They gave sentence pairs of this sort to subjects to read, measuring the amount of time they spent on each sentence. Garrod and Sanford found that subjects took longer to read the second sentence of (1), which has the atypical category member as the antecedent. Furthermore, if the sentences exchanged the category terms, as in (3),

(3)   A vehicle came roaring around the corner.
       The tank/bus nearly flattened a pedestrian.

an analogous result was found: When the second sentence included *tank*, it was more difficult to understand than when it included *bus*. (The first demonstration is more convincing, because it is the exact same sentence that is being compared across conditions.)

In this experiment, then, normal comprehension of sentences was sensitive to the typicality of category items, suggesting that in understanding what *the vehicle* referred to, readers were accessing conceptual information about vehicles and then comparing it to information about tanks or buses. Because more typical things are more similar to their category representations, the anaphoric connection is easier to establish for them.

Studies of word learning have long found that children tend to learn typical referents of words before atypical ones. For example, Anglin (1977) found that children could correctly label typical animals, but not atypical ones, as *animal*. In fact, they were able to classify unfamiliar, yet typical animals like wombats and anteaters when they were not able to classify familiar but atypical animals (from the child's perspective) like butterflies or ants as being animals.

In sum, the findings of typicality throughout the concept literature have parallels in studies of language comprehension, learning, and production. Indeed, many of the first demonstrations of typicality effects, by Rosch, Smith, and their colleagues, were done with linguistic stimuli. Although not focusing on experimental evidence, Taylor (1995) has written an entire book on typicality effects in language (mostly in semantics, but also in phonology and syntax). (This is in fact a very useful introduction to category structure from a linguistic perspective. It is especially good at discussing cases other than noun concepts, which are almost the only topic in the psychological literature.) All these examples provide evidence for the view that word meaning is represented in the conceptual system.

Basic Level Effects

Another important phenomenon of conceptual structure is that of the basic level (see chapter 7). Although objects can usually be described at a number of levels of specificity, there is usually one that is preferred, for example, table, rather than more general categories (superordinates) like furniture or object, and rather than more specific categories (subordinates) like work table, dining room table, or wooden dining room table. Even artificial categories can have a basic level (see Murphy 1991; Murphy and Smith 1982), and so it is not a linguistic phenomenon. Nonetheless, it is found in a number of tasks involving words for categories.

The most fundamental finding is that in object labeling, people prefer to use the basic-level name to other names. That is, when shown a table, they prefer to call it *table* than to use a more specific or general name (see Rosch et al. 1976; and also Cruse 1977; Lin, Murphy, and Shoben 1997; Morris and Murphy 1990). In text, basic-level names are by far the most likely label for a single object, whereas superordinates are typically used only to refer to multiple objects (Wisniewski and Murphy 1989). One can also see basic-level effects in the language as a whole. Linguistic anthropologists have noted that there is usually a preferred level of names in the language, such that basic-level categories have a single-word name (like *table*), whereas more specific categories often involve multiple morphemes (like *dining-room table* or *speckled trout*) (Berlin, Breedlove, and Raven 1973). Another difference is that basic-level names are usually count nouns whereas superordinates are often mass nouns (Markman 1985). For example, I can say "I have two couches," but not "I have two furnitures," because *furniture* is a mass noun, like *sand* or *water*. So, I can say "I have some furniture" (with no plural) just as I can say "I have some water" (with no plural). But I can't say "I have some table." Markman (1985) showed that this difference is found in a number of different languages and is not just a quirk of English.

Finally, children find it much easier to acquire basic-level categories than more general or more specific categories. This is true both in novel category-learning experiments (Horton and Markman 1980) and in everyday vocabulary acquisition (Anglin 1977; Rosch et al. 1976, Experiments 8 and 9; and many other studies—see chapter 10). Thus this aspect of conceptual structure influences vocabulary acquisition. However, it is also true that parents tend to use basic-level names in talking to their children (Brown 1958a)—perhaps that accounts for the acquisition data. It is likely that this is the cart rather than the horse (see chapter 10 for discussion). That is, children would find it difficult to understand other terms, and so parents speak in a way that allows them to be understood. As a general rule, the concepts that are most useful and easiest to learn are the ones that children learn the words for first. This provides further evidence that meaning is based on conceptual structure.

Conceptual Combination

The main question of conceptual combination is how people understand phrases like *apartment dog, mountain stream, peeled apple*, and *sport that is also a game*. The very definition of conceptual combination, then, is in linguistic terms—how people understand phrases. As I will discuss in chapter 12, it is difficult to tell whether conceptual combination is a question of concepts or of language understanding. The two perspectives melt together here, suggesting that there is a very close connection between them. Rather than repeat the information in that chapter, I will simply point out how it relates to the issue at hand.

Typicality raises its head again here, as one of the main topics of study in conceptual combination is in predicting the typicality of items in combined categories (Hampton 1988a,b; Smith et al. 1988). Murphy (1990) found that it was more difficult to understand an adjective-noun phrase when the adjective was rated as atypical of the noun than when it was rated as typical: For example, *loud museum* was more difficult than *quiet museum*. So, typicality is found in this linguistic domain as well. I argue in chapter 12 that an understanding of conceptual combination would require background knowledge of the sort referred to in the knowledge approach to categorization. This is another similarity. Wisniewski and Love (1998) have argued that the alignment of conceptual structures is important in understanding conceptual combinations, just as it is in other conceptual tasks.

Summary of Evidence

When one starts looking for it, there is a very large body of evidence showing that conceptual properties influence linguistic tasks just as much as they do nonlinguistic thought or artificial categories. Indeed, in the concept literature, little theoretical distinction is made between experiments using known words and those using artificial materials. There isn't one theory of concept learning or representation for dot patterns and a qualitatively different one for nouns, say. The reason is that, as just documented, the same phenomena occur in nonlinguistic concepts and in word use, and so any theory of one will serve to a large degree as a theory of the other.

For any one of these cases, it is possible to devise a counterargument, and occasionally one will read such counterarguments about a single such issue in the literature. For example, perhaps linguistic categories don't really reflect typicality structure, but instead typicality differences are due to associations (e.g., *robin* is more associated to *bird* than *chicken* is). Perhaps the early acquisition of basic-level categories is a result of word frequency (parents using basic-level names more than others). And so on. However, to put it briefly, these arguments are unconvincing. Unless there is a competing theory that says how word meanings are represented and that also can independently find evidence for an explanation of each of these effects, a much more powerful explanation is that word meanings are represented by concepts. In this way, *every* conceptual effect that is also found with linguistic materials is automatically explained. If word meaning is not based on concepts, the findings of many parallels between the two is an unbelievable coincidence. So, I would suggest that we not believe it.

Learning Word Meanings

Word learning and conceptual development are discussed at some length in chapter 10. What I would like to do here is to discuss some theoretical questions that arise about word learning when one takes the conceptual approach. This discussion is largely speculative, rather than covering a well-specified area of empirical research. However, I believe that discussion is warranted, given that there are some potentially confusing problems relating word meanings and concepts in early childhood, when both are undergoing rapid development. Those who want to know facts should consult the earlier chapter.

From the perspective of a conceptual model of word meaning, there are two very general (oversimplified) ways that we can think of a word's meaning as being learned. The first is that one could already have a concept and then learn its a name. Mervis (1987), for example, argues that children already have concepts for a number of words that they learn. The word learning corresponds primarily to associating the verbal label to this concept. For example, when her son learned the word *duck*,

Mervis believed that he already knew what ducks were, because of their distinctive shapes and behaviors and the constrained context in which he encountered them (at the lake in the park). When he learned the word, it was just a matter of acquiring the label for this kind of thing.[4] Furthermore, Ari's initial use of the word *duck* did not correspond to what he heard from adults, but to his own (immature) understanding of what ducks are. There is experimental evidence that children will acquire categories without labels and then associate a new label to them when it is provided (Merriman, Schuster, and Hager 1991). On this view, then, the name is associated to an existing concept. E. Clark (1983) argued that children often identify lexical gaps—things in the world that they do not know the name for—which they then try to learn the names for or even make up their own name, if necessary. When this occurs, the concept is driving the word-learning process.

The second general way that a word meaning could be learned is that a new concept could be formed as a result of initial word learning. For example, if you went to a baseball game for the first time, you might not have the concept of a home run.[5] However, in the context of hearing people talk about home runs, you might start to look for the distinctive attributes of home runs. By virtue of trying to understand what people meant by *home run*, you would be forced to form a new concept. In so doing, the usual processes of concept formation would be likely to hold. For example, you would find it easier to learn the new word's meaning if you viewed typical examples rather than atypical examples; if you were exposed to contrast categories, you would also learn how to distinguish that word's use from another's; if you saw a number of examples, you would learn the meaning better than if you only viewed one example; and so on. So, on this second story, you don't already know the concept of home runs and then learn the label. Instead, you hear the label a number of times and then try to work out what the concept behind it must be.

I would argue that the typical word-learning situation combines aspects of both ways of learning a new word. It is probably relatively rare that we have the *correct* already-formed concept ready to attach to a word; it is also probably rare that we really have no inkling of the concept before we hear the word. For example, imagine that you are a young child living in a big city. Further suppose that you are taking a trip to the country with your parents, and that you are going to learn the words *cow* and *horse* as a result of this trip. It is unlikely that you have no concepts at all corresponding to these things, because no doubt you have seen pictures of them, heard the words used, seen them on TV, and so on. On the other hand, you may not know much about them besides the fact that both are large four-legged mammals. Some of these animals appear to be fatter and slower than others, but that's true of many kinds of animals—it doesn't necessarily put them in different categories.

On your trip to the country, then, you'll see cows and horses up close, and you may now be better able to spot some of the intrinsic differences between them. You can start to notice important differences based solely on exposure to the objects. (As we know from chapter 9, even infants can do this.) At the same time, your parents will name some of these animals for you. Since the labels *cow* and *horse* that you hear probably do not map perfectly onto any pre-existing classes you may have formed, you will look for differences between the objects so labeled (Clark 1983). That is, the use of distinctive names may force you to distinguish these somewhat similar concepts, whereas you might not have done so or might have taken longer to do so if you had not been learning the names. So, name-learning can influence or cause category acquisition, based in part on differences you were already noticing in any case: The fat animals with the udders seem somewhat different from the thinner ones without the udders; the first sometimes moo and the second neigh. The influence of the word does not in this case cause you to form an entirely new concept but may help you learn which of the apparent distinctions are important. For example, you can't distinguish which things are called *cow* and which *horse* based on their color, but you can based (partly) on the presence of horns. You can't distinguish them based on location, but you can (partly) based on whether they are being ridden. So, the names focus your attention on the features that are most useful for distinguishing the things being named and thereby influence the categories you form.

In this way, category learning and name learning can go hand in hand, sometimes over a very extended period. There is no simple relationship between the learning of the name and learning of the concept. In some cases, the categories are probably learned as a response to hearing different names. In other cases, children may notice an interesting difference between categories and then ask about it or realize that it corresponds to a naming difference. For example, a child may notice that a chihuahua looks different from other dogs and therefore become very receptive to learning a new name for it, or may even ask "What's that?" The linguistic input now might just be a label for the concept he or she has already formed. In most cases, the full meaning of the word is probably not acquired immediately, as some categories can take much time to fully grasp (e.g., the distinction between geese, ducks, and swans), especially if their members are not encountered that often. All this is due to the fact that children are learning about the world—and in particular, the classes of entities in the world and their properties—at the same time they are learning language. What they learn in one feeds back to the other in an interactive way. This story would be much simpler if only children would first learn all about the world without learning any words. Perhaps after passing a standardized test, they would be deemed ready to learn the words for the things they know. Then language acquisition would be a simple case of paired-associate learning, in which a new label would have to be learned as the name of a known concept. However, language is so useful as a tool of learning that it would be very difficult to learn all one's concepts without it. But this makes our story much more complex because when children first acquire the meaning of a word, they are likely not to have the full concept yet.

In short, both vocabulary learning and concept acquisition are moving targets. As conceptual structure develops, word meanings have to change to reflect that development. But as word learning progresses, this also creates changes in conceptual structure.

A final complication of the relation between concepts and word learning involves certain peculiar errors children make in using words, especially at the very beginning of word use. It is well known that children make *overextensions* and *underextensions*, or applying a word too widely and too narrowly, respectively. In fact, for any word, a child is likely to do both—include some objects that are not correctly labeled by the word, and exclude some objects that should be included (Anglin 1977; Clark 1973). Some of these errors are perfectly understandable as limitations of the child's concepts (Mervis 1987). For example, if a European child does not recognize an ostrich as a bird, this would be completely consistent with the concept of birds that the child has formed based on his or her everyday experience.

In fact, such developments point out one advantage of the conceptual view, namely that as concepts change, word use will automatically change along with them. For example, as a child learns what the critical properties are to being a bird (or to being any biological kind), his or her use of the word *bird* will change along with it. So, when the child begins to understand the importance of feathers to birds, he or she now knows not to call planes or bats *birds*. Learning new facts will be reflected in language use, since the facts are incorporated into conceptual structure, which is the basis of word meaning.

Harder to explain are cases in which children use words to refer to objects that are of drastically different types. Clark (1973) provides a summary of many diary studies of early word use, and some of the children's overextensions are worrisome. For example, a child's word for the moon was also applied to cakes, round marks on a window, writing on windows and books, round shapes in books, and the letter O. Another child used the word *fly* to refer to flies, specks of dirt, dust, small insects, his own toes, crumbs, and a toad. If we take these referents to indicate the child's categories, this would suggest that children's concepts are profoundly and qualitatively different from those of adults, a conclusion that is at odds with most studies of children's concepts (see chapter 10). So, one could argue, this means that the word meanings are not truly picking out the child's concepts.

There are two problems with this conclusion. The first is that the concept the child may be using could be perfectly normal but simply the wrong one. For the case of *moon* described above, the child is probably using the word to refer to an adjective concept of roundness rather than as an object concept referring to a type of celestial body. The child does not really think that the letter O, cakes, and the moon are all the same thing, but she does think that they are all the same shape. Similarly, the *fly* example suggests that the child is using this word to refer to some category of small, dirty things. The fact that the child used the word *fly*, which normally refers to a category of insects, makes us look for a similar object category behind his uses of this word. But there is no reason to assume that the child is using the word to refer to an object category, as it could be an adjective concept (presence of dirt?) instead.

The second problem with this conclusion is that children's intentions often go beyond mere labeling of an object, but this is often difficult to tell when they are capable of saying only one or two words in an utterance. For example, if a child points at a bare foot and says "shoe," she might be indicating that she has a strange word meaning that consists of feet and shoes. However, the child also might not be labeling the foot but could be making a comment, such as "You don't have your shoe on," or "You put shoes on your feet." The child could intend a directive, such as "Put your shoe on!" On the basis of a single short utterance, it is sometimes hard to tell what the child thinks the word really means. For example, the child who used *fly* to refer to a toad could have been talking about the toad eating a fly. There is a general problem that young children with few words must adapt the words they know to refer to a much wider range of meanings that they would like to communicate. So, even a child who can plainly see that a cow is not a dog may call the cow *doggie*, because that is the only word he or she has for any mammal. However, the same child may show good discrimination of cows and dogs in a comprehension task (see Anglin 1977; Clark 1983; Gelman et al. 1998).

In short, children's spontaneous labeling should not be taken as direct evidence of conceptual structure, especially when their vocabulary is very small. When they seem to be evincing some peculiar category structure, a more careful test needs to be done to discover whether the labeling is due to a reasonable, but incorrect meaning, to communicative pressure, or to the intention to make a comment about something rather than label it.

Elaborations of Word Meaning

Now that the reader is fully convinced that word meanings are constructed from conceptual structures (or is at least tired of reading about it), I will turn to more specific phenomena and models of the psychology of word meanings. Much of this discussion is an attempt to bridge the gap between the static representation of words in the head and the dynamic process of comprehension, which colors our interpretations of words in actual discourse and text.

For the most part, I have been talking here as if each word is related to a single concept. If only this were true! I am not worried here about ambiguous words like *bank*. These are not really a problem, because their meanings are so distinct that there is little chance of confusing them. Most linguists would argue that the different uses of *bank* (financial institution and side of a river) are simply different words that happen to have the same phonology, for historical reasons. Therefore, its different meanings do not have to be coordinated in the lexicon. What *is* a problem for us to explain is unambiguous words that have complex meanings.

Much of this complexity falls under the rubric of *polysemy*, which means "many meanings," and which refers to a word having a number of senses[6] that seem to be related but that are also distinguishable. *Polysemy* should not be used to indicate true ambiguity of the *bank* sort, where the meanings are unrelated. Virtually every content word of English is polysemous to some degree. Let's consider some examples. The word *table* appears to be a straightforward, simple word. However, if we start to think about it (and, I confess, if we consult a dictionary), we can come up with a number of distinct senses of this word, including:

- a four-legged piece of furniture: "Put it on the table."
- the class of all such items: "The table is America's most popular furniture."
- a painting, sculpture or photograph of the piece of furniture: "The table is painted very soulfully."
- the stuff that makes up a table: "After the explosion, there was table all over the ceiling."
- the setting of a dinner table: "The table is not suitable for company; get the good silverware."
- food served at the table: "Count Drago keeps the best table in the country."
- the company of people eating at a table: "The entire table shared the paté."

• a flat or level area: "The ranch sits on a table of land south of the mountains."
• an arrangement of words or numbers, usually in columns: "Table 3 shows the results of the experiment."
• a synopsis: "The table of contents is incomplete."
• (verb) to propose something *and* (verb) to put something aside (depending on dialect):[7] "That motion has been tabled."

In addition to these common senses, there are also a number of technical ones (listed in the dictionary), which are presumably known to some speakers if not to all.

• the leaves of a backgammon board
• a facet of a cut precious stone
• the front of the body of a musical instrument
• a raised or sunken rectangular panel on the wall

   Imagine, then, that we have a subject who is a backgammon-playing jeweler who is also a native speaker of English. What is her meaning for the word *table*? It must include the central, specific uses (as in kitchen table), uses related to the central ones (people sitting at the table), representations (pictures of tables, presentations of results), technical uses (parts of diamonds), verb meanings, and so on. This meaning is a mess. It is not a single concept by any stretch of the imagination. Furthermore, among common words in English, this is a very typical situation.[8] For example, Caramazza and Grober (1976) analyzed the word *line* and found 26 senses. They reported finding 40 senses for *run*. Perhaps surprisingly, it is the most common words that tend to be the most polysemous (Zipf 1945). (You can check this by looking up common and uncommon words in the dictionary and just counting the number of entries they have. The difference is obvious.) So, this is not a phenomenon that can be swept under the carpet, because it must be solved by language users every time they encounter a polysemous word. That is, if I say "I'm putting this on the table," you must identify which sense of *table* I intend here, as it is a very different thing to add data to an array of numbers than to put an object on a backgammon board or to submit something for consideration.

   There are two main questions to be asked here, and it is important not to confuse them. One is a purely psychological question, namely, how you represent the meaning of *table* so that you can understand its different uses. The second is why and how it is that word meanings get extended to have these different senses. The latter is not a purely psychological question but a question about the process of meaning change in a language—that is, part of linguistics (see Sweetser 1990, for an interesting discussion). Although I think that the second is also subject to psychological constraints (Murphy 1997a), we will focus on the first question here. How-ever, the fact of polysemy reveals that it is apparently easier for people to take old words and extend them to new meanings than to invent new words (see also Markman and Makin 1998). Over the course of the history of English, it was found to be efficient to extend the word *table* from its usual meanings to the meaning of a face of a jewel and a display of information. Speakers could have invented a new word, or borrowed one from another language, or used a longer expression ("half of a backgammon board"), and so on. But given the very high level of polysemy in the language, using the old words is apparently the preferred route even if it results in very complex word meanings.

One thing to notice about the different senses of a polysemous word is that al-though they are related, they can end up picking out very different things (Nunberg 1979; Taylor 1995). There is an obvious relation between the piece of furniture and the people seated around that piece of furniture, but these are also very different kinds of entities. One is a single object, and the other is a set of individuals; one is inanimate, the other is animate; one is defined by its shape and function, the other by its present location. To put it another way, these senses pick out entirely different categories. The same is true of the representation sense (a painting of a table would not make a good table), the table-setting sense, the jewelry sense, and the verb senses. Although it is not entirely clear whether we should consider the noun and verb forms of *table* as belonging to the same word (Caramazza and Grober 1976 argue that we should, but the forms must be separated at some level for syntactic processing), one can see that they are related meanings, even though they are very different categories (objects vs. actions).

Given this difference in the kinds of things picked out by different senses, it is in-escapable that the word *table* must pick out a number of different concepts. Rather than there being some constant meaning across all uses of *table*, there must be at least a few different concepts being used. This process has sometimes been called *chaining* (Lakoff 1987; Taylor 1995). The idea is that a word with a certain use might then be extended to refer to a related kind of thing; this new use can then be extended to something that is related to that; and so on. With enough links in the chain, one word can get extremely different senses, even though the adjacent senses are related (Nunberg 1979). For example, Cruse (1986, p. 73) pointed out:

In the case of *mouth*, if one knew what an animal's mouth was, and one were to hear, for the first time, a reference to *the mouth of a river*, I surmise that there would be little difficulty in construing the meaning; but suppose one were familiar only with *mouth* used to refer to the mouth of a river, and one heard a reference to *the horse's mouth*, it is by no means certain that one's attention would be directed to the appropriate end of the horse!

Similarly, a word like *paper* can refer to a substance made of wood pulp ("This shirt is actually made of paper") and also to the editorial policy of a newspaper ("That paper is biased against the president"). It is easy to reconstruct the chain of meanings that leads to these two senses (i.e., from the wood pulp substance to sheets printed from that substance, to a publication printed on those sheets, to the management that produces that publication, to their editorial policy), but it is striking that two extremely different concepts get picked out by the same word. In anyone's concepts, wood pulp is not much like editorial policy. It is perhaps not surprising, then, that subjects rarely treat different senses of the same word as being in the same category in a standard category sorting task (Klein and Murphy, in press).

A few linguists have argued that different senses of a word really reflect a common core meaning, which is found in every use of the word (most notably Ruhl 1989). However, examples of the sort given above cast strong doubt on this theory (Rice 1992). In fact, these kinds of examples make one wonder if there is any limit on what senses could be stuck together in a single word. Generally, we can assume that a word will only be extended to something that is related to its other uses. But words that have very distant senses like *line* or *paper* show that all of the meanings do not need to be similar. Rather, it seems necessary only that any sense be predictable from the other senses you know (Nunberg 1989). That is, if you knew only the meaning of *chicken* referring to a barnyard animal, could you understand what someone meant when they said that there was chicken in the stew? Even though the stew does not appear to contain a whole chicken of the sort you are familiar with, you could infer that it is the meat of the chicken that has been incorporated into the stew, rather than the whole animal.[9]

The process of chaining has been supported by the findings of Malt et al. (1999), who looked at the names given to a set of objects they collected from supermarkets, kitchens, and magazines. All of these were containers of some sort, but they received a variety of different names, such as *bottle, container, jar, jug,* and *box.* In many cases, these items were variations on older technology, and so they did not exist when these words first came into use. That is, a plastic juice container in the shape of a cartoon character (labeled a *juice box* by subjects) is something that did not exist ten years ago, much less when the words *bottle* or *box* first came into use. Thus, using one of these words to refer to this new object is an example of chaining. The invention of an object leads to a change of meaning when an old word is extended to cover this new thing.

Malt et al. found that the names for these objects could be best predicted by the names of their neighbors via a chaining process. It was not generally the case that all boxes were similar to a prototypical box. Rather, the plastic cartoon-character juice container was thought to be similar to other plastic juice boxes (without the cartoon character but containing juice and a straw), which were similar to cardboard juice boxes, which were similar to the most typical box (e.g., an open, squarish cardboard box). Malt et al. suggested that when a new form of packaging was developed, it took its name from the most closely related item. In some cases, it is not clear whether this is an on-going psychological process, or a historical process. That is, do people looking at a novel shampoo container think (in essence) "It's very much like other shampoo bottles, so I'll call it a bottle"? Alternatively, perhaps the manufacturer, which has been putting shampoo into bottles for 25 years, decides to call its new containers *bottles* as well, which therefore becomes the conventional name for it. Perhaps a small number of individuals decide on the name, which is then adopted by the community at large, without considerable thought on their part.

What does all this mean in terms of psychological representation? First, as noted, the word meaning is not a single concept or conceptual core. At least, no such core has been suggested for words like *table*, *paper* or *line* that would cover all their meanings. For such words there must be a one-to-many mapping from words to concepts. Given that, the learning problem is not exactly as we have been assuming earlier in the chapter, in which one simply (ha!) had to figure out which concept a word corresponded to. Now, one has to distinguish different senses and identify the concepts for each of them. So, after learning the word *table* as referring to kitchen, dining room, and coffee tables, the child also has to learn the sense in which it refers to people seated at the table. And in some cases, these senses must be kept separate, because they are fairly distinct. That is, one usually doesn't use the word *table* to simultaneously refer to the conglomeration of the people and the object (a restaurant server wouldn't say "The table is wobbly and wants to share the appetizers"; see Cruse 1986).

It is likely, however, that learning each specific sense is not necessary for all sorts of polysemy. Some patterns of polysemy are very common across the language (Nunberg 1979), and they can be immediately extended to other words. Imagine that you just saw an unusual animal at the zoo, about which you overheard someone say "Look at the zork." Although you have only heard this word used to refer to a single animal, you would no doubt immediately understand uses that refer to the entire class of animals ("Zorks have only one kidney"), to representations of the animal ("My zork is the best sculpture in the show"), or to the meat of the animal ("Zork tastes kind of like chicken"). This is because these types of polysemy are found over and over in the language.

Indeed, Murphy (1997) found that people are very willing to extend new words in familiar ways of this sort, even though they had never heard them used in such uses—analogous to the zork example. These extensions may be driven by a kind of meaning-extension schema, for example, one that says that the name of an individual object can be used to refer to the whole class of such objects. In Murphy's experiment these senses could not have been learned from observation, because the words had never been observed in these uses. So, some of our meaning extensions are not directly learned and encoded in memory but are *derived* on the spot. To give a real-life example, it seems extremely likely that once DVDs (Digital Video Discs) become popular (as of this writing, they are not quite yet), people will spontaneously say things like "I saw a great DVD last night," referring to the content of the DVD. That is, they will use the word *DVD* polysemously to refer to the object and its content, just as they do with *CD*, *book*, or *film*.

Confusing matters somewhat are cases in which one cannot extend a word in the way one might expect to be able to. For example, we often extend the meaning of a name for a tool to mean the normal action of using that tool. You can *hammer* a nail with your shoe; or you can *truck* a package across town in your car. Such extensions are productive and predictable, yet some such extensions are not possible. We do not say that we *ovened the bread* or that we *carred the passengers*. The reason for this is the phenomenon of *preemption* (Clark and Clark 1979; Lehrer 1990), namely that one cannot give a word a meaning that another word already has. The word *bake* already means to cook something in an oven; therefore, we cannot use *oven* as a verb with this meaning. We cannot say that we *carred the passengers*, because the verb *drive* would do perfectly well in this situation. So, one constraint on extending a word to new senses is that the sense cannot match the meaning of another word.

The psychological question that arises from this discussion is how stored and derived meanings combine to produce the correct sense of a word when it is used. That is, do people have a listing in their mental lexicon for *chicken* of the sense "meat of a chicken" or do they derive it from the possibly more basic meaning of the animal? In the zork example (hearing the word only once in a zoo), we can be sure that people derive the meat sense from the animal sense, because we know they have never heard the word used in the meat sense. The new sense could not have been stored in the lexicon, and so it must have been derived from a more general principle. Perhaps this approach is quite general. Even very conventional meanings might be derived from more general reasoning about what the word must mean. For example, Clark (1991) discusses the example of names for skin color. Typically, people of different races are referred to as having *white, black, yellow,* or *red* skin in spite of the fact that actual skin color is generally not at all close to these colors. How is it that *white* can be the name of a skin color (in addition to its normal usage), when in fact the people described are often pink or beige or a motley collection of colors? Clark argues that of the skin colors we are familiar with, one color is closest to being white, and so we can identify it as being the one talked about. Furthermore, the word *white* is probably more familiar and shorter than a more accurate color description would be. Finally, the interpretation of *white* as a skin color depends in part on the other familiar skin color terms, so that it includes fairly dark-skinned Mediterranean peoples, for example, because they are not covered by *black* or *red.*

Clark does not turn this point into a specific proposal for processing of these words, but if we were to do so, it would suggest that most polysemy is not stored in the lexicon but is figured out on the fly, using the kind of reasoning process just described. However, I suspect that Clark's analysis is more likely to apply to the question of how conventional word senses develop historically in the language rather than to explain how people understand the words in fast-moving conversations. That is, people have heard the words *white* and *black* used to refer to skin colors hundreds or even thousands of times. It would be peculiar if they did not at some point develop a memory structure that stored this particular word sense but instead kept deriving it time after time. It seems unlikely that people will think, even implicitly, when they hear someone described as *white,* "Although his skin is not actually white, the light skin of Caucasians is closer to being white than it is to other basic color terms, and *white* is a more familiar word than...." Above I noted that we could use the word *zork* to refer to the meat of a zork even if we had never heard the word used that way. But with very common uses, we may bypass this derivation process and simply store the result. Since we talk about chicken meat more often than we talk about the animal (in my house, anyway), it is likely that we have formed the specific representation of *chicken* meaning chicken meat, rather than drawing an inference something like "She could not mean for me to chop up a whole live chicken here, so perhaps she is just referring to the meat of the breast of a chicken, which I happen to have in the refrigerator," every time *chicken* is used to refer to meat. Again, after a few hundred uses of the word to refer to meat, people probably have learned this convention, even if it is derivable from general principles (Kawamoto 1993).

Experiments by Klein and Murphy (2001) suggest that some senses of a polysemous word are stored separately, rather than derived. They found priming when a word was used twice in the same sense and interference when the word was switched from one sense to another. These results seem most consistent with the idea that the senses are represented and accessed separately rather than being derived each time they are encountered. In fact, the priming pattern for polysemous words like *paper* was very similar to that of homonyms like *bank* (though cf. Pickering and Frisson 2001).

The linguistic literature has generally focused on two possibilities: whether the different senses of a polysemous word are stored in the lexicon or are derived (e.g., Rice 1992; Ruhl 1989). However, it is possible or even likely that there is a continuum between these situations. Clearly, if you extend the new words *DVD* or *zork* to have a different meaning than you have ever heard before, you are deriving the new meaning. If you daily use the word *chicken* to indicate a kind of meat, you have probably stored this sense in your lexicon. But in between these cases may be words that have been extended only a few times and so are somewhat familiar in a different sense but are not very strongly represented in that sense. For example, perhaps you have only heard a few times the word *elm* to refer to a type of wood, but have often used it to refer to a type of tree. If I said to you "This table is made from elm," you would have two ways of understanding this: the general principle that a name for a plant can also be used to refer to the substance that makes up that plant and retrieving the lexical entry saying that *elm* can refer to a kind of wood. Because the use of *elm* to refer to a kind of wood is not very well established in your lexicon, it may not dominate the comprehension process. That is, it may be that both of these processes are used in understanding the word in this way. There is as yet no experimental evidence that illuminates how these different sources of information are combined during comprehension.

It should be pointed out that at least some uses of words must be derived, namely what are often called *nonce uses*, in which a word or expression is used to have a meaning that is peculiar to that particular occasion (Clark 1983). For example, consider the case of a man who mainly paints still-lifes as his hobby. His wife mainly paints gardens and farms. If the man's wife was trying to get him to change, he might say, "She wants us to paint the same things. She's trying to turn me into a farmer" (Gerrig 1989, p. 199). Here, *farmer* doesn't mean anything that is stored in our lexicon: It means "someone who paints farms." This, however, is a use that can only be understood within that particular context, rather than being derivable from the meaning of *farm* on general principles. Not surprisingly, such innovations are usually somewhat harder to understand than using the word in its usual sense (for *farmer*, "someone who runs a farm") (Gerrig 1989). However, they can nonetheless be understood, and in some situations are very common indeed. For example, it is common (in English) to take a noun and turn it into a verb, as in "The boy has been porching the newspaper recently" (Clark and Clark 1979; Clark 1983). The ease with which such innovations get uttered and understood reflects the constructive aspects of meaning, in which information from the discourse itself (say, a discussion about newspaper delivery) and from general world knowledge (that boys often deliver newspapers by tossing them near the front door) are accessed to construct a specific meaning that is not already in the lexicon (toss onto the porch). Such constructive processes are probably the same sort that are used in contextual modulation more generally, as will be discussed in the next section.

In summary, then, polysemy creates a real problem for any theory of word meaning, because it can result in radically different senses being picked out by the same word. Even though the senses are usually related to one another, perhaps through a chain of similarities, the categories of things being referred to can be very different. Polysemy has not received the attention it deserves in psychological theories of word meaning, and this is why this section of the chapter is heavy on linguistic examples and general pronouncements, and light on evidence. My analysis suggests that both main proposals for how polysemy could be handled are probably true. In some cases, the sense must be derived, and in others it is most likely retrieved from the lexicon. But the variables influencing each and the interaction of the two processes are simply unknown. The field will need to address this problem, because theories of word meaning that neglect polysemy cannot be complete. Furthermore, any attempt to build a computational language-comprehension device obviously cannot be successful if it ignores this issue. Perhaps it is from this direction that more concrete suggestions for handling the problem will come.

Indeed, Kawamoto (1993) touched on polysemy in his connectionist model of ambiguity resolution. The model represents semantics as a kind of space of features and feature combinations, and a given concept is a location in space corresponding to its particular set of features. This location is not a single point, however, but an area that encompasses all the related uses of the word. Although *dog* might refer to animals of a single species with many common properties, the individuals referred to also differ in size, color, personalities, behaviors, and so on, and so different uses of the word *dog* might pick out slightly different locations in space. According to Kawamoto, different senses of a polysemous word will become established in the lexicon when they are distinct enough and frequent enough to establish their own "local minimum" in that space. If there is a clump of uses of a word that is noticeably distinct from another clump of uses (e.g., *chicken* referring to an animal vs. the meat), the model will act as if there are two different senses. If the uses are infrequent and evenly spread throughout the space, then the model will not distinguish different senses. Although Kawamoto (1993) did not implement his ideas about polysemy in his running model, this is an interesting proposal that has the prospect of dissolving some of the fuzzy distinctions of senses that arise in this topic. That is, rather than worrying about whether two similar uses of a word are the same or different senses and therefore whether they are represented separately, the model would directly represent the continuum of word uses.

A final issue is how the phenomenon of polysemy speaks to the question of the conceptual basis of word meaning. Clearly, it complicates matters considerably. However, the complication is not due to representing meanings by concepts but is in the actual structure of the lexicon. The fact that people use words like *paper* to refer to a substance, a copy of a daily publication, and an editorial policy means that the word's representation must be complex. The conceptual theory provides some basis for the complexity of the meaning, because one can see the relation between the senses in terms of their content. That is, it is because a publishing company establishes its editorial policy, which it prints in individual copies of a newspaper, which are made up of that substance, that the same word can be used to refer to all these things (see Pustejovsky 1995). In contrast, imagine we had a referential theory in which words were defined by the objects they picked out. There is no overlap between newspaper companies and copies of a newspaper or between editorial policy (indeed, it is not clear what its reference would even be) and a paper presented at a conference. Thus, the referential theory cannot explain why it is that the same word is used to refer to these different concepts, whereas the conceptual basis of word meaning at least has some basis for explaining the phenomenon of polysemy. This is not to say that it is completely understood, as linguistic study of the topic continues, and psychological study is just beginning. However, the conceptual basis of meaning at least provides a way of addressing the problem.

Modulation of Meaning

As we have already seen, words do not mean the same thing in different situations. Usually, it is the context, the setting and speakers or the rest of the sentence, that tells us which sense is the right one. If I say "The dog is in the yard," it is easy to infer that I must be intending *dog* to refer to an individual dog rather than to the class of all dogs, because it is very likely that an individual dog but not the entire class of dogs is in the yard. Furthermore, if I own a dog, and the person I'm talking to knows this, then the person can further infer that I am talking about my particular dog. Similarly, a reference to *chicken* made in the kitchen probably picks out the meat sense, but outside on a farm, the animal sense is more likely. So, context can act to select the intended word sense. However, context can also specify in much more detail what is meant by a word, as I will discuss.

Interactional Effects on Meaning

Before getting to that, however, these issues must be put into a broader context. There is a tradition within experimental psychology of studying language in highly decontextualized settings. Typically, words or sentences appear on a computer screen with no apparent speaker, and the subject must make a judgment about the stimuli rather than responding as if the text were part of a normal conversation. Such a situation removes many critical aspects of language use, which some researchers have argued distorts our understanding of language processing. Clark (1996) describes many of these aspects. One concern that is relevant to our present discussion has to do with the differences in word meanings across communities. People who share experiences, specialized knowledge, hobbies, religion, and so on, may use words in a different way than those who do not share those things. If you and I are both jewelers, then you may understand my use of the word *table* to refer to a facet of a gem rather than a piece of furniture. If you didn't think I was a jeweler, you might not understand my using the word in this way. People choose the vocabulary appropriate to the situation and their audience, and listeners understand words in the appropriate senses for those situations. In the most specific case, a word's meaning is only fully known to the people involved in the conversation. For example, Garrod and Anderson (1987) had pairs of subjects solve a maze task. Different pairs used different and incompatible terms to describe the parts of the maze. If a sentence said by a speaker in one pair had been heard by a different pair, they would have misunderstood what was being described. More generally, during referential communication tasks, speakers start with long descriptions but soon shorten them to abbreviated versions that could not be understood without having heard the earlier, complete version (Clark and Wilkes-Gibbs 1986; Krauss and Weinheimer 1966). It is the earlier history of the conversation that allows the shortened version to be understood.

Exactly how people manage to keep track of all these different influences is a matter of some controversy (see Keysar et al. 2000; Polichak and Gerrig 1998). The controversy surrounds how fast and accurate people are at keeping track of all the information they share with people they are speaking with (e.g., Paul is a psychologist, soccer fan, and father, like me, but isn't at my university or town, doesn't share my religion or interest in beer, etc.). Does the jeweler who hears someone refer to a *table* mistakenly think that a jewel face is being referred to before realizing that the speaker is not a jeweler? Such psychological issues surrounding the production and comprehension of words are not yet settled. However, it is nonetheless clear that speakers and listeners use words differently depending on their shared communities and prior discourse.

Having said all that, I must point out that the psychology of concepts is of limited help in explaining some of these phenomena. If word meaning is built out of conceptual structures, this tells us that the senses of *table* must all be represented in conceptual units, for universally known senses as well as novel meanings that have arisen in a discourse. However, the psychology of concepts simply is little help in explaining the nature of personal interactions, episodic memories, and the prior discourse that influences meaning, because these are not conceptual factors. As a result, the remainder of this section focuses on factors more directly related to one's conceptual and world knowledge. These influences arise not from interactions with a specific person but from more general knowledge of words in a sentence. Ultimately, both this sort of knowledge and information about one's interlocutor will need to be integrated in a complete model of language use.

Contextual Modulation

In many cases, a word that has a general meaning is actually understood in a more specific way when it occurs in a conversation. For example, Anderson and Ortony (1975) contrasted the sentences, "The accountant pounded the stake" and "The accountant pounded the desk." The action of pounding that we get from these sentences is somewhat different. And indeed, Anderson and Ortony found that a word like *hammer* was a better recall cue for the first sentence than for the second in a later memory test.[10] This suggests that when the subjects read these sentences, they elaborated the meaning of *pounded* so that it had a more detailed representation, based on the situation that the sentence evoked. This process is called *contextual modulation* (Cruse 1986) or *modification*. In the first case, *pounded* is modulated to include hitting with a mallet or hammer, whereas in the second case, the same word is understood to involve hitting with a fist, though neither of these is explicitly said.

Roth and Shoben (1983) used measures of category structure to study contextual modulation. They presented subjects with sentences containing a category name and then asked them to rate the typicality of different category members. For example:

(4)   During the midmorning break, the two secretaries gossiped as they drank the beverage.

(5)   Before starting his day, the truck driver had the beverage and a donut at the truck stop.

Roth and Shoben predicted that tea would be a more likely beverage than milk for sentence (4) but that milk would be more typical than tea for sentence (5). Indeed, when subjects were asked to rate the typicality of items as being in the category named in the sentence, this is just what was found. More importantly, when subjects read a subsequent sentence referring to tea or milk, the *tea* sentence was easier following sentence (5) above, but the *milk* sentence was easier following sentence (4). That is, even though the same category name, *beverage*, is used in (4) and (5), readers apparently interpret this word more specifically, based on what particular beverages they think are more likely to be drunk in the described situation. This particular result is therefore directly related to category structures, suggesting that the Garrod and Sanford (1977) result described earlier can be modulated by context. That is, people will not simply read the word *tank* more slowly than *bus* when they are thinking of a vehicle; this result can be changed depending on which kind of vehicle seems more likely in the described situation. (See also Barsalou 1991, for more on contextual changes in category structure, though not specifically related to language.)

This process of contextual modulation of word meaning is not confined to general category terms like *beverage*. In fact, Cruse (1986) suggests that "the meaning of any word form is in some sense different in every distinct context in which it occurs" (p. 51). We should not overplay this point, as some of the differences in meanings can be very subtle indeed. However, we should not ignore the effect, either, which is more often done. Let's just consider a few examples to get a sense of the differences in meaning:

(6)   Audrey is visiting her mother in San Diego.

(7)   Audrey is visiting her friend this evening.

(8)   Audrey is visiting her bank.

(9)   Audrey is visiting Madagascar.

Although the same verb *visiting* is used in each case, the act of visiting is somewhat different, due to the differences in the object of the verb and in the time specified (if any). So, Audrey's visiting her mother in San Diego (said in Illinois) probably involves staying at her mother's house and spending considerable time on and off with her mother over the course of several days. But in visiting her friend this evening, Audrey is probably spending a continuous, but much shorter time with her friend, perhaps engaged in a specific activity (dinner, a video). Both (6) and (7) suggest that visiting is primarily a social occasion, but when Audrey visits her bank, it may be for a business meeting, for a brief period of time. Finally, to visit Madagascar, Audrey must have been gone for a fairly long time, and must have been continually in Madagascar during the visit. Furthermore, she obviously did not socially interact with "Madagascar," but viewed the countryside, met the people, ate the food (or tried to avoid it), and so on. There is nothing particularly insightful or unusual in these observations. They simply point out that a word placed into different sentences can yield very different interpretations. So, it is a mistake to think that one can store a single word meaning that will exhaust the word's significance in most contexts.

Cruse (1986, p. 52) describes the process of contextual modulation as "... A single sense can be modified in an unlimited number of ways by different contexts, each context emphasising certain semantic traits, and obscuring or suppressing others." Consider the following example (based on one of Cruse's):

(10) Carl poured the butter over the vegetables.

Here, we clearly understand the butter to be liquid, and therefore hot. As Cruse points out, however, it is unlikely that we have distinguished these different aspects of butter in our lexical entry for the word *butter*. We could make innumerable distinctions between different forms of butter, but we don't have one lexical entry for butter that is cold and solid, another that is hot and melted, one that is in a big stick, one that is molded into little pieces shaped like leaves, and so on. Similarly, we may not have different entries in our mental dictionaries for *visit* in which one is a continuous, short social occasion, another is a long-term, discontinuous social occasion, another is a short, continuous business occasion, and so on. At least some of these contextual modulations are probably derived on the fly.

Murphy and Andrew (1993; see also chapter 12) asked subjects to provide synonyms or antonyms for adjectives. The words, however, were presented as parts of phrases, such as *fresh water, fresh air, fresh bread*, and so on. The results showed that the antonyms and synonyms supplied changed depending on the other word in the phrase. For example, a synonym for *fresh water* might be *spring water*, yet clearly *spring bread* is not a synonym for *fresh bread*. The adjective *fresh* seems to take on somewhat more specific meanings depending on the noun it modifies. The specific meanings led subjects to provide different synonyms in different contexts.

The effects of context, as noted in Cruse's examples, or in Roth and Shoben's experiment, give evidence for a knowledge-based interpretation process. Roth and Shoben's subjects apparently believe that secretaries are more likely to drink tea than milk during their breaks; and they also believe that people are more likely to have milk with donuts than tea. This kind of information is part of our general knowledge of beverages, donuts, social activities in an office, and so on. Such information must become readily available from hearing the word during sentence comprehension. Similarly, Murphy and Andrew (1993) discussed examples that suggest that the antonyms and synonyms that subjects provided were not based on simple lexical associations but rather depended on a complex understanding of the situation being described. For example, one subject gave as a synonym for *dry cake* the phrase *overcooked cake*. Although *dry* and *overcooked* are clearly not synonyms in general (most dry things have never been cooked, much less overcooked), a cake could become dry through overcooking. So, this person accessed knowledge about the possible causes of a cake being dry in this apparently purely linguistic task of providing a synonym. (See also Hörmann's 1983 experiments on the interpretations of quantified phrases like *a few crumbs* and *a few children*.)

Modulation is also found in verbs. Gentner and France (1988) presented subjects with simple subject-verb sentences that were somewhat anomalous, such as "The lizard worshipped" or "The responsibility softened." Often such sentences can be understood if one or more parts are interpreted metaphorically. Gentner and France found, using a number of different measures, that the verb was much more likely to be interpreted metaphorically or undergo some other kind of meaning change than the noun was. For example, one paraphrase for "The lizard worshipped" was "The chameleon stared at the sun in a daze." Here, *lizard* is interpreted literally, but *worship* has been changed so that it is something that a lizard might do. The authors propose that nouns have more cohesive meanings, at least when they refer to objects like lizards and cars. Verbs are often more relational and so are more susceptible to their meanings being stretched by the objects that they relate. Another reason, which the authors didn't consider, has to do with word order. Since the word *lizard* appears first, with no context to suggest that it has anything other than its expected meaning, readers may be less likely to try to reinterpret it. In contrast, *worship* appears later and so may have to adjust itself to the meanings that have already been evoked.

Cruse (1986, p. 152) also suggests that contextual modification is greater for verbs and adjectives, because their meanings depend on the nouns that they are associated with. Saying that John crawled across the floor does not describe the same motion as saying that a centipede did. However, whether there is more or less such modification for nouns vs. adjectives and verbs is very hard to say. For example, Cruse (p. 74) also points out that nouns can have different interpretations in contexts, as in (I have added some examples to his):

(11)   the handle of ...
   a door
   a drawer
   a suitcase
   an umbrella
   a sword
   a saw
   a shopping bag
   a car door

As can be seen, the precise shape, function, and material making up these handles differs greatly, but this information can only be determined by the subsequent prepositional phrase. Thus, although verbs and adjectives may change their precise meaning depending on what they describe, nouns can undergo considerable contextual modulation as well.[11]

Throughout the linguistic literature, there has been a debate on whether the lexicon is more like a dictionary or an encyclopedia. That is, does the meaning associated with *dog* include only the most critical (perhaps "defining") information relevant to the use of this word, or does it include the entire store of what we know about dogs? The concept view I have been proposing is closer to the encyclopedia view, because the concept of dog is what we know about dogs in the world, rather than some specifically linguistic information. However, this does not mean that every piece of information that one knows about dogs is actually retrieved and used every time one hears the word *dog*. One reason for taking an encyclopedic view, however, is to account for contextual modulation of the sort described here. For example, one can only know that the handle of a sword is a long thing, continuous with the sword's blade, by using one's knowledge of what swords are usually like. Similarly, the handle of a shopping bag is likely to be made of string or plastic, and to be an enclosed semicircular shape. We know this through our world knowledge of shopping bags. (Not very long ago, the expression "handle of a shopping bag" would have described something made of string, whereas now it would probably be made of plastic. This is a change in the world, which is reflected in our concepts of shopping bags, which thereby changes our interpretation of the phrase.)

Through the years, many linguists have become very exercised about the distinction between "real" (dictionary) meaning and other aspects of meaning that they thought were not truly linguistic. Such researchers might claim that the difference between the different kinds of handles is not one of linguistic meaning, but of something else (reference, discourse models, or interpretation). However, there is no psychological evidence supporting this distinction. If you eliminate the encyclopedic knowledge, pure dictionary meaning has great trouble in explaining the phenomena discussed here: how polysemy is resolved, how contextual modulation occurs, and how people come to more specific meanings for sentences than the linguistic meanings of individual words include. These are all important processes that must be dealt with in almost every utterance. (Keep in mind that conceptual variables are only part of the answer to these problems, as conversational interaction also plays a part.) Thus, it is not the case that "real" meaning is somehow more important than the encyclopedic meaning, because both must be invoked to explain comprehension. To my mind, this debate has become a dated terminological dispute, in which writers try to argue that some information is, but other information is not, part of the linguistic meaning of a word based on their prior theories of semantics instead of any empirical motivation. Nonetheless, even writers who believe that meaning is (or should be) like a dictionary must admit that real-world knowledge has enormous effects on how sentences in actual utterances are interpreted. Until there is clear evidence that the dictionary meaning is accessed and used separately from the encyclopedic meaning, there is little psychological point in distinguishing them. More detailed reviews of this debate may be found in many standard discussions of semantics and psycholinguistics, including Clark and Clark (1977), Cruse (1986), J. D. Fodor (1977), and Taylor (1995).

The encyclopedic aspect of meaning can be seen in the claim that many words' meanings only make sense when they are taken in the context of a background of knowledge and practice that is shared within a community. This point was probably first made most explicitly in the writing of Fillmore (1982) and was later taken up by Lakoff (1987). Fillmore pointed out that even when verbs seem to be well defined by a listing of simple semantic features, they often can only be used properly when it is understood what kind of situation they were intended to apply in. So, verbs like *buy* and *sell* only make sense in a society that has a conventional notion of economic transactions. For example, if I happened to give you a pen at the same time you gave me a gold coin, I could not describe this as "I sold my pen to you for a gold coin." To truly buy and sell something, the actors need to have certain intentions within a system of exchange, and these intentions are difficult to specify, because they take place in the context of an elaborate economic system. In another example, J. A. Fodor (1981) pointed out that the verb *paint* does not simply mean to cause paint to be applied to a surface. For example, if I put a small bomb in a jar of paint, and it blew up all over Jerry Fodor, I should not say "The bomb painted Jerry Fodor." This is not the notion of painting one has in mind. Rather, painting takes place within a general idea of decoration and protection of surfaces, in which the paint is carefully applied by an agent to a given surface in order to achieve certain results. Other physical actions that might happen to result in the same effect would not really be called painting, because they are not done within the context of decoration that is assumed when talking about painting.[12]

In a final example, the word *bachelor* applies within a societal system in which men and women normally marry at a certain age. In this frame, a bachelor is a man who is eligible to marry but never has. But the Pope is an eligible adult male, and yet he does not seem to be a very good bachelor. Similarly, a gay male couple that has been together for 15 years does not seem to consist of two bachelors, even though they fit the definition. In both cases, the primary features of the word are fulfilled, but the assumptions and background underlying the word are not, as the people have removed themselves from the normal assumptions of marriage as it has traditionally occurred in our society—the Pope, by virtue of having taken a vow of chastity, the gay couple by their sexual orientation.

Thus, there is an argument to be made that word meanings cannot fully be represented by typical feature lists used to describe a single concept. These lists presuppose a certain understanding of the domain, and they only apply within that framework. For those of us who live within that framework, it can be very difficult to see its importance to the word's meaning, because its assumptions are not explicitly represented in each word, but within our overall conceptual structure. In short, word meanings may rely on more complex kinds of assumptions and knowledge than one might think on first glance.

The same thing can be found in concepts more generally. For example, we might tell a child that a dog is something that barks and has four legs. This is sufficient to pick out many dogs. However, we realize that if we were to take a cow and modify it so that it barked, or if we were to build a four-legged mechanical robot, we would not actually have a dog. Instead, a number of deep biological properties are involved in making something a dog or cat—biological properties responsible in part for generating the four legs and barking. People are sensitive to these properties even if they can't explicitly state them (Keil 1989). Such background knowledge is exactly the sort of thing emphasized by the knowledge approach to concepts and reviewed in chapter 6. So, the claims made by Fillmore and others about word meaning are consistent with this approach to concepts.

Associative-Computational Approaches to Word Meaning

I have been focusing on a conceptual approach to word meaning here, but this has not always been the major approach to word meaning in linguistics and psychology. Given the nature of this book, it is not possible to do justice to the history of psychological models of meaning or to fully discuss alternative views. However, one general approach that has been important in the history of psychology has been based on word associations. That is, the meaning of a word is the set of other words (or perhaps words plus other mental entities) it is associated to. This approach has become more prominent again, due to some high-profile computational models that use text association to specify the meaning of a word. These approaches may seem at odds with the conceptual view proposed in the present chapter, and so I will review and critique them here.

Past Computational Models of Meaning

Before discussing the newest associative model, it is useful to consider early computational models of meaning and why they were found to be inadequate. Charles Osgood and his colleagues (e.g., Osgood, Suci, and Tanenbaum 1957) made one of the first quantitative attempts to measure meaning by asking subjects to rate words on 50 different scales of adjective contrasts, such as happy-sad or slow-fast. This test was called the *semantic differential*. A quantitative analysis showed that the 50 scales could be effectively reduced (through a factor analysis) to three orthogonal factors, which Osgood et al. called *evaluative* (e.g., good-bad), *potency* (e.g., strong-weak), and *activity* (e.g., tense-relaxed). Many words could be distinguished based on their values on these scales, and experimental work showed that words with similar scores were behaviorally similar in some respects. Furthermore, once the three factors were identified, Osgood et al. were able to find specific scales that measured each one, so that each word would not have to be rated on all 50 scales. This procedure could not be a total representation of meaning simply because it does not provide the information necessary to tell one when to use a word and what the word means when it is used. For example, if you didn't know the word *zork* but did know its values on the three scales (slightly negative, somewhat active, very potent), you wouldn't have a clue what to call a zork or what someone was talking about when they mentioned zorks to you. The three factors are far too vague to represent the many components of word meaning.[13] In spite of this shortcoming, Osgood's work was very well known, because it was one of the first attempts to quantitatively model semantic information.

A more general and potentially useful attempt to represent meaning came about with the development of scaling procedures in the 1960s, such as multidimensional scaling and various clustering techniques. These procedures require information about the similarity of different words, which was most often obtained by asking subjects to rate the similarity of pairs of words. For example, how similar are *dog* and *cow*? *dog* and *cat*? *cow* and *cat*? and so on. These similarities between all pairs of words being studied would be input into a program, which would output a structure. In the case of multidimensional scaling, this structure would be a *similarity space*. That is, it would create something like a map in which words were the points, and the distance between them represented how similar they are. An example is shown for a set of food names in figure 11.3 (from data reported by Ross and Murphy 1999).

There are two general ways to interpret such scaling solutions. The first is to look for interpretations of the dimensions. Is there some overall difference between the items on the left and the items on the right and between the items on the top and those on the bottom? Sometimes one can find a consistent difference, which would suggest that this dimension is an important one in people's representations of the words. (One can also rotate the entire solution, since the model only determines the distances between the items, not the specific orientation of the whole solution. Rotating the solution can often reveal meaningful dimensions.) For example, Dimension 2 in figure 11.3 might represent the time when these foods are normally eaten. Breakfast foods appear at the top, and dinner entrees at the bottom, with desserts and snacks in between. Foods that might be eaten with any meal (like water, milk, and butter) are in the middle. In a famous use of multidimensional scaling, Rips, Shoben, and Smith (1973) found that mammals differed primarily in size and ferocity. On one dimension, mice and cats differed from deer and bear (size), but on another dimension, the cat appeared with the lion and bear but was distant from vegetarians like sheep and cows. When one can find interpretable dimensions (which is not always the case), it suggests that this kind of variation is important in the domain under investigation.

Another use of such solutions is to look for clusters of objects. In figure 11.3, one can clearly see groups of meats, sweets, fruit, vegetables, and breakfast foods that are fairly distinct from the other clusters. In some cases, these clusters correspond to obvious categories that might well have been guessed in advance (like fruit and

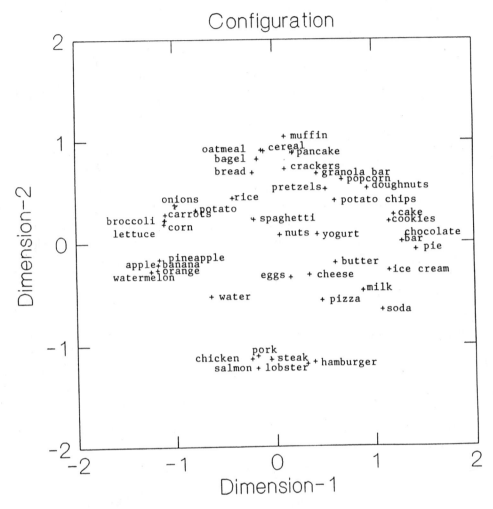

Figure 11.3
A multidimensional scaling solution for the data of Ross and Murphy (1999) on similarity of different foods. (Although it is based on the data in that article, this solution was not published there.) Thanks to Larry Hubert for providing the solution.

meats), but in others, there might be surprising groupings that would not have been expected (like breakfast foods).

When such techniques were developed, there was some hope that they could provide a more quantitative basis for representing word meaning. One could find underlying bases for word meaning that subjects might not overtly express, and one might also discover surprising clusters of words that one did not realize would go together. In fact, both of these things do happen with some of these techniques. However, they also have severe limitations as representations of word meaning.

One of the limitations is much like the one described for the semantic differential, namely that the solutions obtained simply do not represent much of the meaning. Typically, multidimensional scaling, for example, results in two to four dimensions. However, word meaning is extremely complex, and no small set of dimensions can account for how words are used. For example, even if the scaling solution suggests that muffins and cereal are thought of as breakfast foods, this does not explain what the differences are between them, what should be called a muffin as opposed to cereal, that cereal usually has milk poured on it, but muffins do not, and so on. All of this information is used in deciding when to use the words *muffin* and *cereal*, but it cannot all be represented in such scaling solutions. Similarly, although pigs and goats are similar on the size and predacity dimensions, they differ greatly on other dimensions, which was not revealed in Rips et al.'s solution. If people only knew what the solution shows, they couldn't distinguish actual pigs and goats. In short, scaling solutions often do not provide sufficient detail to account for people's semantic knowledge.

Another limitation is that the solutions obtained depend greatly on the particular set of items tested. For example, Rips et al. tested only mammals and found that size and predacity were important dimensions. However, if they had tested only plant-eating animals, it is likely that predacity would no longer be a dimension, and some other difference among the animals would have become more salient and would have appeared in the solution (e.g., domesticated vs. wild), even though it was not present in Rips et al.'s original solution. The scaling solutions are context sensitive for two reasons. First, people's similarity judgments are context sensitive. If one is judging many different kinds of foods, muffins and cereal may seem quite similar. However, if one were judging only breakfast foods, muffins and cereal would now seem quite different, as the differences between baked goods and loose cereals would be much more salient. Second, the scaling procedures are also context sensitive in that they attempt to account for the largest differences in the data. That is, muffins and cereal are extremely far from lobster and hamburger in people's judgments, and the scaling solution must move these items as far apart as possible in order to account for these differences. Smaller differences within clusters (e.g., bagels are a bit more similar to bread than to muffins) are not accounted for as well, because they do not account for as much variance in the ratings. If one were simply to remove the meats from the data included in figure 11.3, one might find a better representation of the breakfast foods.

In any case, the result is that quantitative scaling solutions have been useful for some purposes, especially in exploring unfamiliar domains. However, as a representation of people's knowledge of words, these techniques have not been as helpful as was originally hoped for when they were developed. Their main problem is that they do not provide enough detail to account for word use. For reviews of such scaling techniques, see Van Mechelen et al. (1993) and Shepard (1974). As we will now see, somewhat different, more powerful techniques have recently been developed that may overcome the problems of these scaling techniques.

Recent Associative Models of Semantic Memory

Fast processors and large computer memories have spurred the development of a new form of semantic analysis, called *Latent Semantic Analysis* (*LSA*, Landauer and Dumais 1997) or *Hyperspace Analogue to Language* (*HAL*, Lund and Burgess 1996). This computational technique is based on an associative approach to word meaning. Associationism has a very long history in psychology, most importantly dating from the work of British nineteenth-century philosophers who believed that all thought could be explained by strings of associations. In the early twentieth century, associationistic approaches to meaning were popular because they required reference to little internal cognitive processing. Within the context of American behaviorism, the free association task seemed to be an excellent measure of stimulus-response learning, and many psychologists were able to convince themselves that actual language production and comprehension were simply a matter of stringing together longer and longer series of associations. As a result, mental representations and complex mechanisms would not be needed to explain language use. The failure of such theories was a major event in the founding of cognitive psychology (Chomsky 1959), but associations between words is a fact of life that is still studied (perhaps over-studied) by many researchers in lexical processing.

The recent associative enterprises go beyond the simple idea that word 1 is connected to word 2 by an associative link. They suggest that a word can be characterized by its entire set of associations to all other words. That is, people are exposed to tens of thousands of word types,[14] within millions of sentences that they read and hear. Certain words tend to occur together and other words hardly ever co-occur in people's experience. On this view, these patterns of co-occurrence represent meaning: Words with similar patterns have similar meanings.

Both the models mentioned above use very large text corpora as sources of information about how words are associated. For example, Landauer and Dumais (1997) input 4.6 million words from a student encyclopedia to their LSA model, finding 60,768 word types. They calculated how often each word type occurred with each other word type in the same article in the encyclopedia, creating a 60,768 × 60,768 matrix of co-occurrences. (Lund and Burgess's technique weights co-occurrence scores by how close the two words are in the text.) A complicated mathematical technique was used to reduce this matrix to a more reasonable size of 300 dimensions. (Burgess and colleagues do not always reduce the matrix.) Each word had a value on each of these 300 dimensions, which represented the association information in the entire text. Using these dimensions, the semantic similarity between two words can be calculated as the cosine between the two vectors (a bit like a correlation, going from −1 to 1, showing how similar the two words are across these dimensions). Words with nearly identical patterns of co-occurrences would have cosines near 1, whereas those with orthogonal patterns would have cosines of 0.

Why should this work? That is, why should this procedure result in a measure of semantic similarity? Some words that occur together often are not semantically similar. For example, *knife* and *butter* might co-occur pretty often, but they are semantically very different. However, LSA does not use only the information about how often *knife* and *butter* occur together but also how often they occur with all the other words in the corpus. For example, *butter* might occur with a lot of other foods on shopping lists or in discussion of dairy products, and *knife* would not occur in such lists. Similarly, *knife* might occur with other words describing weapons or cutting, and *butter* would not occur with such words. Because LSA looks at the entire pattern of co-occurrences, it tends to find that words are similar if they are found in similar sentences, and, it is hoped, this will be a good measure of semantic similarity.

Landauer and Dumais (1997) and Lund and Burgess (1996) report a number of experiments and tests of their models, some of which are fairly impressive. Landauer and Dumais tested their system on a synonym test from the Test of English as a Foreign Language (TOEFL), which is used as a college admission test for nonnative speakers of English at American universities. The model got 64.4% correct, which was almost identical to the performance of a large sample of college applicants who took the test. Although these applicants did not all know English very well,

Landauer and Dumais report that such a score would allow admission to many American universities. Lund, Burgess, and Atchley (1995) showed that their model can predict results in word priming experiments of the sort that are often performed in the study of lexical access. In an extremely controversial move, Landauer and his colleagues are adapting LSA to be used as an automatic grading tool for student papers. Essentially, the more the pattern of lexical co-occurrences in the student paper is like that of the course materials, the higher the student's grade. There is evidence that the model may have some validity as a measure of the amount of learning (see Wolfe et al. 1998; and Rehder et al. 1998). A readable article describing the grading system and including outraged howls of critics who object to grading by machine may be found in Thompson (1999).

The success of such models could be taken as undermining the conceptual approach to meaning taken in this chapter. If these models can truly account for how words are used, then word meaning may be a large associative network that merely encodes patterns of co-occurrence. Landauer and Dumais (1997) suggest that such a network would help to explain how it is that children are able to acquire so many words so quickly. When an unfamiliar word appears in a sentence context, children can assume that it is similar in meaning to other words that have appeared in similar contexts. Because the only input to the model is words, meaning would be represented through links to other words rather than through the knowledge underlying those words—that is, concepts. LSA's success in some tests may indicate that conceptual information is simply not that necessary to explaining meaning.

Before we get too carried away, however, we need to see more of the semantic structures that these models create. Landauer and Dumais do not provide examples of the semantic structures that their model arrives at (a fact that is itself worrisome). Lund and Burgess (1996, table 2) are more helpful. In their text base (consisting of 160 million words from newsgroup messages), the closest neighbors to *jugs* were the words *juice, butter, vinegar, bottles,* and *cans.* The closest neighbors to *monopoly* were *threat, huge, moral, gun,* and *large.* (A later paper by Burgess, Livesay, and Lund 1998, suggests that these kinds of neighborhoods are common.) Clearly, these words are related in some ways to their neighbors. However, the meaning of *jugs* is simply not similar to the meaning of *juice, butter,* or *vinegar; monopoly* is not semantically like *threat* or *gun.* Even though monopolies are *large,* and may be considered a *threat,* the fact that these two words are related to monopoly is not very informative. Is the monopoly a threat, or is someone threatening it? Who is it a threat to, and how does it threaten them? If one just knows that *monopoly* and *threat* are "similar," one does not really understand what monopolies are and do. Similarly, are monopolies large like elephants or buildings, or like something else? There is nothing in this set of neighbors specifying that a monopoly is an illegal activity by a company that controls a certain commodity in order to unfairly raise prices for it and stifle competition. Once one knows this, one can easily understand how monopolies are large (in the sense of controlling nearly the entire supply of the commodity), are threats (to other companies or to consumers, but in economic terms), might not be moral (why isn't *immoral* the related term?), and so on. Having the concept explains why these words are related, rather than vice versa.

The general problem with nets of associations is that knowing what words are associated to one another does not specify what the meaning of an individual word is. First, there is an overall problem that one simply cannot understand the meanings of words by reference to other words (as discussed by Johnson-Laird 1983, for example). If one only knows *dog* by its similarity to *cat* and *cow* and *bone* ... and *cat* by its similarity to *dog* and *cow* and *bone* ... and *cow* by its similarity to *cat* and *dog* and *bone* ... and so on, one is caught in a circle of similar words. One simply does not know enough from similarities to other words to know what should be called *cat* and what *dog*. Words must be connected to our knowledge of things in the world, not just other words.

A more specific problem is that the model does not specify the basis for each association. Although *jugs* may be related to both *vinegar* and *bottles*, these relations are extremely different, and an overall similarity score does not represent these differences. One wouldn't know from the scores that "Put it in the jugs" is similar to "Put it in the bottles" but not "Put it in the vinegar." Apparently the similarity score is good enough to allow LSA to pass a synonym test or even to grade student papers, but it will not be enough to represent the very detailed knowledge people have about the referents of words, which is used in speech and comprehension.

These shortcomings are exactly the things that the conceptual approach does well. Since concepts are our nonlinguistic representation of the world, by connecting words to these representations, we can explain how people can connect sentences and words to objects and events in the world. Concepts are just the things that are evoked by our perceptual systems and that control our actions. Thus, by hooking up words to concepts, we can break out of the circle of words connected to words and tie language to perception and action. Furthermore, since one's concept of a jug, say, would include detailed information about its origins, parts, materials, functions, and so on, the concept is more than sufficient to distinguish the meaning of *jugs* from that of *vinegar* and, for that matter, *bottles*, and it directly represents the information that allows one to see that *jug* and *bottle* are near synonyms, but *jug* and *vinegar* are not.

In short, even the more recent associationistic approaches do not cast doubt on the overall conceptual approach I have been proposing here. I think that it is likely that children can learn words by using the context that novel words appear in, as Landauer and Dumais (1997) argue. And it is certainly possible that a system that accumulates massive numbers of associations through a large text base will be able to do a number of useful tasks. However, as a psychological model of word use, the associationistic approaches do not seem likely to replace the conceptual approach.

These programs are still new (as of this writing), and it is possible that they will overcome what now appear to be shortcomings. For example, the accuracy of the models' behavior depends greatly on how many words they are exposed to. It is only with *very* large samples of text that they can accurately represent the meaning of individual words. Although they have in fact been run on large text corpora, the sizes of these corpora are still much less than the verbal experience of a college student, say. So, perhaps with a few more hundred exposures to real-life occurrences of *jugs*, HAL would no longer list it as being similar to *vinegar*. However, it is important for contrast to remember that children can figure out much of the meaning of a word from a single reference, which arguably provides better information than even thousands of word co-occurrences.

Another possibility is that (again, with sufficient input) the 300 dimensions that LSA uses could turn out to be meaningful semantic dimensions. That is, rather than just providing a global measure of similarity between *cat* and *horse*, LSA might allow us to examine the dimensions on which they are similar and dissimilar and thereby specify the properties of cats and horses. For example, dimension 129 might be size, and cat might have a moderately low value on that; and dimension 212 might be tail, and both cat and horse might have high values on that. Although current implementations of such systems do not generally result in many interpretable dimensions, it is again possible that future versions will. If so, then we might be able to use LSA representations to derive more familiar conceptual representations of feature lists or schemata. And unlike Osgood's semantic differential, or most scaling procedures, the large number of dimensions used in LSA could conceivably be enough to represent many different aspects of meaning. At that point, LSA would not necessarily be a different theory of word meaning but could be seen as a way of implementing conceptual knowledge. In the meantime, such models do not pose a threat to the conceptual approach to meaning.[15]

Linguistic Determinism

One of the most popular issues in the psychology of thought and language is whether our concepts are determined by the language we speak. This notion of *linguistic determinism* is often called the *Sapir-Whorf hypothesis* (usually shortened to the *Whorfian hypothesis*). A complete account of the history of the psychology of meaning would give considerable coverage to this theory. However, this view has had little concrete support and as a result has had little influence on psychological theories of word meaning, regardless of its hold on the public's imagination.

In everyday life, one often hears statements of the sort "Eskimos have 50 different words for snow," along with the suggestion that this makes them see and think about snow differently than do, say, people living in New Jersey. Such a statement is a kind of arctic legend rather than a claim about a specific language (e.g., what Eskimos exactly are being talked about, what language, and what exactly are the words?), and it seems, insofar as one can tell with such legends, not to be true (Pullum 1991). But this claim can serve as a prototypical example of the idea that languages differ in ways that might influence thought. Similarly, when one travels, one may notice that people in different lands think about some things differently than we do. And if one learns the language, one sees that they also have a somewhat different way of talking about those things—often having more or fewer words, using different metaphoric expressions, or dividing up the world differently than English does. All this can lead to the conclusion that when learning one's native language, one's thoughts are largely determined. That is, when learning English, one learns only the single word *snow*, and so one sees snow as being one kind of thing; when learning Eskimo, one must now see 50 different things instead of just snow. The idea is that our concepts are fairly malleable relative to language, which is imposed by one's culture, and which no single individual can change very easily. As a result, language acquisition forces a certain conceptual structure on the individual.

There is certainly a note of plausibility to this story. As pointed out earlier, during language acquisition, children are forced to learn distinctions that they might not have spontaneously noticed, because the word meanings depend on them. Although children would probably notice the difference between geese and ducks at some point, their parents' use of two different labels for these birds can accelerate the process. However, behind such straightforward examples lie some much stronger claims that are more controversial. For example, in saying that language determines thought, is one saying that people *cannot* notice the distinction unless it is in the language? Such a statement would clearly be too strong. Indeed, as I have just reviewed, most content words have different senses, which refer to things that are different, but that we perfectly well distinguish, such as *table* referring to a kind of furniture and to the people who are seated at such a piece of furniture. We are not fooled by the use of a common name to treat these things identically (e.g., try to polish the people or to feed the furniture). The importance of polysemy within a language is seldom recognized when considering differences between languages. If words had such a large effect on our concepts, one would not expect to have such drastically different senses referred to by the same word within a language.

Even to say that people would find it harder to notice distinctions that are not marked in the language is a strong claim. So far as I know, there is no verified result that shows this difference (see below). Sometimes the existence of different names is itself taken as evidence for cognitive or perceptual differences: How could the Eskimos use 50 different words for snow unless they had 50 different concepts, in contrast to our one concept? However, this is obviously a completely circular argument. To demonstrate an effect of language on cognition, there must be some evidence that Eskimos conceive of snow differently than those who have a more snow-deprived vocabulary, and that evidence should be a nonlinguistic task.

Furthermore, consider the question of why these linguistic differences come about. Why is it that the Eskimos happen to have 50 different names for snow? Why do the French have 100 different terms for the taste of wine (using another example heard on the street)? If linguistic determinism is true, then it would just be an accident of the language. That is, the Eskimo language happens to have a lot of names for snow, and therefore Eskimo children are forced to form many different concepts of snow, whereas French children are off the hook as regards snow, but are arbitrarily forced to learn the wine terms. (The French seem to have the better end of the deal.) However, these linguistic differences have very good nonlinguistic reasons. For example, if Eskimos did have 50 words for snow (again, see Pullum 1991), this is likely because they live in a very snowy area and need to make different distinctions in order to carry out their everyday activities. And France has many more varieties of wine than do the Northern Territories. Historically, then, it seems much more likely that their activities and thoughts determined the vocabulary than vice versa. Furthermore, even within English, there are experts who have many different words for snow, namely skiers. Clearly, this is not due to linguistic determinism either (given that standard English doesn't include these terms) but arose through the need of skiers to communicate different qualities of snow to one another. They wanted to communicate these qualities because different types of snow have different implications for skiing, such as whether it is fast or slow and whether one can steer on it. It was the need to describe known distinctions that drove the development of a vocabulary, rather than vocabulary determining the concepts skiers have.

In spite of this discussion, one might argue that for a child born into a society where the vocabulary makes certain distinctions, the child is stuck with learning those distinctions and with not learning others that could be made. And so, even if historically the vocabulary came about through conceptual reasons rather than vice versa, the child must learn the language now, and, as a result, the child's concepts are driven by the language. Nonetheless, there is very little evidence that language changes our perception of things in a very deep way, independently of experience and societal interests. This has been most studied within the domain of color. For example, people who come from a language with only two color names (essentially *light* and *dark*) appear to have color perception and memory similar to people who know many color names, like English speakers (Rosch 1973). The perceptual structure of color space and processing of colors in memory do not seem to rely on language. Linguistic determinism has also been studied in more complex nonperceptual domains such as counterfactuals, statements about events that did not occur, such as "If I had won the lottery, I would have paid my rent." Although some languages distinctively mark counterfactuals and others do not, this does not turn out to influence their speakers' counterfactual reasoning, in spite of claims to the contrary (Au 1983).

There is strong resistance to giving up the notion of linguistic determinism in some circles. For example, Lucy (1992) gave a book-long defense of the Whorfian hypothesis, which largely amounted to criticizing all the evidence that had been found against it. However, his defense could not cite actual, strong evidence in favor of the hypothesis—it could only attack the evidence contradicting it. Surely this is very weak support for a scientific hypothesis.

If there is any truth to linguistic determinism, I think that it is most likely to be in simpler domains than the ones typically studied in the psychology of concepts. Recent writers on linguistic determinism have emphasized the importance of grammaticized features rather than lexical domains like words for snow and wine tastes (see Gumperz and Levinson 1996; Lucy 1992). For example, Slobin (1996) points out that verbs in Turkish are marked for whether the speaker directly observed the action or only knows about it second hand. Turkish speakers therefore must keep track of this information when speaking, and perhaps do so in general. I have heard Chinese speakers complain that they found it annoying to have to continually keep track of everyone's gender, so that they could distinguish *he* and *she* when speaking

English. The fact that I don't find this difficult may indicate that English has focused my attention on gender more than Chinese would have. Finally, Bowerman (1996) points out that speakers of Tzeltal, a Mayan language, must use different verbs to say that *X* is on *Y*, depending on *X*'s shape. Perhaps Tzeltal speakers focus on shape or even perceive it somewhat differently than English speakers.

All of these things may well be true, though most of them do not have direct, nonlinguistic evidence to support the notion that language has changed speakers' concepts.[16] These grammaticized distinctions are often based on broadly applied features (like gender, spatial relations, or plurality) instead of conceptual informa-tion relevant to the domains that we have been focusing on (animals, plants, arti-facts), and they may result in greater attention or emphasis placed on some of the relevant features, rather than a change in conceptual organization. For example, Chinese speakers clearly categorize people in terms of gender, but perhaps English speakers do so faster and even in situations when it is not very relevant, because of their need to specify gender in personal pronouns. This would be a quantitative rather than a qualitative difference.

Another possibility, proposed by Slobin (1996), is that when people are planning to speak, they attend to the categories that their language requires in order to plan their utterances. For some languages, this will be plurality, gender, or tense; for other languages, it will be object shape, social distance, or the duration of the event. However, when simply observing events or in their general knowledge about the world, people may be little influenced by these same properties.

Discussions of linguistic determinism in the past have given rise to more heat than light, and the topic is still emotionally charged for many. At this point, I think that some good ideas and good techniques for studying linguistic determinism have been developed. However, the core evidence that one would want for linguistic determinism—adequate description of linguistic differences, followed by indepen-dent demonstrations of parallel conceptual differences—is still largely lacking. The newer approaches represented in the Gumperz and Levinson (1996) book hold out some promise that such evidence will be found, if it exists. However, the domains being looked at by such researchers are not closely related to the main topics inves-tigated in the psychology of concepts, and so it is still an open question about how much language determines adult concepts of objects, events, and so on.

In this context, it is interesting to consider a proposition that is essentially the opposite of the Whorfian hypothesis, that certain linguistic categories are due to universal conceptual and communicative constraints. For example, it is often said that nouns and verbs are found in every language, and adjectives in most languages.

But how does one identify the category of noun in different languages? One can attempt to answer this question syntactically: Nouns are things that take plural and case markings, whereas verbs take tense or aspect markings. However, even this is problematic, as different languages have different syntactic rules for the parts of speech. For example, Chinese does not normally inflect nouns for the plural, and English does not use case markings, whereas Latin does both. How can we say, then, that Chinese, English, and Latin all have the syntactic category of nouns? The traditional answer has been a semantic one, that nouns refer to persons, places, or things, verbs refer to actions or events, and adjectives refer to properties. However, this basis is not perfect either, as some nouns refer to events or properties, like *the party* or *whiteness*, and some adjectives refer to entities, like *corporate*.

Croft (1991) suggests an interesting resolution to this problem. He argues that nouns, adjectives, and verbs arise from a basic communicative need to refer to entities, to modify those references, and to predicate something about those entities, respectively. Therefore, there is a semantic core to nounness and verbhood, based on typical properties of objects and predicates. But rather than a well-defined category, these are prototype categories, with the typical objects and events at their center, and less typical things at the periphery. The particular syntactic properties of each category are related to these conceptual differences, Croft argues. For example, nouns are often inflected for number, topicality, and case, whereas verbs are often inflected for tense and aspect. This is because objects can be counted, are often the topics of conversation, and have different relations to one another, whereas verbs often refer to actions, which happen at a particular time and have other process distinctions (being complete or incomplete; being essentially instantaneous or lasting for some time) marked by tense and aspect. As a result, it is no coincidence that English and Spanish both mark nouns for plurality and have verbs that are marked for tense. It is our basic concepts of objects, event, and properties that lead languages to tend to have similar morpho-syntactic properties. Croft also notes that items that are semantically dissimilar to the category prototypes also often fail to have the typical syntactic properties. For example, although *whiteness* and *water* are both syntactically nouns, they cannot be pluralized, because they do not refer to objects.

In summary, Croft's analysis suggests that language may reflect conceptual universals. Rather than concepts following language, some linguistic structures may arise from conceptual structures combined with communicative needs. I cannot do justice to Croft's theory here, but it provides an interesting contrast to the Whorfian emphasis on the reverse direction of influence.

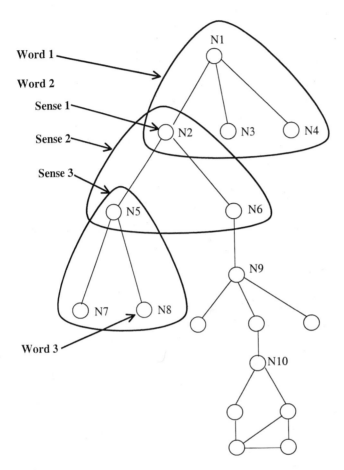

Figure 11.4
A final attempt to illustrate how word meanings are built out of concepts.

Final Summary of the Conceptual Approach

After all the discussions, arguments, and data presented in this chapter, where does this leave us with regard to the relation between concepts and word meaning? It is clear that conceptual structures are deeply involved in word meaning, given all the conceptual effects found in language use and learning. However, the simple relations depicted in figures 11.1 and 11.2 do not adequately represent the relation, as they do not account for phenomena such as polysemy and contextual modulation. An attempt at a more complete picture is made in figure 11.4, but it must be admitted that a complete model of word meaning cannot be represented in a simple diagram, because the number of variables and complexity of the structures involved precludes a simple depiction. In the figure, the nodes and their connections represent conceptual structure, and words are connected to a node or substructure.

The notion here is that an individual (unambiguous) word usually has a number of different senses, like word 2 in the figure (the others don't, for purposes of clarity). These senses are overlapping subparts of the conceptual structure. As it is likely that many of these senses (or at least the most common ones) are explicitly represented, instead of being derived from a core meaning (Klein and Murphy 2001), there must be a number of explicitly marked links between the word form and conceptual structures. The meaning of the word then consists in coherent subparts of conceptual knowledge that are picked out by the lexical item. However, note that the conceptual component also includes other information from the general domain, including superordinates, coordinates (nodes that share an immediate superordinate), and other related concepts. For example, sense 1 of word 2 picks out a single node, N2, in the conceptual structure. N2 has superordinate N1, coordinates N3 and N4, and subordinates N5 and N6 represented in the structure. Although such concepts are not directly picked out by the word, they are important for specifying the meaning by providing contrast, background knowledge, and underlying assumptions (e.g., Fillmore 1982). For example, the exact meaning of the word picking out N2 depends in part on distinguishing it from the related concepts N3 and N4. And since background knowledge is apparently critical for categorization and reasoning about concepts (see chapter 6), word use can draw on such resources as well. Figure 11.4 also attempts to illustrate the general pattern of chaining of word senses, as the parts of conceptual structure picked out by different senses overlap to a large degree. Sense 1 of word 2 is included in sense 2, which overlaps with sense 3. There are also some senses that are not themselves overlapping but are related by intermediate overlapping senses (like the material and editorial policy senses of the word *paper*), as in senses 1 and 3 of word 2 in the figure.

What cannot be represented in such a figure are the processes by which the senses are identified and represented, the way that related concepts and background knowledge constrain senses, and the processes by which an interpretation is constructed each time a word appears in a particular context. However, figure 11.4 certainly does serve to indicate the complexity of the picture relative to that envisioned in figures 11.1 and 11.2. And in fact, part of the reason concepts have been criticized as representations of word meaning is, I believe, because researchers assumed the simple relations of the sort shown in those figures. Unfortunately, the relation is quite complex, which is hardly surprising when one considers the complexity of word meaning itself.

One particular process that the figure cannot display is how new senses are derived for a word. For example, if I have only heard the word *DVD* used to refer to the physical disks, when I hear a new sentence like "This DVD is very boring," I must derive the sense meaning the disk's content. Imagine that my original sense is like that of sense 2 of word 2 in the figure, a fairly complex meaning structure indicating a physical device of a certain shape that contains audiovisual content, if played by a decoder through a TV. However, the "boring DVD" refers only to the content, a substructure of the original sense, perhaps the node picked out in sense 1 in the figure. Thus, I must be able to shift from understanding the word as referring to the larger structure to understanding it as referring to a subpart of that structure. Pustejovsky (1995) formally describes how such operations could be carried out. No doubt other cases exist in which one must go in the other direction—extending a word from a narrow sense to a broader one. Understanding the meaning of a word in context, then involves not only retrieving prestored structures, but more constructive processes based on those structures.

Even a model at this level of generality does help us to understand some long-standing questions in the psychology of word meaning. One question has to do with whether word meanings are decomposed during use. Theories of semantic representation often suggested that word meaning was a list of semantic components (Katz and Fodor 1963), and therefore theories of comprehension suggested that understanding consisted of retrieving each word's components when it was understood. One problem with this is that it is very difficult to provide a simple set of components that is a word's meaning, as I have already suggested (in the *paint* and *buy* examples). Rather diffuse background knowledge can be a necessary part of interpretation even if it does not (and could not) appear in the list of features. An empirical problem is that words that appear to be more complex, in the sense of having more components, are not generally more difficult to understand as measured in a variety of experiments (Johnson-Laird 1981, chapter 10 provides a readable review of this literature), though one exception is that negative words are harder to understand than their positive counterparts (like *absent-present*, Clark 1974). Nonetheless, it is difficult to understand exactly what it would mean to comprehend a word if it is not to bring to mind its components. Although some have proposed that a word meaning is a holistic entity that is not analyzable (J. A.

Fodor 1981), every concrete theory of semantic representation does use components of some kind, because there is no other obvious way to represent the meaning.

By relating words to conceptual structure, we are now less tempted to talk about lexical "decomposition." First, we have acknowledged that a word has a number of senses—not just one decomposition (see figure 11.4)—and coordinating and selecting among those senses is an important aspect of comprehension, which cannot be predicted by the number of components of the word in general. Second, as figure 11.4 also reveals, the substructure being picked out by the word is not a simple list of components, but a possibly elaborate structure. It is in general hard to know how to count up the number of nodes, links, and their relations in order to determine each word's overall complexity. One would have to know the structure very precisely in order to obtain an accurate measure, more precisely than we typically do know. Third, the conceptual structure being picked out by the word is closely integrated with related structures, and these probably have considerable influence on the use of the word. For example, the word *dog* is embedded in biological knowledge of animals in general as well as knowledge of pets, the differences between dogs and cats, and so forth, and this knowledge might be activated to various degrees on some occasions in which one hears the word *dog*—even though it is not an "official" part of the meaning.

Finally, it is worth pointing out that we need not assume that every aspect of conceptual knowledge is retrieved when a word is understood. In fact, it would be very difficult to do so. It has long been known that when a sentence emphasizes one aspect of a word meaning, that aspect is more activated, and other aspects may not be activated (McKoon and Ratcliff 1988; Tabossi 1988). So, it is likely that not all conceptual knowledge associated with a word is retrieved into memory when the word is encountered, but some knowledge is picked out as being particularly relevant. Thus, one would not always expect more complex words to be harder to understand than simple words, as the amount of information explicitly encoded would likely vary across conditions.

Theoretical Implications

The literature on word meaning has not been directed towards distinguishing theories of concept representation. As a result, the phenomena that have been discussed here are generally not very probative in evaluating different accounts of how concepts are represented. For example, although typicality effects have been found in linguistic data, in sentence comprehension, speech production, and rating studies, these studies have not investigated whether people's representations of word meanings are exemplar-based or some kind of prototype representation. (Of course, such phenomena do reinforce the severe problems with the classical view described throughout this book.) Often such studies appear to assume a prototype representation, but it seems likely that exemplar models could explain most of the data just as easily. For example, if reading the word *vehicle* activates memories of specific vehicles, it is more likely that a bus exemplar would be activated than a tank exemplar would be. Thus, the Garrod and Sanford (1977) anaphora data could possibly be accounted for by an exemplar-based representation. Of course, there are some phenomena that I have already identified as being somewhat problematic for exemplar models (e.g., hierarchical classification, see chapter 7), and they are equally problematic when they are applied to words and word meaning.

The phenomenon of chaining is particularly important here. That is, as emphasized by Taylor (1995; and Lakoff 1987), broadly applied words often do not have a simple prototype structure but can be understood as a chain of meanings that are pairwise related (e.g., the examples of *paper* and the juice *box* discussed above). This process has a very exemplarish quality to it (as noted by Malt et al. 1999), because it is similarity to a particular past use that is important, just as exemplar theory says that it is similarity to known exemplars that is important. However, it is not yet clear whether the chaining is taking place between exemplars or summary representations. The plastic cartoon-character juice box is not just similar to a particular plastic squarish juice box—it is similar to a whole class of such juice boxes. Perhaps it is because this novel item is similar to a *subcategory* of boxes (rather than to an exemplar) that it can be called a box. If plastic juice boxes form a subcategory of boxes, they might be represented by a prototype-like summary representation of that subcategory rather than as individual exemplars. So, chaining could involve either summary representations or exemplars.

Thus, it does not seem that the main phenomena of word meaning can be chalked up to either the prototype or exemplar model very clearly.

The knowledge approach comes off well in this analysis, however, from a number of sources. First, it has long been known that in order to understand language, one must make innumerable plausible inferences to fill in what the speaker or writer intended to say (e.g., Bransford, Barclay, and Franks 1972; Gibbs 1984; Grice 1975; Haviland and Clark 1974; Schank and Abelson 1977; among many others). For example, the sentence "Carl poured the butter" requires one to infer that the butter must be hot and in liquid form. Such inferences obviously involve our knowledge of the world (e.g., only liquid can be poured, butter is liquid only when melted, and therefore is hot), which is apparently activated very quickly and continually during real language comprehension.

Knowledge effects can be seen more specifically in conceptual combination (see chapter 12), contextual modulation, typicality shifts (Roth and Shoben 1983), determining the intended sense in polysemy, and the use of background assumptions in determining word meaning (Fillmore 1982). That is, there is no way to tell from the word *table* by itself whether one is talking about the piece of furniture or the collection of people eating dinner. But when embedded in a sentence such as "The table left only a 10% tip," there is only one plausible choice—only one choice compatible with our world knowledge. Although one can argue that such knowledge is not really part of the word meaning but is more general domain knowledge, it effectively becomes part of the meaning, because the knowledge is used to determine the specific interpretation of that word in that context. Indeed, it is in lacking such everyday knowledge that computerized translation and language comprehension devices have often had great difficulty, as well as their difficulty in using pragmatics and knowledge of the speaker. Thus, it can be very difficult to know where to draw the line between what is part of the word meaning per se and what is "background" knowledge. It is not clear to me that drawing this line will be theoretically useful.

In short, insofar as background knowledge and plausible reasoning are involved in determining which sense is intended for a polysemous word for contextual modulation and for drawing inferences in language comprehension, this provides further evidence that background knowledge is involved in the conceptual representations underlying word meaning.

12

Conceptual Combination

Most of the psychology of concepts considers concepts in isolation, such as dog, book, movie, psychiatrist, or party. However, these concepts can be combined into new ones productively, as in dog book, movie psychiatrist, book party, dog psychiatrist, or party movie. In everyday language, words are continually combined into phrases of this sort in the making of sentences. If one thinks of word meanings as picking out concepts (see chapter 11 for a detailed development of this idea), then one can think of a phrase such as *dog book* as picking out a more complex concept. Indeed, a sentence like *The party dog jumped over the psychiatrist* could be thought of as being a very large concept or idea, made up of smaller constituents. To understand the meaning of this sentence, we would need to access our individual concepts in order to understand what parties, dogs, jumping, and psychiatrists are like. Then we would build them up into larger structures. Although we have a general idea of jumping, jumping over something adds more detail—for example, it involves horizontal movement, rather than only vertical translation. Furthermore, we can think about what it would be like to jump over a psychiatrist in particular—probably the psychiatrist was recumbent, since it would be difficult to jump over a standing one. We can also combine *party* and *dog* to come up with a guess about what *party dog* means (perhaps a dog who does tricks at parties), and then we can combine this with the predicate to understand that it was this kind of dog who jumped over the psychiatrist. This gives us more information both about the dog and about the jumping event (a dog jumps over things differently than people do). At the end of this process, you would have an interpretation of the sentence that consists of a structure of complexly elaborated and related concepts. An important part of language comprehension, then, is the combination of concepts into larger and larger structures, as guided by the syntax of the language.

To avoid confusion, I will continue to use the term *concept* to refer to the individual constituents of this complex thought (like dog, party, jump, etc.), and will use *conceptual combination* to refer to the larger structures built out of these components, although they are also concepts. I will not be discussing very complex examples of combinations into whole sentences, paragraphs, and stories, but will be focusing on phrases such as *party dog, movie psychiatrist*, and so on. These are noun phrases, with a noun or adjective modifying another noun. If a phrase becomes standardized, it would be called a *noun compound*, as in *hot dog* or *houseboat*, and in some cases would be written as one word. Because these are already familiar concepts, they would not be considered to be conceptual combinations per se. I will focus on less conventional combinations here, though it is often hard to know where to draw the line. A final bit of terminology is that the first word is called the *modifier*, and the final word, the *head noun* (because it is the head of the noun phrase in syntactic terms).

The question, then, is how people construct a more complex concept out of its parts. One traditional answer to this question derived from older linguistic analyses was an *extensional analysis*. (This general approach was discussed in the previous chapter.) The extension of a word is the set of things that it refers to. For example, the extension of *dog* is the set of all dogs; the extension of *red* is the set of all red things. When two concepts are combined, this view proposed, the resulting concept is a function of their extensions. In general, phrases like XY could be understood as the intersection of the set of Xs and the set of Ys (written as $X \cap Y$), that is, things that are both X and Y (Osherson and Smith 1981). For example, *red dog* probably picks out the set of things that are both red and dogs. This analysis seems to work for some adjectives whose meanings can be determined independently of the noun. *Wet* may mean the same thing when it is applied to different nouns, and so *wet dog* is the intersection of wet things and dogs. However, *relative adjectives* do not refer to an absolute property or relation, but are determined relative to a standard that is imposed by the noun. *Large caterpillar* does not refer to the intersection of large things and caterpillars (presumably this intersection is the null set). Instead, a large caterpillar is one that is large relative to other caterpillars, rather than being large in a neutral sense. Terms like *hot, smooth, loud, dark*, and *dirty* are all relative to some degree (e.g., a loud jet is much louder than a loud cat, though no more annoying). Since the relevant sets cannot be specified in advance, the intersection rule does not work with relative adjectives.

Other adjectives, called *nonpredicating adjectives*, also pose a problem for the extensional approach. Nonpredicating adjectives are ones that cannot be turned into predicates (and maintain their meaning). Predicating adjective-noun phrases like *cold water* and *loud jet* can be turned into sentences like *The water is cold* and *The jet is loud*. However, phrases like *atomic engineer* or *musical clock* do not mean the same as *The engineer is atomic* (which doesn't mean anything very sensible) or *The clock is musical*. These adjectives, then, cannot be placed into the predicate position and hence are nonpredicating. The interpretation of *atomic engineer* as someone who runs equipment to make atomic energy is not the intersection of atomic things (whatever they are) and engineers. If one were to define the set of musical things, it is doubtful that the musical clock that plays the song "Feelings" would be included. In all these cases, then, the intersection of the two sets does not define the combined concept.[1]

Finally, noun-noun combinations are very seldom accurately explained by the extensional view. For example, a movie psychiatrist is not the intersection of movies and psychiatrists; a party dog is hardly the intersection of dogs and parties. In both these cases, there is no real intersection of these sets—nothing is both a movie and a psychiatrist, or both a dog and a party. Although there are noun-noun phrases that can be analyzed intersectively (e.g., when the first noun describes the material that the second noun is made of, as in *stone wall* or *leather wallet*), these are in the small minority. Note also that the extensional view predicts that noun-noun concepts are symmetric, because $X \cap Y$ is the same as $Y \cap X$. However, phrases of the sort XY usually have very different meanings than their YX counterparts (e.g., *houseboat* vs. *boat house*; *bird dog* vs. *dog bird*; *desk lamp* vs. *lamp desk*). A desk lamp is a kind of lamp, but a lamp desk is a kind of desk. The extensional view cannot explain this difference.

For all these reasons, then, theories based on the extensions of the concepts have been dropped in psychology, although they are still somewhat popular in linguistics (in more complex forms than the intersection rule discussed here). Murphy (1988) discusses extensional models and the various kinds of phrases outlined above in greater detail.[2] All the current theories of conceptual combination therefore start with a claim about how concepts are represented and then go on to say how these representations are mentally combined. One reason to study conceptual combination, then, is that it may provide a further way of evaluating theories of concepts. If a prototype model, for example, cannot explain conceptual combination, then it may have to be given up in favor of a model that can explain it.

I start by describing an influential model of adjective-noun combination and will continue by discussing other models that have attempted to explain increasingly more complex forms of combination.

The Selective Modification Model

The most clearly specified model of conceptual combination is that of Smith, Osher-son, Rips, and Keane (1988; first described in incomplete form by Smith and Osherson 1984). One reason that the model is so well specified is that it confines itself to only one kind of conceptual combination, namely, adjective-noun phrases of the sort *long vegetable* or *red dog*. (They did not consider nonpredicating adjectives like *atomic* or *musical*, and it will be seen that their analysis has problems with these adjectives.) One important contribution of their work was to document a number of phenomena in conceptual combination that their own and later models have tried to account for. Before describing their theory, then, I will first describe some of these data.

Smith and Osherson (1984) pointed out that conceptual combination has some interesting typicality effects. Consider a phrase like *pet fish*. What makes something a typical pet fish? If one had an extensional theory, one might think that a typical pet fish would be something that was a typical pet and a typical fish. In fact, though, typical pet fish like goldfish or guppies are not very typical as pets and are quite atypical as fish (Osherson and Smith 1981). So, the typicality of a combination is not a simple function of the typicality of the component concepts.

More positively, Smith and Osherson (1984) noted a *conjunction effect*. When an item is well described by a conceptual combination, it is usually more typical of that concept than of the two components. For example, when shown a picture of a normal red apple, subjects rated it fairly highly as an apple (7.81 on a 0–10 scale) and as a red thing (8.5). However, they rated it highest of all as a red apple (8.87). This effect is even larger when an item is not typical of the head noun. Their subjects rated a brown apple as somewhat typical of brown things (6.93), not typical of apples (3.54), but extremely typical of brown apples (8.52). So, how is it that something that is not very typical of apples can become extremely typical of a sub-type of apples?[3]

To explain these results, Smith et al. (1988) started by assuming a schema structure of concepts. As shown in table 12.1, a schema concept consists of a set of dimensions and values (or features) for those dimensions. (Smith et al. called their dimensions *attributes*. This was an unfortunate choice of terminology, however, because this term is used as a synonym for *feature* in the rest of the concept literature, a usage that is also more consistent with its dictionary definition. Thus, I will use the term *dimension* here.)[4] The concept apple, then, has slots for color, shape, and texture (among others), and possible apple colors are grouped under the color slot. Readers may recall that such a schema representation was described as an

Table 12.1.
Examples of Smith et al. (1988) Conceptual Structures.

Apple		Red Apple	
1	Color	4	Color
	red 25		red 30
	green 5		green
	brown		brown
	...		...
.50	Shape	.50	Shape
	round 15		round 15
	square		square
	cylindrical 5		cylindrical 5
	...		...
.25	Texture	.25	Texture
	smooth 25		smooth 25
	rough 5		rough 5
	bumpy 5		bumpy 5
	...		...

Note: The left columns illustrate the schematic structure for the concept apple, and the right columns illustrate the same concept when it has been modified by the concept red. The numbers to the left of the dimension names are diagnosticity values, and the numbers to the right of the features are the number of votes for each feature.

elaboration of the prototype view in chapter 3. This schema is a summary representation of the category of apples. Rather than just listing features, however, it structures the properties so that the relations between them are more apparent. For example, although apples can be round, crispy, green, sweet, sour, red, brown, and soft, some of these properties are alternatives (green, red, and brown; sweet and sour; crispy and soft) that are usually not simultaneously found in the same entity. Structuring the concept this way also allows representation of possible relations among dimensions (though the selective modification model does not discuss these), as when people know that there is a relation between the color of an apple and its taste, say.

As shown in table 12.1, each dimension has possible values listed for it (e.g., for the dimension color, the values red, green, and brown are listed). In addition, the typicality of each value is indicated by a number of *votes* to its right. These are like the weights given to features in the feature-list representation discussed in chapter 3. Because we think of apples as primarily red, that feature gets most of the votes. Because apples are often green, this feature also gets some votes. Other, unusual colors get few or no votes. Table 12.1 also shows a number in front of each dimension name. This is the *diagnosticity* of each dimension. If a dimension is important to a concept, useful for distinguishing it from other related concepts, then it has a high diagnositicity weight. If the dimension is not important, it has a low weight. In the example shown, color is assumed to be most diagnostic, with shape next, and texture last. I think of apples as coming most often from Michigan, but the place where a fruit comes from is not a very reliable indicator of what kind of fruit it is, so this dimension would have a low weight in my representation. Diagnosticity is not the same as a feature's frequency. All birds breathe, giving this feature many votes, but this dimension does not help to separate birds from other animals, so it would get a low diagnosticity score. In contrast, having wings is fairly distinctive, and so its dimension would get a high diagnosticity score in the bird concept.[5]

These representations are used in categorizing items in a way similar to weighted feature lists. If you see an object that is round, green, and smooth, it might be an apple. To calculate its typicality to apples, you would count the number of votes for each feature that are shared by the object and concept, minus the distinctive features—those in the object not found in the concept, and those in the concept not found in the object. Each of these values for each dimension would be multiplied by the dimension weight. Thus, more important dimensions count more in the typicality calculation. Whichever concept received the highest score would be the one you would categorize the object into. Items with higher scores in the concept would be considered more typical.

Why is all this apparatus needed? Smith et al. argue that it is all necessary to capture the changes made to concepts by modification. Consider the concept red apple. Mentioning the color of apples has two important effects. First, all the votes on the color dimension are moved to the value red (the number of votes is now 30 in the representation of red apple in table 12.1). Second, the diagnosticity of the color dimension is increased (changed to 4 in table 12.1—the exact value would be determined empirically). These changes correspond to two intuitions. First, although apples can be many colors, a red apple has only one color (red), and so all the votes that normally go to other colors accrue to this value. Second, by mentioning the color of the apple, the importance of this dimension has been increased. That is, color is more important to *red apple* than it is to *smooth apple*.

This way of modifying the concept can explain the conjunction effect described above. A red apple is more typical of the concept red apple than it is of the concept apple because (1) it gets more votes from the matching color, and (2) the color dimension has a higher weight, and so the matching color counts for more in the combination than in the single concept apple. Why do we need the change in diagnosticity? Why not just move the votes to the red feature, which would account for the conjunction effect? The reason has to do with mismatching items. Consider a brown apple. It is already atypical of apples, as brown has few or no votes in the apple concept. However, it is even more atypical of red apples; in fact, it is a horrible example of red apples. This effect (see Smith et al. 1988, table 3), called the *reverse conjunction effect*, requires the notion of diagnosticity. A brown apple is a horrible red apple not only because it does not have the correct color, but because the color dimension is the most salient part of the red apple concept. This is modeled by the change in diagnosticity. Without that change, a brown apple would be equally atypical of apples and red apples.

Smith et al. give a formal description of conceptual combination and mathematically model their predictions, showing a good deal of success with the combinations they studied.[6] Since much of the next discussion will be picking on the Smith et al. model, I think it is important to indicate what about this theory seems to be exactly right. We can divide the theory up into two parts. The first is the description of the combination process, in which an adjective works by moving votes onto its value and increasing the diagnosticity. The later criticisms will suggest that this account cannot be extended to other kinds of modifiers. The second part of the model is the explanation of the conjunction and reverse conjunction effects. This part is well supported by the evidence, and later theories have had to accept the Smith et al. account. In general, a modifier appears both to change something about the head concept (though exactly what it changes is controversial) and to increase the importance of what has been changed in the resulting concept. So the critical thing about a dog psychiatrist is not the person's height or age or even professional training, but the fact that the psychiatrist treats dogs. Someone who primarily treats married couples, say, would be a somewhat typical psychiatrist, but would be a very bad example of a dog psychiatrist. In this respect, Smith et al.'s insights about concept combination, as well as the evidence that they provided for these effects, have stood the test of time.

Difficulties with the Selective Modification Model

One of the reasons to make a specific model in psychology is that even if it turns out to be wrong, it may generate critical experiments that provide important new phenomena in the field. This has been the case with the selective modification model. The main problem with this theory that later writers have criticized is its assumptions about modification. Consider the way modification works for the concept red apple. The adjective *red* finds its match in the schema: There is a feature with the same name (see table 12.1). That feature now gets all the votes, and its dimension gets a higher diagnosticity rating. However, there are more complex cases that aren't so easily accommodated. It has been argued that sometimes the exact feature would not be present in the concept already, and yet people can figure out how to modify it. Indeed, there may not be an obvious dimension for the modifier to affect. Furthermore, sometimes more than one dimension is altered. Thus, the modification process itself has been argued to be much more complex than Smith et al. (1988) let on.

To some degree, these arguments rely on using different kinds of modifiers than the ones Smith et al. used. For example, Murphy (1988) discussed the adjective *corporate* (which is a nonpredicating adjective, as defined above). Which dimension in a noun concept do you think *corporate* will modify? Before going any further, try to identify that dimension. Now consider the following examples: corporate stationery, corporate account, corporate car, corporate building, corporate lawyer, and corporate donor. Although these all involve a corporation in some way, the exact relation between the corporation and the noun is somewhat different. Corporate stationery is *used by* the corporation and has the corporate logo on it; a corporate account is an account that is *charged to* the corporation; a corporate car is *owned by* a corporation and used for business travel; a corporate building is *where* the business is carried out; a corporate lawyer is one who *works for* a corporation; and a corporate donor is a donor who *is* a corporation. Clearly, different dimensions are being modified here: works for, does business at, used for travel, and so on. One could argue that there is one basic relation, something like "a corporate X means X that has something to do with a corporation," but this is much vaguer than the real interpretations that people give to these phrases. Such definitions are so vague that *corporate X* might include all Xs: Almost all stationery has something to do with a corporation (e.g., it is manufactured by one, used by one, sent to one, written on by a corporation employee, etc.), so by this definition, almost all stationery would be corporate stationery. However, people's interpretations are richer and more specific (see Downing 1977; Levi 1978, p. 84).

In short, it is not the case that an adjective can automatically pick out a single dimension to modify. The dimension depends on the noun it is paired with. For *car*, the adjective *corporate* primarily modifies the "owned by" dimension, whereas for *building*, the adjective primarily affects the "location" dimension. Murphy (1988) argued from such examples that conceptual combination is a knowledge-laden process. In understanding these combinations, people must decide which dimension is the best fit to the modifier. It does not make sense to talk about a corporation being located in a car, but it does make sense for it to own a car for business activities. It does not make sense for a corporation to use a building for transportation, but it does make sense for it to have its offices located in a building. The dimension being modified depends on an interaction of the modifier and head noun; you can't tell how the modifier will have its effect without knowing the head noun and what head-modifier interactions are plausible.

Another shortcoming of the selective modification model is that modifiers often modify multiple dimensions at once. This was shown most convincingly by Medin and Shoben (1988). They set up quartets of adjectives, consisting of two contrasting pairs, like *light colored–dark colored* and *summer–winter*, all modifying the noun *shirt*. Clearly, *light* and *dark* should modify the color dimension of a concept according to the selective modification model. Similarly, *summer* and *winter* should modify the time of year when the shirt is worn. However, Medin and Shoben argued that such dimensions are often correlated with other dimensions, so that modifying one of them would require modification of the other. To demonstrate this, they had subjects rate the typicality of *light colored shirt* and *dark colored shirt* as examples of winter shirts and summer shirts. They found that *light colored shirt* was much more typical of summer shirt, but *dark colored shirt* was much more typical of winter shirt. Other quartets of items showed similar results. For example, although gravel streets are atypical as streets in general, they are typical of empty streets, whereas paved street is much more typical of busy streets. If the effect of an adjective is to pick out one dimension and modify it as described earlier, then it is unclear why an adjective that manifestly refers to one dimension affects other dimensions. Medin and Shoben argued that people have knowledge about the causal connections of these dimensions, as well as real-world examples of the concepts, which they use to make such decisions. In short, other knowledge leads to multiple dimensions being affected.

Murphy (1988) provided a similar demonstration with a systematic creation of noun phrases. He chose a set of 10 very common nouns and adjectives and made the 100 phrases resulting from their pairings. This provided a less biased way of testing different phrases, since it did not involve preselecting combinations that might support or disprove any particular theory. Murphy then asked subjects to define each of these phrases. He collected together the meanings of each adjective across the 10 different nouns and examined them to see if they had the same meaning or different meanings across the nouns. Although counting something as the same or different meaning is somewhat arbitrary, he found that subjects gave an

Table 12.2.
One subject's meanings for the adjective *open*, for 10 nouns (from Murphy 1988).

Noun	Meaning of *open* when combined with that noun
year	flexible, in which plans are made
people	revealing of thoughts, opinions, feelings
world	full of opportunities and choices
life	having no secrets, hiding nothing
hand	dealt face up
house	a period of time when people can drop by to visit
problem	having many solutions
word	having more than one interpretation
eye	alert, keenly aware
city	lively, welcoming visitors and transients

average of 7 different meanings for each modifier across those 10 contexts. This analysis was performed separately for every subject, so it does not reflect disagreements among subjects but rather variation within every subject's interpretation of the adjective. Table 12.2 shows one subject's meanings of the adjective *open* for the 10 nouns. It can be seen that very different relations are used in each case. Thus, people could not be simply choosing which dimension to modify based on the adjective meaning. Instead, they must be combining the adjective and the noun in a more interactive way. In fact, table 12.2 shows that the noun itself may be affected by the adjective. For example, *open hand* was interpreted by this subject as referring to a hand of cards, whereas for other modifiers, *hand* was understood as the body part.

In summary, the adjective-modification process that Smith et al. (1988 and Smith and Osherson 1984) proposed appears unable to capture many cases of conceptual combination. As I noted earlier, it does a very good job at describing one part of the modification process, namely the typicality phenomena. The mechanisms of dimensional weight change and votes on those dimensions seem necessary to account for the important typicality effects in conceptual combination. The model is weaker as an explanation of the combination process itself. First, it has difficulty in explaining why a single adjective modifies very different dimensions on different nouns. In particular, it usually does not seem to work for nonpredicating adjectives (nor for noun modifiers, as will be seen shortly). Second, it suggests that adjectives modify only a single dimension of a noun concept, whereas they may modify a number of dimensions. There are apparently a number of complexities in the combination process that go beyond the feature voting and dimension weighting that the modification model includes. More recent models attempt to address these shortcomings as well as encompassing a wider variety of combination types.

The Concept Specialization Model

The second main model in this area also starts with the assumption that concepts should be represented by schemata (specific evidence for this assumption was given by Murphy 1990, Experiment 3). Cohen and Murphy (1984) argued that conceptual combination is a process in which a head noun concept was specialized by one or more of its slots being filled by the modifying concept. The *concept specialization model*, as elaborated in Murphy (1988, 1990), is thus far quite similar to the Smith et al. (1988) view. However, it differs in a few important respects. First, it suggests that knowledge is involved in choosing the best-fitting slot. This is especially evident when noun modifiers are considered, because they do not pick out any particular dimension to be modified. What dimension (or slot) is picked out by the concept dog? Our knowledge of dogs is considerable, and it therefore allows us to use it to modify other concepts in a number of different ways: dog magazine, dog trainer, dog food, dog sculpture, and so on. Magazines are usually about a specific kind of topic, and the concept of dog could be a topic of a magazine, but it could not be the reader of the magazine, or the publisher of the magazine, or what the magazine is printed on. Therefore, in understanding *dog magazine*, people choose the slot of the magazine schema that makes the most sense with dog as the filler. In contrast, the concept food does not have a topic slot, but the concept of dogs could easily fit into the agent (eater) slot. In discovering the relation between dogs and magazines or between dogs and food, then, people use their general background knowledge to choose the slot that seems best. This explains why the same modifier can have very different relations to different nouns.

The concept specialization model differs from the Smith et al. view in a second way, which is that after selecting the correct slot, further interpretation and elaboration of the concept occurs. For example, once people realize that a magazine about dogs is being talked about, they can infer other properties of this concept. A dog magazine probably is directed toward dog owners and breeders; it probably contains ads for dog food; it probably has articles on training dogs; unlike many other magazines, it probably does not contain holiday recipes, weight-loss plans, or revelations of the secrets your lover will never tell you. The detail and depth of these features depend to some degree on the task demands. If one is not thinking much about dog magazines, one might not get much further than "magazine about dogs."

On the other hand, if one thinks for a while about this concept, one could have an extremely detailed, rich concept. Importantly, these kinds of properties (like directed toward dog breeders or lacks holiday recipes) are not themselves properties of the concepts of dog or magazine but arise through the interaction of the two (see below).

It is this second stage of elaboration that explains the data that were so troublesome to the selective modification model. For example, in thinking about summer shirts, one thinks not only that they are worn in the summer, but also that they are probably short-sleeved, light colored, loosely woven, more informal, and so on. There are two kinds of knowledge that can enter into this process. One is general background knowledge and reasoning. For example, even if one did not know about summer shirts specifically, one might infer that they would be made of lighter colored cloth than winter shirts, since they should reflect the sun. The second way in which knowledge affects this process is through the use of remembered examples, once the basic interpretation of the phrase is achieved. That is, once you realize that a summer shirt is a shirt worn in the summer, you might think back to your yellow L. L. Bean knit cotton shirt, and use this as one source of inference about summer shirts in general. This kind of information, called *extensional feedback* by Hampton (1987) can only be used once part of the interpretation has been constructed. (You must know which of your remembered shirts to use and which not to use as sources of information, so you must already have a basic interpretation of the phrase in order to retrieve the right shirts from memory. So even extensional feedback may require some prior use of general knowledge.)

In addition to the data discussed earlier, Murphy (1988) provided further evidence for the use of knowledge in conceptual combination. He documented cases in which a combination has a property that is not true of either of its components. For example, *unshelled peas* (an item from Smith and Osherson 1984) are thought by subjects to be long, but they do not think that peas or unshelled things are generally long; *empty stores* are thought to lose money, but empty things do not usually lose money, and most stores do not lose money. These *emergent features* thus give evidence that information from outside the concepts themselves is influencing the combination process. (See also the discussion of Hampton's work below.)

Murphy (1990) provided a test of some aspects of this theory. He argued that different modifiers should make it easier or harder to find the correct slot. For example, adjectives like *red* are often easy to interpret, since they usually denote the dimension they modify, in this case, color. In interpreting *red X*, then, one is usually safe in thinking that it is an X that is colored red. Nouns like *dog* should be hard to use as modifiers, because they are conceptually much more complex and can pick out a number of different dimensions of a noun, as described above. What about the nonpredicating adjectives, like *corporate, atomic,* or *musical?* In many cases, these are simply adjectival forms of noun concepts. That is, *corporate* means having to do with corporations; *musical* means pertaining to music. In some cases one can turn the adjective-noun phrase into a synonymous noun-noun phrase such as *atomic bomb–atom bomb* (Levi 1978). Thus, if these nonpredicating adjectives are based on noun meanings, they should also be more difficult to understand than predicating adjectives that are conceptually simpler. One piece of evidence for this is that people differ more in their interpretations of concepts with these terms. Murphy (1990) found that subjects gave more different interpretations of noun-noun phrases than for adjective-noun phrases. He also found more interpretations for nonpredicating adjective-noun phrases than for predicating adjective-noun phrases. Thus, there is presumably more uncertainty in how to modify a concept when the modifier is complex.

These differences created processing effects as well. Murphy (1990) measured how quickly subjects could comprehend phrases of this sort, and he found that noun and nonpredicating adjective modifiers took significantly longer to understand than simple adjective modifiers. Perhaps not surprisingly, these differences can be eliminated if a context is provided that already activates the relevant slot. That is, if people are thinking about the topic of different magazines, they will more quickly understand *dog magazine* than if magazines are just mentioned neutrally (see Gagné 1997; Gagné and Murphy 1996; Gerrig and Murphy 1992; Murphy 1990; Wisniewski and Love 1998; for other demonstrations of context effects). Such findings supply further support for the idea that background knowledge is involved in conceptual combination, because contexts are simply a highly activated subset of background knowledge.

Problems for the Concept Specialization Model

Wisniewski's Critique

According to both the concept specialization and selective modification models, conceptual combination proceeds by finding a slot or relation of the head noun that the modifier can best fit into. In his recent work, Wisniewski (1997) has adopted the basic framework of that model but also criticized it as being incomplete. Through an analysis of many different conceptual combinations, he found both a simpler form of combination and a form that is more complex than concept specialization.

The simpler form of combination is that of *property mapping*, in which a property of the modifier is attributed to the noun. For example, concepts like tiger squirrel and skunk cabbage are interpreted by most people as a squirrel that has stripes and a cabbage that smells bad. But these are not cases of the modifier filling a preexisting slot of the noun. For example, we can feel certain that the concept of squirrel does not have a slot "has the stripes of ...," nor does the concept of cabbage have a slot like "smells like a...."[7] Instead, it seems that one aspect of the modifier is being attributed to the head noun. Although one can get concept specialization interpretations of these same concepts (e.g., skunk cabbage = cabbage that a skunk eats), they are not the preferred interpretations. Wisniewski (1996) found that such property mapping concepts are most likely to be found when the modifier and head are similar. So, tigers and squirrels are both four-legged mammals. He argues that the differences between two similar concepts are easily noticed (a tiger is larger, carnivorous, and has stripes), and so they become salient properties that could be attributed to the head noun. Furthermore, when concepts are very similar, it may be difficult to find a plausible relation between them as required for concept specialization, perhaps because the concepts are likely to play similar roles in thematic relations (e.g., slot-filling relations between tiger and squirrel may be rather implausible: a squirrel that eats tigers, a squirrel that lives in/on/around tigers, a squirrel that gathers tigers for the winter, etc., are not very likely). In short, the concept specialization model does not accommodate these kinds of interpretations. This finding suggests that there may be a diversity of ways in which concepts are combined. Wisniewski and Love (1998) discovered that the property mapping interpretations accounted for about 30% of the interpretations of real phrases that they found in a variety of printed sources.

Given that almost any property could be transferred from one concept to another, how do people decide that a skunk cabbage is a cabbage that smells bad, rather than one with a white stripe or one with two ears, like a skunk? One important variable is the salience of the property in the modifier. The ears of a skunk are not very salient, but its smell is most salient. Estes and Glucksberg (2000) showed that the property interpretations of phrases were much more common when the property was a salient one of the modifier. Sometimes these properties are conventional, as when we use the words *skunk* and *elephant* to refer to a bad smell and large size. Estes and Glucksberg found that the relevance of a dimension in the head noun also increased property interpretations. For example, they found that subjects interpreted the phrase *feather luggage* to refer to light luggage more than they interpreted *feather storage* to refer to light storage, because the dimension of weight is more relevant to luggage than to storage (see also Murphy 1990, Experiment 3). Again, we see that properties of both concepts are critical to determining the interpretation.

Simply identifying the property to be mapped is not sufficient, however, as the property often has to be modified and placed into the correct location in the head noun. For example, Wisniewski and Middleton (2002) have argued that people attempt to spatially align the modifier with the head noun and to place the property of the first into the analogous spot of the second. For example, a bucket bowl is interpreted as having a handle that goes over the top of the bowl rather than being attached on the side. Because buckets have handles on the top, people attribute the bucket bowl's handle to the same location. In contrast, a coffee cup bowl also is a bowl with a handle, but the handle is on the side.

More radically, Wisniewski (1997) has argued that many noun-noun concepts involve a process of *construal*, in which one or both of the concepts is modified so that it does not have its usual, literal meaning. If you interpret *plastic truck* as being a child's toy, you are not in fact taking the object as being a real truck but are construing the concept of truck as referring to a toy. Another popular construal is when a word is taken as referring to a representation of the thing rather than to the thing itself. For example, if *stone squirrel* is interpreted as referring to a statue, then clearly the squirrel is not a real squirrel but a representation of one (Wisniewski 1997, p. 169). Wisniewski points out that such interpretations can be found in familiar phrases and compounds like *piggy bank*, *animal crackers*, and *chocolate bunny*.

These radical changes in meaning (e.g., from a living animal to an inanimate statue) are not the only kinds of construal that are necessary. Wisniewski argues that the properties and relations used in conceptual combination are often subtly modified during the combination process. For example, some people interpret a *fork spoon* as being a spoon-like thing with small tines at the end of the spoon's bowl (see figure 12.1). (Some readers already may know this kind of thing as a *spork*. However, people of my generation who have managed to avoid fast food restaurants still think of this as a fork spoon and a somewhat novel combination.) This, then, is an example of property mapping, in which a fork's tines are attributed to a spoon. However, it is not just that fork tines are added to a typical spoon. Such an object would be very peculiar. Furthermore, it is not that the tines replace the bowl of the spoon, because this would now become a fork rather than a fork spoon. Instead, the tines and the bowl are both modified so that the tines do not greatly change the shape of the bowl. This subtler form of construal is generally consistent with the concept specialization model's emphasis on using real-world knowledge to

Figure 12.1
A fork-spoon, courtesy of Edward Wisniewski.

choose a slot to be modified and then to clean up and augment the concept after the basic combination has been done (though construal is not done after the basic interpretation but as part of it). However, the articles describing that model (Murphy 1988, 1990) certainly did not emphasize this construal process, especially in the radical form in which the head noun is reinterpreted as something quite different. Nonetheless, such construals are apparently ubiquitous: Wisniewski (1997, p. 169) reports that of 3,003 interpretations he collected for 224 different combinations, "an astonishing 70% involved the construal of a noun's referent as something other than the typical category named by the noun."

In short, it seems that conceptual combination may be richer than any of the individual theories allows. Wisniewski's work has been important in specifying these different forms of combination and in beginning an account of what factors influence the selection of one vs. another form of interpretation. What is not yet known is the online process by which one of these interpretations is constructed/selected. It is clear that people do not always prefer to use a slot-filling interpretation whenever it is possible to do so, since they will choose feature-mapping interpretations for similar concepts that would have made sensible slot-filling concepts (see Wisniewski and Love 1998). But given that these ways of combining concepts are so different, it is not clear how they could be carried out in parallel. The feature-mapping process involves comparing the two concepts, identifying a feature of the modifier that could be plausibly transferred over to the head noun, and carrying out that transfer. The slot-filling process involves seeing whether there is a relation available in the head noun that the entire modifier could fill, and then constructing that relation. Furthermore, both of these are complicated by the possibility of construal (e.g., interpreting *skunk* as referring to a bad smell), which allows many more ways of possibly relating the concepts. How all these alternatives are considered (or if they aren't, how they are ruled out) is at this point not clear.

Feature-Verification Studies

Another concern for the concept specialization model—and, indeed, most theories—is a phenomenon from reaction-time (RT) tests of conceptual combination. Springer and Murphy (1992, following up earlier work by Hampton and Springer 1989) attempted to get more insight into the combination process by testing specific features of combined concepts. Consider the following sentences:

(1)   Boiled celery is green. (True-Noun)

(2)   Boiled celery is soft. (True-Phrase)

(3)   Boiled celery is blue. (False-Noun)

(4)   Boiled celery is crisp. (False-Phrase)

The first two sentences are true, and the second two are false. However, the source of the information about these features (green, soft, blue, crisp) is different in these cases. The fact that boiled celery is green is stored in our concept of celery—it is part of the noun concept, which is also true in the combination. The fact that boiled celery is soft, in contrast, is *not* part of the noun concept—in fact, celery is normally crisp. So, to know that boiled celery is soft, one has to combine the boiling and celery concepts and "cancel out" the crisp feature usually found in celery and substitute the soft feature. So, softness is true of the whole phrase but not of the noun, whereas greenness is directly associated with the noun (and also is true of the phrase). Thus, "green" is called a *noun feature* and "soft" a *phrase feature*. According to most theories of conceptual combination, it should be harder to respond correctly to sentence (2) than to (1)—more generally, harder to verify phrase features, because (2) requires considerable combination processing, including the use of world knowledge to get rid of the crisp feature normally associated with celery.

A similar argument can be made for the false sentences. Boiled celery is not blue, and neither is celery, so no special combination process needs to be done here. In contrast, celery normally is crisp, but boiled celery isn't. To decide that (4) is false should be quite difficult, then, since one must cancel out the usual property of celery. It is not only the concept specialization model that would make these predictions. For example, Smith et al. (1988, pp. 525–526) suggest that if knowledge is involved in adjective-noun combinations, it would occur after the basic weighting process they describe: "That is, our model may describe a rapid composition process, which is sometimes followed by a slower composition process that uses general knowledge." Since the phrase features in (2) and (4) are not already present in the noun concepts, it would presumably take considerably longer to make decisions about them. Indeed, it is hard to think of a reasonable model that would predict otherwise.

It is very interesting, then, that the results do not come out as expected. Springer and Murphy (1992) found that it took significantly longer for subjects to judge the true noun properties like (1) than the true phrase properties like (2)—the opposite of the theories' predictions. The false properties tested in (3) and (4) took virtually identical times to verify. Surprisingly, then, features that required knowledge to be incorporated into the combination did not take longer to judge than features that were already present in the individual concepts. As Smith et al. suggested, perhaps there was an initial combination process in which the noun features were first activated but then the phrase features came to predominate. If so, the observed RTs would not reflect the basic combination process but only the final result. Springer and Murphy addressed this possibility in two ways. The first was to present the sentence very quickly using the RSVP procedure (i.e., presenting words in the middle of the screen in rapid sequence). Similar results were found there. The second experiment used a procedure in which the predicate was presented first (e.g., subjects saw "crisp," and then "boiled celery"). Even here, the phrase features were verified faster (in fact, the effect was strongest under these circumstances). This is quite mystifying, because one would think that seeing a noun feature first, like "crisp," would be immediately consistent with the word *celery* when it was encountered, and so would make it very difficult to respond "false" (boiled celery is not crisp). Instead, subjects were faster for the phrase features.

At the moment, there is no adequate explanation of why these results are obtained. There are two general possible explanations. The first is that they accurately represent the order in which features are activated in conceptual combination. This is somewhat paradoxical, because it suggests that emergent features resulting from the two concepts are activated before the features of the component concepts.

Yet, how can one know what emergent features there are without first activating the features of the component concepts themselves? Of course, we must not assume that every feature of every concept is activated whenever one reads the concept name. When reading the word *celery*, one does not necessarily think of crisp, long, green, curved vegetables, used in salads and for dipping, with leaves at the top, grown in California, and so on. It may be that only a few general properties come to mind (celery is an edible vegetable), or only those that are relevant in the context. So, it is possible that the results paint a true picture of which features are first activated, with the emergent properties getting special attention. However, we do not as yet have an adequate story of exactly how that happens.

The second explanation is that the results do not really reflect the order in which features are activated, but instead reflect something about the verification process. Springer and Murphy suggested that the result was a kind of discourse effect. When one is asked whether boiled celery is green, the implication seems to be that although celery is green, *boiled* celery might not be. But this is incorrect (both are green), and so the statement is somewhat infelicitous. In contrast, boiled celery is soft and regular celery isn't, so saying "boiled celery is soft" is felicitous. More generally, when one qualifies the noun by the adjective, one is suggesting that the adjective is relevant to the decision, and when it isn't (as in the noun features in (1) and (3) above), the sentence sounds strange. At present, the evidence for this explanation is mixed (Gagné and Murphy 1996; Glucksberg and Estes 2000). Again, although this effect is intriguing, most theories do not know what to make of it yet.

Relation Preferences

A final critique of the concept specialization model has been made by Gagné and Shoben (1997). They analyzed noun-noun concepts as filling one of a small number of critical relations, first identified for linguistic analysis by Levi (1978).[8] Thus, concepts like tool drawer would be represented as a drawer FOR tools; mountain stream would be a stream LOCATED AT a mountain; and flu virus would be a virus that CAUSES the flu. Gagné and Shoben analyzed the interpretation of a number of noun-noun phrases that they systematically constructed. When they analyzed their own interpretations of these phrases, they discovered that different nouns tended to be associated with some relations more than others.[9] For example, when used as a modifier, the word *mountain* tended to be associated with the LOCATION relation, as in mountain cloud, mountain stream, mountain house, and so on. When used as a head noun, some words also had preferences. For example, *magazine* tended to have the ABOUT relation, as in dog magazine, fashion magazine, crime magazine, and so on. However, these preferences were not absolute. A mountain painting is not a painting LOCATED AT a mountain; and a lawyer magazine is more likely to be FOR lawyers than ABOUT them.

Gagné and Shoben (1997) had subjects evaluate their phrases for sensibility, measuring the time it took them to do so. They constructed phrases that had their preferred relations and those that did not. Since the preferences could be measured for modifiers and head nouns separately, there were four possible conditions: phrases that had the relation preferred by both the modifier and head noun, by the modifier alone, by the head noun alone, or by neither. However, there were not enough phrases to make up the last condition, and so it was dropped. To understand the other three conditions, consider these examples. Mountain cloud uses the LOCATED AT relation, and this is the preferred relation for both *mountain* and *cloud*. (That is, across all their items, it was the most frequent relation for *mountain* used as a modifier and *cloud* used as a head noun.) Mountain magazine, in contrast, uses the ABOUT relation, which is preferred only for the head noun. And chocolate *rabbit* would use the IS relation (rabbit that is chocolate), which is preferred for the modifier but not the head noun.

The results revealed that the relational preference made a difference for the modifier but not the head noun. Items like mountain cloud and chocolate rabbit (where the modifier's preferred relation was correct) were easier than items like mountain magazine (where the modifier's preferred relation was incorrect). So, when the modifier was used in its preferred form, the phrase was easier to understand. The fact that the modifier has an effect on RT but the head noun doesn't may be due to the order of reading the phrase. For example, when reading *mountain magazine*, subjects first encounter *mountain* and begin to think about locations. Thus when this interpretation must be dropped, it is more difficult to interpret the phrase. In contrast, the head noun is encountered only after the modifier has been processed to some degree. It should be pointed out though, that this explanation requires that the head noun also have an important effect on the interpretation of the phrase. That is, subjects must have realized that magazines are not normally located in one geographic location, which caused them to reject "magazine located in the mountain" as an interpretation. That is why, on Gagné and Shoben's own account, it takes longer to decide that *mountain magazine* makes sense. If the head noun did not constrain the interpretation, subjects would have accepted the "magazine located in the mountain" interpretation and quickly responded that it made sense. Gagné and Shoben assume that the ABOUT relation is the correct interpretation, which is largely driven by the fact that magazines are often about a single topic. So, the head noun has a critical role to play in spite of the ineffectiveness of preferred relation of the head noun in determining RT in that task.[10]

Gagné and Shoben (1997) argued that people must track for each word what relations it prefers when it is a modifier. When reading *mountain* ..., people access the list of likely relations for the word *mountain* (most likely LOCATED AT, possibly FOR) and use this to create an initial interpretation of the phrase. When the phrase can be interpreted using a likely relation, comprehension is faster than when it can't. The authors point out that current models of conceptual combination do not have such a mechanism and conclude that they cannot account for their results.

Although keeping track of these relations would explain Gagné and Shoben's data, there are some difficulties with this explanation. First, the reliance on Levi's (1978) categories is problematic. Although Levi argued that these were basic semantic relations that could account for noun-noun phrases, there is no independent evidence that these are the only or indeed the main relations that exist. In fact, it has often been noted that these relations are extremely vague, whereas interpretation of such phrases is often very detailed (e.g., H. Clark 1983; Downing 1977; Murphy 1988). Clearly, a mountain stream is not located at a mountain in the same way that a mountain goat or a mountain house are. One of them runs over the mountain as a permanent geographical feature; one lives on the mountain; one is built on the mountain. Thus, the relation LOCATED AT does not do justice to the relation between the concepts. It would be somewhat surprising, then, if people stored these rather nondescriptive relations for each noun. Second, this storage of preferred relations seems wasteful of lexical memory: In addition to the usual semantic information stored for a word, one would also have to store the relations it frequently uses when it is a modifier, even though nouns are mostly not modifiers.

There is a different explanation of Gagné and Shoben's data, which is more in keeping with the concept specialization model. To begin with, let us ask where these preferences come from. Why does mountain want to modify a noun by LOCATED AT, and why does magazine want to be related to (as a head noun) by ABOUT? If these are purely arbitrary facts about the words, then perhaps they do need to be stored in the mental lexicon. However, it does not require much semantic analysis to realize that a mountain is a geological entity and geographical location, which is why it prefers the LOCATED AT relation. Mountains cannot eat things or cause events or be about anything, but they can be a place where something happens to be, or where something lives, because of their nature as geographical locations. The concept of a mountain, then, can be combined with other concepts in some ways more plausibly than other ways, and this is what accounts for its preference for certain relations. The reason, on this view, why phrases like *mountain magazine* are hard to understand is not because people have stored the LOCATED AT relation with the word *mountain*, but because the concept of mountain, which is encountered first in the phrase, starts to bring to mind a certain kind of location with certain properties. Subjects attempt to integrate the subsequent word in the phrase with this concept, which is easy to do if the relation involves locations but is difficult to do if it involves something very different. In short, I am suggesting that the preferences Gagné and Shoben found are not stored with the word but arise out of its semantic representation and the properties that are involved in interpreting such phrases (for which there is plenty of independent evidence).

The jury is still out on this question. Gagné and Shoben's (1997) data are important in showing the asymmetry in the processing of the phrase, which past work (mostly not using timed tasks) did not reveal. However, replication of their results using a more objective measure of modifier preference would strengthen the evidence for this finding. So far, no experiment has contrasted their view with the proposal that these preferences are not stored but arise naturally out of their conceptual content. Their results do not seem to pose an insuperable problem for the concept specialization model. It is possible that the model (and more generally, models of the lexicon) would have to be augmented by these relation preferences. If my alternative suggestion turns out to be correct, then modifier preferences simply fall out of the semantic content of modifiers, and no change in the model is required. That is, since a mountain is a particular kind of location, *mountain* will tend to modify locative slots for different nouns. However, since the available slots differ in different head nouns, producing different modifications as in *mountain magazine*, it seems that people attempt to find the best-fitting slot, just as the concept specialization theory predicts.

Conjunctive and Disjunctive Concepts

The research on conceptual combination discussed above has focused on combinations expressed by modifier-noun phrases. Another kind of combination has been studied extensively by James Hampton, phrasal categories of the sort "X that is also a Y," and "X or Y." Although this may be a less frequently occurring kind of combination (the modifier-noun combinations are ubiquitous), it is interesting in part because it offers the best opportunity for an extensional theory. I pointed out earlier that phrases like *typewriter tables* were not the intersection of typewriters and tables, but phrases of the sort *sport that is also a game* could well be understood as the intersection of the sets of sports and games. In fact, that seems to be the exact meaning of the combination. Thus, one of the main points of interest of these concepts is the fact that the extensional model does not work here either.

Hampton has studied conjunctive concepts through two main approaches. The first is to investigate the categorization and typicality of items in conjunctive concepts. For example, how can we predict which things will be members of categories like sports that are also games? And how can we predict the typicality of their category members? The second approach has been to study the properties of the conjunctive concept as a function of the properties of the two components. How can we predict what features are in sports that are also games, based on the features of sports and of games?

The first question, that of category membership, is a clear test of the extensional view. Sports that are also games should consist exactly of the things that are both sports and games. Furthermore, the classical view of concepts (see chapter 2) makes the same prediction. It assumes that sports and games are concepts that have definitions. Therefore, the concept of sports that are also games could be formed by combining the definitions of the two concepts. If games require competition, and if sports require physical activity, then games that are also sports would require *both* competition and physical activity.

Hampton (1988b) tested these predictions by determining the membership of items in the two component categories and in the conjunctive category. Subjects judged whether the category was a member or not and then rated their confidence in their judgment on a 3-point scale. Hampton turned these ratings into a −3 to +3 scale, with the +3 items being very typical category members, and −3 items being nonmembers that were unrelated to the category. A 0 would mean an item that is truly borderline. In testing a number of categories of this type, Hampton discovered many violations of the conjunctive rule. These violations were primarily *overextensions*, cases in which an item was not in one of the components but was judged to be in the conjunction. For example, chess is not considered to be a sport, but it was considered to be a sport that is also a game. Overextensions of this sort—items that were a member of one component and not the other—were quite common for some categories (e.g., as high as 45% of the items). There were even a few cases in which an item was in *neither* of the component categories but was considered to be in the conjunction. That would be a double violation of the extensional intersection rule. Less frequent than the overextensions were *underextensions*, when an item was considered to be in the two component categories but not in the conjunction. However, they also occurred about 8% of the time. Some of these cases might arise simply through errors or inattention. Perhaps a subject wasn't thinking very carefully when saying that chess was not a sport and then was more accurate when deciding that it was a sport that is also a game (or vice versa). Hampton showed that such errors could not account for the pattern of results. In particular, such errors should have produced many fewer overextensions than were actually observed. If one takes underextensions as indicating simple errors or changes in people's opinion, then this rate of changes cannot explain the much higher rate of overextensions. Conversely, if the overextensions are taken as indicating errors, then there should have been many more underextensions.

In addition to these explicit conjunctive concepts, Hampton (1988b, Experiment 1) showed that similar effects were found for noun-noun concepts like school furniture and sports vehicles. That is, subjects sometimes rated items as examples of school furniture even though they did not rate them as a kind of furniture. For example, a blackboard is considered to be an example of school furniture but not of furniture alone. If school furniture is the intersection of furniture with some other category (things that are found in schools, perhaps), then such overextensions should not have occurred. Yet 24% of the items tested were overextended in this way.

Why do we get these overextensions? There are two related answers. One answer requires a discussion of the feature-listing experiments to be discussed shortly. The other answer is based solely on the typicality data. Basically, when an item is a typical member of one category, perhaps this can "pull up" the score in the conjunction even when it is not a member of the other category. That is, rather than requiring that an item be in both categories, people are almost taking an average of the typicality scores of the two categories. A bad score in one category can be made up by a very good score in another. For example, items that were rated −2 in games (recall that the negative scores mean that the item was not a category member) were generally not considered to be in sports that are also games. However, if an item was rated −2 in games but +3 in sports, then it was generally thought to be in the conjunction after all. If an item was rated a −1 in games, then a rating of +2 or +3 in sports was sufficient to pull it into the conjunction (Hampton 1988b, table 3). Rather than applying two definitions to the item to get the conjunctive category, people may be averaging their criteria. Although chess is a pretty crummy sport, it is an excellent game, and this makes it close enough to be a sport that is also a game. Perhaps, then, people are literally averaging typicality (though another explanation is possible, to be discussed shortly).

Hampton (1996) provided further evidence for this typicality explanation by using visual categories that did not involve complex knowledge or interacting properties (as discussed below). Therefore, the only cause of overextensions was the typicality structure of the concepts. For example, he created stimuli that varied in shape from A to H and that varied in color from blue to green. For such items he found that subjects overextended the letter value 36% of the time. That is, some items that were not called As were nonetheless called blue As (when they were very blue) or green As (when they were very green). Thus, people are not following a logical rule in which something is in the category X *and* Y only when it is independently verified as being in the category X and in the category Y.

The second explanation has to do with the conceptual representation that people construct out of descriptions like "sport that is also a game." Hampton (1987) asked subjects to list properties of combinations and their components, and then other subjects rated their importance to the categories. He argued from these data that the combinations have many of the features of the old concepts, weighted by their importance in the old categories. If a feature was considered to be very important in one of the components, it was much more likely to be included in the conjunctive concept than if it wasn't considered important. Best yet was when it was considered to be important in both categories (so, pets that are also birds would have to be living creatures, since this is true of both categories). This results in a new concept that is not exactly the same as either one of the originals, and so it is possible for an item to be more typical of the conjunctive concept than it is of either of the components.

Hampton (1987) found some evidence for emergent features (similar to the properties true of combinations that are not true of the components in modifier-noun concepts, discussed above). For example, people said that birds that are also pets have the property "talks," even though birds and pets by themselves did not have that property. The opposite pattern, *feature cancellation*, can also occur. For example, subjects list "migrates" as a property for birds, but do not think that it is a property for birds that are also pets. Hampton (1987) argues that such features arise through extensional feedback and coherence preservation. The extensional feedback occurs as one thinks of examples of pets that are birds that one has known ("I remember my aunt's parakeet that she used to feed by hand"). These examples can be used to provide properties for the concept ("fed by hand") that were not stored with the component concepts. Coherence preservation works in a number of ways. One is to exclude incompatible features. Although pets are usually cuddly, fish by their nature are not. Therefore, subjects reason that pet fish could not be cuddly. Simply making a fish a pet does not affect the sliminess of its surface. (I am assuming that slimy things cannot be cuddly. If your intuition is otherwise, I advise you to keep it to yourself.) Similarly, although most birds migrate, an animal cannot be a pet if it is allowed to fly away for half the year, and so this aspect of birds must be cancelled in birds that are also pets. Hampton (1987, p. 66) provided some evidence that subjects were indeed engaging in reasoning about the consistency of different properties in making their property lists for the conjunctive concepts. Of course, the degree to which this occurs probably depends on the particular concepts. Some concepts may have few feature interactions (e.g., red and square), whereas others may have many complex interactions, due to the large amount of knowledge we have about both (e.g., intellectual and salesperson).

Social concepts seem likely to involve such complex interactions, as shown by Kunda, Miller, and Claire's (1990) study of combinations such as feminist bankteller, Harvard-educated carpenter, and blind marathon runner. They found evidence of many emergent properties, which could not be explained based on the component concepts. They further argued that such properties arose through the construction of causal narratives, in which people attempted to answer questions such as "Why would someone with a degree from Harvard become a carpenter?" The answers to these questions produced emergent properties that were not previously associated to the two concepts (e.g., "perhaps the person became dissatisfied with the rat race"). Interestingly, they found that such emergent features were most likely when the combination was surprising. For example, Harvard-educated lawyer did not generate emergent features, but Harvard-educated carpenter did. Thus, the novel features may come about through an attempt to explain a surprising combination. They suggest that Hampton would have found more emergent properties if he had used more surprising combinations than sports that are also games.

Theoretical Evaluations

Models of Conceptual Combination

The selective modification model of Smith and colleagues provides a good account of typicality phenomena, and it does well with certain simple adjectives. However, many other phenomena of conceptual combination simply cannot be accommodated by this model. Adjectives appear to modify a number of dimensions of the head noun, and which dimension they modify depends on the noun. Nonpredicating adjectives and nouns do not directly pick out a slot to modify, and so the model cannot say which slot they might modify. The conceptual combination process, then, is more complex than this model allows, even if it is correct in terms of explaining certain typicality phenomena.

Hampton's model has a similar problem, in that it addresses conjunctive and disjunctive concepts well, but it does not seem to handle other forms of modification, such as those using nonpredicating adjectives and noun modifiers. For example, a typewriter table does not have the most important properties of typewriters; a tiger squirrel may have stripes, but it lacks the other important features of tigers. Hampton's suggestion that combinations have features of the components, weighted by their importance in each component, may hold for phrases like *typewriters that are also tables* but not for most noun-noun phrases like *typewriter table*.

The concept specialization model (Murphy 1988) admits of many more kinds of modifiers and forms of modification. By allowing knowledge processing into the basic decisions of which slot to modify and by referring to elaboration of the concept, many of the phenomena that troubled the selective modification model could be accounted for. However, Wisniewski's (1997) property mapping interpretations do cause a problem. In *tiger squirrel*, the tiger concept does not fill a slot of the squirrel concept; instead, one of its attributes is applied to the concept. Furthermore, the radical cases of construal that Wisniewski mentions seem somewhat inconsistent with all models.

At this point, then, an even broader and more powerful theory of conceptual combination seems called for—one that can change the concepts involved (e.g., a plastic truck is not a real truck, but a toy) and that can permit very different forms of combination, including property and relational interpretations. Wisniewski's (1997) proposal is a kind of parallel model in which different sorts of interpretations are considered at the same time (and see Wisniewski and Love 1998). However, as these are very different kinds of interpretations, this does not seem to be a very coherent kind of model—not that I have any better suggestion. One problem in building a more powerful model is that eventually such a model could come up with interpretations that are too remote. For example, what is to stop such a model from claiming that a tiger squirrel is a statue of a squirrel that is made from a tiger, or a kind of toy squirrel that tigers like to play with? Once one allows the modifier and head noun to be construed as meaning different things, and if one allows many different relations to connect the two concepts, the model may generate more different interpretations for a phrase than people would accept. The answer is probably that multiple constraints (property salience, availability of alternative interpretations, plausibility) combine to rule out some interpretations and favor others. The difficulty is in incorporating all those constraints simultaneously into a single model. This is a problem for the future, however, as the current problem is that no model handles all the forms of combinations that people generate.

Finally, the detailed time-course of interpreting combinations needs much more work. The surprising results of Springer and Murphy (1992) do not fit very well with any model either. It is possible that such results can be explained away (e.g., as a function of the task of feature verification rather than a true reflection of the construction of a concept), but that also needs to be demonstrated more fully.

In short, most of the proposed models do seem to have a grain of truth in them. What is lacking is a more comprehensive model that can explain the many different forms of interpretations that have been observed in real-life conceptual combination.

Implications for General Models of Concepts

The most prominent models of conceptual combination assume a schema structure for concepts (Murphy 1988; Smith et al. 1988; Wisniewski 1997). Although researchers like Gagné and Shoben (1997) do not propose a specific conceptual representation, it is clear that they are assuming a summary representation of the concept as a whole. As described in chapter 3, schemata are a more elaborate and structured form of a prototype. They include the typical properties of items, weighted by their frequency and/or distinctiveness, but the relations between the properties are more directly represented and constrained than in the simple feature list of earlier models (Smith and Medin 1981). Hampton (1987, 1997) also appears to be assuming a prototype representation, as he refers to lists of features in describing category representations. Although such lists may be adequate for the conjunctive and disjunctive categories he has investigated (like games that are also sports), more elaborate structures are probably needed for more complex concepts like skunk cabbage, corporate stationery, or fork spoon. In general, though, all of these proposals are consistent with some version of prototype theory, in which a new concept of some kind is constructed from the summary representations of the component concepts.

The construction of a new prototype appears able to account for the overextensions and underextensions found by Hampton (1988b). Typicality averaging by itself cannot account for all the data, because it says nothing about the feature inheritance of conceptual combinations just described (e.g., why birds that are pets do not migrate). Therefore, we might ask if we can do away with the notion of typicality averaging and account for the main results through the formation of a conjunction prototype. Consider an apparent case of typicality averaging: the item that is not generally recognized as an A but that is accepted as a blue A. This item could be more similar to the blue A concept than it is to the A concept alone, because it matches the color feature of the former (which is particularly emphasized in the combination), but the latter has no such feature. Thus, construction of a new combination prototype can explain the overextension and underextension data without requiring that subjects calculate typicalities to each component concept and then average them.

More generally, these kinds of phenomena are consistent with a prototype model in which concepts are represented as a summary description, probably a structured one like a schema.

Notable by its absence in this chapter is any sign of exemplar models. The most natural exemplar theory of conceptual combination would be a kind of extensional model. That is, the concept of pet dogs would be the intersection of remembered dogs and remembered pets. However, as has become clear, this sort of intersection is simply wrong for the majority of noun-noun concepts, as well as for most non-predicating adjective-noun concepts, as a typewriter table is not the intersection of typewriters and tables, and corporate stationery is not the intersection of corporations and stationery (nor is it the intersection of "corporate things" and stationery, as discussed above).

One would expect that in cases where the concepts *could be* intersective, they would be, if the exemplar view were true. For example, one could argue that the category of red apples is simply the intersection of remembered red things and apples. No one has investigated whether an exemplar model could predict the typicality findings of Smith et al. (1988), whose adjective-noun phrases are of this sort. It is possible that by taking the intersection of remembered red things and remembered apples, one could arrive at a set of red apples that would then produce the conjunction and reverse conjunction effects. That is, an actual red apple might be more similar to this set than to the entire set of apple exemplars one remembers. Smith et al. predicted their typicality data by a very different means, more in keeping with prototype views (i.e., looking at how often people listed features for a concept as a whole), but that does not mean that an exemplar model could not also account for these data. However, such models would have considerable problems with the cases of overextension and underextension, as when school furniture includes objects that are not categorized as furniture. Hampton's research has documented many such cases. Similarly, the many cases documented by Hampton, Murphy, and others of emergent features are inconsistent with exemplar views, since features could not make their way into the combination unless they were in the component exemplars to begin with. Furthermore, the effects of context on interpretation of combinations are more consistent with the activation of general knowledge rather than specific exemplars (see Gagné 1997; Gerrig and Murphy 1992; Murphy 1990).

My conclusion is that conceptual combination very often requires abstract representation of an entire category, and so an exemplar representation is simply not going to be the right sort of thing to understand a novel concept that may not pick out a class of objects that we have encountered, or even thought of before. We need this abstract representation of concepts in order to understand that a typewriter table is a table designed to support a typewriter (at the correct height for typing, with a place to put material being typed, etc.)—that is, to represent the relation between tables and typewriters. This is an abstract kind of relation that does not refer to a relation between particular exemplars (e.g., the fact that my typewriter is in a closet that is 30 feet away from my dining room table). To represent this kind of abstract idea, we need more representational detail than exemplar models have so far provided.

The knowledge approach to concepts comes out quite well in this chapter. It is generally acknowledged that in order to understand many noun-noun concepts, people must find a relation between the nouns that is plausible with respect to whatever else they know. An apartment dog is certainly not a dog that has an apartment for a head, nor is it a dog that eats apartments, nor is it a dog used as an apartment. Linguists have argued that there is in principle an infinite number of interpretations of any noun-noun phrase (see Clark 1983; Kay and Zimmer 1976). Somehow, people find a relationship between the two that makes sense, often without even noticing that other interpretations would be possible.[11] If Wisniewski and Love (1998) are right that feature interpretations and relational interpretations are considered in parallel, background knowledge may be an important variable in deciding which one is best. Knowledge effects can be most easily seen when one takes the same word as a modifier and then combines it with different nouns (or vice versa)—as in table 12.1. Here, one can see that the interpretation of the word varies as it is combined with different terms, in order to make the resulting concept more coherent. This process of construal (Wisniewski 1997; and see examples in Murphy 1988) is a direct reflection of the use of general knowledge. One knows that a stone squirrel is likely to be a statue rather than a real squirrel, because of one's knowledge of animals and statues, and the fact that it is possible to carve a squirrel shape out of stone. One does not think that a tiger squirrel is a statue of a squirrel carved out of tiger. Furthermore, even the simple feature-listing task for conjunctive concepts shows some effects of knowledge in making the combination more coherent than it would be if features were simply added to the concept willy-nilly (Hampton 1987).

Direct evidence for knowledge being used in constructing conceptual combinations was found by Johnson and Keil (2000). I describe it here, because it focuses more on how knowledge is involved than on any particular model of conceptual combination.

Johnson and Keil argued that representing combinations as lists of features can be somewhat misleading about the conceptual structure underlying them. In particular, theoretical knowledge, which often explains and links different properties, is likely not to appear in such lists, since it is difficult for people to access and write down in a brief phrase. To demonstrate this, Johnson and Keil started off with 12 noun-noun combinations consisting of a modifier that was an environment (e.g., mountain, laboratory), and a head noun that was a natural kind or artifact (e.g., mouse, bicycle). In an initial study, they asked subjects to list features of either the nouns or the combination. They found a large number of emergent features with their items. In fact, 40% of the combination features that subjects listed were not mentioned by *any* subject for their nouns. For example, arctic bicycles were said to have spiked tires, but this was not listed by subjects for either individual concept.

Johnson and Keil suspected that many of these emergent features were generated by underlying explanations. For example, for a bicycle to work in an arctic environment, it would have to maintain traction somehow on ice and snow. Therefore, its tires must be modified from usual bicycle tires—hence, spiked tires. Subjects simply list the outcome of such reasoning processes, but Johnson and Keil argued that the knowledge behind this reasoning is part of the conceptual structure. To discover what kind of reasoning was used, Johnson and Keil selected an emergent feature for each combination and asked new subjects to explain why it was true. They did this by giving subjects problems of the form:

Since the ARCTIC _____

and since BICYCLES _____

then arctic bicycles have spiked tires.

Subjects had to fill in the relevant facts about the arctic environment and bicycles. Not surprisingly, most of the features listed here had not been listed in the first experiment. That is, subjects listed properties like "require traction to move" for bicycles, but this was not a feature listed for bicycles in isolation. Johnson and Keil noted that many of these properties were longer phrases that included terms like "need to," "requires," "enables," "in order to," and so on. These are exactly the sort of causal links involving underlying knowledge that they had proposed.

Table 12.3.
Procedure of Johnson and Keil (2000), Experiment 3.

---

1. Rate:
   "Arctic rodents are white"
2. Rate either:
   (Theory) "Arctic rodent must blend in"
   (Feature) "Arctic rodent has fur" .
3. Read fact discounting the feature in part 2.
   (Theory) Arctic rodents' smell repels predators.
   (Feature) Arctic rodents have a naked hide.
4. Re-rate original statement:
   "Arctic rodents are white"

But these features were listed after specific elicitation, given the emergent feature (spiked tires). This does not mean that people thought of these underlying properties *while* generating the emergent properties initially. Perhaps they were only generated after the fact. One way to discover if one property is part of a causal connection to another property is to deny it. When a causally relevant property is eliminated, the effect should be reduced or eliminated. If heat is necessary to start a fire, then reducing the heat should reduce the probability of a fire starting. Following this reasoning, Johnson and Keil's last experiment asked subjects to rate emergent properties before and after one of the causal links was denied. If subjects were using the causal links, then denying them should eliminate the emergent features.

As table 12.3 shows, the procedure involved first rating the critical feature (e.g., arctic bicycles have spiked wheels) and the underlying causal feature derived from the previous study. Then subjects were told (in the experimental group) a "fact" that discounted that function for the feature. For example, subjects might be told that arctic bicycles are propelled by jets (so they wouldn't need traction to move—though this was not pointed out). Then subjects were asked to rate the critical feature again, in light of this new fact. The control condition denied another property of the concept, which was not causally related to the emergent feature. (The causal and control features were equally true of the concepts.) The main dependent measure was how much the rating of the critical feature changed after the discounting fact was presented. The results showed that subjects lowered their ratings of this feature by about 3 points on 9-point scale after the discounting, but there was little effect of discounting an unrelated feature.

Thus, although rather complex in its design, the Johnson and Keil study is important in that it gives strong evidence for the importance of explanation-type background knowledge or theories in constructing combinations. They showed (as have many others) that conceptual combinations have emergent features that are not true of their components. But they went further in showing that these combinations appear to arise from relational, causal explanations from the background knowledge of the domain. This work is reinforced by the findings of Kunda et al. (1990) mentioned above, who found emergent properties in social categories like blind marathon runner. They argued that these properties arose through causal reasoning (evoked by asking questions such as "how could a blind person run a marathon?"). Finally, Murphy and Andrew (1993) found evidence for causal reasoning in a task in which subjects provided opposites of adjectives in combinations. For example, one subject said that the opposite of *bloody face* was *untouched face*. This response gives evidence of causal reasoning. *Untouched* is not the opposite of *bloody* in isolation, but it would form part of a causal explanation. If a face were untouched, it would not become bloody, and so *untouched* would contradict a causal antecedent of *bloody*.

In summary, conceptual combination seems to be a knowledge-intensive process that involves coordinating rich conceptual representations. In particular, causal reasoning may be an important determinant of the new concept. Thus, this domain is one of the strongest pieces of evidence for prototype models and knowledge approaches. As pointed out earlier, knowledge may be involved in a number of ways in conceptual combination. First, for relational concepts such as typewriter table, knowledge is involved in deciding what slot of the head concept the modifier fits. Second, when there are a number of different possible interpretations available, knowledge may be used to choose the most plausible one. And third, knowledge is involved in elaborating the concept and deriving novel features for it, including some which may not be represented in the constituent concepts. Based on the evidence described here, then, conceptual combination is a process that is saturated with causal reasoning and knowledge-based processing.

13

Anti-Summary and Conclusions

Those readers who have struggled along through the whole book deserve to hear the answer now about the correct theory of concepts, which has no doubt clearly emerged from the review of the major topics in the field. Or maybe it hasn't. Before the answer is revealed, it would be traditional to summarize the main points that have arisen through the reviews in the preceding chapters. However, such a summary would be extremely heterogeneous, given the wide range of topics the book has covered, and would be rather less comprehensible than the original reviews. Therefore, I would like to do an anti-summary at this point instead. That is, I will summarize some things that have *not* in fact been reviewed in the book—at least, not in the detail they deserve. This is partly to alleviate some of my guilt in ignoring them but also to warn the unwary reader of the biases and limitations of the present review that should not be attributed to the field as a whole. The conclusions offered later in this chapter are based on the review in the rest of the book, and issues that were not covered in that review have had less impact on the conclusions than perhaps they ought. Those who are less interested in finding out what they have missed can skip to the next section.

Topics Uncovered

As this book has been organized around major phenomena involving concepts (see chapter 1), a number of perspectives on concepts have fallen between the cracks. In some cases, this is due simply to lack of space and time. But in many cases, it is due to the topic not fitting into the book's overall structure and narrative. For example, certain theoretical battles that have received a lot of attention in the field may not have received as much attention here, if the battle was not related to a particular topic or empirical issue.

Models

There are a number of interesting and important models of categorization, category learning, induction, and other conceptual processes. (By *model*, I mean a mathematical, computational, or other formal statement of a theory.) I have mentioned a few of them in passing, but I have mostly not attempted to cover the details of current models. The context model and the Generalized Context Model were discussed in some detail as the standard ways of embodying exemplar theory. However, Hintzman's (1986) Minerva model (which unfortunately has not been updated recently) and Kruschke's (1992) ALCOVE models are two other exemplar models that I have not addressed. ALCOVE has been especially successful and is well deserving of study. Estes (1994) presents a book-long description of his array model. There have been a few prototype-based models as well, many within a connectionist framework, such as Anderson and Murphy (1986), Gluck and Bower (1988), McClelland and Rumelhart (1985), and Smith and Minda (2000). The work of Ashby, Maddox, and colleagues on decision-boundary models does not fit in with the main themes of the book and has unfortunately been almost entirely omitted; see Ashby and Maddox (1993) and Ashby, Alfonso-Reese, Turken, and Waldron (1998).

One reason I have not spent more time on such models, which are of intense interest to the contemporary researcher, is that they are all wrong. Of course, that is true of all our current theories, and developing a model for a theory is one way of finding out just how it is wrong. More important, most of the models are limited to a single kind of situation or concept type. Most are directed toward concept learning but have nothing to say about induction, hierarchical structure, word meaning, or conceptual combination. Similarly, models of induction, say, like those of Osherson et al. (1990) or Sloman (1993) do not attempt to account for concept learning, word meaning, or conceptual combination.

The researchers who make these models seem to recognize their limitations, because some of them have also built different models with apparently contradictory assumptions about how concepts are represented (e.g., Nosofsky's RULEX model, Nosofsky, Palmeri, and McKinley 1994; and Kruschke's ADIT model, Kruschke 1996). There is nothing wrong with making different models to suit different situations. This may be a necessary step in coming to an ultimate explanation of conceptual structure. However, to draw conclusions about concepts in general, it is necessary to look more broadly than at a single paradigm. Indeed, it will be seen below that one of the main problems with current theories is that they are not applied to enough of the available phenomena for us to know exactly what their predictions are in each area. Thus, the goal for many approaches at this point is not to develop more detailed models but to broaden their scope so as to account for more phenomena.

That said, readers should be aware that many publications in today's journals are of the sort "I found phenomenon X, which so-and-so's model cannot explain." It is just this use of models to generate new phenomena and ideas that makes them important, even if the lifespan of most models is short.

Perception

There is a lot of action in perception. There are two aspects to this. One is that much interesting research is being done on categorization and perceptual judgments and how they interact with concepts. The research of Goldstone (Goldstone 1994a, 2000; Goldstone and Steyvers 2001; Schyns, Goldstone, and Thibaut 1998) is one good example. Goldstone has shown how learning concepts can change perceptual units. For example, perceptual discrimination is heightened along category boundaries. He argues that category learners can form new perceptual dimensions that correspond to the (otherwise arbitrary) discriminations necessary to learn categories. Similarly, the research of Schyns and his collaborators has addressed the interaction of perceptual units with concept acquisition (e.g., Schyns and Murphy 1994; Schyns and Rodet 1997). Other work has looked at lower-level visual properties, such as spatial frequency scales, and categorization (Oliva and Schyns 1997).

Much of this work criticizes the view that perceptual features precede concepts. In most theories, the concept-learning device takes in category exemplars as described by a preexisting vocabulary of features, and it then outputs a category description in terms of those features. Instead, these researchers argue that learning must occur at the perceptual level as well; the features themselves must be constructed, often in parallel with category learning.

I think that this work is important and fascinating. I described some of it in chapter 6, and the only reason I did not dwell on it further is because much of the research addresses real-time categorization and perceptual processes that are not the focus of this book. Readers interested in those issues could take Schyns et al. (1998) as a starting point.

A second approach to perception is a more theoretically controversial one. This is the notion that concept representations should be thought of as perceptual rather than symbolic. In varying ways, these concerns have been raised by Linda Smith and her collaborators (Jones and Smith 1993; Smith and Heise 1992) and by Barsalou and his students (Barsalou 1999; Barsalou et al. 1993). Part of this approach is a reaction to the rise of knowledge-based research, and part of it is a question about where symbolic thought comes from. If our symbolic representations are not all innately given, it is argued, then they may well come from perceptual representations.

I have incorporated parts of this debate when it came up in chapter 10, but I haven't dealt with it in and of itself. I suspect that the argument about whether concepts and knowledge are really perceptual or symbolic will turn out not to be a substantive issue, but instead an argument about what should be called "perceptual." Jones and Smith (1993), for example, argue that what have been seen as inferences from knowledge ("it's an animal, so it probably has a distinctive color") could be thought instead of as context effects on the salience of perceptual dimensions, thereby being a perceptual phenomenon. Again, this strikes me as a difference in how the effect is talked about—not the underlying explanation. In either case, people draw different conclusions based on some information they have, and the mechanism underlying that effect must be elucidated.

However, the question of how abstract categories may develop out of perceptual origins (Barsalou et al. 1993; Mandler 1998; Quinn and Eimas 1997) is a very important one, although it is not something that we yet know very much about. If it can be shown that abstract symbols develop from simpler image schemata, this would provide an important explanation of development. Another concern in this area is whether theories of concepts adequately represent conceptual features. We often simplify features by treating as identical things that are called by the same name. For example, I have a leg, and so does a dog, and so does the desk I'm working at. In most experiments, these legs would be considered the same feature in all three concepts, in part because subjects would list them using the same word ("has two/four legs"). However, these things look very different, in spite of their common name (see discussion of polysemy, chapter 11). Are such perceptual differences important? Solomon and Barsalou (2001) have found evidence that the particular perceptual configuration of the leg is accessed when we think about the concept. That is, when you think about whether a dog has a leg, you think of a dog-leg, not a person-leg or desk-leg. And once you've thought of the dog's leg, you find it somewhat harder to confirm that desks have legs, because they look so different. What is impressive is that their effects were not achieved with pictures, but with words, suggesting that the perceptual representation of legs was accessed even when the verbal label was used.

Related to this issue is the claim that categories often have perceptual properties that do not appear in feature lists, because they are abstract or not easily verbalizable. For example, animals and artifacts may differ in their texture, and the motion of animals may look different from that of machines (Massey and Gelman 1988;

Smith and Heise 1992). It is possible that there is much more perceptual common-ality to natural categories than we realize from feature lists and than many experi-mental situations reflect.

In short, the emphasis on perception and the perceptual structure of concepts and their features is an up-and-coming topic. My guess is that if this book is revised in 10 years, this topic might deserve its own chapter or (even better) that the findings on perceptual coding and learning would be interleaved with the other topics in this book.

Similarity

The study of concepts has long been tied up with the study of similarity, because of the general notion that concepts contain entities that are similar (see Murphy and Medin 1985). In fact, one way to organize a more theoretically oriented review of concepts would be to start with theories of similarity and use them as the motivation for various theories of concepts (I have used this organization in a course on con-cepts). For example, traditional exemplar and prototype theory are generally con-sistent with Tverskian conceptions of similarity as consisting of overlapping features (Tversky 1977). Knowledge-based approaches may be more consistent with recent approaches that view similarity as a constructive process in which two representa-tions are structurally compared (Markman and Gentner 1993; Medin, Goldstone, and Gentner 1993).

I have not presented the material in this way, largely because it requires taking a certain theoretical stance about how concepts should be explained, whereas the book is organized around phenomena (see chapter 1). So, similarity has come up from time to time but has not been a major focus of discussion. However, the reader should be warned that to be fully literate in this field one must also be familiar with the research on similarity, starting from Tversky's seminal paper, and going through the more recent research by Gentner, Goldstone, Arthur Markman, and Medin.

Other Cultures

As in all psychology, the vast majority of research done on concepts has used American undergraduate students as its subjects. Assuming that the principles of concept learning are fairly constant, there is no harm done. But, to the degree that they aren't, then this fact can only hide the full richness of conceptual struc-tures. Perhaps related to this narrowness of subject selection is the use of simple, abstract materials such as dot patterns, color patches, or circles with lines through them. Again, if concept learning is constant across materials, then no harm is done.

Unfortunately, much of this book has shown that concept learning can change across domains, and a number of examples of differences across subject populations have been found as well (e.g., induction, use of taxonomic categories, and the basic level). There has recently been a very welcome increase in research studying such population differences, much of it carried out by Douglas Medin and his colleagues. In some respects, principles of categorization are fairly constant across cultures (see Malt 1995, for a review). However, in other respects, specific understandings of a domain and specific reasoning practices lead to important differences between populations (e.g., Coley, Medin, and Atran 1997; Proffitt, Coley, and Medin 2000; see Medin and Atran 1999, for a collection of papers). For example, as discussed in chapter 8, Proffitt et al. (2000) found that tree experts did not rely on similarity to draw inductions about disease possession but instead used a more thematic reasoning strategy based on ecosystems and patterns of disease transmission. One intriguing interpretation of their results is that the more subjects knew about the domain, the less likely they are to rely on similarity of categories as specified in the standard theories of induction. That is, the more people are involved in a domain, the less our experiments apply to them.

The anthropological nature of this work makes it difficult to carry out, but I think is is critical to do so in order to understand the limitations of our theories developed in the lab with middle-class American subjects. I have discussed this anthropological work at various points as it became relevant, and so it was not really "uncovered" in the way that some of these other topics were. However, this work is important enough that it could have received its own chapter, and since it didn't, I want to bring readers' attention to it here.

Some people object to anthropological approaches on the grounds that we cannot explain differences in cultures and populations in any coherent way (cf. Fodor's 1983, "First Law of the Nonexistence of Cognitive Science"). If we need separate theories to explain the Tzeltal Mayans, American undergraduates, French vintners, tree experts, and so on, then we will not really have a theory of concepts. Of course, this argument is telling us not to ask the question because we won't like the answer—it is not an argument that the question itself is not worth asking. Furthermore, the idea that if we study N cultures we may end up with N theories of concepts is overly pessimistic. With any luck, there will be an overarching explanation of how and why such differences exist—not separate theories for each population. For every culture to have a unique set of principles underlying their concepts is unbelievable. However, if we simply stay within one kind of setting, it will be impossible to see the influence of factors that are constant within that setting. It may only be by studying different settings that one can even notice that there is variation on some dimension and that that dimension is important (e.g., see the discussion of cultural differences in chapter 6). Thus, the anthropological approach can greatly broaden our understanding of all the variables that eventually result in our conceptual system.[1]

Summary[2]

No book can cover everything in any field of psychology—no field that it is worth writing a book about, anyway. The omissions and emphases of the present book reflect my current beliefs about what is most important in the field, my own knowledge and interests, and my decision to structure the book around phenomena rather than current theorizing. I believe (i.e., hope) that this decision will make the book more relevant and useful years from now than if I had taken the opposite tack, as even the most significant theories often have a tendency of becoming less and less relevant over the years. Nonetheless, a major goal of the present book has been to see how the main theoretical approaches explain each of the phenomena presented, and it is their evaluation that I address next.

Theoretical Evaluations

Well, it can't be put off forever: How do the main theoretical alternatives stand up to the topics I have reviewed? In answering this question, I will refer to the conclusions of the individual chapters without citing specifics, which would cause unbearable redundancy. If some of these judgments seem puzzling, refer to the relevant chapter for the complete discussion.

First, everyone can agree (albeit briefly) that the classical theory, claiming that concepts are represented by definitions, is a total flop. Not only did it fail in the respects it has traditionally been criticized for—unclear category members and typicality judgments—it also has not generated a clear story of other major topics such as the basic level, conceptual development, exemplar effects, and so on. In some cases, this failure could possibly arise because no one has tried to provide such an explanation, but in others it is likely that there is no plausible account starting from the classical view.

The three main theories under consideration, the exemplar, prototype, and knowledge approaches, all do somewhat better. In comparing them, it must be understood that there is no full-scale theory coming from any of these approaches that encompasses all the topics I have discussed. That is, there is no specific prototype theory, for example, instantiated in a computational model or just a set of assumptions, that provides an account of induction, infant concepts, typicality, the basic level, word meaning, and so on. Instead, researchers working on infant concepts, say, have developed explanations of their data, which we can look at and identify as being consistent with the prototype view. A different researcher has developed explanations of induction, which also appear to be consistent with the prototype view. However, there is no guarantee that the prototype explanation suggested for infant concepts is consistent with the induction explanation. They could make different assumptions about the nature of the conceptual representation, the causes of typicality effects, exactly what information is stored in the prototype, and so on. It may be that such assumptions could be reconciled, or that some are not truly necessary to explain the phenomena in one case. But maybe not. In this way, all three approaches are a bit suspect, because the lack of an integrated theory means that contradictions may not be identified. This situation is probably to be expected at the field's present level of development. Nonetheless, absence of an integrated theory is a large grain of salt which should be savored throughout the subsequent discussion.

Both prototype and exemplar views do well in accounting for the general phenomena of typicality effects that caused trouble for the classical view, so that does not distinguish them. The exemplar view seems to have the majority of the evidence in its favor when category-learning experiments are considered. That is, the majority of the comparisons of the two approaches have come out in favor of the exemplar model over the prototype model. Also, one must count the existence of exemplar-reminding effects in categorization as generally supporting an exemplar view, though exemplar-reminding during learning (e.g., Ross's experiments) was not as supportive. One could object to both these conclusions, and the recent research of J. David Smith and Paul Minda (2000) suggests that the preponderance of evidence currently in favor of the exemplar view may not hold up indefinitely. Furthermore, it does seem to be the case that exemplar models do particularly well in situations that encourage the learning of specific exemplars—i.e., the typical category-learning experiment with a difficult structure and a small number of items to be learned. We need to go beyond this traditional head-to-head comparison to consider how each view accounts for the rest of the phenomena covered here.

Exemplar Approach
In the other areas covered by the book, the exemplar model has not done as well. Knowledge effects of all sorts do not seem to be explainable by exemplar knowledge as a general rule. I will expand on this point below. A major problem is the difficulty

in coming up with *any* exemplar account of hierarchical structure. The fact that people know that all dogs are mammals (and use this kind of information spontaneously in induction, for example) is surprisingly difficult to represent in terms of exemplars, except through some unpleasant assumptions, such as every exemplar being encoded with all its potential categories. No one has made that assumption in print (that I know of), and for good reason. Furthermore, even if this problem is ignored, it is not clear that the similarity principles underlying exemplar learning of categories can explain the basic-level advantage in categorization. The problem is not to find some set of parameters that can produce the advantage (e.g., see Palmeri 1999) but to find a set of parameters that can allow categorization at very abstract and very specific levels simultaneously *and* that generate the basic-level advantage.

Induction also poses a problem for exemplar models. First, the fact that people spontaneously use superordinate categories in solving induction problems means that the lack of a story about hierarchical structure causes a corresponding problem here. Furthermore, the approach is computationally suspect, because in order to determine inductions, one must compare exemplars of a number of different categories. Given that these categories can be very large, comparison times would have to be extremely long, and they are not. Finally, the model simply has no very easy way of representing novel information like "All birds have sesamoid bones" in order to draw conclusions. I do not feel confident in saying that the exemplar view cannot do these things, as exemplar theorists have not addressed the main phenomena in induction. It is possible that some clever solution is out there but has not yet been published.

In the area of infant concepts, I suspect that exemplar models could explain the results, because the experiments are mostly just the sort that the models were designed to explain: category-learning studies of a small set of items. For cognitive development of older children, the picture is less clear, in part because few attempts have been made to explain the phenomena in this large field by exemplar models. The findings of Markman, Keil, Carey, Gelman, and others showing that children use knowledge and may be essentialists about category membership do not comport well with the exemplar view. Children's ability to learn a category based on one or two exemplars also seems to go beyond the assumptions of the exemplar view (i.e., they are actively hypothesizing about the category, not just using similarity to the given exemplar). To the degree that the exemplar view has trouble with hierarchical classification and induction in adults, it will have trouble explaining them in children as well. In short, although the exemplar view might be able to explain a number of the phenomena here, the necessary theorizing and empirical support have not been given. I don't believe that any major researcher in conceptual development is an exemplar theorist, which could be a reflection of how well researchers in this area believe an exemplar theory would explain their own data.

The exemplar view has serious problems with conceptual combination and word meaning. In conceptual combination, it is often the case that the exemplars picked out by the combination are not the intersection of the exemplars picked out by the components. Furthermore, the exemplar view does not do well in explaining the changes in the features of the component concepts (e.g., why pet birds talk, if most pets and birds don't talk; why an apartment dog is smaller than a normal dog). It has nothing to say about the difference between relational and property-mapping modification. In terms of word use more generally, I don't see how an exemplar view will provide a theory of polysemy, because the exemplars of different senses of a word are often not overlapping or even similar. For example, the exemplars of the furniture sense of *table* will not overlap with or have much similarity with the exemplars of the textual presentation sense ("Table 1"). There is an abstract semantic relation between these senses, rather than a relation among the exemplars that the senses pick out. Similarly, the notion of contextual modulation does not seem to have an exemplar explanation. Here I do not think that it is a matter of insufficient attention being paid to the question by exemplar theorists but that such phenomena fall outside the realm of any reasonable exemplar view. The relations among word senses and the modulation of context must be explained in terms of semantic structures and not in terms of the referents of a word.

Prototype Approach

The prototype view (obviously) explains the phenomena of typicality and fuzzy categories, which were the reasons it was brought into existence. Prototypes themselves do not handle exemplar effects particularly well, though I suggested that one might consider exemplar effects on categorization as reflecting an implicit categorization process rather than explicit use of the category. However, the head-to-head battles of exemplar and prototype theory in category-learning experiments are clearly the theory's weakest point.

Prototype theories in and of themselves do not explain knowledge effects. However, as I shall discuss below, they are more consistent with those effects than the exemplar view is, because conceptual knowledge is generally about entire categories of things. Biological knowledge is knowledge about entities like the class of mammals or of carnivores—summary representations just like prototypes. As prototypes are summary representations of an entire category (indeed, this is the critical difference between them and exemplars), integrating these two sources of information about concepts is easily done.

The prototype view has no trouble with either hierarchical structure or explaining basic categories. Indeed, the first studies of these topics were done by Rosch as part of her prototype theory of concepts. The differentiation explanation of the basic level I described is phrased in terms of summary representations. As pointed out in the induction chapter, virtually every theory of category-based induction has implicitly assumed a summary representation of concepts, so this work is consistent with prototypes. Similarly, research on concepts in infants and children have predominantly been phrased in terms of prototypes rather than exemplars. Thus, there would be no problem in integrating those accounts with prototype theory more generally.

Meaning and conceptual combination provide strong evidence for prototypes. I think that exemplar accounts of conceptual combination are demonstrably wrong, because the meaning of a phrase has to be composed from the meaning of its parts (plus broader knowledge), and it cannot be composed as a function of exemplars. Similarly, the relations among polysemic senses are based on descriptions of the senses (e.g., newspaper is printed on paper) rather than on similarity of the exemplars of the senses. These "descriptions of the senses" and "meanings of the parts" are basically the summary descriptions that prototype theory talks about.

Knowledge Approach

The virtues and defects of the knowledge approach can be summarized fairly succinctly. Almost every topic covered in this book has had some demonstration of knowledge effects. (Perhaps the only exception was the chapter on infant concepts, not surprisingly.) These effects are not accounted for by traditional exemplar and prototype approaches. In a number of places, it was shown that knowledge effects "beat out" purely empirical aspects of category structure (e.g., in category learning, see chapter 6; in induction reversals; and in Keil's transformation studies), suggesting that in some cases at least, knowledge effects can be more powerful than empirical category structure. Plausible reasoning's influence on conceptual combination and word meaning were ubiquitous. Indeed, in the linguistic domains, knowledge seems to be a driving factor. On the opposite side of the ledger, however, are those effects that do not appear to require knowledge. For example, the basic family resemblance analysis of typicality or the structural analysis of basic categories simply do not refer to knowledge, and yet do very well.[3] Some exemplar effects do not seem to involve knowledge. In general, the results accounted for by knowledge complement those accounted for by the other theories.

Analysis

If you've been keeping score, there is no clear, dominant winner. The prototype and knowledge approaches both have a number of victories notched on their belts, but by no means does either one account for everything. The exemplar approach has not done as well. It has a persistent edge in the traditional category-learning experiment but has gaps in its story in a number of phenomena and is disconfirmed by others. I will attempt to explain this entire pattern, but I must warn you that the result is not pretty.

Starting broadly, I will propose that our theory of concepts must be primarily prototype-based. That is, it must be a description of an entire concept, with its typical features (presumably weighted by their importance). However, this description must be part of a broader knowledge-representation scheme in which the concept is positioned both within a hierarchy (subordinates, superordinates, and coordinates) and within a theoretical framework (or frameworks) appropriate to that domain. The concept and its attributes will play a part in generalizations and hypotheses about the domain as a whole and in turn will be shaped by them. This proposal integrates the prototype and knowledge views so that it can account for the majority of the results reviewed in this book. The prototype aspect takes care of the purely structural findings, such as basic-level structure and some typicality effects, but when knowledge is useful in a task, the same representation leads to the activation of the relevant knowledge structure, which it is part of.

One way to think of this proposal is a simple division of labor in which there are category prototypes and there is knowledge, and each part takes care of its own portion of the data—prototypes handling the structural effects, and background knowledge handling the knowledge effects. However, I believe that a more integrated view of concepts is going to be required. That is, rather than considering the two parts as independent contributors, I suspect that we will have to consider prototypes as being integrated with and influenced by the knowledge. This influence goes in the other direction, too, as prototypes themselves constitute a major portion of our knowledge of the world. Although I am phrasing my proposal as "prototypes plus knowledge," the actual theory may be one in which conceptual information is a large knowledge structure, and the major concepts we use are simply nodes or subsections of that structure. These subsections would be summary representations of categories of objects that follow the usual rules that prototype theorists have developed.

The integration of prototypes and background knowledge is possible just because domain knowledge appears to be about classes of objects rather than about exemplars. For example, all mammals breathe. Furthermore, we know that mammals must breathe because all animals need some means of gas exchange, to take away waste products and take in oxygen. This kind of reasoning uses class names (mammal, animal, gas exchange, waste products) rather than being knowledge about one or two or even a large number of specific exemplars. In fact, for a particular exemplar, say the cat Max, I do not really know that he breathes and takes in oxygen, except by inference from the more general class of animals. Just as important, information about causal links (which seem especially important in knowledge; Ahn 1998) often cannot be verified for individuals, because it requires testing a number of counterfactual conditions. For example, to be sure that Max needs to breathe, I would have to see what happens when he does not breathe, and no one wants that. Instead, I accept the fact that mammals in general must breathe, which has been adequately tested and confirmed so far as I know, and then apply it to individuals as necessary. The locus of knowledge is not our experience with individuals but the facts we represent of entire classes of things. For this reason, a theory of concepts that is based on summary representations is easily integrated into a knowledge-based approach, but an exemplar theory is not.

In order to emphasize the relation between knowledge and prototypes, I would suggest that the schema representation is more appropriate than the simple list of features that is often used (see chapter 3). A schema is a simple knowledge structure, and as such, it is easier to see how it could be integrated into a larger domain knowledge structure. Recall that a schema represents the dimensions of an entity and the possible features that are values of that dimension, in some kind of ordering. One can weight the diagnosticity of the dimension and the strength of each feature, as suggested by Smith et al. (1988). More important, relations between the dimensions (e.g., if the animal flies, it probably has wings) can be directly stored with the schema, as can information on the possible values of any dimension. These possibilities encourage us to include the knowledge of a concept in addition to the simple list of its most common properties. Although the feature list is a very useful simplification of reality for purposes of calculating family resemblance or typicality, it tends to lead us away from thinking about how the concept's properties are constrained and explained by one another and by more general knowledge.

What has to be worked out in this proposal is a coordination of knowledge components and the purely structural components of the prototype in different tasks. Sometimes only the prototype is needed, as when one sees an extremely typical cat and identifies it as a cat. In other cases, more elaborate knowledge is necessary, as in the complicated stories in which a cat is operated on to look like a raccoon, or when one is categorizing based on very limited information (the sound of a glass tipping over in the kitchen—must have been the cat). There is no working model that incorporates these two components,[4] simultaneously providing some knowledge effects along with the usual structural effects such as typicality advantages. I do not see any particular reason that this cannot be done, except for the usual difficulty of representing the large amount of knowledge people have in a domain.

The Role of Exemplars

If one accepts my analysis (and I have a feeling that many will not), the exemplar approach appears to be on the losing end of things. There are simply too many conceptual phenomena for which it does not provide a ready explanation. It is certainly possible that exemplar explanations could be generated for these phenomena, but one major problem with the approach is that it has been far too narrow, focusing on a small number of paradigms and not attempting to address the other conceptual phenomena that the prototype and knowledge views do.

In spite of this conclusion, there is a persistent finding that exemplar models can account for certain category-learning results better than prototype models can. There is also a set of exemplar effects that suggest that individual exemplars are retained and used in learning and categorization. I think that one can criticize the category-learning experiments as potentially deviating from "normal" category learning in a number of respects (see chapter 4). However, even that criticism suggests that there is some (albeit abnormal) category learning for which exemplar memory is useful and is used. And one would be unwise to bet that there are no real-life situations like those category-learning situations. Furthermore, recall that a number of studies that looked at individual subjects' performance have concluded that different subjects follow different strategies, some relying primarily on prototypes and some on exemplars. Smith and Minda (1998) propose that in some such experiments, subjects start out attempting to form prototypes but then switch to exemplars as this process fails, and as the exemplars are learned better and better. The opposite probably happens in other situations, in which the first few exemplars of a category are remembered before they blend in with the others that are encountered later (Homa 1984; Knapp and Anderson 1984).[5] In fact, I noted early on that even a prototype model must claim that exemplar memory exists for the first few category members, before the prototype is abstracted.

Where does this leave us? First, everyone must admit that there is memory for exemplars, if only as normal episodic memory (e.g., I remember what I had for breakfast this morning, and so I can remember at least one exemplar of breakfast food). Second, people may rely on these exemplar memories for making category decisions in some situations. Third, exemplar memory seems to underlie fast categorization of some new category members (as in Brooks's exemplar effects). Fourth, people also attempt to form prototypes, learn rules, and use domain knowledge when possible.

I think that these points can be explained by a parallel memory for exemplars, in addition to the more purely conceptual prototype memory. That is, people attempt to form prototypes or general descriptions for classes, and they can rely on such summary representations in many cases. However, at the same time, they are learning and remembering exemplars, and these also have an effect when the situation encourages it, namely, when category structure is weak (no prototype can be formed), with few exemplars in each category, when exemplars are distinctive and interesting, and when there has been only a short delay since exposure to an exemplar. Mixed models of this sort are notoriously unpopular, and for good reason, because as two very different principles are mixed together in a single explanation, the model becomes almost impossible to disconfirm. However, the problem as I see it is not in disconfirming the present proposal but in figuring out how to account for all the data currently available. Since exemplar explanations have an edge in one important setting, it is difficult to avoid them. Furthermore, no one would deny that people do sometimes remember exemplars, again, as part of their episodic memory abilities. So, one does not gain any points for parsimony by leaving exemplars out of one's explanation, because there is independent reason for thinking that people remember them. The question for our theory of cognition is not whether people remember a particular dog sometimes—obviously they do—but whether that memory influences conceptual behaviors and judgments. (In fact, at least one exemplar theorist has proposed a mixed model for category learning—RULEX, Nosofsky, Palmeri and McKinley 1994—although it uses simple rules rather than prototypes.)

The goal for future exemplar theorists, on this view, is to specify in greater detail when exemplars will and will not influence categorization, and perhaps to integrate that account with theories of episodic memory. Furthermore, it is important on any account to explain how potentially conflicting sources of information are used in conceptual tasks. Prototype or exemplar information will need to be combined (or one of them selected) when both are available. For example, if a large object is reminiscent of an exemplar of category X, but my prototype says that category X is generally small, how is this conflict resolved? More detailed processing models are called for, models that go beyond the mere demonstration that individual exemplars can have an effect (see chapter 4).

Why So Messy?

On the proposal I am making, people attempt to form prototypes as part of a larger knowledge structure when they learn concepts. But at the same time, they remember exemplars and these memories may influence them in a variety of ways. In short, concepts are a mess. (After much thought, I rejected this as the title of this book.) I for one would be much happier to be able to summarize my theory by saying something like "People form prototypes of a category by taking an average of the exemplars they see" or "People just remember exemplars and use them to draw inferences about new items." The proposal that I find myself making is a combination of three different kinds of things, although I am putting exemplar memory in a somewhat secondary role. Why is it so messy? This question has two different levels: First, why did *I* come up with such a messy answer, and second, why is the answer so messy? I think both are worth answering.

One reason I have come up with such a messy answer is that this book has addressed a wide range of conceptual tasks and phenomena. It is a lot easier to hold a simple exemplar model if one only looks at category learning of nine artificial stimuli; it is much easier to dwell only on knowledge if one only does experiments on essentialism in natural kinds. If one has to explain *both* of these topics, a very simple answer is no longer going to work. Since journal articles typically present a series of experiments on a narrow topic, using a single paradigm, it is very natural that they provide much more specific, unified explanations. I am by no means saying that all those explanations are wrong. However, if one takes a step back and tries to develop a more general account of conceptual behavior across many different tasks and domains, that explanation may not be sustainable.

It is extremely reasonable, nonetheless, to ask whether the messy (perhaps I should say "diverse" or "eclectic") quality of my proposal itself casts doubt on whether it is correct. Furthermore, one might suggest that the proposal raises doubts about whether there is a single coherent "psychology of concepts." Let me address these points in turn.

I earlier defended the proposal of a "mixed" theory of concepts by pointing out that it seems to arise from fairly clear demonstrations of exemplar memory combined with fairly clear advantages of prototype theory in the higher-level aspects of concepts. Since the first really requires some kind of exemplar memory, and the second rejects it, I do not believe that there is some simpler explanation out there just waiting to be discovered. The reason for this mixture is, I believe, an extremely important fact about concepts: When people are doing tasks such as categorization, understanding a conceptual combination, or induction, they are using whatever information they can to arrive at an answer that is fast (for tasks with time pressure) or accurate. Some of that information may be the traditional prototype sort in which people remember general properties of a class of objects. However, they can also reason about that information based on other things they know, creating knowledge effects. Furthermore, there is nothing to stop them from relying on or drawing an analogy to a specific instance that they remember. Different tasks are differentially susceptible to such influences, so a subject's answer is not randomly chosen from these different possibilities. That is how we can give fairly simple explanations within some of the domains covered in this book. But across different tasks, or even within particularly difficult, high-level tasks (such as language comprehension), very different sources of information can be drawn on.

One way to think about this diversity, for those who are concerned about its messiness, is to consider which of these sources of information are really concepts. If one likes, one may think of prototypes as the conceptual knowledge and exemplars as part of episodic memory. One could also admit that the prototypes are embedded in broader knowledge of a domain but prefer not to consider this knowledge to be part of the concept. This way, one doesn't have a mixed theory of concepts: The prototype is "the concept," and the other things are represented separately and can even be thought of as being in a different memory system (episodic rather than semantic memory). I think that this kind of view would be consistent with how earlier researchers thought of concepts, and it may restore some clarity to the field to think of things in this way.

That division may make us feel a bit better, but we must simultaneously recognize that the division is in some ways artificial. If what we're trying to explain is people's behavior in various conceptual tasks, such as induction, categorization, and conceptual combination, and if people normally rely on multiple sources of information (perhaps under different conditions or with different materials) in each task, then defining the concept as only including prototype information does not make our theory unmixed or simple. If people's behavior is based on multiple sources of information, then our theory of their behavior must be somewhat messy.

Saying that prototypes, exemplars, and background knowledge are all part of the conceptual system does not mean that they are psychologically similar. I am by no means claiming that they are all the same thing mushed together. There may well be different laws regarding the formation and forgetting of prototypes and exemplar memories, for example. One may well be able to study one component of the system separately from the others, and in fact, one might be well advised to do so. My point is simply that it seems that a number of different components are involved in conceptual tasks, and so the simplest, most parsimonious explanation we may be able to develop for them might well be a mixed theory of this sort.

To try to pull a silk purse out of this messy situation, I will point out that the diverse nature of conceptual behavior is itself an empirical discovery. One might have expected that concepts arise from a module that embodies a self-contained set of principles, with regular input-output relations. In fact, I think that this was the standard assumption in the field for some time. If one were to look at the concept literature of the 1950s through the mid-1970s, one would have read nothing about exemplar memories or knowledge influences. The assumption then was that concept formation was a kind of rule-learning or abstraction that was separate from exemplar memory (and reasoning from knowledge was never considered). The conclusion, if it is true, that people will draw on many different sources of information, including abstractions, episodic memories, and reasoning, to perform conceptual tasks is not a self-evident or necessary result, nor was it researchers' first guess. Sorting out these different influences may make our lives as psychologists a bit harder. But no doubt *using* these diverse influences to answer questions or direct our behavior actually provides greater flexibility and perhaps greater accuracy than people would otherwise achieve.

"Real" Concepts

The dismayed exemplar theorist, or for that matter, possibly the prototype theorist, could object to my proposal in the following way. "Look, my theory is meant to describe the simple, basic processes of category learning. And it does! In fact, it accounts for the following data quite well [list of references—suppressed]. Now you're trying to attack my theory because of data from a lot of different areas, like conceptual combination and induction. But this is not *categorization* or *category learning*! It's ... well, I don't know what, but it certainly isn't real categorization, and so I don't see why my theory should be responsible for it." I have in fact heard such remarks by someone whose theory was being criticized at a conference: These linguisticy or higher-level judgments just weren't part of the domain he was trying to explain. Anderson (1991) is one of the few who had the courage to put this position in print, but I am convinced that this view is widely held among researchers in category learning.

What such researchers may not realize is that theorists from a different perspective have also made a distinction between "real concepts" and other topics in which their favored category-learning experiment falls on the wrong side. Writers with a background in linguistic semantics or philosophy have come to different conclusions about what concepts really are, often with a "classical" flavor—conclusions which are not compatible with the typical results of psychology experiments. For these writers, people may use prototypes or exemplars, or whatever, but these cannot be the essence of their concepts because [long argument, with many citations of Putnam and Quine, or even Frege—suppressed]. In this vein are Armstrong, Gleitman, and Gleitman (1983), J. A. Fodor (1981, 1998), and Osherson and Smith (1981), as well as numerous semanticists and philosophers. Thus, experiments by exemplar theorists are not telling us about real concepts either.

Much as I would enjoy settling this dispute and deciding which is the "real" concept, I feel that we should consider a different way of settling the question: seeing where the data lead us. It is wrong to come up with a definition of concepts based either on prior philosophical work—which simply did not have the empirical knowledge about concepts we have today—or on particular experimental paradigms— which often reflect historical issues of what kinds of studies were popular 25 years ago. Because we cannot derive psychology from first principles, we must follow the phenomena and see what kinds of explanations are necessary for them. That is, we need to take it as an empirical question as to whether the mental entities that we propose to explain psychology experiments are the same kinds of things as the entities that are used in induction by Tzeltal Indians or are the representations behind word meaning. Deciding that one of them is "not what I mean by 'concepts'" or "could not possibly be a word meaning" or "is not a real category" is simply unjustified at our present level of knowledge and seems guaranteed to lead to embarrassment when more is learned. Furthermore, it is just the wrong way to develop a scientific theory, in my opinion. (Can one imagine a physicist saying "That is not what I think of as a real electron"?)

If one takes this claim as an empirical one, it seems very clear that one cannot make such distinctions between the "real" and peripheral concepts. One illustration of this was already given in chapter 11, where I asked whether concepts were the basis of word meaning. What I concluded is that word meaning shows exactly the same kinds of effects as are found in nonlinguistic concepts. This is either an unbelievable coincidence or a demonstration that word meanings are built out of (or based on, etc.) concepts. One could repeat this exercise for other domains as well. For example, why should Jessie, an exemplar theorist, care about knowledge effects in induction? Sure, her theory cannot easily explain these effects, but her theory is about categorization and learning, not about induction or knowledge. The answer is that induction seems to use the same category representations as are used for categorization and other conceptual behaviors. We don't have one concept of birds, for example, formed by learning from exemplars, and another concept of birds that is used in induction. Furthermore, the principles Jessie has observed in her category-learning experiment can also be found in induction: The similarity of the concepts is important for explaining induction; typicality is important; the hierarchical structure of the concepts is used (see chapter 8). The knowledge effects found in induction are similar to knowledge effects found in categorization—both reflect the subject attempting to draw explanatory links. (For example, the use of thematic relations to justify inductions across dissimilar categories, Proffitt et al. 2000, is matched by the use of thematic relations to classify dissimilar items together, Lin and Murphy 2001.) Thus, the results of these two rather different paradigms seem to demand a continuity of the concept construct. One cannot be "real" and the other not, because they are not functionally distinct.

I do not know of any empirical reason to justify the claim that some topic or paradigm reflects different conceptual principles or processes than the rest, and that one of them is more basic (or more "real") than the other. Of course, this is not to say that all concepts are identical or to deny that particular tasks and situations may have unique aspects. Clearly, if one is learning categories of color patches, domain knowledge and linguistic principles are not going to be heavily involved; syntax may influence the learning of word meanings but is simply not available in infant category-learning experiments. The domain of categorization is something of a family-resemblance category itself: Every topic does not have the exact same features as every other. What I am focusing on here is the fact that the representations proposed in each topic share many properties with those proposed in other topics. My argument is that this overlap, which might well not have been expected, leads us to conclude that the same kinds of concept representations, operating under similar principles, are involved throughout the issues I have reviewed. The variations across domains are an interesting topic for research. However, the argument that one topic reveals the true concepts, and so a theory of that topic does not need to worry about its shortcomings in other domains, is simply going against the empirical evidence that there is considerable commonality across topics.

What Is Left to Be Done?

I have sprinkled enough tokens of "future research is needed" throughout this book to give the reader the impression that there is still much to be learned about concepts. I will not repeat those suggestions here but will focus on what needs to be done in a broader theoretical perspective, given the conclusions I have offered of the field above.

First, there needs to be a greater modeling effort by prototype theorists. For many years, exemplar theories have virtually cornered the market in mathematical and computational modeling. Part of the reason for this is the greater perceived success of exemplar models in explaining the traditional category-learning experiment, which is also an easy domain to model. Some of these researchers have also developed prototype models as comparisons, though I feel that their heart was not always in this enterprise. For example, the prototype was almost always identified as a best-example rather than as the weighted-feature or schema models that have actually been proposed by most prototype theorists. If my proposal is correct, then part of the modeling enterprise could be in documenting the interchange between exemplar memory and prototype formation (see Smith and Minda 2000, for a start on this).

Second, researchers need to acknowledge a wide range of data rather than focusing on a single paradigm. In some cases, I believe that researchers have made claims that are clearly disconfirmed in an area outside their particular specialty without a sign of shame. When pointed out, the answer is often "Oh, that's not my kind of category/concept." I have just mentioned the problems with this kind of reply. Claims of important conceptual differences between areas and domains require independent evidence rather than simple stipulation. Indeed, one goal I had in writing this book was to expose workers in one area to the findings of other areas. (I hope those of you who have skipped six chapters feel ashamed now.) If you really believe that concepts are explained by mental images, based on your experiments on gerbils, then how do you deal with conceptual combination or induction? If you find yourself tempted to say "Oh, that's not my kind of concept," then I think you may be both fooling yourself and missing the opportunity of broadening your theory so that it makes contact with other issues and other researchers. It is probably too early to have a Big Theory of Concepts that includes all the topics covered in this book. However, it is not too early to start considering models that do two or three things at once: learn categories and make inductions, or acquire word meanings and use knowledge to categorize. Computational and mathematical models at this level of complexity are within our grasp.

Third, the knowledge approach needs to be better integrated with an empirical learning component. As has become fairly apparent throughout this book, the knowledge approach is not a complete theory of concepts. Instead, it is a claim that concepts are integrated with our general knowledge and are subject to plausible reasoning using that knowledge. It is a research strategy to explore the effects of background knowledge rather than to use meaningless stimuli to avoid them, as in the learning tradition. In the past 15 years, much has been learned so that a knowledge-based *theory* can actually start to be constructed. However, it is clear that empirical modes of concept learning exist as well, and that the knowledge-based aspects affect and are affected by those empirical modes. Studying either one alone may give a misleading picture of the usual case in which people have some limited knowledge that can help concept acquisition (or induction, or conceptual combination, etc.) but also learn truly new and unexpected features. For some time, research on knowledge effects has been directed toward simply demonstrating their existence or showing the inadequacies of a purely empirical approach. It is only recently that specific proposals have been made of how knowledge influences processing, and more work on this is greatly needed. At that time, there will perhaps no longer be "a knowledge approach," but instead all theories of concepts will include knowledge effects, and the theories will differ in terms of their mechanisms for how knowledge is involved in processing.

A Note to Students

In the introduction, I asked the question on behalf of student readers of whether there is still interesting and important work to be done in the psychology of concepts. I think that this conclusion shows that the answer is "yes." Not only is there much to be done on individual topics such as induction, word meaning, infant concepts, and knowledge effects, there is considerable work needed in developing an integrated theory of concepts. Although much of this work can be carried out in the paradigm of traditional experimental psychology (which has constituted the majority of research reviewed here), I think that interdisciplinary techniques will be even more productive. We will need to draw on anthropology, linguistics, and computer modeling in order to understand the rich amalgam that makes up our conceptual abilities. If nothing else, I am sure that my own mixed proposal will provide a useful target for future researchers in this field to take aim at.

Notes

Chapter One

1. I have corrected the punctuation slightly for readability.

Chapter Two

1. For example, I was once unfortunate enough during a blizzard to skid off a highway into a ditch. (Perhaps I should add that I am an excellent driver. It was not my fault.) A state trooper came by and picked me up, but first he went around my car a couple of times asking me "Where's your damage?" As we waited for the tow truck to come pull me out, I asked him why he was asking about the damage. He explained that the state of Illinois defined an "accident" to have occurred if anyone was hurt or if more than $100 worth of damage had been done. Since neither was the case here, I had not had an accident, and he would not have to fill out an accident report. Thus, the state had provided a classical concept for an accident. Sensing an important ontological opportunity, I asked the trooper what it was if it wasn't an accident. At first he didn't seem to know what I was talking about. "Well, *something* happened here, and if it wasn't an accident, what was it?" I asked. He thought about it for a moment and then replied, "Car in a ditch." Whether this was a classical concept he seemed disinclined to discuss. However, even this apparently well-defined concept of an accident would probably have borderline cases, in which one wasn't sure if the damage amounted to $100 or whether a minor injury (bruised knee, bloody nose, or being just shaken up) constituted someone being hurt. Thus, there are typical and atypical accidents even in the state of Illinois.

2. There has been considerable misdescription of Posner and Keele's results in textbooks and secondary sources. In general, they did not find that the prototype was learned *more* accurately or was considered more typical than the items that they had actually been trained on, though this would certainly be a nice result to get. This issue will be discussed more in chapter 3.

3. Rosch and Mervis (1975) and many others after them have attributed the basic family resemblance view to the philosopher Wittgenstein, whose discussion of games was described earlier. However, Ramscar (1997) points out that Wittgenstein did not endorse this

psychological account of concepts. Wittgenstein's real interest in this issue was whether one could provide a traditional philosophical analysis of concepts. As such, his reference to family resemblances had a primarily negative import: He was emphasizing that there were no defining features, even though category members do have some kind of similarity. Wittgenstein was in fact deeply skeptical about the possibility of analyzing concepts at all. Although his philosophy is impossible to summarize here (and is not described very straightforwardly in his writings), he seems to have believed that concepts could only be understood as arising out of our activities and "language games" (talk). That is, he felt that the attempt to describe concepts by their components was doomed to failure. Clearly, this is inconsistent with the goals of the classical view, which holds that concepts can be defined. However, it is also possibly at odds with psychological theories like those of Rosch and Mervis that describe concepts as (nondefinitional) sums of their components. In short, attributions to Wittgenstein as a source for psychological models should be more circumspect than they typically have been, as he was probably more skeptical about concepts than most modern psychological theories are, and he was not proposing a psychological theory in any case. See Ramscar (1997) for a good summary and discussion.

4. The term *natural categories* refers to categories that people naturally and normally use in everyday life—not to categories of nature. They are to be contrasted with *artificial categories*, which are made up by experimenters to test their theories. So, furniture and guns would be considered natural categories, because these are categories people use in everyday life. Unfortunately, there is another term called *natural kinds*, which *does* refer in part to categories of nature. This will make an appearance in the discussion of Barsalou (1985) below. I did not make up these terms and so cannot be held responsible for them.

5. This was probably encouraged by Rosch and Mervis themselves calling the sum of an item's feature weights a *family resemblance score*, even though this does not consider the second component of overlap with other categories. This is puzzling, since they provided the main evidence for the importance of the overlap component in the same article.

6. Strictly speaking, vegetables are not a natural kind, since they are defined by human eating behavior, rather than by a biological property. However, they *are* a natural category. See note 4 for explanation and apology.

7. An illustration of this can be found in the writing of Daniel Osherson and Edward Smith on conceptual combination. They published a very controversial theoretical paper (Osherson and Smith 1981) that, based primarily on examples of conceptual combination along with some logical assumptions, argued that concepts might be well defined after all. (This conclusion was mostly due to an incorrect theory of conceptual combination in my opinion, but that is not the issue right now.) However, in an influential series of empirical papers on conceptual combination, they and their colleagues developed a theory of conceptual combination that was not at all classical but instead allowed continuous variations of typicality and prototype effects (Smith and Osherson 1984; Smith, Osherson, Rips, and Keane 1988). In fact, the main strength of this model is that it predicts typicality effects in combinations—see chapter 12. The change in their theories corresponds to the change in their papers' focus from the theoretical to the empirical: Theoretical concerns made Osherson and Smith embrace the classical view, but empirical data led them in a different direction.

Chapter Three

1. There are a number of ways that one could count missing and mismatching features, ranging from simply ignoring them to using them as evidence against category membership. The issue is complex, however, because it probably makes a difference why the feature doesn't match. For example, if I can see that an animal is tailless, that seems more important than if I can't see whether the animal has a tail, even though in neither case can I count the animal as having a tail. Similarly, if an animal is brown, and the concept has two colors listed, say, brown and green, then do we count it against the item that it isn't green? Since it does have a typical color of the concept, it seems strange to count not being green as negative evidence. For the most part, the situations studied by psychologists have not included or compared such situations, and so there is no single, agreed-upon way to handle these problems.

2. Hintzman's (1986) MINERVA 2 exemplar model has a slightly different way of achieving the same result. A probe is compared to each item in memory, and it gets a score from 0 to 1 for each item, depending on how many features it shares with the item. This score is then cubed, which results in an extremely low number, except for scores close to 1. That is, very close similarity again counts for a lot compared to moderate similarity.

3. The story is somewhat more complex than I am presenting here. When Barsalou et al. took steps to emphasize the individuality of the exemplar or when they got subjects to verbally justify their answers, they then began to treat the types and tokens differently.

4. Traditionally, separable dimensions are said to work best with the city block metric, and integral dimensions with Euclidean distance. If you don't know what these are, don't worry about it.

5. In some versions of the GCM, there is also a bias parameter that takes into account that people may prefer to give some categories as answers more than others. For example, if you like cats, then perhaps you have a tendency to see cats more often than they actually occur, especially when the light is bad or there is little information to go on. The bias is accomplished by multiplying every category's similarity score by a bias parameter, in both the numerator and denominator of equation (3).

Chapter Four

1. Also, I should note that in most exemplar models, an item is compared to multiple exemplars—not just one—and so both old and new items may be categorized by similarity to many exemplars. Thus, an old-new difference is by no means guaranteed in exemplar models. However, the exemplar effect literature discussed here focuses on similarity to a single exemplar rather than to pooled similarity to many exemplars as in most exemplar theories.

2. Hintzman discusses the possibility that generalizations could simply be stored in memory, along with the exemplars. But it seems unlikely that a single item in memory mixed with category exemplars would do the work one expects of a category abstraction.

3. Actually, Smith and Minda (2000) note in the context of related data that exemplar models often become memorization models when they try to simulate experimental results. That is, although the exemplar model requires that a test stimulus be compared to every exemplar, only similar items count for very much in the categorization computation. The degree to

which nonidentical items affect categorization is controlled by the sensitivity parameter (c), as explained in the appendix to chapter 3. Smith and Minda showed that the sensitivity parameter necessary to account for some data sets is so high that the model is essentially using only one stored exemplar to make its judgment.

4. Also, this response ignores the major function of categories, that they tell you the typical features of kinds of things, so that you may reason about them, make predictions and inferences, communicate information, and so on. If categories normally have items that are totally opposites, these goals cannot be served.

5. In particular, in their Experiments 3 and 4, Medin and Schwanenflugel used different instantiations of each item type. Their stimuli were faces, and the dimensions were properties of the faces (which were identified for the subjects), such as long hair, and mouth open or shut. Each stimulus, however, was a different face that instantiated these properties. No doubt the irrelevant differences between the faces made category learning quite difficult. One could argue that the features of real-world categories often have these irrelevant differences, however. Most books have a cover, but the exact color and material making up that cover can vary from book to book; books all have pages, but the exact size and proportions of the pages differ; most books have chapters, but the length of the chapters differ; and so on. The differences between exactly repeating stimulus features in item after item, as is done in the majority of experiments, and using different instantiations of each feature type is now being explored (Yamauchi and Markman 2000). Under the usual classification learning conditions, having different instantiations of features seems to slow learning significantly. But other types of learning tasks are less affected by this manipulation—see Yamauchi and Markman (2000) for details.

6. I am counting here the features listed in Rosch et al. (1976, table 2) as basic-level for nonbiological taxonomies, but the features listed as superordinate level for biological taxonomies, as Rosch et al. discovered that they had guessed incorrectly about the level for biological taxonomies. As a result, tree, bird and fish were (correctly) considered basic categories in my summary. If you count the features listed (incorrectly) as basic level for biological taxonomies, the mean number of features would be even higher than the given figure. Chapter 7 explains this confusion.

7. How is the sensitivity parameter c used to represent forgetting? As exemplar memories decline, the value of c increases (i.e., the model becomes less sensitive) and so reliance on the most similar exemplar to decide categorization declines. As a result the advantage of old over new items will also decrease, which is a measure of forgetting. However, if subjects are truly forgetting the exemplars, then what should change in the model is the exemplar *representation* (i.e., information loss)—not the decision process. What the model is saying is that the exemplars are still perfectly represented over time, but for some reason, people do not use the old exemplar as much to categorize the old items; instead, they rely more on less similar items. I do not think that this is really what the exemplar theorists believe, but their problem is that the model already can account for forgetting this way, and so it may seem unjustified to put in a new mechanism. Unfortunately, this way of dealing with the memory results gives an inaccurate account of the underlying memory processes: If exemplar memories decline over time, then the model's representation should also degrade. Again, there is nothing about exemplar models that prevents them from treating memory in this way, as the Hintzman and Estes models have in fact taken this approach. However, the GCM and other successors to

the context model do not generally represent memory in what I would consider a more accurate way.

Chapter Five

1. For complicated reasons, although these probabilities were used to construct the categories, in fact the probabilities subjects observed were slightly different. I will use the presented probabilities for the sake of simplicity. (For those who are interested: The reason is that there is some probability that a patient would have *no* symptoms for a given category. In fact, if you constructed symptom patterns using the shown probabilities, about 13% of patients in each disease would have no symptoms. Gluck and Bower reasonably enough decided not to present patients who had no symptoms, so this changed the symptom probabilities a bit.)

2. Malt and Smith performed a number of different analyses on their data, and I am reporting the ones they finally settled on as being the best. However, there are many different ways to analyze such data, and many choices must be made along the way. See their article for the details.

3. A more recent study by McRae, de Sa, and Seidenberg (1997) also performed an analysis of features and feature correlations in natural concepts. However, they did not test category structure or use categorization tasks, but instead tested feature verification and similarity judgments of items. Thus their results cannot be directly related to the present issue.

4. Billman and Knutson did not use a category construction task as the other studies discussed in this section did. Instead, they asked subjects questions of the sort, "If an animal has long legs, what time of day would it be found in?" The fact that subjects were able to give correct answers under these conditions (about 75% of the time in Experiments 1 and 2, where 33% would be chance) suggests that they noticed the category structure in the stimuli. We do not directly know how they would perform in a category construction task, but Kaplan and Murphy (1999) used both tasks and found comparable results in them.

Chapter Six

1. Anderson (1991) claims that much knowledge of the sort to be discussed here is book-learned facts that are added on to basic category structure, and as a result, it is not central to concepts. However, more recent research has shown that such knowledge is actually strongest for those who do not have book-learned knowledge but instead experience the domain through living in it or working with it (Coley et al. 1999).

2. However, it should be pointed out that the two categories differ in the properties involved—adult and stretch vs. yellow and small—so the difference between the rules is not as clear-cut as one might like.

3. For reasons that seemed very good at the time, Murphy and Allopenna called this structure *Domain Consistent*, as the features were all from the appropriate domain (vehicles) and were consistent with one another (unlike, e.g., the features in the Murphy and Wisniewski experiment described earlier). However, that label is somewhat opaque and was not used in later studies.

4. Also relevant to this issue is the fact that subjects who have helpful knowledge often learned categories to criterion in two blocks in some published experiments (e.g., Murphy and Allopenna 1994). Although learning was not tracked over time, it is apparent that such very fast subjects must have identified the knowledge in the first block in order to have performed perfectly in the second block. Subjects without knowledge were never able to finish by the second block.

5. The careful reader may have noticed that this result is not entirely consistent with the Wisniewski and Murphy (1989) finding described earlier. The difference may have to do with the overall difficulty of the category and the amount of contradictory knowledge. If the category can be learned empirically fairly easily, then contradictory knowledge may not hurt. Furthermore, if the background knowledge is extremely strong, contradicting it may be worse than if the knowledge is not as compelling. The effect also depends on exactly how the contradiction is instantiated. In Murphy and Kaplan (2000), a small contradiction in most items did not reduce the benefit of knowledge. However, a large contradiction in a couple of items caused the subjects to become very confused. That is, if the knowledge was perfectly consistent almost all the time, a strong inconsistency then throws learners for a loop. As will be discussed below, the match between category structure and knowledge is evidently critical.

6. Of course, tree is already a multidimensional concept, but you might modify it by adding just one new feature. However, this objection demonstrates that real-life categories simply can't be unidimensional.

7. Heit (1998) also presents a mathematical model that combines empirical data and prior knowledge in learning his feature pairs. This model could be expanded to learning categories as a whole, as it is a version of an exemplar model. However, I am not discussing it here, because it is primarily a way of mathematically apportioning empirical and knowledge effects, and it does not provide a psychological model of the latter. For example, it does not specify how the knowledge is represented and show how it is integrated with the experience, or changes as a result of it, and so on. In contrast, the Heit and Bott (2000) model to be discussed next does provide such an account.

8. Mooney (1993) provides an illuminating example that might make the EBL learning situation seem more plausible. He explains that the first time he saw a boot jack, he observed someone use it to remove his boots. Using this as the presumed function of the object, he then determined which aspects of the object were critical (the U-shaped piece for holding the boot, the rear portion that one stands on). He then used these aspects to identify later boot jacks that looked quite different but that had parts that could serve the same functions. In this case, then, the function was directly observed—and then inferred to be the raison d'être of the object. If such situations are typical, then a learner (whether human or machine) would not have to be given the category description in advance of learning but could infer it based on observation.

Chapter Seven

1. These kinds of questions have been widely criticized in part because some of them are very difficult to phrase in a comprehensible manner. For example, children virtually never are asked to compare the size of a subset to its superset (e.g., "Do you have more shirts or more

clothing?"), and so they may not correctly understand such questions when put to them by experimenters. As discussed in chapter 10, this is actually a very strange question to ask. Thus, children's inability to answer them correctly may not really reflect a problem with their understanding of the relative numbers in each category, but may reflect a different interpretation of the question (e.g., they may interpret the question as meaning "Do you have more shirts or more *other* clothing?"—which is in fact a much more reasonable question).

2. For simplicity, I am assuming that these features are true of all the category members. However, as described in chapter 2, this is most likely not the case, and I will in fact have to relax this assumption below. Nonetheless, this assumption is not critical here, if we will allow that the features are generally true of the category members and not require logical certainty of category judgments.

3. I also mentioned as evidence for the hierarchical structure view the finding that it was faster to identify properties associated with a category than properties believed to be associated with a superordinate: Collins and Quillian (1969) found that it took longer to verify statements like "Badminton has rules" (a property true of all games) than statements like "Baseball has innings" a property true of baseball in particular. One problem with the way this prediction was tested, however, was that different features were used in different conditions. "Has innings" was an example of a feature that required no IS-A links to be traversed, and it never was used in a condition that did require IS-A links to be traversed; "has rules" was tested only in the condition requiring multiple IS-A links to be crossed. So, this comparison is of different properties that were not carefully controlled (for length or familiarity, for example), and so it is rather dubious. Furthermore, Conrad (1972) showed that the "long-distance" properties, like badminton having rules were less associated with the category than the "closer" properties. That is, badminton is associated with nets, birdies and rackets, and not so associated to having rules. (We could phrase this in terms of the weights associated with the category's properties, as discussed in chapter 3.) She argued that these differences in association could explain Collins and Quillian's results. Chang (1986) provides a detailed review of the empirical effects and their explanations.

4. Rosch et al. (1976) made an unfortunate choice of terminology in calling these categories "basic level *objects*" (e.g., in their title), a term that was adopted by some subsequent authors as well. However, it is important to realize that it is the *category* that is basic, not the object. The same object is a bulldog, a dog, a mammal, and an animal, so it is not the object that is more or less basic—it is the way of conceiving of this object that is basic (in this case, as a dog) or not (as a bulldog or animal).

5. Unlike the argument about cue validity, it is not *necessarily* true that category validity increase at lower levels of a hierarchy. However, it is apparent that there are some cases in which it is true, and so this measure would not predict the basic level (see Corter and Gluck 1992).

6. More specifically, following a suggestion of Douglas Medin, Mervis and Crisafi took the similarity of objects in the *same* category at a given level and subtracted the similarity of objects in *different* categories at that level. The similarity of objects within a category is a function of how many properties the objects share (i.e., informativeness); the similarity of objects across categories is low if the categories are distinctive. Therefore, the difference between the two measures both informativeness and distinctiveness: To the degree that the first is high and the second low, the difference score will be high.

7. Mervis and Crisafi (1982) presented experiments with artificial categories that have been interpreted as demonstrating the same point. However, in their experiments, subjects did not actually learn the categories—they made judgments about whether pairs of artificial stimuli would be in the same category. As predicted, subjects believed that two items from the same (proposed) basic level category should be in the same category, but subjects were much less consistent in thinking so for superordinates. This result is consistent with the other results cited here, but they do not directly tell us whether such categories would be useful or efficient if they were actually learned.

8. Palmeri (1999) investigated how an exemplar model predicted performance on different levels of categorization, using stimuli from Lassaline et al. (1992). However, these stimuli did not conform to basic and subordinate structures found in natural categories very well, and so they do not address the problems raised here. For example, the higher level categories were purely disjunctive, and the specific categories each had a defining feature but no other features in common.

9. Ignoring the question of whether these categories are similar to real hierarchies (see previous footnote), Palmeri's simulation and discussion does address some important points of how various models might account for hierarchical classification. Palmeri suggested that ALCOVE (Kruschke 1992), a prominent exemplar model, was able to explain the basic-level advantage by developing different attention weights on stimulus dimensions for superordinate and basic-level categorization. Furthermore, unlike the original context model (Medin and Schaffer 1978), ALCOVE uses a nonlinear decision rule such that high-level categorization may not be easily predictable from lower-level categorization. Palmeri's discussion of the different models is much more informative than what I can provide here. However, at least some of the reasons he gives for ALCOVE's success derive from the virtual hierarchies he used. For example, the model was able to give higher weights to different dimensions for basic and superordinate categories because the model never learned both together. If a single simulation was forced to learn both levels of categorization, it could not have had different attention weights for the different levels, since there is only one weight for each dimension. Thus, it is not at all clear whether ALCOVE's success can be generalized from this situation to one in which a learner acquires two or more levels of a hierarchy, as people actually do.

10. Estes (1994, pp 56ff) very briefly describes an exemplar approach to modeling the basic-level advantage that simulates an artificial categorization experiment. He does not directly address the issues raised here. His method of calculating categorization seems to assume that every item is stored with all of its category labels, which are activated on a categorization trial. This is plausible for such an experiment, but perhaps not as plausible for everyday objects that may be in a dozen different categories (e.g., people). However, it would be going beyond his purposes to impute to him a definitive answer to the theoretical questions raised here, which he did not explicitly address.

11. Coley et al. (1997) actually provided what is in some ways a test of pure structural vs. knowledge determinants of the basic level. However, it was in the context of an induction task, which is not one of the main measures of basic-level structure, and so I discuss it in detail in chapter 8. Recall that American college students think of tree and fish as basic-level categories, but many other cultures think of the lower, generic level, such as oak and trout as basic-level categories. Coley et al. asked which of these levels controls induction. If it is the purely structural issue of which category is informative and distinctive, then Americans

should prefer to form inductions around trees, say, rather than around oaks. On the other hand, if even Americans understand that the genus is a much more coherent biological category (although they do not know what its properties are), then they may prefer to form inductions using the genus. And that is what Coley et al. found: American subjects were more willing to infer an unfamiliar property within categories like oaks and trout than they were for their basic-level categories like tree and fish. However, this is not to deny that the same subjects would be slower to identify something as an oak or that oaks and maples are difficult for them to distinguish. It is only in tasks that rely on reasoning that knowledge can overrule category structure.

Chapter Eight

1. This may be because target category typicality is largely redundant with the other two variables, in the limited domains tested. To a large degree, once you know the typicality of the given item and its similarity to the target item, you have determined the typicality of the target item. For example, if the given item is typical, and the target item is similar to it, then it is also likely to be typical. Thus, it is not clear that there was enough independent variance in these stimuli to separate all three variables.

2. There seems to be an assumption that this task is roughly interchangeable with Rips's. (In fact, two readers of a draft of this chapter made just that comment.) However, note that Rips asked subjects to provide the percentage of category members that would have the critical property, whereas in the Osherson-Smith paradigm, subjects are told that *all* category members have a property and are then asked to judge the probability that *all* members of another category have the same property. (The sentences provided did not usually explicitly say "all," but that is the clear implication.) One can imagine circumstances in which the confidence in this induction would be very low, even though one might think that a fairly high percentage of category members would in fact have the property. For example, consider problem (2) below. I might believe that *many* bears do love onions, if grizzly bears and polar bears love onions, but simultaneously think it is extremely unlikely that *all* bears love onions. Thus, I would give different answers to Rips's task and the Osherson et al. task. However, the results of the two paradigms are usually similar, in part, I think, because no one has tried to find induction problems that would distinguish them (see Proffitt et al. 2000).

3. The way that Osherson et al. (1990, p. 190–191) calculate coverage is ingenious, though a bit complex. Imagine that you only know the following mammals: seal, whale, cow, horse, dog, and cat. How well do seal and dog cover this category? For each item in the category, you would calculate the maximum of its similarity to seal and its similarity to dog. Then take the average of these maxima; this is the measure of coverage. You might wonder why you shouldn't just take the average similarity of dog and seal to all mammals. The intuition is that the set dog-and-seal covers mammals well so long as one of the items is similar to each mammal. So, seal covers the water mammals well, and dog probably covers the land mammals well. Together, then, they cover the category. But note that dog is not similar to the water mammals, nor is seal similar to the land mammals. Therefore, if one took the average of all these similarities, one would end up with a mediocre coverage value. When one added more categories to the premise, coverage would not generally go up, because a new category would be similar to some categories and dissimilar to others. Thus, the averaging method would not

explain the effect of premise monotonicity, described below. By first finding the maximum similarity of the premise category and then taking the average, Osherson et al.'s coverage method basically measures whether there is any category in the premises that is similar to items in the category.

4. Alternatively, it is possible that subjects don't interpret premises like "Birds have an ulnar artery" as referring to all birds. If so, then their preference for (10) is not a fallacy, as that arises from the fact that ostriches would necessarily be included in "all birds." However, even if this is not a logical fallacy, the model predicted this preference, which was not a previously known empirical finding.

5. The careful reader (which does not include me, since a reviewer had to point this out to me) might have noticed that this finding suggests that the typicality of the target category makes a difference. As just noted, the preference relies on the fact that ostrich is an atypical bird. This might appear to conflict with Rips's (1975) results showing no effect of target typicality. However, first note that I pointed out a problem with finding such an effect in his experiment (in note 1 of this chapter). Also, keep in mind that this comparison is between a specific category, like ostrich, and its superordinate, bird, and Rips never asked questions about the superordinate category and so never made this comparison. More generally, though, it does seem to be the case that the Osherson et al. model would predict an effect of target typicality under most circumstances, because the premise-target similarity factor would tend to decrease as the target became more and more atypical.

6. Smith, Shafir, and Osherson (1993) proposed an extension to their model to handle some nonblank predicates. However, their model appears to handle only a certain kind of induction, if I understand it correctly, and so it is not a general answer to this question. Interested readers should consult their report.

7. Technically, trees are not even a biological category, as they do not pick out any botanical class. This is in part because being a tree depends on factors such as size, which are not very relevant biological properties.

8. Although I will talk about actual probabilities, it should be understood that this really refers to a psychological variable of how confident or certain one feels about the induction. People do not always correctly understand probability theory, and I am not implying that these psychological probabilities follow the rules of probability theory in mathematics. The important point is that an induction rated as having a probability of .90 would be stronger than one with a .50 rating, and people would be more likely to act on the former induction than on the latter one.

9. For those who can't wait, the conditions were these. First, when *all* the categories were equally probable, subjects used multiple categories. Second, when all the critical figures had the same value, people seemed to notice this. For example, suppose that you are asked who drew a triangle, and what shading it has. Suppose that Bob has drawn the most triangles, and his figures are mostly black. Murphy and Ross (1994, Experiment 11) found that if the triangles in other categories were all black, subjects gave higher estimates for "black" being the correct answer. They suggested that this occurred because subjects noticed the consistent shading of the figures when first trying to decide who drew the figure. In real life, this would only be helpful, then, if the feature was extremely consistent both inside and outside the category.

Chapter Nine

1. This statement is in the context of habituation tasks of the sort discussed in this chapter. With other materials and procedures, infants may prefer items that are somewhat familiar to those that are extremely novel. However, in the literature to be reviewed here, novelty preference is the rule.

2. Note that it is not only perception that is involved here, but also memory. Infants might be able to distinguish the bunnies if placed side by side. However, when seeing items one at a time, with a slight delay in between, infants may not remember the distinctive information from one presentation to the next.

3. One useful aspect of this procedure is that it does not require true habituation (which is why I am calling the first phase *familiarization* now). The infant could still be interested in looking at bunnies at the end of the first phase, but if the mouse is *more* interesting or surprising, then babies will prefer to look at it in the paired test trials. In the single-exposure paradigm, one must wait for the infant to reduce its looking to the training pictures, or else no dishabituation could be found.

4. Some have argued (e.g., Behl-Chadha 1996) that finding such preferences is itself evidence for categorical representation. However, this seems dubious for two reasons. First, such preference can be found without any learning of categories, but may be evident from the first trial of presentation. (In fact, the preference tests to be described shortly do not use any training before taking the preference measures.) Thus, the preference does not itself indicate category *learning*. Second, it is certainly possible to prefer one stimulus to another without placing them in different categories—at least for adults. For example, I have a number of clothes that I would describe as being red, yet one of them seems to me to be a prettier shade of red than the others. That is, I prefer it to the others. Although I could make up an ad hoc description to distinguish this from the others ("bright, highly saturated red"), these colors do not fall into different categories for me. Similarly, I prefer Dexter Gordon to Don Byas, even though I would classify both as "be-bop era tenor saxophonists." So, although a preference for one item over another does indicate that infants can perceive a difference between the items, it does not prove that they categorize them differently.

5. Of course, in some cases, one may not care about this distinction. For example, if you want to know whether infants know the difference between mammals and fish, then you are asking whether they can *both* notice that the items in a series are all mammals and that a fish is not in that category.

6. This point is often ignored in theoretical critiques of the looking measure, such as Haith and Benson's (1998). If one is going to criticize this measure, one must supply an alternative, convincing interpretation of the many findings of novelty preference in the literature.

7. Of course, this in itself could be a very interesting effect. However, to establish it, one would have to compare good with bad figures, or familiar shapes (like Bomba and Siqueland used) with random shapes.

8. One likely reason for this, discussed in chapter 5, is that formal education encourages subjects to search for a single property to divide up category members, rather than learning the category's many properties. The finding that infants learn categories this way is consistent

with that argument, since infants would generally lack a high-school education and so would not have that bias.

9. It should be noted that these subjects were significantly older than Quinn's (1987) subjects, at 10 months. I am not going to attempt to keep careful track of how old infants have to be in order to do these tasks, in part because different studies use different materials and procedures, making it hard to track changes in the ability to learn categories across the first year of life.

10. The tiger data were equivocal, in that children dishabituated to the tiger picture, but a later preference test showed that they had a pre-existing preference for the tiger picture that could have caused this effect.

11. In another experiment, they found that this preference disappeared when infants were given more time to study each picture. This may indicate that infants look at faces first and examine other parts only later. However, this is rather speculative at this stage, and it is possible that the result has something to do with the hybrid test items in particular.

12. One problem with these comparisons and with Mandler and McDonough's logic is that null results are taken as indicating no difference. That is, the pattern that they argue best shows category learning is the one in which trial 8 = trial 9 < trial 10, because this would show that a new category member was treated the same as an old category member, but both were different from a nonmember. However, Mandler and McDonough test this by doing separate tests on trial 8 vs. 9 and 9 vs. 10, so the conclusion that trial 8 = trial 9 is based on not finding a significant difference between them. Examination of the figures in the paper shows that some of the conditions interpreted as "=" are in fact slightly different—occasionally looking about as different as the trials interpreted as "<." Stronger evidence would have been to show that the difference between trials 9 and 10 was significantly greater than that between trials 8 and 9. The paired preference procedure would have avoided this whole issue by giving the child a choice between looking at a category member and nonmember. There, a positive finding inherently reveals that children can tell the difference between members and nonmembers, and no null result is required to interpret the results. That technique also avoids the problems of order effects mentioned above. This reliance on null results weakens Mandler and McDonough's evidence.

13. Actually, Paul Quinn informs me that in his studies, some of the cats did have stripes. Some researchers go to pains to ensure that their categories cannot be distinguished by a simple feature of this sort.

14. Note that this particular finding is at odds with Mandler and McDonough's (1993) explanation of why their subjects distinguished cars and airplanes, which they attributed to the large number of vehicles in the San Diego area. But even in Southern California, children must have had more experience with forks and spoons than with cars and airplanes. In fact, this particular result casts strong doubt on the measure in my view, because I find it impossible to believe that children don't distinguish forks from spoons.

15. The exact relation between concepts and the notion of a sortal is very complex, because some concepts that can be used to count objects cannot individuate them over time. For example, I can count the babies in the room, so the concept baby can be used to individuate entities. However, I cannot decide whether someone is the same individual as someone I've seen before by considering whether both (potential) individuals are babies. That is, a single

individual changes from a baby to an adult without changing identity. In contrast, an individual does not change from a cat to a dog. As a result, we must refer to different subtypes of sortals in order to be able to distinguish these different functions. To be honest, I am not convinced that the philosophical concept of sortals corresponds to a psychological entity. People use many sources of information to individuate objects and to track their identity over time, and category membership is one of them, but not necessarily a special one.

16. The specific results are more complex than one would like, because infants generally look longer at a two-object display. The 12.5-month-olds looked longer at two-object displays during a familiarization period, but equally long at one-object and two-object displays during the test just described. Younger infants always looked longer at two-object displays, which were the unsurprising ones. Thus, Xu and Carey interpret the equal looking at the one- and two-object displays as demonstrating an effect of surprise, which overcomes the natural tendency to look longer at the two-object displays.

17. Technically, Wilcox and Baillargeon's results are consistent with a weaker position in which the infants don't categorize the objects but simply identify their features. That is, rather than seeing a ball and a box, perhaps they see two *objects*, which have different shapes. I think these two possibilities are difficult to distinguish conceptually, much less experimentally, so I will talk somewhat loosely about children using the categories to track the objects.

Chapter Ten

1. Huttenlocher and Smiley (1987) also argued that some cases that look like complexive meanings could not plausibly be complexive. For example, a child who once saw a cookie in a bag later said "cookie" to the closed bag. Does this suggest that the child has a complexive category of cookie-and-bag? Since the cookie had only been seen once in this situation, they argued that the child could not have represented the cookie as cookie-and-bag, but must be making the comment that the bag held cookies, or the like. In fact, a number of times when the child said an object name without the object being present, the utterance appeared to be a request. Simply because a child uses a word in the presence of an associated object does not mean that the child has a thematic category of some kind. The child could be requesting the object or commenting on its absence. Other authors have noted that when children seem to use words thematically, they may be making a comment about the item rather than categorizing it (e.g., Anglin 1977). For example, when pointing at his mother's briefcase and saying "Mommy," the child probably means something like "It's Mommy's." Using a word to comment rather than to label may explain a number of anecdotes that suggest children use words complexively.

2. These anecdotes probably reflect in part a pragmatic strategy (Grice 1975) of the child to give the best name to an object. If someone calls a dog *an animal*, he or she should be informed that it's really *a dog*, because that is a much better name for it. Rejection of the superordinate name is in the service of emphasizing the more specific name. See further description of Blewitt's (1994) study in the next section.

3. This point does not seem to have been understood by some critics who have noted this design flaw, such as Mandler (1998), who argues that the superordinate is in some ways primary. Although the test is incomplete, it still gives evidence for the primacy of the basic over

the superordinate level since superordinate membership was equally present in both conditions. If children relied on superordinate categories, then they should not have done any better in grouping items from the same basic category than from the same superordinate category, when the foil was held constant. In fact, they were almost perfect in the basic grouping and almost at chance with superordinates. Although Rosch et al.'s test could have been designed better, its results still show that superordinates are hard to use.

4. However, Blewitt's (1994) more recent study casts some doubt on this. I suspect that it is not dual identity that causes the problem so much as the abstract nature of superordinate categories.

5. It is no accident on Markman's account that the word *furniture* is a mass term, so that we cannot say "Sit on a furniture" but instead must use a classifier such as "piece of...." See chapter 7 for a discussion of this linguistic phenomenon.

6. Perhaps it is also worth pointing out that many collection concepts require that one specify details of the individual members of the collection. Although terms like *pile* do not care about what makes up the pile, terms like *family* or *army* do care. An army is not just a group of people who happen to be on a battlefield—it is a group of soldiers in a common organizational structure. A family is not just a bunch of people living together—they must have certain biological or socially defined relations. So, even collection concepts specify properties of their individual components. Thus, if children initially think of *furniture*, say, as being a collection term, this does not mean that they do not also represent common features of the things that make up a group of furniture. It may be these common features that turn into a class representation in adults.

7. In fact, labeling the typical examples was better than another condition in which all of the items in each category were named. This is a surprising result which seems at odds with exemplar theory, since it suggests that forming a prototype is better than learning all the category's exemplars. It may be that labeling the typical items makes it easier for children to focus on the most relevant features.

8. It is not entirely clear whether duck is a basic category for most Americans. It may be somewhere between true basic and subordinate status. As pointed out in chapter 7, there is a range of "basicness" rather than a discrete basic vs. nonbasic distinction. It may also be that duck is a basic category when it is interpreted as Ari did (something like water fowl). Or, to put it another way, duck can be a basic category so long as geese and swans are not around—see below.

9. One might also question whether these very complex meanings, like the one possible for *glark* (and the ones used in Goodman's examples), would serve the purposes of language and thought that categories are supposed to serve. That is, a category like rabbits is inductively very rich and useful in the world, but categories of things that are square, green and exist in North America may be less informative in an objective sense, or at least inefficient. The inductions one could derive from glarks would overlap greatly with the inductions one would get from glorks (European glarks), glurks (Australian glarks), and so on. Thus, "green square" may be a better meaning than "green square in North America." Of course even if some possible meanings of *glark* could be said to be objectively substandard, this does not tell us how children avoid considering them.

10. In part for this reason, constraints do not help to solve Quine's problem. For example, perhaps the linguist has certain biases about how to interpret the natives' speech, which sug-

gest that *Gavagai* means "rabbit" rather than "undetached rabbit parts" (assuming that really is a different meaning). However, Quine wishes to solve the problem of translation empirically, not through some unexplained biases of the linguist's, which might not be shared by the natives (Quine 1960, p. 52). Similarly, the child is certainly entitled to jump to the conclusion that I don't mean by *glark* green squares pointed to before noon, but the child has no evidence for this assumption. That's the point of the induction puzzle.

11. When actually discussing word learning in children, he simply states that the child can learn to understand *red* and *ball* as having different meanings, even though both would be uttered in the context of a red ball (p. 84), by learning the respects by which the red ball is similar to other balls or other red things. Elsewhere, Quine makes it clear that much of the meaning of a word can be acquired simply by keeping track of what is constant across its uses (e.g., p. 98). Thus, he does not really address the inductive problem of category learning. Nonetheless, this is the issue that articles referring to Quine in the word-learning literature tend to focus on.

12. One difficulty in carrying out this study is that cultures also differ in the number of superordinate and subordinate names they normally use (Dougherty 1978). Technology has the effect of creating more and more specific categories in order to meet specific needs (as in color names: Berlin and Kay 1969); science may have a similar effect, but it also results in the development of broad categories that share underlying principles, such as arthropods or lipids. I suspect that there is a correlation between the use of motherese and other parental teaching strategies and the general frequency of subordinate and superordinate categories in a culture, which would make it difficult to distinguish the two. Finally, in cultures where parents are not as helpful in their labeling, the children may have other interactions (e.g., with siblings and older playmates) that are more helpful.

13. Though, as I have pointed out, children may have an imperfect grasp of many concepts for some time after initially acquiring them. It is possible that knowledge would aid in the full acquisition of the concept, even if it did not act at very early ages.

14. Krascum and Andrews (1998, p. 335) imply that their categories are basic-level categories. However, especially given that the items' overall shapes were identical, this is not obviously true. Also, as is common in much developmental research, the category structure was not a particularly difficult one, as no feature ever appeared in the "wrong" category, in contrast to Hayes and Taplin's (1992) structure, which was more challenging.

15. As examples will reveal below, these studies included mostly nominal kinds, but a few artifacts and other terms also snuck in. Also, although these concepts seem to be consistent with the Classical View, it turns out that even they can show prototype effects—see Coleman and Kay (1981).

16. This is not to suggest that perceptual similarity has no effect. In fact, in Study 1, Gelman and Markman (1986; and see Gelman and Markman 1987) included a control in which the two items in the same category (two birds) looked more similar than did the two items in the different categories (bird and bat). Subjects were more willing to draw inductions when perceptual and category information agreed than when they conflicted (about 88% vs. 68% of the time). However, this may not indicate a problem with children being "seduced by percepts," but instead may reflect a legitimate basis for induction, since things that look alike may well share nonobvious properties.

17. I call something a *perceptual property* if it is readily identified by one of the senses, as opposed to requiring inference. This is not to say that such properties can be given a very simple perceptual definition.

18. Even if that prediction were true, it would not explain why children use category membership to induce some predicates (like behavioral and biological properties) but not others (like weight). To explain this, one needs to assume that children have some theory about how different properties are related to category membership. A perceptual basis for induction could not explain it.

Chapter Eleven

1. I might also mention that a number of "official" rules of word use that are imposed by publishers or dictionaries are in fact without any good basis. Often they arose from a grammatical misconception or from resistance to a natural change in word use, and long after most people have forgotten the reason for not saying X, they still remember that there is supposed to be something wrong with saying X. For example, the American Psychological Association and some other publishers prohibit using the word *since* as a "causal" connective (e.g., "Since the data were inconclusive, we performed another experiment."). So, this is not part of the official meaning of the word according to them. Yet not only is this usage ubiquitous in educated speech, it has been used in English writing since Chaucer, and even earlier, in Anglo-Saxon (Follett 1970, p. 305). The prohibition seems to be based on a desire to avoid polysemy (confusion between the causal and the temporal senses); however, as I will discuss at length, such polysemy is found in almost every content word. So, if we were to rely on dictionaries and usage experts to tell us what word meaning is, we would by no means be guaranteed to get a reasonable result.

2. Thanks to Cheryl Sullivan for bringing these to my attention.

3. One might interpret the classic semantic feature theory of Katz and Fodor (1972) this way, though they are not entirely clear about what their semantic features are.

4. I am simplifying Mervis's position a bit here, because Ari's concept of ducks was not quite right when he first learned the word, so there was further learning after he acquired the name. This is addressed below.

5. Although *home run* seems to be two words, it must be represented as an item in the lexicon (mental dictionary), because there is no way to figure out what *home run* means based on the meanings of *home* and *run* separately. In general, the lexicon contains not only single words but phrases and idioms with unpredictable meanings.

6. By convention, linguists refer to the different *senses* of a polysemous word, but the different *meanings* of ambiguous words, presumably because the senses could be viewed as variations on the same basic meaning.

7. Bizarrely, British and American English have opposite meanings for this use of the word. In American English, to table an idea is to put it aside; in British English, to table it is to propose it. Given that Americans also say that something is on the table when it is under consideration, their use seems inconsistent.

8. The writer Robert Graves (1926) argued that English was particularly susceptible to polysemy. He discussed historical extensions to word meanings, such as *brazen*, initially meaning

to be made of or like brass, but being extended to meaning strident, shameless, or not very worthy. "It is the persistent use of this method of *'thought by association of images'* as opposed to *'thought by generalised preconceptions'* that distinguishes English proper from the more logical languages" (p. 40), by which he meant particularly French (!). Whether such extensions are more common to English than other languages is not very clear, however. My own impression is that French has a smaller core vocabulary than English does, and so it has greater polysemy.

9. The sense of a chicken referring to the meat is a different sense than that referring to the animal, if only because the former is a mass noun and the latter a count noun. That is, you can say "Have some chicken" when offering meat at the table, but not when offering animals to your farmer neighbor.

10. Unfortunately, it was common in the 1970s to test theories of word meaning and other aspects of language through memory tests. This was a historical holdover from the influence of verbal learning, which was the dominant approach to language until cognitive psychology became popular. Memory tests are not the ideal way to test such things, but nonetheless, their results can usually be replicated in other, more online tasks.

11. Recall that Murphy and Andrew (1993) showed that adjective antonyms and synonyms changed as a function of context. However, in unpublished data, we found identical performance for nouns of these phrases. That is, *water* received different synonyms when it was modified by different adjectives, just as often as *fresh* did when it appeared with different nouns. So, this does not support the idea that adjective meaning is more malleable than noun meaning, though it is obviously a null result.

12. Fodor's (1981) example was in service of a somewhat different point.

13. In retrospect, this problem can be seen as a consequence of Osgood et al.'s procedures. First, by using contrastive adjectives like fast-slow, they could not find out that zorks have hair, have four legs, eat ants, and so on, because such information would not be found in any of the adjective pairs. Second, the factor analysis tends to find the commonalities among the very diverse tested dimensions, which are bound to be very general. As they point out, more specific dimensions like wet-dry did not load very highly on any of the three main factors. In general, specific features that might be important within some domain (e.g., nesting habits for birds) would not be relevant to other domains and so would not emerge as a general factor. Put another way: The three factors were found *because* of their vagueness, rather than in spite of it. I mention these problems in part because more recent writers have sometimes complained that psychological theories of meaning do not include Osgood's factors, which, after all, he found in many different domains. This worry is misguided in my view. Better you should know that cats meow and have whiskers than you should know their potency and evaluation.

14. Note that a word *type* is the abstract word, whereas a word *token* is a particular occurrence of a word. So, in the previous sentence, the word type "word" occurred in three tokens.

15. I am especially indebted to Bob Rehder for pointing out the promise of LSA to me, using simple words that I could understand.

16. In her discussion of Korean spatial words, Bowerman (1996) seems to assume that the fact that the terms are so different between the two languages entails that the speakers must have different concepts. For example, English uses the same word, *in*, to refer to the place-

ment of an apple in a bowl and a videocassette into its case. Korean uses different words for these, because one involves a loose fit and one involves a tight fit (roughly speaking). Thus, "... English- and Korean-speaking children receive different 'instructions' [from their languages] about what spatial actions they should regard as similar" (p. 165). However, as noted in the section on polysemy, often very different senses are included in the same word, and it has been argued that these different senses must be represented separately (Klein and Murphy 2001, in press; Rice 1992, explicitly discusses English spatial prepositions). Thus, children cannot be too naive in thinking that just because a word picks out two kinds of objects, actions, or relations that these two are conceptually identical. And we should not be too fast to assume that just because English describes a number of distinguishable spatial relations with a single term that people view them as being particularly similar. Independent evidence for this claim is needed to avoid a totally circular argument, as noted earlier.

Chapter Twelve

1. There is another kind of nonpredicating adjective, like *mere* and *utter*. You can call someone an *utter fool*, but you can't say *That fool is utter*. However, these adjectives do not refer to categories; there is no class of utter or mere things. Instead, these words are intensifiers or some other kind of discourse operator, similar to *very*. Thus, they fall outside the ambit of conceptual combination.

2. An extensional theory is in some respects anti-psychological, in any case. An extension is a set of objects—not a psychological representation. It should be emphasized that the set here is to be taken literally: the actual set of actual objects, not descriptions of objects or concepts of objects or memories of objects. How are people to manipulate extensions in their heads, when they understand these phrases? Clearly, they don't actually have sets of objects in their minds, and so some other theory is required. So, even if one believed that conceptual combination is compatible with set extension, one would need a different psychological theory to explain how people combine concepts, since what they know is mental descriptions and not extensions. See chapter 11. More realistic extensional models that do not rely strictly on set intersection of the two terms (i.e., that focus on the remembered exemplars of the head noun only) fall afoul of data discussed below in the section on conjunctive concepts.

3. As an aside, this demonstration shows that Jerry Fodor's claim that conceptual combinations do not show typicality differences is false. Fodor (1981) argued that phrases like *grandmother who lives in Chicago* do not admit of typicality differences, which he felt provided an argument against prototype theories of concepts. However, even a moment's thought provides examples of more and less typical exemplars of this concept. The white-haired 65-year-old mother of my father, who lives in the Lincoln Park area of Chicago is prototypical. On the other hand, if she lived in Skokie or Evanston, she would be less typical. A 32-year-old woman whose teenage son has unexpectedly become a father would be an atypical example. If the grandmother likes to bake cookies, go to church, and is socially conservative, she would be considered more typical than if she were a gay arbitrage investment banker. So, it is easy to generate more and less typical examples for grandmothers who live in Chicago and for other combinations. Furthermore, there are now plenty of published data showing typicality differences in conceptual combination, including those of Hampton (1988a,b), in addition to the Smith and Osherson data described here. Perhaps Fodor's claim is a useful example of the dangers of the thought experiment.

4. Note, however, that Smith et al.'s choice of terminology is in keeping with the tradition in the field that every technical term must have at least two incompatible meanings (*attribute* meaning dimension and property), and that every concept must have at least two different names (dimensions being referred to as *attributes, dimensions,* and *slots* in various sources). I think their decision to use the word *attribute* stemmed from a belief that *dimension* refers to quantitative or continuous dimensions only. However, my dictionary makes no such restriction, and *dimension* is often used in nontechnical writing to refer to nonquantitative kinds of variation. In any case, their use of *attribute* seems to have caught on more widely, so that it is now used to mean both a dimension and a value on that dimension.

5. I am not sure that this is Smith et al.'s (1988) intention, but one might think of the votes on features as being related to category validity [i.e., P(feature | category)], whereas diagnosticity is related to cue validity [i.e., P(category | feature)] (see Medin 1981). The latter correspondence is a bit complex, however, because diagnosticity refers to the entire dimension, such as color or size, rather than a single feature.

6. They also considered intensifiers like *very* and *slightly*, as well as negation, attempting to account for concepts like *very red apple* or *slightly non-red apple*. However, this part of the model was noticeably less successful and involved some ad-hoc assumptions that suggest that a different approach may be needed.

7. Such interpretations can be accommodated in a schema view like that advocated by Smith and Osherson or Murphy if one allows inheritance from more general concepts. That is, people know that any object can have a smell and so they can infer a "smells" slot for their cabbage schema. Murphy (1990) provides evidence that such a process can occur but takes considerable time to accomplish. The question is, however, how people know when to perform such an inference process.

8. Current thinking would not attempt to account for the meaning of noun-noun phrases by linguistic analysis because it is so dependent on conceptual knowledge. However, Levi's work was from an earlier paradigm of generative semantics, which still hoped to answer such questions by linguistic rules. For present purposes, it is not relevant whether these relations are really linguistic.

9. A weakness of this enterprise is its reliance on the authors' own intuitions at various points in the experimental design.

10. Gagné and Shoben (1997) appear to forget this point occasionally, when they make remarks such as "one would have thought that the head noun should have exerted some influence on conceptual combination ..." (p. 83). Although the relational preference of the head noun had no significant effect in their task, they themselves are arguing that it did determine the final relation that was selected—that is why they see the slowdown when the modifier preference is not met. It should also be remembered that the head noun typically determines the category of the entire phrase. That is, a mountain magazine is a kind of magazine, not a kind of mountain. It is made of paper and ink, not trees and rocks. So, the head noun is usually (but not always) the semantic basis for the combination, and so it clearly has an enormous effect on the interpretation. See Estes and Glucksberg (2000), Medin and Shoben (1988), and Murphy (1988, 1990), for other effects specifically of the head noun.

11. It can be instructive to think of contexts in which a bizarre interpretation could be justified. For example, if I had stuffed my deceased dog, and then found that a family of mice was living in it, I might refer to it, rather callously, as *an apartment dog*, meaning a dog used as an

apartment. So, it is not that these interpretations are ungrammatical or impossible to get, but just that they describe very unusual states of the world, and so we normally do not think of them.

Chapter Thirteen

1. However, I disclaim any part of the argument that all research should be done in the field. Even when one discovers something new and unknown in anthropological work, it is often necessary to return to the lab to attempt to replicate the results and directly manipulate variables that were only observed in the field, to address the correlation-causation problem. A give and take between the two methods is most likely to lead to progress.

2. Careful readers will note that this is a summary of an anti-summary. It had to happen some day.

3. I did point out some cases in which typicality was influenced by knowledge factors such as that of ideals (Barsalou 1985; Lynch, Coley, and Medin 2000). But my point is that there are purely structural effects of typicality for artificial materials that subjects have no knowledge about. If one does have knowledge about the stimuli, this will of course influence typicality judgments. But in Barsalou's (1985) major study, such structural factors counted for significant variance even when information about ideals was removed. So, there appear to be structural causes of typicality phenomena apart from whatever knowledge effects exist.

4. Since writing this, Heit and Bott (2000) and Bob Rehder and I (2001) have made a start. These models are just first steps at the moment.

5. Part of the reason for this difference is that experimental materials are often very confusable, and so to remember an individual exemplar may take considerable learning. In some real-life categories whose exemplars are distinctive, remembering the individual exemplars may be easier at first than figuring out the category prototype. A simple progression of exemplar-to-prototype or the reverse may not hold across all categories.

References

Adelson, B. (1985). Comparing natural and abstract categories: A case study from computer science. *Cognitive Science*, *9*, 417–430.

Ahn, W. (1990). Effects of background knowledge on family resemblance sorting. *Proceedings of the Twelfth Annual Conference of the Cognitive Science Society* (pp. 149–156). Hillsdale, NJ: Erlbaum.

Ahn, W. (1998). Why are different features central for natural kinds and artifacts? The role of causal status in determining feature centrality. *Cognition*, *69*, 135–178.

Ahn, W., Brewer, W. F., and Mooney, R. J. (1992). Schema acquisition from a single example. *Journal of Experimental Psychology: Learning, Memory, and Cognition*, *18*, 391–412.

Ahn, W., Gelman, S. A., Amsterlaw, J. A., Hohenstein, J., and Kalish, C. W. (2000). Causal status effect in children's categorization. *Cognition*, *76*, B35–B43.

Ahn, W., Kim, N. S., Lassaline, M. E., and Dennis, M. J. (2000). Causal status as a determinant of feature centrality. *Cognitive Psychology*, *41*, 361–416.

Ahn, W. and Medin, D. L. (1992). A two-stage model of category construction. *Cognitive Science*, *16*, 81–121.

Allen, S. W. and Brooks, L. R. (1991). Specializing the operation of an explicit rule. *Journal of Experimental Psychology: General*, *120*, 3–19.

Anderson, J. A. and Murphy, G. L. (1986). The psychology of concepts in a parallel system. *Physica*, *22D*, 318–336.

Anderson, J. R. (1991). The adaptive nature of human categorization. *Psychological Review*, *98*, 409–429.

Anderson, J. R. and Bower, G. H. (1973). *Human Associative Memory*. Washington: Winston.

Anderson, R. C. and Ortony, A. (1975). On putting apples into bottles—A problem of polysemy. *Cognitive Psychology*, *7*, 167–180.

Anglin, J. M. (1977). *Word, Object, and Conceptual Development*. New York: W. W. Norton.

Annett, M. (1959). The classification of instances of four common class concepts by children and adults. *British Journal of Educational Psychology*, *29*, 223–236.

Apostle, H. G. (1980). *Aristotle's Categories and Propositions (De Interpretatione)*. Grinnell, IA: Peripatetic Press.

Armstrong, S. L., Gleitman, L. R., and Gleitman, H. (1983). What some concepts might not be. *Cognition, 13,* 263–308.

Ashby, F. G., Alfonso-Reese, L. A., Turken, A. U., and Waldron, E. M. (1998). A neuro-psychological theory of multiple systems in category learning. *Psychological Review, 105,* 442–481.

Ashby, F. G. and Maddox, W. T. (1993). Relations between exemplar, prototype, and decision bound models of categorization. *Journal of Mathematical Psychology, 37,* 372–400.

Au, T. K. (1983). Chinese and English counterfactuals: The Sapir-Whorf hypothesis revisited. *Cognition, 15,* 155–187.

Baillargeon, R. (1998). Infants' understanding of the physical world. In M. Sabourin, F. Craik, and M. Robert (Eds.), *Advances in Psychological Science, Vol. 2: Biological and Cognitive Aspects* (pp. 503–529). London: Psychology Press.

Baillargeon, R., Spelke, E. S., and Wasserman, S. (1985). Object permanence in five-month-old infants. *Cognition, 20,* 191–208.

Baldwin, D. A., Markman, E. M., and Melartin, R. L. (1993). Infants' ability to draw inferences about nonobvious object properties: Evidence from exploratory play. *Child Development, 64,* 711–728.

Barrett, S. E., Abdi, H., Murphy, G. L., and Gallagher, J. M. (1993). Theory-based correlations and their role in children's concepts. *Child Development, 64,* 1595–1616.

Barsalou, L. W. (1983). Ad hoc categories. *Memory & Cognition, 11,* 211–227.

Barsalou, L. W. (1985). Ideals, central tendency, and frequency of instantiation as determinants of graded structure in categories. *Journal of Experimental Psychology: Learning, Memory, and Cognition, 11,* 629–654.

Barsalou, L. W. (1987). The instability of graded structure: Implications for the nature of concepts. In U. Neisser (Ed.), *Concepts and Conceptual Development: Ecological and Intellectual Factors in Categorization.* Cambridge: Cambridge University Press.

Barsalou, L. W. (1990). On the indistinguishability of exemplar memory and abstraction in category representation. In T. K. Srull and R. S. Wyer, Jr. (Eds.), *Advances in Social Cognition, Vol. III: Content and Process Specificity in the Effects of Prior Experiences* (pp. 61–88). Hillsdale, NJ: Erlbaum.

Barsalou, L. W. (1991). Deriving categories to achieve goals. In G. H. Bower (Ed.), *The Psychology of Learning and Motivation, Vol. 27* (pp. 1–64). New York: Academic Press.

Barsalou, L. W. (1999). Perceptual symbol systems. *Behavioral and Brain Sciences, 22,* 577–660.

Barsalou, L. W., Huttenlocher, J., and Lamberts, K. (1998). Basing categorization on individuals and events. *Cognitive Psychology, 36,* 203–272.

Barsalou, L. W., Yeh, W., Luka, B. J., Olseth, K. L., Mix, K. S., and Wu, L. (1993). Concepts and meaning. In K. Beals, G. Cooke, D. Kathman, K. E. McCullough, S. Kita, and D. Testen (Eds.), *Chicago Linguistics Society 29: Papers from the Parasession on Conceptual Representations* (pp. 400–432). Chicago: Chicago Linguistics Society.

Battig, W. F. and Montague, W. E. (1969). Category norms for verbal items in 56 categories: A replication and extension of the Connecticut category norms. *Journal of Experimental Psychology Monograph, 80* (3, part 2).

Bauer, P. J., Dow, G. A., and Hertsgaard, L. A. (1995). Effects of prototypicality on categorization in 1- to 2-year-olds: Getting down to basic. *Cognitive Development, 10,* 43–68.

Becker, A. H. and Ward, T. B. (1991). Children's use of shape in extending novel labels to animate objects: Identity versus postural change. *Cognitive Development, 6,* 3–16.

Behl-Chadha, G. (1996). Basic-level and superordinate-like categorical representation in early infancy. *Cognition, 60,* 105–141.

Berlin, B. (1992). *Ethnobiological Classification: Principles of Categorization of Plants and Animals in Traditional Societies.* Princeton, NJ: Princeton University Press.

Berlin, B. and Kay, P. (1969). *Basic Color Terms: Their Universality and Evolution.* Berkeley, CA: University of California Press.

Berlin, B., Breedlove, D. E., and Raven, P. H. (1973). General principles of classification and nomenclature in folk biology. *American Anthropologist, 75,* 214–242.

Billman, D. and Knutson, J. (1996). Unsupervised concept learning and value systematicity: A complex whole aids learning the parts. *Journal of Experimental Psychology: Learning, Memory, and Cognition, 22,* 458–475.

Bjorklund, D. F. and Thompson, B. E. (1983). Category typicality effects in children's memory performance: Qualitative and quantitative differences in the processing of category information. *Journal of Experimental Child Psychology, 35,* 329–344.

Blewitt, P. (1983). *Dog* versus *Collie*: Vocabulary in speech to young children. *Developmental Psychology, 19,* 602–609.

Blewitt, P. (1994). Understanding categorical hierarchies: The earliest levels of skill. *Child Development, 65,* 1279–1298.

Bloom, P. (1996). Intention, history, and artifact concepts. *Cognition, 60,* 1–29.

Bloom, P. (2000). *How Children Learn the Meanings of Words.* Cambridge, MA: MIT Press.

Bloom, P. (2001). Roots of word learning. In M. Bowerman and S. C. Levinson (Eds.), *Language Acquisition and Conceptual Development* (pp. 159–181). Cambridge: Cambridge University Press.

Bloom, P. and Markson, L. (1998). Capacities underlying word learning. *Trends in Cognitive Science, 2,* 67–73.

Bomba, P. C. and Siqueland, E. R. (1983). The nature and structure of infant form categories. *Journal of Experimental Child Psychology, 35,* 294–328.

Boster, J. S. and Johnson, J. C. (1989). Form or function: A comparison of expert and novice judgments of similarity among fish. *American Anthropologist, 91,* 866–889.

Bowerman, M. (1996). The origins of children's spacial semantic categories: Cognitive versus linguistic determinants. In J. J. Gumperz and S. C. Levinson (Eds.), *Rethinking Linguistic Relativity* (pp. 145–176). Cambridge: Cambridge University Press.

Boyd, R. (1999). Homeostasis, species, and higher taxa. In R. A. Wilson (Ed.), *Species: New Interdisciplinary Essays* (pp. 141–185). Cambridge, MA: MIT Press.

Bransford, J. D., Barclay, J. R., and Franks, J. J. (1972). Sentence memory: A constructive versus interpretive approach. *Cognitive Psychology, 3,* 193–209.

Brooks, L. R. (1987). Decentralized control of categorization: The role of prior processing episodes. In U. Neisser (Ed.), *Concepts and Conceptual Development: Ecological and Intellectual Factors in Categorization* (pp. 141–174). Cambridge: Cambridge University Press.

Brooks, L. R., Norman, G. R., and Allen, S. W. (1991). Role of specific similarity in a medical diagnosis task. *Journal of Experimental Psychology: General, 120,* 278–287.

Brown, R. (1958a). How shall a thing be called? *Psychological Review, 65,* 14–21.

Brown, R. (1958b). *Words and Things.* Glencoe, IL: The Free Press.

Bruner, J. S., Goodnow, J. J., and Austin, G. A. (1956). *A Study of Thinking.* New York: Wiley.

Burgess, C., Livesay, K., and Lund, K. (1998). Explorations in context space: Words, sentences, discourse. *Discourse Processes, 25,* 211–257.

Callanan, M. A. (1985). How parents label objects for young children: The role of input in the acquisition of category hierarchies. *Child Development, 56,* 508–523.

Callanan, M. A. (1989). Development of object categories and inclusion relations: Preschoolers' hypotheses about word meanings. *Developmental Psychology, 25,* 207–216.

Callanan, M. A. (1990). Parents' descriptions of objects: Potential data for children's inferences about category principles. *Cognitive Development, 5,* 101–122.

Callanan, M. A. and Markman, E. M. (1982). Principles of organization in young children's natural language hierarchies. *Child Development, 53,* 1093–1101.

Cantor, N. and Mischel, W. (1979). Prototypes in person perception. In L. Berkowitz (Ed.), *Advances in Experimental Social Psychology, Vol. 12* (pp. 3–52). New York: Academic Press.

Cantor, N., Smith, E. E., French, R. de S., and Mezzich, J. (1980). Psychiatric diagnosis as prototype categorization. *Journal of Abnormal Psychology, 89,* 181–193.

Caramazza, A. and Grober, E. (1976). Polysemy and the structure of the subjective lexicon. In C. Rameh (Ed.), *Georgetown University Roundtable on Languages and Linguistics. Semantics: Theory and Application* (pp. 181–206). Washington, DC: Georgetown University Press.

Carey, S. (1978). The child as word learner. In M. Halle, J. Bresnan, and G. A. Miller (Eds.), *Linguistic Theory and Psychological Reality* (pp. 264–293). Cambridge, MA: MIT Press.

Carey, S. (1982). Semantic development: The state of the art. In E. Wanner and L. R. Gleitman (Eds.), *Language Acquisition: The State of the Art* (pp. 347–389). Cambridge: Cambridge University Press.

Carey, S. (1985). *Conceptual Change in Childhood.* Cambridge, MA: MIT Press.

Chang, T. (1986). Semantic memory: Facts and models. *Psychological Bulletin, 99,* 199–220.

Chi, M. T., Feltovich, P. J., and Glaser, R. (1981). Categorization and representation of physics problems by experts and novices. *Cognitive Science, 5,* 121–152.

Chi, M. T. H., Hutchinson, J. E., and Robin, A. F. (1989). How inferences about novel domain-related concepts can be constrained by structured knowledge. *Merrill-Palmer Quarterly, 35,* 27–62.

Chierchia, G. and McConnell-Ginet, S. (1990). *Meaning and Grammar: An Introduction to Semantics.* Cambridge, MA: MIT Press.

Chin-Parker, S. and Ross, B. H. (in press). The effect of category learning on sensitivity to within-category correlations. *Memory & Cognition.*

Chomsky, N. (1959). Review of Skinner's *Verbal Behavior. Language, 35,* 26–58.

Church, B. A. and Schachter, D. L. (1994). Perceptual specificity of auditory priming: Implicit memory for voice intonation and fundamental frequency. *Journal of Experimental Psychology: Learning, Memory, and Cognition, 20,* 521–533.

Clark, E. V. (1983). Meaning and concepts. In J. H. Flavell and E. M. Markman (Eds.), *Manual of Child Psychology: Cognitive Development* (Vol. 3, pp. 787–840). New York: Wiley.

Clark, E. V. (1973). What's in a word? On the child's acquisition of semantics in his first language. In T. E. Moore (Ed.), *Cognitive Development and the Acquisition of Language* (pp. 65–110). New York: Academic Press.

Clark, E. V. (1993). *The Lexicon in Acquisition.* Cambridge: Cambridge University Press.

Clark, E. V. and Clark, H. H. (1979). When nouns surface as verbs. *Language, 55,* 767–811.

Clark, H. H. (1974). *Semantics and Comprehension.* The Hague: Mouton.

Clark, H. H. (1983). Making sense of nonce sense. In G. B. Flores d'Arcais and R. J. Jarvella (Eds.), *The Process of Language Understanding* (pp. 297–331). New York: John Wiley.

Clark, H. H. (1991). Words, the world, and their possibilities. In G. R. Lockhead and J. R. Pomerantz (Eds.), *The Perception of Structure.* Washington, DC: American Psychological Association.

Clark, H. H. (1996). *Using Language.* Cambridge: Cambridge University Press.

Clark, H. H. and Clark, E. V. (1977). *Psychology and Language.* New York: Harcourt Brace Jovanovich.

Clark, H. H. and Wilkes-Gibbs, D. (1986). Referring as a collaborative process. *Cognition, 22,* 1–39.

Cohen, L. B. and Caputo, N. (1978). Instructing infants to respond to perceptual categories. Paper presented at the Midwestern Psychological Association Convention, Chicago, May.

Cohen, B. and Murphy, G. L. (1984). Models of concepts. *Cognitive Science, 8,* 27–58.

Coleman, L. and Kay, P. (1981). Prototype semantics: The English word *lie. Language, 57,* 2644.

Coley, J. D., Medin, D. L., and Atran, S. (1997). Does rank have its privilege? Inductive inferences within folkbiological taxonomies. *Cognition, 64,* 73–112.

Coley, J. D., Medin, D. L., Proffitt, J. B., Lynch, E., and Atran, S. (1999). Inductive reasoning in folkbiological thought. In D. L. Medin and S. Atran (Eds.), *Folkbiology* (pp. 205–232). Cambridge, MA: MIT Press.

Collins, A. M. and Loftus, E. F. (1975). A spreading-activation theory of semantic processing. *Psychological Review, 82,* 407–428.

Collins, A. M. and Quillian, M. R. (1969). Retrieval time from semantic memory. *Journal of Verbal Learning and Verbal Behavior, 8,* 241–248.

Collins, A. M. and Quillian, M. R. (1970). Does category size affect categorization time? *Journal of Verbal Learning and Verbal Behavior, 9,* 432–438.

Conrad, C. (1972). Cognitive economy in semantic memory. *Journal of Experimental Psychology, 92,* 149–154.

Corter, J. E. and Gluck, M. A. (1992). Explaining basic categories: Feature predictability and information. *Psychological Bulletin, 111*, 291–303.

Croft, W. (1991). *Categories and Grammatical Relations: The Cognitive Organization of Information*. Chicago: University of Chicago Press.

Cruse, D. A. (1977). The pragmatics of lexical specificity. *Journal of Linguistics, 13*, 153–164.

Cruse, D. A. (1986). *Lexical Semantics*. Cambridge: Cambridge University Press.

DeJong, G. F. and Mooney, R. J. (1986). Explanation-based learning: An alternative view. *Machine Learning, 1*, 145–176.

Dougherty, J. W. D. (1978). Salience and relativity in classification. *American Ethnologist, 5*, 66–80.

Downing, P. (1977). On the creation and use of English compound nouns. *Language, 53*, 810–842.

Dowty, D. R., Wall, R. E., and Peters, S. (1981). *Introduction to Montague Semantics*. Dordrecht, Holland: D. Reidel.

Eimas, P. D. and Quinn, P. C. (1994). Studies on the formation of perceptually based basic-level categories in young infants. *Child Development, 65*, 903–917.

Estes, W. K. (1986). Memory storage and retrieval processes in category learning. *Journal of Experimental Psychology: General, 115*, 155–174.

Estes, W. K. (1994). *Classification and Cognition*. Oxford: Oxford University Press.

Estes, Z. and Glucksberg, S. (2000). Interactive property attribution in concept combination. *Memory & Cognition, 28*, 28–34.

Federmeier, K. D. and Kutas, M. (1999). A rose by any other name: Long-term memory structure and sentence processing. *Journal of Memory and Language, 41*, 469–495.

Fillmore, C. J. (1982). Frame semantics. In Linguistics Society of Korea (Ed.), *Linguistics in the Morning Calm: Selected Papers from SICOL-1981* (pp. 111–137). Seoul: Anshin Publishing Co.

Fisher, C. (2000). Partial sentence structure as an early constraint on language acquisition. In B. Landau, J. Sabini, J. Jonides, and E. L. Newport (Eds.), *Perception, Cognition, and Language: Essays in Honor of Henry and Lila Gleitman* (pp. 275–290). Cambridge, MA: MIT Press.

Fodor, J. (1972). Some reflections on L. S. Vygotsky's *Thought and Language. Cognition, 1*, 83–95.

Fodor, J. A. (1975). *The Language of Thought*. New York: Crowell.

Fodor, J. A. (1981). The present status of the innateness controversy. In *Representations: Philosophical Essays on the Foundations of Cognitive Science*. Cambridge, MA: MIT Press.

Fodor, J. A. (1983). *The Modularity of Mind*. Cambridge, MA: MIT Press.

Fodor, J. A. (1998). *Concepts: Where Cognitive Science Went Wrong*. Oxford: Clarendon Press.

Fodor, J. D. (1977). *Semantics: Theories of Meaning in Generative Grammar*. New York: Crowell.

Follett, W. (1970). *Modern American Usage*. New York: Grosset and Dunlap.

Franks, J. J. and Bransford, J. D. (1971). Abstraction of visual patterns. *Journal of Experimental Psychology, 90,* 65–74.

Gagné, C. L. (1997). Use of recently-encountered examples during the interpretation of noun-noun phrases. Unpublished Ph.D. thesis, Psychology Department, University of Illinois.

Gagné, C. L. and Murphy, G. L. (1996). Influence of discourse context on feature availability in conceptual combination. *Discourse Processes, 22,* 79–101.

Gagné, C. L. and Shoben, E. J. (1997). Influence of thematic relations on the comprehension of modifier-noun combinations. *Journal of Experimental Psychology: Learning, Memory, and Cognition, 23,* 71–87.

Garrod, S. and Anderson, A. (1987). Saying what you mean in dialogue: A study in conceptual and semantic co-ordination. *Cognition, 27,* 181–218.

Garrod, S. and Doherty, G. (1994). Conversation, co-ordination and convention: An empirical investigation of how groups establish linguistic conventions. *Cognition, 53,* 181–215.

Garrod, S. and Sanford, A. (1977). Interpreting anaphoric relations: The integration of semantic information while reading. *Journal of Verbal Learning and Verbal Behavior, 16,* 77–90.

Gelman, R. (1990). First principles organize attention to and learning about relevant data: Number and the animate-inanimate distinction as examples. *Cognitive Science, 14,* 79–106.

Gelman, S. A. (1988). The development of induction within natural kind and artifact categories. *Cognitive Psychology, 20,* 65–95.

Gelman, S. A., Coley, J. D., and Gottfried, G. M. (1994). Essentialist beliefs in children: The acquisition of concepts and theories. In L. A. Hirschfeld and S. A. Gelman (Eds.), *Mapping the Mind: Domain Specificity in Cognition and Culture* (pp. 341–365). Cambridge: Cambridge University Press.

Gelman, S. A., Croft, W., Fu, P., Clausner, T., and Gottfried, G. (1998). Why is a pomegranate an *apple*? The role of shape, taxonomic relatedness, and prior lexical knowledge in children's overextensions of *apple* and *dog*. *Journal of Child Language, 25,* 267–291.

Gelman, S. A. and Markman, E. M. (1986). Categories and induction in young children. *Cognition, 23,* 183–209.

Gelman, S. A. and Markman, E. M. (1987). Young children's inductions from natural kinds: The role of categories and appearances. *Child Development, 58,* 1532–1541.

Gelman, S. A. and Wellman, H. M. (1991). Insides and essences: Early understandings of the non-obvious. *Cognition, 38,* 213–244.

Gentner, D. and France, I. M. (1988). The verb mutability effect: Studies of the combinatorial semantics of nouns and verbs. In S. L. Small, G. W. Cottrell, and M. K. Tanenhaus (Eds.), *Lexical Ambiguity Resolution: Perspectives from Psycholinguistics, Neuropsychology, and Artificial Intelligence*. San Mateo, CA: Morgan Kaufman.

Gentner, D. and Stevens, A. L. (Eds.) (1983). *Mental Models*. Hillsdale, NJ: Erlbaum.

Gerrig, R. J. (1989). The time course of sense creation. *Memory & Cognition, 17,* 194–207.

Gerrig, R. J. and Murphy, G. L. (1992). Contextual influences on the comprehension of complex concepts. *Language and Cognitive Processes, 7,* 205–230.

Gibbs, R. W., Jr. (1984). Literal meaning and psychological theory. *Cognitive Science, 8,* 275–304.

Glass, A. L. and Holyoak, K. J. (1975). Alternative conceptions of semantic memory. *Cognition, 3,* 313–339.

Gluck, M. A. and Bower, G. H. (1988). From conditioning to category learning: An adaptive network model. *Journal of Experimental Psychology: General, 117,* 227–247.

Glucksberg, S. and Estes, Z. (2000). Feature accessibility in conceptual combination: Effects of context-induced relevance. *Psychonomic Bulletin & Review, 7,* 510–515.

Goldstone, R. L. (1994a). Influences of categorization on perceptual discrimination. *Journal of Experimental Psychology: General, 123,* 178–200.

Goldstone, R. L. (1994b). Similarity, interactive activation, and mapping. *Journal of Experimental Psychology: Learning, Memory, and Cognition, 20,* 3–28.

Goldstone, R. L. (2000). Unitization during category learning. *Journal of Experimental Psychology: Human Perception and Performance, 26,* 86–112.

Goldstone, R. L. and Steyvers, M. (2001). The sensitization and differentiation of dimensions during category learning. *Journal of Experimental Psychology: General, 130,* 116–139.

Golinkoff, R. M., Shuff-Bailey, M., Olguin, R., and Ruan, W. (1995). Young children extend novel words at the basic level: Evidence for the principle of categorical scope. *Developmental Psychology, 31,* 494–507.

Goodman, N. (1965). *Fact, Fiction, and Forecast (2nd ed.).* Indianapolis: Bobbs-Merrill.

Graves, R. (1926). *Impenetrability or the Proper Habit of English.* London: Hogarth Press.

Grice, H. P. (1975). Logic and conversation. In P. Cole and J. L. Morgan (Eds.), *Syntax and Semantics 3: Speech Acts* (pp. 41–58). New York: Academic Press.

Gumperz, J. J. and Levinson, S. C. (Eds.). (1996). *Rethinking Linguistic Relativity.* Cambridge: Cambridge University Press.

Haith, M. M. and Benson, J. B. (1998). Infant cognition. In D. Kuhn and R. S. Siegler (Eds.), *Handbook of Child Psychology, Vol. 2: Cognition, Perception, and Language* (pp. 199–254). New York: John Wiley.

Hall, D. G. and Waxman, S. R. (1993). Assumptions about word meaning: Individuation and basic-level kinds. *Child Development, 64,* 1550–1570.

Hampton, J. A. (1979). Polymorphous concepts in semantic memory. *Journal of Verbal Learning and Verbal Behavior, 18,* 441–461.

Hampton, J. A. (1982). A demonstration of intransitivity in natural categories. *Cognition, 12,* 151–164.

Hampton, J. A. (1987). Inheritance of attributes in natural concept conjunctions. *Memory & Cognition, 15,* 55–71.

Hampton, J. A. (1988a). Disjunction of natural concepts. *Memory & Cognition, 16,* 579–591.

Hampton, J. A. (1988b). Overextension of conjunctive concepts: Evidence for a unitary model of concept typicality and class inclusion. *Journal of Experimental Psychology: Learning, Memory, and Cognition, 14,* 12–32.

Hampton, J. A. (1993). Prototype models of concept representation. In I. Van Mechelen, J. Hampton, R. Michalski, and P. Theuns (Eds.), *Categories and Concepts: Theoretical Views and Inductive Data Analysis* (pp. 67–95). New York: Academic Press.

Hampton, J. A. (1995). Testing the prototype theory of concepts. *Journal of Memory and Language, 34*, 686–708.

Hampton, J. A. (1996). Conjunctions of visually based categories: Overextension and compensation. *Journal of Experimental Psychology: Learning, Memory, and Cognition, 22*, 378–396.

Hampton, J. A. (1997). Conceptual combination: Conjunction and negation of natural concepts. *Memory & Cognition, 25*, 888–909.

Hampton, J. A. and Springer, K. (1989). Long talks are boring. Paper presented at the 30th annual meeting of the Psychonomic Society, November, Atlanta, GA.

Hart, H. L. A. (1961). *The Concept of Law*. Oxford: Clarendon Press.

Haviland, S. E. and Clark, H. H. (1974). What's new? Acquiring new information as a process in comprehension. *Journal of Verbal Learning and Verbal Behavior, 13*, 512–521.

Hayes, B. K. and Taplin, J. E. (1992). Developmental changes in categorization processes: Knowledge and similarity-based modes of categorization. *Journal of Experimental Child Psychology, 54*, 188–212.

Hayes, B. K. and Taplin, J. E. (1993). Developmental differences in the use of prototype and exemplar-specific information. *Journal of Experimental Child Psychology, 55*, 329–352.

Hayes-Roth, B. and Hayes-Roth, F. (1977). Concept learning and the recognition and classification of exemplars. *Journal of Verbal Learning and Verbal Behavior, 16*, 321–328.

Heibeck, T. H. and Markman, E. M. (1987). Word learning in children: An examination of fast mapping. *Child Development, 58*, 1021–1034.

Heit, E. (1994). Similarity and property effects in inductive reasoning. *Journal of Experimental Psychology: Learning, Memory, and Cognition, 20*, 411–422.

Heit, E. (1997). Knowledge and concept learning. In K. Lamberts and D. Shanks (Eds.), *Knowledge, Concepts and Categories* (pp. 7–41). Hove, England: Psychology Press.

Heit, E. (1998). Influences of prior knowledge on selective weighting of category members. *Journal of Experimental Psychology: Learning, Memory, and Cognition, 24*, 712–731.

Heit, E. and Bott, L. (2000). Knowledge selection in category learning. In D. L. Medin (Ed.), *Psychology of Learning and Motivation* (pp. 163–199). San Diego: Academic Press.

Heit, E. and Rubinstein, J. (1994). Similarity and property effects in inductive reasoning. *Journal of Experimental Psychology: Learning, Memory, and Cognition, 20*, 411–422.

Hintzman, D. L. (1986). "Schema abstraction" in a multiple-trace memory model. *Psychology Review, 93*, 411–428.

Hintzman, D. L. and Ludlam, G. (1980). Differential forgetting of prototypes and old instances: Simulation by an exemplar-based classification model. *Memory & Cognition, 4*, 378–382.

Hirschfeld, L. A. (1996). *Race in the Making: Cognition, Culture, and the Child's Construction of Human Kinds*. Cambridge, MA: MIT Press.

Hirschfeld, L. A. and Gelman, S. A. (Eds.) (1994). *Mapping the Mind: Domain Specificity in Cognition and Culture*. Cambridge: Cambridge University Press.

Homa, D. (1984). On the nature of categories. In G. H. Bower (Ed.), *The Psychology of Learning and Motivation, Vol. 18* (pp. 49–94). New York: Academic Press.

Homa, D., Sterling, S., and Trepel, L. (1981). Limitations of exemplar-based generalization and the abstraction of categorical information. *Journal of Experimental Psychology: Human Learning and Memory, 7*, 418–439.

Homa, D. and Vosburgh, R. (1976). Category breadth and the abstraction of prototypical information. *Journal of Experimental Psychology: Human Learning and Memory, 2*, 322–330.

Hörmann, H. (1983). The calculating listener, or How many are *einige, mehrere* and *ein paar* (some, several, and a few)? In R. Bäurle, C. Schwarze, and A. von Stechow (Eds.), *Meaning, Use, and Interpretation of Language* (pp. 221–234). Berlin: de Gruyter.

Horton, M. S. and Markman, E. M. (1980). Developmental differences in the acquisition of basic and superordinate categories. *Child Development, 51*, 708–719.

Hull, C. L. (1920). Quantitative aspects of the evolution of concepts. *Psychological Monographs, XXVIII*.

Huttenlocher, J. and Smiley, P. (1987). Early word meanings: The case of object names. *Cognitive Psychology, 19*, 63–89.

Inhelder, B. and Piaget, J. (1964). *The Early Growth of Logic in the Child: Classification and Seriation*. London: Routledge and Kegan Paul.

Jacoby, L. L. (1983). Remembering the data: Analyzing interactive processes in reading. *Journal of Verbal Learning and Verbal Behavior, 22*, 485–508.

Jacoby, L. L., Baker, J. G., and Brooks, L. R. (1989). Episodic effects on picture identification: Implications for theories of concept learning and theories of memory. *Journal of Experimental Psychology: Learning, Memory, and Cognition, 15*, 275–281.

John, O. P., Hampson, S. E., and Goldberg, L. R. (1991). The basic level of personality-trait hierarchies: Studies of trait use and accessibility in different contexts. *Journal of Personality and Social Psychology, 60*, 348–361.

Johnson, C. and Keil, F. C. (2000). Explanatory understanding and conceptual combination. In F. C. Keil and R. A. Wilson (Eds.), *Explanation and Cognition* (pp. 328–359). Cambridge, MA: MIT Press.

Johnson, K. E. and Mervis, C. B. (1994). Microgenetic analysis of first steps in children's acquisition of expertise on shorebirds. *Developmental Psychology, 30*, 418–435.

Johnson, K. E., Scott, P., and Mervis, C. B. (1997). Development of children's understanding of basic-subordinate inclusion relations. *Developmental Psychology, 33*, 745–763.

Johnson, S. C. and Solomon, G. E. A. (1997). Why dogs have puppies and cats have kittens: The role of birth in young children's understanding of biological origins. *Child Development, 68*, 404–419.

Johnson-Laird, P. N. (1983). *Mental Models*. Cambridge, MA: MIT Press.

Jolicoeur, P., Gluck, M., and Kosslyn, S. M. (1984). Pictures and names: Making the connection. *Cognitive Psychology, 19*, 31–53.

Jones, G. V. (1983). Identifying basic categories. *Psychological Bulletin*, 94, 423–428.

Jones, S. S. and Smith, L. S. (1993). The place of perception in children's concepts. *Cognitive Development*, 8, 113–139.

Jones, S. S., Smith, L. S., and Landau, B. (1991). Object properties and knowledge in early lexical learning. *Child Development*, 62, 499–516.

Kalish, C. W. and Gelman, S. A. (1992). On wooden pillows: Multiple classification and children's category-based inductions. *Child Development*, 63, 1536–1557.

Kaplan, A. S. (1999). Alignability and prior knowledge in category learning. Unpublished Ph.D. thesis, Department of Psychology, University of Illinois.

Kaplan, A. S. and Murphy, G. L. (1999). The acquisition of category structure in unsupervised learning. *Memory & Cognition*, 27, 699–712.

Kaplan, A. S. and Murphy, G. L. (2000). Category learning with minimal prior knowledge. *Journal of Experimental Psychology: Learning, Memory, and Cognition*, 26, 829–846.

Katz, J. J. and Fodor, J. A. (1963). The structure of a semantic theory. *Language*, 39, 170–210.

Katz, N., Baker, E., and Macnamara, J. (1974). What's in a name? A study of how children learn common and proper names. *Child Development*, 45, 469–473.

Kawamoto, A. H. (1993). Nonlinear dynamics in the resolution of lexical ambiguity: A parallel distributed processing account. *Journal of Memory and Language*, 32, 474–516.

Kay, P. and Zimmer, K. (1976). On the semantics of compounds and genitives in English. *Sixth California Linguistics Association Proceedings*. San Diego: Campile Press.

Keleman, D. and Bloom, P. (1994). Domain-specific knowledge in simple categorization tasks. *Psychonomic Bulletin & Review*, 1, 390–395.

Keil, F. C. (1989). *Concepts, Kinds, and Cognitive Development*. Cambridge, MA: MIT Press.

Keil, F. C. (1994). The birth and nurturance of concepts by domains: The origins of concepts of living things. In L. A. Hirschfeld and S. A. Gelman (Eds.), *Mapping the Mind: Domain Specificity in Cognition and Culture* (pp. 234–254). Cambridge: Cambridge University Press.

Kelly, M. H., Bock, J. K., and Keil, F. C. (1986). Prototypicality in a linguistic context: Effects on sentence structure. *Journal of Memory and Language*, 25, 59–74.

Kemler, D. G. (1981). New issues in the study of infant categorization: A reply to Husaim and Cohen. *Merrill-Palmer Quarterly*, 27, 457–463.

Kemler Nelson, D. G. (1995). Principle-based inferences in young children's categorization: Revisiting the impact of function on the naming of artifacts. *Cognitive Development*, 10, 347–380.

Keysar, B., Barr, D. J., Balin, J. A., and Brauner, J. S. (2000). Taking perspective in conversation: The role of mutual knowledge in comprehension. *Psychological Science*, 11, 32–38.

Klein, D. E. and Murphy, G. L. (2001). The representation of polysemous words. *Journal of Memory and Language*, 45, 259–282.

Klein, D. E. and Murphy, G. L. (in press). Paper has been my ruin: Conceptual relations of polysemous senses. *Journal of Memory and Language*.

Klibanoff, R. S. and Waxman, S. R. (2000). Basic level object categories support the acquisition of novel adjectives: Evidence from preschool-aged children. *Child Development, 71,* 649–659.

Knapp, A. G. and Anderson, J. A. (1984). Theory of categorization based on distributed memory storage. *Journal of Experimental Psychology: Learning, Memory, and Cognition, 10,* 616–637.

Kolers, P. A. and Ostry, D. J. (1974). Time course of loss of information regarding pattern analyzing operations. *Journal of Verbal Learning and Verbal Behavior, 13,* 599–612.

Krascum, R. M. and Andrews, S. A. (1998). The effects of theories on children's acquisition of family-resemblance categories. *Child Development, 69,* 333–346.

Krauss, R. M. and Weinheimer, S. (1966). Concurrent feedback, confirmation, and the encoding of referents in verbal communication. *Journal of Personality and Social Psychology, 4,* 343–346.

Kruschke, J. K. (1991). Dimensional attention learning models of human categorization. In *Proceedings of the Thirteenth Annual Conference of the Cognitive Science Society* (pp. 281–286). Hillsdale, NJ: Erlbaum.

Kruschke, J. K. (1992). ALCOVE: An exemplar-based connectionist model of category learning. *Psychological Review, 99,* 22–44.

Kruschke, J. K. (1993). Three principles for models of category learning. In G. V. Nakamura, R. Taraban, and D. L. Medin (Eds.), *Categorization by Humans and Machines: The Psychology of Learning and Motivation,* Vol. 29 (pp. 57–90). San Diego: Academic Press.

Kruschke, J. K. (1996). Base rates in category learning. *Journal of Experimental Psychology: Learning, Memory, and Cognition, 22,* 3–26.

Kruschke, J. K. and Johansen, M. K. (1999). A model of probabilistic category learning. *Journal of Experimental Psychology: Learning, Memory, and Cognition, 25,* 1083–1119.

Kunda, Z., Miller, D. T., and Claire, T. (1990). Combining social concepts: The role of causal reasoning. *Cognitive Science, 14,* 551–577.

Lakoff, G. (1987). *Women, Fire, and Dangerous Things: What Categories Reveal about the Mind.* Chicago: University of Chicago Press.

Lamberts, K. (1995). Categorization under time pressure. *Journal of Experimental Psychology: General, 124,* 161–180.

Lamberts, K. (2000). Information-accumulation theory of speeded categorization. *Psychological Review, 107,* 227–260.

Landau, B., Smith, L. B., and Jones, S. S. (1988). The importance of shape in early lexical learning. *Cognitive Development, 3,* 299–321.

Landauer, T. K. and Dumais, S. T. (1997). A solution to Plato's problem: The latent semantic analysis theory of acquisition, induction, and representation of knowledge. *Psychological Review, 104,* 211–240.

Lasky, R. E. (1974). The ability of six-year-olds, eight-year-olds, and adults to abstract visual patterns. *Child Development, 45,* 626–632.

Lassaline, M. E. (1996). Structural alignment in induction and similarity. *Journal of Experimental Psychology: Learning, Memory, and Cognition, 22,* 754–770.

Lassaline, M. E. and Murphy, G. L. (1996). Induction and category coherence. *Psychonomic Bulletin & Review, 3*, 95–99.

Lassaline, M. E. and Murphy, G. L. (1998). Alignment and category learning. *Journal of Experimental Psychology: Learning, Memory, and Cognition, 24*, 144–160.

Lassaline, M. E., Wisniewski, E. J., and Medin, D. L. (1992). The basic level in artificial and natural categories: Are all basic levels created equal? In B. Burns (Ed.), *Percepts, Concepts and Categories: The Representation and Processing of Information*. Amsterdam: Elsevier.

Lehrer, A. (1990). Polysemy, conventionality, and the structure of the lexicon. *Cognitive Linguistics, 1*, 207–246.

Lesgold, A. M. (1984). Acquiring expertise. In J. R. Anderson and S. M. Kosslyn (Eds.), *Tutorials in Learning and Memory: Essays in Honor of Gordon Bower* (pp. 31–60). San Francisco: W. H. Freeman.

Levi, J. N. (1978). *The Syntax and Semantics of Complex Nominals*. New York: Academic Press.

Lin, E. L. and Murphy, G. L. (1997). The effects of background knowledge on object categorization and part detection. *Journal of Experimental Psychology: Human Perception and Performance, 23*, 1153–1169.

Lin, E. L. and Murphy, G. L. (2001). Thematic relations in adults' concepts. *Journal of Experimental Psychology: General, 130*, 3–28.

Lin, E. L., Murphy, G. L., and Shoben, E. J. (1997). The effect of prior processing episodes on basic-level superiority. *Quarterly Journal of Experimental Psychology, 50A*, 25–48.

López, A., Atran, S., Coley, J. D., Medin, D. L., and Smith, E. E. (1997). The tree of life: Universal and cultural features of folkbiological taxonomies and inductions. *Cognitive Psychology, 32*, 251–295.

López, A., Gelman, S. A., Gutheil, G., and Smith, E. E. (1992). The development of category-based induction. *Child Development, 63*, 1070–1090.

Lucy, J. A. (1992). *Language Diversity and Thought: A Reformulation of the Linguistic Relativity Hypothesis*. Cambridge: Cambridge University Press.

Lund, K. and Burgess, C. (1996). Producing high-dimensional semantic spaces from lexical co-occurrence. *Behavior Research Methods, Instruments, & Computers, 28*, 203–208.

Lund, K., Burgess, C., and Atchley, R. A. (1995). Semantic and associative priming in high dimensional semantic space. In *Proceedings of the Seventeenth Annual Conference of the Cognitive Science Society* (pp. 660–665). Hillsdale, NJ: Erlbaum.

Luria, A. R. (1976). *Cognitive Development: Its Cultural and Social Foundations*. Cambridge, MA: MIT Press.

Lynch, E. B., Coley, J. B., and Medin, D. L. (2000). Tall is typical: Central tendency, ideal dimensions, and graded category structure among tree experts and novices. *Memory & Cognition, 28*, 41–50.

Macnamara, J. (1986). *A Border Dispute: The Place of Logic in Psychology*. Cambridge, MA: MIT Press.

Maddox, W. T. (1999). On the dangers of averaging across observers when comparing decision bound models and generalized context models of categorization. *Perception & Psychophysics, 61*, 354–374.

Madole, K. L. and Cohen, L. B. (1995). The role of object parts in infants' attention to form-function correlations. *Developmental Psychology, 31,* 637–648.

Malt, B. C. (1989). An on-line investigation of prototype and exemplar strategies in classification. *Journal of Experimental Psychology: Learning, Memory, and Cognition, 15,* 539–555.

Malt, B. C. (1995). Category coherence in cross-cultural perspective. *Cognitive Psychology, 29,* 85–148.

Malt, B. C., Ross, B. H., and Murphy, G. L. (1995). Predicting features for members of natural categories when categorization is uncertain. *Journal of Experimental Psychology: Learning, Memory, and Cognition, 21,* 646–661.

Malt, B. C., Sloman, S. A., Gennari, S., Shi, M., and Wang, Y. (1999). Knowing versus naming: Similarity and the linguistic categorization of artifacts. *Journal of Memory and Language, 40,* 230–262.

Malt, B. C. and Smith, E. E. (1982). The role of familiarity in determining typicality. *Memory & Cognition, 10,* 69–75.

Malt, B. C. and Smith, E. E. (1984). Correlated properties in natural categories. *Journal of Verbal Learning and Verbal Behavior, 23,* 250–269.

Mandler, J. M. (1992). How to build a baby: II. Conceptual primitives. *Psychological Review, 99,* 587–604.

Mandler, J. M. (1998). Representation. In D. Kuhn and R. S. Siegler (Eds.), *Handbook of Child Psychology (5th ed.), Vol. 2: Cognition, Perception, and Language* (pp. 255–308). New York: Wiley.

Mandler, J. M., Bauer, P. J., and McDonough, L. (1991). Separating the sheep from the goats: Differentiating global categories. *Cognitive Psychology, 23,* 263–298.

Mandler, J. M. and McDonough, L. (1993). Concept formation in infancy. *Cognitive Development, 8,* 291–318.

Mandler, J. M. and McDonough, L. (1996). Drinking and driving don't mix: Inductive generalization in infancy. *Cognition, 59,* 307–335.

Markman, A. B. (1999). *Knowledge Representation.* Mahwah, NJ: Erlbaum.

Markman, A. B. and Gentner, D. (1993). Structural alignment during similarity comparisons. *Cognitive Psychology, 25,* 431–467.

Markman, A. B. and Makin, V. S. (1998). Referential communication and category acquisition. *Journal of Experimental Psychology: General, 127,* 331–354.

Markman, A. B. and Wisniewski, E. J. (1997). Similar and different: The differentiation of basic-level categories. *Journal of Experimental Psychology: Learning, Memory, and Cognition, 23,* 54–70.

Markman, E. M. (1985). Why superordinate category terms can be mass nouns. *Cognition, 19,* 31–53.

Markman, E. M. (1989). *Categorization and Naming in Children: Problems of Induction.* Cambridge, MA: MIT Press.

Markman, E. M. and Callanan, M. A. (1984). An analysis of hierarchical classification. In R. Sternberg (Ed.), *Advances in the Psychology of Human Intelligence, Vol. 2* (pp. 325–365). Hillsdale, NJ: Erlbaum.

Markman, E. M., Cox, B., and Machida, S. (1981). The standard object-sorting task as a measure of conceptual organization. *Developmental Psychology*, 17, 115–117.

Markman, E. M., Horton, M. S., and McClanahan, A. G. (1980). Classes and collections: Principles of organization in the learning of hierarchical relations. *Cognition*, 8, 227–241.

Markman, E. M. and Hutchinson, J. E. (1984). Children's sensitivity to constraints on word meaning: Taxonomic vs thematic relations. *Cognitive Psychology*, 16, 1–27.

Markson, L. and Bloom, P. (1997). Evidence against a dedicated system for word learning in children. *Nature*, 385, 813–815.

Massey, C. M. and Gelman, R. (1988). Preschooler's ability to decide whether a photographed unfamiliar object can move itself. *Developmental Psychology*, 24, 307–317.

Mayr, E. (1982). *The Growth of Biological Thought: Diversity, Evolution, and Inheritance*. Cambridge, MA: Harvard University Press.

McCarrell, N. S. and Callanan, M. A. (1995). Form-function correspondences in children's inference. *Child Development*, 66, 532–546.

McClelland, J. L. and Rumelhart, D. E. (1985). Distributed memory and the representation of general and specific information. *Journal of Experimental Psychology: General*, 114, 159–188.

McCloskey, M. E. and Glucksberg, S. (1978). Natural categories: Well defined or fuzzy sets? *Memory & Cognition*, 6, 462–472.

McCloskey, M. and Glucksberg, S. (1979). Decision processes in verifying category membership statements: Implications for models of semantic memory. *Cognitive Psychology*, 11, 1–37.

McKoon, G. and Ratcliff, R. (1988). Contextually relevant aspects of meaning. *Journal of Experimental Psychology: Learning, Memory, and Cognition*, 13, 331–343.

McRae, K., de Sa, V. R., and Seidenberg, M. S. (1997). On the nature and scope of featural representations of word meaning. *Journal of Experimental Psychology: General*, 126, 99–130.

Medin, D. L. (1983). Structural principles of categorization. In T. Tighe and B. Shepp (Eds.), *Perception, Cognition, and Development: Interactional Analyses* (pp. 203–230). Hillsdale, NJ: Erlbaum.

Medin, D. L., Altom, M. W., Edelson, S. M., and Freko, D. (1982). Correlated symptoms and simulated medical classification. *Journal of Experimental Psychology: Learning, Memory, and Cognition*, 8, 37–50.

Medin, D. L. and Atran, S. (1999). (Eds.), *Folkbiology*. Cambridge, MA: MIT Press.

Medin, D. L. and Bettger, J. G. (1994). Presentation order and recognition of categorically related examples. *Psychonomic Bulletin & Review*, 1, 250–254.

Medin, D. L., Dewey, G. I., and Murphy, T. D. (1983). Relationships between item and category learning: Evidence that abstraction is not automatic. *Journal of Experimental Psychology: Learning, Memory, and Cognition*, 9, 607–625.

Medin, D. L. and Edelson, S. M. (1988). Problem structure and the use of base-rate information from experience. *Journal of Experimental Psychology: General*, 117, 68–85.

Medin, D. L., Goldstone, R. L., and Gentner, D. (1993). Respects for similarity. *Psychological Review, 100,* 254–278.

Medin, D. L., Lynch, E. B., Coley, J. D., and Atran, S. (1997). Categorization and reasoning among tree experts: Do all roads lead to Rome? *Cognitive Psychology, 32,* 49–96.

Medin, D. L. and Ortony, A. (1989). Psychological essentialism. In S. Vosniadou and A. Ortony (Eds.), *Similarity and Analogical Reasoning* (pp. 179–195). Cambridge: Cambridge University Press.

Medin, D. L. and Schaffer, M. M. (1978). Context theory of classification learning. *Psychological Review, 85,* 207–238.

Medin, D. L. and Schwanenflugel, P. J. (1981). Linear separability in classification learning. *Journal of Experimental Psychology: Human Learning and Memory, 7,* 355–368.

Medin, D. L. and Shoben, E. J. (1988). Context and structure in conceptual combination. *Cognitive Psychology, 20,* 158–190.

Medin, D. L. and Smith, E. E. (1981). Strategies and classification learning. *Journal of Experimental Psychology: Learning, Memory, and Cognition, 7,* 241–253.

Medin, D. L., Wattenmaker, W. D., and Hampson, S. E. (1987). Family resemblance, conceptual cohesiveness, and category construction. *Cognitive Psychology, 19,* 242–279.

Meints, K., Plunkett, K., and Harris, P. L. (1999). When does an ostrich become a bird? The role of typicality in early word comprehension. *Developmental Psychology, 35,* 1072–1078.

Merriman, W. E., Schuster, J. M., and Hager, L. (1991). Are names ever mapped onto preexisting categories. *Journal of Experimental Psychology: General, 120,* 288–300.

Mervis, C. B. (1987). Child-basic object categories and early lexical development. In U. Neisser (Ed.), *Concepts and Conceptual Development: Ecological and Intellectual Factors in Categorization* (pp. 201–233). Cambridge: Cambridge University Press.

Mervis, C. B., Catlin, J., and Rosch, E. (1976). Relationships among goodness-of-example, category norms, and word frequency. *Bulletin of the Psychonomic Society, 7,* 283–284.

Mervis, C. B. and Crisafi, M. A. (1982). Order of acquisition of subordinate, basic, and superordinate level categories. *Child Development, 53,* 258–266.

Mervis, C. B., Johnson, K. E., and Mervis, C. A. (1994). Acquisition of subordinate categories by 3-year-olds: The roles of attribute salience, linguistic input, and child characteristics. *Cognitive Development, 9,* 211–234.

Mervis, C. B. and Pani, J. R. (1980). Acquisition of basic object categories. *Cognitive Psychology, 12,* 496–522.

Mervis, C. B. and Rosch, E. (1981). Categorization of natural objects. *Annual Review of Psychology, 32,* 89–115.

Miller, G. A. and Johnson-Laird, P. N. (1976). *Language and Perception.* Cambridge, MA: Harvard University Press.

Mooney, R. J. (1993). Integrating theory and data in category learning. In G. V. Nakamura, R. Taraban, and D. L. Medin (Eds.), *The Psychology of Learning and Motivation, Vol. 29: Categorization by Humans and Machines* (pp. 189–218). San Diego: Academic Press.

Morris, M. W. and Murphy, G. L. (1990). Converging operations on a basic level in event taxonomies. *Memory & Cognition, 18,* 407–418.

Murphy, G. L. (1982). Cue validity and levels of categorization. *Psychological Bulletin, 91,* 174–177.

Murphy, G. L. (1988). Comprehending complex concepts. *Cognitive Science, 12,* 529–562.

Murphy, G. L. (1990). Noun phrase interpretation and conceptual combination. *Journal of Memory and Language, 29,* 259–288.

Murphy, G. L. (1991a). Meaning and concepts. In P. Schwanenflugel (Ed.), *The Psychology of Word Meaning* (pp. 11–35). Hillsdale, NJ: Erlbaum.

Murphy, G. L. (1991b). Parts in object concepts: Experiments with artificial categories. *Memory & Cognition, 19,* 423–438.

Murphy, G. L. (1993). A rational theory of concepts. In G. V. Nakamura, R. M. Taraban, and D. L. Medin (Eds.), *The Psychology of Learning and Motivation, Vol. 29: Categorization by Humans and Machines* (pp. 327–359). New York: Academic Press.

Murphy, G. L. (1993). Theories and concept formation. In I. Van Mechelen, J. Hampton, R. Michalski, and P. Theuns (Eds.), *Categories and Concepts: Theoretical Views and Inductive Data Analysis* (pp. 173–200). New York: Academic Press.

Murphy, G. L. (1997). Polysemy and the creation of new word meanings. In T. B. Ward, S. M. Smith, and J. Vaid (Eds.), *Creative Thought: An Investigation of Conceptual Structures and Processes* (pp. 235–265). Washington, DC: American Psychological Association.

Murphy, G. L. (2000). Explanatory concepts. In F. C. Keil and R. A. Wilson (Eds.), *Explanation and Cognition* (pp. 361–392). Cambridge, MA: MIT Press.

Murphy, G. L. and Allopenna, P. D. (1994). The locus of knowledge effects in concept learning. *Journal of Experimental Psychology: Learning, Memory, and Cognition, 20,* 904–919.

Murphy, G. L. and Andrew, J. M. (1993). The conceptual basis of antonymy and synonymy in adjectives. *Journal of Memory and Language, 32,* 301–319.

Murphy, G. L. and Brownell, H. H. (1985). Category differentiation in object recognition: Typicality constraints on the basic category advantage. *Journal of Experimental Psychology: Learning, Memory, and Cognition, 11,* 70–84.

Murphy, G. L. and Kaplan, A. S. (2000). Feature distribution and background knowledge in category learning. *Quarterly Journal of Experimental Psychology A: Human Experimental Psychology, 53A,* 962–982.

Murphy, G. L. and Lassaline, M. E. (1997). Hierarchical structure in concepts and the basic level of categorization. In K. Lamberts and D. Shanks (Eds.), *Knowledge, Concepts and Categories* (pp. 93–131). London: UCL Press.

Murphy, G. L. and Medin, D. L. (1985). The role of theories in conceptual coherence. *Psychological Review, 92,* 289–316.

Murphy, G. L. and Ross, B. H. (1994). Predictions from uncertain categorizations. *Cognitive Psychology, 27,* 148–193.

Murphy, G. L. and Ross, B. H. (1999). Induction with cross-classified categories. *Memory & Cognition, 27,* 1024–1041.

Murphy, G. L. and Smith, E. E. (1982). Basic level superiority in picture categorization. *Journal of Verbal Learning and Verbal Behavior, 21*, 1–20.

Murphy, G. L. and Wisniewski, E. J. (1989). Categorizing objects in isolation and in scenes: What a superordinate is good for. *Journal of Experimental Psychology: Learning, Memory, and Cognition, 15*, 572–586.

Murphy, G. L. and Wisniewski, E. J. (1989). Feature correlations in conceptual representations. In G. Tiberghien (Ed.), *Advances in Cognitive Science, Vol. 2: Theory and Applications* (pp. 23–45). Chichester: Ellis Horwood.

Murphy, G. L. and Wright, J. C. (1984). Changes in conceptual structure with expertise: Differences between real-world experts and novices. *Journal of Experimental Psychology: Learning, Memory, and Cognition, 10*, 144–155.

Needham, A. and Baillargeon, R. (2000). Infants' use of featural and experiential information in segregating and individuating objects: A reply to Xu, Carey and Welch (2000). *Cognition, 74*, 255–284.

Newport, E. and Bellugi, U. (1979). Linguistic expression of category levels. In E. S. Klima and U. Bellugi, *The Signs of Language*. Cambridge, MA: Harvard University Press.

Nosofsky, R. M. (1984). Choice, similarity, and the context theory of classification. *Journal of Experimental Psychology: Learning, Memory, and Cognition, 10*, 104–114.

Nosofsky, R. M. (1986). Attention, similarity, and the identification-categorization relationship. *Journal of Experimental Psychology: General, 115*, 39–57.

Nosofsky, R. M. (1988). Similarity, frequency, and category representations. *Journal of Experimental Psychology: Learning, Memory, and Cognition, 14*, 54–65.

Nosofsky, R. M. (1992). Exemplars, prototypes and similarity rules. In A. Healy, S. Kosslyn, and R. Shiffrin (Eds.), *From Learning Theory to Connectionist Theory: Essays in Honor of W. K. Estes* (Vol. 1, pp. 149–168). Hillsdale, NJ: Erlbaum.

Nosofsky, R. M. (2000). Exemplar representation without generalization? Comment on Smith and Minda's (2000) "Thirty categorization results in search of a model." *Journal of Experimental Psychology: Learning, Memory, and Cognition, 26*, 1735–1743.

Nosofsky, R. M. and Palmeri, T. J. (1997). An exemplar-based random walk model of speeded categorization. *Psychological Review, 104*, 266–300.

Nosofsky, R. M., Palmeri, T. J., and McKinley, S. C. (1994). Rule-plus-exception model of classification learning. *Psychological Review, 101*, 53–79.

Nosofsky, R. M. and Zaki, S. R. (1998). Dissociations between categorization and recognition in amnesic and normal individuals: An exemplar-based interpretation. *Psychological Science, 9*, 247–255.

Nunberg, G. (1979). The non-uniqueness of semantic solutions: Polysemy. *Linguistics and Philosophy, 3*, 143–184.

Oakes, L. M., Coppage, D. J., and Dingel, A. (1997). By land or by sea: The role of perceptual similarity in infants' categorization of animals. *Developmental Psychology, 33*, 396–407.

Oliva, A. and Schyns, P. G. (1997). Coarse blobs or fine edges? Evidence that information diagnosticity changes the perception of complex visual stimuli. *Cognitive Psychology, 34*, 72–107.

Osgood, C. H., Suci, G. J., and Tannenbaum, P. H. (1957). *The Measurement of Meaning.* Urbana, IL: University of Illinois Press.

Osherson, D. N. and Smith, E. E. (1981). On the adequacy of prototype theory as a theory of concepts. *Cognition, 9,* 35–58.

Osherson, D. N., Smith, E. E., Wilkie, O., López, A., and Shafir, E. (1990). Category-based induction. *Psychological Review, 97,* 185–200.

Osherson, D. N., Stern, J., Wilkie, O., Stob, M., and Smith, E. D. (1991). Default probability. *Cognitive Science, 15,* 251–269.

Palmeri, T. J. (1999). Learning categories at different hierarchical levels: A comparison of category learning models. *Psychonomic Bulletin & Review, 6,* 495–503.

Palmeri, T. J. and Blalock, C. (2000). The role of background knowledge in speeded perceptual categorization. *Cognition, 77,* B45–B57.

Pazzani, M. J. (1991). Influence of prior knowledge on concept acquisition: Experimental and computational results. *Journal of Experimental Psychology: Learning, Memory, and Cognition, 17,* 416–432.

Pickering, M. J. and Frisson, S. (2001). Processing ambiguous verbs: Evidence from eye movements. *Journal of Experimental Psychology: Learning, Memory, and Cognition, 27,* 556–573.

Poldrack, R. A., Selco, S. L., Field, J. E., and Cohen, N. J. (1999). The relationship between skill learning and repetition priming: Experimental and computational analyses. *Journal of Experimental Psychology: Learning, Memory, and Cognition, 25,* 208–235.

Polichak, J. W. and Gerrig, R. J. (1998). Common ground and everyday language use: Comments on Horton and Keysar. *Cognition, 66,* 183–189.

Pond, R. (1987, April). Fun in metals. *Johns Hopkins Magazine,* 60–68.

Posnansky, C. J. and Neumann, P. G. (1976). The abstraction of visual prototypes by children. *Journal of Experimental Child Psychology, 21,* 367–379.

Posner, M. I. and Keele, S. W. (1968). On the genesis of abstract ideas. *Journal of Experimental Psychology, 77,* 353–363.

Posner, M. I. and Keele, S. W. (1970). Retention of abstract ideas. *Journal of Experimental Psychology, 83,* 304–308.

Proffitt, J. B., Coley, J. D., and Medin, D. L. (2000). Expertise and category-based induction. *Journal of Experimental Psychology: Learning, Memory, and Cognition, 26,* 811–828.

Pullum, G. K. (1991). *The Great Eskimo Vocabulary Hoax and Other Irreverent Essays on the Study of Language.* Chicago: University of Chicago Press.

Pustejovsky, J. (1995). *The Generative Lexicon.* Cambridge, MA: MIT Press.

Quine, W. v. O. (1960). *Word and Object.* Cambridge, MA: MIT Press.

Quinn, P. C. (1987). The categorical representation of visual pattern information by young infants. *Cognition, 27,* 145–179.

Quinn, P. C. and Eimas, P. D. (1996). Perceptual cues that permit categorical differentiation of animal species by infants. *Journal of Experimental Child Psychology, 63,* 189–211.

Quinn, P. C. and Eimas, P. D. (1997). A reexamination of the perceptual-to-conceptual shift in mental representations. *Review of General Psychology, 1,* 271–287.

Quinn, P. C., Eimas, P. D., and Rosenkrantz, S. L. (1993). Evidence for representations of perceptually similar natural categories by 3-month-old and 4-month-old infants. *Perception,* 22, 463–475.

Quinn, P. C. and Johnson, M. H. (1997). The emergence of perceptual category representations in young infants: A connectionist analysis. *Journal of Experimental Child Psychology,* 66, 236–263.

Rakison, D. H. and Butterworth, G. E. (1998). Infants' use of object parts in early categorization. *Developmental Psychology, 34,* 49–62.

Ramscar, M. (1997). Wittgenstein and the representation of psychological categories. In M. Ramscar, U. Hahn, E. Cambouropolos, and H. Pain (Eds.), *Proceedings of SimCat 1997: An Interdisciplinary Workshop on Similarity and Categorisation* (pp. 205–211). Edinburgh: Department of Artificial Intelligence, University of Edinburgh.

Randall, R. (1976). How tall is a taxonomic tree? Some evidence for dwarfism. *American Ethnologist, 3,* 543–553.

Reed, S. K. (1972). Pattern recognition and classification. *Cognitive Psychology, 3,* 382–407.

Regehr, G. and Brooks, L. R. (1993). Perceptual manifestations of an analytic structure: The priority of holistic individuation. *Journal of Experimental Psychology: General, 122,* 92–114.

Regehr, G. and Brooks, L. R. (1995). Category organization in free classification: The organizing effect of an array of stimuli. *Journal of Experimental Psychology: Learning, Memory, and Cognition, 21,* 347–363.

Rehder, B. and Hastie, R. (2001). Causal knowledge and categories: The effects of causal beliefs on categorization, induction, and similarity. *Journal of Experimental Psychology: General, 130,* 323–360.

Rehder, B. and Murphy, G. L. (2001). A knowledge resonance (KRES) model of category learning. In *Proceedings of the 23rd Annual Convention of the Cognitive Science Society.* Mahwah, NJ: Erlbaum.

Rehder, B, Schreiner, M. E., Wolfe, M. B. W., Laham, D., Landauer, T. K., and Kintsch, W. (1998). Using latent semantic analysis to assess knowledge: Some technical considerations. *Discourse Processes, 25,* 337–354.

Rey, G. (1983). Concepts and stereotypes. *Cognition, 15,* 237–262.

Rice, S. A. (1992). Polysemy and lexical representation: The case of three English prepositions. In *Proceedings of the Fourteenth Annual Conference of the Cognitive Science Society* (pp. 89–94). Hillsdale, NJ: Erlbaum.

Rifkin, A. (1985). Evidence for a basic level in event taxonomies. *Memory & Cognition, 13,* 538–556.

Rips, L. J. (1975). Inductive judgments about natural categories. *Journal of Verbal Learning and Verbal Behavior, 14,* 665–681.

Rips, L. J. (1989). Similarity, typicality, and categorization. In S. Vosniadou and A. Ortony (Eds.), *Similarity and Analogical Reasoning* (pp. 21–59). Cambridge: Cambridge University Press.

Rips, L. J., Shoben, E. J., and Smith, E. E. (1973). Semantic distance and the verification of semantic relations. *Journal of Verbal Learning and Verbal Behavior, 12,* 1–20.

Roberts, K. (1988). Retrieval of a basic-level category in prelinguistic infants. *Developmental Psychology, 24*, 21–27.

Roediger, H. L., III (1990). Implicit memory: Retention without remembering. *American Psychologist, 45*, 1043–1056.

Roediger, H. L., III and Blaxton, T. A. (1987). Effects of varying modality, surface features, and retention interval on priming in word fragment completion. *Memory & Cognition, 15*, 379–388.

Rosch, E. H. (1973). On the internal structure of perceptual and semantic categories. In T. E. Moore (Ed.), *Cognitive Development and the Acquisition of Language* (pp. 111–144). New York: Academic Press.

Rosch, E. (1975). Cognitive representations of semantic categories. *Journal of Experimental Psychology: General, 104*, 192–233.

Rosch, E. (1977). Human categorization. In N. Warren (Ed.), *Advances in Cross-Cultural Psychology (Vol. 1)* (pp. 177–206). London: Academic Press.

Rosch, E. (1978). Principles of categorization. In E. Rosch and B. B. Lloyd (Eds.), *Cognition and Categorization* (pp. 27–48). Hillsdale, NJ: Erlbaum.

Rosch, E. and Mervis, C. B. (1975). Family resemblance: Studies in the internal structure of categories. *Cognitive Psychology, 7*, 573–605.

Rosch, E., Mervis, C. B., Gray, W., Johnson, D., and Boyes-Braem, P. (1976). Basic objects in natural categories. *Cognitive Psychology, 8*, 382–439.

Rosch, E., Simpson, C., and Miller, R. S. (1976). Structural bases of typicality effects. *Journal of Experimental Psychology: Human Perception and Performance, 2*, 491–502.

Ross, B. H. (1984). Remindings and their effects in learning a cognitive skill. *Cognitive Psychology, 16*, 371–416.

Ross, B. H. (1990). Reminding-based category learning. *Cognitive Psychology, 22*, 460–492.

Ross, B. H. (1989). Remindings in learning and instruction. In S. Vosniadou and A. Ortony (Eds.), *Similarity and Analogical Reasoning* (pp. 438–469). Cambridge: Cambridge University Press.

Ross, B. H. (1996). Category representations and the effects of interacting with instances. *Journal of Experimental Psychology: Learning, Memory, and Cognition, 22*, 1249–1265.

Ross, B. H. (1997). The use of categories affects classification. *Journal of Memory and Language, 37*, 240–267.

Ross, B. H. (1999). Postclassification category use: The effects of learning to use categories after learning to classify. *Journal of Experimental Psychology: Learning, Memory, & Cognition, 25*, 743–757.

Ross, B. H. (2000). The effects of category use on learned categories. *Memory & Cognition, 28*, 51–63.

Ross, B. H. and Murphy, G. L. (1996). Category-based predictions: Influence of uncertainty and feature associations. *Journal of Experimental Psychology: Learning, Memory, and Cognition, 22*, 736–753.

Ross, B. H. and Murphy, G. L. (1999). Food for thought: Cross-classification and category organization in a complex real-world domain. *Cognitive Psychology, 38*, 495–553.

Ross, B. H., Perkins, S. J., and Tenpenny, P. L. (1990). Reminding-based category learning. *Cognitive Psychology, 22,* 460–492.

Roth, E. M. and Shoben, E. J. (1983). The effect of context on the structure of categories. *Cognitive Psychology, 15,* 346–378.

Ruhl, C. (1989). *On Monosemy: A Study in Linguistic Semantics.* Albany: SUNY Press.

Rumelhart, D. E. and McClelland, J. L. (1986). *Parallel Distributed Processing: Explorations in the Microstructure of Cognition. Vol. 1: Foundations.* Cambridge, MA: MIT Press.

Rumelhart, D. E. and Ortony, A. (1977). The representation of knowledge in memory. In R. C. Anderson, R. J. Spiro, and W. E. Montague (Eds.), *Schooling and the Acquisition of Knowledge.* Hillsdale, NJ: Erlbaum.

Schank, R. C. and Abelson, R. P. (1977). *Scripts, Plans, Goals and Understanding.* Hillsdale, NJ: Erlbaum.

Schneider, W. and Bjorklund, D. F. (1998). Memory. In D. Kuhn and R. S. Siegler (Eds.), *Handbook of Child Psychology (5th ed.), Vol. 2: Cognition, Perception, and Language* (pp. 467–521). New York: Wiley.

Schyns, P. G., Goldstone, R. L., and Thibaut, J. (1998). The development of features in object concepts. *Behavioral and Brain Sciences, 21,* 1–54.

Schyns, P. and Murphy, G. L. (1994). The ontogeny of part representation in object concepts. In D. L. Medin (Ed.), *The Psychology of Learning and Motivation, Vol. 31* (pp. 305–349). New York: Academic Press.

Schyns, P. G. and Rodet, L. (1997). Categorization creates functional features. *Journal of Experimental Psychology: Learning, Memory, and Cognition, 23,* 681–696.

Sharp, D., Cole, M., and Lave, C. (1979). Education and cognitive development: The evidence from experimental research. *Monographs of the Society for Research in Child Development, 44,* serial #148, nos. 1–2.

Shaver, P., Schwartz, J., Kirson, D., and O'Connor, D. (1987). Emotion knowledge: Further explorations of a prototype approach. *Journal of Personality and Social Psychology, 52,* 1061–1086.

Shepard, R. N. (1974). Representation of structure in similarity data: Problems and prospects. *Psychometrika, 39,* 373–421.

Shepard, R. N. (1987). Toward a universal law of generalization for psychological science. *Science, 237,* 1317–1323.

Shepard, R. N., Hovland, C. I., and Jenkins, H. M. (1961). Learning and memorization of classifications. *Psychological Monographs: General and Applied, 75* (13, whole no. 517).

Shepp, B. E. (1983). The analyzability of multidimensional objects: Some constraints on perceived structure, the development of perceived structure, and attention. In T. J. Tighe and B. E. Shepp (Eds.), *Perception, Cognition, and Development: Interactional Analyses* (pp. 39–75). Hillsdale, NJ: Erlbaum.

Shipley, E. F. (1993). Categories, hierarchies, and induction. In D. L. Medin (Ed.), *The Psychology of Learning and Motivation, Vol. 30* (pp. 265–301). San Diego, CA: Academic Press.

Shipley, E. F., Kuhn, I. F., and Madden, E. C. (1983). Mothers' use of superordinate category terms. *Journal of Child Language, 10,* 571–588.

Simons, S. (Ed.). (1993). *No One May Ever Have the Same Knowledge Again: Letters to Mount Wilson Observatory, 1915–1935.* Los Angeles: Society for the Diffusion of Useful Information Press.

Slobin, D. I. (1996). From "thought and language" to "thinking for speaking." In J. J. Gumperz and S. C. Levinson (Eds.), *Rethinking Linguistic Relativity* (pp. 70–96). Cambridge: Cambridge University Press.

Sloman, S. A. (1993). Feature-based induction. *Cognitive Psychology, 25,* 231–280.

Sloman, S. A. (1998). Categorical inference is not a tree: The myth of inheritance hierarchies. *Cognitive Psychology, 35,* 1–33.

Smiley, S. S. and Brown, A. L. (1979). Conceptual preferences for thematic or taxonomic relations: A nonmonotonic age trend from preschool to old age. *Journal of Experimental Child Psychology, 28,* 249–257.

Smith, C. (1979). Children's understanding of natural language hierarchies. *Journal of Experimental Child Psychology, 27,* 437–458.

Smith, E. E. (1978). Theories of semantic memory. In W. K. Estes (Ed.), *Handbook of Learning and Cognitive Processes, Vol. 6* (pp. 1–56). Potomac, MD: Erlbaum.

Smith, E. E., Balzano, G. J., and Walker, J. (1978). Nominal, perceptual, and semantic codes in picture categorization. In J. W. Cotton and R. L. Klatzky (Eds.), *Semantic Factors in Cognition* (pp. 137–168). Hillsdale, NJ: Erlbaum.

Smith, E. E. and Medin, D. L. (1981). *Categories and Concepts.* Cambridge, MA: Harvard University Press.

Smith, E. E. and Osherson, D. N. (1984). Conceptual combination with prototype concepts. *Cognitive Science, 8,* 337–361.

Smith, E. E., Osherson, D. N., Rips, L. J., and Keane, M. (1988). Combining prototypes: A selective modification model. *Cognitive Science, 12,* 485–527.

Smith, E. E., Rips, L. J., and Shoben, E. J. (1974). Semantic memory and psychological semantics. In G. H. Bower (Ed.), *The Psychology of Learning and Motivation, Vol. 8* (pp. 1–45). New York: Academic Press.

Smith, E. E., Shafir, E., and Osherson, D. (1993). Similarity, plausibility, and judgments of probability. *Cognition, 49,* 67–96.

Smith, E. E. and Sloman, S. A. (1994). Similarity- versus rule-based categorization. *Memory & Cognition, 22,* 377–386.

Smith, J. D. and Minda, J. P. (2000). Thirty categorization results in search of a model. *Journal of Experimental Psychology: Learning, Memory, and Cognition, 26,* 3–27.

Smith, J. D. and Minda, J. P. (1998). Prototypes in the mist: The early epochs of category learning. *Journal of Experimental Psychology: Learning, Memory, and Cognition, 24,* 1411–1436.

Smith, J. D., Murray, M. J., Jr., and Minda, J. P. (1997). Straight talk about linear separability. *Journal of Experimental Psychology: Learning, Memory, and Cognition, 23,* 659–680.

Smith, L. B. and Heise, D. (1992). Perceptual similarity and conceptual structure. In B. Burns (Ed.), *Percepts, Concepts, and Categories: The Representation and Processing of Information* (pp. 233–272). Amsterdam: Elsevier.

Smoke, K. L. (1932). An objective study of concept formation. *Psychological Monographs*, *XLII* (whole no. 191).

Solomon, K. O. and Barsalou, L. W. (2001). Representing properties locally. *Cognitive Psychology*, *43*, 129–169.

Soja, N. N., Carey, S., and Spelke, E. S. (1991). Ontological categories guide young children's inductions of word meaning: Object terms and substance terms. *Cognition*, *38*, 179–211.

Solomon, G. E. A., Johnson, S. C., Zaitchik, D., and Carey, S. (1996). Like father, like son: Young children's understanding of how and why offspring resemble their parents. *Child Development*, *67*, 151–171.

Spalding, T. L. and Murphy, G. L. (1996). Effects of background knowledge on category construction. *Journal of Experimental Psychology: Learning, Memory, and Cognition*, *22*, 525–538.

Spalding, T. L. and Murphy, G. L. (1999). What is learned in knowledge-related categories? Evidence from typicality and feature frequency judgments. *Memory & Cognition*, *27*, 856–867.

Spalding, T. L. and Ross, B. H. (1994). Comparison-based learning: Effects of comparing instances during category learning. *Journal of Experimental Psychology: Learning, Memory, and Cognition*, *20*, 1251–1263.

Spencer, J., Quinn, P. C., Johnson, M. H., and Karmiloff-Smith, A. (1997). Heads you win, tails you lose: Evidence for young infants categorizing mammals by head and facial attributes. *Early Development and Parenting*, *6*, 113–126.

Springer, K. and Keil, F. C. (1991). Early differentiation of causal mechanisms appropriate to biological and nonbiological kinds. *Child Development*, *62*, 767–781.

Springer, K. and Murphy, G. L. (1992). Feature availability in conceptual combination. *Psychological Science*, *3*, 111–117.

Starkey, D. (1981). The origins of concept formation: Object sorting and object preference in early infancy. *Child Development*, *52*, 489–497.

Strange, W., Keeney, T., Kessel, F. S., and Jenkins, J. J. (1970). Abstraction over time of prototypes from distortions of random dot patterns. *Journal of Experimental Psychology*, *83*, 508–510.

Strauss, M. S. (1979). Abstraction of prototypical information by adults and 10-month-old infants. *Journal of Experimental Psychology: Human Learning and Memory*, *5*, 618–632.

Sutcliffe, J. P. (1993). Concept, class, and category in the tradition of Aristotle. In I. van Mechelen, J. Hampton, R. S. Michalski, and P. Theuns (Eds.), *Categories and Concepts: Theoretical Views and Inductive Data Analysis* (pp. 35–65). London: Academic Press.

Sweetser, E. E. (1990). *From Etymology to Pragmatics: Metaphorical and Cultural Aspects of Semantic Structure*. Cambridge: Cambridge University Press.

Tabossi, P. (1988). Effects of context on the immediate interpretation of unambiguous nouns. *Journal of Experimental Psychology: Learning, Memory, and Cognition*, *14*, 153–162.

Tanaka, J. W. and Taylor, M. E. (1991). Object categories and expertise: Is the basic level in the eye of the beholder? *Cognitive Psychology*, *15*, 121–149.

Taylor, J. R. (1995). *Linguistic Categorization: Prototypes in Linguistic Theory (2nd ed.)*. Oxford: Oxford University Press.

Thompson, C. (1999, July/August). New word order: The attack of the incredible grading machine. *Lingua Franca*, *9(5)*, 28–37.

Thompson, L. A. (1994). Dimensional strategies dominate perceptual classification. *Child Development*, *65*, 1627–1645.

Tversky, A. (1977). Features of similarity. *Psychological Review*, *84*, 327–352.

Tversky, A. and Kahneman, D. (1982). Judgments of and by representativeness. In D. Kahneman, P. Slovic, and A. Tversky (Eds.), *Judgment under Uncertainty: Heuristics and Biases* (pp. 84–98). Cambridge: Cambridge University Press.

Tversky, B. and Hemenway, K. (1983). Categories of environmental scenes. *Cognitive Psychology*, *15*, 121–149.

Tversky, B. and Hemenway, K. (1984). Objects, parts, and categories. *Journal of Experimental Psychology: General*, *113*, 169–193.

Vallecher, R. R. and Wegner, D. M. (1987). What do people think they're doing? Action identification and human behavior. *Psychological Review*, *94*, 3–15.

Van Mechelen, I., Hampton, J., Michalski, R., and Theuns, P. (Eds.) (1993). *Categories and Concepts: Theoretical Views and Inductive Data Analysis*. New York: Academic Press.

Vygotsky, L. S. (1965). *Thought and Language*. Cambridge, MA: MIT Press.

Ward, T. B. (1993). Processing biases, knowledge, and context in category formation. In G. V. Nakamura, R. M. Taraban, and D. L. Medin (Eds.), *The Psychology of Learning and Motivation (Vol. 29): Categorization by Humans and Machines* (pp. 257–282). New York: Academic Press.

Ward, T. B., Becker, A. H., Hass, S. D., and Vela, E. (1991). Attribute availability and the shape bias in children's category generalization. *Cognitive Development*, *6*, 143–167.

Wattenmaker, W. D. (1993). Incidental concept learning, feature frequency, and correlated properties. *Journal of Experimental Psychology: Learning, Memory, and Cognition*, *19*, 203–222.

Wattenmaker, W. D. (1995). Knowledge structures and linear separability: Integrating information in object and social categorization. *Cognitive Psychology*, *28*, 274–328.

Wattenmaker, W. D., Dewey, G. I., Murphy, T. D., and Medin, D. L. (1986). Linear separability and concept learning: context, relational properties, and concept naturalness. *Cognitive Psychology*, *18*, 158–194.

Waxman, S. R. (1990). Linguistic biases and the establishment of conceptual hierarchies: Evidence from preschool children. *Cognitive Development*, *5*, 123–150.

Waxman, S. and Gelman, R. (1986). Preschoolers' use of superordinate relations in classification and language. *Cognitive Development*, *1*, 139–156.

Waxman, S. R. and Klibanoff, R. S. (2000). The role of comparison in the extension of novel adjectives. *Developmental Psychology*, *36*, 571–581.

Waxman, S. R. and Kosowski, T. D. (1990). Nouns mark category relations: Toddlers' and preschoolers' word-learning biases. *Child Development*, *61*, 1461–1473.

Waxman, S. R., Lynch, E. B., Casey, K. L., and Baer, L. (1997). Setters and samoyeds: The emergence of subordinate level categories as a basis for inductive inference in preschool-age children. *Developmental Psychology*, *33*, 1074–1090.

Waxman, S. R. and Markow, D. B. (1995). Words as invitations to form categories: Evidence from 12- to 13-month-old infants. *Cognitive Psychology, 29*, 257–302.

Waxman, S. R. and Markow, D. B. (1998). Object properties and object kind: Twenty-one-month-old infants' extensions of novel adjectives. *Child Development, 69*, 1313–1329.

Waxman, S. R. and Namy, L. L. (1997). Challenging the notion of a thematic preference in young children. *Developmental Psychology, 33*, 555–567.

Waxman, S. R., Shipley, E. F., and Shepperson, B. (1991). Establishing new subcategories: The role of category labels and existing knowledge. *Child Development, 62*, 127–138.

Wellman, H. M. (1990) *The Child's Theory of Mind*. Cambridge, MA: MIT Press.

Wells, H. G. (1930). *The Island of Dr. Moreau*. New York: Dover Books.

Whittlesea, B. W. A. (1987). Preservation of specific experiences in the representation of general knowledge. *Journal of Experimental Psychology: Learning, Memory, and Cognition, 13*, 3–17.

Wilcox, T. and Baillargeon, R. (1998a). Object individuation in infancy: The use of featural information in reasoning about occlusion events. *Cognitive Psychology, 37*, 97–155.

Wilcox, T. and Baillargeon, R. (1998b). Object individuation in young infants: Further evidence with an event-monitoring paradigm. *Developmental Science, 1*, 127–142.

Wilson, R. A. and Keil, F. C. (2000). The shadows and shallows of explanation. In F. C. Keil and R. A. Wilson (Eds.), *Explanation and Cognition* (pp. 87–114). Cambridge, MA: MIT Press.

Wisniewski, E. J. (1995). Prior knowledge and functionally relevant features in concept learning. *Journal of Experimental Psychology: Learning, Memory, and Cognition, 21*, 449–468.

Wisniewski, E. J. (1996). Construal and similarity in conceptual combination. *Journal of Memory and Language, 35*, 434–453.

Wisniewski, E. J. (1997). When concepts combine. *Psychonomic Bulletin & Review, 4*, 167–183.

Wisniewski, E. J., Imai, M., and Casey, L. (1996). On the equivalence of superordinate concepts. *Cognition, 60*, 269–298.

Wisniewski, E. J. and Love, B. C. (1998). Relations versus properties in conceptual combination. *Journal of Memory and Language, 38*, 177–202.

Wisniewski, E. J. and Medin, D. L. (1994). On the interaction of theory and data in concept learning. *Cognitive Science, 18*, 221–281.

Wisniewski, E. J. and Middleton, E. (2002). Of bucket bowls and coffee cup bowls: Spatial alignment in conceptual combination. *Journal of Memory and Language, 46*, 1–23.

Wisniewski, E. J. and Murphy, G. L. (1989). Superordinate and basic category names in discourse: A textual analysis. *Discourse Processes, 12*, 245–261.

Wittgenstein, L. (1953). *Philosophical Investigations*. Oxford: Blackwell.

Wolfe, M. B. W., Schreiner, M. E., Rehder, B., Laham, D., Foltz, P. W., Kintsch, W., and Landauer, T. K. (1998). Learning from text: Matching readers and texts by latent semantic analysis. *Discourse Processes, 25*, 309–336.

Woodward, A. L. and Markman, E. M. (1998). Early word learning. In D. Kuhn and R. S. Siegler (Eds.), *Handbook of Child Psychology (5th ed.), Vol. 2: Cognition, Perception, and Language* (pp. 371–420). New York: Wiley.

Xu, F. (1997). From Lot's wife to a pillar of salt: Evidence that *physical object* is a sortal concept. *Mind & Language, 12,* 365–392.

Xu, F. and Carey, S. (1996). Infants' metaphysics: The case of numerical identity. *Cognitive Psychology, 30,* 111–153.

Xu, F. and Carey, S. (2000). The emergence of kind concepts: A rejoinder to Needham and Baillargeon (2000). *Cognition, 74,* 285–301.

Xu, F., Carey, S., and Welch, J. (1999). Infants' ability to use object kind information for object individuation. *Cognition, 70,* 137–166.

Yamauchi, T. and Markman, A. B. (1988). Category learning by inference and categorization. *Journal of Memory and Language, 39,* 124–148.

Yamauchi, T. and Markman, A. B. (2000a). Inference using categories. *Journal of Experimental Psychology: Learning, Memory, and Cognition, 26,* 776–795.

Yamauchi, T. and Markman, A. B. (2000b). Learning categories composed of varying instances: The effect of classification, inference, and structural alignment. *Memory & Cognition, 28,* 64–78.

Younger, B. A. (1992). Developmental change in infant categorization: The perception of correlations among facial features. *Child Development, 63,* 1526–1535.

Younger, B. A. and Cohen, L. B. (1985). How infants form categories. In G. H. Bower (Ed.), *The Psychology of Learning and Motivation, Vol. 19* (pp. 211–247). New York: Academic Press.

Younger, B. A. and Gotlieb, S. (1988). Development of categorization skills: Changes in the nature or structure of infant form categories? *Developmental Psychology, 24,* 611–619.

Zipf, G. K. (1945). The meaning-frequency relationship of words. *Journal of General Psychology, 33,* 251–256.

Name Index

Abelson, R. P., 440
Adelson, B., 228
Ahn, W., 128, 133, 140, 161–162, 192, 194, 489
Allen, S. W., 81–83, 85–88, 92
Allopenna, P. D., 38, 104, 150–151, 154, 183, 189, 192–183, 503–504
Altom, M. W., 123
Anderson, A., 414
Anderson, J. A., 55, 478, 490
Anderson, J. R., 258, 264, 494, 503
Anderson, R. C., 415
Andrew, J. M., 417–418, 475, 515
Andrews, S. A., 359–361, 379, 513
Anglin, J. M., 213, 295, 319, 327, 330, 336, 363, 396–397, 402–403
Annett, M., 322
Apostle, H. G., 11
Aristotle, 11, 39
Armstrong, S. L., 24, 25, 38, 64, 495
Ashby, F. G., 478
Atran, S., 211, 254, 482
Au, T. K., 433
Austin, G. A., 16, 149

Baillargeon, R., 272, 283, 305–308, 313, 511
Baker, E., 353
Baker, J. G., 81, 86
Baldwin, D. A., 310, 314, 371–372
Balzano, G. J., 23, 166, 212
Barclay, J. R., 440
Barrett, S. E., 126, 358–359, 379

Barsalou, L. W., 35–38, 44, 59, 62–63, 113, 172–173, 189, 338, 479–480, 500–501, 518
Battig, W. F., 23
Bauer, P. J., 294, 311
Becker, A. H., 348–349, 357
Behl-Chadha, G., 299, 509
Benson, J. B., 273, 509
Berlin, B., 204, 211, 229, 397, 513
Bettger, J. G., 79, 89–91
Billman, D., 132
Bjorklund, D. F., 336, 377
Blalock, C., 168, 171, 179, 184
Blaxton, T. A., 86–87
Blewitt, P., 325, 329, 351, 511–512
Bloom, P., 188, 336, 340, 348, 352, 354–355
Bock, J. K., 23, 395
Bomba, P. C., 55, 285–288, 310–312, 314
Bott, L., 153, 186–188, 192–193, 195, 504, 518
Bower, G. H., 46, 116, 478, 503
Bowerman, M., 434, 515
Boyd, R., 144
Bransford, J. D., 79, 440
Breedlove, D. E., 211, 397
Brewer, W. F., 194
Brooks, L. R., 73, 80–83, 85–88, 90, 92, 128–130, 161
Brown, A. L., 319, 322
Brown, R., 210, 217, 330, 353, 398
Brownell, H. H., 23, 166, 212, 218, 222–224, 231, 238

Subject Index

ALCOVE, 67
Artificial intelligence models of concepts, 193–196

Base-rate neglect in category learning, 115–118
Basic level of categorization, 200, 210–223
  in children's concepts, 327–331
  differentiation explanation of, 218–223
  in nonobjects, 228–229
  in word meaning, 397–398
Baywatch model, 186–187
Blank predicates, 182, 245–246

Category-based induction, 180–182, 243–269
  by children, 371–375
Category construction, 126–134
  and knowledge, 171–173
Category production, 23
Category use, 134–140
Category validity, 214
Central tendency, 35
Children's concepts
  vs. adults' concepts, 337–340
  domain specificity of, 370–371
  perceptual vs. conceptual accounts, 380–382
Classical view of concepts, 15–40, 73
  revisions of, 24ff
Cognitive economy, 204
Cognitive reference point, 24

Collections vs. classes, 332
Concept, vs. *category*, 5
Concept specialization model of conceptual combination, 453–455
  criticisms of, 455–459
Conceptual combination, 443–475
  conjunctive and disjunctive concepts, 464–468
  feature-verification studies, 459–461
Conceptual development, 317–383
Configural cue model, 46
Conjunction effect in conceptual combination, 446
Conjunctive and disjunctive concepts, 149
Core and identification procedures, 24
Cue validity, 213–216
Cultural influences on concepts, 481–483

Definitions, 11
  problems with, 17, 25–28
Dishabituation technique (in infants), 273–279
Domain specificity in children's concepts, 370–371
Dot pattern categories, 28–30

Elbonics, 389
Essentialism, 366–369
Exemplar, definition of, 58–60
Exemplar effects, 75–94
  in categorization, 80–85
  in learning, 76–80
Exemplar models, tests of, 94–112